Praise for Vincent Bugliosi's *Reclaiming History*

"What Bugliosi has done is a public service. This book should be applauded. . . . A delight to read. . . . *Reclaiming History* . . . is more than a critical analysis [of the Kennedy assassination]. . . . [It is] the literary equivalent of World War I, a kind of trench warfare for the mind."
—*New York Times Book Review*

"This is quite simply a book that will be read for centuries."
—Scott Turow, author of the
New York Times #1 bestseller *Presumed Innocent*

"Vincent T. Bugliosi in *Reclaiming History* clearly has written the definitive book on the assassination of President John F. Kennedy. . . . A voluminous book, encyclopedic in scope, capacious enough not only to include a thorough explanation of the facts . . . of the JFK assassination, but also to expose the faults and debunk the arguments of the conspiracy community. . . . From the date of its publication . . . this stupendous [book] became the seminal work for future JFK assassination studies and essays." —*The International Criminal Justice Review*

"*Reclaiming History* is important not just because it's correct, though it is. It's significant not just because it is comprehensive—surely, no one will deny that. It is essential, first and foremost, because it is conclusive. From this point forward, no reasonable person can argue that Lee Harvey Oswald was innocent; no sane person can take seriously assertions that Kennedy was killed by the CIA, Fidel Castro, the Soviets, [etc.]. . . . *Reclaiming History* may finally move these accusations beyond civilized debate. . . . It is a book for the ages. No serious scholar of the president's assassination will ever write again on the subject without citing Bugliosi. . . . [He] is an American master of common sense, a punishing advocate and a curmudgeonly refreshing voice of reason."
—*Los Angeles Times Book Review*

"[Bugliosi has] made a pretty airtight case. [There is] the sense that Bugliosi's [book] is the final word."   —*Los Angeles Times*

"*Reclaiming History* is by far the most accurate and detailed non-governmental account of the assassination. Bugliosi's epic book is of great historical significance and should . . . be the final account of the facts surrounding the assassination. His work is irrefutable. Not only is the book monumental in scope, it is well-written. I . . . found the account engrossing. It is hard to believe that a work of this length on a well-plowed subject could still be a page-turner."—Richard Mosk, member of the Warren Commission staff, in the *Los Angeles Daily Law Journal*

"*Reclaiming History* presents a stronger case against Lee Harvey Oswald than the Warren Commission Report and a much more compelling one that Oswald acted alone with no conspiracy behind the assassination."—Robert K. Tanenbaum, deputy chief counsel, United States House of Representatives Select Committee on Assassinations

"This encyclopedic work is a bargain. Unlike any other book on the assassination ever produced by a single author, *Reclaiming History* [should] probably be shelved alongside the two massive federal investigations of the assassination."   —*Wall Street Journal*

"Absent a trial proving [Oswald's] guilt, Bugliosi has offered the next best thing: a prosecutor's air-tight brief that leaves no reasonable doubt. . . . If you read, or even read around in this book and still come to the conclusion that Oswald was part of a conspiracy to kill Kennedy, you are likely to believe that black helicopters have been sent by the feds to enforce the Endangered Species Act. . . . Bugliosi is right that this case is, and ought to be, closed."   —*Washington Post*

"The most exhaustive book yet written about the Kennedy assassination, *Reclaiming History* is a magnificent . . . achievement. . . .

[Bugliosi] exhilarates the reader with rat-a-tat annihilations of others' false premises and shaky inferences. . . . [*Reclaiming History*] will be a kind of eternal flame. . . . There is no question that Bugliosi succeeds in scorching the conspiracy theory terrain with ferocious, even definitive, plausibility." —*The Atlantic*

"*Reclaiming History* is Proustian in its conception, scope and design. . . . Bugliosi's book, which denies all conspiracies, has the ring of truth—scrupulous, irrefutable truth—and I predict will be the line that historians a hundred years from now will take on this story. . . . If any one book can make you believe the assassination was performed by Lee Harvey Oswald acting alone . . . this is that book. Few books are as gripping in their narrative, or as telling in their fine detail. This is a book that will make you weep. Powerfully, *Reclaiming History* evokes the confusion and awful fatefulness, a feeling of the world ripped asunder, that gripped millions then." —*Philadelphia Inquirer*

"*Reclaiming History* is the final word on the Kennedy assassination. It sets out to recapture the assassination from the conspiracy theorists, and succeeds so triumphantly that only the most demented reader could doubt its conclusions." —*Telegraph* (London)

"[Bugliosi is] a prosecutor on a mission, armed with both the sense of moral outrage that wins over juries and the dispassionate ability to keep millions of details straight. . . . Point by point, fact by fact, Bugliosi demolishes his opponents' arguments. And yet, even with this incredible detail, the story as well as its teller are compelling."—*Legal Times* (Washington, DC)

"With indignation crackling on every page . . . Bugliosi aims to redress, once and for all, what he sees as an outrageous imbalance between the books that deal with the assassination responsibly and those that do not. . . . [Bugliosi's] richly textured book is as engrossing as it is convincing." —*Boston Globe*

"What Bugliosi has done is reframe the narrative in such a compelling manner, in such an original writing voice, that he essentially shuts the conspiracy theorists down cold. *Reclaiming History* is the unrushed version of the Warren Commission Report, with all the wrinkles ironed out. . . . Bugliosi lays [the Kennedy assassination] out on a legal pad, pros and cons, discrepancies and all, and comes up with what amounts to an airtight prosecution brief."   —*Oregonian*

"*Reclaiming History* . . . sets the record straight forever and always. [Bugliosi] takes apart every single conspiracy theory ever perpetrated."
                                                                —*New York Post*

"Such a tome would seem to be for conspiracy geeks only, were it not written by Vincent Bugliosi, who knows how to construct airtight paragraphs as well as cases. Bugliosi is a very convincing man."
                                                                —*San Diego Tribune*

"Bugliosi whacks the wacky conspiracy theorists and demolishes the arguments of serious writers who have sought to prove that there had to be a conspiracy."   —*St. Louis Post-Dispatch*

"Bugliosi argues persuasively. . . . There's a reward in *Reclaiming History* for anyone with a passing interest in the topic, and anyone with a yen [for] seeing familiar arguments cross-examined and taken to their logical conclusions by a relentless, take-no-prisoners prosecutor. . . . A truly massive case against both the basic notion that JFK was done in by a conspiracy, and virtually every major conspiracy theory individually."
                                                                —*San Antonio Express News*

"Compulsively readable . . . an essential buy for all large public libraries."   —*Library Journal*

"A monumental critique. Bugliosi's best-selling cachet gains him the audience; his direct, energetic prose keeps it; and his journey through the evidence might sway it. Bugliosi's study will provoke controversy and debate." —*Booklist*

"In *Reclaiming History,* Vincent Bugliosi identifies and dismantles the conspiracy theories that still abound in discussions of the Kennedy assassination. . . . Critics, after an obligatory remark on the book's astounding length, generally concede that the author's exhaustive efforts have paid off, making this weighty tome *the* encyclopedic source for readers interested in reliving the events of November 1963."

—*Bookmarks* magazine

"Bugliosi's *Reclaiming History* is all-inclusive and unquestionably definitive." —*Chicago Sun-Times*

"The ultimate Kennedy assassination conspiracy debunking book. It lays waste to the uncountable conspiracy theories that have sprouted over the years." —*Washington Times*

"Bugliosi, the author of the magisterial *Reclaiming History*, is perhaps better qualified than anyone else to determine if there was a conspiracy in the Kennedy assassination. *Reclaiming History* is a great book and is the definitive account of the assassination." —*Assassinology*

"*Reclaiming History* is a towering masterpiece, achieving what many experts consider the 'final word' on the Kennedy assassination. It is a carefully written reconstruction and exhaustive study of the case."

—Mary Whipple, *Seeing the World through Books* blog

"The definitive tome on the Kennedy assassination is Vincent Bugliosi's Edgar-winning *Reclaiming History: The Assassination of President John F. Kennedy*." —Peter Canon, *Publishers Weekly*

"*Reclaiming History* is an indispensable and irreplaceable analysis of the facts and theories relating to President Kennedy's assassination. It

is truly a book for the ages." — Howard P. Willens, assistant counsel,
Warren Commission

Leading longtime members of the JFK assassination conspiracy community weigh in on *Reclaiming History*:

"It is likely that *Reclaiming History* will stand forever as the magnum opus of this case. . . . It is a masterpiece." —Dr. David W. Mantik,
Assassination Research Book Review

"Vince Bugliosi's masterful *Reclaiming History* is a devastating knockout blow to those who, like me, once believed there was a conspiracy in the death of JFK. Bugliosi finishes and completes, in exhaustive and impressive detail, the work of the Warren Commission, the House Select Committee on Assassinations, and, quite frankly, all the other writers who have ever delved into the crime of the twentieth century. It is time to get a life, America: Oswald did indeed kill Kennedy, acting alone. Vince Bugliosi has done what I once thought was the impossible: he has convinced me of this notion. The conspiracy community was able to survive the Warren Commission Report, as well as the Report of the House Select Committee on Assassinations. The question is whether it will be able to survive Bugliosi's *Reclaiming History*."
—Vince Palamara, Secret Service
expert and former JFK conspiracy theorist

Parkland

Helter Skelter (with Curt Gentry)

And the Sea Will Tell (with Bruce Henderson)

Till Death Do Us Part (with Ken Hurwitz)

The Phoenix Solution: Getting Serious about Winning
America's Drug War

Outrage: The Five Reasons Why O.J. Simpson Got Away with Murder

No Island of Sanity: Paula Jones v. Bill Clinton:
The Supreme Court on Trial

The Betrayal of America: How the Supreme Court Undermined the
Constitution and Chose Our President (with forewords by
Molly Ivins and Gerry Spence)

Reclaiming History: The Assassination of President John F. Kennedy

PARKLAND

Vincent Bugliosi

W. W. NORTON & COMPANY

NEW YORK · LONDON

Previously published under the name *Four Days in November*

Drawn from an earlier work, *Reclaimining History: The Assassination of President John F. Kennedy* (W. W. Norton, 2007)

Manufacturing by RR Donnelley, Bloomsburg
Book design by Chris Welch
Production manager: Devon Zahn

Library of Congress Cataloging-in-Publication Data

Bugliosi, Vincent.
[Four days in November]
Parkland / Vincent Bugliosi.
pages cm
"Previously published under the title Four days in November"—T.p. verso.
"Drawn from an earlier work, Reclaiming history : the assassination of President John F. Kennedy (W. W. Norton, 2007)"—T.p. verso.
Includes bibliographical references and index.
ISBN 978-0-393-34733-3 (pbk.)
1. Kennedy, John F. (John Fitzgerald), 1917–1963—Assassination. 2. Oswald, Lee Harvey. 3. Conspiracies—United States. I. Bugliosi, Vincent. Reclaiming history. II. Title.
E842.9.B835 2013
973.922092—dc23
2013024350

W. W. Norton & Company, Inc., 500 Fifth Avenue, New York, NY 10110
www.wwnorton.com

W. W. Norton & Company Ltd., Castle House, 75/76 Wells Street, London W1T 3QT

1 2 3 4 5 6 7 8 9 0

To the historical record, knowing that nothing in the present can exist without the paternity of history, and hence, the latter is sacred, and should never be tempered with or defiled by untruths.

Contents

Editor's Note

Parkland is the closely documented and gripping narrative of the assassination of President John F. Kennedy on November 22, 1963. It covers the shattering event in Dealey Plaza, the futile efforts to save the president's life, the apprehension and interrogation of Lee Harvey Oswald, his subsequent murder by Jack Ruby, and the funerals of Kennedy and Oswald on the fourth day following the assassination.

As exciting as this account undoubtedly is—and utterly persuasive of Oswald's guilt—it is but a part of Vincent Bugliosi's magnum opus, *Reclaiming History*, an extraordinary and historic book of a million and a half words that required twenty years to research and write. That book goes beyond the fascinating narrative of events to confront and destroy every one of the conspiracy theories that have grown up since the assassination, exposing their selective use of evidence, flawed logic, and outright deceptions. So thoroughly documented, so compellingly lucid in its conclusions, *Reclaiming History* is, in a sense, the investigation that completes the work of the Warren Commission. In it, Bugliosi, the nation's foremost prosecutor, takes on every aspect of the most important murder in American history. No one imagined that such a book would ever be written: a single volume that once and for all resolves, beyond any reasonable doubt, every lingering question as to what happened in Dallas and who was responsible. Bugliosi's irresistible logic, command of the evidence, and ability to draw startling inferences shed fresh light on this American nightmare. At last it all makes sense.

Readers who enjoy *Parkland*, or who have unanswered questions about conspiracy theories and the various investigations of the assassination, will want to consult Bugliosi's masterwork, *Reclaiming History*, which has raised scholarship on the assassination to a new and final level, one that far surpasses all other books on the subject.

—Starling Lawrence

Author's Note

All times noted are derived, when possible, from reliable sources (e.g., Dallas police radio recordings, television videotapes with times on screen). When not, times are inferred from the unfolding events and the totality of witness statements. This methodology is necessary because the time estimates given by, for instance, a single witness would often change every time the witness was interviewed and nearly always be in conflict with those given by other witnesses. All of this, of course, is normal and to be expected. I believe the following chronology to be the most accurate reconstruction to date. Throughout this chronology, the times, unless stated otherwise, are those of Central Standard Time.

Parkland

Friday, November 22, 1963

6:30 a.m.

Marina Oswald awakens in the dark. This late in November the sun doesn't rise until seven, even as far south as Irving, Texas. The young Russian woman, born Marina Nikolaevna Prusakova, is still tired from an uneasy night. She and her American husband, Lee, argued the night before, not as intensely as usual, but unpleasantly enough, particularly as they hadn't seen each other for nearly two weeks. And their newborn, Rachel, awoke twice, as babies will.

Lee usually woke up before the alarm went off, but this morning he didn't, sleeping through the sound, and Marina awakened him about ten minutes later. In the other bedroom Marina's friend Ruth Paine, the owner of the house, is still asleep with her kids.[1]

Lee has changed a lot in the two and a half years since Marina first met him at a dance at the Palace of Culture in Minsk, the capital city of the Soviet province of Byelorussia. She was only nineteen then, he was twenty-one and just a few months out of the U.S. Marines. Marina thought him to be very well dressed in his gray suit, white shirt, and white tie.[2] When she found out later that he was an American defector to the Soviet Union, it only increased her attraction to him. She still finds him good looking, in some ways even more so since he has been losing weight

1

and some of the babyish plumpness of cheek that made him look a bit like a chipmunk. At five foot nine inches and less than 150 pounds, Lee is rather small of build. But he's wiry, and his hands and arms are unusually strong. He is hardening into a man, and Marina is still Lee's woman, despite his crazy imagination. Honestly, some of his ideas would make the cat laugh. He told her not long ago that in twenty years he would be the "prime minister."

The lingering squabble from the night before is nothing out of the ordinary. They have been bickering from the first day of their marriage, and Lee isn't above hitting her when he loses his temper. They quarrel when they live together, they quarrel when they live apart. Marina has plenty of reason to want to live apart, but now he wants her to come back to live with him. He wants to take an apartment near his job, in Dallas, so they can all be together again—quite a turnaround from the pressure he had been putting on her to return to the Soviet Union, unless he is just trying to manipulate her again for some hidden reason of his own. Marina can never be quite sure. She knows she will eventually have to go back to him—she can't presume upon the hospitality of Ruth much longer—but she isn't ready yet. She is particularly outraged that Lee has been living in Dallas under an assumed name—more of his foolishness. She doesn't even know where in Dallas—some cheap furnished room somewhere, she supposes—and it was more or less an accident that she found out about the phony name at all.

Lee didn't come out to Irving last weekend. He didn't call her either. Perhaps he was angry because she had asked him not to come. Ruth, an intellectually inclined Quaker, was having a birthday party for her daughter on Saturday, her estranged husband Michael would be there, and Marina felt Lee's presence would be an intrusion on what ought to be a family day.

Then on Sunday, baby June, their two-year-old, was playing with the telephone dial, and Marina, perhaps feeling a little guilty, impulsively asked Ruth to call Lee. After seventeen months in the United States, Marina still doesn't speak English, so she had Ruth call for her. The man who answered the phone told Ruth that no one by the name of Lee Oswald lived at that number. Neither she nor Ruth knew that he was living there under an assumed name, and when he finally did call on Monday, Marina let him know she was furious that he was up to his childish tricks again. He got very angry and ordered her to remove his name and phone number from Ruth's address book. She said she wouldn't, and they argued about it. He claimed he did it because he didn't want the landlady to know his real name. She might, he said, read in the paper that he had defected to Russia. He told her he also didn't want the FBI to know where he lived because his contacts with the bureau were unpleasant. He never did tell her what name he had registered under at the rooming house.[3]

She is further aggravated by the fact that Lee came out to Irving last night—Thursday—instead of Friday, in violation of their understanding with Ruth. Lee is allowed to come out on Friday evening and stay over the weekend, but this week he'd come out a day early, which he had never done before, claiming he'd gotten "lonesome for my girls." But he wanted more, begging her to come live with him again, in Dallas, with their two girls.[4]

For all his faults, Lee loves the children. Last night he played with them out on the lawn in the gathering dusk—Ruth's children, the neighbors' kids, and his and Marina's own toddler, June. He loved that. They were still out on the lawn and it was nearly dark when he asked Marina for the third and last time to come back to him. He even agreed to buy her a washing machine, an unusual gesture for Lee, who was always so close with the little money he had. Marina nearly did give in. If he'd waited until Friday evening, she might have said yes. The truth of the matter is, despite their sorry marriage, he's all she's got. Even the warm friendship and support of Ruth, who only speaks sufficiently serviceable Russian to teach it part-time at a private high school and is delighted to have Marina around the house to pick up better Russian from her, doesn't make up for Lee's absence. But she isn't ready to give in yet. For once, she enjoys having the upper hand, however slight.

Lee didn't sleep well last night, although he'd turned in at ten o'clock, an hour earlier than usual. She could tell he was very upset when he retired for the evening and wasn't really asleep when she crept into bed after a late, hot bath. Around three in the morning she rested her foot on his leg, but he shoved her foot away hard. "My, he's in a mean mood," she thinks, believing he's angry at her for not coming back to him right away. She senses he may not have slept at all until about five o'clock in the morning.[5]

His mood has changed since last night, as it so often does. He seems upset rather than angry. Marina, at the mercy of his moods, knows the difference well. He is quiet and calm. He doesn't ask her to come to live with him in Dallas anymore.

As Lee finishes dressing, he comes over to the bed.

"Have you bought those shoes you were going to get?" he asks.

"No, I haven't had time," Marina answers.

"You must get those shoes, Mama," Lee tells her, then adds, "Don't get up, I'll get breakfast myself."

It was an odd comment for him to make, since there was little danger that she would. Lee rarely ate breakfast, it was usually just a cup of instant coffee, which he had this morning, and she certainly had never fixed him anything before. Why would he say that? she wondered.[6]

Before he leaves the bedroom, Lee kisses the children, as he always does, then walks to the bedroom door. He stops and returns to the side of the bed. He has always kissed his wife good-bye and Marina assumes he will do so now. But this time, she only hears his voice.

"I've left some money on the bureau," he says in his odd, if fluent, Russian. "Take it and buy everything you and Junie and Rachel need."

In the dark he has left $170 in bills, and something else—his wedding ring, quietly placed in a little china teacup that had belonged to Marina's grandmother. She won't find it until later that day.

"Bye-bye," he says, then turns and goes out the door.

Marina is surprised at her husband's sudden and unexpected kindness. She knows his $1.25-an-hour job doesn't really allow for a lot of new shoes, much less everything she and the children need. He certainly had never said such a thing before. But she is used to his erratic behavior, and it doesn't keep her from drifting back to sleep.[7]

7:21 a.m.

Linnie Mae Randle fixes a lunch at the kitchen counter for her nineteen-year-old brother, Wesley Frazier, to take to work. She sees a man crossing Westbrook Street. She doesn't recognize him at first but realizes he is heading to where her brother's automobile is parked in the carport.

"Who was that?" Linnie Mae's mother asks from the breakfast table, having caught a glimpse of him as he looked in the kitchen window.

"That's Lee," Wesley says.

He looks at the clock. It's late. Wesley likes to leave the house by 7:20 for the fifteen-mile drive into Dallas, even if that means getting there a few minutes early. He finishes off his coffee and jumps up from the table, where he has been having breakfast with his mom and his sister's kids, and hurries to get his lunch and a jacket. It is a gray, cold, miserable morning, and he will probably need that jacket.[8]

Linnie Mae, at the back door, watches Lee go over to Wesley's beat-up '59 Chevy four-door, open the right rear door—the sticky one with the broken window—and lay the package he's carrying on the backseat. She doesn't pay much attention to the light brown paper package. It's a couple of feet long, and wider at the bottom than at the top, where he carries it in the fashion soldiers call "trail arms."[9]

It isn't so surprising that she didn't recognize Lee, even though in a way she was responsible for getting him his job. She has only caught a couple glimpses of him when he came by to ride into work with Wesley. Linnie Mae knows that he is the husband of that Russian girl who has been staying with Ruth Paine, a neighbor who lives up the street from her. He came up in a conversation one afternoon at another neighbor's house. In early October, just about the time Marina's baby was due, Ruth and Marina were there drinking coffee. They were talking about Marina's husband being out of work at the worst possible time. Linnie Mae told them about the job Wesley had just found at the Texas School Book Depository, a private company at 411 Elm Street near downtown Dallas that warehoused and shipped school textbooks for various publishers. She thought there might be another vacancy there,[10] so Ruth called the Depository and was told to have Lee come on in for an interview.[11]

Linnie Mae doesn't have a lot of time to think about Marina's husband, although she realizes vaguely that it is out of the ordinary for
him to be out in Irving on a Friday morning. She's heard about the
odd arrangement where he lives in Dallas and only visits his wife and
kids on the weekend. She was surprised to see him coming back with
Wesley the night before when she was on her way to the store. Wesley told her Lee had come in a day early to get some curtain rods or
something.[12]

Wesley is relieved when the old Chevy finally fires up. It has been raining off and on all night and the battery is really weak. He notices that Lee
doesn't have a lunch bag with him, something he has always had before
on trips back into Dallas.[13]

"Where's your lunch?" Wesley asks.

"I'm going to buy it today," Lee replies.

Wesley figures Lee will get something from the catering truck that
comes around the warehouse at ten o'clock. A lot of the boys do that.[14]
As Wesley backs the car out, he glances over his right shoulder and notices
a brown paper package on the rear seat.

"What's the package, Lee?" he asks.

"Curtain rods," Oswald says.

"Oh, yeah," Wesley nods, shifting into forward. "You said you were
going to go get them last night."[15]

Lee doesn't have a lot to say. He rarely does. Lee is one of those guys
who just doesn't talk very much. Wesley, on the other hand, feels it's
important to make friends. That's why he introduced himself to Lee when
Lee came on the job in mid-October.

"We're glad to have you," he had told Lee. Wesley, a self-described
country boy from Huntsville, Texas, had only been on the job four or five
weeks himself, but he felt like a veteran. He already knew that Lee's wife
was living up the street from him, so he told Lee, "Any time you want to
go, just let me know."[16]

Lee told him he had an apartment in Dallas and wouldn't be going
home every night like most men do. He said he didn't drive either. That's
when he asked Wesley if he could ride out with him "on Friday afternoon

on weekends and come back on Monday morning," and Wesley said that would be just fine with him.

Wesley knows Lee's wife is from Russia but doesn't think anything about that. Lee said something about being in Russia, Germany, and France, and Wesley figured he had been in the service or something. Wesley doesn't know much more than that. Come to think of it, he doesn't even know Lee's last name.[17]

Back in Dallas, nightclub operator Jack Ruby is still asleep. Jack's day starts when most people are thinking about going home from work. Today he will get up around ten to get his ad into the offices of the *Dallas Morning News*, but that's early for him. Jack's Carousel Club, on Commerce Street halfway between the county jail and the police station, stays open until two every morning, even though the curious Texas liquor laws require customers to stop drinking at a quarter past midnight. This is kind of a pain in the behind, but Jack is scrupulous about keeping drinks off the table after hours. He runs a clean joint, which everyone knows. Even that vice-squad dick Gilmore has never cited him, and, as one of Jack's girls says, Gilmore would cite his own mother.

Dallas is a "dry" town, meaning that hard liquor cannot be sold in a public bar. So Jack's profit is in beer and champagne. His beer is the cheapest money can buy, and it is served in a glass with a bottom that works like a lens to magnify the modest quantity inside. His bartender also sells "setups," nonalcoholic beverages to which the customer may add his own liquor from the bottle he brought to the club in a paper bag, which is legal but not very profitable. The real dough is in champagne. Jack sells his champagne, which costs him $1.60 a bottle, for $17.50, and the waitress usually gets the change from a twenty as a tip. The champagne girls get $2.50 for each bottle they persuade their customers to buy. There are over a dozen of Jack's girls—waitresses, champagne and cigarette girls, and strippers. The strippers work under the American Guild of Variety Artists (AGVA) contract, but the others live on their tips and the commissions on the champagne.[18]

The champagne or cocktail girls are called B-girls, companions to the male customers to induce them to buy drinks, but Jack is proud of them. They aren't hookers. He's hell on any girl he suspects of making dates with the customers. His girls have class. He really cares about that. So what if most of his customers think his B-girls are hookers and keep buying Jack's rotgut champagne for them, while the girls keep pouring the stuff into bar towels and ice buckets to avoid drinking it. They are provided with "spit glasses," frosted tumblers ostensibly filled with ice water, really just ice, that they use to spit the champagne in their mouth into. Jack doesn't want the girls to drink any more than they absolutely have to. He doesn't like drunks any more than hookers. Jack's girls are a major preoccupation. He is always flying off the handle at them, browbeating, bullying, firing them. Diana Hunter, a veteran, reckons Jack has fired her two hundred times. But he's good to them too, always there with a bit of cash or even a pint of blood when they're really in trouble. They scream back at him when he loses his temper and turns cruel and mean, but they also know that a short time later he will have forgotten all about it. The girls love Jack in some odd way. Jack is a mensch.[19]

Jack Ruby lives in a low-rent district south of downtown, Oak Cliff. Though he is a neat dresser and his personal hygiene is high—taking two or three showers a day—he lives in an apartment full of litter, dirty clothes, unread newspapers, unwashed glasses—an apartment as implacably disordered, out of control, and marginal as his life.[20] Jack has troubles. His rock-and-roll joint out on Oak Lawn in North Dallas, the Vegas Club, which his sister Eva runs for him, is in trouble. With Eva out sick, he has to get the kid, Larry Crafard, to look after things out there, but who knows how long that's going to last—Crafard is a drifter. He was working as a roustabout with Bob Craven's carny show, "How Hollywood Makes Movies," until it folded in Dallas last month. Jack lets Larry sleep in the room down at the Carousel and gives him a buck or two for his meals at the Eat Well Café in return for doing odd jobs around the Carousel. So who knows how long Larry will last? Larry's a good kid, but no way is he going to get back together with that ballsy wife of his, and Jack knows he won't be around Dallas long.[21]

Not only is Eva sick, but Little Lynn is too—that's one of his strippers, out the whole damned weekend, probably. Drank too much champagne and passed out over at Nichols Brothers garage, but wouldn't let Jack drive her to the hospital.[22] He'll probably have to send her a couple of bucks, wire it to her over in Fort Worth. She's most likely pregnant, and that salesman boyfriend of hers is out of work because his car broke down.[23]

Jack has his own problems. Like recently with the stripper Jada? He goes to all sorts of trouble and expense to bring her up from New Orleans because she's supposed to be such a class act, and he's paying her way over scale, and then she gets out of line, starts doing front bumps and other kinds of things that could get his club shut down in a place like Dallas, and Jack has to douse the lights when it gets too raunchy. Jack screams at Jada and, she says, threatens her. Her agent calls the cops, and Jada files a "threats warrant" for Jack's arrest. At the peace-bond hearing, Jada tells the judge that Jack was trying to get out of paying her on the rest of her contract by threatening to cut up her wardrobe if she gives him trouble. Her wardrobe, she says, is worth $40,000. Jack's own arresting officer tells Jada, "Young lady, how in the world could you have $40,000 worth of G strings because that's all I've ever seen you in?"[24] And where's Jack going to get the dough to pay if old Judge Richberg ends up giving him a stiff fine when he's way behind on the union welfare payments for his dancers?[25]—particularly with the feds after him for delinquent income taxes,[26] and the competition, the Weinstein brothers, beating him to death with their fake "amateur nights" at Abe's Colony Club and the Theatre Lounge? They have pros there pretending to be housewives and working for ten or fifteen bucks a show,[27] way under scale, and you can't get the AGVA to do anything about it, probably because someone's paying them off or something. Jack spends his whole time trying to get the AGVA off the dime and start protecting its artists the way it should, but that bunch is so crooked they'd cheat God. In the meantime, Jack has just paid the rent on the Carousel, five hundred bucks, by certified check,[28] so he can breathe easy for another little while anyway. People go and tell you show biz is the life, but listen to Jack. Jack knows—it's tough, really tough.

Jack's favorite dachshund, Sheba, snuffs and begins to snore, but Jack sleeps on. Jack really loves Sheba. He tells some people she's his wife. Sheba is always with Jack, goes everywhere with him, even sleeps in his bed. The four dachshunds he's now keeping in a room off the kitchen at his club (he's had as many as ten dogs at a time) he calls his children. He gets really pissed off if you take that as a joke, tilting his head in a menacing way.[29]

7:30 a.m.

In Fort Worth's dowdy, brown-brick Texas Hotel, George Thomas enters the small foyer of suite 850 and raps lightly on the door of the master bedroom. He hears a stirring beyond the door and then the word "okay," a communication from the president that the First Lady had not slept in her husband's bedroom that night. If she had, like at the White House, the president's response would have been a cough if he didn't want to disturb her in her slumber.

"Mr. President," the portly black valet calls gently, then pushes the door open and steps across the threshold.

"It's raining," Thomas says.

A voice, with a distinctive Boston accent, groans from under the covers, "That's too bad."[30]

President John F. Kennedy throws back the comforter and swings his legs over the side of the bed, planting his feet on the icy floor. His first appearance of the day is out of doors, and later, several motorcades are planned—useless for vote-getting if the president and his wife have to be driven past sodden, disgruntled crowds, hidden beneath the limousine's plastic bubble top. While the president showers, Thomas lays out his clothes—a blue-gray, two-button suit, a dark blue tie, and a white shirt with narrow gray stripes.[31]

If, for a few moments in this blandly impersonal hotel room, he seems like just another American head of a household getting up to go to work, that's an illusion, for Jack Kennedy is the chief executive of the most powerful government on earth, the commander of its most powerful military machine, the most powerful man alive. Even the impression that this nondescript eighth-floor suite* in Fort Worth is far from the White House is an illusion. The White House is there, in the hotel with him, in the suite, never beyond the sound of Jack Kennedy's voice. To make sure that none of the far-flung people and agencies of the American government are out of range of that voice, an elite group of Signal Corps technicians from the White House Communications Agency travels ahead of the president to install a jungle of special telephone circuits, relays, and networks that are tied back to the key switchboard in the east basement of the executive mansion, and Jack Kennedy is never allowed to be more than five minutes away from that network.

Many of his enormous entourage are already awake and waiting for him to emerge from the shower. Some who watched through the night, like the nine Secret Service agents of the White House detail† on the twelve-to-eight shift, will sleep only after passing their responsibilities on to the next shift. John F. Kennedy's presidency is in fact a collection of special teams that never sleep, teams with code names: an S team for communications, a D team for the Secret Service, a W team for the president's staff, a V team for the vice president's staff. The L team is the president and his family—Jack is Lancer, Jackie is Lace, their children Lyric and Lark, and they all live in the Crown (or Castle), a code name for the White House. There are political advisers, medical men, the military, secretarial pools, and a luggage crew, and every individual has a precisely worked-out itinerary and schedule specifying his transportation, accommodations, and duties for every moment of the three-day trip through Texas.[32]

A peculiarly inconspicuous but nonetheless vivid symbol of the pres-

---

*It was not the most expensive and plush suite in the hotel. That was the Will Rogers Suite on the thirteenth floor, normally going for $100 a night, but rejected by the Secret Service because there was more than one access to it. So LBJ and Lady Bird stayed in that suite. (Gun, *Red Roses from Texas*, p.24)

†Twenty-eight Secret Service agents accompanied the president on his trip to Texas (HSCA Report, p.228).

ident's power is Warrant Officer Ira D. Gearhart, the man with the "satchel," or the "football." The football is a locked metal suitcase jammed with thirty pounds of codes and equipment that Kennedy can use to launch America's nuclear strike force. In the event of a missile attack on America or Europe the president will have only fifteen minutes to make up his mind on how to respond. Kennedy's military aides will actually operate the equipment, but it is Gearhart's lugubrious duty to be there with the football—and to remember the combination of the lock—if Kennedy decides to push the button. Gearhart, known to the president's staff as "The Bagman," is never far from the president.[33]

7:52 a.m.

In Dallas, the drizzle from a gray sky has stopped by the time Wesley Frazier and Lee Oswald exit Stemmons Freeway. The Pacific cold front that rolled in from New Mexico last night is moving faster than predicted and is already on the way out of central Texas, taking its scattered thundershowers with it. The air behind it is cold, but it looks as though the day will turn fair after all.[34]

Wesley circles around up Record Street to McKinney and down to the wire-fenced parking lot reserved for employees at the corner of Munger and Broadway, across the street from the Texas School Book Depository Warehouse. It's about a twelve-hundred-foot walk back to the Depository's rear door, but they'll be able to get there for the workday, which starts at 8:00 a.m. and ends at 4:45 p.m., with a forty-five-minute lunch period starting at noon.[35]*

Lee gets out, takes his package from the backseat, and starts toward the rear of the Depository Building. Wesley stays in the car for a minute or so to rev the engine so his car battery will have a good charge when they quit

---

*The Texas School Book Depository Company had two buildings: an administrative office and storage area at 411 Elm Street (at Houston), and a warehouse four blocks north at 1917 North Houston (between Munger and McKinney). Parking lot 1, designated for "employees and publishers," was located across the street from the warehouse (Frazier parked there). Parking lots 2 ("company officials and customers") and 3 ("publishers and managers") were located on the west side of the Depository Building.

work. Trains are switching back and forth in the train yards off to the west. Lee waits for him at the end of the cyclone fence, and Wesley notices that Lee is carrying the long, paper package in his right hand.[36] When Wesley cuts the engine and gets out, Lee starts off toward the Depository again. As Wesley begins to follow, Oswald quickens his pace, keeping an ever-increasing distance between them. It's the first time that Lee has walked ahead of him; usually they walk together.[37]

Wesley doesn't bother to catch up. They've got plenty of time and he likes to watch the switch engines shunting freight cars around the yards. He stops to watch some guys welding a section of track. You have to be careful crossing the tracks here, because you never know when a string of boxcars might be bearing down on you. Wesley steps over the rusty rails, avoiding the puddles, and spots Lee, fifty feet ahead, still carrying the package, as he goes in the back door of the Depository, the one near the Houston Street loading dock. By the time Wesley gets there, Lee is nowhere in sight. Wesley goes downstairs, hangs up his coat, puts up his lunch, and goes to work filling orders for schoolbooks.[38]

8:00 a.m.

In a Fort Worth hotel bathroom, the president can hear the murmur of the crowd awaiting him eight floors below as he drags a razor across his face. In the mirror he looks good. He has to. Americans want their president to be the picture of robust health. They will never know how much it costs him to give them that image. Although muscular and well developed, the president has been bedeviled all his life by an endless series of debilitating illnesses, starting in his early childhood when he had all the traditional childhood illnesses, including scarlet fever, as well as high fevers and allergies. "Jack was sick all the time," a boyhood friend would say. He was thirty before the doctors figured out that most of his health problems stemmed from Addison's disease, an extremely grave disorder of the adrenal glands that weakens the immune system, leaving the victim unable to fight off infection. The first crisis occurred on a trip to England in 1947. The British doctor who first diagnosed the disease in Kennedy gave him a year to live. He was taken off the ship that brought him home, the *Queen Mary*, on a stretcher, so near death that he had to be given the Catholic Church's sacrament of extreme unction—the last rites.[39]

Even though the disease has been brought under control by a relatively new (1939) hormone derived from the adrenal gland, cortisone, the hormone causes odd fat deposits, such as a slight upper-back "buffalo hump" and full cheeks, both of which the president exhibited, and he is forced to keep himself well tanned to hide its typical brownish discoloration of the skin. His frequent bouts of fever are explained away as recurrences of the malaria he caught during the war. In fact, he is extremely prone to infection and takes various medications, including painkillers, every day— including some that had never been prescribed by his White House doctors[40] and might earn anyone else a stretch in jail.

The most painful of his multiple disabilities is his back, which never ceases tormenting him and even causes him to use crutches or a cane in private.[41] One of his shoes has a quarter-inch riser in it, he wears a stiff, six-inch-wide elastic corset to immobilize his lower back, and he sleeps on a special bedboard of thick plywood with a five-inch horsehair pad. Two of these Spartan devices follow him wherever he goes. By 1954, Kennedy's back pain "had become almost unbearable. X-rays showed that the 5th lumbar vertebra had collapsed, most likely the consequence of the corticosteroids he was taking for the Addison's disease. He could not bend down to pull a sock on his left foot and he had to climb and descend stairs moving sideways."[42] In 1954, he again was given the last rites when he fell into a coma after a risky operation to fuse the deteriorating vertebrae— with no better than a fifty-fifty chance of surviving. Because of his condition, the family has stashed small quantities of deoxycorticosterone acetate, or DOCA, the powerful corticoid drug that might save his life in the event of another crisis, in safe deposit boxes all over America.[43] His brother Robert, the attorney general, is one of the few who knows that Jack spends half the hours of his life in pain.[*]

---

[*]Presidential historian Robert Dallek, the first scholar to examine Kennedy's medical records on file at the Kennedy presidential library in Boston, reported in 2002 that Kennedy had

The president finishes shaving and begins the arduous task of wrapping himself firmly in his back brace.[44] As he slips on his shirt, he decides to have a look at the crowd in the parking lot eight floors below. He can't see them from where he is, so he tiptoes into his wife's bedroom.

"Gosh, look at the crowd!" he beams.

About five thousand people are down there, hemmed in by two loan companies, two bus stations, a garage, a theater, and mounted police in rain-wet yellow slickers. The politician in him is pleased. It looks like a great crowd, mostly working men—Texas senator Ralph Yarborough's constituency—tough men who don't mind a bit of rain, with a few secretaries from nearby office buildings. They had begun to gather about two hours before dawn to see and hear the president. He appreciates every opportunity to show himself to ordinary people. He needs every one of their votes. He tells Jackie he'll see her later at breakfast in the hotel, where he is meeting with the Fort Worth Chamber of Commerce. In the meantime she can catch another hour of sleep.[45]

---

nine previously undisclosed hospital stays between 1955 and 1957 and took a substantial amount of medication during his presidency on a daily basis. Included on the list were painkillers for his back, steroids for his Addison's disease, antispasmodics for his colitis, antibiotics for urinary-tract infections, antihistamines for allergies, and, on at least one occasion, an antipsychotic for a severe mood change that Mrs. Kennedy believed was brought on by the antihistamines. According to Dallek, three doctors were treating Kennedy, including the famous "Dr. Feelgood," Max Jacobson, who was giving him amphetamine shots during his first summit with Soviet premier Nikita Khrushchev. Although Dallek suggested that Kennedy and his advisers had recklessly deceived the public by not telling voters in 1960 just how sick he really was, Ted Sorenson, one of Kennedy's closest advisers, and reporter Hugh Sidey, who followed Kennedy from 1957 to 1963, denied that the president's medication kept him from performing his duties. Both reported that the president never faltered during the grueling 1960 presidential campaign, one that left them, and everyone else, absolutely exhausted. Sidey wrote that the newly released medical records were indisputable, "but they don't give the whole picture and do leave the impression that Kennedy was little more than a chemical shell ready to self-destruct. I have my doubts. John Kennedy was a strong, determined President partly handicapped by a weakened body. But he was never an invalid." In 1970, long before Dallek's revelations, Kennedy's two closest assistants, Kenneth P. O'Donnell and David F. Powers, wrote of Kennedy's "tireless energy and stamina which wore out everybody following him on an average eight-hour day of campaigning." (Lawrence K. Altman and Todd S. Purdom, "In J.F.K. File, Hidden Illness, Pain and Pills," *New York Times*, November 17, 2002, pp.1, 28; see also Dallek, *Unfinished Life*, pp.213, 262, 398–399, 471; Lacayo, "How Sick Was J.F.K.?" pp.46–47; Sidey, "When It Counted, He Never Faltered," pp.46–47; Peggy Noonan, "Camelot on Painkillers," *Wall Street Journal*, November 22, 2002, p.A12; O'Donnell and Powers with McCarthy, *Johnny, We Hardly Knew Ye*, p.116)

Jackie is still recovering from the death of their infant son Patrick, who died just forty hours after his birth in August. Only those close to the First Family know how devastating the loss was for both of them. Jack had wept hard, and in his grief had put his arms around the small white casket at the grave site. Jackie didn't leave the hospital until four days after the funeral, and her emotional convalescence was long. Once, when Jack was comforting her, she told him, "There's just one thing I couldn't stand—if I ever lost you."[46]

Jackie has tried hard to put the trauma of that sorrowful event behind her, and even though she has never campaigned with him before, the dark-haired beauty with a European elegance who disdains the vulgarity of politics can muster a practical gesture on occasion, and she volunteered to make this trip to Texas. To everyone's delight, she actually seems to be enjoying herself, prompting the president to ask her if she would like to accompany him on a forthcoming trip to the West Coast, and she said yes. After leaving the White House the previous morning, the president and Jackie had flown to San Antonio, where Vice President Johnson and his wife, Lady Bird, joined the presidential party, and the president had dedicated new research facilities at the U.S. Air Force School of Aerospace Medicine. The four had then flown to Houston in the late afternoon for a testimonial dinner that evening for U.S. Representative Albert Thomas. (There had been motorcades through both San Antonio and Houston.) They arrived in Fort Worth after 11:00 p.m., leaving very little time to sleep and get ready for another vigorous day that would end that night with a fund-raising dinner in Austin. Then back to Washington, D.C., on Saturday morning in time for their son John-John's third birthday on Monday.[47] Jack is grateful to Jackie for accompanying him on the trip and being such a trooper. He knows her presence is an enormous plus, but doesn't want to put her under any more strain than absolutely necessary. He slips out of her bedroom and quietly pulls the door shut.

The president, who loves a good cigar from time to time, reaches a friend, James Chambers Jr., on the phone. "Can you get me some Macanudo cigars?" Kennedy asks. "They don't have any over here in Fort

Worth." Chambers, president of the *Dallas Times Herald*, is delighted to hear from the president and answers, "Sure." "Well, get me about a half a dozen." "Fine," Chambers says. He goes to the United Cigar store in Dallas and gets the president six expensive Macanudo cigars. He'll give them to the president at the luncheon scheduled that day at the Trade Mart.[48] The president finishes a light breakfast consisting of coffee and a roll, and is knotting his tie and fastening it with the obligatory PT 109 tie clip when David F. Powers, one of his closest friends and confidants, enters the suite. The president lets him know how thrilled he is over the crowd awaiting him below, speaks of the great crowds in San Antonio and Houston yesterday, and the brilliant reception accorded Jackie, who is turning into the star of the whole show. It seems that most of the crowds have come to see her rather than the president.[49]

8:30 a.m.
Brigadier General Godfrey McHugh, Kennedy's air force aide, comes into the president's suite with the CIA situation report on Saigon, Cyprus, and Korea, which the president looks over. He also scans the leading metropolitan dailies.[50]

The news for November 22, 1963, is pretty light: a Labour victory in a British by-election; a Soviet note complaining about American convoys to Berlin; the death of the "Birdman of Alcatraz" at the age of seventy-three; the trial of Jimmy Hoffa in Nashville—brother Bobby's doing; and the removal of a portrait of the president from an American Legion Post wall in Abilene because he is "controversial." The crucial news—for a president all too aware that his trip to the South to shore up support for next year's election, and how he is received in Texas, represent the real beginning of the campaign for his reelection—is the squabble in the Texas Democratic Party between its conservative and liberal wings.

An editorial in the *Chicago Sun-Times* confirms his instinct about the value on this matter of the enthusiastic reception Jackie has received thus far on the Texas trip: "Some Texans, in taking account of the tangled Texas political situation, have begun to think that Mrs. Jacqueline Kennedy may turn the balance and win her husband this state's electoral vote." Other papers are less reassuring. The front-page headline stories in the *Dallas Morning News* hammer the point home: "Storm of Political Controversy Swirls around Kennedy on Visit"; "Yarborough Snubs LBJ"; and "President's Visit Seen Widening State Democratic Split."[51] But one of the main purposes behind the Texas trip was to narrow this split, bridge the gap between the two factions, which would help not only the Democratic Party in Texas, but, with a united front, Kennedy's own reelection effort in the state.[52*]

In recent days and weeks, although Dallas's morning paper has been carrying plenty in its front pages about the widening chasm in the state's Democratic Party, the paper's emphasis this morning in its lead editorial is simple, extending a welcoming hand to the young president as he arrives in a city, it says, "with a substantial Republican representation."[53] The previous day, former vice president Richard Nixon, in town for a bottler's convention, urged Dallas residents to give President and Mrs. Kennedy "a courteous reception."[54] United States Attorney Barefoot Sanders says he is investigating whether certain scurrilous leaflets—apparently mugshots of Kennedy captioned "Wanted For Treason,"[55] five thousand of which appeared on the streets the previous day and that morning—violate federal laws. Dallas police chief Jesse E. Curry says anybody caught distributing them will be arrested for littering,[56] and in a press conference on Wednesday, November 20, says that "nothing must occur that is disrespectful or degrading to the President of the United States. He is entitled to the highest respect, and the law enforcement agencies of this area are going to do everything possible to insure that no untoward incident" takes place. "We will take immediate action if any suspicious conduct is observed, and we also urge all good

*The *Dallas Morning News*, Texas's largest circulation daily at the time, with a readership of over a quarter of a million, was no friend of JFK's, its editorials consistently being anti-Kennedy because of the right-wing inclination of its publisher, E. M. "Ted" Dealey. Indeed, in a White House meeting in the autumn of 1961 between Kennedy and a contingent of Texas media leaders, Dealey bluntly told JFK, "You and your administration are weak sisters," adding that the country needed "a man on horseback to lead the nation, and many people in Texas and the Southwest think that you are riding Caroline's tricycle." (Aynesworth with Michaud, *JFK: Breaking the News*, pp.6–7)

citizens to be alert for such conduct . . . Citizens themselves may take preventative action if it becomes obvious that someone is planning to commit an act harmful or degrading to the president . . . I am sure that all but a handful of our citizens will cordially welcome the president of the United States to Dallas." Curry said 350 Dallas policemen, about a third of the force, would be assigned to the Kennedy guard detail, and this would be supplemented by forty state police and fifteen Dallas deputy sheriffs. Police officials said it was the largest security detail ever assembled in Dallas.[57]*

The businessmen of Dallas, not natural Kennedy supporters, have nonetheless made it clear to Curry that they want his eleven-hundred-man force to do everything possible to ensure that there be no incidents, however trivial, during the presidential visit. A front-page article in the *Dallas Morning News* of November 17, 1963, was captioned "Incident-Free Day Urged for JFK Visit," and quoted Dallas leaders such as the president of the Dallas Chamber of Commerce and the county Republican chairman asking Dallas citizens to put aside politics and accord the president of the United States a very warm and hospitable welcome. Dallas, a notorious hotbed for right-wing conservatives, simply couldn't afford any repetition of last month's Stevenson incident. What happened to UN Ambassador Adlai Stevenson in Dallas shocked America and gave Dallas a black eye. On October 24, UN Day, after speaking optimistically about world peace through the United Nations to an audience of five thousand people, Stevenson was jeered by a mob of unruly demonstrators, hit in the head with an anti-UN picket sign carried by a woman, and spat upon as he left Dallas's municipal auditorium and was being escorted to his limousine.[58] The following day, one hundred Dallas civic and business leaders sent a telegram to Stevenson apologizing profusely and saying the city was

*Ultimately, 447 Dallas police officers were used on specific assignments associated with the president's visit, 178 of them assigned to the motorcade route. The biggest assignment (one would think inappropriately from a priority standpoint) was to the Trade Mart, where 63 were assigned to work the parking area outside and 150 under the command of a deputy chief were to provide security inside. (King Exhibit No. 5, 20 H 464)

"outraged and abjectly ashamed of the disgraceful discourtesies you suffered at the hands of a small group of extremists."[59] Mayor Earle Cabell lashed out at the "right wing fanatics" responsible for the Stevenson incident, saying these "so-called patriots" were "not conservatives" but "radicals" who had become "a cancer in the body politic."[60]

And it's not just the lunatic right-wing fringe that was capable of the Stevenson kind of incident. Back in 1960, then-senator Lyndon Johnson (years before his civil rights legislation, when few perceived him as liberal) and his wife Lady Bird had been spat upon at Dallas's Adolphus hotel—and the Johnsons were Texans. Some members of Kennedy's staff opposed his visiting Dallas, being the cauldron of conservatism it was, and indeed the state itself, much of Texas not being favorably disposed to the president. And Stevenson, as well as Byron Skelton, the National Democratic committeeman from Texas, urged Kennedy not to make the trip. From 1961 to 1962, the Secret Service had recorded thirty-four threats on the president's life from Texas.[61]

Kennedy overlooks another article about Nixon in the same paper—"Nixon Predicts JFK May Drop Johnson."* Jack Kennedy, though elected by a mere handful of votes over Nixon in 1960 (Kennedy's margin of victory was one-tenth of 1 percent, receiving 34,221,355 votes to Nixon's 34,109,398), has nevertheless been popular with most Americans from the beginning of his administration. His approval rating soared to 83 percent in April 1961, ironically in the wake of his biggest failure, the abortive invasion of Cuba at the Bay of Pigs. By now, though, three years after his election, it has slumped to 59 percent. Just last month, in October, *Newsweek* estimated that Kennedy's pro-black position on the civil rights issue had cost him 3.5 million votes and reported that no Democratic president had ever been so disliked in the South. In Georgia the

---

*In the spring of 1964, Robert Kennedy stated, "There was no plan to dump Lyndon Johnson. It didn't make any sense . . . And there was never any discussion about dropping him." The president himself told a close confidant in October 1963 that the idea of dumping Johnson was "preposterous on the face of it. We've got to carry Texas in '64, and maybe Georgia." (Schlesinger, *Robert Kennedy and His Times*, p.605)

marquee of a movie theater showing the film *PT 109* read, "See how the Japs almost got Kennedy."[62] Indeed, less than two months earlier, the chairman of the Georgia Democratic Party had persuaded JFK to cancel a speech in Atlanta because of the political climate in his state resulting from JFK's pending civil rights bill.[63] However, Kennedy did include Florida on the trip that took him to Dallas, since Florida had gone Republican in 1960.[64] The South, overwhelmingly Democratic in presidential elections since the Reconstruction era following the Civil War, was more conservative than any other region of the country. But the long-standing distrust by southerners for the Republican Party (northern Republicans were largely responsible for Reconstruction, which brought the former Confederate states back into the United States and was unpopular in the South) was showing signs everywhere of melting away.

Kennedy can ill afford to lose those southern votes to Barry Goldwater, the conservative senator from Arizona who appears to have a lock on the Republican nomination for president. Texas voted for Kennedy over Nixon in 1960 by a mere 46,233 votes out of more than two million cast (he lost in Dallas, the only large American city to vote for Nixon over Kennedy), mostly owing to Lyndon Johnson's presence on the ticket. Texas, being conservative, had voted for Eisenhower in 1952 and 1956.[65] Texas's senior senator, Ralph Yarborough, also accounted for a lot of votes by appealing to the state's dwindling, old-style liberals and unionists. Texas, three years later, now looks weak for the Kennedy ticket, and it is Kennedy's own suggestion and desire to come to Texas to raise money and to try to appeal to the business community (which was suspicious of him) and the conservative wing of the Democratic Party, thereby enhancing his political fortunes there.[66] He couldn't have a better forum to appeal to that group than at the luncheon that noon. The Dallas Citizens Council, an informal organization of the leading businessmen of Dallas which had been a "behind-the-scenes force in Dallas affairs" for years, was the main sponsor of the luncheon.[67] Governor Connally tells his wife and others, "Nellie, if the people of Texas can just get a look at him, up close, I know they will vote for him."[68]

However, Johnson, Connally (Johnson's conservative protégé and ally), and the liberal Yarborough are at each other's throats, hacking the Democratic Party right down the middle. If they and their factions cannot be reconciled soon, or at least made to look as though they are, the Democrats could lose all twenty-five of the state's electoral votes in the 1964 election, an unthinkable disaster.

Kennedy, angered by the story which suggests that his visit is widening the split in the state's party, grabs the phone to call Kenneth P. O'Donnell, one of his principal political advisers and the one responsible for all the arrangements of the Texas trip. O'Donnell, whose official title is appointments secretary, is Kennedy's political right hand, troubleshooter, devil's advocate, and, per White House press secretary Pierre Salinger, "the most powerful member" of the president's staff.[69] Another member, Dave Powers, has been with Kennedy the longest, ever since he emerged from Boston's Eleventh District to back young Jack's first campaign for the Senate in 1946, one of several young World War II veterans who helped shape the "new generation" rhetoric that Kennedy continues to employ into the 1960s.[70] O'Donnell and Larry O'Brien are of more recent vintage, dating from the 1952 senatorial campaign which saw the creation of the "Kennedy machine." O'Donnell, one of Bobby's classmates and friends at Harvard, where he captained the football team, has a reputation for cool, ruthless efficiency that rivals Bobby's own, and Jack means to employ it now.[71]

Kennedy has had enough of the childish antics of Connally, Yarborough, and Johnson. For weeks, ever since the Texas trip was first suggested, the three of them have been arm wrestling each other for the symbolic trappings of political power, freezing each other out of seats at ceremonial dinners, refusing each other places in the Texas trip motorcades, and bending the president's itinerary to suit their own agendas and to humiliate their rivals. None of this has gone unnoticed by the Texas papers, which are watching and reporting on the day-to-day ups and downs of the embattled Yarborough: "Yarborough Seating Pondered"; "Yarborough Gets JFK Table Spot"; "Yarborough Invited to Travel with JFK"; "Demo Factions to Be Pacified, Salinger Says"; "New Fuss Erupts over JFK Tickets."[72]

Kennedy may indeed have widened the rift between Johnson and

Yarborough when he acceded to Johnson's demand for half of Yarborough's senatorial patronage—the right to select judges, postmasters, and other presidential appointments in Texas—but the quarrel has to end now, before it brings the Texas party down with it. Kennedy orders O'Donnell to tell Yarborough to get in the vice president's limousine today. O'Donnell and O'Brien have to make it clear to the senator that he no longer has any choice.

"You tell him," Kennedy barks at O'Donnell, "it's ride with Lyndon or walk."[73]

8:50 a.m.

The president starts down to the parking lot, meeting Fort Worth congressman Jim Wright and his party in the corridor. He speaks briefly to his Secret Service bodyguards who fall in behind him, pauses for a word with an elderly woman in a wheelchair, and graciously offers to be introduced to some Dallas friends of his personal secretary, Evelyn Lincoln.

As the president moves toward the parking lot, his entourage snowballs. He picks up Vice President Johnson, Governor Connally, Senator Yarborough, several congressmen, and Raymond Buck, president of the Fort Worth Chamber of Commerce. Bill Greer, his veteran Secret Service driver, dashes up with the president's raincoat—it's drizzling again—but Kennedy shrugs it off. He walks out under the marquee that reads "Welcome, Mr. President" and "Welcome to Fort Worth, where the West begins,"[74] and around to the parking lot to mount the flatbed truck awaiting him there.[75]

After a brief introduction by the vice president, Jack Kennedy steps to the microphone to address the crowd that has waited in the rain for three and a half hours to see him. "There are no faint hearts in Fort Worth!" he says gaily to the crowd, which manages a cheer in spite of the drizzle. "Mrs. Kennedy is [still] organizing herself. It takes her a little longer"—the crowd breaks into laughter as the president grins broadly—"but, of course, she looks better than we do when she does it."[76]

Upstairs in her bedroom, Jackie hears her husband's voice booming over the public address system. She is glad it is still raining. She hopes the

Plexiglas bubble top will be on the presidential limousine for the noon motorcade in Dallas. Then her hair won't get mussed in the open car. She sits at her dressing table and looks into the mirror. She looks tired.

"Oh, God," she moans to an attendant, "one day's campaigning can age a person thirty years."[77]

9:10 a.m.

Bolstered by the enthusiastic Fort Worth crowds, the president reenters the hotel and climbs aboard the elevator to take him to the next event on the schedule, a formal breakfast. However, in the elevator, Acting Press Secretary Malcolm Kilduff[*] persuades Kennedy to make a slight detour. Kilduff has read the newspapers and shares the president's political concerns. To improve the situation, he has convinced Governor Connally to hold a press conference and thought that the president might want to discuss it with the governor first. The president agrees and is escorted to the Longhorn Room, down the mezzanine from the Grand Ballroom, where hundreds of breakfast guests await his presence.

Kennedy reviews the governor's prepared statement and finds it rather bland and meaningless. Nevertheless, the president endorses it and returns to the hallway, where he runs into Senator Yarborough and bluntly tells him to ride in the vice president's car. When the senator starts to object, the president lets him have it.

"For Christ's sake cut it out, Ralph," he snaps. Yarborough responds that he *had* ridden to the hotel with Johnson. Kennedy shook his head. It wasn't good enough. He had no intention of being thwarted by evasions.

The president turns and makes his way into the kitchen of the Grand Ballroom, leaving the chastised senator to lick his wounds. For a moment, the entourage stands wedged between a corridor of stainless-steel sinks and gigantic pots and pans. Kennedy looks over his shoulder. One member is missing.

---

[*]Kilduff was the acting press secretary in the absence of Pierre Salinger, who was en route to Hawaii at the time of the assassination.

"Where's Mrs. Kennedy?" he asks a nearby Secret Service agent. "Call Mr. Hill. I want her to come down to the breakfast."

The guests in the Grand Ballroom are on their tiptoes, straining their necks in the direction of the kitchen entrance. Amid a spattering of applause, Governor Connally, Vice President Johnson, Senator Yarborough, and other dignitaries file into the ballroom. As they stand at attention at the head table, the band breaks into the familiar "Hail to the Chief," and a smiling John F. Kennedy strolls into the ballroom. Now the cheers are loud and sustained, although many present must be disappointed that the First Lady is not with him.[78]

Upstairs, Jackie Kennedy is putting the finishing touches to her outfit, a navy blue blouse and matching purse and a rose pink suit with a navy collar and matching pink pillbox hat. The president wants her to be elegant in Dallas and she means to be, although it does take time. She wavers over two pairs of white gloves, one short and one long. She decides the short ones are more restrained, and holds up her wrists while her attendant buttons them for her. She has become so preoccupied with the idea of going to Dallas that she forgets all about the breakfast reception downstairs. When the elevator arrives at the mezzanine floor, she is confused.

"Aren't we leaving?" she asks Secret Service agent Clint Hill, who accompanies her on the ride down.

"No, you're going to a breakfast," he says.[79]

9:20 a.m.

In the Grand Ballroom, the anticipation that the First Lady may appear is tremendous. The crowd has been keeping an eye on the kitchen entrance throughout breakfast and the subsequent performance by the Texas Boys Choir. When toastmaster Raymond Buck spots Agent Hill peering from the kitchen entrance, he steps to the microphone at the head table and introduces the First Lady like a ringmaster: "And now—an event I know you have all been waiting for!" Buck sweeps his arm toward the kitchen door as Clint Hill leads Mrs. Kennedy into the ballroom. Two thousand businessmen and their wives leap to their feet and cheer enthusiastically. The First Lady spots her husband smiling from behind the

head table and is drawn toward him through the cheers and smiles of a
generous crowd. As the spontaneous response dies down, the president
is introduced and steps to the microphone.

"Two years ago I introduced myself in Paris as the man who had accompanied Mrs. Kennedy to Paris," he says. "I'm getting somewhat that same
sensation as I travel around Texas."*

The crowd cheers wildly as the president grins.

"Nobody wonders what Lyndon and I wear—"

A wave of laughter sweeps again over the crowd. The president is hitting all the right notes and the guests are loving every minute of it.[80]

After what one reporter described as a "ripsnorting political speech"†
by the president, in which he emphasized national defense,‡ the president
of the Fort Worth Chamber of Commerce provides a jovial moment when
he presents the President and First Lady with parting gifts. "Mr. President, we couldn't let you leave Fort Worth without providing you with
some protection against the rain," he says, and offers the president a ten-
gallon hat. The audience shouts for him to put it on. Jack, who dreaded
the idea of looking ridiculous, has always managed to avoid putting on a
cowboy hat, sombrero, or Indian headdress. He grins and dodges the gesture, responding, "I'll put it on in the White House on Monday. If you'll
come up there you'll have a chance to see it then."[81]

---

*The president's exaggeration was not great. Jacqueline Kennedy, traveling abroad to thir-
teen countries, alone or with the president, and speaking fluent French, Spanish, and Italian as
she went, "soon carved for herself a niche of fame" independent of JFK. Described by many as
beautiful, cultured, and imperious, "she drew crowds by the thousands and became a good-will
ambassador for America on her own." (Associated Press, November 26, 1963)

†Kennedy had unquestionably become an effective politician, but unlike most in his chosen
profession, he wasn't inordinately ambitious, was famous for never taking himself too seriously,
and once said that he only started in politics "because Joe died. [Joseph P. Kennedy Jr., JFK's
older brother, was the one of the four sons of Joe Sr. who was being groomed for high political
office; he and his copilot died during the Second World War when their plane, laden with explo-
sives to be dropped on a German bomb-launching base in France, exploded in midair over the
English Channel on August 12, 1944.] If something happened to me tomorrow, my brother Bobby
would run for my seat in the Senate. And if Bobby died, Teddy would take over for him." (*New
York Times*, November 23, 1963, p.13)

‡The president received a long, standing ovation when he referred to the controversial TFX
jet fighter, built at the General Dynamics plant in Fort Worth, as a powerful force for freedom
(*Dallas Morning News*, November 23, 1963, p.11).

9:45 a.m.

Lee Harvey Oswald ostensibly continues to go about his work. His job is
to pick up orders for schoolbooks on the first floor, fix them to his clipboard, take one of the two big freight elevators at the back of the Depository Building up to the sixth floor, search out the requested books from
the thousands of titles stored there, take them back down in the elevator
to the order desk on the first floor for eventual shipping, and pick up the
next lot of orders. He's a human conveyor belt, not particularly distin-
guishable from the fourteen other "order fillers," or stock boys in the
warehouse crew.[82] But this particular morning, only one order was known
to have been worked on by Oswald.[83]

The Texas School Book Depository Company is, in spite of the official
ring to its name, private, with no connection to the state of Texas. The
seven-story building, which has been occupied by the company since January of 1962, is an old, rust-colored brick structure at the corner of Elm
and Houston, not the original building at this location. That building,
erected in 1883, was home to the Southern Rock Island Plow Company.
In 1901, the building was struck by lightning and almost burned to the
ground. It was rebuilt that same year to look identical to the previous structure, only the new building had seven stories instead of five.[84]*

In view of the enormous number of titles handled by the company, the
stock boys tend to specialize. Since starting work at the Depository, Lee
has been focusing on the books of Scott, Foresman & Company, some of
which are kept on the first floor, which is handy to the shipping department, with the vast majority up on the sixth floor. The women in the office
write orders and drop them down a sort of dumbwaiter to the men below,
who carry them to a little table by the checking stand and sort them out
by publisher and location. If there aren't enough orders for Scott, Foresman & Company to keep him busy, Lee will fill orders for one of the

---

*For years prior to its occupancy by the Texas School Book Depository Company, when it
became known as the Texas School Book Depository Building after its principal occupant, the
building was known as the Sexton Building, and many old-timers continued to call it that for
years thereafter.

smaller publishers, like Gregg Publishing Company, but that doesn't happen often.[85]

Most of the people working in the Depository Building this day are not aware of Oswald, he goes about his work so unobtrusively. Lee's boss, Roy S. Truly, did happen to notice him earlier in the morning.

"Good morning, Lee."

"Good morning, sir," Lee answered.

Truly likes that, the word "sir," one which a lot of the other stock boys don't use. Truly is pleased with Lee, who is "quiet and well-mannered, a nice young fellow." The job is only temporary, but when he hired him, Truly assumed that Lee was just out of the Marines—Lee had mentioned no other employment history—and the young man certainly needed work, with his second child due shortly after he took the job. In fact, the baby was born at Dallas's Parkland Memorial Hospital just five days later. Mr. Truly remembers that well, because Lee asked for and got a few days' grace in filling out his withholding tax deduction form, which allowed him to claim the new dependent. Truly occasionally asked about the baby, and Lee would respond with a big smile, but that was about the extent of any conversation he'd ever had with him. Lee is a loner, working day after day on his own, taking the orders up, bringing the books down, keeping to himself, but that's fine with Roy Truly.[86]

One of the few other employees in the Depository who even notices Lee this morning is the order checker, James Jarman Jr. It's "Junior" Jarman's job to make sure the books brought down to the first floor by the order fillers match those on the order forms. He saw that Lee was already at work when he came in that morning around eight, and later had occasion to send him back upstairs to correct a botched order.[87]

It's between 9:30 and 10:00 a.m. when Jarman sees Lee at one of the windows between two of the long book bins on the first floor. Outside, people are already beginning to gather on the corner of Elm and Houston and Lee asks Jarman why. Jarman tells Lee they're picking spots to watch the presidential motorcade, which is supposed to pass right by the building this afternoon.

"Do you know which way he's coming?" Lee asks.

Junior explains that the motorcade will be coming down Main, turning right onto Houston, then left onto Elm, passing right under their windows.

"Oh, I see," Lee says, and walks off.[88]

10:15 a.m.

The president and his wife don't make it back to suite 850 until after ten o'clock, but find they have nearly an hour before the flight to Dallas. Kennedy takes time to call former vice president John Nance Garner to wish him a happy ninety-fifth birthday while Jackie spends a moment looking around the suite. She discovers something they were all too busy to notice until now, that the paintings aren't the usual by-the-yard hotel-room art, but real paintings—a Monet, a Picasso, a Van Gogh, a dozen others, and some bronzes, all borrowed from the local museum for the pleasure of America's First Couple. From a specially prepared catalog they find the name of the woman who made it all possible, Ruth Carter Johnson. The First Couple telephone Mrs. Johnson, the wife of a newspaper executive, and thank her for her kindness. Mrs. Johnson is both flabbergasted and touched by the graciousness of the gesture, one she will never forget.[89]

Ken O'Donnell shows the president what is at best a disrespectful advertisement in the *Dallas Morning News*. It's a full-page ad draped with a funeral black border, and headlined "WELCOME MR. KENNEDY TO DALLAS." Placed by the "American Fact-Finding Committee," chaired by one Bernard Weissman, the ad, with twelve questions for Kennedy, rapidly moves from inane innuendo—"WHY has Gus Hall, head of the U.S. Communist Party, praised almost every one of your policies and announced the party will endorse and support your re-election in 1964?"—to outright accusation of treason—"WHY has the Foreign Policy of the United States degenerated to the point that the C.I.A. is arranging coups and having staunch Anti-Communist Allies of the U.S. bloodily exterminated?"[90]

"Can you imagine a paper doing a thing like that?" Jack says to O'Donnell, and then, making light of it to Jackie, who is sickened by the hate behind the ad, he adds, "Oh, we're heading into nut country today."[91]

Of course, Jack Kennedy knows that the presidency is a vulnerable position, just as every chief of state is aware of the special hazards he faces, but he simply refuses to accept the notion that an American president can't go into any American city. He prowls the room restlessly.[92]

"It would not be a very difficult job to shoot the president of the United States," he says to nobody in particular. "All you'd have to do is get up in a high building with a high-powered rifle with a telescopic sight, and there's nothing anybody could do."[93]

10:30 a.m.

The motorcade that will take the presidential party to Fort Worth's Carswell Air Force Base—long lines of limousines, cars, and press vehicles stacked three abreast—is clogging Eighth Street. O'Donnell and O'Brien are lying in wait outside the hotel, determined to make sure Senator Yarborough gets into the car with the vice president, as the president has ordered.[94] They are relieved to see that the drizzle is finally clearing, and O'Brien even hopes for what he likes to call "Kennedy weather."

Vice President Johnson and his wife, Lady Bird, emerge from the Texas Hotel to a smattering of applause. O'Brien escorts them to the waiting convertible, with a grumpy Yarborough walking closely behind. The political orchestration pays off. When the motorcade finally pulls out just after eleven o'clock for the short drive to Carswell, a bit behind schedule, Senator Yarborough and the vice president are seen smiling and riding together by the media. Although neither man may be happy about the close contact, the needs of the Democratic Party have been served.[95]

11:00 a.m.

It usually takes Jack Ruby a good while to get going in the morning. For one thing, he is really meticulous about his physical appearance. In addition to his morning shower and shave, he takes care to dress in a good suit, tie, and hat. He tries to keep in shape too, exercising every day at the YMCA and working out with weights he keeps both at his office and in his apartment. Keeping up his appearance is a daily struggle. He worries about creeping baldness and his weight. He is five foot eight (five foot nine inches by some accounts), weighs 175 pounds, and is brawny in the arms and shoulders. He is always dieting, usually with the help of pills.[96]

It is around eleven before Ruby gets to the offices of the *Dallas Morning News* at the corner of Houston and Young streets.[97] The building is only five blocks from the Texas School Book Depository.[98] Since there are no high buildings on the west side of Houston, one can actually see the Depository Building from the northwest corner windows of the advertising department's second floor.[99]

The morning visit to the *News* is a regular Friday event for Jack, one he looks forward to. He takes particular pains composing the weekend ads in the classified-ad office of the *News* for his two clubs, because the weekend is "very lucrative," and Jack has a way of making his ads, as he says in his strange way of talking, "where they have a way of selling the product I am producing or putting on the show." It's not always easy to figure out what Jack is saying. "It's been a lovely, precarious evening," he might say, or, to an attractive woman, "You make me feel very irascible." A favorite expression is "In lieu of the situation, let's do this."[100]

On his way to the elevator in the lobby, he spots a *News* employee he's always friendly with and has recently dated, Gladys Craddock, who works in the classified-ad department on the first floor, and cheerily shouts out to her across the lobby, "Hi, the president is going to be here today."[101] He gets a quick breakfast in the building's cafeteria on the second floor[102]—part of his Friday routine.

Jack then saunters over to the advertising and promotion department, also on the second floor. He could walk around the department blindfolded. He knows its big bullpen for the ad-space salesmen, and the cubicles along the sides for the executives. He knows every employee, and he knows the routine: how to leave his ad copy in the box if John Newnam (not Newman), his designated salesman, isn't there and how to get help if he needs it in preparing his ad.

Newnam isn't there today. This morning a lot of the twenty-six ad salesmen are adjusting their schedules to take in the presidential motorcade when it cuts through the downtown on Main Street a few blocks away.[103]

The fact that Newnam isn't there is no problem for Jack. It gives him time to go up to Tony Zoppi's office on the third floor of the building.[104] Zoppi, the paper's nightclub editor, is one of Jack's preoccupations. He has known Zoppi for a dozen years—Zoppi will never forget being introduced to the audience in one of Ruby's clubs, the night they first met, and hearing Ruby explain how "superfluous" it was to have Tony Zoppi there.[105] Ruby is always trying to get Zoppi to mention his clubs in his daily column or his television show. That's worth far more than any amount of advertising, and what's more, it's free, while the ads have to be paid for in cash. At least Jack's ads do. His credit with the *News*, in spite of the fact that he's a steady customer, is not terrific. In fact, it's nonexistent.

Zoppi isn't there either—someone tells Jack he's in New Orleans for a couple of days—but Jack sees the brochure he left for Zoppi a few days before about the emcee at the Carousel, Bill DeMar. Jack is annoyed with Zoppi, who promised him a story, which amounted to a "build" of one or two lines. Picking up the brochure, Jack meanders back to Newnam's desk to work up the copy for his weekend ads when Don Campbell turns up to distract him.

Campbell is not just another ad-space salesman, but a friend and a colleague, so to speak. Campbell operates and manages the Stork Club, a supper club out on Oak Lawn across from another club called the Village, and they often talk shop. Jack particularly wants to apologize for the other evening, when Campbell came over to Jack and his friend, Ralph Paul, as they were having dinner at the Egyptian Lounge to invite them to come along with him to the nearby Castaway Club. Jack, still seething over the way the Castaway Club had once pirated his whole band from the Vegas, turned down the invitation, and now wants to be sure Campbell's feelings weren't hurt.

Jack has a lot on his mind: his troubles with Jada, the crazy stripper from New Orleans who's going to get him closed down if she doesn't clean up her act; the struggle to keep his two clubs afloat. Campbell has known Jack for three or four years, and it's not the first time he has heard Jack's complaints about the lousy business they are in, running nightclubs. Jack moans about the fights he gets into with what he regards as undesirable customers, "characters" or "punks," as he calls them. Fortunately, Jack is, he tells Campbell, a very capable fighter. Also, anytime he is fixing to have trouble with someone, he gets a gun and keeps it on his person.

Neither Campbell nor Ruby mentions the presidential motorcade, which will be passing within four blocks of the *News* building in a few minutes. When Campbell goes off to see another client about 12:25, Jack is still sitting at Newnam's desk, working on his ad copy.[106]

11:25 a.m.

The flight from Carswell Air Force Base in Fort Worth to Love Field, Dallas's airport, is just thirty miles and takes but thirteen minutes. The presidential party could easily have driven the distance in half an hour, but presidential aide Ken O'Donnell vetoed that. It would cut out the welcome at the airport for the president and Jackie, and O'Donnell knows that the airport arrival, with the inevitable cameras recording the enthusiasm of the crowd, is as important to modern political campaigns as all those whistlestop appearances on the rear platform of the cross-country train were to Harry Truman's astonishing upset victory in 1948.

Short as the flight is, O'Donnell and the president use the fleeting minutes to put the squeeze, as O'Donnell puts it, on Governor Connally, who is aligned with LBJ against Yarborough in the state's Democratic bloodletting. The president motions at Texas congressman Albert Thomas from the doorway of his cabin and asks him to "give Kenny a hand with Connally." Thomas is glad to oblige, and the governor begins to wilt under their pressure.

Senator Yarborough was particularly incensed about a deadly slight Governor Connally had in store for him—after selling $11,200 in tickets to tomorrow night's dinner in Austin, there was no place for his wife. Worse, he hadn't been invited to the Connally's formal reception for the Kennedys.[107]

"It was my wife who didn't want the senator at the reception, not me," Connally tells O'Donnell and Thomas, taking advantage of Nellie's temporary absence. "She said she wouldn't let that man in her house, and when your wife says something like that, what can you do?"

At a strategic moment O'Donnell nudges the governor and the senator into the president's cabin, and watches his boss expertly wield the
overwhelming Kennedy charm to solve the problem in three minutes. The
governor finds himself agreeing not only to invite Senator Yarborough to
the reception at the Governor's Mansion, but to seat him at the head table
for the dinner.

The president, who has already changed suits once that morning,
excuses himself to change his shirt. The governor mutters to the smug
O'Donnell, "How can anyone say no to that man?"

"So we land in Dallas with everybody on the plane in love with each
other and the sun shining brightly," O'Donnell thinks. The day is looking up.[108]

11:40 a.m.

Air Force One, code-named Angel, touches down at Love Field, just
north of downtown Dallas, and rolls across the puddled tarmac to the
red and green terminal building.[109]* The last U.S. Weather Bureau temperature reading at Love Field, at 10:55 a.m., was fifty-seven degrees.
But by the next reading, at 11:55, sixteen minutes after the president
arrived, it had risen to sixty-three degrees.[110] The president is pleased at
his first glimpse of the waiting crowd from the plane's window. He says
to O'Donnell, "This trip is turning out to be terrific. Here we are in
Dallas, and it looks like everything in Texas is going to be fine for us."[111]

The stage directions for the airport welcome call for the vice president's
plane to land ahead of the president's by a minute or two, enough time
to allow Johnson and his wife to position themselves to greet President

---

*The $8.6 million Boeing 707 jet, tail number SAM26000, was delivered to the air force on
October 10, 1962. Though not the first Air Force One, it is the first jet aircraft designed specifically for presidents, JFK being the first one to make extensive use of a jet for presidential travel.
(James Sawa, "JFK Air Force One: Conspiracy or Not," self-published, 2004) When JFK first
saw the new Air Force One, he exclaimed, "It's magnificent! I'll take it." President Gerald Ford
would later say, "When they fly you on Air Force One, you know you're the president." (Ter-
Horst and Albertazzie, *Flying White House*, p.13)

and Mrs. Kennedy at the foot of the ramp, as though they hadn't just left them a quarter hour earlier in Fort Worth.[112]

Aura, though a reality, cannot be adequately described. It just is. And JFK's aura was legendary. Reporting live for radio KBOX in Dallas, reporter Ron Jenkins waits for the door to Air Force One to open. When it does, no one emerges for several moments. "And then all of a sudden President Kennedy appeared," he would later recall. "And he had a way of doing this like no one I had ever seen before. And it was a presence bigger than life. I never knew how tall the man was, or anything else, but he looked about 7 feet tall when he came out of that door all by himself."[113] Unwittingly, Jenkins's words contained their own validation. He was so struck by Kennedy he had forgotten that Jackie Kennedy, someone few overlooked, had emerged from the plane door ahead of the president.

Texas governor John Connally and his wife, Nellie, followed Kennedy and Jackie down the stairs of Air Force One in the dazzling sunlight. "We were two couples in the prime of our lives," Nellie Connally recalled. "We were two women, so proud of the men we loved . . . That day, November 22, 1963, the autumn air was filled with anticipation."[114]

11:45 a.m.

Police Chief Jesse Curry, waiting in the open door of the motorcade's lead car, checks on communications with Deputy Police Chief George L. Lumpkin. A few minor problems are solved.

"Ervay Street is completely blocked with pedestrians and is completely out of control," Sergeant Campbell informs Inspector J. H. Sawyer.

"I've got two reserves I'm bringing down now," Sawyer says.

"I have two 3-wheels [a three-wheel police motorcycle] with me," Campbell adds, "and we still can't get the pedestrians off of Ervay, so Ervay is completely closed."

"Ten-four [radio jargon for "acknowledged"]. I'm on my way."

Captain J. M. Souter asks the dispatcher for a progress report. The dispatcher contacts the driver of the pilot car, Deputy Chief Lumpkin, who is assigned to drive over the motorcade route a quarter of a mile ahead of the main body of the procession in an effort to spot and avert any potential trouble.

"Are they moving yet?" the dispatcher asks him.

"No," Lumpkin replies.

"Have not started yet," the dispatcher relays to Captain Souter.[115]*

Bill Greer, the president's Irish-born driver and, at age fifty-four, the oldest man in the Secret Service's White House detail, will drive the waiting presidential limousine—a 1961 Lincoln Continental convertible built at Ford Motor Company's Wixom, Michigan, plant and customized to rigid Secret Service specifications for the president by the Hess & Eisenhardt Company in Cincinnati. The car was leased to the White House in June of 1961. Its Secret Service designation was SS-100-X.[116] Weighing about seventy-five hundred pounds with its special build and heavy armor, and being a full twenty-one feet eight inches long, it is a big chore to deliver it to every place the president intends to be—which is why they didn't have it in Fort Worth. A government C-130 cargo plane—the kind they fly tanks around in—brought it from Washington, D.C., down to San Antonio. From San Antonio they flew it down to Dallas, skipping the president's stop in Houston and overnight stay in Fort Worth.[117]

In addition to the armor, the car is fitted with jump seats behind the front seat, effectively making the car comfortable for seven passengers and allowing the president to accommodate guests without having them obscure the crowds' view of him on the slightly higher backseat. There is also an electrical system, operable by the president himself provided the top is down, to raise that seat and its footrest by as much as eight inches from their normal positions.[118] Over the back of the front seat, a

*Variations in transcripts of both channels 1 (regular) and 2 (presidential motorcade) of the Dallas police radio transmissions are common. In 1982, the National Academy of Science's Committee on Ballistic Acoustics (NAS-CBA) created a new recording of the channel 2 radio traffic at the time of the assassination directly from the original Gray Audograph disk. This recording proved to be the best to date, avoiding many of the skips and repeats inherent in previous recordings. Throughout this book, the most complete versions of channel 1 and 2 radio traffic conversations, primarily from the recordings themselves, are utilized.

sort of roll bar, fitted with handholds, allows the president to ride standing up for certain occasions. On the back bumper, on each side of the
elegant spare-tire housing at the rear of the car's trunk, are two steps,
each large enough to permit a Secret Service agent to ride there while
holding on to the special handgrip fitted to the trunk. Dashboard-
controlled, retractable running boards run along each side of the limousine and can accommodate additional agents, but unlike prior presidents
who had agents riding on the side running boards of their limousines,
Kennedy does not want this, and these side running boards are never
used. It is also possible to bolt a bubble top—six panels of clear plastic
kept in the trunk—to the frame, with a black canvas-type cover that buttons over the top of the plastic. Neither plastic nor canvas are bulletproof, or even bullet resistant, just protection from the weather.[119]

Today, the car is without the bubble top. Kennedy never wanted it
when the weather was clear. This morning in Fort Worth, Ken O'Donnell told Secret Service agent Roy Kellerman that with the weather
breaking, there would be no need for the bubble top. Kellerman passed
the word on to the Secret Service's advance man in Dallas, Winston G.
Lawson.[120]

11:47 a.m.

Some of the stock boys in the Texas School Book Depository Building
are laying new flooring up on the sixth floor. The schoolbook business is
a little slow this late in the year, and rather than lay the boys off entirely,
Bill Shelley, a Depository manager, put them to work resurfacing the
upper floors, where most of the books are stored.[*] Half a dozen of them
are at it—Bill Shelley himself, Bonnie Ray Williams, Charles Givens,
Danny Arce, Billy Lovelady, and occasionally Harold Norman, when he
has time to give them a hand.

The work is pretty straightforward. They have to move the heavy car-

---

[*]The Depository had previously been occupied by a wholesale grocery company engaged in
supplying restaurants and institutions, and during the time it occupied the building, the floors
became oil-soaked and this oil was damaging the books that were now being stacked on the floor
(CD 205, p.135).

tons of books from one side of the floor to the other, then back, as they lay new flooring over the old planks. It took them about three weeks to do the fifth floor, and they're just starting in on the sixth, moving as many cartons as they can from the west side of the open floor over to the east. Given the number of books they have to move, they aren't very far along. They're still working on the first section, on the westernmost portion of the sixth floor.[121]

At one point, Bonnie Ray Williams thought he saw Lee Oswald, though he is not sure, messing around with some cartons near the easternmost freight elevator on the sixth floor, during the half hour before noon. He didn't pay much attention though. Oswald is always messing around, kicking and shoving cartons around.[122]

The warehouse crew usually knocks off about five minutes before noon to give themselves time to wash up for lunch, but today, anxious to see the president, they quit a little earlier. In high spirits, the young men commandeer both of the big freight elevators for a mock race to the bottom. Bonnie Ray, Billy, Danny, and Charlie all pile into the east elevator and head for the bottom. The rest of them take the west elevator. It isn't really much of a race. The east elevator is faster, and they all know it.[123]

Charlie Givens notices Lee Oswald in front of the elevator shaft on the fifth floor as they flash past on their way to the ground floor.[124]

"Guys!" Oswald calls after them. "How about an elevator?"

Givens tosses his head back as the freight elevator plunges down.

"Come on, boy!" Givens calls out, suggesting Oswald come down to the bottom floor too, though apparently not on their moving elevator.

"Close the gate on the elevator," Oswald shouts down the shaft, "and send the elevator back up."[125] Oswald means the west elevator. The east elevator has to be manned, but the west one can be summoned from any floor if its gate is closed.[126] When they get to the first floor, however, no one bothers with Oswald's request.

Out at Ruth Paine's house in Irving, Marina Oswald, who still hasn't dressed for the day, watches television alone. Ruth has left to run some errands. Marina doesn't understand much of what the announcers are saying, but the live images speak for themselves.[127] She sits on the edge of the couch and watches as Air Force One taxies up close to the reception line at Dallas Love Field. Crewmen run under the wings and throw down the chock-blocks as the jet comes to a halt and the engines wind down. A ramp is pushed up to the back entrance of the jet as the door is propped open. The excited crowd watches the back door, giggling with anticipation. Suddenly, Jackie's pink suit comes into view.

"There is Mrs. Kennedy and the crowd yells," the TV announcer says, a smile in his voice, "and the President of the United States. And I can see his suntan all the way from here!" The President and First Lady descend the ramp and shake hands with the official welcoming party, one of whom, the Dallas mayor's wife, Mrs. Earle Cabell, presents Mrs. Kennedy with a brilliant bouquet of red roses.* The sunshine is blinding, the weather absolutely beautiful. They look like Mr. and Mrs. America.[128]

Robert Donovan, Washington bureau chief of the *Los Angeles Times*, thinks to himself that if Hollywood had tried to cast a president and his wife, it could never have dreamed up John F. Kennedy and Jacqueline Kennedy. They were just two beautiful, glamorous people, and were receiving a screaming reception. (He would later add that "there was never a point in the public life of the Kennedys, in a way, that was as high as that moment in Dallas.")[129]

Marina can see the presidential party making its way toward the cars. Suddenly, the President and First Lady turn toward the cheering crowds hugging the fence line.

"The press is standing up high, getting a lot of shots of this!" the television announcer says excitedly. "This is great for the people and makes the eggshells even thinner for the Secret Service whose job it is to guard the man."

Secret Service agent Roy Kellerman, the assistant special agent in

---

*Jackie would later recall that three times on the Texas trip "we were greeted with bouquets of the yellow roses of Texas. Only in Dallas they gave me red roses. I remember thinking: How funny— red roses for me" (Gun, *Red Roses from Texas*, unnumbered p.5).

charge of the White House detail for this trip to Texas, slips up close to the fence, scrutinizing every hand that reaches over toward the president. The happy and loudly exuberant crowd, perhaps two thousand strong,[130] is tightly packed behind the fence at gate 28. The president can't seem to soak up enough of their warmth. He moves along the fence line, his image growing larger on local television screens as he nears the pool camera setups. The eager, outstretched hands reach for him. Jackie follows closely behind, radiant and gay, her beauty enhanced by the bouquet of red roses.[131]

"And here they come, right down toward us!" the TV announcer gushes. "I can see Mrs. Kennedy, and they're going to come right on down and shake hands with *everybody*. Mrs. Kennedy gave a lovely wave and a smile that time. There's the president shaking hands with the people. He's waving at a lot of people. Smiling. Secret Service men all around. Boy, this is *something!*"[132]

But there is palpable tension at Love Field too. Those on the scene are all too aware of the discordant placards among the signs of welcome. "IN 1964, GOLDWATER AND FREEDOM"; "YANKEE GO HOME"; "YOU'RE A TRAITOR." Liz Carpenter, Jackie's assistant, thought some of them were the ugliest she had ever seen.[133]

Roy Kellerman follows the president by inches, ready, like the other nearby agents, to use his body as a human shield. Any contact with the public is a nightmare for the Secret Service, but the agents also know that it is the lifeblood of electioneering. So far, they have been unable to persuade Jack Kennedy to be more cautious on these occasions.[134]*

Bill Greer, noticing how far down the fence the president is getting, drives the armored Lincoln at a crawl alongside him. Other Secret Service men are trying to get everyone to take his or her place in the long line of vehicles strung out along the fence behind the president's car. The

---

*The president's personal style causes the Secret Service deep concern. Not only does he travel more frequently than any previous president, but he relishes contact with crowds of well-wishers. The problem is compounded by the fact that Kennedy is not receptive to many of the measures designed to protect him, treating the danger of assault philosophically. (HSCA Report, p.228)

radio networks are alive with reports, queries, and advisories. Security men strung out for miles along the route all the way to the Trade Mart know from their radios that the president is on the ground, that the next forty-five minutes, as the motorcade threads its way across the city, will require their utmost alertness and preparedness.

The president and Mrs. Kennedy finally step toward the presidential limousine, where Governor Connally and his wife wait, standing just in front of the jump seats. *Newsweek* White House correspondent Charles Roberts manages to get in a quick question to Jackie: "How do you like campaigning?" "It's wonderful, it's wonderful," she says, sounding as if she almost means it.[135] The president places his hand in the small of Mrs. Kennedy's back and helps her into the backseat first. She moves to the left side as the president steps in and takes his seat on the right. Mrs. Kennedy places the bouquet of red roses on the seat between her and the president. The governor and his wife fold the jump seats back and sit down, the governor in front of the president, and Nellie in front of Mrs. Kennedy. Secret Service agent Roy Kellerman takes his position in the front passenger seat next to the driver, Special Agent Bill Greer.

Television cameras zoom in on the limousine as the president and Mrs. Kennedy continue waving to the cheering crowds.

"The party is now leaving Love Field," the announcer tells television viewers. "And of course thousands will be on hand for that motorcade now, which will be [through] downtown Dallas, down Cedar Springs to Harwood, and on Harwood it will turn on Main, from which point it will go all the way down to the courthouse area, which is the end of Main, it'll turn on Houston Street to Elm, under the Triple Underpass, out to the Mart, where the president talks at approximately one o'clock, which will also be carried live right here on most of these channels. And then we'll be back here, as we told you, at about two-fifteen for the president's departure."[136]

11:55 a.m.

The motorcade finally gets underway on its scheduled nine-and-one-half-mile journey to the Trade Mart, driving right through an opening in a section of the Love Field fence that Special Agent Forrest Sorrels has had removed. Sorrels has been working on the presidential visit since November 4, when Special Agent-in-Charge Gerry Behn of the White House detail alerted him to the likelihood of the visit, and he is reasonably sure that the arrangements they've made are satisfactory under the circumstances.[137] An advance car, driven by Dallas police captain Perdue D. Lawrence, head of the Traffic Division, is already a half mile out in front of the motorcade watching for any potential problems.

First through the opening in the fence is the so-called pilot car, a white Ford sedan driven by Deputy Chief Lumpkin, who scouts the route a quarter of a mile ahead, on the lookout for motor vehicle accidents, fires, obstructions, or any other problem necessitating a last-instant change of route or procedure. Along for the ride are two Dallas homicide detectives, B. L. Senkel and F. M. Turner, and Lieutenant Colonel George Whitmeyer, commander of the local Army Intelligence reserve unit.[138] Three two-wheel Dallas police motorcycle officers under the command of Sergeant S. Q. Bellah are next, followed by five two-wheel motorcycle officers under the command of Sergeant Stavis Ellis. The "lead car," an unmarked white Ford police sedan driven by Dallas police chief Jesse Curry, follows a short distance behind. Accompanying Curry are Secret Service agents Lawson and Sorrels, and Dallas sheriff Bill Decker.

Five car lengths back, and the third car in the motorcade, is the presidential limousine with four motorcycle escorts, two on each side, flanking the rear bumper. Although, as indicated, the president's car is equipped to allow Secret Service agents to ride on the running boards or rear bumper steps, no agents are there this day. Kennedy is weary of seeing bodyguards hovering behind him every time he turns to see the crowds.[139]

Less than a car length behind is the Secret Service follow-up car, a black 1955 four-door modified Cadillac convertible touring car—"Halfback" to the agents—with Agent Sam Kinney at the wheel. Emory Roberts, the car's commander, is at his side. Agent Clint Hill is standing on the left running board, Agent Bill McIntyre right behind him. Agent

John Ready stands on the right running board, Agent Paul Landis behind him. President Kennedy's close friends and advisers, Dave Powers and Ken O'Donnell, are seated in the right and left jump seats. Agent George Hickey sits in the left rear seat, Agent Glen Bennett on the right. Between them is an AR-15 .223 caliber automatic rifle, capable of blowing a man's head off.

Two and a half car lengths behind Halfback is the vice presidential limousine, a light blue 1961 Lincoln convertible carrying the vice president and Mrs. Johnson, Senator Yarborough, Secret Service agent Rufus Youngblood, and the driver.

Immediately behind the vice president is another Secret Service follow-up car, a yellow Ford Mercury four-door hardtop nicknamed "Varsity." Driven by Texas Ranger Hurchel Jacks, the car contains vice presidential aide Cliff Carter and three Secret Service agents. Dallas mayor Earle Cabell and his wife ride in the next vehicle, a white Ford Mercury convertible, along with Congressman Ray Roberts.

The national press pool car, a blue-gray Chevrolet sedan on loan from the telephone company, complete with driver, follow through the fence opening next. Assistant Press Secretary Malcolm Kilduff and United Press International (UPI) correspondent Merriman Smith occupy the front seat, with Smith in the middle, next to the radiophone mounted on the transmission hump under the dashboard. Jack Bell of the Associated Press (AP), Robert Baskin of the *Dallas Morning News*, and Bob Clark of the American Broadcasting Company (ABC) are in the backseat.

The rest of the motorcade follows: two camera cars carrying local motion and still photographers; two Dallas police motorcycle escorts (H. B. McLain and Marrion L. Baker); a third camera car; three cars full of congressmen; a VIP staff car carrying a governor's aide and the military and air force aides to the president; two more motorcycle escorts (J. W. Courson and C. A. Haygood); a White House press bus; a local press car with four *Dallas Morning News* reporters; a second White House press bus; two more Dallas police motorcycle escorts (R. Smart and B. J. Dale); a Chevrolet sedan carrying the president's physician, Admiral George G. Burkley, and the president's personal secretary,

Evelyn Lincoln; a 1957 black Ford hardtop carrying two representatives from Western Union; a white 1964 Chevrolet Impala containing White House Signal Corps officer Art Bales and Army Warrant Officer Ira Gearhart ("Bagman"); a 1964 white-top, dark-body Chevrolet Impala; a third White House bus carrying staff and members of the Democratic Party; a 1963 black-and-white Ford police car; and at the rear, a solo three-wheel Dallas police motorcycle escort.[140]

In a long procession the motorcycles and cars turn left out of Love Field onto Mockingbird Lane, then almost immediately southeast onto Lemmon Avenue, heading for downtown. There aren't many people along this first long straightaway down Lemmon Avenue, which is flanked by those low, nondescript structures characteristic of the light industry near airports. Clumps of people, mostly workers from the factories, have gathered to watch the procession flash past, but there are long barren stretches too. Mostly, the road looks much like any avenue through a suburban industrial park in the middle of an ordinary workday.

Jackie, squinting in the bright sunshine, looks forward to the looming Cotton Belt overpass—cleared of onlookers by police orders—for the fleeting moment of shade it will provide. She tries to put on her sunglasses, but the president asks her not to—the people have come to see her, and the dark glasses might make her look distant and aloof. She keeps them in her lap, though, and sneaks them on for a moment or two whenever there is no one along the road to see.[141]

12:00 p.m.

At the Book Depository, some of the stock boys wade into their lunches in the small, first-floor employee's lounge, which the architects designated as the recreation room and which employees call the "domino room," after their favorite pastime, while others eat while standing in front of the building. Charlie Givens discovers he left his cigarettes in the pocket of his jacket up on the sixth floor. The thirty-eight-year-old navy veteran goes back up on the elevator. The sixth floor appears deserted as he crosses the wide space they cleared for the new flooring, but when he gets back to the elevator with the cigarettes and prepares to go down, he is startled to see Lee Oswald, whom he had seen a few minutes earlier on the fifth floor, now on the sixth floor, walking along the east aisle, away from the southeast corner of the room, clipboard in hand.

"Boy, are you going downstairs?" Givens calls out. "It's near lunchtime."

"No, sir," Oswald replies. Oddly, he again asks for the west elevator gate to be closed when Givens gets back downstairs.

"Okay," Givens shrugs.[142]

When he returns to the first floor on the east elevator, he turns to close the west elevator gate, as Oswald requested, but finds it missing—it's up on some other floor.[143] After eating lunch in front of the building, he joins Harold Norman and James Jarman inside at a first-floor window looking onto Elm Street, but after a bit they decide to go outside for the motorcade. Later, Norman and Jarman change their minds and go back in to watch from the fifth floor, while Givens walks over to the corner of Main and Record to watch the motorcade with a couple of friends.[144]

12:06 p.m.

At the corner of Lemmon and Lomo Alto Drive, the president's eye catches a group of children with a large placard: "MR. PRESIDENT, PLEASE STOP AND SHAKE OUR HANDS."

"Let's stop here, Bill," Kennedy calls to the driver.

The car is immediately mobbed by the squealing, ecstatic kids. People as far as a block away start to run toward the car. When he realizes that the president has stopped, Chief Curry stops the lead car and begins to back up. The motorcycle escorts in front of him wheel around and head back toward the limousine. It's all Secret Service agent Kellerman and the men from the follow-up car can do to restore some order and get the motorcade moving again.

A few blocks farther on, the president stops again, this time for a bunch of little children and a nun—an irresistible temptation for America's first Catholic president. The nervous agents don't interfere, partly out of tact and partly because they are satisfied with their progress so far. They still have every chance of getting to the Trade Mart in good time.[145]

At the Book Depository Building, Bonnie Ray Williams had picked up his lunch in the domino room on the first floor, gotten a Dr. Pepper from the soda machine, and taken the east elevator back up to the sixth floor, expecting to find some of the other guys up there. Billy Lovelady said he was going to watch the motorcade from there, and Bonnie had more or less agreed with Danny Arce that they would too—but he doesn't see anyone on the sixth floor when he gets there.

Bonnie settles down anyway, in front of the third double-window from the southeast corner overlooking Elm Street, to eat his lunch—a piece of chicken on the bone, two slices of bread, and a bag of Fritos. No one else shows up. After a while he gets up and perches on a "two-wheeler," one of the hand trucks they use to buck the heavy boxes of books around. It's dead quiet up here, nothing moving but specks of dust in the air. To his right he can see the west wall, because that's where they cleared the books out to resurface the floor. His view to the left is blocked by the unusually high piles of boxes the workers moved there in preparation for the reflooring job. It's so quiet he can hear the pigeons on the roof above and someone moving around on the floor below—someone walking, then moving a window. He hears the traffic and growing murmur of the crowd in the street below. It's finally clear that no one else is coming up to watch from the sixth floor. He finishes off his Dr. Pepper, puts the chicken bones back in the paper sack, leaves the bottle and sack there, and goes back to the elevator to see who's on the floor below.[146]

12:12 p.m.
Howard L. Brennan, a forty-four-year-old steamfitter, watches the crowd gathering outside the windows as he finishes his lunch in the cafeteria at the corner of Record and Main streets. Brennan could join the crowd right there on Main Street, but folks are already jostling for position, and he reckons he'll walk back toward the railroad yards near Elm and Houston, where he's been working on a pipeline for Wallace and Beard Construction for the past seven weeks.[147]

12:15 p.m.

Arnold Rowland and his wife Barbara find a place to watch the motorcade on the sidewalk in front of the Criminal Courts Building on Houston Street, near the west entrance to Sheriff Decker's office. The young couple are still students at Dallas's Adamson High School, but both got off early today and came downtown to shop for a while before Arnold goes to his job at the Pizza Inn on West Davis Avenue.[148]

A hundred yards to the west the Rowlands can see policemen on the railroad bridge over the Triple Underpass and another two-dozen or so uniformed officers in the streets around the plaza. Arnold and Barbara remember the nasty incidents involving Adlai Stevenson and Lyndon Johnson not too long ago and understand that security will be tight for the motorcade.[149] Arnold knows the building on the next corner very well—several times he has been to the Texas School Book Depository to get books, including a physics notebook he bought there two or three weeks ago.[150] He and his wife take note of a number of people looking out the windows of the building, including a black man hanging out of one of the southeast corner windows.[151]

A nearby police radio squawks out the progress of the motorcade.

"What's the location?" Inspector J. H. Sawyer asks.

"Now turning onto Cedar Springs Road off of Turtle Creek," the dispatcher informs him.

"Ten-four," Sawyer replies.[152]

Arnold Rowland can tell from the conversation that the motorcade is about two miles away now.[153] As he continues to scan the upper floors of the Depository, Rowland would later say he spotted a man holding a high-powered rifle at port arms (across his chest) in the window at the west end of the sixth floor. That's some distance away, but Arnold knows his way around guns, and he can tell by the relative proportion of the scope to the rifle that it's a heavy piece, no .22 caliber. Though the rifleman is a couple of feet back in the shadows, Arnold, whose eyesight is better than 20/20,[154] sees him very clearly, a slender man in his early thirties, with a light complexion and either well-combed or close-cut dark hair, wearing a light-colored, open-collared shirt over a T-shirt.[155]

"Hey, you want to see a Secret Service man?" he asks his wife Barbara.

"Where?" she asks, staring intently at a commotion developing across the street.

"In the building there," Arnold says, pointing back up at the Depository. His wife, however, is paying no attention and instead directs him to look across the street at a couple of police officers assisting a young black man who's having some sort of epileptic fit. By the time Arnold gets his wife's attention and points out the open window, the man with the rifle has disappeared.

"What did he look like?" she asks, disappointed to have missed him.

Arnold describes the man and how he was holding a rifle with a scope.

"Oh," she sighs, "I wish I could have seen him. He's probably in another part of the building now, watching people."

Her attention returns back to the action across the street, where an ambulance arrives to take the epileptic to Parkland Hospital. Although Arnold continues to scan the upper floors of the Depository every thirty seconds or so, hoping to catch another glimpse of the man he assumes is a Secret Service agent so that he can point him out to his wife, he doesn't see the rifleman again. Nor, to his later regret, does he bother to mention what he saw to a nearby police officer.[156]

Bonnie Ray Williams steps off the elevator onto the fifth floor of the Depository. He discovers Harold Norman and James "Junior" Jarman there.[157] With seven big double-windows across the Elm Street face of the building, there's plenty of room for the three of them to watch the motorcade. Harold squats at the window in the southeast corner, and Bonnie Ray joins him there, taking the second window of the pair. Junior kneels at the second double-window, leaning over the low sill. If they lean out far enough, they can talk to each other outside. The view is terrific, since from their perch they can see south to the corner of Houston and Main and beyond, as well as all the way west down the curving sweep of Elm to the Triple Underpass, with nothing in their line of sight but the thick foliage clustered on the branches of an oak tree[158] nearly right below them along the north side of Elm. Except for that oak, they will get a pretty good view of the motorcade from the moment it turns off Main Street until it disappears into the shadow of the underpass leading to the Stemmons Freeway.[159]

12:20 p.m.
In the pilot car, Deputy Chief Lumpkin rolls closer to the downtown area. As each block passes, the skyline of Dallas grows taller and larger and the crowds increase in size. Already, police officers are finding it nearly impossible to keep people back onto the sidewalks and behind the barricades.

"Need some motorcycles—just to kinda keep the crowd over to Harwood and Ross," Chief Lumpkin warns Curry over the radio. "They're kinda getting out into the street here."

"We've got 'em," Curry answers.

"[Unit] One [Curry], are you approaching Ross?" the dispatcher asks.

"Just approaching at this time," Curry says over the roar of the crowd.[160]

Governor Connally had feared some ugly incident occurring in this most conservative of cities. But these fears have fallen away as the people are friendly, waving, smiling. And it is plain the president is enjoying himself.[161]

12:21 p.m.
Charles F. Brehm is very pleased with his position for the motorcade, on the northwest corner of Main and Houston. Compared to the throngs on Main Street, there are relatively few people here, and a better chance that his son will get a clear view of the president. Joe is five years old. He doesn't really understand the significance of it now, but his father feels he is old enough to remember seeing John F. Kennedy and his wife for the rest of his life. It's a story he will be able to tell his own grandchildren one day. The position has another advantage. If the motorcade is moving slowly enough, Brehm may be able to run diagonally across the

adjacent plaza to Elm Street for a second bite of the cherry. Little Joe is too big to carry for long, but not too big for a quick sprint down the grassy slope to Elm.[162]

12:22 p.m.
Deputy Chief Lumpkin turns the pilot car right off Harwood onto Main Street and gets his first good look at the crowds awaiting the motorcade. "Crowd on Main Street's in real good shape," he tells Chief Curry over the police radio. "They've got 'em back off on the curb."

"Good shape," Curry says, barely audible over the shrieks and screams of the cheering crowds. "We're just about to cross Live Oak."

"Ten-four," Lumpkin replies.[163]

At Live Oak Street, two and a half blocks from Main, where the high buildings of downtown turn the streets into deep canyons, the motorcade plunges into an avalanche of roaring cheers from people standing eight and ten deep and hanging out the windows high above. Curry's men are helpless against the press of the crowd, which closes in, narrowing the passage for the cars and forcing Greer to drop his speed from twenty miles an hour to fifteen, to ten.

"There's certainly nothing wrong with this crowd," O'Donnell says to Powers, beside him on the jump seat of the Secret Service follow-up car. The steady roar from the crowd is deafening. It is by far the happiest and most enthusiastic crowd they've seen in Texas. They also see the faces of the president and his wife in the car immediately ahead when they turn to wave to the swarms of people pushing past the police barricades into the street. The president seems thrilled by the unexpected warmth of the welcome, and O'Donnell is pleased to note that Jackie is following his last-minute instruction to keep turned toward her own side of the street, to make sure that the crowds on both sides get at least a glimpse of one or the other of the country's most famous couple.[164]

12:23 p.m.
Seven minutes from Dealey Plaza, the crowds on Main are the heaviest. This is the mouth of the bottle. Ahead lies a twelve-block-long forest of

humanity nestled between the tall buildings and eight skyscrapers of downtown Dallas. Fifteen hundred yards of screaming, whistling, cheering pandemonium. The throngs of people on both sides of the street are so heavy they threaten to choke it off entirely.

Governor Connally thinks it looks like about a quarter of a million people have turned out to greet the Kennedys in Dallas, an enormous crowd for a city with a population of around three-quarters of a million in 1963.[165]* Connally's estimate of the crowd is almost assuredly overblown, but by all accounts, it's the largest and friendliest crowd so far on Kennedy's Texas trip. And the crowd is certainly more than Captain Perdue Lawrence expected. As the Dallas police officer in charge of crowd control for the day, he began to realize early on that things are a bit out of hand. The Dallas police simply don't have enough men, barricades, or rope to handle this kind of reception.[166]

Secret Service agent Greer slows the presidential limousine to a crawl as the crowds press in. The motorcycle escorts find their handlebars bumping people standing out in the street.

"Escort, drop back," Curry commands. "Have to go at a real slow speed now."[167]

A teenage boy dashes from the crowd, camera in hand, and chases after the limousine. Running between the motorcycle escorts on the right and the president's car, the boy raises the camera to his eye. Before he can get a picture off, a Secret Service agent jumps from the follow-up car, overtakes the boy, and throws him back into the crowd, causing people to tumble to the ground.[168] Chief Curry can see that the lead motorcycle escorts are too far ahead, allowing the crowd to close in behind them.

"Hold up escort," Curry orders, then a moment later, "Okay. Okay, move along."[169]

The reception is phenomenal. The First Lady lifts her white-gloved hand and flutters her fingers at the faces on her left, evoking a nearly hysterical "Jackiiieee!" from the crowd. The president is working the right

---

*According to U.S. Census records, the population of the city of Dallas was 679,684 in 1960. In 1970, it had increased to 844,401.

side of the street with equal results. It is the crowning moment of the parade.[170]

Howard Brennan's hunch was right—he does indeed find a great spot, at the corner of Houston and Elm, right across the street from the Book Depository. He even has a seat, a low, ornamental wall curving around the end of the long reflecting pool—or "lagoon," as Dallas folk call it—along the west side of Houston Street. His aluminum hardhat shields his head from the sun, and he reckons he will have, in a couple of minutes, a good view of the First Family.

His eyes rove over the swelling crowd. There's quite a bunch on the steps of the Depository Building across the street, and more people turning up every moment. If the crowd gets too thick he can always stand up on top of the low wall to see well over their heads. He notices quite a few people in the windows of the Texas School Book Depository, in particular three black men on the fifth floor near the southeasternmost side of the building, leaning way out of their windows to chatter to each other, and a fellow just above them on the sixth floor, who for a moment sits sideways on the low windowsill.[171] It strikes Brennan as odd that this guy is alone, while almost everyone else is with someone. The man in the sixth-floor window seems to be in his own little world, unsmiling, calm, with no trace of excitement. Brennan, who is farsighted, has especially good vision at a distance, and sees him very clearly.

12:25 p.m.

It took Abraham Zapruder a while to find the right spot. At the urging of his secretary, the fifty-eight-year-old Dallas dressmaker, a bespectacled, balding man wearing his trademark fedora and bowtie, had returned home earlier in the morning and retrieved his new 8-millimeter Bell & Howell movie camera. At first he thought he would use the telephoto lens to shoot pictures from his office in the Dal-Tex Building, across the street from the Texas School Book Depository, but after he came back to the office he realized his office window was too far away. So, he and Mar-

ilyn Sitzman, his receptionist, went down into the plaza. He tried standing on a narrow abutment along the north side of Elm, but it was too
narrow and he was afraid that he'd lose his balance trying to shoot pictures from there. A bit farther down Elm Street he found the perfect
spot—a larger, square abutment about four feet high at the west end of
the ornamental pergola. The perch would place him right in the middle
of that stretch of Elm, and high enough to give him a pretty clear view of
the motorcade from the corner of Houston and Elm on his left, down to
the Triple Underpass on his right. There is even enough room for Marilyn to stand behind him on the abutment and help steady him if he gets
dizzy looking through the telescopic lens.[172]

As the limousine proceeds down Main between Ervay and Akard, all eyes
in the car instinctively turn to the left to see the giant display windows of
Neiman Marcus, the pride of Dallas and, indeed, the premier luxury
retail store in the world. As elegant and expensive a shopper as Jackie is,
nothing in New York City, London, and Paris, her normal shopping
grounds, quite compares to it. The store caters not only to the oil zil-
lionaires of Texas but to those with very deep pockets everywhere. They
tell the story about the oil magnate who approached the store's owner,
Stanley Marcus, one day before Christmas and said, "I'll buy all the win-
dow-displays as they stand. Just shift the lot to my ranch, around my
wife's window—it's my Christmas present to her."[173]

12:26 p.m.
FBI special agent James P. Hosty Jr., the man responsible for monitoring
right-wing political activists in Dallas, watches the motorcade rumble past
from the corner of Field Street, about halfway down Main. Hosty is really
pleased to see the tumultuous welcome. As a Kennedy Democrat he
doesn't like the radical rightist atmosphere of the city at all, but it's clear
that Dallas has turned out for the president with real enthusiasm. As soon
as the motorcade passes, he crosses the street to a restaurant to get some
lunch.[174]

Senator Yarborough, riding two cars behind the presidential limousine, is astonished at the enthusiasm of the crowds on the sidewalks. But the people looking out the windows on the floors high above the street are a different story. The senator doesn't see a single smile there, and he imagines that some of those faces express sheer dislike. As the motorcade approaches Dealey Plaza[*] at the end of Main Street, and he sees the open area sloping down to the Trinity River beyond, he starts to feel relief about leaving the high-rise buildings behind. "What if," he wonders uneasily, "someone throws a flowerpot down on top of Mrs. Kennedy or the president?"[175]

There is a lot of good-natured grumbling in the Chevrolet convertible to which Bob Jackson has been assigned. The twenty-nine-year-old *Dallas Times Herald* staff photographer sits on the top of the backseat and wrestles with one of his two cameras, trying to rewind and unload the film he shot at Love Field and during the motorcade procession so he can toss it to the *Times Herald* staffer who will be waiting for it at the corner of Main and Houston. He and the others—Jim Underwood of KRLD-TV; Tom Dillard, chief photographer for the *Dallas Morning News*; and a couple of newsreel guys from WFAA, the *Dallas Morning News*'s radio station, and Channel 11—figure they might as well be in the next county. They are *eight* cars behind the president. They know because they counted. That far back, their chance of getting a lens on anything worth printing or broadcasting is just about nil. Even from his perch on the rear deck, Jackson catches only occasional glimpses of the president's limousine. He hopes things will be better at the Trade Mart.[176]

---

[*]Dealey Plaza is a three-acre, well-manicured patch of land with concrete pergolas and peristyles, reflecting pools, and some office buildings. It is called "The Front Door of Dallas" and was named in 1935 after George Bannerman Dealey, a Dallas civic leader and the founder of the city's main paper, the *Dallas Morning News*. The plaza is in the form of a triangle, with three main thoroughfares, Main Street in the middle having east and westbound lanes, and flanked by Elm to the north having only westbound lanes, and Commerce to the south with only eastbound lanes. The three arteries converge at a triple underpass built in 1936 beneath the Union Terminal Railroad overpass at the southwestern tip of the plaza. (CE 877,17 H 897–898) The site of the Texas School Book Depository Building at the northwest corner of Houston and Elm in the plaza was originally owned by John Neely Bryan, the founder of Dallas.

12:28 p.m.

"Crossing Lamar Street," Chief Curry says into the lead car's radio microphone.

"Ah, ten-four, [Unit] One [Curry]" the dispatcher replies. "Is there a pretty good crowd there?"

"Big crowd, yes," Curry replies.

The dispatcher knows there must be. He can hear the squeals of delight in the background of the chief's transmission. Deputy Chief Lumpkin cuts in, "Uh, notify Captain Souter . . . [of] the location of the convoy now."

"Fifteen, car two [Souter]," the dispatcher calls. "On Main, probably just past Lamar."

"Just crossing Market Street," Curry says, updating the motorcade's progress.

"Now at Market, car two [Souter]," the dispatcher quickly repeats.[177]

The president is now just two blocks from the open sky of Dealey Plaza.

On the southwest corner of Elm and Houston, directly across the street from the Book Depository, Ronald Fischer, a young auditor for Dallas County, and Bob Edwards, a utility clerk from the same office, wait at the curb for the motorcade. Edwards notices a white man, on the thin side, among the boxes at the sixth-floor southeast corner window of the Depository Building. "Hey, look at that guy in the window," Edwards says, poking Fischer. "He looks like he's uncomfortable."[178]

He does look uncomfortable, Fischer thinks, when he spots the man in the window, a slender man with brown hair in his early twenties, casually dressed. Oddly enough, even though the motorcade is likely to appear at any moment now, this guy isn't watching out for it. Instead of looking south toward the corner of Main and Houston like most of the crowd, he's staring west toward the Triple Underpass, or maybe even beyond to the Trinity River. He is curiously still too, not moving his head or anything else. He appears to be kneeling or sitting on something, literally

boxed in by the high wall of boxes behind him. Edwards laughs, wondering who the guy is hiding from. Fischer goes on watching him for a
while, but never sees a movement. The man seems "transfixed." It's very
strange.[179]

On the southeast corner of Houston and Elm, diagonally across the
street from the Book Depository Building, young James Crawford, a
deputy district clerk in the Records Building, anxiously awaits the motorcade with his friend and coworker Mary Ann Mitchell. They had left their
office on Houston Street just a few minutes earlier but had no trouble
getting a good position along the parade route.[180]

A sudden jolt of excitement hits the crowd. The pilot car driven by
Deputy Chief Lumpkin, its red lights flashing, sweeps around the corner off Main onto Houston Street. They can hear the crowd near Main
and Houston begin to break into applause, screams, and whistles. The
presidential limousine can't be more than a minute away now.

12:29 p.m.

Five lead motorcycles round the corner from Main onto Houston followed by the white 1963 Ford sedan driven by Chief Curry, its red front
grill lights pulsating rhythmically. Suddenly, the presidential limousine
bursts into view, the two flags mounted on its front fenders fluttering
majestically in the breeze. The crowd in Dealey Plaza breaks into spontaneous applause. As the limousine makes the slow right turn onto Houston Street and heads north, Mrs. Kennedy reaches up and steadies her
bright pink hat against the strong wind that whips across the open grass
of the Plaza. Two motorcycle escorts flank each rear fender, with the
Secret Service follow-up car and its jumble of agents following only a few
feet behind them.

The crowds lining both sides of Houston Street cheer wildly. Nellie
Connally is overwhelmed by the unexpected response of the people of
Dallas. She turns and beams brightly at the president.

"Mr. President," she says, as the president leans toward her, "they can't
make you believe now that there are not some in Dallas who love you and
appreciate you, can they?"

The president leans back, waves, and flashes the famous Kennedy smile at the passing faces.

"No, they sure can't," he grins.[181]

The limousine moves slowly up Houston toward the large brick Texas School Book Depository Building looming over them just ahead, and to the left. Mrs. Kennedy, looking to her left across the reflecting pools onto Elm Street, can see that the pilot car of the motorcade is heading toward an underpass and thinks how cool the shade will feel after basking in the warm rays of the Texas sun.[182] As the first three of the five lead motorcycles round the corner at Elm and Houston, Abraham Zapruder begins filming. After a few seconds, he stops his home movie camera and waits until the president comes into view.[183] Chief Curry, right behind the three motorcycle escorts, swings the lead car left off Houston, through the hairpin turn, and onto the gently curving downslope of Elm Street.

"Approaching the Triple Underpass," Curry tells the dispatcher.

"Ten-four, [Unit] One [Curry]," the dispatcher responds.[184]

Secret Service agent Winston Lawson, in Chief Curry's car, contacts the agents waiting at the Trade Mart.

"Five minutes away," he says into his radio.[185]

Charles Brehm, with little Joe in his arms, runs down the lawn of Dealey Plaza from Houston to Elm, and arrives well before the presidential limousine. He puts Joe down and tells him to get ready to wave to the president. There's hardly anyone that far down Elm, and he and his five-year-old boy have a completely unobstructed view as Chief Curry's lead car sweeps past them—the presidential limousine just beginning the turn onto Elm.[186] It is sunny and the temperature is sixty-five degrees.[187]

While the NBC television affiliate covered the president's appearance in Fort Worth that morning and the CBS and ABC affiliates covered the president's landing at Love Field, no live TV cameras are even remotely close to Dealey Plaza, and there is also no live radio coverage of the motorcade in the plaza.

As noted earlier, President Kennedy had requested that Secret Service agents not ride on the two steps built into the rear bumper of the

presidential limousine, but Clint Hill, the Secret Service agent riding on
the left running board of the follow-up vehicle just five feet behind had
disregarded this request for four separate but brief moments since the
motorcade left Love Field when he felt the situation created an increased
danger, all of which happened on Main Street, where the crowds were
the greatest. (Since Mrs. Kennedy was Hill's primary responsibility this
day, he got on the left rear step.) On at least one of the four occasions,
when the limousine stopped for the president to shake hands with people
alongside the road, Secret Service agent John Ready, Hill's counterpart
riding on the right running board of the follow-up car, had left the running board and gotten on the rear step on the president's side of his limousine.[188] But the crowds are lighter now and neither Hill nor Ready see
any need to stand on the two rear steps of the presidential limousine.

12:29:45 p.m.
The glistening, dark blue limousine carrying the president of the United
States—license plate number GG300 under District of Columbia reg-
istry—approaches the Texas School Book Depository Building. Cheers
from the crowd ripple across the plaza as the president's limousine commences its turn onto Elm Street.

Bonnie Ray Williams, Harold Norman, and James Jarman, the three
black stock boys seen by people on the street below, have a perfect view
of the president from their fifth-floor Depository perch. Sunlight glints
run down the length of the chrome trim as the presidential limousine
completes its turn onto Elm Street, straightens out, and passes directly
below their window. Bonnie Ray and Harold can see the president brush-
ing his chestnut hair back from his face.[189]

Zapruder points his camera at the approaching limousine and again
presses the camera's release button, which sends film shuttling through
the camera with a soft, whirling sound. The clock on the Hertz sign high
atop the Texas School Book Depository reads twelve-thirty.[190]

12:30 p.m.
First Shot—:00.0 seconds BANG!—The loud crack is quickly swal-
lowed up by the sound of sputtering motorcycles. The three stock boys in

the Depository think it's a firearm salute for the president, or maybe, Bonnie Ray Williams thinks, it's a motorcycle backfire. The thought that it could be anything more serious is beyond their imagination.[191]

Virgie Rachley, a young bookkeeper for the Texas School Book Depository, watching from the curb in front of the Depository, is startled to see sparks fly off the pavement in the far left lane, right behind the presidential limousine. She thinks it's a firecracker thrown by some boys who are fixing to get in a lot of trouble.[192]

Secret Service agent Paul Landis, riding on the right running board of the Secret Service follow-up car, knows immediately what the sound is—the report of a high-powered rifle coming from over his right shoulder. Landis snaps his head back toward the Depository. Nothing. He begins scanning the crowd but doesn't see anything unusual.

"What was it?" Agent John Ready says. "A firecracker?"

"I don't know," Landis answers, beginning to doubt his own senses. "I don't see any smoke." Landis now starts to wonder whether it was a blowout and glances at the tires on the right side of the presidential limousine. The one he can see, the right front, seems all right. The doubts unnerve him and he draws his gun.[193]

Secret Service agent Rufus W. Youngblood, riding in the front seat of the vice president's car, isn't sure what the sound is either—some kind of explosive noise. Vice President Johnson is equally puzzled. Youngblood quickly surveys the crowd, then the Secret Service follow-up car ahead of him, and notices the agents aboard making "unnatural movements." Fear suddenly consumes him. In a flash, Youngblood turns and hits the vice president on the right shoulder, shoving him down into the backseat. "Get down!" he shouts.[194]*

Governor Connally knows *exactly* what the sound is—the report of a high-powered rifle. An avid hunter all his life, Connally knows it isn't a firecracker or a blowout or anything else. It's a rifle shot. He turns and looks over his right shoulder, in the direction of the sound. Faces in the crowd blur past, but he sees nothing out of the ordinary. There is only

---

*There is no evidence that the two Secret Service agents in the president's limousine, Greer and Kellerman, were as alert as Youngblood and directed the president to get down.

one horrific thought that crosses his mind—this is an assassination attempt. In despair, thinking that such a beautiful day and warm reception are about to end in tragedy, Connally blurts out, "Oh no, no, no!"[195]

Mrs. Kennedy, who is looking to her left, mistakes the sound for a motorcycle backfire. Suddenly, however, she hears the governor's exclamation of "Oh no, no, no" and turns to her right, toward him.[196] Nellie Connally is turning too, startled by the loud frightening noise that emanates from somewhere to her right.[197]

Motorcycle escort Marrion L. Baker is seven cars back behind the presidential limousine, having just turned north onto Houston, and knows exactly what the sound is too. He just came back from deer hunting, where he heard the firing of a lot of high-powered rifles. He sees a great number of pigeons flying around the top of the Texas Book Depository Building and suspects a sniper is firing from the roof. Baker instinctively revs his Harley-Davidson, rumbles past the faltering motorcade press cars, and races toward the building two hundred feet in front of him.[198]

Twenty-year-old high school dropout James R. Worrell Jr. is standing right in front of the Book Depository, his back to the building from watching the motorcade come up Houston. When he hears the first shot, Worrell throws his head back, looks straight up, and sees six inches of gun barrel with the forepart of the stock sticking out a window high overhead on the southeasternmost side of the building.[199]

Across the street, ninth-grader Amos Euins thinks it's a car backfire and begins looking around, then up. He spots a pipelike object sticking out of the southeasternmost window of the sixth floor.[200]

A few feet away, Howard Brennan sits on the low stone wall of the reflecting pool. He thinks it's the backfire of a motorcycle, or a firecracker thrown from the Depository. Those around him must be thinking the same thing, because there's no immediate reaction by the crowd. He looks up. The man he saw earlier in the sixth-floor window is aiming a rifle straight down Elm Street toward the presidential limousine. Brennan sees him from the waist up with awful clarity, the rifle braced against his right shoulder as he leans against the left window jamb. The gunman's motions are deliberate and without panic. After a few seconds, he fires again.[201]

Second Shot—:02.7 seconds BANG!—The report is so loud inside the fifth floor of the Texas School Book Depository Building that the windows rattle, and loose plaster and dirt fall from the ceiling onto Bonnie Ray Williams's hair.[202]

The car is very close to Charles Brehm and his son, maybe twenty feet away, so they can see the president's face very well when the shot rings out. The president stiffens perceptibly, and his hands swoop toward his throat. "My God," Brehm thinks, "he's been shot."[203]

Secret Service agent Glen Bennett, sitting in the right rear seat of the follow-up car, is looking right at the president when the second shot hits him, he estimates, "about four inches down from the right shoulder."[204] "He's hit!" Bennett shouts, and reaches for the Colt AR-15 assault rifle on the seat, but Agent George Hickey has already got it. Hickey cocks the rifle and spins toward the right rear, from where the shots appear to have come. Bennett draws his own side arm but there is nothing to shoot at.[205] Special Agent Clint Hill leaps off the running board of the follow-up car and dashes toward the president's limousine.[206] Special Agent Roy Kellerman, riding in the front passenger seat of the president's limousine, turns back to his right, the direction from which he hears the firecracker-like pop. He believes he hears the president say, "My God, I am hit!"[207]* Kellerman sees the president's elbows have flown up higher than his shoulders, hands lower, fists clenched. He immediately turns his body back to the front and turns to his left to look into the backseats, where he sees Connally in clear distress.[208]

Unable to see the president over his right shoulder, and deeply concerned for his safety, Governor Connally is in the middle of a turn to look back over his left shoulder into the backseat, to see if Kennedy has been hit, when he feels a hard blow to the right side of his own back, like a doubled-up fist. Driven down into the seat by the shot, Connally spins back to his right, a gaping, sucking wound in his chest drenching his shirt with blood.

*Kellerman is the only one in the car who heard this remark. In 1964 he testified that he spoke often with the president during the three years he served him, and would not have mistaken the president's Boston accent (2 H 75). But it's unlikely the president *could* have spoken after the bullet penetrated his throat.

"My God," he cries out, "they're going to kill us all!"[209]

His wife, Nellie, reaches out and pulls her wounded husband down into her arms and out of what she believes is the line of fire. She puts her head down over his head and doesn't look up.[210]

Mrs. Kennedy turns toward her husband, who has a strange, quizzical look on his face—almost like he has a slight headache.[211]

Greer had thought the sound of the first shot was a backfire from one of the police motorcycles accompanying the motorcade, but when he heard the second loud sound, he glances over his right shoulder, momentarily slowing the car down, and sees Governor Connally in the process of slumping down. He turns back facing the front again, but knows something is very wrong now. At the same time, his partner, Kellerman, yells at him, "Let's get out of here. We're hit."[212]*

In the vice president's car, Agent Youngblood vaults over the front seat and sits on top of the crouched-down figure of the six-foot four-inch Lyndon Johnson as Mrs. Johnson and Senator Yarborough collapse toward the vice president. There is no doubt in Youngblood's mind what the sound is now—gunshots![213]

Abraham Zapruder hears the shot. The thought flashes in his mind, as he sees the president jerk and slump to his left against Jackie, that it's a joke, the president clowning around like people sometimes do when they hear a shot, "Oh, he got me." But even his confused mind is already telling him that the president of the United States does not make jokes like this.[214]

Across the street, Mary Moorman and her friend, schoolteacher Jean Hill, watch as the president's limousine glides toward them, curiously unaware that shots have already been fired. Mary knows she will have only

*Back at Love Field, where Air Force One pilot Colonel James B. Swindal is listening to the radio chatter of the Secret Service agents in the motorcade (the plane's communication center was linked with the White House Communications Agency's temporary signal board in the Sheraton Dallas Hotel, which in turn was linked to the Secret Service radio frequency), he hears two loud shouts over the radio frequency around 12:30 that he recognizes as the voice of Roy Kellerman. Then he hears a third sharp cry from Kellerman: "*Dagger* cover *Volunteer*," the code names, respectively, for Rufus Youngblood, the chief Secret Service agent in LBJ's limousine, and Vice President Johnson. But the radio immediately becomes a "babel of screeching voices. Then it fell silent." (TerHorst and Albertazzie, *Flying White House*, pp.199, 210–211)

one chance to get a picture of the president with her Polaroid camera, which takes about ten seconds to recycle, and fears he will be looking away from her, to his right, at people on the north side of Elm street. As the limousine draws closer, Jean thinks that President and Mrs. Kennedy are looking down at something in the seat. She calls out to the president so Mary can get a good snapshot, "Hey, we want to take your picture!"[215]

From the moment he looked up after the first shot, James Worrell hasn't taken his eyes off the barrel of the rifle sticking out the window, and when he sees it fire again he sees a little flame and smoke coming out of the barrel. There is a lot of commotion, people screaming and saying, "Duck." Frightened, he turns and starts to run toward Houston, just feet away, intending to run to the back of the building, which he feels is the safest place.[216]

Amos Euins scuttles for cover behind a bench near the reflecting pool. From there he can see that the pipelike object sticking out of the southeasternmost window of the sixth floor of the Depository is a rifle. He can see a good portion of it, from the trigger housing to the front sight. The fifteen-year-old can't take his eyes off the rifleman as he again takes aim.[217]

Third Shot—:08.4 seconds BANG!—A final shot rings out. Howard Brennan, who is also looking directly at the gunman as he fires, turns quickly to his left to see if it hit, but his view of the president's car is blocked by part of the concrete peristyle.[218]

Zapruder's view, on the other hand, is clear and unobstructed. He pans his camera with the limousine as it rolls inexorably on down the long slope, the angle changing from three-quarter frontal to near broadside. As it draws abreast of him and only a few yards away, he hears a shot and sees, through the viewfinder, to his horror, the right side of the president's head explode.[219] His receptionist, Ms. Sitzman, sees the president's "brains come out, you know, his head opening . . . between the eye and the ear." It must have been a "terrible shot," she says, "because it exploded his head, more or less."[220]

Mrs. Kennedy is six inches from her husband's face when the bullet strikes, driving pieces of his skull into the air. His limp body bounces off the back of the seat and topples onto her shoulder in one horrifying, violent motion. She cries out, "Oh, no, no no. Oh my God, they have shot my husband. I love you, Jack."[221]

Just as Agent Clint Hill's hand reaches for the handhold on the trunk of the limousine, he hears the sound of a fired bullet smacking into a hard object.[222] In the front seat, Special Agent Roy Kellerman feels a sickening shower of brain matter blow into the air above his head and hears Mrs. Kennedy shout, "What are they doing to you?"[223]

From the follow-up car, Agent Paul Landis hears a muffled exploding sound—like shooting a bullet into a five-gallon can of water or a melon. He sees pieces of flesh and blood flying through the air and thinks, "My God, the president could not possibly be alive after being hit like that." He is not certain from which direction this shot came, but senses it came from the president's right front.[224]

Governor Connally, grievously wounded, is nonetheless still conscious at the moment of the head shot and knows all too well that the president has been hit. He and his wife are even more horrified to hear Jackie, somewhere behind them, saying, "They've killed my husband. I have his brains in my hand."[225]

At the same time that Kellerman yelled to Greer they were hit and to take off, Kellerman had grabbed the microphone used to access the Secret Service radio network linking the cars of the motorcade.

"Lawson, this is Kellerman," he shouts into the mike. "We're hit. Get us to the hospital immediately!"[226] But as he's starting to talk to Lawson and before Greer accelerates, a third shot rings out. Greer stomps on the gas pedal and the massive limousine lunges forward.[227]

Agent John Ready, who had jumped off the running board of the Secret Service follow-up car when the limousine had slowed and had started to run across the asphalt for the president's car, doesn't make it in time as the limousine speeds up, and Special Agent Emory Roberts orders Agent Ready back to the follow-up car.[228] As soon as he's aboard, Halfback's driver, Agent Sam Kinney, hits the accelerator and releases the car's siren as they shoot after the presidential limousine.[229]

Clint Hill, his hand grasping the trunk handhold, loses his footing, but jumps onto the back of the car just as it lurches forward.[230] Mrs. Kennedy has already climbed out of the backseat and is crawling toward him.* Hill senses that she is probably reaching for something coming off the right rear bumper of the car. He thinks he sees something come off the back of the car too, but he cannot be sure.[231] Hill pushes the First Lady back into the seat. "My God, they have shot his head off," she cries. Hill climbs toward her, clinging to the trunk as the limousine picks up more speed.

An instant after the head shot, Mary Moorman, on the grass fifteen feet away near the south curb of Elm Street, snaps a picture of the presidential limousine passing by. She quickly falls to the ground and tugs on Jean Hill's slacks, shouting, "Get down, they're shooting." Despite her pleas, Jean Hill is too stunned to move and just stands there for a moment, transfixed, before she slumps to the grass.[232]

A few feet away, Charles Brehm instinctively throws himself on his young son, covering him with his body. Brehm, a former army staff sergeant, knows about gunfire. Nineteen years before, at Brest in Normandy, not long after D-day, a German bullet went through his chest and blew his elbow joint apart. Now, despite his desperate hopes, he is positive that the president was also hit.[233]

"They've killed him, they've killed him!" Abraham Zapruder cries, his finger frozen on the movie camera's button. He pans to his right, following the presidential limousine as it lunges toward the Triple Underpass. Only after it disappears into the shadows of the underpass does Zapruder release the switch.[234]

Before James Worrell makes the left turn to start running north on Houston, he pivots and looks back over his shoulder before the window with the rifle in it is out of sight and sees the rifle fire a third time. Crossing Houston he runs north nearly a block along the east side of the Depos-

---

*Mrs. Kennedy would later have no recollection of crawling on the trunk of the car. Looking at still frames from the Zapruder film while working with author William Manchester, she said they brought nothing back to her. It was as though she were looking at photographs of another woman. (Manchester, *Death of a President*, p.161 footnote)

itory, stopping finally at the corner of Pacific to catch his breath. All he can think of is the sight of that gun barrel firing over his head.[235]

Across from the Depository, Howard Brennan dives off the stone wall. Caught up in the confusion and hysteria around him, he half expects bullets to start flying from every direction. His eyes swing back to the sixth-floor window. He watches as the gunman pulls the rifle back from the window as though drawing it back to his side. The gunman pauses another second as though to assure himself that he hit his mark, and then he disappears.[236]

Press photographer Bob Jackson, twenty-nine, saw the gun being withdrawn from the window too. All the press guys in Jackson's car (James R. Underwood, Thomas Dillard, Jimmy Darnell, and Malcolm O. Couch) were still laughing at a reporter chasing a canister of film across the street when the gunfire had broken out. Jackson had tossed it to him, as scheduled, at Main and Houston but it got caught in a strong gust of wind and started bouncing away from its pursuer. The press car was halfway up the block toward Elm when its occupants heard the first shot. Dillard told his companions that it sounded like a firecracker, but the words were barely out of his mouth when they heard the other two shots and realized it was gunfire. Jackson looked straight ahead at the Book Depository. He noticed two black men in the southeast corner window of the fifth floor leaning out to look up to the floor above. Jackson followed their gaze and saw the better part of a rifle barrel and stock being withdrawn, rather slowly, back out of sight behind the right edge of the window.

"There's the gun!" Jackson shouts.

"Where?" the others ask.

"It came from that window!" he says, pointing at the southeast corner window of the sixth floor.[237]

WFAA-TV cameraman Malcolm Couch, hearing Jackson, catches a one-second glimpse of "about a foot of a rifle" barrel being brought back "into the window" on the "far right" of "the sixth or seventh floor." He snatches his camera up from his lap and starts shooting the window, but there's nothing more to be seen there, just stacks of cartons.

The press car rounds the corner onto Elm, and Couch finds his camera's viewfinder filled with people running in all directions. Dillard, Underwood, and Darnell jump out at the corner, leaving Couch and Jackson to wonder whether they should follow them or stay with the motorcade.[238]

James Crawford had thought the first loud sound he heard to be a backfire of a car, but he quickly realized that the quality of the cars in the motorcade would not be the type to have backfires. Then he heard the second sound and began to look around, thinking someone was firing firecrackers. As the report from the third shot sounded, he looked up and saw a very quick, indistinct movement in the southeasternmost window on the sixth floor of the Book Depository Building. It was a profile, somewhat from the waist up, of something light colored, perhaps caused by the reflection of the sun, and what came to his mind automatically was that it was a person having moved out of the window. He also saw boxes stacked up behind the window. Crawford turned to his friend Mary Ann Mitchell, and pointing to the window, tells her, "If those were shots, they came from that window," but she is unable to see anything. Neither Crawford nor Mitchell saw or was aware of the president being hit and they soon returned to their office to listen to the radio to learn what had taken place.[239]

Aftermath Agent Bill Greer pulls the president's car to the right as he charges the lead car, overtaking it in the cool darkness of the underpass. Chief Curry accelerates the lead car to catch them. As the two cars emerge into the sunlight on the west side of the underpass, Agent Clint Hill, spread over the trunk of the president's car, looks into the backseat. The sight sickens him. The president's head is covered in blood, a portion blasted away. Hill can see a chunk with hair on it lying on the seat next to him. There is blood everywhere. Hill looks forward to the jump seats and notices Governor Connally's chest covered in blood. Only then does he realize that the governor, too, has been shot. But for Hill, the heart-wrenching scene is in the backseat, where Mrs. Kennedy is cradling the president's head, whimpering over and over, "Jack, Jack, what have they done to you?"[240]

Hill looks back to his left rear toward the lead car they are passing and yells as loud as he can, "To the hospital, to the hospital!"[241]

The Secret Service follow-up car rockets out of the shadow of the underpass. From the right running board, Agent Paul Landis looks toward the president's limousine just ahead. He can see Clint Hill lying across the back of the trunk. Hill looks back toward Landis, shakes his head back and forth, and gives a thumbs-down sign with his hand.[242] In the follow-up car's front seat, Agent Emory Roberts picks up the car radio.

"Halfback to Lawson," Roberts hollers, "the president has been hit. Get us to the nearest hospital!"

The Secret Service men in the follow-up car turn back to the vice president's car trailing a half block behind them and begin waving frantically, motioning the driver to close the gap. Roberts looks over at Agent William McIntyre, who's clinging to the follow-up car's left running board, the wind whistling through his hair.

"They got him! They got him!" Roberts shouts. "You and Bennett take over Johnson as soon as we stop!"

Roberts eyes Agent Hickey as he waves the AR-15 assault rifle aimlessly.

"Be careful with that!" he warns.[243]

Dallas police officers James M. Chaney and Douglas L. Jackson, the two motorcycle officers who had been flanking the right rear of the president's limousine, catch up with Chief Curry's lead car as they accelerate up the entrance ramp leading to Stemmons Freeway.[244]

"What happened?" Curry calls out.

"Shots have been fired," Chaney shouts.

"Has the president's party been hit?" Curry asks.

"I'm sure they have," Chaney confirms, as Curry grabs the radio microphone.[245]

"We're going to the hospital!" Chief Curry shouts frantically into his radio transmitter. "Parkland Hospital.* Have them stand by. Get men on

---

*Parkland Memorial Hospital, a ten-story county hospital about four miles from Dealey Plaza, was the largest and best hospital in Dallas County, a distinction it holds to this very day. Taking its name from the wooded parkland it sat on, the hospital opened on May 19, 1894. The present Parkland Hospital, on a new site, was dedicated on October 3, 1954.

top of that there over—underpass. See what happened up there. Go up to the overpass. Have Parkland stand by."[246] But Officer J. W. Foster, who was *on* the overpass at the time of the shooting, is convinced the shots came from the Book Depository Building, and indeed, he sees some officers running toward the building. He immediately gets off the overpass and runs toward the building, where he will assist in blocking it off.[247]

Officer Marrion L. Baker, who had been pretty sure the shots came from the roof of the Book Depository, wheels his motorcycle to a stop at the curb in front of the building. Quickly dismounting, Baker looks to his left and notices people lying on the grass in Dealey Plaza, others rushing to grab their children. A woman near him is screaming, "Oh they shot that man, they shot that man!"[248] He turns and runs toward the front steps of the Depository, pushing his way through the spectators crowding the entranceway.[249]

Roy Truly, the building superintendent, sees Baker coming and immediately understands that the young motorcycle officer is looking for a way to the roof. Truly follows him up the front steps, through the glass front doors, and into the vestibule, where he finds Baker asking people in the lobby where the stairs are.

"I'm the building manager," Truly tells him.

"Where is the stairway?" Baker asks.

"This way," Truly says, pushing his way through another set of double-doors.

Officer Baker is right on his heels and bumps into Truly's back when they start to cut through a little swinging door at the call counter. A bolt has slid out of place and keeps the door from opening. Truly frantically fumbles with the latch, pushes the door wide, and plunges diagonally toward the freight elevators at the back of the building, Officer Baker in hot pursuit.[250]

The chaos and confusion in the plaza is indescribable. The remainder of cars, motorcycles, and buses that make up the motorcade bunch up at the corner of Elm and Houston, then speed away toward the underpass. People are running every which way. Some who aren't running lie on the ground in fear. A motorcycle policeman, seeing some people on the ground pointing to the railroad yards, lets his bike fall at the north curb of Elm just east of the Fort Worth road sign and dashes up the grassy slope toward the yards.[251] Several police officers and a number of civilians run toward the area of the grassy knoll and retaining wall.[252]

The three stock boys on the fifth floor of the Depository peer down at the confusion unfolding below them. With the last shot still ringing in his ears, James Jarman jumps up and moves toward Bonnie Ray Williams and Harold Norman.

"That's no backfire," Jarman says. "Someone's shooting at the president."

"No bullshit!" Bonnie Ray says rising to his feet, still in disbelief.[253]

"I think it came from above us," Norman says. "I'm sure of it." Jarman and Williams agree.[254]

The three stock boys run toward the west side of the building where Jarman yanks a window open so they can see what's going on below. Jarman can see police officers and people running across the railroad tracks to the west of the building, the area behind the pergola, and the police "searching the boxcar yard and the passenger train."[255]

It doesn't take long for Jarman to also see the plaster dust in Bonnie's hair.

"That shot probably did come from above us," Jarman concedes.

"I *know* it did," Norman answers excitedly. "I could hear the action of the bolt and the cartridges hitting the floor."[256] Norman is very familiar with the sound of the bolt being pushed backward and forward because he has fired a bolt-action rifle before.[257]

12:31 p.m.

In the lead car, Sheriff Decker takes the radio microphone from Chief Curry and identifies himself to the police dispatcher.

"Go ahead, Dallas One [Decker]," the dispatcher replies crisply. Decker blurts back instructions over the wail of police sirens.

"Have Station Five [call sign for the sheriff's radio dispatch room] move all men available out of my department," Decker says, "back into the railroad yards there in an effort to try to determine just what and where it happened down there, and hold everything secure until the homicide and other investigators can get there."

"Ten-four, Dallas One. Station Five will be notified," the dispatcher says.[258]

By now the motorcade is flying at top speed[*] along Stemmons Freeway, all sirens screaming, past the stunned and puzzled onlookers scattered along both sides of the freeway to see the president. Curiously, the motorcade is still on its planned route, although now, when the cars turn off Stemmons onto Industrial Boulevard, they will pass their original destination, the Trade Mart, and go straight to Parkland Memorial.[†] In the backseat throughout the ride to the hospital, Jackie Kennedy cradles the president's head in her lap, bending over him and saying, "Jack, Jack, Jack. Can you hear me? I love you Jack." As she would later recall, "I kept holding the top of his head down, trying to keep his brains in . . . but I knew he was dead."[259]

At police headquarters, the dispatcher asks Chief Curry for any information he can give him.

"Looks like the president's been hit," Curry shoots back. "Have Parkland stand by."

"Ten-four. Parkland has been notified."[260]

Bob Jackson doesn't know what happened, or where the press car is going now, or why, only that it is following the rest of the motorcade toward Stemmons Freeway at a high speed. He is still holding his empty camera in his lap. The other one, which is loaded, is still strapped around his neck.[261] It all happened so fast he didn't get a single photograph. If he

---

[*]Later estimates of the speed vary. Two of the motorcycle escorts gave estimates of the speed on Stemmons Freeway ranging from 80 to 90 mph (Savage, *JFK First Day Evidence*, p.364; Sneed, *No More Silence*, pp.129, 156). Dallas police radio recordings (NAS-CBA DPD tapes, C2, 12:34 p.m.) indicate approximately four minutes were required to cover the four-mile ride to Parkland, which computes to an average speed of 60 mph over the entire route, which accounts for the slowing down of the limousine once it got off the Stemmons Freeway onto Industrial and then Harry Hines Boulevard.

[†]Not all pass the Trade Mart. The first press bus in the motorcade, unaware the president has been shot, proceeds to the Trade Mart, where the bus passengers soon learn he's been shot and is at Parkland Hospital (Semple, *Four Days in November*, pp.591–592).

had only gotten a picture of the rifle barrel in the window, he undoubtedly would have won the Pulitzer Prize for the best news photograph of
the year.*

Journalist Merriman Smith is sitting beside the driver of the press pool
car, which puts him in control of the car's only radio telephone. He grabs
it and calls the Dallas bureau of United Press International and tells the
bureau operator, "Three shots were fired at President Kennedy's motorcade in downtown Dallas." He goes on talking as the press car shoots forward, trying to catch up with the rapidly vanishing motorcade. He has
little to add to his one-liner, except to say that there are "no casualties"
to report, but the longer he can keep the phone out of the hands of Associated Press reporter Jack Bell, sitting directly behind him in the center
of the backseat, the bigger his "beat" of the rival wire service. On an event
as big as this, getting the story even a couple of minutes ahead of the competition is a coup. Smith, stalling, asks the bureau operator to read back
his dictation. Bell is beside himself, but Smith claims that nearby, overhead electric wires could have caused interference and he has to be sure
his news bureau got the story. Bell, by now furious, tries to grab the phone.
Smith, hanging onto it, crouches under the dash, while Bell flails at him.
When Bell finally gets the phone, it goes dead in his hands.[262]

Deputy Sheriff E. R. "Buddy" Walthers and dozens of sheriff deputies
are sprinting across the lawn in Dealey Plaza. They were out on the sidewalk on Main Street, in front of the Dallas County Criminal Courts
Building, when they heard what sounded like shots. Some run toward the
Book Depository Building, but Walthers and others, like Deputy Sheriff Eugene Boone, dash across Houston Street and run toward the grassy
knoll area, Walthers going over the stockade fence, Boone the concrete
retaining wall, into the train yards and parking area to the rear to search
for the gunman.[263]

---

*Jackson redeemed himself two days later when he took a Pulitzer Prize–winning photo-
graph of the murder of Lee Harvey Oswald by nightclub owner Jack Ruby.

Roy Truly and Officer Baker arrive at the back of the Depository, having crossed the first-floor shipping area, and find that neither freight elevator is there. Truly looks up the shaft and sees that both elevators appear to be on the fifth floor. He punches a nearby button, trying to summon the west elevator. A bell rings, but nothing happens—the elevator gate has been left open on the fifth floor.

"Turn loose the elevator!" he shouts up the shaft. He punches the button and hollers again. Nothing.

"Let's take the stairs!" Baker says, impatiently.

"Okay," Truly replies, and in a wink, spins and bolts up the northwest stairwell.[264]

Baker draws his service pistol and races up behind him. Truly is already pounding up the flight of stairs leading to the third floor when Baker reaches the second-floor landing. Just as the officer leaves the stairway and steps out onto the second floor, his eyes sweep across the area to his right through the window of the second-floor door, and he catches a glimpse of a man inside, walking away from him. Baker opens the door and runs through the doorway, then sees the man more clearly through a little window in the door to a vestibule that leads to a lunchroom. The man, twenty feet away, continues to walk away from Baker inside the lunchroom. Baker opens the vestibule door and walks through the vestibule about five feet to the door frame of the lunchroom. Leveling his gun waist-high at the man, he commands, "Come here."[265]

The man turns and walks back to within three feet of the officer. He appears calm, expressionless.[266]

Meanwhile, Roy Truly, who realizes that the officer is no longer following him, comes back down the stairs to the second floor, hears voices in the lunchroom, and steps into the vestibule behind Baker. He sees that the officer has drawn a gun on Lee Oswald, one of his employees. Oswald doesn't seem to be excited, overly afraid, or anything. He might be a bit startled, like Truly might have been if someone had confronted him with a gun, but otherwise Oswald's expression doesn't change one bit.[267]

"Do you know this man?" Baker asks, turning slightly to look at Truly over his left shoulder.

"Yes," the building superintendent says, "he works here."[268]

Officer Baker doesn't waste another second. He doesn't even bother to look back at Oswald. He brushes past Truly, makes his way back to the stairwell, and continues toward the roof, the building superintendent close behind him.[269]

Thomas P. Alyea, a camera-reporter for WFAA-TV in Dallas, is stopped (with his partner, Ray John) at the traffic light located at Commerce and Houston streets listening to Dallas police radio as well as the WFAA commercial radio. He hears a voice (Chief Curry) over the police radio instructing officers to go to Parkland Hospital. He has no reason to associate this with President Kennedy, but twenty seconds or so later he hears newsman John Allen over the commercial radio announce that shots had been fired at the president. Alyea immediately grabs Ray John's fully loaded camera and three extra cans of film, gets out of the car, and runs toward the intersection of Houston and Elm, filming the emerging, chaotic scene along the way. He notices several people pointing toward the upper floors of the Depository Building and runs inside along with a number of others who appear to be plainclothes detectives. Right behind him is *Dallas Morning News* reporter Kent Biffle. Biffle with his pencil and pad and Alyea with his camera would end up being the only two newsmen in the building during the period after the shooting. While Alyea starts filming, and Biffle recording on his notepad, the police search for the assassin on the various floors of the building.[270]

Newsman Robert MacNeil, of later *MacNeil/Lehrer News Hour* fame, far down the motorcade in the first press bus, is jolted out of a half sleep by the sound of a shot, but he isn't sure. Working on three and a half hours of shut-eye, a light breakfast, and then an unwise Bloody Mary on the flight to Dallas from Fort Worth, he has been finding it hard to stay awake. MacNeil was only recently made the number-two man on NBC's White House detail covering the president's Texas trip because Sandy Vanocur chose to accompany most of the cabinet on a mission to the Far East.

From his seat in the bus he has only been catching glimpses of the president's limousine seven cars ahead, and when he hears two more very distinct explosions, he knows they are shots, and he shouts out, "Stop the bus! Stop the bus!"

The driver opens the door as he turns the corner onto Elm Street, and MacNeil jumps out. People are down on the grass on both sides of the street, covering their children, and the air is filled with screaming. The sun is so bright it makes his eyes ache. Seeing some people run toward the far end of the grassy slope right next to the railroad overpass, MacNeil dashes after them—they may be chasing the sniper. But he really can't imagine that the president was hit. It must be some right-wing nut making some kind of crazy demonstration.

MacNeil climbs up on the bottom ledge of the concrete railroad bridge alongside many other spectators and looks over the top with them. He sees nothing of significance except police searching the area and realizes he had better find a telephone, fast.

He runs back and into the first building he comes to, the Texas School Book Depository, running into a young man in shirtsleeves coming out whom he would later come to believe may have been Oswald. He asks for a phone. The young man points inside to a man talking on a phone near a pillar. "Better ask him," he says.

Inside, MacNeil asks another young man, who steers him to another phone in an office, four of its five lines occupied. Mercifully, he gets through to the radio news desk in New York, but, infuriatingly, is asked to wait. He screams into the phone until Jim Holton comes on the line. "This is MacNeil in Dallas. Someone shot at the president."

Holton switches on a tape recorder and MacNeil records all he knows so far: "Shots were fired as President Kennedy's motorcade passed through downtown Dallas. People screamed and lay down on the grass as three shots rang out. Police chased an unknown gunman up a grassy hill. It is *not* known if the shots were directed at the president. This is Robert MacNeil, NBC News in Dallas."

Outside again, MacNeil rushes over to a policeman listening to the radio on a motorcycle. "Was he hit?"

"Yeah. Hit in the head. They're taking him to Parkland Hospital."

MacNeil dashes out into the street, dodging the police cars whose wailing sirens are pulling up from all directions, bouncing over curbs, flowerbeds, and lawn. Not a taxi in sight. Traffic is beginning to jam. He sprints across Dealey Plaza to Main Street and leaps out in front of the first car that comes along.

"This is a terrible emergency," he tells the driver. "The president's been shot. I'll give you five dollars to take me to Parkland Hospital."

The driver, about thirty, not too swift, smiles and says, "Okay." The car is filled with packages that look like cake boxes. "Yeah, I heard something about that on the radio a couple of minutes ago," he says.

"Where's the radio?"

"I put it in the backseat."

MacNeil grabs the little transistor and holds it out the window to clear the antenna. They are already bogging down in the rapidly jamming traffic. He begs the driver to speed, take risks, run red lights, anything—MacNeil will pay the fines. All the police cars are headed in the opposite direction, back toward the Texas School Book Depository.[271]

12:32 p.m.

Mrs. Robert A. Reid, a clerical supervisor, had been watching the motorcade from in front of the Book Depository Building. Right after the shots were fired she runs into the building and is returning to her desk in the big central office space on the second floor of the Depository as Oswald cuts through the office from the lunchroom, a full bottle of Coke in hand.

"The president has been shot," she tells him as he walks past her, "but maybe they didn't hit him."

Oswald mumbles something in reply, but what it was does not register with her. She feels it is a little strange for a stock boy to be up in the office at that time. Indeed, the only time she had seen Oswald in the office before is when he needed change, presumably to get a drink from the soda machine in the lunchroom. But this time, Oswald already has a Coke. She takes off her jacket and scarf as Oswald heads toward the stairs leading to the front entrance of the building.[272]

Baker and Truly round the stairwell on the fifth floor and discover one of the freight elevators. They take it to the top floor—the seventh—then climb one more flight of stairs to come out, through a little penthouse over the stairhead, onto the roof. Officer Baker trots over to the west side of the roof and immediately realizes the parapet, five feet high, is too high to look or shoot over. He has to stand on tiptoes to even see the street and the railroad yards below. He starts to check the huge Hertz sign atop the Depository roof, but after climbing ten feet up the ladder attached to it, Baker rules that out too—there's nothing to hold onto up there.[273]

The motorcade rockets along Stemmons Freeway, the president's car right on the tail of motorcycle escorts Stavis Ellis, Jim Chaney, and B. J. Martin. They know if they lose control of their motorbikes, they'll be run down by the four-ton monster behind them. They try to put some distance between themselves and the president's car but each time they accelerate and look back, limousine driver Bill Greer has increased his speed and closed the gap.[274]

Secret Service agent Rufus Youngblood is still crouching in the backseat of the vice president's car, trying to shout to Johnson over the roar of the wind and wailing sirens.

"When we get to the hospital," he hollers, "I want you and Mrs. Johnson to stick with me and the other agents as close as you can. We don't know the extent of the emergency in the president's car, but it may be necessary for you to be acting president. We are going into the hospital and we aren't gonna stop for anything or anybody. Do you understand? We will separate from the other party the moment we stop!"

"Okay, pardner," Johnson says.[275]

From his vantage point next to Mrs. Johnson, Senator Yarborough can see Clint Hill, sprawled over the back of the speeding presidential limousine, beating his fist on the trunk, his face contorted by grief, anguish, and despair. Whatever has happened, Yarborough knows it is serious.[276]

There is little movement in the president's car. The governor lapses into unconsciousness, believing, as he closes his eyes, that he is dying. So does his wife. Nellie puts her lips to his ear and whispers, "It's going to be alright, be still," though she can scarcely believe it herself. For a moment, she thinks he is dead. Then, his hand trembles slightly. She can only hold on tighter.

Behind them, they hear the muted sobs of the First Lady, "He's dead—they've killed him—oh Jack, oh Jack, I love you." There is a pause, then, in shock, she begins again.[277]

The motorcade exits the freeway onto the service road, barely slowing to make the right turn onto Industrial Boulevard, where the entrance to the Trade Mart is located. Sergeant Striegel and some other officers are there trying to flag them down, unaware that there's been a shooting. Striegel steps into the street and waves frantically for them to stop as the lead motorcycles accelerate and blast past him at a frightening speed for a surface street.[278]

The motorcade fast approaches Harry Hines Boulevard, where they'll have to navigate a forty-five-degree left turn toward Parkland Hospital. Just before Harry Hines, the road rises sharply to cross a railroad grade. The motorcycle escorts are familiar with the turn, but limousine driver Bill Greer is not, and he pushes the president's car faster, moving dangerously close to the motor jockeys. With the limousine's front grill barking at their heels, the police escorts hit the rise wide open, go airborne, and nearly lose control as they slam to earth in the middle of the boulevard, thirty feet away. On contact, the Harley-Davidson motorcycles bank hard into the left turn, sparks kicking up from their footstands dragging across the pavement. The president's car is right behind them, hitting the rise with a *Whump!*, then into the turn on squealing tires. Greer is doing all he can to handle the careening limousine, which bumps J. W. Courson's motorcycle briefly into the curb.[279] The men frantically pull out of the turn and accelerate toward the emergency entrance of Parkland Hospital three-quarters of a mile up the road. It's a wonder they haven't wrecked yet.

12:34 p.m.
Just four minutes after the shooting, United Press International, getting the story from the Dallas office after its reporter, Merriman Smith, called

it in from the radiophone on the dashboard of the White House press pool car in the motorcade, flashes the news, "Three shots were fired at President Kennedy's motorcade today in downtown Dallas," to its vast network of subscribers—newspapers, radio and television stations, and business offices all over the world. It is the first word to the outside world of what has happened in Dallas.[280]

As word of the shooting starts to spread throughout the land into every city and town, and every hamlet with a phone, radio, or TV set, people everywhere are physically staggered and stricken by the news. Groups of people gather everywhere, even around parked automobiles waiting for the next news bulletin over the car radio. Telephone switchboards light up like never before. The news spreads quickly across the Atlantic and Pacific oceans and the whole civilized world becomes "one enormous emergency room."[281]

12:35 p.m.

In Dealey Plaza, motorcycle officers and squad cars are swarming the Book Depository Building.[282] In the railroad yard, Deputy Sheriff Buddy Walthers encounters many police and spectators rummaging around, many beginning to doubt whether shots had been fired at all.

"Well, they sounded like rifle shots to me," Walthers tells the other officers. Walthers is familiar with the freight yards, having chased a couple of escapees from the county jail over here before, and knows that there's nowhere to hide. It's a wide-open river-bottom area as far as anyone can go, and he quickly begins to question whether anyone would be foolhardy enough to shoot from back here. Deputy Walthers walks back down the grassy slope to Elm Street and begins checking around a sewer cover off the south curb, where it appears that a bullet has chugged through the turf.[283]

Nearby, Dallas police motorcycle officer B. W. Hargis has located an eyewitness to the shooting, grabs his radio, and contacts the dispatcher.

"A passerby standing under the Texas School Book Depository stated that the shots came from that building," Hargis tells him.[284] This is the first police broadcast pinpointing the Book Depository as the source of the shots, but it will not be the last.

The reports are coming in fast now. The next one is from Officer C. A. Haygood.

"I just talked to a guy up here at the scene of this, where these shots were fired at, and he said that he was sitting here close to it, and . . . he thought they came from the Texas School Book Depository Building here, with that Hertz rental sign on top."

"Ten-four," the dispatcher says. "Get his name, address and phone number, and all the information you can. 12:35 p.m."[285]

12:36 p.m.

Sergeant D. V. Harkness, standing at the west end of the Elm Street extension, is asking for witnesses when young Amos Euins walks up, points to the Depository, and tells him he saw a man shooting from that building.[286] Harkness puts Euins on his three-wheel motorcycle and shuttles him to the front door of the Depository.[287] Harkness asks Euins which window he saw the man firing from. The teenage boy tells him it was the easternmost window of the floor "under the ledge"[288]—which makes it the sixth floor.

"It was a colored man," Euins says excitedly, "he was leaning out of the window and he had a rifle."[289]

Sergeant Harkness grabs the radio on his motorcycle and notifies headquarters, "I have a witness that says it came from the *fifth* floor of the Texas . . . ah . . . Depository Bookstore at Houston and Elm. I have him with me now. I'm gonna seal off the building."[290]*

As Harkness hangs up the radio mike, Inspector J. Herbert Sawyer, a twenty-three-year veteran of the Dallas Police Force, pulls his car to the curb in front of the Depository. For the last few minutes, the forty-seven-

---

*Harkness testified that Euins told him, "It was under the ledge," which referred to the sixth floor (6 H 313). Photographs of the building show a decorative ledge separating the sixth and seventh floors. Harkness further testified that "it was my error in a hasty count of the floors" (6 H 313) that led to his broadcast reference to the "fifth floor." Harkness's error is understandable in light of the fact that in 1963 the Depository's first-floor windows were covered with decorative masonry. Persons unfamiliar with the building could easily mistake the second floor for the first, third for the second, and so on—making the sixth floor appear as if it were the fifth floor. This is apparently what Harkness did during these initial confusing moments.

year-old plainclothes officer has been working his way toward the shooting scene from Main and Akard, where he had been in charge of crowd control.[291] Sawyer jumps from the car, and Harkness tells him that he's got a witness who says that shots were fired from the fifth floor of the Depository.[292]

"The building is sealed off," Harkness tells him. "There are officers all around the building."[293] The inspector grabs two officers. "Come with me," he says, and heads for the front door, intent on going to the fifth floor to check out Euins's story. Meanwhile, Harkness puts Euins in the back of Sawyer's car and tells him to stay put until someone can get a statement from him.[294]

Howard Brennan, standing across the street from the Depository, watches as the officers seem to be directing their search to the west side of the Book Depository Building and down Houston Street. He runs across the street toward Officer W. E. Barnett, who is at the front of the building.

"Get me someone in charge," Brennan tells Barnett, who had just come from searching the north and east sides of the Depository Building. "You're searching in the wrong direction. The man is definitely in this building. I was across the street there and I saw the man in the window with a rifle."

"Which window?" Barnett asks.

"One window from the top," Brennan says, pointing to the southeasternmost window on the sixth floor of the Depository Building.[295]

When Sawyer returns to the street after his cursory search found nothing, he takes two patrolmen and stations them at the front door to the Depository Building with instructions not to let anyone in or out.[296]

James R. Underwood, the assistant news director of KRLD-TV and radio, who had been riding in the motorcade and bailed out at the sound of the shots, approaches the squad car where Amos Euins sits in the backseat.

"Did you see someone with a rifle?" Underwood asks.

"Yes, sir," the fifteen-year-old boy answers.

"Were they white or black?"

"It was a colored man," Euins says.

"Are you sure it was a colored man?" Underwood presses.

"Yes, sir," Euins replies.[297]*

At Parkland Hospital, the presidential limousine pulls up abruptly at the emergency entrance. Secret Service agent Roy Kellerman leaps from the car and opens the back door. Not a gurney or a hospital orderly is in sight. Almost by the time it took the Dallas police to notify Parkland of the president's imminent arrival, the limousine was already at the back entrance.[298] The Secret Service follow-up car skids to a stop and a half-dozen agents tumble out.

"Go get us two stretchers on wheels!" Kellerman yells to them.[299]

The governor, lying face up in his wife's lap, begins to regain consciousness.

"Governor, don't worry," Kellerman says, "everything is going to be all right."

Special Agent Winston Lawson is the first into the building. He spots two gurneys at the end of a long corridor being pushed toward him. He dashes down and helps Nurse Diana Bowron and an orderly, Joe Richards, race them back to the entrance.[300]

Dave Powers and Ken O'Donnell jump from the follow-up car and bound toward the Lincoln. Powers hears Secret Service agent Emory Roberts shouting at him to stop, but he ignores him. When Powers reaches the side of the limousine, he half expects to hear the familiar voice say, "I'm all right." He and Jack Kennedy have been through so much. He finds his friend in Jackie's arms, his eyes open, and for a moment thinks he's conscious.

"Oh, my God! Mr. President, what did they do?"

Jackie looks up at him and shakes her head, "Dave, he's dead."

---

*Later that afternoon, Euins told the Dallas County Sheriff's Department in a sworn and signed statement that the shooter "was a white man" (CE 367, 16 H 963).

Suddenly, he realizes that the open eyes are in a fixed, vacant stare—the left eye bulging from its socket. Powers breaks down in tears.

Ken O'Donnell can only turn away.[301]

The vice president's car pulls up and agents hustle Lyndon Johnson, seen lightly rubbing his arm,* into the safety of the building. Senator Yarborough hears one of the Secret Service agents refer to Johnson as the "president," and he knows that John Kennedy must be dead. He runs over to the president's limousine and sees Mrs. Kennedy there in the backseat covered in blood, her head bowed.

"They murdered my husband," she moans.

Ralph Yarborough is devastated. It is the most tragic sight of his life.[302]

Emory Roberts opens the left rear door of the limousine. He sees the First Lady covering the president's body with hers and tells her they have to get the president out of the limousine, but she doesn't move. "Mrs. Kennedy, you've got to get out," an unidentified Secret Service agent shouts imploringly.

"There's no need," she replies faintly.

Roberts lifts her elbow for a close look at the president, then drops it.

"You stay with Kennedy, I'm going to Johnson," Roberts says to Kellerman, undoubtedly aware of the cruelly insensitive mechanical transfer of power.[303]

Nellie Connally grows agitated at the men fussing over the president. To her the situation is clear. The president is dead. She saw the gore; no one could live through that. Everyone is fretting over a dead man instead of helping her husband.[304] The governor, conscious enough to realize that his jump seat is blocking access to the president in the backseat, tries to get out, then collapses in pain.

"My God, it hurts," he groans.[305] A gurney rolls up to the side of the car.[306] A Dallas police motorcycle officer and two Secret Service agents lift

---

*The gesture, witnessed by a spectator, became the basis for an early report that Johnson had been wounded or suffered a heart attack (Associated Press wire copy, November 22, 1963, 1:18 p.m.; Manchester, *Death of a President*, p.169).

Connally's body onto the stretcher.[307] Hospital attendants push him quickly inside as Mrs. Connally stumbles after them.

Roy Kellerman folds the jump seats out of the way, as agents turn their attention to the president. Agent Paul Landis grabs Mrs. Kennedy by the shoulders and tries to help her up, but she resists, "No, I want to stay with him!"[308]

It is the most pitiful sight. The First Lady refuses to budge, crooning softly as she huddles over the mess in her lap. Agent Clint Hill mounts the rear bumper behind her and touches her gently on her trembling shoulders.

"Please, Mrs. Kennedy," he says tenderly.

Everyone around her is quiet. Seconds pass. Her moans are barely audible.

"Please," Hill mumbles again. "We must get the president to a doctor."

"I'm not going to let him go," she finally manages to say.

"We've got to take him in," Hill pleads.

"No, Mr. Hill. You *know* he's dead," she answers. "Let me alone."

Now, Hill thinks he realizes why Jackie isn't moving. She doesn't want everyone around to see the horror she is cradling. He quickly removes his suit coat and covers the president's head and upper chest with it to shield the horror from photographers, and Jackie releases her husband as a second gurney is pushed closer to the side of the limousine. Several agents pull the president toward them, struggling to lift the lifeless body onto the stretcher. The stretcher is quickly wheeled into the emergency entrance, a flock of people running alongside of it. Mrs. Kennedy is one of them; Jackie's hat and the red roses she'd been given at Love Field heaped on top of the president's body.[309]*

---

*There was one red rose from the bouquet that did not make it into the hospital. Stavis Ellis, one of the Dallas police cyclists who had led the close-tailing presidential limousine to Parkland is among the large crowd of people who have swarmed around the emergency area in back of the hospital. After President Kennedy's body and Connally have been removed from the limousine he can't resist the temptation to look inside the car. He sees several puddles of blood on the rear seat and floorboard. Right in the middle of one of the puddles lay a beautiful red rose. Years later he would recall, "I never forgot that. I can still see it, that red rose in that blood." (Sneed, *No More Silence*, p.147)

The national press pool car and several other motorcade vehicles left behind in Dealey Plaza begin to arrive at the hospital. Doors fly open and UPI correspondent Merriman Smith runs up and grabs Clint Hill.

"How is he?" Smith asks.

Hill curses, then says, "He's dead."

The reporter dashes into the hospital, bursts into the emergency room's cashier's cage, and snatches a telephone. "How do I get outside?" he demands.

"Dial nine," she stutters.

He calls the local UPI office.

"Kennedy has been seriously wounded—perhaps, fatally," Smith tells them.[310]

12:38 p.m.

The emergency room* is sheer bedlam. Roy Kellerman, moving as quickly as he can, enters a doctor's office and asks the medic there, "Can I use either one of these phones to get outside?"

"Yes, just pick one up."

Kellerman calls Gerald Behn, chief of the Secret Service White House detail, in Washington. "Gerry, . . . the president and the governor have been shot. We're in the emergency room of Parkland Memorial Hospital. Mark down the time."

Kellerman notes it as 12:38, Behn as 12:41 p.m.[311] Officially, the president is logged into the hospital register at 12:38 p.m. as "No.24740, Kennedy, John F."[312]

---

*Inside the emergency area at Parkland were four emergency rooms, Trauma Rooms One, Two, Three, and Four. They were located on what was called the ground floor, not the first floor, at Parkland Hospital. Kennedy was immediately taken to Trauma Room One. (3 H 358–359, WCT Dr. Charles James Carrico) Above the ground floor were floors one through ten. The operating rooms were on the second floor. Though Governor Connally, who was taken to Trauma Room Two, was eventually brought up to an operating room on the second floor, Kennedy never left Trauma Room One. The entire emergency area at Parkland has since been reconstructed, and the Trauma Room One that Kennedy was brought into is no longer in existence. (Telephone interview of representative of Parkland's Corporate Communication section by author on January 21, 2004)

12:39 p.m.

Dallas police are quickly mobilizing in Dealey Plaza. More reports are coming in, each focusing on the building commanding the northwest corner of Elm and Houston.

"Get some men up here to cover this building, this Texas School Book Depository," Officer Clyde A. Haygood radios in. "It is believed these shots came from [there]."[313]

Officer E. D. Brewer cuts in with another report: "We have a man here that saw [a gunman] pull a weapon back through the window off the second floor* on the southeast corner of that Depository building."[314]

Cecil McWatters, an eighteen-year veteran bus driver for the Dallas Transit Company, has been driving the Marsalis-Munger route for about two years now, zigzagging diagonally across the city from the Lakewood Addition out in the northeast to Oak Cliff in the southwest, and back again. There's only a handful of people in the forty-four-passenger bus as he heads west on Elm in downtown Dallas, but McWatters more or less expects that, since so many folks went into town earlier for the presidential motorcade.[315]

While at a complete stop in traffic on Elm at Murphy (just before Griffin), which is seven blocks east of the Depository, a man bangs on the door and McWatters lets him board, collecting the twenty-three-cent fare, even though, as indicated, he is not at a bus stop. The man takes the second seat back, on the right. From that seat he will be passing right by the scene of the assassination.[316]

Mary E. Bledsoe is sitting right next to the front door of the bus. She turns her face away as the man gets on, hoping he doesn't recognize her. It's Lee Oswald and there is just something about him that she has never liked. Mary's been divorced for a good many years, but

---

*Photographs show this second-floor window to be closed at the time of the shooting. Brewer no doubt meant the sixth-floor sniper's nest window, which would have been at the southeast corner, *second floor down from the roof*.

she's managed to scrape by and raise her two boys on a little money her doctor father had left her and by renting out two or three of the four bedrooms in her house on North Marsalis. Back in October she had rented a room to Oswald for seven dollars a week, then five days later asked him to leave the premises. He was always fussing with someone over the phone looking for a job. And she didn't like his big-shot attitude or the fact that while using the telephone once she heard him talking in a foreign language. She told a lady friend of hers, "I don't like anybody talking in a foreign language."[317]

His appearance now—a hole in the right elbow of his brown shirt, which is "undone," his trousers "all ragged" in the waist area, and a "bad" look on his "distorted" face—reaffirms her opinion of him. He passes right in front of her and sits somewhere behind her.[318]

12:40 p.m.

Harry McCormick, a veteran police reporter at the *Dallas Morning News*, pulls into Dealey Plaza and jumps from his car, which is filled with fellow newsmen. They were scheduled to cover the president's luncheon at the Trade Mart, but after hearing of the shooting they immediately raced to the scene of the crime. One of the first people McCormick encounters is Abraham Zapruder, who is highly agitated, almost weeping.

"I saw it all through my camera," Zapruder half sobs to himself.

"What happened?" McCormick asks.

"I got it all on film," Zapruder replies. "There were three shots. Two hit the president and the other Governor Connally. I know the president is dead. His head seemed to fly to pieces when he was hit the second time."

McCormick knows that if Zapruder really did capture the assassination on film, it could be the most important film in history.

"The Secret Service will want to see those films," McCormick says. "Where are you going?" Zapruder tells him that he's going back to his office, across the street from the Book Depository. Thinking fast, McCormick assumes the authority of an officer.

"Go ahead," he tells Zapruder. "I'll find Forrest Sorrels, head of the Secret Service here, and we'll be back to talk with you."

McCormick didn't have a clue where he was going to find Sorrels, whom he had known personally for many years, but he knew he'd have to find him fast, before his competition found out about Zapruder's film.[319]

Zapruder stumbles back to his office in a state of shock, muttering, "They killed him, they killed him." At his office, Zapruder calls his twenty-six-year-old son, Henry, a government lawyer. "The president is dead," he says. Henry suggests his father is wrong, that he had just heard over the radio the president was wounded and on his way to the hospital. "No," the elder Zapruder says, "he's dead," explaining he had seen the president's head exploding through the lens of his camera.[320]

James Tague, who had witnessed the shooting from the mouth of the Triple Underpass, walks up to plainclothes deputy sheriff Buddy Walthers, combing the grass near the south curb of Elm Street.

"Are you looking to see where some bullets may have struck?" Tague asks.

"Yes," Walthers replies, barely paying attention.

"I was standing right there where my car is parked," Tague says, pointing to where Commerce meets the underpass, "when those shots happened. Well, you know, now I recall something stung me on the face while I was standing down there."[321]

Walthers looks up.

"Yes, you have blood there on your cheek," he says, rising to his feet.

Tague reaches up and wipes his fingers through a few drops of blood.

"Where were you standing?" Walthers asks.

"Right down here," Tague says, leading him toward a concrete strip that runs between Commerce and Main Street just east of the Triple Underpass.[322]

Twenty-three feet from the east face of the underpass,[323] along the south curb of Main Street, Walthers spots a mark on the top of the curb. It is quite obvious to both of them that the fresh gash was made by a bullet, and from the angle of the mark, it came from the direction of the Texas School Book Depository.[324]

Across America, housewives are following the fortunes of the characters of *As the World Turns*, the CBS network's popular soap opera. Actress Helen Wagner turns to fellow actor Santos Ortega and says, "And I gave it a great deal of thought, Grandpa." Suddenly, the program is cut off, replaced by a blank screen with the words "CBS NEWS" and in larger, white type, the single word "BULLETIN." Over it comes the sound of the network's leading newscaster, Walter Cronkite, his voice charged with emotion.[*]

"Here is a bulletin from CBS News. In Dallas, Texas, three shots were fired at President Kennedy's motorcade, in downtown Dallas. The first reports say President Kennedy has been seriously wounded by this shooting."

Cronkite fumbles momentarily with a fresh sheet of wire copy handed to him.

"More details just arrived," he says, scanning it quickly. "These details about the same as previously. President Kennedy shot today just as his motorcade left downtown Dallas. Mrs. Kennedy jumped up and grabbed Mr. Kennedy. She called, 'Oh no!' The motorcade sped on. United Press International reports that the wounds perhaps could be fatal."

The network suddenly returns to *As the World Turns*, the actors, working live in their New York studio, unaware of the interruption. Shocked viewers who switch to ABC or NBC are treated to similar bulletins, equally terse, equally alarming. All three networks will soon cancel all programming and commercials for coverage of the event in Dallas.[325]

At Parkland Hospital, thirty-four-year-old Dr. Malcolm O. Perry is enjoying a quiet lunch with Dr. Ronald C. Jones in the main dining room. They hear Dr. George Shires being paged.

---

[*]At the time, CBS did not have the capability of putting a commentator on camera immediately. "It took nearly twenty minutes to set up the cameras so Cronkite's voice could be joined by his face, and because of that experience, CBS would later install a 'flash studio' to enable visual, as well as audio, bulletins to be transmitted immediately." (Gates, *Air Time*, p.3)

Perry knows that Shires, chief of the emergency surgical service at the hospital, was actually delivering a paper to a medical conference in Galveston that morning and may not be back yet. When Shires is paged a second time, Perry asks Jones to pick up the page to see if it's a matter on which they might be of some assistance.

Jones rushes back to their table to report that the president has been shot and is being brought to emergency, not knowing the president had already arrived by the time he received the message from the hospital operator. The two surgeons bolt from the dining room and, too rushed to wait for the elevator, gallop down the flight of stairs to the emergency room.[326]

12:41 p.m.

Out in Irving, Marina Oswald and Ruth Paine, who has returned from her errands, are taking care of some household chores. When Ruth goes into the kitchen to fix lunch for them, Marina retires to her bedroom to get dressed. She hears a sudden, loud, puzzling commotion from the television set in the living room, but makes no sense of it—until Ruth appears in the doorway, ashen. Someone shot at the president.

They run to the living room and stare at the television, waiting for it to tell them something, anything. There are no images of the event, nothing but a news announcer who seems to be at a loss too, obviously marking time until some real information comes in, and it's clear that he knows little more than they do. Ruth is crying as she translates the essential information—President Kennedy's been taken to Parkland Hospital. Marina knows Parkland—she had baby Rachel there just a month ago.

Lunch is forgotten. No one feels like it now. Ruth lights some candles, and lets her little girl light one. Marina, who knows that her friend takes her Quaker religion very seriously, asks, "Is that a way of praying?"

"Yes, it is," Ruth says, "just my own way."

Marina goes to her room and cries.[327]

D r. Charles Carrico is standing in Trauma Room One, a narrow room with gray-tiled walls and a cream-colored ceiling, when the president is wheeled in on an emergency cart. Carrico is only twenty-eight and still doing his residency in surgery, but he has already seen nearly two hundred gunshot wounds at Parkland Hospital.[328] He rapidly assesses the president's condition—his color is "blue white, ashen," an indication of failing blood circulation; his respiration is slow, agonal (death throes), and spasmodic, with no coordination; there are no voluntary movements at all; his eyes are open and staring, with no reaction to light, his pupils dilated; and there is no palpable pulse. With the assistance of Drs. Don T. Curtis and Martin G. White and Nurse Diana Bowron, Dr. Carrico opens the president's suit coat and shirt and puts his ear to the president's chest. He listens for a few seconds and detects a faint heartbeat. Other nurses arrive and continue to remove Kennedy's clothing. Carrico slips his hands under the president's midsection and runs them up his back past his back brace.*

---

*After eliciting from Carrico and other Parkland doctors that the president was wearing a back brace, nowhere did Warren Commission counsel go on to ask the doctors just what they did with the famous brace, although one could assume they would have removed it at some point. One doctor testified he saw it "lying loose" (6 H 66, WCT Dr. Gene Coleman Akin), though another said he "pushed up the brace" to feel the president's femoral pulse (3 H 368, WCT Dr. Malcolm O. Perry), suggesting it wasn't removed. In less-than-clear testimony, Secret Service agent William Greer suggested that the brace was among the items of the president's belongings he was given in two shopping bags by a Parkland nurse when the body was ready for removal (2 H 125), but this wouldn't tell us when, if at all, it was removed by the Parkland doctors *during* their effort to save his life. Almost thirty years later, Dr. Marion T. "Pepper" Jenkins, one of the Parkland doctors, said the president "must have had really severe back pain judging by the size of the back brace *we cut off.* [Again, not when, though the natural assumption would be at the beginning of the effort to save the president. But Dr. Paul Peters, who arrived at least five minutes after the president entered Trauma Room One, said the brace was still on, and he only refers to his removing "an elastic bandage wrapped around his pelvis," but says nothing about removing the back brace (6 H 70).] He was tightly laced into this brace with wide Ace bandages making figure-of-eight loops around his trunk and thighs" (Breo, "JFK's Death, Part II," p.2805). A Parkland doctor described it as a "corset-type" brace with "stays . . . and buckles" (3 H 359, WCT Dr. Charles James Carrico).

Dr. John Lattimer, who studied the assassination for years, researched the entire brace issue and concluded it may have been responsible for Kennedy's death. He writes that Kennedy had "bound himself firmly in a rather wide corset, with metal stays and a stiff plastic pad over the sacral area, which was tightly laced to his body. The corset was then bound even more firmly to his torso and hips by a six-inch-wide knitted elastic bandage, which he had wrapped in a figure eight between his legs and around his waist, over large thick pads, to encase himself tightly . . . He apparently adopted this type of tight binding as a consequence of the painful loosening of his joints around the sacroiliac area, probably a result of his long-continued cortisone therapy." The result? When he and Connally were hit by the same bullet, the "corset prevented him from

He can feel blood and debris, but no wounds. He looks briefly at the president's head wound—a gaping hole, oozing with blood and shredded scalp and brain tissue—then turns his attention to restoring the president's breathing and circulation.[329]

Carrico orders Drs. Curtis and White to do a cutdown on the president's right ankle—a small incision to lay bare a large vein into which they can insert polyethylene catheters through which fluid, medicine, and blood can be administered to maintain the body's circulatory system.[330] The president is losing so much blood that the trauma room is already awash with it. Meanwhile, Carrico inserts a plastic endotracheal tube down

---

crumpling down out of the line of fire, as Governor Connally did. Because the president remained upright, with his head exposed, Oswald was able to draw a careful bead on the back of his head." (Lattimer, *Kennedy and Lincoln*, p.171; Lattimer, "Additional Data on the Shooting of President Kennedy," p.1546)

Since the first bullet that struck Kennedy passed through soft tissue and did not penetrate any organ of the body, it was the opinion of Dr. Perry, Kennedy's chief attending surgeon, that "barring the advent of complications, this wound was tolerable, and I think he would have survived it" (3 H 372). Writer James Reston Jr. captioned his article on this issue, "That 'Damned Girdle': The Hidden Factor That Might Have Killed Kennedy" (*Los Angeles Times*, November 22, 2004, p.B9). If this is true, the Japanese destroyer that sunk Kennedy's PT boat in World War II and killed two of his crewmates, only injuring Kennedy's already fragile back when he was hurled backwards onto the deck (Leaming, *Jack Kennedy*, p.139; O'Donnell and Powers with McCarthy, *Johnny, We Hardly Knew Ye*, p.48), finally claimed Kennedy as its third victim twenty years later.

If there is no certainty as to the role the president's back brace played in his death, there is something closer to certainty that caused his death and which he himself was responsible for. As indicated earlier, President Kennedy did not want Secret Service agents riding on the steps attached to the right and left rear bumper of the presidential limousine. Gerald A. Behn, special agent in charge of the White House Secret Service detail, said that shortly after assuming his job in late 1961, President Kennedy had told him this. No fewer than five Secret Service agents gave statements to the Warren Commission that it was common knowledge among the White House detail that this was Kennedy's desire, which he reiterated twice in the summer of 1963, once in Rome on July 2, 1963, the other time in Tampa, Florida, just four days before the assassination. Kennedy's desire was not etched in stone, and since the Secret Service has the right to do whatever is necessary to protect the president, in Tampa, on November 18, Special Agent Donald Lawton was standing on the right rear step, Special Agent Charles Zboril on the left rear. Kennedy told Special Agent Floyd Boring, who was seated in the right front seat of the limousine, to have the two agents return to the follow-up car. When the limousine slowed through downtown Tampa about three minutes later, the two agents dismounted. (CE 1025, 18 H 805–809; "Kennedy Barred Car-Step Guards," *New York Times*, November 24, 1964, pp.1, 33)

The likelihood is high that if Kennedy had not been opposed to Secret Service agents riding on the back of his car—the agent standing on the *right rear* step would have blocked Oswald's sight on Kennedy's head.

the president's throat into the trachea (windpipe) in order to create an adequate air passage. He notices a small ragged tear to the right of the larynx (voice box) and ragged tissue below, indicating tracheal injury. Carrico steers the plastic tube deep into the throat and begins connecting the cuff inflator (a latex cuff designed to prevent air leakage) to a respiratory machine.[331]

Just then, Drs. Perry and Jones arrive. Perry sheds his dark blue glen-plaid jacket and wristwatch in the corner, and takes charge.[332] Dr. Charles Baxter, another thirty-four-year-old assistant professor of surgery at the school, and director of the emergency room at Parkland, arrives around the same time, having made a dead run from the school as fast as he could when he heard the news.[333]* The trauma room is now filled with law enforcement officers and several members of the president's party. Supervising nurse Doris Nelson has already arrived and is struggling to clear them from the room.[334]

Dr. Perry steps over toward the ambulance gurney where the president is lying under the hot glare of an overhead lamp, a sheet over his lower extremities and trunk. He is surprised to find the president a bigger man than he thought, and is momentarily awed by the thought, "Here is the most important man in the world." Perry quickly notes the deep blue color of his face and the short, jerky contractions of his chest and diaphragm as he struggles to draw a breath.[335]

12:43 p.m. (1:43 p.m. EST)
Robert Kennedy, the nation's attorney general, had been in a good, even bouncy mood this morning. He called a meeting in his office with U.S. attorneys from around the country to report to him on his war against organized crime in their respective districts. As was his style, he loosened his tie, and with his suit coat hanging over a nearby chair, rolled up his shirt sleeves and got down to work with his associates. The news he

---

*Per the Warren Report, "As the President's limousine sped toward the hospital, 12 doctors rushed to the emergency area." The report named the twelve (four surgeons, one neurologist, four anesthesiologists, one urological surgeon, one oral surgeon, and one heart specialist), but omitted at least two doctors, Dr. Carrico and Dr. Charles Crenshaw. (WR, p.53)

received was encouraging. The mob was on the run. Breaking for lunch he got into his car with the U.S. attorney for the Southern District of New York, Robert Morgenthau, and Morgenthau's chief deputy, Silvio Mollo, and drove to his Hickory Hill home in a Virginia suburb of Washington, D.C. It was an unseasonably warm day for November 22, and the men and RFK's wife, Ethel, took their lunch of clam chowder and tuna-fish sandwiches at an outdoor patio. When a pool-side extension phone rings nearby, Ethel leaves the table to answer it.

"It's J. Edgar Hoover," she says, holding the phone out toward her husband.

He knows something extraordinary has happened; Hoover never calls him, and certainly not at home. It is an open secret that there is no love lost between Hoover and RFK. Hoover had never been in a position before of having an attorney general who was closer to the president than he was, and he resented this. Also, RFK's strong offensive against organized crime was, in effect, a slap in the face to Hoover in that it implied that the FBI had not been the gangbusters everyone had been brought up to think they were. RFK rises and crosses over to take the phone, "Hello?"

Morgenthau sees one of the workmen painting the new wing of the house spin and race toward them, clutching a transistor radio. He's shouting something unintelligible.

"I have news for you," Hoover says formally. "The president's been shot. It's believed to be fatal. I'll call you back when I find out more."

Bobby Kennedy turns away, his hand to his mouth. There is a look of shock and horror on his face. Ethel rushes to his side. For a few seconds he can't speak. Then, he forces the words out: "Jack's been shot. It may be fatal."[336]

On the other side of Washington, the U.S. Senate press liaison officer, Richard Riedel, darts onto the Senate floor and gives the message of the president's shooting to the first senator he encounters, S. L. Holland of Florida. He repeats the message to Senator Wayne Morse and then spots Senator Edward Kennedy on the dais, presiding over the chamber in a desultory debate over a bill on federal library services. He immediately rushes to the young senator.

"The most terrible thing has happened!" Riedel exclaims.

The senator, who is signing correspondence, looks up.

"What is it?"

"Your brother, the president," Riedel says. "He's been shot."

Ted Kennedy gasps.

"No!" he says. "How do you know?"

"It's on the ticker. Just came in on the ticker."

Senator Kennedy quickly gathers up his papers and runs from the chamber. He knows he must get his sister Eunice and fly immediately to Hyannis Port to be with his mother and father. When Majority Leader Mike Mansfield learns the news, he is too overcome with grief to make a motion for adjournment.[337]

With the Senate in recess, senators and reporters rush to the "marble room," the lobby behind the Senate chamber where UPI and AP printers ("tickers") are slowly delivering the tragic and unfolding story on paper. A young CBS reporter, Roger Mudd, sees Richard B. Russell, the conservative, states-rights senator from Georgia who opposed civil rights legislation, bent over the cabinet enclosing the UPI ticker, reading the Teletype out loud to the crowd around him as tears are streaming down his face.[338]

At Parkland Hospital in Trauma Room Two, across the hall from the president, Dr. Robert R. Shaw attends to Governor Connally. Shaw, chief of thoracic surgery at Parkland, saw the motorcade fly past the intersection of Harry Hines and Industrial boulevards as he drove back to Parkland from Children's Hospital. Continuing on to the medical school,[*] where he expected to have lunch, he heard the news of the shooting on

---

[*]The medical school, so often referred to in assassination literature, is the University of Texas Southwestern Medical School located right next door to Parkland Hospital. In fact, the first floors are connected by a long corridor. The two institutions are separately owned and governed but have an extremely close relationship, Parkland being the "teaching hospital" for the medical school. In fact, many of the doctors on the Parkland staff are professors at the school, and most of the school's graduates do their residency at Parkland.

his car radio. At the medical school, he overheard a student telling three others that the president was dead on arrival at Parkland.

"You're kidding, aren't you?" one of the three asked.

"No, I'm not. I saw him. And Governor Connally has been shot through the chest."

Shaw sprinted over to the hospital's emergency room, where he found the governor being attended by three doctors. Now, Connally complains of difficulty breathing due to a deep pain in the right side of his chest. He has apparently been conscious, except for brief moments, since the shooting. Shaw notes that the team has already put a tight occlusive dressing over the large sucking wound in the chest, and a rubber tube, connected to a water seal bottle, between the second and third ribs—an attempt to expand the collapsed right lung. Shaw steps outside for a moment to relay to Nellie Connally that a sample of the governor's blood has been sent for cross-matching, and that a regular operating room two floors above has been alerted. A few minutes later, the team transports the governor upstairs by elevator.[339]

Across the hall, in Trauma Room One, Dr. Perry orchestrates the treatment of the president. Dr. Carrico finishes hooking up the respirator and flips the switch, pumping air into the president's lungs. Carrico listens briefly to the president's chest. His breathing is better, but still inadequate. Air is leaking from the small hole in the throat.[340] Dr. Perry examines the chest briefly but can see no wound. He pushes up the body brace on the president's left side to feel for his femoral pulse.* There is none. Perry can see that the president is still struggling to breathe, despite the endotracheal tube Dr. Carrico inserted in his throat. Perry knows that a more effective air passage must be made immediately. He asks someone to bring him a tracheotomy tray as he snaps on a pair of surgical gloves, but finds there is already one there. Perry gestures toward a small hole in the throat. "Did you start a tracheotomy?" he asks Carrico.

"No," Carrico replies, shaking his head. "That's a wound." Carrico had previously observed foamy blood oozing, with each attempt at respiration,

---

*The femoral artery is the main artery of the thigh and can be felt in the pelvic area.

from a small, fairly round wound in the front of the president's throat just below and to the right of the Adam's apple.[341]

Commencing a tracheotomy (incision into the windpipe), Dr. Perry grabs a scalpel and makes a quick, large incision directly through the hole in the throat.[342]*

Other doctors are now arriving en masse. Dr. William Kemp Clark, the hospital's senior neurosurgeon, pushes his way in and helps to withdraw Dr. Carrico's endotracheal tube as Dr. Perry is about to insert a plastic tracheotomy tube directly into the windpipe.[343] Drs. Charles R. Baxter and Robert N. McClelland, both general surgeons, along with urologist Dr. Paul C. Peters, assist Perry in inserting the tracheotomy tube, while Dr. Marion T. Jenkins, professor and chairman of Parkland's Department of Anesthesiology, and his assistant, Dr. Adolph H. Giesecke Jr., hook up the tube to an anesthesia machine, which they had brought down from the Anesthesia Department on the second floor in order to better control the president's circulation.[344]

Perry asks Dr. Peters to make an incision in the chest and insert a tube to drain any blood or air that might be accumulating in the right side of the chest cavity.[345] Meanwhile, Dr. Ronald C. Jones inserts a chest tube into the left side of the chest, then, along with several other doctors (including surgery interns and residents Drs. Don T. Curtis, Kenneth E. Salyer, Martin C. White, and Charles A. Crenshaw),[346] makes additional cutdowns on the president's right and left arms and legs in order to quickly infuse blood and fluids into the circulatory system.[347] The pace is very quick and intense. Dr. Clark works his way around closer to the president's massive head wound. He exchanges a desperate glance with Perry. Both know there is no chance of saving the president. They are only going through the motions.[348]

Admiral George Burkley, the president's personal physician, rushes into the room and immediately sees that the president's condition is hopeless and death is certain. Whatever life might still exist in the motionless

---

*The bullet wound happened to be located in the precise place where a tracheotomy is normally performed.

body on the gurney will be impossible to sustain no matter what the Parkland doctors do. He sees that the surgical team is working to supply type
O RH-negative blood. He informs them that Kennedy's type is O RH-
positive[349]* and asks Dr. Peters to administer steroids to the president,
essential because of the president's adrenal deficiency, which leaves his
body unable to cope with stress and trauma. He hands over three 100-
milligram vials of Solu-Cortef, muttering, "Either intravenously or
intramuscularly."[350] Burkley knows there is really no need for it, but knows
also that they have to do everything they can.[351]

The president's personal physician steps out into the corridor, where
Mrs. Kennedy is sitting on a folding chair, dazed. Afraid that her husband's death is imminent, she wants to go into the operating room.

"I'm going in there," she murmurs.

Doris Nelson, the strong-muscled supervising nurse with plenty of
starch in her collar, hears her and bars the door, the policy of the hospital, as with most hospitals, being not to allow relatives into an operating
room.

"You can't come in here," she says sharply, setting her rubber-soled
shoes against the frame of the door.

"I'm coming in, and I'm staying," Mrs. Kennedy says and pushes. The
nurse, considerably stronger, pushes back. Jackie Kennedy always used
to bow to medical advice. She was young, and the doctors, she thought,
always knew best. When she heard her husband calling her after his back
operation in 1954, she tried to go to him, but no one would admit her and
she backed off. Then, after the operation, when a specialist's treatments
began to fail, they talked her out of bringing in a consultant. The president subsequently suffered through four months of intense pain. She
vowed then and there not to allow doctors and nurses to intimidate her.

"I'm *going* to get in that room," she whispers fiercely to the nurse
blocking the door.

*The Parkland doctors chose type O RH-negative blood because it is safe to give to anyone,
regardless of his or her type, as it causes no adverse reaction.

The commotion attracts Admiral Burkley, who suggests that Mrs. Kennedy take a sedative.

"I want to be in there when he dies," she tells him, and she refuses the sedation,[352] wanting, it seems, to soak up as much pain as she can. To cheat pain at a moment like this, when her husband has suffered the most horrible wounds and was near death, would have diminished her and what they had meant to each other.

The admiral nods understandingly.

"It's her right, it's her prerogative," he says as he leads her past the nurse, who mistakenly believes he is a Secret Service agent.

Looking shell-shocked, Mrs. Kennedy aimlessly circles the hospital gurney where technicians work feverishly on her husband's body. Her hands are cupped in front of her, as if cradling something. As she passes Dr. Jenkins, she nudges him with her elbow and hands him what she has been nursing—a large chunk of brain tissue. Jenkins quickly gives it to a nearby nurse.[353] The president's physician ushers Mrs. Kennedy into a corner of the trauma room, now overflowing with people. She rests her cheek on Admiral Burkley's shoulder, then drops briefly to the floor, closes her eyes and prays.[354]

The McWatters bus carrying Lee Oswald rumbles west on Elm Street, the smell of diesel exhaust permeating the floorboards. Between Poydras and Lamar, the driver pumps the air brakes as the bus rolls up behind traffic that is stalled for four blocks from the assassination scene. From the looks of it, they won't be going anywhere soon. A man climbs out of a car stopped in front of the bus, and walks back. McWatters pulls the lever next to him and the front doors hiss open.

"I heard over my car radio that the president has been shot," the man says.

The passengers are astonished. Some don't believe it.

The woman across from Mrs. Bledsoe realizes in panic that the bus may not move for a very long time, and she has to catch a train at Union Station, four blocks away. She decides to walk, even if it means lugging her suitcase all that way. She asks McWatters if she can have a transfer so she can get back on the bus if it breaks free from traffic, and McWatters is happy to oblige.

Oswald gets up and asks McWatters for a transfer too, following the woman off the bus. He walks right past his former landlady again, and this time Mary Bledsoe thinks he might have recognized her. In any event, she is happy enough to see the last of him.[355]

The area around the entrance to the Depository is quickly growing chaotic. Dealey Plaza witnesses are offering various bits of information. Inspector Sawyer knows he will need help to handle the situation, and reaches for his car radio.

"We need more manpower down here at this Texas School Book Depository," he says and instructs the dispatcher to have some squad cars pick up the officers stationed along the motorcade route and bring them down to the Depository.[356]

Officer E. W. Barnett, with Howard Brennan in tow, tells Sawyer that he has an eyewitness who saw the gunman.

"What did you see?" Sawyer asks Brennan.

The steelworker gives him a description of the man in the window and the inspector mashes the button on his car radio again: "The wanted person in this is a slender white male about thirty. Five foot ten. A hundred and sixty-five. And carrying a—what looked like—a 30-30 or some type of Winchester."

"It was a rifle?" the dispatcher asks.

"A rifle, yes," Sawyer replies.

"Any clothing description?"

"The current witness can't remember that," Sawyer says.[357]

The dispatcher immediately throws a switch in the radio room that allows him to broadcast simultaneously on both channels of the Dallas police radio, effectively reaching every officer in the city. "Attention all squads. Attention all squads. The suspect in the shooting at Elm and Houston is reported to be an unknown white male, approximately thirty. Slender build, height five feet, ten inches. Weight one hundred sixty-five pounds. Reported to be armed with what is thought to be a thirty caliber rifle." The dispatcher repeats the message, adding, "No further description or information at this time. 12:45 [p.m.] KKB-364, Dallas."[358]*

12:45 p.m.

In Irving, Marina is hanging up clothes in the backyard when Ruth comes out and joins her with the latest news: "They're reporting that the shots were fired from the Texas School Book Depository."

Marina's heart drops. She thinks about the rifle she knows that Lee has stored in Ruth Paine's garage, about the last time he used it—a few months earlier in trying to murder Dallas John Birch Society figure Major General Edwin Walker—and whether that might have been the real reason he came out to the house last night. She hopes that Ruth can't see the fear in her face.

As soon as she can do it inconspicuously, Marina slips into the garage. She knows exactly where the rifle is, wrapped in a green and brown wool blanket, near the garage door, by some suitcases. She saw the blanket there in early October and unwrapped it then and found the rifle inside. Is it still there? When she gets inside the garage, she sees the familiar bundle laying in the same place it had been before, and feels a great weight lift from her shoulders.

"Thank God," she thinks.[359]

William Whaley, a squat, burr-haired former navy gunner who won a Navy Cross during the battle of Iwo Jima, pulls his cab up to the cabstand at the Greyhound bus station on the northwest corner of Jackson and Lamar, four blocks south of Elm Street, and realizes that he's out of cigarettes. He's about to go inside the terminal to get a pack when he sees a fare walking toward him down Lamar Street.[360]

---

* "KKB-364" is the radio call sign of the Dallas police radio station.

"May I have the cab?" the man asks.

"You sure can," Whaley says. "Get in."

To Whaley, Lee Oswald looks like a wino who has been off his bottle for about two days, like he's been sleeping in his clothes, although he isn't actually dirty or nervous or anything.[361] Oswald gets in the front, which is allowed in Dallas, and Whaley's got nothing against it. A second later an elderly woman pokes her head in the passenger's window and asks if she can get in his cab.

"There'll be a cab behind me in a few moments that you can take," Whaley tells her, and he vaguely recalls that Oswald may have told the woman something similar.[362] As he pulls the 1961 Checker sedan out into Lamar and turns west into Jackson, he asks his fare where he wants to go.

"Five hundred North Beckley."

Police cars, their sirens wailing, are crisscrossing everywhere.

"I wonder what the hell is the uproar," Whaley muses, but Oswald doesn't answer and Whaley figures he's one of those people who doesn't like to talk, which is fine with him.[363]

Whaley, who has been driving cabs for thirty-seven years, notices Oswald's silver ID bracelet. He always takes note of watchbands and identification bracelets because he makes them himself, and this one is unusual. Most of them are made with chain links, not stretch bands, like this one.[364] They drive in silence, turning left at the first corner, Austin, and then onto Wood. They catch the light at Lamar and Jackson and several others as they move smartly through traffic down to Houston, the street they call the "old viaduct," which is the fastest way to Oak Cliff.[365]

Dallas police radio dispatcher Murray J. Jackson can see from the callboard in front of him that many of the patrolmen assigned to the Oak Cliff area (south of the Trinity River, which separates it from downtown Dallas, and before the emergence of North Dallas in later years, perhaps the biggest area of Dallas) have gone downtown to help in the assassination investigation.[366] He knows that if an emergency such as an armed robbery or a major accident occurs in that area, there might not be anyone to respond quickly to the call. He decides to pull two of the outermost patrol units in Oak Cliff closer to central Oak Cliff just in case something comes up. Units 78 and 87 (radio call numbers for Dallas Police Districts 78 and 87)* get the call—J. D. Tippit and Ronald C. Nelson.[367]

"[Units] 87 and 78, move into central Oak Cliff area," Jackson orders, basically giving Tippit and Nelson a blank check to move at will within the roughly five or six police districts that could be considered as Oak Cliff.

Tippit, cruising his beat alone in south Oak Cliff on the 7:00 a.m. to 3:00 p.m. day shift, lifts the radio microphone first.

"I'm at Kiest and Bonnieview," Tippit replies.

But Nelson shoots back, "[Unit] 87's going north on Marsalis, [at] R. L. Thornton."[368]

Dispatcher Jackson knows from Nelson's location that he is already on his way downtown to join other units. He decides to let him go. Tippit can handle anything that might come up, he figures. Jackson has known "J. D."† for eleven years and in that time they've become close friends. In fact, it was Tippit who originally got Jackson interested in police work. In 1952, Murray was a high school graduate working at a Mobil filling station where Tippit and his partner used to stop occasionally. Tippit was his image of a hero, and through J. D.'s encouragement, Jackson was successful at joining the force. After a promotion to patrolman, Jackson and Tippit were partnered for eight months and the bond between the two men strengthened.

One night in the early 1960s, Jackson was working temporarily with new partner Bill Johnson when they arrested seven teenagers for being drunk and disorderly. En route to the Oak Cliff substation, the teenagers

---

*The city of Dallas was broken down into eighty-six police districts. Each day was broken down into three eight-hour shifts ("platoons"). Most districts only had one patrolman assigned to it, although "hot districts" (those with a higher incidence of crime) had two. The number "78" was Tippit's radio call number because it was the police district, number 78, he was assigned to. (Eighty-six districts: "Dallas Police Department Squad Districts as of January 1, 1960," DMA, box 7, folder 10, item 3; Telephone interview of Jim Bowles by author on March 25, 2004)

†The author of the only book on the Tippit murder case wrote that "the initials [J. D.] he was known by didn't have any particular meaning. To everyone he was just J. D." Tippit's brother, Wayne, told the author that reports that his brother's initials stood for "Jefferson Davis" were incorrect. (Myers, *With Malice*, pp.28, 588 note 20) However, at least as to the first initial, a fellow officer who worked with Tippit for a while referred to him as John (Sneed, *No More Silence*, p.463).

decided they didn't want to go to jail and a fight broke out in the squad car. Jackson put out a call for assistance and J. D. was the first to arrive.

"Thanks, partner," Jackson told him, "you saved my life."

The humor of the situation wasn't lost on Tippit, who joked and chided Jackson, "I turn you loose one time and I got to come down here and save your life." Of course, Jackson's life wasn't really in any danger. It was just Tippit's way of kidding his former police apprentice.

It was with this incident in mind that Jackson called on Tippit to help him out again, this time by covering an area outside his own assigned district.[369]

But it obviously wasn't necessary for Jackson to have this prior relationship with Tippit to get him to go into central Oak Cliff. Tippit was on duty and had to go wherever assigned. Moreover, Tippit was not the type of officer to complain about much, being easy to get along with. Not overly ambitious, and with only a tenth-grade education, he wasn't "sharp enough," as one Dallas detective who knew Tippit said, to pass department promotional exams. However, the shy officer loved his job and seemed more than satisfied to remain a patrolman, resigned to his inability to advance because of his limited education. Well liked by his fellow officers, his immediate supervisor on the force, Sergeant Calvin B. Owens, described Tippit as a "good officer" who used "good common sense." A Dallas police officer, Donald Flusche, said that Tippit and he "worked together in West Dallas. He was really a good and decent man . . . He was pretty much a country boy . . . He was kind of bashful, thought a little slow, moved a little slow, but there was nothing dishonest about him."[370] Seldom talking about politics, Tippit, age thirty-nine, had voted for John F. Kennedy in the 1960 presidential election. On this day, Tippit had come home to have lunch with his wife, Marie, around 11:30 a.m., hurried through his food, and reported back for duty by 11:50 with a "78 clear" transmission from his car radio to the police dispatcher.[371]

12:50 p.m.

Forrest Sorrels, the agent in charge of the Dallas Secret Service office, arrives at the side of the Texas School Book Depository and walks to the same backdoor used by Frazier and Oswald that morning.[372] There is a black employee on the loading dock who doesn't seem to realize what's happened.

"Did you see anyone run out the back?" Sorrels asks him, as he approaches.

"No, sir," the man replies.

"Did you see anyone leave the back way?" Sorrels probes.

"No, sir," the man says again.[373]

The agent proceeds to the first floor by the rear loading-dock door, and to his surprise there's nobody in law enforcement there to challenge him.

"Where is the manager here?" he asks upon entering the building.

Someone directs him to Roy Truly. Sorrels pulls out his Secret Service credentials.

"I want to get a stenographer," he tells him, "and we would like to have you put down the names and addresses of every employee in the building."[374] Sorrels has not yet learned that shots have been fired from the building. He simply wants to establish the identity of everyone present at the time of the shooting so that they can be interviewed later.[375] Sorrels heads for the front of the building, pushes open the glass front doors, and steps out onto the concrete landing, "Is there anyone here that saw anything?"

"That man over there," a voice calls out, pointing to Howard Brennan standing nearby.

Sorrels bounds down the steps and identifies himself to the construction worker. "What did you see?" he asks.

Brennan tells him what happened and how he glanced up at the building and saw the man take deliberate aim and fire the third shot. "He just pulled the rifle back in and moved away from the window, just as unconcerned as could be," Brennan says.

After Brennan gives him a description of the gunman, Sorrels asks him if he thought he could identify him and Brennan says, "Yes, I think I can."

"Did anyone else see it?" Sorrels asks Brennan, who points out Amos Euins.

Sorrels questions the boy and learns that Euins also saw the gunman for a few brief seconds, but now Euins isn't sure if the man he saw was white or black. Asked if he, too, thought he could identify the man if he saw him again, Euins says, "No, I couldn't."[376]

Eventually, Sorrels escorts the two eyewitnesses over to the sheriff's office across the street to give a statement.[377]

12:52 p.m.

"This will do fine," Oswald tells the cabdriver. William Whaley pulls over to the curb at the northwest corner of Neely and North Beckley, which is the 700, not the 500 block Oswald had first requested, but it's all the same to Whaley.[378] The meter on the six-minute trip has just clicked over to ninety-five cents, about two and a half miles. Oswald gives Whaley a buck, gets out, and crosses the street in front of the cab, and that's the last Whaley sees of him. A big tipper.[379]

When he finally gets around to entering the trip in the passenger manifest required by the Dallas authorities, he writes it up as 12:30 to 12:45 p.m. Nobody at the cab company really cares about exact time, so when he gets a chance Whaley just marks it to the nearest quarter-hour or so.[380]

12:53 p.m. (1:53 p.m. EST)

All three networks headquartered in New York are gearing up for exclusive coverage of the shooting in Dallas for what will turn out to be over three consecutive days. A representative network is NBC, which, at 1:53 p.m. EST, cancels all regular programs to devote all of its time and resources to the unfolding events in Dallas. This will continue until 1:17 a.m. Tuesday morning, November 26.[381]

12:54 p.m.

Police dispatcher Murray Jackson checks in with patrol Unit 78—Officer J. D. Tippit.

"You are in the Oak Cliff area, are you not?" Jackson asks.

"Lancaster and Eighth," Tippit responds affirmatively.

"You will be at large for any emergency that comes in," Murray says.

"Ten-four," J. D. replies.[382]

The patrolman cruises north on Lancaster. He's a long way from his roots in Red River County. Born and raised south of Clarksville, Texas, J. D. Tippit grew up during the Great Depression on the family farm, where electricity and running water were only dreams. The Tippits were sharecroppers, renting farmland to raise cotton. The work was hard and the tools of the day primitive. J. D., the oldest of five brothers and two sisters, spent many days behind a mule team and plow. He grew to become a crack horseman and although outsiders found him quiet and reserved, his family knew him as fun-loving. As World War II entered its last bloody year in Europe, J. D. joined the U.S. Army, volunteering to become a member of the elite paratroopers. In 1945, he landed in France as an ammo bearer with the Seventeenth Airborne Division as it fought its way through the Rhine Valley. Like many men, the war made deep impressions on him and he returned with a renewed sense of duty and honor. Tippit's background was similar to that of many other officers on the force who came from small Texas towns with names like Athens, Palestine, and Ferris. Not a lot of academics, many not quite making it through high school. A lot of military service, which is good—guys who knew something about discipline and teamwork and were comfortable with firearms and uniforms.

In December 1946, at the age of twenty-two, J. D. married his high school sweetheart, Marie Frances Gasaway, age eighteen. They briefly moved to Dallas to find work after the war, but soon returned to Red River County, where they hoped to farm and raise a family. Nature's wrath took its toll on J. D.'s dreams of farming, and in July 1952 he joined the Dallas Police Department to feed his growing family. At $250 a month, Tippit soon found himself moonlighting to make ends meet. In early 1961, J. D. took a part-time job as a security guard from 10:00 p.m. until 2:00 a.m. every Friday and Saturday night at Austin's Barbeque in Oak Cliff, a popular teen hangout, and every Sunday afternoon at the Stevens Theater located in a shopping center. Tippit enjoys the free time he spends with his family—enjoying his three young children, taking dance lessons with his wife, listening to the music of Bob Wills and the Texas Playboys, or horsing around with his boyhood pal and brother-in-law, Jack Christopher.

In fact, J. D. has plans to see Jack and his family tonight. Earlier this morning, J. D. stopped at his sister's house on the way to work and got a ticket to the South Oak Cliff High School football game, where his niece, Linda, will be performing with the Golden Debs cheerleading squad. As he's done on Friday nights past, he'll have to beat it over to Austin's Barbeque before the game gets out and a good part of the grandstand shows up. It'll be another busy Friday night keeping the high school rowdies in line at Austin's.[383]

12:57 p.m.

In a second-floor operating room at Parkland, an anesthesiologist rapidly evaluates Connally's condition and starts to put the governor under for an operation that will last well over three hours.[384]

Dr. Robert Shaw and Dr. Charles F. Gregory, chief of orthopedic surgery, enter the operating room, where Connally lies ready for surgery. Dr. Shaw removes the temporary dressing and inspects Connally's chest wounds. After three years with the U.S. Army Medical Corps in the European Theater of Operations, Shaw is no stranger to bullet wounds.[385]

The surgeons place an endotracheal tube into the pharynx and trachea to control the governor's breathing, then roll him over to inspect the entrance wound just behind his right armpit, a roughly elliptical puncture with relatively clean-cut edges. Turning to the large and ragged exit wound below the right nipple, Shaw excises its edges, and then carries the incision back along the right side of the governor's chest and finds that about four inches of the fifth rib have been shattered and carried away from what appears to have been a glancing strike by the bullet. Several small fragments of the rib are still hanging to bits of partly detached tissue from the rib's lining. An X-ray reveals no metallic fragments left behind by the bullet in the area of the ribs. There's a lot of damage to the right lung, which is engorged with blood and rib fragments. It will have to be closed and sutured, along with the muscles surrounding the rib cage, but the diaphragm is uninjured, and the wounds are far from fatal. The governor has also sustained wounds on both sides of his right wrist and a superficial wound in his left thigh. X-rays reveal a shattering of the radius bone just above the right wrist and the presence of a number of small metallic fragments. There's several hours of work to do, but it's clear to the surgeons that Governor Connally will survive his injuries.[386]

12:58 p.m.

An unmarked squad car pulls up to the front of the Book Depository, and Police Captain Will Fritz, Detectives Sims and Boyd, and Sheriff Bill Decker climb out. An officer in front of the building tells them that the man who did the shooting is believed to be still in the building. Several officers take out their shotguns and follow Fritz and his men as they enter the Depository. They quickly locate an elevator and go up to the second floor, where they see several officers already there. They continue up, finding officers already stationed on the third and fourth floors.

This particular elevator only goes to the fourth floor, so Fritz and his men exit the elevator and cross over to the freight elevators near the northwest corner of the building, and take one up to the fifth floor. They make a hurried search along the front and west side windows, then, joined by some other officers, go up to the sixth floor. A few officers get off on the sixth, and Fritz, Sims, and Boyd continue up to the seventh floor and start to search along the front windows.[387]

Father James Thompson drives into Parkland in the black Ford Galaxie belonging to Holy Trinity Church. Parkland is only three miles from the church, but the traffic is brutal. Even though he took a "secret route" taking advantage of back streets, he and Father Oscar Huber found themselves held up by what seemed like endless traffic delays. Both of them are worried because they know that the last rites of the Catholic Church, to be valid, must be administered to the dying before the soul has left the

body. Father Huber, like many parish priests, takes a liberal view of that—
to his way of thinking, there can be quite a long time between what the
doctors call clinical death and the eventual flight of the soul, but that's
no reason to dally. As they pull up, Father Thompson tells Father Huber
to jump out of the car and hurry into the hospital while he finds a place
to park.[388]

Father Huber saw Jack Kennedy, it seems to him, only minutes ago.
He knew that the president's motorcade would pass within three blocks
of Holy Trinity, and when he rose at five this morning in his room at the
rectory, he resolved to go down to see it. He was disappointed that he
couldn't interest any of the other priests in the project.

"Well, I'm going," he told them. "I'm seventy years old and I've never
seen a president. I'll be danged if I'm going to miss this chance."

Huber, a short, stocky man, had to leap up and down to see over the
heads of the dense crowd, but managed to get a glimpse of Kennedy, who
turned and seemed to look right at him. Now he hurries to the emergency
entrance to give the last rites to this once-vibrant man. The significance
of his arrival is not lost on anyone.

"This is it," Congressman Henry Gonzalez thinks as he sees Huber arrive
at the hospital. Malcolm Kilduff, the president's acting press secretary, whispers to Congressman Albert Thomas, "It looks like he's gone."[389]

In Oak Cliff, at 1026 North Beckley, Earlene Roberts tugs at the "rabbit
ear" antennas trying to get a clear picture on the television set when the
young man she knows as "O. H. Lee" enters, walking unusually fast, in
shirt sleeves.

"You sure are in a hurry," the housekeeper says, but he goes straight
to his room without saying a word.[390]

That isn't so strange. Since renting the room in mid-October, "O. H.
Lee" has hardly said two words to anyone. Once, Mrs. Roberts said "good
afternoon" to him and he just gave her a dirty look and walked right past
her. At night, if one of the other boarders had the television on in the living room, he might stand behind the couch for a couple of minutes, but

then he'd go to his room and shut the door without a word. For the most part, "O. H. Lee" has kept to himself, which is why Mrs. Roberts doesn't really know anything about him, least of all the fact that his real name is Lee Harvey Oswald.[391]

Oswald is in his room just long enough to get his revolver and his jacket. He comes out of his room, zipping up his jacket, and rushes out.[392] Mrs. Roberts glances out the window a moment later and notices Lee standing at the curbside near a bus stop in front of the rooming house. That's the last she sees of him.[393] He apparently doesn't wait to board any bus since there is no record of anyone seeing him on a bus after one o'clock, and if he had boarded a bus in front of his home, it would take him in a direction away from where we know he was next seen.

1:00 p.m.

At Parkland Hospital, Dr. Kemp Clark feels the carotid artery in the president's neck for a pulse. There is none. Clark asks that a cardio-tachyscope (a cardiac monitor that measures heartbeat) be connected to the president's body, and starts external heart massage,[394] an unsophisticated physical procedure practiced by physicians from the sixteenth century, even before they understood anything about the circulation of blood in the body.

The anesthesiologists, Drs. Jenkins and Giesecke, now report a carotid pulse in the neck, and Dr. Jones reports a pulse in the femoral artery in the leg. After a few moments, Dr. Perry takes over for Dr. Clark, who is in an awkward physical position to continue the rigorous cardiac massage.[395]

"Somebody get me a stool," Dr. Perry commands. A stool is slid near the table and Perry stands on it to get better leverage as he works the livid white flesh beneath his palms. Drs. Jenkins and Clark watch the cardio-tachyscope. The green dot suddenly darts across the screen trailing a perfectly smooth line of fluorescence, without the tiniest squiggle of cardiac activity.[396] Dr. Clark shakes his head sadly, "It's too late, Mac." Perry slowly raises himself up from the body, steps down off the stool, and walks numbly away. Dr. Jenkins reaches down from the head of the cart and pulls a white sheet up over the president's face as Dr. Clark turns to Mrs. Kennedy.

"Your husband has sustained a fatal wound," he says solemnly.

Her lips move silently, forming the words, "I *know*."

It is one o'clock and it's all over. The thirty-fifth president of the United States is dead.[397]*

As the senior neurosurgeon, Dr. Clark will sign the death certificate, and the cause is so obviously the massive damage to the right side of the brain.[398] It is what they call a four-plus injury,† which no one survives, even with the five-star effort they made. Clark knows what Carrico and the others knew from the outset—medically, the president was alive when he entered Parkland Hospital, but from a practical standpoint he was DOA, dead on arrival.[399] As *New York Times* White House correspondent Tom Wicker, who was in Dealey Plaza at the time of the shooting, put it, Kennedy probably died way back on Elm Street a half hour earlier. He "probably was killed instantly. His body, as a physical mechanism, however, continued to flicker an occasional pulse and heartbeat."[400]

Dr. Jenkins starts disconnecting the multitude of monitoring leads running to the lifeless body and removing the intravenous lines. Admiral Burkley begins to weep openly. Mrs. Kennedy moves toward the hospital cart where her husband lies, and Jenkins retreats quietly to a corner of the room. Looking pale and remote, she leans down and kisses the president through the sheet on the foot, leg, thigh, abdomen, chest, and finally on the partly covered face.[401]

Father Oscar Huber enters the room out of breath and walks directly to Jackie Kennedy. He whispers his sympathies, draws back a sheet that

---

*The Parkland doctors had worked on the president in the emergency room for twenty-two minutes before he expired. (But see also *New York Times*, November 23, 1963, p.2)

Dr. Charles Baxter, one of the many surgeons attempting to save the president, would later recall, "As soon as we realized we had nothing medical to do, we all backed off from the man with a reverence that one has for one's president. And we did not continue to be doctors from that point on. We became citizens again, and there were probably more tears shed in that room than in the surrounding hundred miles" ("Surgeon Who Operated on JFK in Dallas Dies," Associated Press, March 12, 2005).

†In emergency medicine, injuries are described as one-plus, two-plus, et cetera. A four-plus injury is a worst-case scenario.

is covering the president's face, pulls the purple and white stoll over his shoulders, wets his right thumb with holy oil and administers in Latin the last rites of the Catholic Church, the sacrament of extreme unction, including the anointing of a cross with his thumb over the president's forehead. Because the president was dead, a "short form" of absolution was given, and in a few minutes he finishes and steps back.

"Is that *all*?" Admiral Burkley blurts out, offended at the brevity of the ceremony. The death of a president deserves more, he thought. "Can't you say some prayers for the dead?"

Father Huber quickly obliges with a recitation of the Lord's Prayer and a Hail Mary, joined by the widow and Admiral Burkley, while the nurses who are cleaning up the appalling mess in the room remain still, their heads bowed. Father Thompson, having parked the car outside, steps in just as they are finishing.

Mrs. Kennedy turns and walks back out into the corridor, slumping into the folding chair just outside the door. The two priests follow.

"I am shocked," Father Huber says to her, his body beginning to tremble. "I want to extend my sympathy and that of my parishioners."

"Thank you for taking care of the president," she whispers. "Please pray for him."

"I am convinced that his soul had not left his body," he assures her. "This was a valid last sacrament."

Mrs. Kennedy's head drops down as she struggles to keep from fainting. Father Thompson signals a passing nurse.

"Do you want a doctor?" Father Huber asks Mrs. Kennedy.

"Oh, no," she mumbles. The nurse brings her a cold towel anyway. The First Lady presses it to her forehead and leans over until the spell passes.[402]

Across the hall from Trauma Room One, the two priests confer briefly. What will they say to the horde of reporters outside as they leave? It's clearly not their role to make any statement at all. In fact, as they head for the exit a Secret Service agent warns Huber, "Father, you don't know anything about this."

Just as they feared, they are besieged in the parking lot by the news media. Father Thompson refuses to give his name, but Father Huber is unable to remain silent.

"Is he dead?" Hugh Sidey of *Time* magazine asks.

"He's dead all right," Huber answers.[403]

1:05 p.m. (2:05 p.m. EST)
At his Virginia home, Robert Kennedy is in an upstairs bedroom with his wife, Ethel, preparing to leave for Dallas. The White House extension phone rings and he practically dives for it. It's Captain Taz Shepard, the president's naval aide, with news from Parkland.

"Oh, he's dead!" Bobby cries out in anguish.

"Those poor children," Ethel says in tears.

The attorney general stares out the window.

"He had the most wonderful life," he finally manages to say.

Bobby Kennedy descends the stairs and pokes his head into the living room where Robert Morgenthau and several others are watching television coverage.

"He died," Kennedy says in a low voice and walks toward the pool, where the extension phone has rung. It's J. Edgar Hoover again. He informs the attorney general, in a cold and unsympathetic manner characteristic of the FBI director, that the president is in "very, very critical condition." Bobby Kennedy listens politely, then says, "It may interest you to know that my brother is dead."[404]

RFK is plunged into a staggering gloom and depression by his brother's murder, one from which his intimates said he never recovered. For months thereafter, a biographer wrote, he "seemed devoured by grief. He literally shrank, until he appeared wasted and gaunt. His clothes no longer fit, especially his brother's old clothes—an old blue topcoat, a tuxedo, and a leather bomber jacket with the presidential seal—which he insisted on wearing and which hung on his narrowing frame. To close friend John Seigenthaler, he appeared to be in physical pain, like a man with a toothache or on a rack. Even walking seemed too difficult for him, though he walked for hours, brooding and alone . . . On many winter nights he arose before dawn and drove, too fast, in his Ford Galaxie convertible with the top down, sometimes to see his brother's grave." That is why it is all the more remarkable that within an hour of his brother's death, and in the trancelike midst of his dark abyss, the protective concern over his dead brother's well-manicured image enables him to extricate himself enough to call JFK's national security adviser, McGeorge Bundy, over at the White House. He instructs Bundy to immediately change the locks on his brother's personal files in the event that Lyndon Johnson decides to comb through them, and transport them to the offices of the national security staff located in the Old Executive Office Building, with a round-the-clock guard. And though he has no jurisdiction over the Secret Service, he has them dismantle and remove the secret taping system his brother had installed in the Oval Office and Cabinet Room.[405]

1:06 p.m.

It doesn't take long for Captain Fritz, Detectives Sims and Boyd, and other police officers to assure themselves that there's no one hiding on the seventh floor of the Book Depository and no sign that anyone fired at the president from there. The whole floor is one big open space with a few stacks of books here and there, some shelves, and not much else. A storage room in the southeast corner yields nothing but a collection of forgotten desks, chairs, and other office space odds and ends. The windows facing Elm Street are still closed, as they were at the time of the shooting.[406]

On the sixth floor below, Dallas police officers and deputy sheriffs are systematically searching the entire floor—from the cleared space on the west side, where the new flooring is going down, toward the stacks of boxes that have been piled into rows on the east side.

Deputy Luke Mooney is near the southeastern corner of the floor when he whistles loudly and hollers to his fellow officers.[407] He's inside the sniper's nest, a roughly rectangular screen of boxes stacked around the southeasternmost window. Anybody sitting or crouching behind them would be completely hidden from anyone else on the floor. Two more cartons on top of each other are right in front of the window. A third box lies closer to the window, resting in a canted position on the windowsill. In the corner, a long, handmade, brown paper bag is bunched up. On the floor, at the baseboard beneath the window, are three spent cartridge casings—"hulls," as they call them in Texas.

Dallas police sergeant Gerald L. Hill walks over to an adjacent window, sticks his head out, and yells down to the street for the crime lab, but fears that no one can hear him over the sirens and crackling police radios. He starts down himself to report the find and meets Captain Fritz and Detectives Sims and Boyd at the freight elevator on the sixth floor. They had heard Mooney's and Hill's shouts through the cracks in the floorboards and came down to investigate. Hill tells them he's going down to the street to make sure the officers know where to send the crime-lab boys.[408]

Fritz, Sims, and Boyd work their way across the sixth floor over to the southeast corner window, where Deputy Mooney stands and other officers begin to congregate. Mooney tells Captain Fritz that everything is just as he found it. Fritz orders Detectives Sims and Boyd to stand guard and don't let anyone touch anything until the crime lab can get there, then Fritz turns to the officers present and instructs them to turn the sixth floor upside down. If there's a weapon here somewhere, he means to find it.[409]

1:07 p.m.

At the New York Stock Exchange, news of the president's shooting has brought about a wave of selling that reaches panic proportions, and the Dow Jones Industrial Average plummets 21.16 points.[410]

1:08 p.m.

Officer J. D. Tippit, probably traveling south on Beckley or southeast on Crawford in the general direction of Jefferson Boulevard in central Oak Cliff, spots Oswald walking on the right side of the street in front of him and sees that he vaguely fits the physical description of the suspect in the Kennedy assassination that he heard over the police radio in his squad car, it having been broadcast over channel 1 at 12:45 p.m., 12:48 p.m., and again at 12:55 p.m.[411] Slowly tailing Oswald from behind, he tried to call the radio dispatcher for a further description of the suspect. "Seventy-eight" (Tippit's call number, the police district he is assigned to), he says into his radio microphone, but he is not acknowledged by the dispatcher. Seconds later, he calls in "seventy-eight" again, but once again is not acknowledged by the dispatcher, he assumes because of the heavy radio traffic due to the assassination, and he continues to slow-tail Oswald.[412]*

*The few minutes leading up to Tippit's murder were only known to Tippit and Oswald. (Witnesses to the murder were only aware of the previous minute, not minutes.) So we have to infer what happened from what little we do know. Looking at the map in the photo section, we know that to get to Tenth and Patton, where Tippit was murdered, Oswald had to have at least started out by going south on Beckley. We also know that the last time we heard from Tippit was at 1:08 p.m. when he called the channel 1 police dispatcher twice to communicate but was never acknowledged. Since this time is so close to the time of his death, in February of 2004 I called the person I felt would be most qualified to confirm or dispel my suspicion that the 1:08 p.m. transmission by Tippit was related to his death, Dallas sheriff Jim Bowles, a fifty-three-year member of Dallas law enforcement—thirty years with the Dallas Police Department, twenty-three with the Dallas sheriff's office, the last twenty as sheriff. Responding to my amazement over his fifty-three years in law enforcement, Bowles said, "Most police officers have starved to death [on their low pay] by that time." Just as important as Bowles's long experience in law enforcement is the fact that he was a Dallas police radio dispatcher supervisor in November of 1963. (Because of his father's stroke, Bowles was off duty on the day of the assassination.) Indeed, it was Bowles who transcribed the recordings on the police radio tapes for the Warren Commission. "Oh, I don't think there's too much question the two 1:08 transmissions from Tippit pertained to Oswald," Bowles said. I asked Bowles when would the 1:08 transmissions have likely been made, shortly before the murder or earlier? "Most likely earlier, when Tippit first saw Oswald walking like the devil possessed, probably back on Beckley or Crawford, and he just slow-tailed him to Tenth." (Confirmation of Bowles's analysis that Tippit was slowly following Oswald comes from witness William Scoggins, who said that when he saw Tippit's car cross the intersection of Tenth and Patton, Tippit was traveling "not more than ten or twelve miles an hour" behind where Oswald was walking on Tenth [3 H 324]. And Helen Markham also noticed that the police car was "going real slow . . . real slow" [3 H 307].) I asked Bowles, "Tippit wouldn't have pulled his squad car over to the curb next to Oswald shortly after spotting him, and was calling in at 1:08 to let the dispatcher know he was leaving his patrol car [and radio, since in 1963 the Dallas Police never had walkie talkies] to approach Oswald?" Bowles, who worked for ten years in the Dallas police radio dispatcher's office, said, "Possible, but that wouldn't be the norm for an officer under these circumstances, particularly Tippit. I knew Tippit. He was a slow, cautious, deliberate guy. The norm would have been for him to call in for a further description of the suspect from the dispatcher. But not being acknowledged, after following Oswald for a few minutes he pulled over to see what this person [Oswald] is up to." "You don't think Tippit had enough PC [not as in *probable cause* for an arrest, but still used as a loose way of referring to a reasonable suspicion of criminal activity justifying a police officer to stop a pedestrian or driver of a car for questioning] to stop Oswald because Oswald vaguely fit the general description of the suspect sent out over police radio?" "Possibly," Bowles said, "but his PC was probably the description coupled with some overt behavior by Oswald like walking too fast, looking over his shoulder, walking in some

1:10 p.m.

At Parkland Hospital, Ken O'Donnell, acting as a stoic messenger between Trauma Room One and Lyndon Johnson, enters the vice president's cubicle in Minor Medicine.

"He's gone," O'Donnell says.

The vice president finds the whole thing hard to believe. A few hours ago he was having breakfast with John Kennedy; he was alive, strong, and vigorous. Now, he is dead.[413] Mrs. Johnson turns to her husband, her eyes filled with anger and sorrow, her voice choked with emotion. "*I must* go see Mrs. Kennedy and Nellie," she says.

Johnson nods and wishes to go with her. Agent Youngblood, however, refuses to let him leave the ward.[414] Agent Emory Roberts and Congressman Jack Brooks escort Lady Bird Johnson to the hall outside Trauma Room One, where Mrs. Kennedy stands, "quiet as a shadow," as Lady Bird later remembered. Mrs. Johnson always thought of the president's wife as a woman insulated, protected, and is now struck by the realization that in this moment she is terribly alone. "I don't think I ever saw anyone so much alone in my life," she would later recall. She goes to Jackie, puts her arm around her, and says, crying, "Jackie, I wish to God there was something I could do." But there is nothing she can do and eventually she slips away.

On the second floor of the hospital, Lady Bird greets her close friend of a quarter century, Nellie Connally. They hug each other tightly, both giving in to tears.

"Nellie, he's going to be all right."

"He *is*, Bird," Nellie says. "He's going to be all right."

Mrs. Connally's eyes well up and Jack Brooks, sensing they're about to spill over, hands her his handkerchief.

"Oh, he'll be out there deer hunting at ninety," he quips.

She dabs her eyes and smiles.[415]

---

erratic, jerky way. Remember, Oswald had just killed the president. He probably wasn't walking in a normal, casual way and a police officer would pick up on this more than someone else would." (Telephone interview of Dallas sheriff Jim Bowles by author on February 23, 2004)

In the corridors below, the Kennedy staff stands numb and stricken. No one seems to be in charge or knows what to do.

Mac Kilduff seeks out Ken O'Donnell.

"This is a terrible time to have to approach you on this," Kilduff says, "but the world has got to know that President Kennedy is dead."

O'Donnell looks at him, incredulous. "Don't they know it already?"

It seems like Kilduff's been carrying the burden of the death for a hundred years.

"No, I haven't told them," Kilduff says.

"Well, you're going to have to make the announcement," O'Donnell replies. He thought about the new order of things a moment, then added, "Go ahead, but you'd better check it with Johnson."

An agent leads Kilduff through the maze of cubicles in Minor Medicine until they round a corner and Mac spots Lyndon Johnson sitting on an ambulance cart, head down, legs dangling. Kilduff swallows hard, "Mr. President . . ."

Johnson's head snaps up sharply. It's the first time Lyndon Johnson has been addressed that way; the first time he *knows* he is the thirty-sixth president of the United States.

Kilduff proceeds to ask Johnson if he can announce President Kennedy's death. Johnson nods yes, then says, "No. Wait. We don't know whether it's a Communist conspiracy or not. I'd better get out of here and back to the plane." Kilduff and Johnson agree that he will not announce Kennedy's death until after Johnson leaves the hospital.[416]

Ken O'Donnell enters the ward and finds Johnson, frightened and nervous, conferring with the Secret Service agents. Emory Roberts, the ranking agent in the room, jumps up when O'Donnell comes in: "What'll we do, Kenny, what'll we do?"

"You'd better get the hell out of here," O'Donnell replies, "and get back to Washington right away. Take Air Force One."[*]

---

[*] The Kennedy loyalists felt it was in the worst of taste for President Johnson to take the former president's plane back to Washington instead of flying back on Air Force Two, the plane he had come to Texas in. And indeed, when Warren Commission counsel asked O'Donnell if, after he informed LBJ that the president had died, there was "any discussion about his taking the

"Don't you think it might be safer if we moved the plane to Carswell Air Force Base and took off from there?" Johnson asks.

O'Donnell doesn't like it. It would take time to get one of the jets from nearby Love Field to the air force base, and the thirty-five-mile drive from Dallas to Carswell would be risky. He suggests that Johnson should head to Love Field and take off for Washington as soon as he gets there.

"How about Mrs. Kennedy?" Johnson asks.

"She will not leave the hospital without the president," O'Donnell says.

There is no doubt about which president he is referring to. Afraid that the public might view his departure as deserting the Kennedys, Johnson digs his heels in.

"I don't want to leave Mrs. Kennedy like this," he says.

O'Donnell tells Johnson that he will stay behind with Mrs. Kennedy until the president's body is ready to be moved to the airport.

"You take good care of that fine lady," Johnson says.[417]*

Secret Service agents are already arranging for a couple of unmarked

---

presidential plane, AF-1, as opposed to AF-2?" O'Donnell replied, "There was not" (7 H 451). And he reiterated this in his book (O'Donnell and Powers with McCarthy, *Johnny, We Hardly Knew Ye*, p.40). But one wonders if O'Donnell found it convenient to deny the conversation when he thereafter heard the sentiments of his associates about Johnson flying on Air Force One. President Johnson told the Warren Commission that after O'Donnell informed him that Kennedy had died, O'Donnell "said that we should return to Washington and that we should take the president's plane" (5 H 563). And Secret Service agent Rufus Youngblood, special agent in charge of the vice presidential detail for the Texas trip, testified before the Warren Commission that "O'Donnell told us to go ahead and take Air Force One. I believe this is mainly because Air Force One has better communications equipment and so forth than the other planes [Air Force Two and the cargo plane]" (2 H 152–153). *U.S. News & World Report* sought to confirm this and was told by a former White House official that, at the time, the three jet planes in the presidential fleet were being "regeared for communications of a classified nature. Naturally, the first plane to be re-equipped was AF-1. Most of the new gear had been installed in AF-1. The other two jet planes had not been completed" ("Fateful Two Hours without a President," p.73).

Another reason to believe LBJ and Youngblood on this point is that the weight of the evidence (see later text) is that LBJ was very sensitive to the feelings of the entire Kennedy camp following the assassination.

*O'Donnell thought that he had convinced Johnson to depart immediately upon his arrival at Love Field; however, Johnson wasn't about to fly back to the capital alone, with a dead president and a grieving widow on a following plane. He agreed to return to Love Field but was determined to wait for Mrs. Kennedy and the president's body before departing for Washington. (5 H 563, WC statement of President Lyndon Baines Johnson; O'Donnell and Powers with McCarthy, *Johnny, We Hardly Knew Ye*, p.34; Bishop, *Day Kennedy Was Shot*, pp.193–194; Telephone interview of Assistant Special Agent-in-Charge Lem Johns by author on June 28, 2005)

police cars to spirit Johnson and his party away to Love Field. The agents at the airfield have taken extraordinary measures to secure the area around the two presidential planes, directing local police and airport people to clear all the buildings, hangars, and warehouses of both employees and civilians. It seems bizarre to prepare such a departure for the president of the United States, in his own country, but the fact is, none of them know where the assassin or assassins are, or what they plan to do next.[418]*

William W. Scoggins, a forty-nine-year-old cabdriver, eats a sandwich in his taxi and ponders the shooting of the president. He's just dropped a fare from the airport, and after a brief stop at the Gentleman's Club, a domino parlor and lunch spot on Patton (on the other side of the street from where Scoggins parked his car, about a half a block south in the direction of Jefferson Boulevard), to watch coverage of the assassination on TV, he returns to his parking spot at the corner of Tenth and Patton. The area is a "scruffy, working-class residential neighborhood of aging frame houses" about four miles from Dealey Plaza. He's only been there a few seconds when he notices Dallas police car number 10—J. D. Tippit's squad car—crossing left to right a few yards in front of him as it

---

*Although the FBI and other members of law enforcement first suspected that the nation's right wing was behind the assassination, Warren Commission chronicler and assassination researcher Max Holland writes, "For officials whose instincts were honed by national-security considerations, the Soviet-American rivalry loomed over what had happened and dictated what immediately needed to be done. The overwhelming instant reaction among these officials was to suspect a grab for power, a foreign, Communist-limited conspiracy aimed at overthrowing the U.S. government. The assassination might be the first in a concerted series of attacks on U.S. leaders as the prelude to an all-out attack . . . When Major General Chester Clifton, JFK's military aide, arrived at Parkland Hospital, he immediately called the National Military Command Center and then switched to the White House Situational Room to find out if there was any intelligence about a plot to overthrow the government. The Defense Department subsequently issued a flash warning to every U.S. military base in the world and ordered additional strategic bombers into the air. General Maxwell Taylor [chairman of the Joint Chiefs of Staff] issued a special alert to all troops in the Washington [D.C.] area, while John McCone, director of Central Intelligence, asked the Watch Committee to convene immediately at the Pentagon. The committee, an interdepartmental group organized to prevent future Pearl Harbors, consisted of the government's best experts on surprise military attacks" (Holland, "Key to the Warren Report," pp.52, 54).

prowls very slowly eastbound on Tenth Street. Scoggins takes another bite of his sandwich and swigs a Coke.[419]

A woman stands on the corner diagonally across from Scoggins, waiting for traffic to clear so she can cross the street. A pair of work shoes in her hand, Helen Markham, forty-seven, is on her way to catch the 1:15 p.m. bus at the next corner (the corner of Patton and Jefferson), the same one she takes every day to the Eatwell Restaurant on Main Street downtown, where she works as a waitress.[420] She sees "this police car slowly cross [the intersection] and sorta ease up alongside the man."[421]

1:11 p.m.

Scoggins watches the police car stop around 120 feet down Tenth Street to his right, and it is then that he also notices a man in a light-colored jacket standing on the sidewalk. The man walks over toward the police car, passing out of Scoggins's sight behind some shrubs.[422] Markham has an unobstructed view and sees the man go over to the squad car, lean over, and place his arms on the ledge of the open front window on the passenger side. She observes him "talking to the officer through the open window" and assumes it is a friendly conversation.[423]

Jack Ray Tatum, a twenty-five-year-old medical photographer for Baylor University Medical Center, turns onto Tenth Street from Denver and heads west in his red Ford Galaxie. Tatum's boss has given him an afternoon off and he's been spending it running errands and buying a watch and ring for his wife, on a lay-a-way, at Gordon's Jewelers on Jefferson. Approaching Patton, he sees a squad car driving east on Tenth Street and a young white male "was also walking east, the same direction the squad car was going." When the squad car pulls over to the curb, he sees the man approaching the squad car on the passenger side. As Tatum drives past, he can see the police officer in the front seat leaning over toward the man, whose hands are crammed into the pockets of his light-gray zipper jacket. He gets the impression they are talking. Tatum wonders why the cop has stopped him.[424]*

_____

*The conventional wisdom and that of the Warren Commission is that Tippit pulled his squad car over to talk to Oswald because Tippit must have heard the description of the suspected killer

Domingo Benavides is in his pickup truck a half-dozen car lengths behind Tatum. The mechanic from Dootch Motors is pretty annoyed with himself. He was on his way to the auto parts store at Marsalis and Tenth to get a carburetor and was damned near there when it dawned on him that he'd forgotten the part number. He's heading back west on Tenth Street when he sees the police car ahead on the left.[425] (See photo section for diagram of Tippit murder scene with location of Tippit's car, Oswald, and witnesses.)

1:12 p.m.

Just after Tatum passes the squad car, Helen Markham watches the driver's door open and the police officer climb out. He doesn't seem to be in a hurry, and has not drawn his weapon.[*] The officer starts walking toward the front of the car, not keeping his eyes on Oswald but looking down at the ground,[†] his right hand, like a western sheriff, on his gun butt as the young man on the passenger side puts his hands in his pockets and takes two steps back. Suddenly, the young man pulls a gun out from under his jacket.

BANG! BANG! BANG! BANG! Bullets fly across the hood of the car.[426]

Scoggins looks up from his sandwich and sees the policeman grab his stomach, then fall.[427] Benavides is almost abreast of the squad car when the shooting erupts. He jerks the wheel hard right, bumps his '58 Chevy pickup into the curb, and throws himself down on the front seat.[428]

Tatum is passing through the intersection of Tenth and Patton when

---

of the president, which was sent out over Dallas police radio at 12:45, 12:48, and 12:55 p.m., that he was a "white male, approximately thirty, slender build, height five foot ten inches, weight 165 pounds," and Oswald's description was similar to the suspect (WR, p.165). The argument of conspiracy theorists, seeking to link Oswald to Tippit before Tippit's murder, that Oswald wasn't similar enough for Tippit to have stopped him, is a very weak one. If there ever was a time when a police officer would stop someone if he even remotely resembled a suspect, surely this was it.

[*]We will never know what words Oswald and Tippit exchanged that caused Tippit to leave his patrol car and start to approach Oswald. But we can safely assume that there was something about Oswald's words, appearance, or demeanor that made Tippit want to check Oswald out further, but that was not suspicious enough at that point for him to have drawn his gun on Oswald.

[†]Tippit had a bad habit, which his fellow officers unsuccessfully tried to break him of, of never looking anyone straight in the eye, looking down or sometimes sideways when he approached a person on duty. This may have accounted for how Oswald got the jump on him.

he hears the crack of several pistol shots behind him. He jams on the brakes and turns to look back. The police officer is lying on the ground beside the left front tire of the squad car. Tatum sees a man in a light tan-gray jacket start off in Tatum's direction, hesitate at the rear of the police car, then step back into the street and fire one more shot, right into the head of the officer on the ground.[429]*

Mrs. Markham is screaming. The man walks calmly away, back toward Patton Street, fooling with his gun.[430]

Tatum, realizing the gunman is coming his way, drives off, with an eye on his rearview mirror.[431]

The gunman spots Mrs. Markham across the street and looks straight at her. She thinks he's fixing to kill her too. She falls to her knees and covers her face with her hands, but when she pulls them down enough to see, she realizes that he is veering off, cutting across the yard of the corner house.[432]

Barbara and Virginia Davis are babysitting when they hear the shots. The young women (nineteen and sixteen, respectively) have been sisters-in-law for a couple of months, ever since they married brothers. Their husbands are in the home-repair business, and the two couples each live in an apartment in the corner house at Tenth and Patton. Barbara slips on her shoes and rushes to the screen door, Virginia on her heels. She sees Mrs. Markham across the street on the corner, screaming and pointing toward the man coming across her yard, "He killed him! He killed him!" Barbara glances to her right and sees a Dallas police car parked in front of the house next door. The gunman is now less than twenty-five feet away as he cuts across her front walk. He looks at her coolly as he shakes spent cartridges from an open revolver into his hand. She dashes to the phone and calls the police.[433]

Scoggins has been driving a cab for less than two years, but if there's one thing he's learned, it's to get as far away from the cab as possible when

---

*I have asked Tatum if he got "a good look" at the man who shot Tippit and whom he identified at the trial. "Very good look," Tatum responded. I asked if there was "any question in your mind" that the man was Oswald. "None whatsoever," he answered. (Transcript of *On Trial*, July 23, 1986, p.200)

trouble starts. He doesn't fancy being commandeered by some nut with a gun. Scoggins is already getting out when he sees the gunman cutting across the yard of the house on the corner, and realizes he'd better get out of sight, fast. He starts to cross the street, but there's no time to run and hide. He quickly crouches down behind the cab, then steals a look as the man runs through the bushes of the corner house. Scoggins can see the side of the man's face as the killer looks back over his shoulder and mutters, "Poor damn cop," twice. Or maybe it was "poor dumb cop." Scoggins isn't sure.[434]

1:13 p.m.

Ted Callaway is in his office, a small clapboard building at the back of Dootch Motors, the used-car lot on the northeast corner of Jefferson and Patton, when he hears five shots. The office boys with him laugh about the "firecrackers," but the forty-seven-year-old Callaway, knowing instantly what it is, says, "Firecrackers, hell! That's pistol shots!"[435]

The used-car manager is a Marine Corps veteran who fought on the Marshall Islands during World War II, and later trained recruits during the Korean War. He's on his feet in a flash, running out to Patton Street. He looks to his right, up toward Tenth and the sound of the shots. He can see the cabdriver Scoggins crouched down next to his taxi as a man leaps through the bushes and cuts across Patton, running toward him. The fleeing man has both of his hands on a pistol he holds straight up, elbow high—what the Marines call a "raised pistol position." As the gunman gets kitty-corner across the street—less than sixty feet away—Callaway hollers to him, "Hey, man, what the hell is going on?"

The killer slows, almost stops, says something unintelligible, shrugs his shoulders, and walks briskly on toward Jefferson Boulevard, then turns right and proceeds in a westerly direction down Jefferson.[436]

Callaway turns to B. D. Searcy, a car-lot porter, and tells him, "Keep an eye on that guy, follow him. I'm going to go down there and see what's going on!"

He takes off on the double, a good hard run.

"Follow him, hell," Searcy calls after him. "That man will kill you. He has a gun." Searcy proceeds to find refuge behind the office building.[437]

Warren Reynolds is standing on the balcony of the two-story office building at his brother's used-car lot—Reynolds Motor Company—across Jefferson Boulevard from Dootch Motors. Three men are on the lot below him—Harold Russell, L. J. Lewis, and B. M. "Pat" Patterson. They all heard the shots and now see a man running down Patton toward them. As he nears the corner, they can see he is reloading a pistol, which he promptly tucks into his belt. As he heads west on Jefferson, Reynolds descends the stairs and tells the others that he's going to trail the guy. Patterson goes with him, Lewis runs back to the office to phone police, and Russell trots down toward the scene of the shooting.[438]

On Tenth Street, when the killer is about half a block away, Mrs. Markham runs over to the policeman's body to see if she can help. The gurgling sounds coming from Tippit's body lead Markham to think he may be trying to say something. But it's only death gasps. Markham screams in despair, "Somebody help me!" but she is all by herself, and no one responds to her pleas for what seems to her like several "minutes."[439]

Frank Cimino, who lives at 405 East Tenth Street, directly across the street from the shooting, had been listening to his radio at the time he heard "four loud noises that sounded like shots," after which he heard a woman scream. He puts on his shoes, runs outside, and sees a woman dressed like a waitress (Markham) shouting, "Call the police." She tells him the man who shot the police officer had run west on Tenth Street and pointed in the direction of an alley between Tenth and Jefferson off Patton, but he sees no one when he looks in that direction. Cimino approaches the officer, who is lying on his side with his head in front of the left front headlight of the police car. Cimino can see that Tippit has been shot in the head. Tippit's gun is out of his holster, lying by his side. Tippit moves slightly and groans but never says anything that Cimino can understand. Soon people start coming from all directions toward the police car.[440]

1:15 p.m.

Benavides has been sitting in his truck for two or three minutes, very afraid that the gunman lives in the corner house and might come back shooting. He finally gets out, walks across the street, and cautiously approaches the fallen officer. A big clot of blood bulges at the officer's right temple, his eyes sunken into his skull. It makes Benavides feel sick, and "really" scared.[441]

1:16 p.m.
The mechanic gets into the squad car, grabs the microphone, and tries to call the police dispatcher. Unfortunately, Benavides has no idea how the radio works. He fumbles with the controls and keeps clicking the button on the mike, but from the chatter on the police radio he can tell they can't hear him.[442]

A small crowd has gathered at the squad car by the time Ted Callaway gets there, closely followed by Sam Guinyard, a porter at Dootch Motors, who had been waxing and polishing a station wagon at the back of the lot when he saw the gunman run by. More people from the neighborhood are arriving every minute.[443] Callaway kneels down next to the body. He doesn't have to look very hard to see the officer has been hit at least three times, once in the right temple. Callaway had seen a lot of dead men during the Korean War. This officer looks just like them.[444]

In New York, CBS News anchor Walter Cronkite tells the nation for the first time that the president has reportedly died. Calling it "only a rumor," he leads to Eddie Barker, the news director of CBS's Dallas affiliate KRLD, who is on the scene at Parkland Hospital. Barker says, "The word we have is that President Kennedy is dead. This we do not know for a fact . . . The word we have is from a doctor on the staff of Parkland Hospital who says that it is true. He was in tears when he told me just a moment ago. This is still not officially confirmed, but . . . the source would normally be a good one."[445]

1:17 p.m.
T. F. Bowley, who just picked up his twelve-year-old daughter at the R.L. Thornton school in Singing Hills and was on his way to pick up his wife

from work at the telephone company at Ninth and Zangs, drives up on the scene at Tenth and Patton. Bowley tells his young daughter to wait in the car as he walks over to see what's happened. He takes one look at the officer and knows there is nothing anyone can do for him. He walks over to the open driver's door of the squad car. Benavides looks up and says, "I don't know how it works."[446] Benavides gets out of the car and hands the mike over to Bowley, who calls in the shooting, "Hello, police operator?"

"Go ahead," dispatcher Murray Jackson answers. "Go ahead, citizen using the police—"

"We've had a shooting out here," Bowley blurts out.

"Where's it at?" Jackson asks.

Bowley hesitates. He isn't sure.

"The citizen using police radio—" Jackson continues.

"On Tenth Street," Bowley cuts in.

"What location on Tenth Street?"

"Between Marsalis and Beckley," Bowley answers. "It's a police officer. Somebody shot him—what—what's this?" Someone at the scene tells Bowley the address and he repeats it to the dispatcher, "404 Tenth Street."*

Jackson knows his friend, Officer J. D. Tippit, is in that general area and immediately calls over the police radio, "[Unit] 78?"

Bowley says, "You got that? It's in a police car." Someone at the scene tells him the number of the police car. Bowley repeats it: "Number ten."

Now Jackson knows. That's Tippit's squad car number. In fact, he and J. D. had once partnered in that same car. He can't believe what appears to have happened. He doesn't want to believe it. Both he and the other dispatcher working channel 1, C. E. Hulse, shout into their mikes, "Seventy-eight."

Seconds tick by. No response. It can't be true, Jackson thinks. But it is.

"You got this?" Bowley asks the stunned dispatcher.

---

*Actually, Tippit pulled over and stopped his squad car on the street in front of the driveway between 404 and 410 East Tenth Street (CE 523, 17 H 229; photo of car parked on East Tenth: Barnes Exhibit D, 19 H 114).

Hulse takes command, "Attention all units—"

"Hello, police operator? Did you get that?" Bowley asks, talking over the dispatcher.

"—Signal 19 [police call number for a shooting] involving a police officer, 510 East Jefferson."[*]

"The citizen using the police radio, remain off the air now," Jackson orders, as he recovers from the shocking news.

"[Unit] 91?" Hulse calls, trying to contact Patrolman W. D. Mentzell, who checked out a few minutes earlier at a traffic accident near the Tippit shooting scene. No response.

"[Unit] 69's going out there," Patrolman A. R. Brock calls in to Jackson.

"Ten-Four, 69," Jackson replies, relieved to know that help is on the way.[447]

It isn't long before law officers throughout the city learn that one of their own has been shot. First, it was the president. Now, for the Dallas police, it's personal.

On the street in front of the Texas School Book Depository Building, Sergeant Gerald Hill had run into Lieutenant J. C. "Carl" Day of the crime lab, just as he arrived at the scene. Hill told him about finding spent cartridges up on the sixth floor, and Day had gone on up. Now, Hill is giving Inspector Sawyer the same information, as *Dallas Morning News* reporters James Ewell and Hugh Aynesworth stand nearby, listening intently to the conversation. Hill, a former newsman, knows how tough it is to gather facts without good police sources. He speaks clearly so the newsmen get it right.

Sergeant C. B. "Bud" Owens and Assistant District Attorney Bill

[*]Hulse has gotten the 510 East Jefferson address (the site of Reynolds Motor Company) from the call sheet passed through the conveyor belt to the dispatch room from the adjacent room manned by civilian employees of the police department taking calls from other civilians—the result of the phone call made by L. J. Lewis from that location. The confusion resulting from the two addresses given for the shooting delayed the arrival of many police officers in getting to the shooting scene.

Alexander join the group. In a moment, Sheriff Bill Decker walks up. He's grimfaced. Decker was in the lead car of the motorcade and had seen the carnage at Parkland Hospital. But all he says is, "It looks bad."[448]

They are all standing there but a moment when they hear T. F. Bowley's voice break in on a nearby police radio with the news that a Dallas police officer has been shot.

Sergeant Owens, acting lieutenant in charge of the Oak Cliff area, listens with growing horror to the dispatcher calling in vain for Unit 78. He knows immediately that it's one of his men, J. D. Tippit—a longtime friend.[449] Owens jumps into his car as Hill and Alexander pile in behind him. Owens puts the pedal to the floor and the car squeals away toward Oak Cliff.[450] Hill grabs the radio in the front seat: "Give me the correct address on the shooting."

"501 East Tenth," dispatcher Jackson replies, giving an address from another call sheet just handed to him from an officer who had received this address from a telephone operator who in turn had been given the address by a resident calling in from East Tenth Street. The police are being flooded with call sheets—notations that record telephone calls from citizens.

Patrolmen Joe Poe and Leonard Jez, also racing to the scene, are equally confused by the multiple addresses.

"Was 519 East Jefferson correct?" Poe asks.

"We have two locations, 501 East Jefferson and 501 East Tenth," Jackson says, not mentioning the correct address of 404 East Tenth Street (Tenth and Patton) that he had also been given. "[Unit] Nineteen [Owens], are you en route?"

"Ten-four," an unknown officer says, "nineteen is en route."[451]

At 1:18 p.m., the channel 2 dispatcher, Gerald D. Henslee, informs "all squads" of the correct address of the shooting.[452]

Back in front of the Depository, reporters Ewell and Aynesworth confer briefly. The shooting in Oak Cliff *has* to be connected to the president's death, they think. They decide to split up—one will stay at the

Depository and the other will go out to Oak Cliff. Aynesworth draws the Oak Cliff assignment. After he runs off, Ewell has second thoughts about staying behind. He spots Captain W. R. Westbrook, in charge of the Dallas Police Department's Personnel Bureau, running for his car. He's headed for Oak Cliff too. Ewell asks permission and joins him.[453]

At Tenth and Patton streets, ambulance attendants J. C. Butler and William "Eddie" Kinsley swing their 1962 Ford ambulance around in front of the squad car and jump out. (Though they had received the incorrect address of 501 East Tenth Street from the police, they had no trouble spotting the squad car, and people around it, less than a block to the east.) They've been dispatched from the Dudley Hughes Funeral Home, less than three blocks away, but there's nothing they can do for Tippit. Ambulance attendants at that time are basically just drivers whose job is to get victims to a nearby hospital as quickly as possible. Their ambulance is equipped with little more than a stretcher.

Butler kneels next to Tippit's body and rolls him on his back as Kinsley pulls the stretcher cot from the back of the station wagon. Tippit's pistol is out of its holster, lying on the pavement near his right palm. Ted Callaway moves the gun to the hood of the squad car, then, with Scoggins and Guinyard, helps the attendants lift the body onto the stretcher. As they do so, the first Dallas police officer to arrive at the murder scene, reserve sergeant Kenneth Croy, pulls up. Butler and Kinsley push the cot into the back, slam the door, and are off in a flash to Methodist Hospital about a mile away.[454]

1:20 p.m.
Out at Parkland, the hospital's senior engineer, Darrell Tomlinson, has been manually operating the elevator, shuttling it between the emergency room on the ground floor and the operating rooms on the second floor. Coming down from the second floor, Tomlinson notices that on the ground floor a gurney, which was left in the hallway, has been pushed out into the narrow corridor by someone who may have used the men's room.

There is barely enough room in front of the elevator doors as it is, so Tomlinson pushes the gurney back. As it bumps the wall, Tomlinson hears a "clink" of metal on metal. He walks over and sees a bullet lying between the pad and the rim of the gurney.[455]

O. P. Wright, personnel officer of Parkland Hospital, has just entered the emergency unit when he hears Tomlinson call to him. Wright walks over and Tomlinson points out the bullet lying on the edge of the stretcher.[456] Wright, a former deputy chief of police for the city of Dallas, immediately looks for a federal officer to take charge of the evidence. At first, Wright contacts an FBI agent, who refuses to take a look at the bullet, saying it wasn't the FBI's responsibility to make the investigation, in apparent deference to the Dallas Police Department. Next, Wright locates a Secret Service agent, but he too doesn't seem interested in coming to look at the bullet on the stretcher. Frustrated, Wright returns to the stretcher, reluctantly picks up the bullet, and puts it into his pocket. There it remains for the next half hour or so, until Wright runs into Secret Service agent Richard E. Johnsen, who agrees to take possession of the bullet, which will later become a key piece of evidence in the assassination.[457]

In Oak Cliff, Ted Callaway can hear the confusion and desperation of the police over Tippit's car radio as they struggle to locate the scene of the officer's shooting. He lowers his big frame into the patrol car and grabs the mike, "Hello, hello, hello!"

"From out here on Tenth Street," he continues, "five-hundred block. This police officer's just shot, I think he's dead."

"Ten-four, we [already] have the information," dispatcher Jackson replies, exasperated. "The citizen using the radio will remain *off* the radio now." The last thing he needs is some gung-ho citizen tying up the airwaves.[458]

Ted Callaway climbs out of the squad car and spots his mechanic, Domingo Benavides.

"Did you see what happened?"

"Yes," Benavides says.

Callaway picks up Tippit's service revolver.

"Let's chase him," he says.

Benavides wants no part of it. Callaway snaps the revolver open—and Benavides can see that no rounds have been fired. Callaway tucks the gun in his belt and turns to the cabdriver, Scoggins.

"You saw the guy, didn't you?" the former marine asks.

Scoggins admits he had.

"If he's going up Jefferson, he can't be too far. Let's go get the son of a bitch who's responsible for this."

In his blue suit and white shirt, Callaway looks like some kind of policeman, or Secret Service agent. Scoggins doesn't find out until later that he's simply a used-car manager. They go back to Scoggins's cab and set off to cruise along Jefferson, the last place Callaway saw the gunman.[459]

Two blocks away, Warren Reynolds and Pat Patterson wonder whether the gunman went into the rear of one of the buildings near Crawford and Jefferson. They've been tailing him since he headed west, walking briskly along Jefferson Boulevard. They saw the killer turn north and scoot between a secondhand furniture store and the Texaco service station on the corner.

Eventually, they approach Robert and Mary Brock, the husband and wife employees of the service station, and ask if they've seen a man come by. Both say, "Yes." They last saw him in the parking lot behind the station. Reynolds and Patterson run back and check the parking lot, then the alley behind it. Nothing. He's escaped. Reynolds tells them to call the police, then heads toward Tenth and Patton to tell the others.[460]

1:21 p.m. (2:21 p.m. EST)

In Washington, FBI Director J. Edgar Hoover calls James J. Rowley, chief of the Secret Service, to offer any assistance. He tells Rowley it has been reported that a Secret Service agent has been killed, but he had not been able to get his name. Rowley states he did not know one of his agents had been killed. Hoover says the information he has is that the shots came from the "fourth floor of a building" and that "apparently a Winchester rifle was used." The two speculate about who was behind the shooting, Rowley mentioning subversive elements in Mexico and Cuba, Hoover mentioning the Ku Klux Klan.[461]

At the Dallas FBI office, Special Agent-in-Charge Gordon Shanklin, a chain-smoker who buys cartons of cigarettes by the grocery bag, is on the telephone with the third in command at FBI headquarters in Washington, Alan Belmont. With his thin hair, glasses, and comfortable attire, Shanklin looks like a rumpled professor, but all the agents understand his nervousness. It isn't easy to work for J. Edgar Hoover, with his whims and moods. Shanklin tells Belmont that from the information available, it appears the president has died of his wounds and that Governor Connally is in fair condition. He adds that, contrary to prior reports, a Secret Service agent has not been killed in Dallas.

"The director's specific instructions on this," Belmont says, "are that we should offer all possible assistance to the Secret Service and local police, and that means exactly that—give *all* possible assistance."

"Do we have jurisdiction?" Shanklin questions.

"The question of jurisdiction is not pertinent at the moment," Belmont replies. "The Secret Service will no doubt regard this as primarily their matter, but the essential thing is that we offer and give all possible assistance. In fact, see if the Secret Service wants us to send some laboratory men down to assist in identifying the spent shells found in the Depository."

"I've already made the offer," Shanklin tells him. "I've got our men with the Secret Service, the Dallas police, and the sheriff's office. I've even got a man at the hospital where Mrs. Kennedy is."

Shanklin fills Belmont in on the latest developments—shots appear to have been fired from the fifth floor of a five-story building at the corner of Elm and Commerce, where a Winchester rifle was reportedly used.* Shanklin tells him that the building has been roped off and the Secret Service and police are going through it.

"Has anyone been identified?" Belmont asks.

"No, not yet," Shanklin answers.

"We'll send out a Teletype to all offices to check and account for the whereabouts of all hate-group members in their areas," Belmont tells him. "If you need more manpower down there, let us know and we'll send it."

"Okay," Shanklin says, and hangs up.

Belmont promptly starts working on a Teletype to alert all FBI offices to immediately contact all informants and sources regarding the assassination and to immediately establish the whereabouts of bombing suspects, Klan and hate-group members, racial extremists, and any other individuals who on the basis of information in bureau files might have been involved.[462]

1:22 p.m.

The cavernous sixth floor of the Texas School Book Depository is crawling with officers looking for evidence. Since the discovery of the sniper's nest, the search has been concentrated there.[463] They have all heard about the shooting out in Oak Cliff and are tense, jumpy. *Dallas Morning News* reporter Kent Biffle, caught up with the officers involved in the search, wonders whether he risks getting shot by a nervous officer.[464]

A flashbulb pops in the southeast corner window as crime-lab investigators Lieutenant Carl Day and Detective Robert Studebaker photograph the three spent cartridges lying on the floor of the sniper's nest. Nearby, Captain Will Fritz of homicide converses with Detectives L. D. Montgomery and Marvin Johnson, who've just arrived.[465] Across the floor, in the northwest corner, near the top of the back stairwell, two sheriff deputies comb through a stack of boxes for the umpteenth time.

---

*This, and Hoover's statement about a Secret Service agent being killed, are two examples of the kind of erroneous information that was being passed along immediately after the assassination during the initial phases of the investigation. Shanklin's source was apparently the Dallas police radio where similar information had just been broadcast.

Deputy Eugene Boone shines his high-powered flashlight into every gloomy crack, crevice, and cranny, looking in, under, and around the dusty boxes and pallets. Alongside him is Deputy Constable Seymour Weitzman, who has been over this area of the sixth floor twice already, though without the aid of a flashlight. Now the bright beam of light picks up something on the floor stuffed down between two rows of boxes, another box slid on an angle over the top of it. Weitzman crawls down on the floor, as Boone shines the light down into the crevice from the top. They spot a rifle at the same moment.

"There it is!" Weitzman shouts.

"We got it!" Boone hollers to other officers across the sixth floor. It was pretty well concealed from view—eight or nine searchers must have stumbled over it before they found it. Boone checks his watch—1:22 p.m.[466]

Captain Fritz tells Detectives Montgomery and Johnson to stay with the hulls, while he and Detectives Sims and Boyd walk over to where the rifle has been found. They can see it down among the boxes. Detective Sims goes back to the area of the sniper's nest and tells Lieutenant Day that they need him, the camera, and the fingerprint dust kit over where the rifle has been found. Detective Studebaker takes another picture of the position of the three empty cartridges lying below the half-open window as Day tells him they've got the pictures they need.

Detective Sims reaches down and picks up the empty hulls and drops them into an evidence envelope that Lieutenant Day is holding open. With the empty hulls secured, Day packs up the camera and dust kit and immediately goes to the officers gathering around the rifle near the stairwell in the northwest corner of the sixth floor. As Day leaves, Detectives Montgomery and Johnson start to collect other evidence in the area of the sniper's nest, including the long, brown paper bag. The bag has been folded twice and is lying to the left of the sniper's nest window. As Montgomery unfolds it, he and Johnson speculate that it may have been used to bring the rifle into the building.[467]

Within minutes, Lieutenant Day and Detective Studebaker are photographing the rifle from several points of view. When they're satisfied they have enough, Fritz carefully lifts the weapon out by its homemade sling. A local TV cameraman records the scene for posterity.[468]

None of the officers crowding around, many of them gun enthusiasts, are able to identify the rifle positively, although it's clearly an infantry weapon with a Mauser action. It is stamped "Made Italy," with a date of 1940 and serial number C2766. Along with some other more arcane markings, it bears the legend "Caliber 6.5" across the top of the rear iron sight. It has the distinctive magazine—designed by Ferdinand Ritter von Mannlicher, who worked on the Mauser bolt action—built on the leading edge of the trigger guard, and capable of holding up to five rounds, or six of a smaller caliber. Day notices that the detachable cartridge clip in the magazine is empty. The rifle has been fitted with a cheap Japanese telescopic sight and an improvised, homemade sling. Whatever the sling came from, it didn't start out as a rifle sling.

Before the rifle is touched or moved, Captain Fritz has Day photograph the rifle and surrounding boxes. Fritz then gingerly opens the bolt and finds one live cartridge in the chamber, which he ejects.[469] The cartridge is printed with the caliber, 6.5 millimeter, and the make, "WW"— symbol of the Western Cartridge Company of Alton, Illinois.[470]

Sergeant Bud Owens races his car south on Beckley with passengers Gerald Hill and Bill Alexander. In Dallas law enforcement at the time of the assassination, two names stood out: Captain Will Fritz, who headed up the Homicide and Robbery Bureau of the Dallas Police Department, and Bill Alexander, the chief felony prosecutor for the Dallas district attorney's office. Alexander had been with the office for eleven years, had had ten murderers he convicted or helped convict executed at the state prison in Huntsville, and had a 93 percent conviction rate in felony jury trials, above average in his office of twenty-five assistant district attorneys. Both men, though not social friends, liked and respected each other and worked closely on the major homicide cases in Dallas. Both liked their respective bosses, Police Chief Jesse Curry and District Attorney Henry Wade, but viewed them charitably as administrators (though both, particularly

Wade, had distinguished careers in their respective departments before leading them) who really didn't know what the hell was going down in the cases handled by their offices.

Alexander, an infantry captain during the Second World War who saw combat in Italy, to this day wears a "John B. Stetson" hat—"with embroidered lining," he hastens to add—and carries a .380 automatic underneath his belt on his left side. Perhaps no other incident illustrates the lore of Bill Alexander more than one involving a Dallas con-artist named "Smokey Joe" Smith. It seems that Smith had the practice of reading obituaries and then preying on and swindling the decedents' vulnerable widows. Alexander did not take kindly to this and started to investigate Smith. One day, word got back to Alexander that Smith was in the Courthouse Café (a popular hangout for court regulars across the street from the courthouse) flashing his .45 and saying he was going to put a few holes in Alexander. There's always been an element of Texas justice that pronounces the word *justice* as "just us," and Alexander walked into the busy coffee shop, jerked Smith's "overfed" body off the counter stool, and with Smith on his knees, put his automatic to Smith's head and said, "Beg me for your life you no good son of a bitch or I'll kill you right here." After first pleading with Alexander, "Don't kill me. Please put the gun away," Smith, becoming more brazen when no projectile was on its way, told Alexander, "I'm going to tell the sheriff." "Well, go ahead and tell that one-eyed, old son of a bitch [Dallas sheriff Bill Decker]. That won't help you if you're gut-shot." Alexander left Smith with this cheerful admonition: "If you ever walk up behind me, I'll kill you dry." Smith, in fact, did call Decker, who called Alexander with this friendly advice: "You really shouldn't talk like that, Bill. Don't kill him."

But anyone led into thinking that because of Alexander's tough talk he was just a raw-boned hick who happened to have a law degree would be wrong. One can't spend more than a few minutes with Alexander without sensing that he is very intelligent and has a dry and pungent wit that he enjoys just as much as the person he's sharing it with.

On the day of the assassination, Alexander was returning to his office from a lunch-hour trip to a hardware store in the Oak Cliff section of

Dallas to get supplies for the deer-hunting season coming up, when he heard sirens and saw traffic gridlock near his office in the old Records Building off Dealey Plaza. Learning the president had been shot, he went to his office on the sixth floor. It was virtually empty, since Wade, in view of the president's visit and motorcade, had told his office to take the afternoon off. Knowing there would be a flood of calls coming in, Alexander asked the switchboard operator to stay on the job, and immediately went to the sheriff's office in the Jail Building, which was joined to the Records Building, to "see what was going on." Within minutes he walked to the assassination scene, where his friend, Dallas deputy chief Herbert Sawyer, was coordinating things from a makeshift command post he had set up on Elm in front of the Book Depository Building. When a call came in that a Dallas officer had been shot in the Oak Cliff area, as indicated, he got in the squad car with Bud Owens and Gerald Hill and went to the scene. Alexander knew what all good prosecutors know. If at all possible, you join in the police investigation. It's much easier to present a case in court that you helped put together than to rely solely on the police. If you do the latter and they do a good job, fine. But if they don't, it's legal suicide. Alexander was at ground zero and starting to put his case together against the killer of Officer Tippit.[471]

As Owens, Hill, and Alexander proceed to the Tippit murder scene, they see an ambulance, sirens wailing, cross in front of them, a police car close behind. The officers know it's heading for the emergency unit at Methodist Hospital.[472] The ambulance bearing Tippit's body had picked up a patrol car, driven by Officer Robert Davenport and partner W. R. Bardin, a block earlier. In a moment the two are wheeling into the emergency entrance. When Butler and Kinsley open the back of the ambulance, Officer Davenport is shocked to see J. D. Tippit, whom he knew well and had worked with for three years. Davenport and Bardin help get Tippit into the emergency room. Though he appears to be dead, the officers observe "the doctors and nurses trying to bring [Tippit] back to life."

Up in the call-room of the hospital, Dr. Paul C. Moellenhoff, a twenty-nine-year-old surgery resident, is watching TV coverage of the presidential shooting. Someone from the emergency room calls and asks for the doctor on duty. He's out, so Dr. Moellenhoff runs down to cover for him.[473]

At Tenth and Patton, Officer Roy W. Walker pulls to the curb and recognizes an old school friend, Warren Reynolds, who gives him a description of the suspect.[474] Officer Walker grabs his radio mike as more police cars approach.

"We have a description on this suspect," Walker broadcasts, "last seen about 300 block of East Jefferson. He's a white male, about thirty, five-eight, black hair, slender, wearing a white jacket, white shirt, and dark slacks."

"Armed with what?" dispatcher Jackson asks.

"Unknown," Walker replies.[475]

Patrol partners Joe Poe and Leonard Jez pull up just as Walker finishes the broadcast. Owens, Hill, and Alexander are right behind them. Police cars are now arriving at Tenth and Patton en masse.[476] Sergeant Owens takes command of the area, instructing Officers Poe and Jez to talk to as many witnesses as possible and guard the crime scene. Someone at the scene informs them that the gunman had cut through a parking lot on Jefferson and dumped his jacket. Sergeant Owens and Assistant District Attorney Alexander and a posse of officers leave in search of the gunman.[477]

Sergeant Hill tells eyewitness Harold Russell to come with him. Hill takes Poe's squad car and drives off with Russell in the hopes of spotting the gunman in flight.

Eyewitness Jack Tatum walks up to Officers Poe and Jez with Mrs. Markham in tow. Hysterical, incoherent, and on the verge of fainting, Mrs. Markham recounts the brutal murder for police. It's tough to understand Markham's story through her tears. She keeps telling them that she'll be late for work, and they reassure her that everything will be okay.[478]

Ted Callaway and cabdriver William Scoggins return to the scene after failing to find the gunman. Callaway swears he would have shot him if he had found him. Police are just glad to get Tippit's service revolver back from this gung-ho Dallas citizen.[479]

1:23 p.m.

At Methodist Hospital, Dr. Moellenhoff is joined in the emergency room by Dr. Richard A. Liquori. The physicians make no further effort to resuscitate J. D. Tippit. Dr. Liquori thinks the bullet wound in the temple could have caused instant death. He turns to Officer Davenport and tells him he's declaring Tippit dead on arrival. Davenport shakes his head in despair and leaves the room to notify police headquarters. Tippit's body will be transported to Parkland Hospital for an autopsy. Before it is, Captain Cecil Talbert asks Dr. Moellenhoff to remove a bullet from Tippit's body, one that had not penetrated deeply, so the police can determine what caliber weapon was used in the shooting. "One 38 [caliber] slug and a button from Tippit's shirt" are removed from the wound.[480]

1:25 p.m.

FBI agent James P. Hosty Jr. hurries into the FBI squad room on the eleventh floor of the Santa Fe Building in downtown Dallas. He scans the room for Kenneth C. Howe, his immediate supervisor. Hosty was eating a cheese sandwich in a café when he heard that Kennedy had been shot. He's already been out to the Trade Mart, Parkland Hospital, and now, under orders from Howe, back at the bureau offices.

Hosty sees that Howe, in his fifties, is visibly close to the edge.

Because of Kennedy's progressive civil rights stance, Howe, like so many, suspects that the right wing may be behind the assassination, and Hosty is the only Dallas agent that monitors the right-wing groups. He knows he's in the hot seat now. Just then, Agent Vince Drain calls from Parkland Hospital to report that the president is dead of a gunshot wound to the head. Silence falls over the FBI office. A few secretaries start to sob quietly.

Hosty jumps on the telephone and calls Sergeant H. M. Hart, his counterpart in the Dallas police intelligence unit. In a matter of minutes, they agree to coordinate their investigation of right-wing extremists. As he hangs up the telephone, Hosty, like most of the law enforcement officers involved, can't help but think that the shootings of Officer Tippit and President Kennedy are somehow connected. But how?[481]

———

In the 400 block of East Jefferson, Sergeant Owens climbs from the squad car and directs a flock of arriving officers into the parking lot behind the Texaco service station. Another group of lawmen, including Assistant District Attorney Alexander, storm into two large vacant houses on Jefferson used for the storage of secondhand furniture. Warren Reynolds had told the police he saw the gunman running toward the houses. *Dallas Morning News* reporter Hugh Aynesworth is with the police searchers. A handful of cops run up a flight of rickety stairs, while another posse paws through the clutter of furniture, weapons cocked.

"Come out of there you son of a bitch, we've got you now!" one of them hollers.

Suddenly an officer falls through a weak section of the second-story flooring with a thunderous sound, his descent stopping at his waist. Before witnessing the humorous sight of the officer being half in and half out of the ceiling, all of them had instantly drawn their guns. Aynesworth, realizing he's the only one in there without a gun, runs for the exit, leaving police to do their duty. It doesn't take long for police to determine that there's nothing but junk in either building.[482]

Captain Westbrook and several officers proceed to the adjacent parking lot behind the Texaco service station, where the suspect lost his civilian pursuers, to conduct a further search. Quickly, an officer points out to Captain Westbrook a light-colored jacket tossed under the rear bumper of an old Pontiac parked in the middle of the parking lot. Westbrook walks over and inspects the clothing. Looks like their suspect has decided to change his appearance.[483] Motorcycle officer J. T. Griffin reaches for his police radio to notify the dispatcher, and fellow officers, of the discovery.[484]

"We believe we've got [the suspect's] white jacket. Believe he dumped it on this parking lot behind this service station at 400 block East Jefferson."[485] A moment later, dispatch supervisor Sergeant Gerald Henslee contacts Captain Westbrook on police radio channel 2.

"Go ahead," Westbrook says as he reaches a nearby radio.

"D.O.A. [dead on arrival], Methodist [Hospital]."

"Name?" Westbrook asks.

"J. D. Tippit."[486]

1:26 p.m.

At the makeshift headquarters in Parkland Hospital's emergency section, Secret Service agent Lem Johns reports to Agent Youngblood that he has lined up two unmarked police cars, along with Dallas Police Chief Curry and Inspector Putnam, who'll act as drivers, to get Johnson back to Love Field.

"Let's go," Johnson says.

They rush out in a football formation, Johnson the quarterback surrounded by a wedge of agents, those at the rear walking backward, hands on their guns. A second formation comprising Mrs. Johnson and two congressmen, Jack Brooks and Homer Thornberry, are close behind. The bewildered crowd at the emergency entrance scarcely has time to react before Johnson dives into the rear seat of Chief Curry's car. Youngblood crowds in behind him, as Thornberry slides in front. Mrs. Johnson and Congressman Brooks and a bevy of agents jump into the second car. As the cars begin to pull away, Congressman Albert Thomas runs up, calling out, "Wait for me!" Youngblood, not eager to present a sitting target right in front of the hospital, tells Curry to drive on, but Johnson overrules him. "Stop and let him get in."

The cars are stopped momentarily by a delivery truck on the access road to the hospital, but the police motorcycle escort gets them through, and they are off again, sirens wailing. Both Youngblood and Johnson ask Curry to turn off the sirens. They don't want to attract any more attention than absolutely necessary. Youngblood radios ahead to have Air Force One ready to receive them. They will be coming on board immediately.[487]

Malcolm Kilduff stands outside Parkland Hospital watching as the new president heads for Love Field. He turns and heads back into the hospital, where he knows he'll have to make the hardest announcement of his life. A crowd of journalists crazy for something official, anything at all, flock around him. All of them know, from Father Huber's indiscretion, that President Kennedy is dead. Someone has already lowered the flag out in front of the hospital to half-mast. Kilduff refuses to oblige them, repeating mechanically that he will make no further statement until the press conference begins.[488]

1:29 p.m.

For the first time, Dallas police headquarters learns that there may be a connection between the Kennedy and Tippit shootings. When Deputy Chief of Police N. T. Fisher calls into channel 2 police radio dispatcher Gerald Henslee and asks if there is "any indication" of a connection between the two shootings, Henslee radios back, "Well, the descriptions on the suspect are similar and it is possible."[489]

1:30 p.m.

Vernon B. O'Neal, proprietor of O'Neal's Funeral Home, and his book-keeper, Ray Gleason, arrive at Parkland's emergency entrance and open the back of the Cadillac ambulance. Secret Service agents and White House correspondents spring forward to help lug the four-hundred-pound casket requested by the Secret Service out onto the undertaker's lightweight, portable cart assembled there.* Ken O'Donnell gets the signal that the casket has arrived. He returns to the corridor outside Trauma Room One and finds Jackie Kennedy still sitting on the folding chair surrounded by Clint Hill and members of President Kennedy's staff.

"I want to speak to you," he says to Mrs. Kennedy, motioning for her to follow him. They move a short distance down the passageway, away from the casket being wheeled in. The First Lady guesses that he doesn't want her to see it. Dr. Kemp Clark appears beside O'Donnell, and Jackie pleads with him, "Please—can I go in? Please let me go back."

---

*Seventeen of O'Neal's eighteen employees are out to lunch when he got a call from Secret Service agent Clint Hill, shortly after 1:00 p.m., who wanted him to bring the best casket he had to Parkland Hospital. His most expensive model, at $3,995, was the Elgin Casket Company's Handley Britannia, a four-hundred-pound, double-walled, hermetically sealed, solid-bronze coffin manufactured by the Texas Coffin Company. O'Neal had to wait until three more of his men came back from lunch before he could wrestle the behemoth into his 1964 Cadillac hearse. (ARRB MD 131, Texas Coffin Company reorder card; Bishop, *Day Kennedy Was Shot*, p.267; Manchester, *Death of a President*, pp.291–292)

"No, no," he said softly.

Finally, she leans toward him.

"Do you think seeing the coffin can upset me, Doctor? I've seen my husband die, shot in my arms. His blood is all over me. How can I see anything worse than what I've seen?"

There is nothing left for Clark to do but accede to her wishes.

Mrs. Kennedy is right behind Vernon O'Neal as they push the casket into Trauma Room One. She wants to see her husband one more time before they close the coffin, to touch him and give him something. She moves to the president's side, takes off her wedding ring, which he had bought her in Newport, Rhode Island, just before their grand wedding there, lifts her husband's hand, and slips it on his finger. She wants desperately to be alone with him, but she knows it cannot be. She steps into the passageway outside.

"Did I do the right thing?" she asks Ken O'Donnell. "I wanted to give him something."

"You leave it right where it is," he says.

"Now I have nothing left," she says.[*490]

After seeing the condition of the president's body, Vernon O'Neal knows that it's going to take some time to make sure that the casket's expensive pale satin lining isn't irretrievably stained. Nurses Margaret Henchliffe and Diana Bowron, along with orderly David Sanders, line the coffin with a sheet of plastic, then wrap the body in a white sheet before placing it in the casket. Additional sheets are wrapped around the head to keep it from oozing more blood. The whole process takes twenty minutes.[491]

Meanwhile, Dr. Earl Rose, the Dallas County medical examiner, with an office at Parkland Hospital, rushes into the emergency area and grabs a phone off the wall of the nurses station.

"This is Earl Rose," he says into the mouthpiece, presumably to a Park-

---

[*]At 1:00 a.m. the next morning at Bethesda Hospital, O'Donnell slipped into the room where Kennedy's body lay, removed the ring, and brought it back to Jackie (O'Donnell and Powers with McCarthy, *Johnny, We Hardly Knew Ye*, p.35; *New York Times*, December 5, 1963, p.32).

land Hospital official. "There has been a homicide here. They won't be able to leave until there has been an autopsy."

He hangs up and turns to leave when Roy Kellerman, who overheard Rose's directive, blocks the door.

"My friend, I'm the special agent in charge of the White House detail of the Secret Service," he says. "This is the body of the president of the United States and we are going to take it back to Washington."

"No, that's not the way things are," Rose snaps, waving his finger.

"The president is going with us," Kellerman argues.

"You're not taking *the body* anywhere," Rose lashes back. "There's a law here. We're going to enforce it!"

"This part of the law can be waived," Kellerman insists, every muscle tightening.

Rose shakes his head, no.

"You'll have to show me a lot more authority than you have now," Kellerman says.

"I will!" Rose shoots back, reaching for the phone.

The law, of course, is on the medical examiner's side. The president was murdered on a Dallas street, and unbelievably, killing a president was not a federal crime at the time unless it was committed on federal property, which wasn't the case here.[*] Also, since Texas law required an

---

[*]One of the most prominent misconceptions that has been parroted by virtually everyone, including the Warren Commission, is that in 1963 it wasn't a federal crime to murder the president. "Murder of the president has never been covered by federal law," said the Warren Commission in 1964 (WR, p.454). "At that time it was not a federal crime to assassinate a president," said Chief Justice Earl Warren in his memoirs (Warren, *Memoirs*, p.355). Indeed, even FBI Director J. Edgar Hoover said that "it is not a federal crime to kill the president" (5 H 98, WCT, Hon. J. Edgar Hoover). For *almost* all practical intents and purposes, this is true, but the statement, technically, is not. Under Section 1111 of Title 18 of the U.S. Code, murder was, of course, a federal crime in 1963. And just as obviously there was no language in Title 18 that said, "However, if the victim of the murder is the president of the United States, then it's not a federal crime." Where the limitation came in is in subdivision (b) of Section 1111, which provided (and still does) that for there to be federal prosecutorial jurisdiction over any murder, it has to take place "within the special maritime and territorial jurisdiction of the United States," which the courts have held to be places owned, possessed, or controlled by the U.S. government (most importantly, the president's residence, the White House, but also, for example, federal buildings like the Pentagon, military installations, U.S. highways, national parks, islands like Palmyra in the Pacific that are U.S. possessions, etc.). Since a Dallas street is not a U.S. highway and would

inquest by a justice of the peace for all homicides, and then, if ordered—
as it automatically would have been done in this case—an autopsy,[492] Rose
has a legal obligation to Dallas County to make sure an autopsy is conducted. Telephone calls to the sheriff's office and police department
assure him that he is right, that an inquest and autopsy are mandatory.

Ken O'Donnell and others in the presidential party, imagining the
ordeal for the widow if she has to remain in Dallas for another day or two,
take turns arguing with the medical examiner. This is not an ordinary
homicide, but an assassinated president. He has been examined by doctors and will certainly undergo a federal-level autopsy on his return to
Washington, D.C. Further delay will serve no purpose and could cause
undue misery for his widow. And so on.

Dr. Rose concedes that he could legally release the body to a Texas justice of the peace functioning as a coroner, but without that, there's no

not qualify, there could not be a federal prosecution of Oswald for having killed Kennedy. It is
highly anomalous that even in 1963, if it could have been shown that Oswald had entered into a
conspiracy to murder the president, or even threatened harm to him, since Sections 372 and 871,
respectively, of Title 18 contain no such territorial limitation, federal jurisdiction to prosecute
Oswald for those separate offenses would have existed. But not for the actual act of murdering
the president.

As a direct result of Kennedy's assassination, and pursuant to one of the recommendations
of the Warren Commission (WR, pp.26, 455), this loophole in the federal law was plugged on
August 28, 1965, when Congress enacted Section 1751 of Title 18 specifically making the assassination of a president (or president elect or vice president) murder under Section 1111, and
conveying federal jurisdiction irrespective of where the killing occurred, even if on foreign soil.
Section 1751(k) provides that "there is *extra*territorial jurisdiction over the conduct prohibited
by this section." Also, anomalously, although the jurisdictional limitation wasn't removed for the
president until 1965, in 1963 it already was a federal crime to murder (anywhere) federal judges,
U.S. attorneys and marshals, and other "officers and employees of the United States." (18 USC
§1114; WR, p.454)

Congressional efforts to make, without limitation, the assassination of a president a prose-
cutable federal crime (a House bill in 1901 and Senate bill in 1902 following the assassination of
President McKinley in 1901, and a House bill in 1933 following the attempted assassination of
President Roosevelt on February 15, 1933) failed to be enacted into law (WR, pp.454–455; H.R.
10386, 57th Cong., 1st sess., 1901; S. 3653, 57th Cong., 1st sess., 1902; H.R. 3896, 73rd Cong.,
1st sess., 1933).

Attempted assassination is also covered under Section 1751, and the indictment of Charles
Manson follower Lynette "Squeaky" Fromme for her attempted assassination of President Ger-
ald Ford on September 5, 1975, in Sacramento, California, was the first under the new law.
Fromme was subsequently convicted and is now serving a life sentence.

way he will permit them to remove the body from his jurisdiction. The president's men start making phone calls to find an authority who can overrule him.[493]

At the Texas School Book Depository, police officers are conducting a roll call outside of Supervisor Bill Shelley's office, and collecting the names and addresses of the building's employees. Superintendent Roy Truly notices that Oswald isn't among the dozen or so stockroom boys talking to the police. In fact, Truly hasn't seen Oswald since he and Officer Baker ran into him in the second-floor lunchroom right after the shots. That encounter may be the only reason Truly is thinking of him now.

"Have you seen Lee Oswald around lately?" Truly asks Shelley.

"No," Shelley replies.[494]

Truly approaches O. V. Campbell, the Book Depository vice president.

"I have a boy over here missing," Truly says. "I don't know whether to report it or not."

Truly thinks that another one or two boys are also missing,[*] but the only one who sticks in his mind is Oswald, if for no other reason than that he had seen Oswald on the second floor of the building (when almost all of his other employees were out on the street) just an hour or so earlier.

Truly calls down to the warehouse personnel office to get Oswald's telephone number, home address, and description from his employment application. He jots it all down, and hangs up. Deputy Chief Lumpkin is a few feet away.

---

[*]Actually, only one other of the boys was missing: Charles Douglas Givens (CE 705, 17 H 419; CE 1974, 23 H 873), who went to the corner of Main and Record (two blocks from the Depository) to watch the motorcade. When he returned to the Depository sometime after 12:40 p.m., police wouldn't let him back inside (7 H 382, 385–386, WCT Roy Sansom Truly; 6 H 355, WCT Charles Douglas Givens). Givens, who had a prior police record for narcotics violations, was spotted in the crowd an hour later by Dallas police lieutenant Jack Revill, who recognized Givens from his past dealings with him. Givens was subsequently taken to police headquarters, where he was questioned and gave a statement (5 H 35–36, WCT Jack Revill; 6 H 355, WCT Charles Douglas Givens; CE 2003, 24 H 210).

"I've got a boy missing over here," Truly tells him, instinctively focusing in, again, only on Oswald. "I don't know whether it amounts to anything or not."

"Let's go up and tell Captain Fritz," Lumpkin says as the two head upstairs.[495] They find Captain Fritz on the sixth floor at the top of the stairs, standing with a group of officers and reporters. Lumpkin pulls Fritz aside to listen to Truly, who repeats his story and gives him Oswald's address and general description: age twenty-three (he was now twenty-four), five foot nine, about a hundred fifty pounds, light brown hair.[496]

1:33 p.m.

The large double classroom in the medical school, room 101–102, is jammed with noisy, excited reporters who have difficulty calming down when Malcolm Kilduff takes his place at the teacher's lectern. He starts to speak, then stops. "Excuse me, let me catch my breath." Kennedy has been dead for half an hour and everyone in the room knows it, but Kilduff still can't think of what to say or how to say it. He wonders whether he will be able to control his quivering voice. Finally, he begins, "President John F. Kennedy . . ."

"Hold it," someone calls, as cameras click. Kilduff starts over.

"President John F. Kennedy died at approximately one o'clock Central Standard Time today here in Dallas."

"Oh God!" a reporter blurts out.

Kilduff welcomes a moment of respite as the wire reporters rush out to find a telephone.

"He died of a gunshot wound in the brain," Kilduff continues. "I have no other details regarding the assassination of the president. Mrs. Kennedy was not hit. Governor Connally was not hit. The vice president was not hit."

Reporters will discover Kilduff's error about the governor soon enough.

Tom Wicker, the *New York Times* White House reporter, starts to ask whether Johnson has been sworn in as president, but breaks down. Kilduff's voice also breaks as he tries to answer. Another correspondent asks, "Has the vice president taken the oath of office?"

"No," Kilduff says. "He has left."

The reporters demand a briefing by the attending doctors, and Kilduff, who hadn't thought of it, promises to see what he can do.[497]

1:34 p.m.

In the parking lot in back of the Texaco station, Captain Westbrook turns around and starts toward the Abundant Life Temple, a four-story brick church at the corner of Tenth and Crawford, located right behind the Texaco parking lot. But he sees it's already covered. Officer M. N. "Nick" McDonald was standing at the rear of the Temple and McDonald calls in to the radio dispatcher, "Send me a squad over here at Tenth and Crawford. Check out this church basement."[498]

1:35 p.m.

Dallas police officer Charles T. Walker drops a couple of newsmen off at the Tippit killing scene and drives off to comb the neighborhood. Turning onto southbound Denver, he spots a man, fitting the description of the suspect, running into the library a block ahead, at Jefferson and Marsalis. Walker punches the gas and grabs his radio mike, "He's in the library, Jefferson—East 500 block!"

The radio suddenly comes alive with excited chatter.

"What's the location, 223?" the dispatcher asks.

"Marsalis and Jefferson, in the library, I'm going around the back, get somebody around the front . . . Get 'em here fast!" Walker shouts as he wheels to the curb, tires screeching.

Police and sheriff deputies, including the officers about to search the church, scramble for their cars. Within a minute, the library is ground zero, surrounded by nearly every squad car in the area. Police feel certain they have the cop killer cornered.[499]

1:36 p.m.

Six blocks west of the library on Jefferson Boulevard, twenty-two-year-old Johnny C. Brewer, manager of Hardy's Shoe Store, listened to the president's arrival at Love Field and the motorcade on a little transistor radio, and has been riveted since the first vague reports of the shooting of the president were heard. From what he can gather, a policeman has also been shot, less than three-quarters of a mile away.[500] He's been hearing the periodic wail of sirens for nearly twenty minutes.

Now, Brewer can hear police sirens coming west on Jefferson, their wail growing so strong it sounds like it might land on his doorstep at any moment. Suddenly, a young man walking west on Jefferson steps into the lobby—a large recess, fifteen feet deep, between the sidewalk and the door of the shop, with display windows on either side. The fellow, wearing a brown sports shirt over a white T-shirt, his shirttail out, is behaving very strangely. Brewer is only about ten feet away, just beyond the display window, and is looking directly at his face. Brewer finds it quite unusual that with all the commotion going on outside, the man keeps his back to the street. His hair is messed up, he's breathing heavily and looks like he's been running, and he also looks scared. Brewer thinks he recognizes him as a particular persnickety customer who once took an agonizingly long time to make up his mind to purchase a cheap pair of black crepe-soled shoes.[501] (Police did recover a pair of "black low quarter shoes, John Hardy Brand," from Oswald's Beckley room on November 23, 1963.)[502]*

Just as the man stepped into the foyer, Brewer can see the approaching police cars make a U-turn at Jefferson and Zangs, a few stores away, and head back east on Jefferson toward the library, sirens screaming. The man in the foyer turns and looks over his right shoulder toward the receding police cars, then, seemingly after making sure they have gone by, steps out of the foyer and continues west on Jefferson. The more Brewer thinks about it, the more suspicious he becomes. About a half minute later, curiosity gets the better of him, and Brewer steps out onto the sidewalk

*The Tippit murder occurred at approximately 1:12 p.m. and the murder scene at Tenth and Patton is not even quite seven blocks from the shoe store and Texas Theater. Also, we know Oswald was running at least part of the time after he shot Tippit, yet Oswald doesn't reach the shoe store until close to twenty to twenty-five minutes later. Even given the somewhat circuitous path he must have taken to reach the shoe store area, the likelihood is that although the area was swarming with police officers searching for him, Oswald succeeded, along the way, in secreting himself from human view, where he most likely stayed hidden for several minutes at a time.

to see where this character is going. The suspect is already fifty yards away, walking at a good clip, nearing the marquee of the Texas Theater, which is showing a double-feature, *Cry of Battle* and *War Is Hell.*[503]

Julia E. Postal, the forty-seven-year-old ticket-taker, has been listening to the radio too. Just before the Texas Theater opened for business at 12:45 p.m., her daughter called to tell her that someone had shot the president, and she has been listening right there in the box office ever since. Though most of the police cars had turned around, one continued on, its siren blasting as it shot past the theater box office. John Callahan, the theater manager, who is standing next to Mrs. Postal, says, "Something's about to pop."

They both scramble out onto the sidewalk. The squad car looks like it's stopping up the street. Callahan gets into his car at the curb to go see what's happening.[504]

Shoe store manager Johnny Brewer, on the sidewalk east of the theater, sees the suspicious man, "walking a little faster than usual," slip into the Texas Theater behind Postal's back.[505] For Brewer, it's all adding up.

Postal watches her boss drive off, then turns to go back to the box office. Brewer is standing there, having walked up from the shoe store. He asks her if the man that just ducked into the theater had bought a ticket. "No, by golly, he didn't," she says looking around, half expecting to see him. She saw the man out of the corner of her eye when she walked out with Mr. Callahan.[506]

Brewer tells her the man's been acting suspiciously. He goes inside and checks with concessionaire Warren "Butch" Burroughs, but he was busy stocking candy and didn't see anyone come in. Brewer returns to the box office.[507]

"He *has* to be in there," Postal says. She tells him to go get Butch and have him help check the exits, but don't tell him why because he's "kind of excitable." Brewer goes back in and asks Burroughs to show him where the exits are. The concessionaire wants to know why? Against Postal's advice, Brewer tells him he thought "the guy looked suspicious."[508]

The Texas Theater, an architecturally decorative structure built in 1932, was the very first in a chain of theaters built by inventor Howard Hughes. Upon entering the theater lobby from Jefferson Boulevard, patrons find themselves to the rear of the theater, where a concession stand is set up. A staircase near the stand leads up to a spacious balcony above the main seating area. Another staircase at the far end of the lobby leads to the theater office. Being an L-shaped theater, from the concession stand a theater-goer can only enter the main seating area by walking farther into the lobby and turning right down one of four aisles. The main seating area in the middle of the theater has an aisle on each side of it, and smaller seating areas to the left and right have an aisle adjacent to the left and right walls. The seats descend downward in typical theater style toward a large movie screen rising above a narrow area ("stage") not large enough for live performances, though the theater was built during the vaudeville era. There are five (today, six) fire exits, one to the left of the stage, one at the far end of the lobby, two on the balcony level, and a fifth on the small floor above the balcony, where the projection room is. Four of the fire exits lead directly into an alley running parallel with Jefferson Boulevard.[509]

The flickering images of *War Is Hell* dance across the screen as Brewer and Burroughs check the lock bars on the two ground-floor exits. They are still down, meaning whoever ducked into the theater is still there.[510] There are twenty-four patrons in the theater who have purchased their ninety-cent tickets for the double-feature.[511]

1:38 p.m. (2:38 p.m. EST)
On CBS television, Walter Cronkite again repeats details of the shooting as he awaits official word on the president's death. Viewers can see two newsmen ripping fresh wire-copy from the Teletype machine in the background, then race over to the anchorman, and hand him the sheet. Cronkite slips on his heavy, dark-frame glasses and glances at the copy. Now, for the first time, without equivocation, Cronkite tells a waiting nation, "From Dallas, the flash apparently official, President Kennedy died at one o'clock Central Standard Time—two o'clock Eastern Standard Time—some thirty-eight minutes ago."

The words catch in his throat, and for a moment, the most respected news anchor in the business is about to lose his composure. Choking back tears, Cronkite clears his throat and continues, "Vice President Lyndon Johnson has left the hospital. We don't know to where he has proceeded.

Presumably, he will be taking the oath of office and become the thirty-sixth president of the United States."[512] During a later break, Cronkite answered a network telephone and heard a snobbish-sounding woman caller say, "I just want to say that this is the worst possible taste to have that Walter Cronkite on the air with his crocodile tears when everybody knows that he spent all his time trying to get the president." The newsman shot back, "Madam, *this* is Walter Cronkite and you're a goddamned idiot!" and slammed the phone down so hard he thought for a moment he had damaged it.[513]

With the news of the president's death, men and women across the country "sobbed in the streets of the cities and did not have to explain why," historian Theodore White wrote. "Not until he was dead and all men knew he would never again point his forefinger down from the platform in speaking to them, never pause before lancing with his wit the balloon of an untidy question, did Americans know how much light the young president had given their own lives—and how he had touched them."[514] Comedian Bob Hope wasn't trying to be funny when he said, "The lights had blown out in Camelot and the whole nation was stumbling around in the dark."[515] The *New York Times'* Tom Wicker wrote, "People were unbelieving, afraid . . . desperately unsure of what would happen next. The world, it seemed, was a dark and malignant place; the chill of the unknown shivered across the nation."[516]

Many in America, a nation of 190 million people, "simply stood, stupefied, no longer listening to the staccato voices that sounded unceasingly on the radios. Church bells tolled and the churches began to fill . . . Strangers spoke to each other, seeking surcease," wrote Relman Morin, a Pulitzer Prize–winning correspondent who covered the assassination for Associated Press and was a personal friend of the president's. In Boston, he continued, "the Boston Symphony broke off a Handel concert to play a funeral march by Beethoven. The gong sounded in the New York Stock Exchange, suspending trading. Hundreds of football games to have been played Saturday were postponed. Race tracks closed . . . Sessions in the United Nations came to a halt . . . Television and radio networks announced that they were withdrawing all entertainment programs and commercials from their schedules to devote full time to . . . the assassination; normal programming would not be resumed until after the funeral."[517]

What happened in New York City is a microcosm of the country as a whole. The *New York Times* reported,

> The cry rang across the city, echoing again and again: "Is it true?" Another cry quickly took its place as the news of the death of President Kennedy swept with sudden impact: "My God!" . . . In all parts of the five boroughs, motorists pulled up their cars and sat hunched over their dashboard radios . . . Hundreds of thousands reached for so many telephones that the system blacked out and operators had to refuse calls . . . Uptown, midtown, downtown, work in offices came to an abrupt halt . . . The biggest city in the nation turned into something of a ghost town. All Broadway theaters and all musical events . . . were cancelled . . . One common scene was the tight grasp of one's hand on another's arm as they discussed the assassination . . . Those who had no one familiar at hand walked up to strangers . . . The grief and the acts of mourning knew no special group, no particular section of the city . . . The sorrow and shock were unfolded in the human vignette, the collection of individuals who stared as though in a trance from their subway seats, their stools at luncheon counters, their chairs near television sets . . . A postman . . . encountered many housewives who wept as they told him the news. They talked about it just as if they had lost their son or daughter. . . . A dentist, weeping, said: "I can't work. I've sent two patients home and I've closed my office." . . . A bartender said: "Everybody feels dead, real dead." . . . A department store saleswoman declared: "I would do anything to bring him back." . . . As dusk came, automatic devices turned on the huge, gaudy signs that normally blot out the night in Times Square. Then, one by one, the lights blinked out, turning the great carnival strip into what was almost a mourning band on the city's sleeve.[518]*

---

*The almost reflexive belief was that a southern segregationist had shot the president. "A lawyer in Riverdale commented: 'We have allowed certain factions to work up such furor

It was not too different in most foreign countries, people weeping in the streets of the world's great capitals—Berlin, London, Paris, Rome. Even peoples who did not understand a word of English that Kennedy spoke had sensed that he was special, and he somehow touched the hearts of these millions. "To them, Kennedy symbolized youth, new ideas, a fresh approach, the New Generation. Indeed, he had sounded that chord himself in his Inaugural Address. 'Let the word go forth from this time and place, to friend and foe alike, that the torch has been passed to a new generation of Americans, born in this century, tempered by war, disciplined by a hard and bitter peace.'" Kennedy had come to power after the greatest and most destructive war ever, "only to be followed by the specter of an even greater war in which new weapons could decimate the human race." Because of his leadership, soaring oratory, and innate charisma, millions throughout the planet felt that a peaceful resolution to the world's problems was more likely with him leading the way. People somehow believed in the possibilities of his vision of "a new world . . . where the strong are just, and the weak secure and the peace preserved . . . Let us begin."

"That young man," Kennedy's cold-war counterpart, Soviet premier Nikita S. Khrushchev, reminisced in sorrow, without the need to say another word. West Berlin mayor Willy Brandt said, "A flame went out for all those who had hoped for a just peace and a better life."[*] Eighty-

---

throughout the South with fanatic criticism [of Kennedy] that a demented person can feel confident that such atrocious action is justifiable' " (*New York Times*, November 23, 1963, p.5).

The terrible irony is that the man who killed the president was not the product of that segment of the South that despised the president for championing civil rights for the black population, but someone who admired the president for it.

[*]On the evening of Monday, November 25, 1963, a quarter of a million West Berliners crowded into newly dedicated John F. Kennedy Square, where just five months earlier Kennedy gave his famous "Ich bin ein Berliner" (I am a Berliner) speech, to mourn Kennedy's death, thousands openly crying. The Associated Press reported that "never in memory has this tortured city grieved more than in the last four days since the death of the President." (*Dallas Morning News*, November 26, 1963, p.16)

Earlier on Monday the *Telegraph*, a conservative London paper, said that "few of the 35 American Presidents have touched the minds and hearts of British people as have Abraham Lincoln, Franklin Roosevelt and John Kennedy." The paper opened a fund drive to build a statue of Kennedy in London with a contribution of one thousand pounds. (*Dallas Morning News*, November 26, 1963, p.15)

nine-year-old Winston Churchill, hearing the news in London while peering at his TV set with his Clementine, said, "The loss to the United States and to the world is incalculable." Around the world, "groups divided by deep ideological chasms found common cause in mourning John F. Kennedy . . . . For an hour, at least, he drew men together in universal mourning."[519] In Latin America, grief was pervasive. Brazilian president João Goulart declared three days of official mourning and canceled all of his official engagements. Chilean president Jorge Alessandri Rodriguez declared national mourning, and radio stations replaced all programs with funeral music. Rómulo Betancourt, president of Venezuela, attempting to read to newsmen the message of condolences he had sent to Washington, broke into tears and was unable to go on.[520]

But if one were to think that grief over Kennedy's death was universal, they would be wrong. "An Oklahoma City physician," author William Manchester writes, "beamed at a grief-stricken visitor and said, 'God, I hope they got Jackie [too].' In a small Connecticut city a doctor called ecstatically across Main Street—to an internist who worshiped Kennedy—'The joy ride's over. This is one deal Papa Joe can't fix.' A woman visiting Amarillo, the second most radical city in Texas [after Dallas], was lunching in the restaurant adjacent to her motel when a score of rejoicing students burst in from a high school directly across the street. 'Hey, great, JFK's croaked!' one shouted with flagrant delight, and the woman, leaving as rapidly as she could, noticed that several diners were smiling back at the boy. In Dallas itself a man whooped and tossed his expensive Stetson in the air, and it was in a wealthy Dallas suburb that the pupils of a fourth-grade class, told that the President of the United States had been murdered in their city, burst into spontaneous applause."[521] Similarly, in the fifth grade of a private school in New Orleans, the teacher was called out of the room by another fifth-grade teacher to listen to a transistor radio bearing the news. When he returned to his class to announce that Kennedy had been shot and killed, spontaneously the pupils cheered and applauded—one girl, the exception, cried.[522]

Because of JFK's open support for civil rights for the nation's blacks, as indicated, many in the South had detested him. And when news of the shooting and later the death of the president became known, although most in the South—including those like the former Birmingham police commissioner T. Eugene "Bull" Connor, and John Birch Society founder Robert W. Welch Jr., who opposed Kennedy's civil rights policies— expressed their profound grief over the assassination, some southern newspapers received anonymous, jeering telephone calls: "So they shot the nigger lover. Good for whoever did it." "He asked for it and I'm damned glad he got it . . . trying to ram the damn niggers down our throats."[523] Radio also heard from the racial bigots. Before the announcer cut him off, a man who had called a station in Atlanta got in his belief that "any white man who did what [Kennedy] did for niggers should be shot."[524] And it wasn't just in the South. A young man wearing a swastika on his left arm walked around the state capitol in Madison, Wisconsin, proclaiming that Kennedy's death was "a miracle for the white race" and telling bystanders he was "celebrating."[525]*

Ralph Emerson McGill, publisher of the Atlanta, Georgia, *Constitution*, wrote of the antipathy for Kennedy before his death that spilled over, among some, to his demise: "There were businessmen who, in a time when profits were at an all-time high and the domestic economy booming, nonetheless could speak only in hatred of 'the Kennedys.' There were evangelists who declared the President to be an anti-Christ, an enemy of God and religion. This hatred could focus on almost anything the President proposed. When he asked for legislation for medical aid for the aged, for example, there were doctors who succumbed to the fever of national unreason and began abusing the President. In locker rooms and at cocktail parties, luncheons and dinners, it became a sort of game to tell vulgar and shabby jokes about the President, his wife, and his family. Most of

---

*The venom was flying both ways. Republican Senator John Tower of Texas, regarded as a right-wing conservative, had always been highly critical of Kennedy. When he was informed at a Republican conference in St. Louis that his office in Washington had received about a dozen anonymous and threatening phone calls and a number of similar telegrams, he arranged to have his wife and three daughters stay at the home of friends in Maryland until he returned to the capital. Republican Representative Bruce Alger of Dallas was also reported to have received a number of threatening phone calls and telegrams. (*New York Times*, November 23, 1963, p.7)

these were repeats of stories in vogue at the time Franklin D. and Eleanor Roosevelt were in the White House."[526]*

In Irving, Texas, Marina Oswald and Ruth Paine are sitting side by side on the sofa watching the television coverage when they hear the news.

"What a terrible thing for Mrs. Kennedy," Marina sighs, "and for the children to be left without a father." Ruth walks about the room crying, while Marina is too stunned to cry, although she feels as though her blood has "stopped running."[527]

In Oak Cliff, police order everyone out of the library at Marsalis and Jefferson, hands high. Officer Walker points out the man he saw run in— Adrian Hamby, a nineteen-year-old Arlington State University student who had dashed into the library, where he worked part-time as a page, to tell friends that the president had been shot. Hamby is terrified as the cops realize the truth. A disappointed Sergeant Owens informs the dispatcher, "It was the wrong man."[528]

1:39 p.m. (2:39 p.m. EST)
The FBI dispatches its first Teletype, from Director Hoover, to all fifty-five of its field offices. Stamped "Urgent" it reads:

> All offices immediately contact all informants, security, racial and
> criminal, as well as other sources, for information bearing on assas-

---

*One such story about Roosevelt became a favorite of Roosevelt's, and he delighted in telling it to friendly Democratic audiences. It seems there was a wealthy businessman commuting from heavily Republican Westchester County in New York who would hand the newsboy at the train station a dime every morning for the *New York Times*, glance at the front page, then hand the paper back as he rushed out the door to catch his train. Finally, one day, the newsboy, unable to control his curiosity any longer, asked the man why he always only looked at the front page.

"I'm interested in an obituary," the man said.

"But the obituaries are on the back pages of the paper, and you never look at them," the newsboy retorted.

"Son," the man said, "the son of a bitch I'm interested in will be on page one."

sination of President Kennedy. All offices immediately establish whereabouts of bombing suspects, all known Klan and hate group members, known racial extremists, and any other individuals who on the basis of information available in your files may possibly have been involved.[529]

Meanwhile, at Love Field, because he had been alerted to prepare Air Force One for immediate takeoff if necessary, the pilot, Colonel James Swindal, had had the ground air-conditioner disconnected, and the interior of Air Force One is hot and stuffy.[530] Since the plane's own air-conditioning works only when the engines are running, the interior temperature continues to rise slowly but steadily. The shades have been drawn (Agent Youngblood fears a sniper on the roof of the terminal building), the doors locked, and a Secret Service sentinel posted at each one. More agents ring the aircraft on the ground. The Dallas police are patrolling both inside and outside the terminal. Some of them are checking the departure gates for every youngish man who comes close to meeting the broadcast descriptions of the assassin.[531]

Johnson could have left Dallas three-quarters of an hour ago, but feeling, he said, a "sharp, painful, and bitter concern and solicitude for Mrs. Kennedy," he resolves not to leave without the president's widow, knowing that she would not leave without her husband's body.[532]

He is also anxious to take the oath of office as soon as possible. Johnson's aides and the congressmen present aren't quite sure of the procedure. Two of the congressmen, Jack Brooks and Albert Thomas, are in favor of doing it immediately. The third, Thornberry, advises waiting until they get to Washington. No one is clear on the law as mandated by the Constitution, and no one can think where the actual text of the oath might be found. The steadily rising heat in the stateroom* makes clear thought increasingly difficult. The men loosen their ties, open their shirt collars,

---

*The presidential cabin located toward the rear of the plane consisted of three rooms: the stateroom—the president's "office" on the plane—and an adjacent bedroom and bathroom.

and fan themselves with papers. The question of how to dramatize the presidential succession is more than symbolic—there is already news of a panic on Wall Street that has wiped out eleven billion dollars of stock values in the little more than an hour since the shooting.

Johnson goes into the bedroom of the presidential cabin to make private phone calls. He calls Robert Kennedy at his home in Virginia. Relations between the two men have always been frosty. Johnson offers Kennedy words of condolence, and they briefly discuss what is known and what remains unknown about the assassination. The murder, he says, "might be part of a worldwide plot." Kennedy is unresponsive. He doesn't understand what Johnson is talking about.

"A lot of people down here think I should be sworn in right away," Johnson says, moving closer to the point of the call. "Do you have any objection to that?"

Kennedy is stunned by the question. It has only been an hour since his brother was shot and he doesn't see what the rush is. Johnson forges ahead.

"Who could swear me in?" he asks.

Bobby is in a daze. The events are swirling too fast. He'd like his brother's body to be returned to Washington before Johnson becomes the new president, but he decides that his feelings are all personal.

"I'll be glad to find out," he tells Johnson. "I'll call you back."[533]

Johnson then calls a number of political friends in Dallas, finding few of them in their offices. He is particularly anxious to reach federal district judge Sarah Hughes, an old friend and political protégée, on the assumption that she might be able to administer the oath. Judge Hughes is contacted by phone and she agrees to do so.[534]

Youngblood, national security uppermost in his mind, hates the idea of remaining parked on the apron at Love Field any longer than necessary. He thinks there are several people on board the plane who can administer the oath—anyone who himself has taken an oath of office, even a Secret Service agent, for example—but he has to wait while Johnson makes a few more calls to Washington, one to his chief aide, Walter Jenkins, another to McGeorge Bundy.[535] Neither of them can think where to find the exact text of the oath. Meanwhile, Robert

Kennedy has consulted Assistant Attorney General Nicholas Katzenbach, who finds it easily—in the Constitution itself, Article II, Section 1 [8]. Katzenbach also resolves the question of who is legally empowered to administer the oath—anyone who can take a sworn statement under state or federal laws. Even a justice of the peace will do. Kennedy calls Johnson back with the information, and tells Johnson that the oath should be administered immediately, before taking off for Washington.[536]

At Tenth and Patton, police question Barbara and Virginia Davis. Domingo Benavides and Sam Guinyard are nearby as the two young women describe how the gunman ran across their front walk, shaking shells from his revolver into his hand. It doesn't take long for Benavides to find one of them, near the bushes at the corner of the house. He picks it up in his hand before he thinks that police might check for fingerprints. He drops it, picks it up again with a twig, and puts it into an empty Winston cigarette package. A minute later, he finds a second cartridge shell in a bush. He turns them over to Officer Joe Poe, standing nearby.[537]

1:41 p.m.
Sergeant Gerald Hill takes Patrolman Poe's squad car back to the scene and hands him the keys. Poe shows the sergeant a Winston cigarette package containing the two spent cartridge casings found by Benavides.[538] Hill tells the patrolman to turn them over to the crime lab and radioes the police dispatcher.

"The shells at the scene indicate that the suspect is armed with an automatic thirty-eight, rather than a pistol," Hill informs him, unaware that eyewitnesses saw the gunman manually removing the spent shells.[539] Police are reconverging on the Tippit murder scene after the false alarm at the Jefferson Branch Library when a civilian witness at the scene gives Hill information that he immediately radios in to the channel 2 dispatcher: "A witness reports that he [the gunman] last was seen in the Abundant Life Temple . . . We are fixing to go in and shake it down."[540] (If Hill had called into channel 1, the dispatcher would have told him the church had been checked out just seven minutes earlier by Officer M. N. McDonald.) Two women emerge from inside the church and tell Hill they are employees. He asks them if they had seen anybody enter the church. They say no, nobody entered the church but invite him and his people to go inside and check for themselves,[541] which the police do,[542] finding no one hiding inside.

At the Tippit murder scene, Captain Westbrook and Sergeant Owens question Mrs. Markham to learn exactly what happened before the shooting. She describes how the gunman seemed to lean on the passenger side of the squad car when he spoke to the officer inside. Crime-lab sergeant W. E. "Pete" Barnes arrives and Westbrook orders him to dust the right passenger side of the car for fingerprints.[543] Just below the top part of the right passenger door and also on the right front fender, Barnes finds some smudged prints.[544]*

Nearby, Sergeant Richard D. Stringer contacts the channel 2 dispatcher.

"Could you pass this to someone. The jacket the suspect was wearing over here on Jefferson in this shooting bears the laundry tag with the letter B 9738. See if there is a way you can check this laundry tag."[545]

---

*Barnes told the Warren Commission that after he took the prints he had "lifted" from the right side of Tippit's car back to the crime lab, "no legible prints were found" (7 H 274). Contrary to popular belief, this is typical. In working with the Los Angeles Police Department when I was with the Los Angeles district attorney's office, I learned that approximately only 30 percent of the times that fingerprint experts are dispatched to the scene of a crime are they able to secure clear, readable, latent prints belonging to anyone. In most cases the prints found are just too fragmentary, smudged (the Tippit car), or superimposed with other prints to be used for comparison with a fingerprint exemplar of someone (here, Oswald) taken at a police station. (To compound the problem in the Tippit case, Barnes testified that the exterior surface of Tippit's car was "dirty," making it much more difficult to lift a readable print.) Indeed, even in those cases where readable prints are secured, only 10 percent of the time do those prints match up to those of a suspect. The rest belong either to the victim or to some third party. A simple equation: 10 percent of 30 percent equals 3 percent. Hence, in only 3 percent of the times that fingerprint experts go to a crime scene are they able to secure the latent prints of the accused. Ninety-seven percent of the time they are unsuccessful. As a prosecutor I would present this "negative fingerprint testimony" from my expert, and I found it to be a powerful statistical rebuttal to the common defense argument that since the defendant's prints were not found at the scene, he was never there.

1:44 p.m.

Johnny Brewer and Butch Burroughs come out to the box office. They tell Julia Postal that it was too dark to see anything, but they think the man is still inside.[546]

"I'm going to call the police," Postal tells Brewer. "You and Butch get on each of the exit doors and stay there."[547]

1:46 p.m.

Patrolman Bill Anglin, a close friend and neighbor of the slain officer, leans against his own squad car at Tenth and Patton. He still can't believe it's true. Yesterday afternoon he and Tippit had installed a new wheel bearing on J. D.'s 1953 Ford. Just a couple of hours ago the two of them knocked off for coffee at the Rebel Drive-In, as they often did. Now, J. D. was dead. For Anglin, it's nothing short of a nightmare.[548]

The police dispatcher is trying to contact Sergeant Owens, who Anglin can see is engrossed in conversation with homicide detective James R. Leavelle. Officer Anglin reaches through the car window and picks up the radio mike. "I'm here at [Unit] 19's [Owens] location. Message for him?"

"Ten-four. Have information that a suspect just went in the Texas Theater on West Jefferson," the dispatcher says. "Suppose to be hiding in the balcony."[549]

Anglin hangs up the transmitter and hollers across the street, "It's just come over the radio that they've got a suspicious person in the Texas Theater!"[550]

Everyone sprints for their vehicles, adrenaline pumping.

The Texas Theater, on Jefferson Boulevard, is about six-tenths of a mile from where Tippit was shot. In less than two minutes, every police car in the area descends on the theater's two-dozen or so unsuspecting patrons.

1:48 p.m.

Julia Postal punches the intercom in the box office and tells the projectionist that she has called the police. He wonders whether he should cut the film off, and she says, "No, let's wait until they get here."[551]

It seems the minute she hangs up the intercom, the place is swarming with squad cars, police officers, plainclothesmen, and deputy sheriffs—armed to the teeth.

"Watch him! He's armed!" one of them shouts.

"I'll get that son of a bitch if he's in there," another replies.[552]

Some of the officers remain outside trying to control the excited crowd materializing from nowhere, a real mob scene.[553] Inside the theater, officers order the theater staff to turn up the house lights.[554]

Behind the stage Johnny Brewer is standing near the curtains that separate the audience and the exit door on the left side of the screen. When the house lights come up, he steps to the curtain and scans the astonished audience. There he is—the man he saw slip into the theater. He's sitting in the center section, six or seven rows from the back of the theater. No sooner do the lights come up than the man stands up, and scoots to the aisle to his right. Police are pouring into the lobby. The suspect turns around and sits back down,[555] this time in the third row from the back. Suddenly, Brewer hears someone rattling the exit door from the outside. The shoe store manager pushes the door open and is immediately grabbed by two officers as he is exiting. The alley is crawling with cops, some up on the theater's fire escape.[556]

Officer Thomas A. Hutson puts a gun into Brewer's stomach. "Put your hands up and don't make a move." Brewer is shaking.

"I'm not the one," he stammers. "I just came back to open the door for you. I work up the street. There's a guy inside that I was suspicious of."

The officer can see that Brewer's clothing—sport coat and tie—is different from the description of the suspect.

"Is he still there?" Hutson asks.

"Yes. I just seen him," Brewer tells him, and leads the lawmen into the theater.[557]

1:50 p.m.

Patrolmen M. N. "Nick" McDonald, C. T. Walker, Ray Hawkins, and Thomas Hutson gather around Brewer as he points out the man in the brown shirt sitting in the main section of the theater on the ground floor, three rows from the back, fifth seat over. From the orientation of the stage looking out toward the audience, McDonald and Walker step out from behind the curtain and walk up the left center aisle and approach two men seated near the front—a diversionary tactic—and order them to their feet. They search them for weapons, all the while keeping an eye on the man in the brown sport shirt. McDonald then walks out of the row to the right center aisle and advances up the aisle. Officers Walker, Hawkins, and Hutson are shadowing McDonald from the left center aisle—the suspect between them. McDonald feigns interest in a man and woman seated across the aisle from the man in the brown shirt, but just as he gets even with him, McDonald spins and faces the suspect.[558]*

"Get on your feet," McDonald orders.

The man obeys and starts to raise his hands. Officers Walker, Hawkins, and Hutson are moving toward him from the opposite side. McDonald reaches for the suspect's waist to check for a weapon.

"Well, it's all over now," the suspect says in a tone of resignation. In a flash, the man cocks his left fist and slugs McDonald between the eyes, knocking his cap off and forcing him backward into the seats. McDonald quickly recovers and swings back as they topple into the seats, McDonald shouting out, "I've got him," though they end up with the man on top of McDonald.[559]

---

*The Warren Commission never pinned down what row or seat Oswald was in, and the arresting officers were all in disagreement. McDonald said Oswald was in the "second seat" over from the "right center aisle" and mentions no row (3 H 299); Hawkins said "three or four" seats over from the right center aisle as you face the screen, and "three or four rows from the back" (7 H 93); Walker: "fourth or fifth" row from the back, "third seat" in from where McDonald was (7 H 38–39); Captain W. R. Westbrook: "third or fourth row from the back," seated "in the middle" (7 H 112; see also Sneed, *No More Silence*, p.314). Hutson not only seemed to be the most precise, but on a trip I took to Dallas on September 22, 2004, Ken Holmes, a Dallas student of the assassination with an emphasis on historical detail, said he was very confident, from his studies, where Oswald was seated in the theater, and he pointed out the seat to me. In Hutson's December 3, 1963, report to Chief Curry, Hutson said that Oswald was "sitting in the third row from the back" in the "fifth seat" of "the center section," which he later told the Warren Commission. In his Commission testimony, however, he didn't say fifth seat from what side, but in his report to Curry he did. It was "the fifth seat north of the south aisle [from the stage looking toward the audience, the north aisle is on one's right, the south aisle to one's left] of the center section." (Report from Officer T. A. Hutson to J. E. Curry, Chief of Police, December 3, 1963, p.1; 7 H 31, WCT Thomas Alexander Hutson) That's the same seat Holmes pointed out to me. Holmes, a member of the Dallas Historical Society, has run a popular tour of JFK assassination sites for several years under the name Southwestern Historical Inc.

Officers Hutson, Walker, and Hawkins rush in from the other side. Nick McDonald is trying to push the suspect off, but he's holding Nick down with his left hand and reaching for something in his waistband with the other hand. Hutson, in the row behind, reaches over the seats, wraps his right arm around the suspect's neck and yanks him back until he's stretched over the top of the seat. Officer Walker grabs the suspect's left arm and struggles to hold on to it. McDonald jumps forward and grabs the man's right hand, which is trying to pull a revolver out of his belt-line. For a second or two, McDonald keeps the suspect from getting the gun out, but then it springs free.

"Look out! He's got a gun!" someone yells.

McDonald, on the receiving end of the barrel, quickly grabs the cylinder of the revolver with his left hand to keep it from turning and firing a bullet. The suspect thrashes as the gun waves in McDonald's direction.[560]

The officers are in a frenzy, a half-dozen hands desperately trying to get the damn gun out of the man's hand.

"Let go of the gun!" a cop commands.

"I can't," the suspect says.[561]

Punches fly as an officer slams the butt of a shotgun against the back of the suspect's head. McDonald gets his right hand on the butt of the pistol and starts to rip it out of the man's hand. Just before he jerks it free, McDonald hears what he believes to be the snap of the hammer and feels a sting to the fleshy web of skin between his thumb and forefinger. The gun continues across his left cheek, leaving behind a four-inch scratch, from which blood trickles.[562]

Captain Westbrook can't quite see what's happening. "Has somebody got the gun?" he yells out. McDonald holds the gun out toward the aisle, where Detective Bob Carroll grabs it, saying, "I've got it!"[563]

Officer Walker pulls the suspect's left arm around and Officer Hawkins snaps handcuffs on him.

"Don't hit me anymore. I am not resisting arrest!" the suspect shouts, loud enough for nearby patrons to hear him. "I want to complain of police brutality!"

Captain Westbrook, who's just heard Mrs. Markham tell him how Tippit's killer shot him down like a dog, at point-blank range, can't believe the gall of the man. Westbrook pushes his way into the aisle in front of the suspect and looks him right in the face—less than ten inches away.

"What's your name?" Westbrook asks.

The suspect is silent.

"Get him out of here!" Westbrook shouts above the commotion.[564]

The officers on the suspect's right start to pull him toward the center aisle, but the officers on the left are pulling in the opposite direction—inadvertently stretching the gunman between them.

"They're violating my civil rights!" the suspect screams.

FBI agent Robert M. Barrett, standing nearby, can only shake his head. They're not violating anything, he thinks to himself. Barrett has been observing the police actions since his arrival at the Book Depository nearly an hour ago. As the FBI agent who handles civil rights violations, Barrett knows that he'll have to write a report on what he's just witnessed.[565]

A WFAA-TV cameraman is in the lobby filming the suspect as police hustle him toward the front entrance. The suspect uses the opportunity to berate the police as he passes: "I want my lawyer. I know my rights. Typical police brutality. Why are you doing this to me?"[566]

Julia Postal, though safe in her box office, is shaking. She's never seen a mob like the one on the sidewalk in front of the theater. Since police stormed into the theater, word has spread among the crowd that they've cornered the president's killer. Few know that a police officer was shot nearby—not even Mrs. Postal.[567]

The doors to the theater are slammed open as a wedge of officers bursts into the sunlight. The suspect shuts up quickly when he sees the size of the crowd on the sidewalk in front of the theater—maybe a hundred people. A half-dozen uniformed officers and several deputy sheriffs are doing their best to prevent a lynching by holding the crowd back and clearing a passage to an unmarked police car at curbside, but the crowd is ugly.

"That's him!" they shout as he comes into view. "Murderer! Kill the son of a bitch! Hang him! Give him to us, we'll kill him!"

The flying wedge just keeps moving, pushing the suspect toward the waiting squad car, its back door open. The suspect complains that the handcuffs are too tight. Detective Paul Bentley, on the suspect's left, cigar stub firmly clenched between his teeth, isn't too sympathetic, thinking to himself that Oswald was in much better shape than Tippit was. He reaches back and tightens the cuffs even more. They're actually a little loose, he later recalls, and he doesn't want to take any chances.[568]

An officer squeezes into the box office to use the phone. Mrs. Postal hears him say, "I think we have got our man on both accounts."

"What two accounts?" Postal asks as he hangs up.

The shootings of both the president and Officer Tippit, the officer tells her. Mrs. Postal is shocked. She knew J. D. Tippit. He had worked part-time at the theater on Friday and Saturday nights a number of years ago.[569]

1:52 p.m.

Police push the suspect into the backseat of the four-door sedan, where he's sandwiched between Officer C. T. Walker on the right and Detective Paul Bentley on the left. Three officers pile into the front seat, Detective Kenneth E. Lyons on the right, Sergeant Gerald Hill in the middle, and the driver, Detective Bob Carroll. As Carroll slides behind the steering wheel, he hands a .38 caliber snub-nosed revolver to Hill.

"Is this yours?" Hill asks.

"No, it's the suspect's," Carroll replies.

Hill snaps the cylinder open and sees that it's fully loaded. He grabs the radio transmitter as the car pulls away from the curb.[570] "Suspect on the shooting of the police officer is apprehended. En route to the station," he announces.

"Ten-four. At the Texas Theater?" the dispatcher asks.

"Caught him on the lower floor of the Texas Theater after a fight," Hill confirms.[571]

The suspect is asked his name, but the guy is dead silent.

"Where do you live?" someone asks. Again, nothing.

"Why don't you see if he has any identification?" Hill asks Bentley.

The detective reaches down and feels the suspect's left hip pocket. There's a wallet in it. As Bentley pulls it out, the suspect breaks his silence.

"What is this all about? I know my rights. I don't know why you are treating me like this. Why am I being arrested? The only thing I've done is carry a pistol in a movie," he says.[572]

One of the cops turns to the suspect. "Sir, you've done a lot more. You have killed a policeman."

"Police officer been killed?" the suspect asks innocently.

The cops remain silent, as the squad car rolls along.

"I hear they burn for murder," the suspect adds.

"You might find out," Officer Walker replies.

"Well, they say it just takes a second to die," the suspect answers coolly.[573]

Detective Bentley flips through the billfold and finds a library card.

"Lee Oswald," Bentley calls out from the backseat. In a moment, Bentley thumbs across another name in the wallet—A. J. Hidell. He asks the prisoner which of the two names is his real name, but Oswald is silent.

"I guess we're going to have to wait until we get to the station to find out who he really is," someone remarks.

One thing they all notice is that Lee Harvey Oswald is showing absolutely no emotion.[574]

1:55 p.m.

FBI special agent Gordon Shanklin telephones Alan Belmont in Washington again.

"Dallas police have captured the man who is believed to have shot the policeman," he tells Belmont, "and police think he may be the man who killed the president. They're en route to police headquarters right now. I'll report as soon as I have the facts."

Belmont prepares a Teletype and takes it in to FBI Director Hoover.[575]

1:58 p.m.

As the unmarked squad car carrying Lee Oswald pulls into the basement garage of City Hall, a gray stone structure in downtown Dallas where police headquarters are located, Sergeant Hill tells Oswald that there will be reporters, photographers, and cameramen waiting there, but he doesn't have to speak to them. They will hold him in such a way that he can turn his head down and away from the cameras.

"Why should I hide my face?" Oswald responds. "I haven't done anything to be ashamed of."[576]

The arresting officers form their wedge around the suspect and rush him into the building. Sure enough, photographers and cameramen are there to film the event. The officers take Oswald to a waiting elevator for the ride up to the Homicide and Robbery Bureau on the third floor.[577]

2:00 p.m.

At the sheriff's office, *Dallas Morning News* reporter Harry McCormick, sidetracked in his quest to locate Secret Service agent Forrest Sorrels, telephones his office to report that he's heard a man was captured at the Texas Theater. The paper already has the news. He hangs up the telephone and spots his initial quarry, Agent Sorrels, standing in a nearby office.[578]

"Forrest, I have something over here you ought to know about," McCormick tells him.

"What have you got?" Sorrels says.

"I have a man who got pictures of this whole thing," McCormick answers.

"Let's go see him," Sorrels replies.

The two men make their way over to the Dal-Tex Building, directly across the street from the Book Depository, and up to the office of dress manufacturer Abraham Zapruder. There are already a few magazine and newspaper representatives there, McCormick's worst fear. Zapruder is a basket case. His business partner, Erwin Schwartz, stands nearby, unable to help.

"I don't know how in the world I managed to take those pictures," Zapruder whimpers. "I was down there taking the thing and—my God, I saw the man's brains come out of his head."[579]

"Mr. Zapruder, I wonder if it would be possible for us to get a copy of those films," Sorrels asks politely. "Please understand that it would be strictly for the official use of the Secret Service."

Zapruder was already expecting to sell the film for as high a price as

he could get, and agreed to Sorrels's request with the understanding that
it not be shown or given to any newspapers or magazines. McCormick,
ever mindful of a scoop for his paper, suggested that the *Dallas Morning
News*, just three blocks away, might be able to develop the film for them.
The men agree and Zapruder removes the camera from a small office safe,
where he put it upon his return to the office. Sorrels, McCormick,
Zapruder, and Schwartz hurry down to the street below, where the Secret
Service agent commandeers a Dallas police car.

"Take us to the *Dallas Morning News* building immediately," Sorrels
says.[580]

Back at the Book Depository, crime-lab technicians are focused on completing the evidence-gathering process. It will be several more hours
before they finish dusting the stacks of boxes in the sniper's nest for fingerprints, and combing the sixth floor for possible additional evidence.
Word passes quickly that the suspect in the murder of Officer J. D. Tippit has been arrested in Oak Cliff, but no name is given. Captain Fritz,
still concentrating on the murder of Kennedy, instructs Detectives Sims
and Boyd to come with him; he wants to go out to Irving and check on
this missing employee named Oswald. The three men head downstairs
and are out in front of the Depository when an officer tells Captain Fritz
that Sheriff Decker would like to see him at his office, and he proceeds
to Decker's office a block away at the corner of Main and Houston for a
conference.[581]

2:02 p.m.
Homicide detective C. W. Brown is taking an affidavit from Book Depos-
itory foreman Bill Shelley in a small interrogation room inside the Homi-
cide and Robbery office when the arresting officers bring Oswald in. Mr.
Shelley looks up at the man in custody and remarks to Detective Brown,
"He works for us. I'm his supervisor."[582]

Detectives Richard S. Stovall and Guy F. Rose begin to question
Oswald in the interrogation room as Brown takes Shelley to another room

to complete Shelley's affidavit. When they ask him his name, Oswald replies, "Hidell." Finding two identifications in his billfold, one card saying Hidell and the other Lee Oswald, Rose asks him which of the two is his correct name and Oswald replies, "You find out," but later gives the officers his real name.[583]

In the outer office, Sergeant Hill is showing Oswald's pistol to newsmen. In a corner, Detective Brown finishes taking the statement from Bill Shelley. The telephone rings. It's Captain Fritz calling from the sheriff's office. Brown tells him that the officers just brought in a suspect for the shooting of the police officer and how Mr. Shelley identified him as an employee of the Book Depository. Fritz says, "I'll be right up in a few minutes."[584]

The third-floor hallway at police headquarters is beginning to fill with a flood of reporters from newspapers, television, radio, and the wire services. UPI cub reporter Wilborn Hampton had been out at Parkland, where he felt the situation was chaotic. As he ran across the front lawn of Parkland Hospital to nearby Harry Hines Boulevard, hoping his car, which he had abandoned alongside the road because of the clogged traffic, hadn't been towed away, he paused and leaned on a live oak tree, crying, "He's dead, he's really dead." He then continued on to his car, which was still there. When he arrived at City Hall, he took his press card out of his wallet, ready to show it to anyone who challenges him, but security was so lax no one does. He quickly sees on the third floor that it's not merely chaotic, like Parkland, it's pandemonium, and so crowded he is virtually unable to move. It's as if, he thinks, someone had ordered a fire drill and told everyone in the building to show up at this one place.[585]

Less than a half hour after the shooting of the president—twenty-six minutes after the first news moved on the wires of United Press International—68 percent of all adults in the United States, about seventy-five *million* people, had heard about it. That percentage rises steadily through the afternoon, particularly after the president's death, until it reaches an astounding 99.8 percent. This is the story of the century and it's being followed around the world. Reporters and correspondents are already catching planes that will eventually bring them, in the next few

hours, to as close as they can get to the tiny hallway outside room 317—
Homicide and Robbery Bureau, Dallas Police Department, Dallas,
Texas.[586]

2:04 p.m.
By the time the president's body is ready to be moved from Parkland Hospital, the row over the state of Texas's jurisdiction over the body has turned
into a major imbroglio. Medical examiner Dr. Earl F. Rose refuses to listen to the pleading of Dr. Kemp Clark, the head of neurosurgery, who
sides with the presidential party, or to the advice of Dallas district attorney Henry Wade, who advised him by phone to give it up. Tempers are
at the melting point. Kennedy's men have had about all of Dallas law they
can stand. Rose sees the casket bearing the president's body being pushed
out of Trauma Room One, Mrs. Kennedy at its side. The medical examiner blocks the way with his own body, his hand flying up like a traffic
cop. "We are removing it," Admiral Burkley says, enraged. "This is the
president of the United States and there should be some consideration
in an event like this."

"We can't release anything!" Rose shouts. "A violent death requires a
postmortem! There's a law here. We're going to enforce it."

A crush of forty sweating men are clustered around the wide doorway
as curses fly back and forth. One of them looks like he might belt the
medical examiner at any moment.

Admiral Burkley, in an attempt to calm everyone down, informs the
conclave that a justice of the peace has arrived and has the power to overrule the medical examiner. Theron Ward, a young justice of the peace for
the Third Precinct of Dallas County, makes his way down the corridor.
Too timid to buck the medical examiner, the young justice tells them there
is nothing he can do.

"In a homicide case, it's my duty to order an autopsy," Ward says in a
tone much too weak for Dr. Rose's pleasure. "It shouldn't take more than
three hours."

Special Agent Kellerman tells Ward there must be something inside
of him that tells him it wouldn't be right to put Mrs. Kennedy and all of

the president's people through any further agony in Texas, but Ward can only say, "I can't help you out."

Ken O'Donnell pleads with him, "Can't you make an exception for President Kennedy?"

Incredibly, Ward tells him, "It's just another homicide case as far as I'm concerned."

O'Donnell's response is instantaneous. "Go fuck yourself," he yells. "We're leaving!"

A policeman next to Rose points to the medical examiner and the justice of the peace and says to the president's men, "These two guys say you can't go."

"Move aside," shouts Larry O'Brien, moving toward the officer.

"Get the hell out of the way," O'Donnell hollers. "We're not staying here three hours or three minutes. We're leaving *now*! Wheel it out!" he orders.

The Secret Service men shoulder their way into the patrolman, who wisely capitulates. Rose, overpowered by circumstance, steps out of the way as the casket is wheeled toward the emergency exit, Mrs. Kennedy hurrying alongside, her fingertips touching the bronze finish.

As they move out toward the waiting hearse, Justice Theron Ward dashes to the nurses station and telephones District Attorney Wade and is stunned to hear him say the same thing he told Earl Rose earlier—he has no objection whatsoever to the removal of the president's body.[587]

2:14 p.m.

By the time Jackie Kennedy and the president's men arrive at Love Field with his body in the casket, Secret Service agent Lem Johns, assistant special agent in charge of LBJ's security detail, and the air crew have removed the last two rows of seats from the rear port-side section of the plane,[*] the small area located directly behind the presidential cabin and

---

[*]"We were sort of in a bind," Air Force One pilot Colonel Swindal would later recall, "because there was no place on Air Force One for a casket, and we sure didn't want to put it in the cargo hold" (*Los Angeles Times*, May 2, 2006, p.B11).

to the front of the rear galley (kitchen). There is now room on the port side for the casket to rest on the floor, but no one thought to arrange for a hydraulic lift. Kennedy's men—O'Donnell, Powers, and O'Brien—and the Secret Service agents, all unwilling, for Jackie's sake, to delay the departure, even by as little as the few minutes it would take to fetch a forklift, proceed to carry the heavy bulk by hand up the steep steps of the plane. Since none of them know that such a casket comes with a device that automatically pins it to the floor of the hearse, and a catch that releases the lock, they manage to rip a piece of trim from a hinge and the top of a handle housing as they remove it from the hearse. They struggle with the appallingly heavy bronze casket, which, they learn, is actually wider than the steps of the ramp to the rear entrance. As they shuffle the casket the last few feet, Ken O'Donnell keeps checking over his shoulder for police cars, half expecting the Dallas County medical examiner to roar up waving an injunction.[588]

2:15 p.m.
At the FBI's Dallas office, Agent James Hosty is immersed in putting together a list of right-wing extremists when his supervisor, Ken Howe, grabs his elbow. "They've just arrested a guy named Lee Oswald and they're booking him for the killing of the policeman over in Oak Cliff," Howe tells him. "The officer's name was Tippit."

It takes only a second for Hosty to shift from the pile of right-wingers to Lee Oswald. Hosty is in charge of the active file on both Oswalds—Lee and Marina—whom the FBI has considered to be possible espionage risks since their arrival in the United States in 1962. Hosty had learned on November 1 that Lee worked at one of the Texas School Book Depository buildings in Dallas, but he did not know which one.

"That's him! Ken, that must be him. Oswald has to be the one who shot Kennedy!" Hosty exclaims, having no basis to believe this other than his instinct that the Kennedy and Tippit murders are probably related. Three weeks ago he received a lengthy report from New Orleans special agent Milton Kaack describing Oswald's arrest after an altercation that broke out while he was passing out leaflets for the Fair Play for Cuba Committee. The incident was banal enough. People who pass out flyers on the street, even for kooky organizations, are not necessarily potential assassins.

"Do you have the Oswald file?" Howe asks.

"It should be in the active file cabinet," Hosty replies as they rush over to it. The file is gone, which means the mail clerk probably has it to update it with incoming mail. They hurry to the mail clerk's office and frantically dig for it as another supervisor comes over to help.

In a few minutes, the FBI men find the file. Paper-clipped to the top is a one-page communiqué from the Washington, D.C., field office—and it's a shocker. According to the communiqué, Oswald had written to the Soviet embassy in Washington, D.C., about a trip he had made to Mexico City at the end of September, during which he had a conversation with "Comrade Kostine" at the Soviet embassy there. Hosty had read something about the Mexico City trip in October but was forbidden to question Oswald about it for fear of tipping off Oswald, and presumably the Soviets, to FBI surveillance methods in Mexico.[589]

This was a bombshell—*if* Lee Harvey Oswald was in contact with the Soviet government, he may have been some type of agent for them, which would mean a potentially explosive international situation. Had they been negligent and allowed a Soviet agent to assassinate the president? The press would come down very hard on the bureau, and J. Edgar Hoover would come down even harder on everyone in the bureau who had any responsibility with respect to Oswald.

Hosty takes the file to the special agent-in-charge, Gordon Shanklin. Hosty sits down while Shanklin calls Alan Belmont in Washington and advises him that a suspect named Lee Harvey Oswald is under arrest for the murder of Officer Tippit, and that police are questioning Oswald and have his handgun. Hosty hands him the Oswald file. Shanklin glances over the communiqué regarding Oswald's contacts with the Soviet embassy, then, with no visible reaction, says, "Alan, I've got Jim Hosty here. He's the agent who was working our file on Oswald. He's got the file here with him now."

Over the next few minutes, Hosty assists Shanklin by leafing through the Oswald file, locating pertinent information, and handing it to Shanklin as he talks with Belmont at headquarters.

"Oswald is the subject of an Internal Security-R-Cuba case," Shanklin tells Belmont. "The file shows that Oswald works at the Texas School Book Depository where the rifle and shells were found. The file also shows that three years ago Oswald left the U.S. and went to Russia, where he tried to renounce his American citizenship. He returned to the U.S. on June 13, 1962, and brought with him a Russian bride whom he married in Russia.

"Our agents have interviewed him twice since his return," Shanklin continues, "in an attempt to determine why he went to Russia and whether he was given an assignment by the Russians. He was completely uncooperative. He said he came back because he wanted to; denied being given an assignment; and said that why he went to Russia was his own business.

"He has since lived in Fort Worth, Dallas, New Orleans, and is currently back in Dallas. He was arrested in New Orleans in August 1963 on charges of creating a disturbance by passing out leaflets on the street which were published by the Fair Play for Cuba Committee. He drinks, has a violent temper, and has beaten his wife, who has recently had a baby."

"Do the files show whether Oswald has ever made a threat against the president or any public official?" Belmont asks.

"No," Shanklin says. "The agents who have interviewed him have the impression he is a mental case. He withdraws within himself when being questioned."

"Have you given this file information to the Secret Service?" Belmont asks.

"No, not yet," Shanklin replies.

"Well, get this information to the Secret Service," Belmont commands, "and arrange to have the agents who have questioned Oswald to sit in on the interrogations. They might be helpful to the police."

Shanklin puts his hand over the phone, and tells Hosty, "Belmont wants you to get down to the police department and take part in the interrogation of Oswald. Cooperate fully with the police and give them any information we have on Oswald. Get going. Now."

Hosty's heart starts beating wildly as he heads out the door for City Hall.[590]

2:17 p.m.

The third-floor hallway at police headquarters resembles Grand Central Station when Captain Fritz and Detectives Richard Sims and Elmer Boyd return to the homicide office. The first order of business is to have some officers get a search warrant and go out to Ruth Paine's residence at 2515 West Fifth Street in Irving, the address on Oswald's employment card at the Book Depository. Lee Oswald, the employee who Fritz was told wasn't present at a roll call of employees, supposedly lived there. But before Fritz starts to round up the officers, Lieutenant T. L. Baker tells him that the man who shot Tippit is in the small interrogation room. The homicide captain enters the room and learns from Detectives Stovall and Rose that the man's name is Lee Oswald, the prime suspect in Kennedy's murder. He immediately dispatches Rose, Stovall, and a third detective, J. P. Adamcik, to go to the Paine residence and rendezvous there with three Dallas deputy sheriffs to conduct a search of the residence. (The presence of the Dallas County deputy sheriffs was needed because although the city of Irving was in Dallas County, it was outside the jurisdiction of the Dallas city police.) He then has Oswald brought into his room to be interrogated.[591]

It's pretty clear to the officers in Homicide and Robbery that the man arrested for the murder of Officer J. D. Tippit is most likely responsible for the assassination of the president of the United States.

2:18 p.m.

With the casket safely aboard Air Force One, Ken O'Donnell hurries forward to ask General McHugh, the ranking air force officer on board, to tell the pilot to take off immediately. But McHugh advises O'Donnell shortly thereafter that President Johnson had ordered the pilot to delay taking off until he was sworn in.[592]

Meanwhile, Jackie Kennedy wants to be by herself for a moment. She doesn't want to leave the coffin but knows that the private presidential cabin that she and Jack had last shared was adjacent to the tail compartment, where the coffin lay. With feelings of nostalgia sweeping over her, she thought it proper that she go there to compose herself. Moving quietly down the dim, narrow corridor, she enters the cabin and proceeds to the bedroom. When she turns the latch and opens the door, she sees Lyndon Johnson, reclining across the bed, dictating to his secretary, Marie Fehmer, who sat in a desk chair. Mrs. Kennedy stops dead. The new president scurries to his feet and hurries past her out the bedroom door, his secretary close behind. Jackie stares after them.[593]*

Everyone settles back in the stale air of Air Force One to await the arrival of Judge Hughes. O'Donnell keeps looking out the window, still fearing the sudden arrival of a squadron of howling police cars and an apoplectic medical examiner.[594]

Lady Bird Johnson reenters the presidential cabin by herself to try to offer whatever comfort she can to Jackie, but Jackie is beyond comfort. Seeing that the always exquisitely dressed Jackie had blood on her dress and her right glove was soaked in blood, she asks Jackie if she can get someone in there to help her change. "Oh, no," Jackie says. "Perhaps later . . . but not right now," then tells Mrs. Johnson, "What if I had not been there? . . . I'm so glad I was there."[595]

2:20 p.m.
Detectives Elmer Boyd and Richard Sims move Oswald across the hall, from the small interview room to room 317, the Homicide and Robbery office, and then into Captain Fritz's office, a cozy, nine-and-a-half-by-fourteen-foot room, surrounded by waist-high windows looking out onto the outer office. Venetian blinds offered Captain Fritz privacy when needed. As Oswald settles into a chair beside the captain's desk, Boyd asks him how he bruised his eye.

"Well, I struck an officer and the officer struck me back, which he should have done," Oswald replies.[596]

*It has to be noted that this is Mrs. Kennedy's version of what happened. Although President Johnson never addressed himself directly to the matter, his brief statement to the Warren Commission suggests a different version from what Mrs. Kennedy told author William Manchester. He says that when Mrs. Kennedy and President Kennedy's body arrived, "Mrs. Johnson and I spoke to her. We tried to comfort her, but our words seemed inadequate. She went into the private quarters of the plane" (5 H 564). Mrs. Johnson's version is more directly at odds with that of Mrs. Kennedy. She told the Warren Commission that "we had at first been ushered into the main presidential cabin on the plane, but Lyndon quickly said, 'No, no,' and immediately led us out of there; we felt that is where Mrs. Kennedy should be" (5 H 566).

2:25 p.m.

Captain Fritz enters his office and strolls around behind his desk.[*]
Oswald, handcuffed behind his back, tries to look comfortable in the
straight-back wooden chair adjacent to the homicide captain's desk.
Detectives Sims and Boyd stand guard nearby. They know that Oswald
is about to face a grueling interrogation. One, the other, or both, would
be present at every subsequent interrogation of Oswald.[597][†]

John William Fritz has been a Dallas cop since 1921 and chief of the
Homicide and Robbery Bureau since its inception in 1934. He regards it
as his own private and independent fiefdom. Fritz's Homicide and Robbery Bureau, consisting of two lieutenants and twenty detectives below him,
is the top unit of the department and even has its own sartorial signature,
the "Will Fritz" cowboy hat, always a Stetson. The hat designated one as a
member of the elite homicide unit, since the only people in the Dallas Police
Department who were allowed to wear those types of hats were members
of homicide. If you purchased a hat like that but were not in homicide, you
were told to get rid of it. And if an on-duty detective in Fritz's unit happened to be caught without his Stetson on, even on a very hot Texas summer day, it meant three days' suspension without pay. Three detectives in
Fritz's unit worked on each investigation. Each team of detectives had a
senior officer and a rookie, even though the rookie may have been on the
force for many years. Each homicide detective carried two guns.[598]

Because of Fritz's sober, and many feel intimidating demeanor, and
because he has headed the most important and powerful bureau on the

---

[*]Dallas district attorney Henry Wade, a law enforcement power in his own right, would later
tell the Warren Commission, "Fritz runs a kind of one-man operation there where nobody else
knows what he is doing. Even me, for instance, he is reluctant to tell me, either, *but I don't mean
that disparagingly*. [But, of course, it *is* disparaging.] I will say Captain Fritz is about as good a
man at solving a crime as I ever saw, to find out who did it, but he is the poorest in the getting
[of] evidence that I know, and I am more interested in getting evidence" (5 H 218). Without further explanation, unless Wade was speaking loosely, it is difficult to know how one "solves" a
crime without a successful gathering of evidence, unless Wade meant that Fritz's intuition was
usually accurate.

[†]There would eventually be three more interrogations of Oswald. All four, totaling approximately twelve hours, took place intermittently between 2:30 p.m. on November 22 and 11:10
a.m. on November 24, 1963. (WR, pp.180, 633)

force for over three decades, most officers respect and fear him more than Chief Curry. Fritz was born in Texas, grew up near Roswell, New Mexico, and was a cowhand and mule trader before he started walking a beat in the downtown area of Dallas known as "Little Mexico." He was involved in the hunt for the famed desperados of the early 1930s, Bonnie and Clyde, and won a shootout in an attic with Dagger Bill Pruitt, a robber responsible for several ugly murders, when Pruitt surrendered. Divorced, Fritz has lived alone for years in a hotel room (the White Plaza) located across the street from police headquarters. He has a daughter and some grandchildren, but no one knows much else about his private life, if he has any. His only topic of conversation is whatever case is at hand, and he sometimes works two or three days around the clock to sew up a case. You'd never know his nickname was "Will" because everyone called him Captain Fritz.[599]

Fritz is what one subordinate calls "a straight-laced perfect gentleman" who never uses improper language, is always 100 percent truthful and straightforward, and isn't the least bit political. He has above-average intelligence, understands people very well, seems to be able to know when people are not being truthful with him, and is able to analyze personalities quickly.[600] In particular, Fritz has a phenomenal memory for the details of cases he's worked on over the years, and he's quick to pick up on the contradictions in a suspect's story. If a suspect can't tell his story the same way a second or third time, or a tenth time, Fritz will catch him because he knows exactly what the suspect said the first time.[601]

His style of interrogation is quiet and soothing, a disarming approach for even the most cunning of criminals. His reputation in law enforcement is impeccable and his record of confessions is the best in the Southwest. His men often relate how Fritz even got a confession over the telephone once. An Ohio sheriff had picked up a Texas fugitive wanted for murder. When Fritz was informed, he called the sheriff and asked if the man had confessed. The sheriff told him, "No," then asked Fritz if he wanted to talk to him. Fritz said, "Sure." When the fugitive got on the line, Fritz made small talk, found out they knew someone in common, then told him, "Kind of a bad thing you done here."

"I didn't kill him," the prisoner snapped back.

"You don't strike me as the type that does this every day," Fritz said softly. "Is this the first time you ever killed anybody?"

"Yes, sir, first time" the man answered, without thinking.[602]

Captain Fritz is considered to be the finest interrogator on the Dallas Police Force. This time he faces his ultimate challenge. After asking Oswald his "full" name and Oswald replies, "Lee Harvey Oswald," Fritz begins, as he always does, with casual questions, asking Oswald about where he was from, his background and education, service in the Marines, and so on.[*] His grandfather-like manner almost compels people to talk with him, and in that regard, this young suspect is no different.

"Where do you work?" Fritz asks, getting into the present.

"Texas School Book Depository," Oswald says without hesitation.

"How'd you get the job?" Fritz asks.

[*]Although the Sixth Amendment to the U.S. Constitution has provided since 1791 that an accused has the right to counsel to assist him in his defense, in Texas in 1963 the police did not have to *advise* a suspect or person arrested of this right. In this case, Oswald asked Fritz if he had the right to counsel and Fritz told him he did (4 H 215, WCT John Will Fritz; WR, p.602). However, Texas statutory law at the time *did* require that someone under arrest be advised that he did not have to make a statement, and if he did, it could be used against him. Although there is nothing in the report of Captain Fritz on his interrogation of Oswald (WR, pp.599–611) that he advised Oswald of this right against self-incrimination, Dallas assistant district attorney Bill Alexander, who sat in on many interrogations of arrestees by Fritz through the years, said that Fritz always would comply with Texas law and he assumes the reason this was not in Fritz's notes is that it "went without saying" that he gave Oswald this admonition (Telephone interview of William Alexander by author on February 17, 2002). In any event, once FBI agents James Bookhout and James Hosty joined in Oswald's interrogation, the agents advised Oswald of both rights (WR, p.619; 7 H 310, WCT James W. Bookhout; see also 7 H 353, WCT, Forrest V. Sorrels).

In the landmark cases of *Escobedo v. Illinois* (378 U.S. 478), a year *after* the assassination, and *Miranda v. Arizona* in 1966 (384 U.S. 436), it became a federal constitutional right that a suspect (and certainly an arrestee) has to be advised at the commencement of questioning of his right to have counsel during his interrogation, and if he doesn't have funds for a lawyer, one will be appointed. He also has to be told he has a right to remain silent, and anything he says can be used against him, and if this is not done, any statement made by him thereafter that was elicited by the police during the interrogation cannot be introduced against him at his trial.

It should be noted that even before *Escobedo* and *Miranda*, the widespread practice, particularly by *federal* law enforcement agencies like the FBI and Secret Service, was to tell a suspect or arrestee of these rights and help him get a lawyer by allowing him to make a phone call for this purpose, as Captain Fritz allowed Oswald to do in this case. It's just that there was *no legal requirement* to advise arrestees and suspects of these rights before they were questioned.

"A lady that I know recommended me for the job," Oswald replies. "I got the job through her." Fritz asks about the "Hidell" name found in his wallet, and Oswald says that it was a name he "picked up in New Orleans."[603]

Fritz asks Oswald if he lives in Irving.

"No," Oswald replies. "I've got a room in Oak Cliff."

"I thought you lived in Irving?" Fritz asks, a little confused. Oswald says, no, he lives at 1026 Beckley. Although he doesn't know whether the address is North or South Beckley, Fritz and his detectives can tell from Oswald's description of the area that it's North Beckley.

"Who lives in Irving?" Fritz asks.

"My wife is staying out there with friends," Oswald says.[604] Fritz steps out into the outer office and instructs Lieutenant Cunningham of the Forgery Bureau, along with Detectives Billy Senkel and Walter Potts, to go out to 1026 North Beckley and search Oswald's rented room.[605] The homicide commander then gathers Lieutenants James A. Bohart and Ted P. Wells and Detective T. L. Baker around him.

"We've got a lot of work to do," Fritz tells them. "Who's working Officer Tippit's killing?"

"Leavelle and Graves," Baker answers.

"Fine, let them stay on that," Fritz says. "Everybody else will work on the president's killing."[606] Fritz returns to his office and Oswald.

2:30 p.m.

As federal district judge Sarah Hughes, a kindly faced woman of sixty-seven, climbs aboard Air Force One, someone hands her a three-by-five-inch card on which Johnson's secretary has typed out the text of the oath of office. Only a few minutes after Barefoot Sanders, the U.S. attorney in Dallas, whose office was just a floor below hers, had left a message for her, she had returned to her office. Her old friend Lyndon Johnson wanted her immediately at Love Field. She knew what that meant. Judge Hughes goes on into the stateroom of the presidential cabin and embraces the president, Mrs. Johnson, and several fellow Texans.

"We'll get as many people in here as possible," Johnson says, sending

Jack Valenti, Rufus Youngblood, Emory Roberts, and Lem Johns to round up witnesses. "If anybody wants to join in the swearing-in ceremony, I would be happy and proud to have you."

When O'Donnell comes up from the aft compartment where the casket is stowed, he finds the group around the president sweltering in the increasingly unpleasant air of the small stateroom, a room that can accommodate eight to ten people seated. UPI reporter Merriman Smith, one of two pool reporters on the plane, the other being *Newsweek*'s Charles Roberts, wedges himself inside the door, and for some reason begins counting. There are twenty-seven people in the room. It turns out that Johnson is waiting for Mrs. Kennedy. "She said she wanted to be here when I take the oath," he says. "Why don't you see what's keeping her?"

O'Donnell locates her nearby in the dressing room of the presidential cabin, combing her hair. He tactfully explains that she doesn't need to take part in the ceremony if she doesn't feel up to it.

"I think I ought to," she says. "In the light of history, it would be better if I were there."

She wonders whether she should take the time to change out of her bloodstained suit. O'Donnell urges her not to go to the trouble.[607]

2:38 p.m.

Captain Cecil Stoughton, the official White House photographer, records the crowded scene on Air Force One as Judge Hughes reads the oath, from Article II, Section 1 [8] of the U.S. Constitution, with Johnson resting his left hand on top of a Catholic prayer book,[*] his wife on his right, John Kennedy's widow, her Chanel suit stained with her husband's blood and her white gloves caked with it, on his left. Mac Kilduff

---

[*]Author William Manchester wrote that JFK's Bible, "his most cherished personal possession," was found on the plane, and LBJ had rested his hand on it (Manchester, *Death of a President*, pp.324, 328). But Lady Bird took the "Bible" off the plane with her as a memento, and later inquiry revealed it was not a Bible but a Catholic prayer book or missal, which, to all appearances, had never been opened (Holland, *Kennedy Assassination Tapes*, p.310).

holds a microphone out to catch the words of the swearing-in ceremony on a scratchy Dictaphone.

After the sixty-seven-year-old jurist tells Johnson, "Hold up your right hand and repeat after me," he says, "I do solemnly swear that I will faithfully execute the Office of President of the United States, and will to the best of my ability, preserve, protect and defend the Constitution of the United States."

Judge Hughes impulsively adds the formulaic "So help me God"— not part of the prescribed oath—and the president, in a deep voice, repeats it. In twenty-eight seconds, it's over.[*]

---

[*]Johnson's elevation to president from vice president marked the fourth time in American history when an assassin's bullet has elevated a sitting vice president. Andrew Johnson was the first so elevated when John Wilkes Booth, a fierce proponent of the Confederate cause, shot Abraham Lincoln at the Ford Theater in Washington, D.C., on April 14, 1865. Lincoln died the next day. Booth was shot to death during his capture on April 26, 1865. Next was the elevation to the presidency of Chester Alan Arthur, when Charles Julius Guiteau, a self-styled "lawyer, theologian, and politician" who claimed he had worked for President James A. Garfield's election and was entitled to a prominent foreign service post in payment for it, which he never got, shot Garfield as he was walking to a train in the Baltimore and Potomac Station in Washington, D.C., on July 2, 1881. Garfield did not die from his wound until September 19, 1881, and Guiteau was later hanged, on June 30, 1882. The next vice president to be elevated was Theodore Roosevelt when President William McKinley was shot by Leon F. Czolgosz, an anarchist who said McKinley was "the enemy of the working people," on September 6, 1901, at the Pan American Exposition in Buffalo, New York. McKinley didn't expire until September 14. Czolgosz was electrocuted on October 29. (McConnell, *History of Assassination*, pp.310–312, 314–317; WR, pp.504–510)

That the job of the president of the United States is the most dangerous elected job in the world cannot be too vigorously contested. In addition to the two attempted assassinations of President Gerald Ford in 1975 (by Lynnette "Squeaky" Fromme in Sacramento on September 5, 1975, and Sarah Jane Moore in San Francisco on September 22, 1975), the attempted assassination of President Richard Nixon by Samuel Joseph Byck on February 22, 1974, and the attempted assassination of President Ronald Reagan by William Hinckley in Washington, D.C., on March 30, 1981, two other presidents were attacked before Kennedy, but the attempts failed. Additionally, attempts were made on one president-elect and even one former president. On January 30, 1835, an English-born house painter, Richard Lawrence, fired two pistols, both of which misfired, at President Andrew Jackson. Like William Hinckley, Lawrence was found by a jury to be not guilty by reason of insanity and died in a mental hospital sixteen years later. On November 1, 1950, two Puerto Rican nationalists, Oscar Collazo and Griselio Torresola, attempted to shoot their way into Blair House, where President Harry Truman and his wife were temporarily residing while the White House was being repaired. Torresola was shot to death by White House guards in a hail of gunfire (one of the guards was also killed). Collazo was seriously wounded and sentenced to death, but Truman commuted his sentence to life imprisonment.

The new president then turns to his wife, hugs her around the shoulders, and kisses her cheek. Then he turns to John Kennedy's widow, puts his left arm about her, and kisses her cheek. As others among the group move toward President Johnson, he seems to back away from any act of congratulation. Instead, he says firmly, "Now, let's get airborne."[608] In an oath-taking ceremony approaching, in the uniqueness of its setting, the one that Calvin Coolidge took by lamplight in a Vermont farmhouse in 1923, Lyndon Baines Johnson was now the thirty-sixth president of the United States, an office he had dreamed of attaining—he had even run for the office three years earlier, losing the Democratic nomination in Los Angeles to JFK—but not this way.*

The pilot starts Air Force One's engines as Judge Hughes, Chief Curry, and Cecil Stoughton, who will not be making the flight to Washington, deplane. Johnson and Lady Bird remain in the stateroom, and Jackie excuses herself, returning to her husband's casket in the small aft cabin, where Ken O'Donnell, Dave Powers, Larry O'Brien, Brigadier General Godfrey McHugh, and for awhile, Admiral Burkley, will keep her company.[609]

President-elect Franklin D. Roosevelt was shot at in his car five times at a political rally in Miami's Bayfront Park on February 15, 1933 by Giuseppe Zangara, a thirty-two-year-old bricklayer and stonemason. All five of Zangara's shots missed Roosevelt. However, one of them hit Chicago mayor Anton Cermak, who was riding with Roosevelt. Cermak died of his wound on March 6, and Zangara was electrocuted on March 20, only thirty-three days after his attempt on Roosevelt. The former president who escaped was Theodore Roosevelt, who was running for president again as the candidate of the Progressive or "Bull Moose" Party. On October 14, 1912, a German-born New York bartender, John Schrank, fired one shot at Roosevelt as he entered his car outside a hotel in Milwaukee. The bullet hit Roosevelt in the chest, but a folded manuscript of the speech he was about to make and the metal case for his eyeglasses absorbed part of the bullet's thrust, and he survived. Schrank was found to be insane and died in a mental hospital in 1943. (WR, pp.505, 509–513)

So starting with Lincoln in 1865, approximately one out of every three American presidents either has been assassinated or had an attempt on his life.

*Speaking of his early days in office to his biographer, Doris Kearns, LBJ said, "I took the oath. I became president. But for millions of Americans I was still illegitimate, a naked man with no presidential covering, a pretender to the throne, an illegal usurper. And then there was Texas, my home, the home of both the murder and the murder of the murderer. And then there were the bigots and the dividers and the Eastern intellectuals, who were waiting to knock me down before I could even begin to stand up. The whole thing was almost unbearable" (Kearns, *Lyndon Johnson and the American Dream*, p.170).

Jackie sits in the aisle seat, directly opposite the casket, O'Donnell beside her in the only other seat available. When their eyes meet, she begins to cry hard. When she finally regains her composure, she cries, "Oh, Kenny, what's going to happen?"

O'Donnell knows that she is wondering what is going to happen to all of them now that Jack is dead.

"You want to know something, Jackie?" Ken says. "I don't give a damn."

When Admiral Burkley tries to persuade the young widow to change out of her bloodstained clothes, she says quietly, "*No*. Let them see what they've done."[610]

2:40 p.m.

Over in Fort Worth, Marguerite Oswald, Lee's mother, dressed in her nurse's uniform, is driving to work at the Hargroves Convalescent Center, listening to the news on the radio of her old, run-down Buick. She had been sitting on the sofa at home watching the television coverage, but had to leave at two-thirty if she wanted to get to work by three. Now, just seven blocks from home, she hears that police have picked up a suspect—Lee Harvey Oswald. Stunned, she immediately turns around and goes back home. She must call Robert Oswald, the younger of Lee's two older brothers. Robert works for Acme Brick, a Fort Worth company. He travels a lot, but they'll know how to get in touch with him.[611] She's also going to call the *Fort Worth Star-Telegram*. She figures there's a way to turn this into cash. And maybe someone there can give her a lift to Dallas.

Twenty-six-year-old *Fort Worth Star-Telegram* police reporter Bob Schieffer is lamenting the fact that he wasn't a political reporter covering the biggest story in the world when he picks up the ringing phone on the city desk. A woman wants to know if there is anyone there who can give her a ride into Dallas. "Lady, this is not a taxi company, and besides, the president has been shot." "I know," the woman says. "They think my son is the one who shot him." Schieffer and a colleague, Bill Foster, drive out to Fort Worth's west side and find Marguerite, waiting for them on the front lawn of her small, white stucco bungalow. The short, pudgy woman in large, dark, horn-rimmed glasses gets in the backseat with Schieffer for the close-to-an-hour trip into town.[612] En route, Schieffer is taken aback by Marguerite's attitude. She not only seemed somewhat mentally deranged but for most of the trip he sensed that she was less concerned about Kennedy's death and her son's predicament than she was with herself. She kept railing about the fact that her son's wife would get all the sympathy but no one would "remember the mother" and that she would probably starve.* However, she did cry quietly and her talk was punctuated with sobs. "I want to hear him tell me he did it," she said at one point. Schieffer never did get around to asking her why she had called the paper for a ride but learned later that she had at one time worked briefly as a governess in the home of Ammon Carter Jr., the owner of the paper, but had been discharged because the children complained that "she was mean." Schieffer ends up depositing Marguerite in what looked like some kind of interrogation room at Dallas police headquarters.[613]

Robert Oswald has not seen his brother Lee for a year and hasn't even heard from him for about eight months. He had heard the news of the assassination just as he was leaving Jay's Grill, a steak and seafood restaurant not far from Acme Brick's new plant in Denton, Texas, where he worked as a sales coordinator linking the marketing and plant departments, scheduling production to meet orders, and following through on customer service.[614] Now, Robert is back at the office going over some invoices and wondering whether Lee had taken a few minutes off to watch the motorcade. He goes down to the timekeeper's office to get some of the invoices checked. The receptionist at the front desk has her radio on, and, as he passes by, they both hear a news announcer say the name "Oswald."

---

*Marguerite told her biographer, Jean Stafford, in 1965, "I'm a mother in history. I'm all over the world . . . and *my* son's the one accused. You know, here is Mrs. Kennedy, a very wealthy woman, Mrs. Tippit, a very wealthy woman, Marina, very wealthy [referring to the donations from the public Marina and particularly Mrs. Tippit received], but *I* am wondering where my next meal is coming from. It's almost unbelievable" (Stafford, *Mother in History*, p.54).

Robert stops. He thought someone had called his name until he realizes that the voice came from the radio.

The announcer repeats the name, this time in full—"Lee Harvey Oswald."

Robert is paralyzed. "That's my kid brother," he says, stunned.

He calls his wife Vada and tells her he will be home shortly, but before he can leave he gets a call from the credit manager at the company's Fort Worth office.

"Bob, brace yourself," he says. "Your brother has been arrested."

"I know. I just heard."

The credit manager tells him his mother is trying to reach him. Robert calls her and arranges to meet her in Dallas at the Hotel Adolphus later in the evening.[615]

At the Terminal Annex Building overlooking Dealey Plaza, a box clerk bursts into the office of U.S. postal inspector Harry D. Holmes to tell him it's just come over the radio that police have arrested someone named Lee Harvey Oswald for the murder of Officer Tippit.

"I think you ought to know, Mr. Holmes," the clerk says, "that we rented a box downstairs to a Lee Oswald recently. Box number 6225." The clerk, who has already retrieved the original box application, dated November 1, 1963, hands it to Holmes and tells the inspector that he can't recall what the applicant looked like, but he does remember one thing. The man definitely filled out the application himself.[616]

The form lists "Fair Play for Cuba Committee" and "American Civil Liberties Union" in the space for firm or corporation. Under "kind of business" is the word "nonprofit." No business address is given, but in the space for home address, the applicant has written, "3610 N. Beckley." This is a variation of Oswald's actual address, 1026 North Beckley. At the bottom of the form is the applicant's signature, "Lee H. Oswald."[617]

Inspector Holmes telephones the Secret Service, who order a twenty-four-hour, round-the-clock surveillance of the box to see if anyone attempts to retrieve mail from it.[618]

2:45 p.m.

Secret Service agent Forrest Sorrels is beginning to realize that getting Zapruder's film developed is not going to be easy. The amateur movie camera takes 8-millimeter color film, something that neither the *Dallas Morning News* nor their companion television station, WFAA, can handle. Both are set up for 16-millimeter black-and-white newsfilm.

While the WFAA television news department telephones Eastman Kodak Company, *Dallas Morning News* reporter Harry McCormick manages to arrange a live television interview with Zapruder, who provides a graphic description of the shooting to a stunned Dallas audience.

Sorrels is told that the people at Eastman Kodak Company, located near Love Field, have the capability of developing Zapruder's footage and are standing by right now to assist. Within minutes, the Secret Service agent, with Zapruder, Schwartz, and McCormick in tow, is speeding toward Eastman Kodak in a Dallas police car.[619]

2:47 p.m.

The wheels of Air Force One* clear the runway at Love Field as the pilot takes it to an unusually high cruising altitude of forty-one thousand feet, where at 625 mph the great plane races toward Andrews Air Force Base, just outside Washington, D.C., in Maryland. John Fitzgerald Kennedy, in office for 1,037 days, is going home.[620]

2:50 p.m.

The basement garage of City Hall is an incredible hive of activity. Police cars swing in and out of the cavernous space, shouts and hollers echo over parked cars, and officers rush frantically about. FBI agent Jim Hosty jumps from his bureau-issued '62 Dodge and heads for the elevator. Car doors

---

*Two other planes leave Love Field following Air Force One: Air Force Two, the vice presidential plane, tail number SAM86970, now occupied mostly by Kennedy staffers forced to leave Air Force One to make room for President Johnson and his entourage; and SAM86373, the C-130 cargo jet carrying the blood-spattered presidential limousine and other trappings of the presidency, such as the president's seal and a special American flag (Holland, *Kennedy Assassination Tapes*, pp.48–49; see also TerHorst and Albertazzie, *Flying White House*, pp.210, 212).

slam to his right as Dallas police lieutenant Jack Revill and several detectives emerge from their autos and head briskly toward him.

Although Hosty and Revill, a thirty-four-year-old veteran of the Dallas police narcotics unit who was recently promoted to head the intelligence unit, have disagreed and clashed a number of times over politics and police work, they have remained friends.[621] Revill tells Hosty he's got a "hot lead" on the Kennedy killing, an unaccounted-for employee at the Texas School Book Depository named Lee. Why Revill only knew Oswald's first name when the full name of the unaccounted-for employee (Oswald) was known from the very beginning is not known. But in the frenetic exchange of information in these first minutes of the investigation, incomplete (and, indeed, incorrect) information was the norm.

"Jack, the Lee you're talking about is Lee Harvey Oswald," Hosty blurts out. "He was arrested an hour ago for shooting Officer Tippit. He defected to Russia and returned to the U.S. a year ago. Oswald is the prime suspect in the Kennedy assassination."[622]

A look of doubt crosses Revill's face. Revill, a conservative who saw Kennedy as being soft on Communism, can't believe what he's hearing, particularly that a Communist, of all people, had killed the president. Revill explodes as they get on the elevator that will take them to the third floor. "Jim, if you *knew* all this [about Oswald's background], why the hell didn't you tell us?"

"I couldn't," Hosty replies, referring to the bureau's long-standing need-to-know policy regarding espionage cases, in which local police were not considered by the FBI to be in the need-to-know group.[623]

The third-floor hallway is in an uproar. Cameramen and reporters are crammed everywhere. The giant television cameras of the era are trained on newsmen as they broadcast live reports. Flashbulbs are going off continuously and people are moving quickly in opposite directions, bumping into each other. It's a three-ring circus without a ringmaster.

The elevator doors open and Agent Hosty and Lieutenant Revill wade into the chaos and make their way toward room 317—Homicide and Robbery Bureau. As they push their way inside, they find that Captain Fritz is in his private office, behind closed doors. Revill leads Hosty into Lieu-

tenant T. P. Wells's office across the hall from Fritz's private door, introduces Hosty to Wells, and leaves. FBI agent James Bookhout is already
in Wells's office when Hosty arrives.[624]

2:58 p.m.
In Oak Cliff, Detectives Senkel and Potts and Lieutenant Cunningham
bang on the door at 1026 North Beckley. The housekeeper, Mrs. Earlene
Roberts, answers the door and invites the officers inside, where they meet
the landlady and her husband, Mr. and Mrs. Arthur C. Johnson. The officers ask if they have a boarder registered under the name of Lee Harvey
Oswald or A. J. Hidell.

"No," none of them had heard of either name.

The officers ask to see the register. Earlene Roberts gets out the book
and opens it on the table as Mrs. Johnson tells them that she has seventeen rooms and sixteen boarders at the moment. The officers quickly run
down the list of names in the register. Neither name is listed. They run
through the listings again, this time more carefully. Nothing. There is no
record of either Oswald or Hidell.

"Can I use your telephone?" Detective Senkel asks.

"Sure," Mrs. Johnson replies. The housekeeper leads him to a hall
phone.

"What's he look like?" Mrs. Johnson asks one of the other officers. He
describes the man they have in custody.

"I do have two new tenants that fit that description," Mrs. Johnson says.
"Their rooms are around back, in the basement. Let me get the key."[625]

3:00 p.m.
A telephone rings inside the homicide office. Lieutenant T. L. Baker
answers. It's Detective Senkel out on North Beckley.

"There's no one registered out here as either Oswald or Hidell,"
Senkel tells him.

"Maybe it's under a different name," Baker says.

"She's got sixteen boarders here," Senkel replies.

"Sit tight, I'll get someone out there with a search warrant," Baker
orders.[626]

At the rooming house, Mrs. Johnson returns with a key to the basement rooms and offers to let the police look if they want. Mrs. Roberts and Mrs. Johnson lead the officers out the back door toward a separate entrance to the basement. Meanwhile, in the living room, Mr. Johnson is watching television coverage of the assassination when the screen flashes the image of Lee Harvey Oswald.

"Hey!" he hollers at his wife as she heads out the door. Mrs. Johnson hands the keys to the housekeeper, "Go ahead, I'll see what he wants." Returning to the living room, her husband tells her, "Why, it's this fellow that lives in here," gesturing to the little room a few feet away. "Go tell them."[627]

Mrs. Roberts has unlocked the doors in the basement, and the officers have just stepped in, when Mrs. Johnson comes running up. "Oh, Mrs. Roberts, come quick. It's this fellow Lee in this little room next to yours."[628]

They run back upstairs to the living room, where images relating to the assassination continue to flicker across the television screen. For a moment, they all stand transfixed on the screen. Suddenly, there he is again—Lee Harvey Oswald.

"Yes, that's him," Mrs. Roberts confirms. "That's O. H. Lee. He lives right here in this room."[629]

Mrs. Roberts points to the two french doors off the main living room. There is no number on the door, just the designation "O." The light, aqua-colored room, just five feet wide and thirteen and one-half feet long, is hardly more than a large closet.[*]

The police return to the table and look back through the register. They quickly find the listing for "O. H. Lee," now known to be Lee Harvey Oswald. He had rented the room under the fictitious name on October 14, 1963, and is paying eight dollars a week.[630]

---

[*]But there are five small windows in the room, all with venetian blinds and curtains connected to one five-and-ten-cent-store-type curtain rod. There is a single iron-rail bed, a large wooden movable wardrobe dresser drawer, a small plastic-top table, and a nightstand with a table lamp next to the head of the bed. Two small throw rugs are on the linoleum-tiled floor. (CD 705, pp.1–2, March 28, 1964; CE 2046, 24 H 460–461; 10 H 297, WCT Mrs. Arthur Carl Johnson)

3:01 p.m. (4:01 p.m. EST)

In Washington, D.C., FBI Director Hoover calls Attorney General Robert F. Kennedy at his home to inform him he thinks they have the man who killed his brother in Dallas, that the man's name is Lee Harvey Oswald, that he was working in the building from which the shots were fired, that he left the building and "a block or two away ran into two police officers and, thinking they were going to arrest him, shot at them and killed one of them with a sidearm."[631]

Hoover may have been the head of the nation's most famous law enforcement agency, but that doesn't mean he knows what's going on, in real time, in Dallas.

3:08 p.m.

Inside the inner sanctum of Captain Fritz's private office, where the serious questioning of Oswald was just beginning, the telephone rings. It's the Dallas FBI's Gordon Shanklin and he wants to speak to Agent Bookhout. Fritz steps across the hall to Lieutenant Wells's office and tells Bookhout he can take the call in Wells's office, then quietly picks up an extension in his office to listen in.

"Is Hosty in that investigation?" Fritz hears Shanklin say.

"No," Bookhout replies.

"I want him in that investigation right now!" Shanklin says angrily. "He knows those people [the Oswalds]. He's been investigating them." Shanklin finishes by telling Bookhout what he can do if he doesn't do it right quick, using language that Fritz would later tell the Warren Commission, "I don't want to repeat." Fritz slips the receiver back into its cradle.[632] (Fritz was already aware that the FBI would be sitting in on the interrogations prior to the call from Shanklin. A few minutes earlier, Chief Curry had received a call from Shanklin requesting that they have a representative in on the interrogations. Curry had called Fritz and asked him to permit the FBI to sit in.)[633]

Bookhout hangs up. "We'd better get in there," he tells Hosty.

Before they can make a move, Captain Fritz appears and invites the two agents to sit in on the interrogation.[634] Fritz leads the FBI agents back into his office. Bookhout and Hosty pull out their identification badges and lay them on the desk next to Oswald.

"I'm Special Agent James Hosty of the Federal Bureau of Investigation," the agent begins, "and this is Special Agent James Bookhout."

As soon as Oswald hears Hosty's name, he reacts.

"Oh, so *you're* Hosty," Oswald snarls, clearly agitated. "I've heard about you."

"You have the right to remain silent," Hosty says as Oswald eyes him. "Anything you say may be used against you in a court of law." Hosty can barely finish the words, when Oswald explodes. "You're the one who's been harassing my wife!"

Fritz and his detectives glance at one another. Oswald curses both agents with a string of profanities. Hosty tries to calm Oswald down, but only manages to whip him into a frenzy.

"My wife is a Russian citizen who is here legally and is protected under diplomatic laws from harassment by you or anyone else from the FBI," Oswald argues, his face flush, his voice quivering. "You're no better than the Gestapo of Nazi Germany! If you want to talk to me, you should come to me directly, not my wife."[635]

Fritz jumps in and tries to soothe Oswald with a calm voice. Hosty has struck a nerve, and Fritz doesn't want to lose the trust he's been working hard to establish with Oswald. The fact is, Fritz doesn't like it one bit that the federal agents are horning in on his investigation. Anyone in law enforcement knows that when you conduct an interrogation with large groups of people present, you decrease the likelihood of satisfactory results. But, under the circumstances, Fritz knows he'll have to put up with the unwelcome company.

"What do you mean, he accosted your wife?" Fritz asks, thinking he meant some kind of physical abuse.

"Well, he threatened her," Oswald snaps. "He practically told her she'd have to go back to Russia. He accosted her on two different occasions."[636]

Agent Hosty had indeed spoken briefly to Marina, and at somewhat greater length to Ruth Paine, early in November when, in the course of trying to determine where Lee and Marina were living, he located the two women living together out in Irving. But he's never laid eyes on

Oswald before, and knows him only from the FBI file, which has been building up ever since he attempted to defect to Russia in 1959.[637]

What strikes Hosty at the moment is the realization that it might have been Oswald who had left an angry note for him at the FBI office about ten days earlier. The note was unsigned, but Hosty recalled that it stated in no uncertain terms that Hosty should not "bother my wife," and threatened to "take action against the FBI" if he didn't stop.[638]* At the time, Hosty, who was juggling thirty-five to forty cases simultaneously, had no

*The date that Oswald came to the FBI office is not known, although it is inferable from Ruth Paine's testimony that Oswald indicated to her it was sometime during the week preceding the weekend of November 9–10, 1963 (3 H 18). Hosty, in his 1996 book, *Assignment: Oswald* (p.29), says it was "ten days before" the assassination. And in a July 15, 1975, affidavit given to the FBI, Nannie Lee Fenner, the FBI receptionist to whom Oswald gave the note, said it was around ten days before the assassination. But there seems to be little basis for this certitude. Indeed, when Hosty testified under oath about it in 1975, he said Oswald dropped the note off "probably November the sixth, seventh, or eighth," which would have been sixteen to eighteen days earlier. And Fenner testified in 1975 that "I do not know the exact date . . . It would have been in November. It could have been before that. I have racked my brain up one side and down the other and I cannot come up with the date." Fenner said Oswald, not identifying himself, came to the FBI office during the noon hour and said to her, "S.A. Hosty, please." He had a "wild look in his eye" and was "awfully fidgety." While she was checking to see if Hosty was in, she said the "bottom portion" of the note Oswald was holding was visible to her and she recalls "the last two lines" of the note, which said, "I will either blow up the Dallas Police Department or the FBI office." When Fenner learned, and told Oswald, that Hosty was not in, he gave her the note to give to Hosty. After Oswald left, she decided to see "what was above" those two lines and said it "was something about [Hosty] speaking to his wife and what he was going to do if they didn't stop." Fenner said the note was signed "Lee Harvey Oswald," and when Hosty came back to the office, she gave the note to him. Hosty, who disposed of the note following the assassination (see later discussion), did not recall the note being signed, and said the note did not contain the language Fenner recalls. When asked at a House Judiciary subcommittee hearing in 1975, "It [the note] didn't say anything about the blowing up of the office?" he replied, "No, sir, I would have remembered that." Hosty characterized Fenner as unreliable and someone with "a distinct reputation for gross exaggeration," saying he was "almost certain that Fenner had never even read the note. It is more likely that she heard about it and embellished her knowledge." A coworker of Fenner's, Joe Pearce, gave an affidavit on July 22, 1975, that Fenner had "a tendency to exaggerate." Actually, Fenner's testimony before the House Judiciary subcommittee that when she saw Oswald on TV after the assassination and recognized him as the man who had given her the note, yet told no one at the office about this fact when she came in to work because "there was no one for me to talk to" and "what I didn't know was none of my business," throws her entire story about the contents of the note into question. And of course her recalling that the note said Oswald threatened to blow up the Dallas Police Department for a grievance he had against the FBI has no ring of truth to it. (*FBI Oversight*, December 11 and 12, 1975, pp.37–38, 40–41, 47, 53 [Fenner's testimony on December 11]; pp.129–130, 145–146 [Hosty's testimony on December 12]; Hosty with Hosty, *Assignment: Oswald*, pp.185, 195–199; Telephone interview of James Hosty by author on April 9, 2004; Joe Pearce affidavit: DOJCD Record 186-10006-10077, July 29, 1975; see also Church Committee Report, pp.96–97)

idea who had written the note and simply put it in his file drawer. Now, it seems Oswald may have been the author.

Oswald asks Fritz to take off his handcuffs.

"That sounds reasonable," Hosty quickly interjects, hoping to buddy up. Oswald can only glare at him.

Detectives Sims and Boyd look at Fritz. They know who's in charge here. Fritz tells them he wants Oswald to remain in handcuffs, but tells the detectives Oswald's hands don't need to be cuffed behind his back. As they make the adjustment, Oswald starts to settle down.

"Thank you, thank you," he says to Captain Fritz. He turns to Agent Hosty, and offers an apology, "I'm sorry for blowing up at you. And I'm sorry for writing that letter to you."

Hosty now knows that Oswald was the author of the note. Captain Fritz and the detectives in the tan Stetson hats are wondering just what kind of relationship exists between Oswald and FBI agent Hosty.[639] As Oswald begins to relax, Captain Fritz turns back to the matter at hand. "Do you own a rifle, Lee?"

"No," Oswald says dryly. "But I saw Mr. Truly, my supervisor at work, he had one at the Depository on Wednesday, I think it was, showing it to some people in his office on the first floor."

"Have you *ever* owned a rifle?" Fritz asks.

"Oh, I had one a good many years ago," Oswald says. "It was a small rifle, a twenty-two or something, but I haven't owned one for a long time."[640]

Hosty is eager to find out about Oswald's contacts with the Soviet embassy in Mexico City, which were discussed in the communiqué received by his office that morning. Now that Oswald is somewhat relaxed, Hosty decides to broach the subject.

"Ever been in Mexico City?" Hosty asks, interrupting Captain Fritz's line of questioning.

Oswald hesitates for just a moment, one of the few times he doesn't have an immediate answer.[641]

"Sure," he says. "Sure, I've been to Mexico. When I was stationed in San Diego with the Marines, a couple of my buddies and I would occasionally drive down to Tijuana over the weekend."[642]

Hosty knows he dodged the question, but lets it go, for the moment.

"You said you have a wife who is a Russian?" Fritz asks.

"That's right," Oswald says.

"Have you been to Russia?" Fritz asks.

"Yes," Oswald replies, slightly annoyed. "My wife has relatives over there, and she and I still have many friends."

"How long were you in Russia?" Fritz asks.

"About three years," Oswald says, growing increasingly edgy every time Agent Hosty asks a question.

"Ever own a rifle in Russia?" Fritz asks.

"You know you can't own a rifle in Russia," Oswald smirks, figuring that Fritz probably knows nothing about life in the Soviet Union. "I had a shotgun over there. You can't own a rifle in Russia."[643]

"Do you have any political beliefs, Lee?" Fritz asks.

"No," Oswald replies, "but I'm a supporter of the Castro revolution."[644] Captain Fritz picks up a piece of paper from his desk that was found in Oswald's wallet.

"What is the Fair Play for Cuba Committee?" he asks.

"I was the secretary of that organization in New Orleans a few months ago," Oswald says.

"What is the organization about?" Fritz probes.

"Why don't you ask Agent Hosty?" Oswald replies.[645]

Hosty is itching to grill Oswald about his Soviet contacts in Mexico City and can't understand why Fritz is fooling around with this line of questioning. He jumps in.

"Mr. Oswald, have you been in contact with the Soviet embassy?"

The question instantly unnerves Oswald.

"Yes, I contacted the Soviet embassy regarding my wife," Oswald snaps back. "And the reason was because you've accosted her twice already!"[646]

Oswald is growing steadily out of control, and Captain Fritz knows it. Hosty's questions continually undo the calm and talkative demeanor Fritz is working hard to establish. Hosty presses Oswald further—this time, too far.

"Mr. Oswald, have you ever been to Mexico City? Not Tijuana; Mexico City?"

Oswald jumps up like a live wire and slams his manacled fists down on the desktop.

"No! I've never been there!" he shouts. "What makes you think I've been to Mexico City? I deny it!"[647]

Oswald is shaking and starting to sweat. Hosty has hit a raw nerve. Fritz works quickly to soothe Oswald.

"All right, all right, let's calm down," Fritz says. Oswald sits back down, smoldering, and Hosty wisely retreats to a corner of the office to scribble notes. Fritz steps out to take a phone call. That'll give Oswald a chance to cool off, he thinks.

A detective approaches the homicide captain and tells him that an eyewitness to the Tippit shooting, Helen Markham, may have to be taken to the hospital to be treated for shock. Markham has been across the hall, in the burglary and theft office, for over an hour. The prospect of having to face Tippit's murderer in a lineup has her teetering between vomiting and fainting.

Captain Fritz can't have his key eyewitness leaving the premises, not yet anyway. He needs an identification as soon as possible. Fritz carries some ammonia, which he keeps in the office, across the hall to help get Markham back on her feet. He instructs officers to take her down to the first-aid room in the basement, to get her away from the noise and excitement, and call him when she's ready.[648]

Detective Leavelle follows her downstairs and tries to calm her down. Markham's biggest fear is that Oswald will be able to see her during the lineup.

"Aw, he ain't going to see you," Leavelle tells her. "All you have to do is just stand there and you've got to say just one word—repeat the number over the man's head that you saw shoot the officer. That's all you've got to do. Say one word."[649]

3:14 p.m.
In the morgue at Parkland Hospital, Dr. Earl Rose commences the autopsy on Officer Tippit. Measuring Tippit's height at five feet eleven inches and estimating his weight at 175 to 180 pounds, he finds four

separate bullet entrance wounds in Tippit's body, two in the right side of his chest, one in his right temple, and a fourth superficial wound to his left rib. (The bullet had hit Tippit's uniform button and the button had prevented it from penetrating deeply.) There was extensive damage to the brain and penetration of the lung and liver with massive hemor-rhaging. The three bullets entering Tippit's chest and temple had not exited the body and were removed by Rose, who listed the cause of death as "gunshot wounds of the head and chest." Rose found "no pow-der tattooing at the [wound] margins," tattooing or "powder burns" being the term used to describe an embedding into the skin surround-ing the entrance wound of splayed grains of burned gun powder explod-ing from the muzzle. The absence of powder burns in this case indicates that although Oswald shot Tippit at close range, the revolver's muzzle was probably never closer than three feet.[650]

3:15 p.m.

From Air Force One in flight, twenty-eight minutes after the plane left Dal-las, President Johnson makes his first telephone call as president, to the mother of his murdered predecessor. The conversation, taped by the U.S. Signal Corps, is to Rose Kennedy in Hyannis Port, Massachusetts, but put through the White House line. Above the static and the sound of the jet engines, the president, his wife, and Mrs. Kennedy shout out their words:

Voice: "AF-1 [Air Force One] from Crown [a code name for the White House]. Mrs. Kennedy on. Go ahead, please."

Sergeant Joseph Ayres [chief steward on Air Force One]: "Hello, Mrs. Kennedy. Hello, Mrs. Kennedy. We're talking from the airplane. Can you hear us all right, over?"

Rose Kennedy: "Thank you. Hello?"

Ayres: "Yes, Mrs. Kennedy, I have . . . uh . . . Mr. Johnson for you here."*

---

*Ayres would later tell author William Manchester that he started to say "President" John-son, but checked himself, apparently not wanting to further hurt Mrs. Kennedy with the declared reality that her son was no longer the president (Manchester, *Death of a President*, p.371).

Rose Kennedy: "Yes, thank you."

LBJ: "Mrs. Kennedy?"

Rose Kennedy: "Yes, yes, yes, Mr. President."

LBJ: "I wish to God there was something that I could do and I wanted to tell you that we are grieving with you."

Rose Kennedy: "Yes, well, thank you very much. That's very nice. I know. I know you loved Jack and he loved you."

Lady Bird Johnson: "Mrs. Kennedy, we feel lucky—"

Rose Kennedy: "Yes, all right."

Lady Bird: "We're glad that the nation had your son as long as it did."

Rose Kennedy: "Well, thank you for that, Lady Bird. Thank you very much. Good-bye."

Lady Bird: "—thought and prayers—"

Rose Kennedy: [weeping] "Thank you very much. Good-bye, good-bye, good-bye." [She hangs up.][651]

At Parkland Hospital, two of Parkland's surgeons, Drs. Malcolm Perry and Kemp Clark, hold an impromptu press conference. Dr. Perry bears the brunt of the questioning, manfully trying to impart what he knows in response to a hysterical crossfire of badly put questions. Before he can finish one answer, he is interrupted by another question and another. Answers about complicated medical procedures are shouted down by questions the doctors aren't able to answer. They don't really know how many times the president was struck nor from which direction. Perry can't really answer those questions but thinks the wound in the throat they enlarged for the tracheotomy was an entrance wound.[652] As to the bullet wound to the right side of the president's head, Perry doesn't know if that wound and the wound to the throat "are directly related" (i.e., caused by one bullet) or if the two wounds were caused by "two bullets." Though Perry's conclusions were not categorical, in the headlong rush to print it would be reported by some in the media that at least one of the shots definitely came from the front, not where Oswald was believed to be, to the president's right rear.[653]

At the Eastman Kodak Company near Love Field, Secret Service agent Forrest Sorrels and Abraham Zapruder meet with Phillip Chamberlain, acting laboratory manager, and Richard Blair, customer service representative. Within minutes, the laboratory begins the developing process, which will take about an hour.

Sorrels calls his office for the first time since leaving Love Field that morning in the lead car of the motorcade. He learns that Captain Fritz has been trying to get a hold of him, that he has a suspect in custody. Sorrels hangs up and tells Zapruder that he must leave, but will contact him later about getting a copy of his film. The agent hurries out to the Dallas police car and has the waiting patrolmen take him to Dallas police headquarters.[654]

3:30 p.m.

Across town, six plainclothesmen move quickly toward the small ranch-style, brick home at 2515 West Fifth in Irving. The Dallas police detectives had been waiting up the street for nearly forty minutes until the three Dallas County sheriff deputies arrived.[655]

Detective John Adamcik and Deputy Sheriffs Harry H. Weatherford and J. L. Oxford circle around toward the back door; Deputy Sheriff Buddy Walthers and Detectives Rose and Stovall bound up to the front entrance. The front door is standing open, screen door shut, and the officers can see Ruth Paine and Marina Oswald, a baby in her arms, watching television. Rose knocks on the door and fishes for his credentials.[656]

Ruth Paine answers the door and the officers identify themselves.

"It's about the president being shot, isn't it?" Mrs. Paine asks.

"Yes," Rose responds. "We have Lee Harvey Oswald in custody. He is charged with shooting an officer."

They explain that they want to search the house. Mrs. Paine asks if they have a warrant and they tell her they do not, but can get the sheriff out there right away with one if she insisted.

"That won't be necessary," Mrs. Paine says, as she pushes the screen door open. "Come on in. We've been expecting you. Just as soon as we heard where it happened, we figured someone would be out."[657]

Guy Rose, as the senior detective, does most of the talking. Ruth introduces him to Marina, who is holding June in her arms, and explains that she is Lee's wife, a citizen of Russia.

Detective Stovall goes to the back door and lets the other officers in.[658] They spread out and begin searching the premises.

Detective Rose asks to use the phone and calls Captain Fritz, asking him whether there are any special instructions.

"Ask her if her husband has a rifle," Fritz says.

Rose keeps the line open while he asks her, but she doesn't understand. Mrs. Paine explains that Marina speaks very little English and offers to translate for him. Ruth asks Marina the question in Russian, then turns back to Rose and says, "No." But then Marina says something to Ruth, who suddenly tells Rose, "Yes, he does have."

Rose relays the information to Captain Fritz, who tells him to gather everything they can and bring it downtown. Rose hangs up the phone and asks Marina if she would show him where the rifle is. Mrs. Paine translates the request and Marina indicates the garage.[659] They go to the garage, attached to the house just off the kitchen, and Marina points to a blanket rolled up and lying on the floor near the wall. A piece of white twine is tied around one end of the blanket, the other end is loose. To the detective, it looks like something might still be there, the blanket retaining the outline of a rifle.[660]

"Well, now they will find it," Marina thinks to herself.[661]

Detective Rose reaches down and picks up the blanket. It falls loosely over his arm—obviously empty. Marina lets out an audible gasp.[662] About a week after arriving at the Paine residence from New Orleans, she was in the garage looking for a metallic part to put June's crib together. When she came across the blanket with something wrapped in it, she opened it up and saw the rifle.[663] She knows, now, it was Lee who shot the president. Until that moment, she had thought the rifle was in the garage, and therefore Lee couldn't have done it. She had convinced herself that the police had come out simply because her husband was always under suspicion—something the FBI visits in November had reinforced. Now she knows better.[664]

Ruth Paine looks at Marina and sees that she is pale white. Ruth senses what that means. For a moment, Detective Rose thinks Marina might be about to faint.

"I'm going to have to ask both of you to come downtown with us," Detective Rose tells them.[665]

As they return to the house, Ruth Paine's estranged husband Michael arrives. Seeing only Ruth, he says to her, "I came to help you. Just as soon as I heard where it happened, I knew you would need some help."[666]

When Michael Paine heard the news, his first thought was that Oswald could have been the one who had done it.[667]

3:40 p.m.

Captain Fritz returns to his office and resumes his methodical questioning of Oswald. "Lee, I'm a little confused about why your wife is living in Irving and you're living in Oak Cliff. Can you tell me about that?"

"My wife is staying with Mrs. Paine who's trying to learn Russian," Oswald says, gradually regaining his composure. "My wife teaches her and Mrs. Paine helps her out with our small baby. It makes a good arrangement for both of them."

"How often do you go out there?" Fritz asks.

"Weekends," Oswald says.

"Why don't you stay out there?"

"I don't want to stay there. Mrs. Paine and her husband are separated. They don't get along too well," Oswald answers unresponsively.

Fritz asks Oswald if he has a car and Oswald says, "No," adding that the Paines had two cars but he didn't use either one of them.[668] Asked about his education, Oswald tells Captain Fritz that he went to school in New York for a while, then Fort Worth, then he dropped out of high school to go into the Marines, but eventually finished high school while in the service.

"Did you win any medals for rifle shooting in the Marines?" Fritz asks in an innocent way.

"Just the usual medals," Oswald says, heading off the inquiry.

"Like what?" Fritz asks.

"I got an award for marksmanship," Oswald says matter-of-factly.[669]

Fritz suddenly changes subjects.

"Lee, why were you registered at the boarding house as O. H. Lee?"

"Oh, she didn't understand my name correctly," he shoots back. "I just left it that way."[670]

Fritz leans back in the chair, "Did you work at the Depository today?"

"Yes," Oswald replies.

"How long have you worked there?" Fritz asks.

"Since October fifteenth."[671]

"What part of the building were you in at the time the president was shot?" Fritz quizzes.

"I was having lunch about that time on the first floor," Oswald says dryly. "We broke for lunch about noon and I came down and ate."[672]

"Where were you when the officer stopped you?" Fritz asks, referring to the story that Roy Truly, the building manager, had told him earlier.

"I was on the second floor drinking a Coke when an officer came in," Oswald replies. "There's a soda machine in the lunchroom there. I went up to get a Coke."

"Then what did you do?" Fritz prompts.

"I left," Oswald says, like it's nothing.

"Where did you go when you left work?" the homicide captain asks.

"I went over to my room on Beckley," Oswald says, "changed my trousers, got my pistol, and went to the movies."

"Why did you take your pistol?" Fritz asks.

"I felt like it," Oswald says snidely.

"You felt like it?"

"You know how boys are when they have a gun," Oswald smirks, "they just carry it."

"Did you shoot Officer Tippit?"

"No, I didn't," Oswald says. "The only law I violated was when I hit the officer in the show; and he hit me in the eye and I guess I deserved it. That is the only law I violated. That is the only thing I have done wrong."[673]

The answers seem to be coming easy now for Oswald. Like an experienced cross-examiner, Fritz changes the subject abruptly.

"What did you do during the three years you lived in the Soviet Union?"

"I worked in a factory," Oswald says casually.

"What kind?" Fritz asks as he peers at Oswald through his owlish spectacles.

"A radio electronics factory," Oswald answers.[674]

"Why did you leave the Depository after the shooting?" Fritz asks, returning suddenly to the present. The questions are coming from all angles now, but Oswald handles the changeups with ease.

"I went out front and was standing with Bill Shelley," Oswald tells him, "and after hearing what happened, with all the confusion, I figured there wouldn't be any more work done the rest of the day, so I went home. The company's not that particular about our hours. We don't even punch a clock."

"What kind of work do you do at the Depository?" Fritz asks.

"I fill orders," Oswald says.

"Which floors do you have access to?"

"Well, as a laborer," Oswald replies, "I have access to the entire building."

Oswald explains that the company offices are on the first and second floors and that they store books on the third, fourth, fifth, and sixth floors.[675]

"Did you shoot the president?" Fritz asks.

"No, I emphatically deny that," Oswald snaps. "I haven't shot anybody."[676]

A detective opens the door to Fritz's office and pokes his head in. "Captain Fritz, they're ready downstairs."

"Okay," Fritz says, rising from his chair, "let's take a break."[677] Not the best session Fritz has ever had with a suspect, but certainly not the worst, either. Oswald thinks he is being cagey, answering only the questions he thinks he can answer without being caught, but he's talking too much anyway. Fritz didn't know a damn thing about him except his name, where he worked, and one of his addresses, but now he already knows quite a bit more, a lot of little details his men can check out—and who knows what they'll find?

4:05 p.m.

Secret Service agent Forrest Sorrels and a small group of fellow agents are waiting in the outer office of Homicide and Robbery when Fritz comes out of his office. Sorrels greets Fritz, whom he's known for some time.

"Have you gotten anything out of him?" Sorrels asks the homicide captain.

"No," Fritz replies, "he hasn't made any admissions yet, but I'll be talking to him again very soon."[678]

Sorrels sees two detectives preparing to escort Oswald out of Captain Fritz's office.

"Captain, I'd like to talk to this man when I have the opportunity," Sorrels says.

"You can talk to him right now," Fritz answers, deciding to keep the lineup waiting a few minutes. Fritz makes arrangements to have Sorrels question Oswald in a small squad room tucked behind his private office.[679] When Oswald is led in, the cool demeanor is gone, replaced with an arrogant and belligerent attitude.[680]

"I don't know who you fellows are, a bunch of cops?" Oswald asks.

"Well, I will tell you who I am," the agent begins. "My name is Sorrels, and I am with the United States Secret Service. Here is my commission book [the Secret Service term for the small leather folder that contains the agent's ID on top and badge on the bottom]."

Sorrels holds it out in front of the prisoner.

"I don't want to look at that," Oswald says, holding his head up, refusing to look. "What am I going to be charged with? Why am I being held? Isn't someone suppose to tell me what my rights are?"

"Yes, I will tell you what your rights are," Sorrels replies calmly. "Your rights are the same as that of any American citizen. You do not have to make a statement unless you want to. You have the right to get an attorney."

"Aren't you suppose to get me an attorney?" Oswald asks.

"No," Sorrels says.

"You're not?" Oswald says with surprise.

"No," Sorrels answers, "because if I got you an attorney, they would say I was probably getting a rakeoff on the fee." A slight smile creeps across Sorrels's face. He hopes his bit of humor will help loosen the suspect up. But Oswald will have none of it, not finding Sorrels's attempt at humor amusing.

"You can have the telephone book and you can call anybody you want to," Sorrels continues. "I just want to ask you some questions."

Sorrels asks if Oswald has ever been in a foreign country. Oswald says that he had traveled in Europe and spent a good deal of that time in the Soviet Union. Then suddenly, Oswald says, "I don't care to answer any more questions."[681]

With that, the just-started interview is terminated. Fritz instructs his men to take Oswald down to the basement show-up room, then turns to two plainclothes vice squad officers, William E. Perry and Richard L. Clark, waiting to take part in the lineup. Normally, available prisoners are pulled from jail and used in the lineups. But Captain Fritz is afraid that prisoners might try to hurt Oswald, due to the high feeling in Dallas over the assassination of the president. His own office doesn't have any men the right size to show with Oswald, so he had called down to vice to borrow a couple of their men. Fritz tells Officers Perry and Clark to take off their sport coats, loosen their ties, and generally change their appearance before heading down to the show-up room.[682]

4:10 p.m.

Detectives Sims, Boyd, and M. G. Hall escort Oswald toward the exit that leads out of the Homicide and Robbery office. The door opens and they wade into the crowd of reporters jammed in the corridor outside. Flashbulbs pop incessantly as questions are fired at the prisoner. Oswald raises his manacled fists for the photographers.[683] The crowd is shoulder to shoulder, pressing in as the detectives shuffle Oswald twenty-three feet to the jail elevator at a snail's pace. Reporters, frantic for information, shout questions over each other. The huge TV cameras blocking the corridor manage to catch a few seconds of the young man upon whom the attention of the whole world is now focused. Oswald catches one question from the deafening storm directed at him, "Did you kill the president?"

"No, sir." He answers calmly. "Nobody charged me with that."

When they arrive downstairs in the basement holdover room, Sims and Boyd search Oswald—remarkably, no one has yet. Boyd finds five live rounds of .38 caliber ammunition in the left front pocket of Oswald's trousers.

"What are these doing in there?" the detective asks.

"I just had them in my pocket," Oswald says nonchalantly.[684]

Detective Sims finds a bus transfer issued by the Dallas Transit Company in his shirt pocket.[685] Oswald takes off his silver Marine Corps ring and hands it to Sims.[686] Also recovered from Oswald's pockets are a small white boxtop with the name "Cox's, Fort Worth" printed on the top; a paycheck stub from American Bakeries dated August 22, 1960; a brass key marked "P.O. Dept., Do Not Dup." with the number 1126; eighty-seven cents in change; and thirteen dollars in paper money—a five-dollar bill, and eight singles.[687]

The telephone rings in Shanklin's Dallas FBI office. It's Belmont in Washington. He wants an update.

"Well, Alan, our agents are interviewing the suspect Oswald," Shanklin tells him. "Hosty and Jim Bookhout, a good criminal agent, are in with the police right now."

"If there's any question that a polygraph might be productive," Belmont says, "go right ahead and use it. Have you talked with the Secret Service?"

"They don't appear to be doing much," Shanklin replies. "Most of them have gone back to Washington with the vice president."

"You should make sure that all possible investigative steps are being taken," Belmont orders him. "For example, make sure that the gun is checked for fingerprints; determine Oswald's whereabouts throughout the day; and make sure that the locations where the gun and shells were found is examined carefully."

"Well, I think the police have that covered," Shanklin says.

"Don't assume the police are going to handle this properly," Belmont says. "We must conduct a vigorous and thorough investigation if we expect to get answers."

"Right," Shanklin responds.

"Now, if you need additional personnel to accomplish that," Belmont adds, "you should let us know."

"Well, if it turns out Oswald is not the person who shot the president," Shanklin says, "we're going to need more manpower down here. We should know something very soon."[688]

Returning to his office, Chief Curry finds television trucks all around City Hall, the building itself overrun with newsmen and television cameras, their heavy cables snaking through hallways and offices. The Dallas police have always permitted free movement of the press around City Hall, but they have never been faced with anything like this before, with the national and international press descending on them.

Chief Curry knows that his men have a suspect in the Tippit killing, possibly in the assassination, and from the reports coming in it seems that everything that can be done is being done. Curry calls the personnel office and requests the file on the officer killed in Oak Cliff.

Checking the record of the eleven-year veteran patrolman, Curry finds that J. D. Tippit had two previous brushes with death while on the force. Back in April 1956, he and his partner, Daniel Smith, had intervened in a domestic dispute involving a suicidal husband with an icepick. When the two officers moved in to arrest the man, he managed to stab Smith once in the left shoulder and Tippit twice, in the stomach and again in the right knee. Surgeons later found a half inch of the icepick's tip embedded in his right kneecap. It left him with an occasional slight limp and a much more cautious attitude. Four months later, on September 2, 1956, Tippit and partner Dale Hankins shot Leonard Garland to death at Club 80 in Dallas, after Garland pulled out a semiautomatic pistol, shoved it into Tippit's face, and pulled the trigger. Garland had failed to remove the safety, and luckily for Tippit, the gun didn't fire. Tippit and Hankins returned fire, killing the gunman, who turned out to be wanted

by the FBI. Tippit (as did Hankins) received a Dallas Police Department
Certificate of Merit for his "outstanding judgment and quick thinking."
Bud Owens, Tippit's immediate supervisor for nearly ten years, vouched
for him as a well-liked officer who used good common sense.[689]

4:15 p.m.
Lieutenant Jack Revill, the man in charge of the Dallas Police Department's Criminal Intelligence Section, dictates a memo to one of the
clerks in the Special Services Bureau office. After leaving FBI agent
Hosty in the homicide office, Revill had returned to his office and
immediately reported the conversation with Hosty to his boss, Captain
W. Pat Gannaway, telling Gannaway that Hosty had said the FBI knew
all about Oswald before the assassination and knew he was capable of
it. If true, this was explosive information. Why hadn't the FBI told the
Dallas Police Department about Oswald before the president came to
town? Indeed, why hadn't they and the Secret Service been watching
Oswald?

"Put it in writing," Gannaway told him.

Revill said that he hated to do that. After all, Hosty might have been
simply stating his personal opinion.

"Put it on paper," Gannaway replied adamantly, "and give it to me and
I will take it to Chief Curry."

With the help of an office clerk, Revill follows Gannaway's order:

> On November 22, 1963, at approximately 2:50PM, the undersigned
> officer met Special Agent James Hosty of the Federal Bureau of
> Investigation in the basement of City Hall. At that time Special
> Agent Hosty related to this officer that the Subject was a member
> of the Communist Party, and that he was residing in Dallas. The
> Subject was arrested for the murder of Officer J. D. Tippit and is a
> prime suspect in the assassination of President Kennedy. The
> information regarding the Subject's affiliation with the Commu-
> nist Party is the first information this officer has received from the
> Federal Bureau of Investigation regarding same. Agent Hosty fur-

ther stated that the Federal Bureau of Investigation was aware of the Subject and that *they had information that this Subject was capable of committing the assassination of President Kennedy.*[690]

When the clerk hands Revill the typed copy, he reads it over carefully before signing it.

"Are you sure this is the way you spell *assassination*?" he asks.

"Yes, sir," the clerk replies. "I looked it up in the dictionary."[691]

4:20 p.m.

Bill Alexander had been in a police squad car parked behind the Texas Theater along with many officers who were watching the backdoor of the theater for a possible escape. When word was received that the Tippit murder suspect was apprehended inside, and was being taken to police headquarters at City Hall, Alexander returned to his office. His old friend, Captain Fritz, was on the phone shortly thereafter, asking Alexander to prepare a search warrant pronto for Oswald's Beckley apartment. Alexander prepared the warrant and called Justice of the Peace David Johnston, whom he needed to sign the warrant, to meet him at the sheriff's office for the trip to Beckley. Alexander meets with Johnston and Dallas police detectives F. M. Turner and H. M. Moore at the sheriff's office, and the four immediately leave for Beckley; Johnston, because of the rush, signed the warrant in the squad car en route to Beckley.[692]

4:35 p.m.

The darkened detail room in the basement, where the officers get their assignments at the beginning of each shift, is full of men, some in uniform, others not. At one end of the room is a narrow stage, about two and a half feet high, screened off from the rest of the room by a one-way black nylon scrim. The stage is hotly illuminated by floodlights overhead and at the floor level, making it easy for the witnesses standing in the darkness to see the suspects through the scrim, but impossible for the suspects to see them in the darkness beyond.[693] Detectives Sims, Boyd, and Hall have Oswald in a holdover room next to the stage. They are joined by Officers

Perry and Clark, and a jail clerk (a civilian employee), Don Ables, who will appear in the lineup with Oswald. Each of them is handcuffed to the other.[694]

Helen Markham, who had been close to fainting before being given ammonia, is brought out of the first-aid room and into the darkened area of the detail room by Detectives Leavelle and Graves. Captain Fritz, Chief Curry, and Detective C. W. Brown join them momentarily.[695] Mrs. Markham, who still hasn't recovered from the shock of seeing the murder, is terribly jittery, and the darkened roomful of policemen isn't all that reassuring.

The word is given and Detectives Sims, Boyd, and Hall troop the four men out onto the stage.[696] As soon as Oswald comes out, Mrs. Markham feels cold chills run over her and begins to cry.[697] The four men come to a stop, each positioned underneath a large number. Left to right, from Markham's position, the four men are W. E. Perry (under number 1), Lee Harvey Oswald (2), R. L. Clark (3), and Don Ables (4).[698]

Though Markham is confident Oswald is the man she saw shoot Officer Tippit, she wants to be sure and whispers to one of the policemen that she wants them to turn Oswald sideways, which was standard procedure anyway. Detective Leavelle tells the men to turn to their right, left, to the rear, then back to the front. Each man is then asked a question or two so that Markham can hear them speak. Leavelle doesn't ask Oswald his name because Markham might have heard it since the shooting.

Mrs. Markham can't forget the way the killer looked at her on Tenth Street—the glassy, wild look in his eyes.

"The second one," Markham says.

The police aren't sure what she means—second from the left, or the right?

"Which one?" they ask.

"Number 2," she says.

There's an immediate stirring of voices in the room, and Mrs. Markham, faint again, falls over.[699]

Detectives Sims, Boyd, and Hall march the men off the stage and Oswald is taken back up to Captain Fritz's office on the third floor.[700]

4:45 p.m.

The unmarked squad car pulls up in front of the rooming house on North Beckley in Oak Cliff and four men, armed with a search warrant, climb out.

After showing the search warrant to the landlord, Mr. Johnson, Alexander and the detectives enter Oswald's room. They notice the sagging single bed framed in a metal headboard, and the movable wardrobe, an old blonde oak dresser with missing handles. When they open two dresser drawers, some clothing spills onto the floor. Alexander finds an empty leather holster hanging from a doorknob. A shelf on a wall has some food atop it. The room, Alexander sees, is "messy but not dirty."[701]

The detectives begin piling everything on the bed for the trip downtown: clothing, shoes, a shaving kit; a city map of Dallas with some suspicious pencil markings on it, including some at the Texas School Book Depository and Elm Street; an address book, some paperbacks—*A Study of the USSR and Communism* and a couple of James Bond books—a Gregg shorthand dictionary, a copy of *Roberts Rules of Order*; a pair of binoculars; several pamphlets and handbills; a certificate of Undesirable Discharge from the U.S. Marine Corps, and a lot of other documents.

The detectives are particularly struck and alarmed by the stuff in Russian and the left-wing literature. It's not the kind of thing they find too often in Dallas. There's a letter about photography from Gus Hall, leader of the American Communist Party, one in Russian from the Soviet embassy in Washington, and another from someone called Louis Weinstock of the Communist Party's paper, the *Worker*. There are two letters from the Fair Play for Cuba Committee, sent to Oswald at an address in New Orleans, a letter from the Socialist Workers Party—a Trotskyite organization—regarding membership, and a Russian passport with Oswald's photo in it. Alexander thinks to himself that there's a lot of difference between a homegrown killer and someone who appeared, from what he could see, to be a card-carrying Communist with overseas connections. The possibility of a Communist conspiracy enters his mind. Even the thought of Russian military transport planes, landing in Dallas, flashes across his mind.

Over the next hour and a quarter, they nearly strip the room, using the pillow cases and one of Oswald's own duffle bags to carry everything to the waiting patrol cars. Only a banana peel and some uneaten fruit are left behind when they leave just after 6:00 p.m.[702]

Aboard Air Force One, the flight back to Washington has been abuzz with a continuous and overlapping series of communications with the outside world, some to pick up the threads of the American government so brutally ripped asunder just hours ago, some to let profoundly worried officials and congressmen have a reassuring word with the new president, but most of the conversations are about the fallen president.[703] As Air Force One zoomed through the sky to its Washington, D.C., destination at more than 600 mph, there are conflicting reports about the extent, if any, of the tension existing between the old and the new presidential administrations. At a minimum, the ride to Washington, as Mrs. Johnson says, was "strained."[704] And it's clear that the aides to Kennedy and Johnson were separated on the plane, Kennedy's aides in the rear of the plane with Mrs. Kennedy and the casket. A top Kennedy aide is said to have told a news reporter, "Make sure that you report that we rode in back with our president, and not up front with him [LBJ]."[705] Was a lot more involved? Kennedy assistant press secretary Malcolm Kilduff was quoted as telling one source, "That was the sickest airplane I ever was on." And he told the *Los Angeles Times* that there was friction between Kennedy and Johnson factions on the flight. "I think that there are things that happened that could be embarrassing to both the Kennedys and the Johnsons," he said, though he would not describe the events referred to. Another passenger, wishing to remain anonymous, said, "They refought the battles of 1960," during which Johnson and Kennedy had bitterly contested for the Democratic nomination. But, under the circumstances, much of this seems unlikely, and Jack Valenti, an LBJ aide, remembered no such discussion and acrimony, adding that the extreme grief of Kennedy's top aides, Kenneth O'Donnell and Larry O'Brien, was "simply beyond anything as casual as hostility." Charles Roberts of *Newsweek*, who was aboard, wrote, "As an unbiased witness to it [the transition of power], now that questions have been raised, . . . it was careful, correct, considerate and compassionate."

As far as President Johnson's conduct on the plane, rumors abounded that he had been "rude," "overbearing," and "boorish," one anonymous source even saying he had been impatient with Jackie when she did not "immediately come forward to witness the oath-taking." However, the evidence from named sources contradicts this. William Manchester himself, who, in writing *The Death of a President*, probably interviewed more people, including all the Kennedy entourage on the plane, than anyone else, said, "I think Johnson acted in incredibly difficult circumstances. I think he behaved well," particularly, Manchester said, in being solicitous and caring to Jackie throughout, a view which sounds much more believable to me. And Roberts of *Newsweek* said that although Johnson was very "capable of crudities," the new president's conduct during the four hours of flight was completely proper and "four of Johnson's finest." Indeed, even Kilduff, who spoke of hostility on the plane between the two camps, said in a radio-television interview on November 21, 1966, on the Westinghouse Broadcasting network, "I can't help but feel that he [President Johnson] showed the utmost . . . personal concern for Mrs. Kennedy, all members of the Kennedy family, and the whole Kennedy party that was with us."[706]

About certain things, everyone agrees. As author Relman Morin writes, as the plane thundered toward Washington it was "heavily freighted with grief and horror and memories and the aching sense of loss." Also, that Johnson, with the levers of power now in his hands, started working immediately at his new job. He was on the phone to Washington calling for a cabinet meeting the next morning, requesting that Robert S. McNamara, the secretary of defense, and McGeorge Bundy, the special assistant to the president for national security affairs, be at Andrews Air Force Base when Air Force One landed so they could instantly bring him up to date on the very latest developments flowing from the assassination throughout the world, and so on. The transition of power was also filled with the unavoidable poignancies that strike at the heart. During the flight, in the Oval Office "a sad task was going forward. They were removing some of [JFK's] most prized mementos: the coconut shell in which he had sent the message for help after the Japanese destroyer *Amagiri* rammed and sank PT-109, the framed photographs of his wife and of Caroline and John-John at different ages, the silver calendar that marked the dates of the beginning and end of the Cuban missile crisis, his famous rocking chair."[707]

During the flight, Rufus Youngblood and Roy Kellerman conferred frequently by phone with the head of the White House Secret Service detail in Washington, D.C., Gerry Behn, to arrange security and procedures at Andrews Air Force Base. Behn wanted President Johnson to come immediately to the White House, where both security and communications were best, but Youngblood told him that the president was adamantly against it. "That would be presumptuous on my part," Johnson said. "I won't do it." Instead, Johnson instructs Youngblood to have the Secret Service secure the Johnsons' Washington, D.C., residence instead.[708]

A dispute over how and where to take the body broke out. Admiral Burkley advised Captain Taz Shepard, the president's naval aide, to make arrangements with Bethesda Naval Hospital, while Ted Clifton informed Dr. Leonard Heaton, the army's surgeon general, that the autopsy would be performed at the Walter Reed Army Medical Center, the great hospital in the nation's capital that since 1909 had treated grunts and generals, even presidents and Winston Churchill.[709] General McHugh ordered an ambulance, but was informed that it was illegal in the District of Columbia to move a dead body by ambulance without a coroner's permit. McHugh didn't give a damn.

"Just *do* it," he snapped. "And don't worry about the law. *I'll* pay the fine."[710]

Eventually, the choice of hospital was left to Mrs. Kennedy. Dr. Burkley made his way back to the tiny rear cabin area where she held vigil next to her husband's coffin. He knelt in the aisle beside her, and explained to her that the president's body would first have to be taken to a hospital. "Why?" she asked. To have the bullet removed for evidence, Burkley improvised, not knowing if there was a bullet inside the president's body. He was careful not to use the word *autopsy*, which would conjure up the image of a dissection. Burkley told her that he would be willing to arrange to have it done at any place that she felt it should be done, although for reasons of security it should be done at a military hospital. The president was, after all, the commander in chief. That effectively narrowed the choice down to two hospitals in the Washington, D.C., area: the army's Walter Reed or the U.S. Naval Medical Center in Bethesda, Maryland.

"The president was in the navy," Burkley said softly.

"Of course," Jackie said, "Bethesda."[711]

Then she thought of Secret Service agent Bill Greer, the driver of the limousine in Dallas. Greer had been remorseful all afternoon, feeling that somehow he might have been able to save the president if only he had swerved the car, or sped away before the fatal shot. Mrs. Kennedy felt sorry for him and requested that Greer drive the casket to the naval hospital.[712]

There had been a steady stream of visitors to the cramped cabin in the rear of the plane throughout the flight, but, with the casket at their feet and so many seats removed, there was not enough room for them to stay long. President Johnson, otherwise closeted with his advisers Cliff Carter and Bill Moyers, came back for a visit, telling Kennedy's men that he hoped they would stay on at the White House: "I need you now more than President Kennedy needed you." Later Moyers came back and asked Ken O'Donnell, Dave Powers, and Larry O'Brien to join the president for a conference about arranging a meeting of the congressional leadership, but they didn't want to leave Jackie.

"We understand perfectly," Moyers agreed.

By then, a small Irish wake, full of melancholy reminiscences, had been unrolling in the rear compartment. Jackie recalled how much Jack enjoyed the singing of tenor Luigi Vena at their wedding, and decided to ask Vena to sing "Ave Maria" and Bizet's "Agnus Dei" at the president's funeral mass. Dave Powers and Ken O'Donnell told her about Jack's meeting with Cardinal Cushing at the North American College in Rome a few months ago. Many U.S. cardinals attended the coronation of Pope Paul VI, but only

Cushing was there when the president arrived. "They've all gone home, Jack," the cardinal laughed. "I'm the only one who's for ya! The rest of them are all Republicans." It was decided that Cushing, who married Jack and Jackie, would say the low requiem mass, because Jack liked that better than the solemn high ritual.

Powers told Jackie about the president's last visit to the Kennedy family compound at Hyannis Port on October 30, when he spent the whole day with his crippled and speechless father. The next day, when the president's helicopter arrived, Jack kissed his father on the forehead, started off, and then went back to kiss him again—almost, Dave thought, as though he sensed he would never see his father again. They told how they had accompanied Jack to his son Patrick's grave in Brookline that same afternoon and how they heard him remark, "He seems so alone here."

"I'll bring them together now," Jackie said quietly. At first, Dave and Ken thought she was thinking of burying the president in Boston, but she had already decided on Arlington and planned to have Patrick's body moved from Massachusetts for reburial beside his father.[713]

They told her about their trip to Ireland in June, which Jack had described to her as the most enjoyable experience of his whole life. He was impressed by the drill of the Irish military cadets at Arbour Hill when he placed a wreath on the graves of the leaders of the Easter Rising of 1916. Jackie decides to have them attend the funeral too, if they can, along with the pipers of the Royal Highland Black Watch Regiment, who performed for the president and his family only last week on the grounds of the White House.

Now, as the plane begins its descent into Andrews Air Force Base, O'Donnell, Powers, and O'Brien learn that a detachment of military pallbearers is waiting to carry the coffin from the plane. Overcome with Irish sentiment, Ken O'Donnell speaks up.

"We'll carry him off ourselves."[714]

In a quiet Maryland suburb of the nation's capital, Naval Commander James J. Humes strolls purposefully toward the entrance of Bethesda Naval

Hospital. There is a cordon of marines and military police around the hospital, with additional guards stationed at all three entrance gates to the grounds with instructions to admit only employees, patients in serious condition, their relatives, and cars with White House clearance. The thirty-nine-year-old Humes senses that the president's body must be en route.

Earlier, around noon, he had left Bethesda, where he is director of laboratories of the Naval Medical School, and had gone home to help his wife, Ann, get ready for a dinner party they were having that evening for twenty-four people, almost all of them military colleagues. In addition to the dinner party, they were busy taking care of last-minute details related to their son's First Communion, scheduled to take place the following morning at their parish church. Both Jim and Ann were far too busy to listen to the radio, and neither had any idea of the tragedy gripping the country until a couple of their older children—they have five in school and two at home—came home on the school bus and told their mother, "The president's been shot."

"That's a terrible thing to say," she scolded, only to switch on the television and find that it was true. Jim and Ann both knew the dinner party was off, which meant they had a lot of telephoning to do. But the Washington telephone system had given out, overloaded by thousands of people wanting to talk about and share their grief over news of the tragedy, and Ann was finding it impossible to reach any of their guests.[*] In the interim, Jim decided to take his son out for a haircut. They had just returned when his wife was finally able to get an open line, only to have an operator interrupt her for an emergency call from Admiral Edward Kenney, surgeon general of the navy. "Jim," Kenney told him, "you better hurry over to the hospital."

Humes could hardly have imagined at this time that he would someday be accused by many conspiracy theorists as being an accessory after

---

[*]Most of the nearly one and a half million telephones in service in the Washington metropolitan area on November 22 were used during the first half hour. A staggering quarter-million long-distance calls alone were made on Friday, resulting in overloaded exchanges, delayed dial tones, and intermittent service. Normal telephone operations were not completely restored until 4:15 p.m. EST. (Manchester, *Death of a President*, pp. 205–206, 253–254)

the fact to Kennedy's murder, and indeed, by necessary extension from their arguments, a part of a plot to murder the president.

Now Humes bounds toward Admiral Kenney's office, where the surgeon general gives the commander his orders: "Be prepared to do an autopsy on the late president." As the words sink in, Humes is told that Commander J. Thornton Boswell, the forty-one-year-old chief of pathology at the Naval Medical School, will be assisting him. He can add anyone else to the team he deems necessary in helping him to determine the cause of death, but he's instructed to limit the personnel as much as possible.[715] Retiring to the solitude of his office, Commander Humes gets a phone call from his friend Dr. Bruce Smith, acting deputy director of the Armed Forces Institute of Pathology (AFIP), who offers whatever help he might need. Humes is grateful and tells him he may call him later.

A short time later, Humes gets in touch with Dr. Boswell and together they decide that Dr. Humes should be the senior autopsy surgeon, considering that he was Boswell's superior at the hospital.[716] Both men have performed autopsies, although neither has been trained or certified as a forensic pathologist, a fact that will ultimately be used to great advantage by conspiracy theorists.[717]*

4:58 p.m. (5:58 p.m. EST)
At two minutes before the hour in the East Coast darkness, Air Force One, the superb blue and white plane of the nation's chief executive, touches down at Andrews Air Force Base in Maryland, about fifteen miles southeast of the nation's capital.[718] The plane taxis into the glare of the reception area, now thronged with hundreds of government officials and other VIPs.

The first person to board Air Force One is President Kennedy's

---

*When Boswell was informed that the autopsy would take place at Bethesda, he said, "That's stupid. The autopsy should be done at the Armed Forces Institute of Pathology [AFIP]," located just five miles up the road from Bethesda at the Walter Reed Army Medical Center. The AFIP was "the apex of military pathology and, perhaps, world pathology," according to Boswell. However, his suggestion was rejected. "That's the way it is," he was told. "Admiral Burkley wants Bethesda." (Breo, "JFK's Death—The Plain Truth from the MDs Who Did the Autopsy," p.2796; ARRB MD 26, Memorandum, Andy Purdy to Jim Kelly and Kenneth Klein, August 17, 1977, Notes of interview with Dr. J. Thornton Boswell, pp.1–2)

brother, Attorney General Robert Kennedy, who bounds up the ramp and races from the front of the plane to the rear, ignoring President Johnson's outstretched hand as he passes. Johnson is miffed, but O'Donnell, realizing that Bobby's only thought is to get to Jackie as quickly as possible, doubts whether he even saw the president's gesture.[719]

In the tail compartment, Bobby Kennedy rushes to Jackie's side.

"Hi, Jackie," he says quietly, putting an arm around her. "I'm here."

"Oh, Bobby," Jackie sighs. It is so like him, she thinks. He is always there when you need him.[720]

Most of the civilized world is riveted to the live television coverage of the arrival. A huge "catering bus"—an outsized forklift, roofed and painted a garish yellow, used to load meals aboard military transports—is brought to the left rear of the plane and attached to the exit twelve feet above. A military casket team moves forward to secure the casket but is pushed out of the way by the dead president's friends and aides, who, along with the assistance of Secret Service agents, start to move the casket onto the compartment of the catering bus.[721]

The compartment containing both the casket and the Kennedy entourage slowly begins to descend, then comes to a stop five feet above the ground. Not being designed for such uses, it's the lowest the forklift can go. It is almost impossible to unload the casket from this height, even with two teams of pallbearers, one on the ground, the other on the lift. Television cameras relentlessly record the awkward scene in black and white. The men struggle to move the cumbersome burden into the rear of a gray U.S. Navy ambulance, its rotating beacon throwing flashes of light over their faces, and finally succeed after several minutes. Meanwhile, the men in the Kennedy entourage begin jumping off the catering bus to the ground below. Robert Kennedy, one of the first on the ground, turns back to help Mrs. Kennedy down to the tarmac.[722]*

---

*In spite of all the planning for the landing, the ambulance is waiting there not by design but by order of Captain Robert Canada Jr., USN, commanding officer of Bethesda Naval Hospital. Canada, unaware of the role his hospital would play, had sent the navy ambulance to Andrews Air Force Base in case Lyndon Johnson, a navy veteran, whom Canada had treated after his massive heart attack in July 1955, had suffered another one. (Manchester, *Death of a President*, p.381)

Jackie Kennedy walks toward the navy ambulance. Clint Hill assumes she'll ride in the front seat, but she makes her way to the rear door. She tries to open it but can't. Fastened from the inside, the driver quickly reaches back to release the lock. She and Robert Kennedy climb into the back with General McHugh. Secret Service agent Bill Greer takes the wheel, while Kellerman, Paul Landis, and Dr. Burkley crowd into the front seat beside him.[723]

Still aboard the plane, President Johnson glances at a brief statement on the three-by-five card in his hand. The words were drafted in longhand by Liz Carpenter, the press attaché of Lady Bird Johnson, honed by LBJ aide Bill Moyers, and finally typed up for the president. Studying it on the plane, Johnson reversed the order of the last two sentences.

"Bird?" Johnson inquires of his wife. She is ready. Bareheaded in the freezing November cold, Lyndon Johnson, Lady Bird at his side, moves down the ramp into the glare of the airport and television lights, steps up to a podium encrusted with microphones, and speaks to the world for the first time as president of the United States, amid the deafening thwacking of helicopter rotors, which await the task of transporting the new president to his next destination.

"This is a sad time for all people," Johnson intones solemnly. "We have suffered a loss that cannot be weighed. For me it is a deep personal tragedy. I know the world shares the sorrow that Mrs. Kennedy and her family bear. I will do my best. That is all I can do. I ask for your help—and God's."[724]

Because of this event, television has taken on an important new dimension. In addition to meting out bits of new information about the day's events as the drama unfolds, it has now become a vehicle through which the nation's grief is both shared and amplified. NBC's cameras, filming people's reactions to the news on a New York street, caught a middle-aged woman in dark glasses and a fashionable hat at the moment the news of the president's death came over a nearby car radio. The woman jerked as though hit with a physical object, and cried out loudly in disbelief. Similar responses were caught on camera throughout America.[*]

ABC begins rerunning the footage shot by its Dallas affiliate at Love Field earlier that morning in the sparkling sunshine after the rain cleared, showing Jack Kennedy, trailed by Jackie, working his way along the fence to shake some of the hundreds of hands reaching out to him, his enjoyment so obviously unfeigned, his whole being seeming to exemplify a vibrant hope for the future.

"This," Jim Hagerty, former President Eisenhower's press secretary, says, commenting on the ABC footage, "is the president's way of saying thank you to the people. How can you stop it? I don't think you want to stop it . . . It's rather difficult, while guarding the president, to argue that you can't shake hands with the American people or ride in an open car where the people can see you."

In the world of television, where recording and rebroadcasting somehow erase the distinction between past and present, the event can be shown over and over again, but it remains tragically unstoppable.

Harry S. Truman, contacted in retirement in Missouri, is reported to be so upset he is unable to make a statement. Dwight D. Eisenhower feels not only shock and dismay but indignation. He angrily mentions this "occasional psychopathic thing" in the American people, but expresses his belief that it is nonetheless a nation "of great common sense" that will not be "stampeded or bewildered."

General Douglas McArthur says, "The president's death kills something in me."

Adlai Stevenson, speaking from the UN and for millions, says, "All men everywhere who love peace and justice and freedom will bow their heads," adding later, "It's too bad that, in my old age, they couldn't have spent their violence on me and spared this young man for our nation's work."

---

[*]In a large-sample national poll in March of 1964 by the National Opinion Research Center, an affiliate of the University of Chicago, an astonishing 53 percent of those interviewed said they had wept when they heard the news of Kennedy's death (*New York Times*, March 7, 1964, p.11). This percentage is remarkable by itself, and becomes even more so when you factor in the number of people who, though grieving as much, cannot bring tears to their eyes.

There's footage too of President Johnson being sworn in aboard Air Force One by Judge Hughes, with the stunned but dutiful widow of his predecessor at his side. The nation, as one, sees an orderly transition of government.

The network anchors—Ed Silverman and Ron Cochran of ABC, Bill Ryan, Chet Huntley, and Frank McGee of NBC, Charles Collingwood and Walter Cronkite of CBS—are addressing the largest television audience in history, unconsciously weaving—out of fact, history, and emotion—a shared experience that will hold the nation in its grip into an unforeseeable future.[725]

5:10 p.m.

In Irving, Texas, at the Paine residence, police are just about finished loading everything they have seized into the police cars.

It isn't quite clear to Ruth Paine whether she and Marina are under arrest or not, although it feels as though they are. Earlier, when the officers asked them, as well as Ruth's husband, Michael, to come down to the police station, Ruth, wanting to cooperate, had gone to see whether she could get a babysitter.

As Ruth left to walk next door to her neighbor's house, one of the police officers moved to accompany her.

"Oh," she said, "you don't have to go with me."

He said he would be glad to, and she told him to come along, but with a sinking feeling as she realized he was probably assigned to escort her. She called on Mrs. Roberts next door, but Mrs. Roberts was just on her way out and couldn't help. It was after school by that time, though, so Ruth went to another neighbor's house and managed to get one of her teenage daughters to come stay with the kids. As she came back to her own house, still under police escort, she saw the other officers carrying boxes of things from the house to their cars. In a backseat she spotted three cartons of phonograph records, her old 78s.

"You don't need those," she protested, "and I want to use them on Thanksgiving weekend. I promised to lead a folk dance conference that weekend. I'll need those records, which are all folk dance records, and I doubt that you'll get them back to me by then."

They paid no attention to her. The records went. She complained about her 16-millimeter projector too, but her escort took her by the arm and told her they were wasting "too much time."

The brusque treatment continued inside the house, and Ruth began to resent it more and more. Now, she changes from her slacks to a suit, but the officers prevent Marina from doing the same.

"She has a right to," Ruth explains to them icily, a note of proper Quaker decency in her voice. "She's a woman, she has a right to dress as she wishes before going." She tells Marina in Russian to go to the bathroom to change, but while Ruth is talking to the babysitter, one of the cops opens the bathroom door and tells Marina she has no time to change. Ruth's protests were useless. Marina, her emotions whipsawing, is suddenly angry. "I'm not a criminal," she says to herself. "I didn't do anything."

"We'd better get this straight in a hurry, Mrs. Paine," one of the officers says, "or we'll just take the children down and leave them with Juvenile while we talk to you."

Ruth doesn't take this lying down. She makes a point of saying to her daughter, who, unlike her son Christopher, was up and about, "Lynn, you may come too."

For the trip downtown Michael was put in another car, but Marina and Ruth, Lynn, Marina's little girl, and her baby were all jammed in together with three police officers.

Marina, who had been shaking all over with fright before they got into the car, calms down as they drive toward Dallas, and the two women speak quietly in Russian. One of the officers, Adamcik, tries a little Czech on them, but they don't understand him. Marina can tell how shaken Ruth is. Ruth had never ridden in a police car before, had never even envisioned doing so, and the experience is unnerving.

One of the officers in the front turns back to ask Ruth, "Are you a Communist?"

"No, I am not," she replies firmly, "and I don't even feel the need for the Fifth Amendment."[726]

On the trip downtown, Ruth Paine starts to be tormented by "if only" thoughts. If only she had known that Lee had hidden a rifle in her garage.

If only she had appraised him as someone capable of such terrible violence. If only the job she helped him find had not put him in a building overlooking the president's parade route. If only she had done a dozen things differently, the country might have been spared this tragedy, and Marina, whom she has come to love as a sister, would not have been made into an assassin's wife, bullied by overbearing policemen in a language she doesn't comprehend.

Ruth wonders whether her determination to look for the good in everyone prevented her from seeing Lee clearly. Just three days ago she learned that Lee was using a false name in his Dallas rooming house. How much truth was there in anything he ever told her? What sort of a man was he beyond the confines of Ruth's house, where he was simply Marina's husband and Junie's and Rachel's father?

Is it possible that he is a Soviet agent? She finds that impossible to believe. He's neither bright nor organized enough for such an assignment. Even if he had volunteered his services to the Russians, they wouldn't have accepted him, or they are bigger fools than she ever dreamed.[727]

5:26 p.m. (6:26 p.m. EST)

Just twenty-eight minutes after Air Force One landed at Andrews Air Force Base, a helicopter delivers President Johnson to the south lawn of the White House. The president, his wife, Secretary of Defense McNamara, and McGeorge Bundy, special adviser to the president, walk in the chilly night through the rose garden on the White House grounds on their way to the Oval Office. When they come to the french doors of the president's office, all stop except Johnson, who pauses, then walks in, alone, and stays for but a minute.

After Johnson closed the door behind him and exited the Oval Office, he and his party went across the street (West Executive Avenue, a blocked-off street across from the West Wing of the White House) to his vice presidential office on the second floor of the Executive Office Building, where congressional leaders from both parties stopped by to pledge their bipartisan support for the good of the grief-stricken nation.[728]

Before he meets with anyone though, the president takes the time to pen two notes to a little boy and a little girl, the first two letters of his presidency:

> Dear John—It will be many years before you understand fully what a great man your father was. His loss is a deep personal tragedy for all of us, but I wanted you particularly to know that I share your grief—You can always be proud of him.

He signs it "affectionately," as he does the next letter.

> Dearest Caroline—Your father's death has been a great tragedy for the Nation, as well as for you at this time.
> He was a wise and devoted man. You can always be proud of what he did for his country.

It is 7:30 p.m. as Lyndon Johnson hands the letters to his secretary, gets up, and goes out to the anteroom to meet the men upon whom the continuity of the government of the United States now depends.[729]

5:55 p.m. (6:55 p.m. EST)

It is near dusk as the presidential motorcade, having left Andrews at 6:10 p.m. EST, takes the Suitland Parkway to Bethesda. FBI agent James Sibert, in a car right behind the navy ambulance carrying the president's body, will never forget the sight of people lining the many bridges over the parkway, holding white handkerchiefs to their eyes. At 6:55 p.m., the navy ambulance with its escort of cars and motorcycle police arrives at Bethesda.[730]

By the time the navy ambulance with its escort of cars and motorcycle police arrives at the Bethesda hospital,[731] crowds, alerted by the television coverage of the arrival of the president's body at Andrews, are waiting silently. More than three thousand people have worked their way inside the grounds because of the hopelessly inadequate cordon improvised by Captain Robert Canada Jr., commanding officer of the hospital. Canada had only twenty-four Marine guards at his disposal, so he mobilized all of his off-duty corpsmen, but still hasn't got nearly enough men to keep the ever-growing crowd from surging toward the ambulance.[732] It's one solid mass of humanity, people standing shoulder to shoulder, between the semicircle drive in front of the hospital (which comes off Wisconsin Avenue and returns) and Wisconsin Avenue a few acres away.[733]

The ambulance, now joined by a sedan with a chaplain and nurses, sweeps up to the main entrance. Robert and Jacqueline Kennedy disembark and are met by Captain Canada, Rear Admiral Calvin Galloway, and a chaplain. After a brief exchange, Secret Service agents Clint Hill and Paul Landis accompany RFK and Mrs. Kennedy to one of the two VIP suites on the seventeenth floor of the hospital's high, stone tower.[734] Jackie had been expected to join her children, John-John and Caroline, before their bedtime and tell them of their father's death, but she decides instead to spend the night at the hospital so as not to leave her slain husband. Although the children were shielded from the news throughout the afternoon, Caroline will be told that evening and John Jr. sometime later (see later text).[735]

The hospital suite consists of three rooms—a bedroom and a kitchen facing each other across a small hallway, at the end of which was a long narrow drawing room. While it is comfortable enough, with air-conditioning, wall-to-wall carpeting, and a bedroom television, the walls, furniture, carpet, and drapes were depressing because of their lifeless and uniformly beige color. The entourage is met at the suite by the president's sister, Jean Kennedy Smith; Jacqueline's mother and stepfather, Janet and Hugh Auchincloss; and Ben Bradlee, Washington bureau chief of *Newsweek* and a longtime friend of the president and his family, along with his wife, Toni. Secret Service agents Hill and Landis move quickly to secure the entire floor, taking control of communications and making sure that no one will be allowed to enter without authorization. Since Mrs. Kennedy is determined to wait until the autopsy is over, they know it's going to be a long night.[736]

An overnight bag and makeup case with Jackie's initials, J.B.K. (B is for Bouvier, Jackie's maiden name), on it are brought to Jackie, but both remain unopened in the long hours ahead. Among the friends

who will come to the seventeenth floor to try to console her are political columnist Charles Bartlett and his wife, Martha. It was they who
had contrived to introduce Jackie to JFK at a dinner party in their
Georgetown home in May of 1951. At the time, Jackie was a Georgetown socialite with blue-blood roots (like JFK, her schooling had been
at the best private schools—Miss Porter's, Vassar, the Sorbonne in
Paris) who was excited to be working as an "inquiring photographer"
and celebrity reporter about town for the *Washington Times-Herald*,
and he was a young, dashing war hero who was a member of the House
of Representatives from Massachusetts.[737] It wouldn't be until September of 1953, when JFK had become a U.S. senator, that the two would
wed in Newport, Rhode Island, *the most* correct social address at the
time. A church ceremony attended by over three thousand guests was
followed by a grand, *beau monde* reception at Hammersmith Farm, an
estate overlooking Narragansett Bay. JFK may have been twelve years
her senior (ages thirty-four and twenty-two at the time they met two
years earlier), but Jackie would later say, "I took the choicest bachelor
in the Senate." Few would disagree that by the time JFK was elected
president, "Jack and Jackie were America's royal couple."[738]

Below the seventeenth floor, at the main entrance, Larry O'Brien,
Kenny O'Donnell, General McHugh, and other members of the
Kennedy party are standing in front of the hospital talking. The navy
ambulance carrying the president's body is nearby, with Secret Service
agent Bill Greer still in the driver's seat. Secret Service agent Roy Kellerman has gotten out and gone in to find out where the entrance to the
morgue is located.[739] After several minutes, Baltimore FBI agents James
W. Sibert and Francis X. O'Neill Jr., who had been ordered to accompany the procession from Andrews Air Force Base, witness the autopsy,
take custody of any bullets retrieved from the president's body, and
deliver them to the FBI laboratory,[740] approach the group of men and ask
what the delay is all about. Larry O'Brien says they don't know where the
autopsy room is. The FBI men tell them to follow them around to the
rear of the hospital.

When the caravan reaches the morgue entrance, Secret Service agent

Roy Kellerman comes out onto the rear loading dock. FBI agents Sibert and O'Neill approach him and identify themselves and their mission.

"Yes, I've already been informed," he tells them and moves down the stairs toward the rear of the ambulance, where Secret Service agent Bill Greer waits. First Lieutenant Samuel R. Bird's honor guards quickly assemble and help Secret Service and FBI agents pull the casket out of the back of the ambulance and onto a conveyance cart, and shuffle it toward the steps leading to the small landing at the rear door.[741] At the base of the stairs, the cart is abandoned and the casket is hand-carried up to the loading-dock entrance.[742] Along the way, General McHugh insists on helping to carry the commander in chief into the hospital and relieves one of the casket team members. One end of the casket dips precariously as General McHugh struggles to carry his share of the weight.[743] Just inside the loading-dock entrance, the team returns the casket to the cart and wheels it a short distance down the corridor toward a naval attendant holding open a double-door marked "Restricted—Authorized Personnel Only."

The Bethesda Naval Hospital morgue is stark and spotless. It was newly renovated just four months earlier. They enter an anteroom equipped with eight refrigerated lockers labeled "Remains." To their right is a swinging-type double-door, with glass panels, that leads to the main room where the autopsies are performed. The tiled autopsy room is lined with equipment specialized for postmortem work: scales, a sterilizer, a washing machine, and a power saw. Situated near the center of the room are two eight-foot-long, stainless-steel autopsy tables, their tops perforated with hundreds of drain holes that feed into pipes set in the floor. Against one wall, on a two-step riser, is a small gallery section that contains a short tier of bleacher-style benches, enough for thirty to forty medical students and young doctors to observe autopsies being performed. This night, the students and young doctors are absent.[744]

The casket team rolls the casket through the doors into the autopsy room and veers to the left, where they come face-to-face with Drs. Humes and Boswell and several other Bethesda personnel dressed in surgical garb, who direct the team to move the casket next to autopsy table number one.[745] Major General Wehle orders his aide, Richard Lipsey, "not to leave the body for any reason,"[746] as Lieutenant Sam Bird's casket team takes up guard duty outside the two entrances to the autopsy room, with the assistance of a detachment of marines.[747]

5:57 p.m.

Detectives Stovall, Rose, and Adamcik march Michael and Ruth Paine and Marina Oswald and her two small children up to the third floor to Homicide and Robbery's outer office. They are unaware that Lee Oswald sits a few feet away, behind the closed venetian blinds of Captain Fritz's private office. It is near bedlam in the homicide office, full of the noise of incoming telephone calls and constant traffic. Within a few minutes, the detectives move them to the Forgery Bureau office next door, to get away from the congestion of homicide.

After getting the Paines and Marina Oswald settled and calling for an interpreter, Detectives Stovall and Rose turn their attention to locating Wesley Frazier. If for no other reason than that he had driven Oswald to work that day and his present whereabouts are unknown, Frazier has become a suspect. Although they'd been told that Frazier was at Parkland Hospital visiting his ailing father, it takes the detectives nearly forty-five minutes to determine that he is actually at the Irving Professional Center, a medical facility. The detectives telephone the Irving Police Department and make arrangements for Frazier to be arrested.[748]

6:16 p.m.

In the fourth-floor crime lab, Lieutenant Carl Day examines the rifle carefully, looking for fingerprints that the gunman might have left behind. Captain Fritz walks in and tells Day that Marina Oswald has arrived[*] and is downstairs in the Forgery Bureau office.

"I want her to look at the rifle and see if she can identify it," Fritz says.

---

[*]Despite Marina's suspicion that her husband had murdered the president, as she walked past the media at police headquarters upon her arrival, she said loyally, "Lee good man—he no shoot anyone" (*JFK/Deep Politics Quarterly*, April 2006, p.8).

"But there's an awful mob down there. I don't want to bring her through that crowd. Can you bring the rifle down there?"

"I'm still working with the prints," Day replies, "but I think I can carry it down there without disturbing them."

In a minute, Day is ready and the two of them make their way down-stairs. When they get to the third floor, Day hoists the rifle high over his head and wades into the throng of reporters, who shout questions, "Is that the rifle? What kind is it? Who made it?"

Day says nothing as Fritz clears the way to the Forgery office. They step inside and close the door, shutting out the maddening noise. Marina Oswald is there, holding an infant daughter. Ruth and Michael Paine sit nearby with Detectives Senkel and Adamcik and Russian interpreter Ilya A. Mamantov.[749]

Lieutenant Day shows Marina the rifle as Fritz asks through the inter-preter whether this is the rifle her husband owns. Marina says it looks like it, they both have dark wood, but she can't be sure. She only saw the stock and can't remember if it had a telescopic sight. To her, all guns look the same.[750]

As the two detectives prepare to take affidavits from Marina Oswald and the Paines, Captain Fritz and Lieutenant Day push back into the sea of reporters in the outer hall. Fritz heads back to his office, while Day, rifle again lofted over his head, slowly makes his way toward the elevators that will take him and the weapon back to the crime lab.

At the corner of Commerce and Harwood, two detectives wait patiently for Piedmont bus number 50. Just a few minutes earlier, the bus transfer found in Oswald's pocket was traced to the driver of that bus, Cecil McWatters. The detectives have orders to intercept the bus and bring the driver to City Hall. When it arrives as scheduled, McWatters is shocked to find that two potential passengers are, in fact, police. They tell him they want to ask him a few questions and escort the befuddled bus driver into police headquarters. Once inside, they show him the bus transfer found in Oswald's pocket.

"Do you know anything about this?" they ask.

McWatters surely does. He's absolutely positive that he issued the transfer, number 004459, on the Lakewood run about one o'clock that afternoon, give or take fifteen minutes. Each driver has a distinctive punch mark, registered with the company, and McWatters recognizes the crescent shape mark as one made by his hand punch. He even takes his hand punch out of his pocket and punches a sheet of paper to prove it. McWatters also remembers that he only gave out two transfers on that run, both at the same stop, the first to a lady and the second to a young man who got off right after her.[751]

6:20 p.m.

Captain Fritz enters the homicide office where Detective Jim Leavelle informs him that downstairs he's got two eyewitnesses from a car lot near the Tippit shooting who are ready to view Oswald in a lineup.

"Good," Fritz tells him. "Have the bus driver take a look at him too."

Detectives Sims, Boyd, and Hall lead Oswald out of the office and wade into the madhouse of reporters in the outer corridor. As the door closes behind them, Fritz walks over to Jim Allen, a former assistant DA now in private practice, and Secret Service agent Forrest Sorrels. The agent tells Fritz that he has a witness he has talked to and that he would very much like for him to get a chance to see Oswald in a lineup.

"That'll be fine," Fritz says.

Sorrels turns to Secret Service agent William Patterson and asks him to track down Howard Brennan and bring him to City Hall.[752]

6:30 p.m.

The lights are dim in the back half of the basement detail room at Dallas police headquarters in anticipation of the second lineup police are about to conduct. Ted Callaway, the manager of Dootch Motors in Oak Cliff, one of his porters, Sam Guinyard, and bus driver Cecil McWatters wait nervously as police make the last-minute preparations. Detective Leavelle leans over toward Callaway and speaks in hushed tones.

"When I show you these guys, be sure, take your time, see if you can make a positive identification," Leavelle says. "We want to try to wrap him up real tight on killing this officer. We think he is the same one that shot the president. But if we can wrap him up tight on killing this officer, we have got him."[753] Callaway steps to the back of the detail room so he can view the lineup from a distance similar to the distance from which he had seen the gunman on Patton Street. When everything is ready, Detectives Sims, Boyd, and Hall march the shackled men onto the brightly lit stage—the same men, in the same order as the first lineup.[754] As soon as Oswald comes out, Callaway recognizes him. No doubt about it. Detective Sims puts the men through the routine—turn left, face forward, then answer a few brief questions so the witnesses can hear them speak.[755] Detective Leavelle walks over to Callaway, "Which one do you think it was?"

"He's the number 2 man," Callaway says firmly.

Sam Guinyard agrees. Number 2 is the man he saw run past him while he was waxing and polishing a station wagon.[756]

Bus driver Cecil McWatters is less certain. There's one man in the lineup, number 2 (Oswald), who is about the same height, weight, and complexion as the person who got on his bus, but he tells the police he cannot make a positive identification.[757]

As the four men are led off stage, Detective Leavelle takes Ted Callaway and Sam Guinyard up to the crime lab on the fourth floor, where they both identify the light gray Eisenhower-style jacket found in the parking lot behind the Texaco station as the one the man they saw was wearing.[758]

6:35 p.m. (7:35 p.m. EST)

At the Bethesda Naval Hospital morgue, autopsy pathologists Drs. Humes and Boswell open the bronze casket and find the naked body of John F. Kennedy wrapped in a bloody sheet labeled "Parkland Hospital," lying on a heavy-gauge clear plastic sheet, placed there to prevent the corpse from soiling the satin interior of the coffin. An additional wrapping, soaked in blood, envelops the president's shattered head.[759] Paul K. O'Connor and James Curtis Jenkins, student lab technicians in charge of the admission and discharge of morgue bodies, lift the body out of the casket and place it on the autopsy table, where the bloody wrappings are removed.[760]* In spite of his training, Dr. Humes is still shocked by the sight of the president's body. His eyes are open, one lid hanging lower than the other. His mouth is also open, in sort of a grimace, his hands are knotted in fists, and there is a ghastly head wound. Still, the well-known facial features are intact and Dr. Humes can't help but think that apart from the horrible head wound, John Kennedy, who is only a few years older than he is, looks perfectly normal. In fact, at a little over six feet and 170 pounds, Kennedy was "a remarkable human specimen," he would later put it, who "looked as if he could have lived forever."[761] Humes shrugs off the moment of hypnotic shock and fascination, reminding himself there is a lot of work to do.

Several of the nearly two-dozen people in attendance,† particularly the

---

*Dr. Boswell said Humes was "afraid the sheets would end up in somebody's barn on Highway 66 as exhibits" and immediately threw them into the morgue washing machine to be laundered (ARRB MD 26, Memorandum, Andy Purdy to Jim Kelly and Kenneth Klein, August 17, 1977, Notes of interview with Dr. J. Thornton Boswell, pp.2–3; ARRB Transcript of Proceedings, Deposition of Dr. J. Thornton Boswell, February 26, 1996, p.14).

†FBI agents O'Neill and Sibert noted the following were in attendance at the beginning of the autopsy: Admiral Calvin B. Galloway, USN, commanding officer of the U.S. Naval Medical Center, Bethesda; Captain John H. Stover, commanding officer, U.S. Naval Medical School; Admiral George G. Burkley, USN, the president's personal physician; Commander James J. Humes, chief pathologist; Commander J. Thornton Boswell, chief of pathology at Bethesda; Jan G. Rudnicki, laboratory assistant to Dr. Boswell; John T. Stringer Jr., medical photographer; John H. Ebersole, assistant chief radiologist at Bethesda; Floyd A. Riebe, medical photographer; Paul K. O'Connor, laboratory technologist; James Curtis Jenkins, laboratory technologist; Jerrol F. Custer, X-ray technician; Edward F. Reed, X-ray technician; James E. Metzler, hospital corpsman, third-class; and Secret Service agents Roy Kellerman, William Greer, and John J. O'Leary (who stayed only briefly) (ARRB MD 44, FBI Report of O'Neill and Sibert, November 26, 1963, p.2). Admiral George Burkley reported that Admiral Edward Kenney, the surgeon general of the navy; Captain Robert O. Canada, commanding officer of Bethesda Naval Hospital; and Brigadier General Godfrey McHugh, air force aide to the president, were also present when the president's body was moved to the autopsy table (NARA Record 189-10001-10048, Report of George Burkley, November 27, 1963, 8:45 a.m., p.7, ARRB MD 48). During the course of the autopsy Pierre A. Finck, chief of the wound ballistics pathology branch at Walter Reed medical center, arrived to assist Humes and Boswell. In addition, Lieutenant Commander Gregory H. Cross, resident in surgery, and Captain David Osborne, chief of surgery, entered the autopsy room. (ARRB MD 44, FBI Report of O'Neill and Sibert, November 26, 1963, p.2) At one point, Major General Philip C. Wehle, commanding officer of the U.S. Military District of

military officers in command of the naval hospital, retreat to the benches in the gallery as Drs. Humes and Boswell begin an initial examination of the body.[762] In addition to the cutdowns (i.e., small incisions for the insertion of tubes) on the arms, ankles, and chest, Dr. Humes notes a tracheotomy incision in the throat. The body is then rolled briefly onto its side and Humes notes a bullet wound in the president's right upper back. As they complete the initial examination, Admiral Burkley reminds the pathologists that the president's brother and wife are waiting upstairs and that they should expedite the autopsy procedure.

"They've captured the guy who did this, all we need is the bullet," Burkley tells them.

Drs. Humes and Boswell disagree. They feel a complete and thorough autopsy is needed. A discussion ensues, one that Burkley ultimately wins—for the moment.[763]

Dr. Humes requests that all nonmedical personnel leave the autopsy room and retire to the adjacent anteroom so that X-rays and photographs of the body can be made.[764] At Humes's instruction, medical photographer John T. Stringer Jr. begins taking photographs of the body from a variety of angles in both color and black-and-white, being careful to bracket the exposures* of the large (four-by-five-inch) images.

As soon as the photographs are complete, John H. Ebersole, assistant chief radiologist at Bethesda Naval Hospital, begins taking X-rays of the president's skull, with help from X-ray technicians Jerrol F. Custer and

---

Washington, D.C., entered the autopsy room to make arrangements with the Secret Service regarding the transportation of the president's body back to the White House. Near the end of the autopsy, Chester H. Boyers, chief petty officer in charge of the pathology division, entered the room to type up receipts for items given to the FBI and Secret Service. At the end of the autopsy, John VanHoesen, Edwin Stroble, Thomas E. Robinson, and Joe Hagan (personnel from Gawler's Funeral Home) prepared the president's body for burial. Also in attendance at that time were Brigadier General Godfrey McHugh and Dr. George Bakeman, USN. (ARRB MD 44, FBI Report of O'Neill and Sibert, November 26, 1963, pp.2–3) The HSCA also noted that Richard A. Lipsey, personal aide to General Wehle, and Samuel A. Bird were also present at various times (7 HSCA 9).

*This is a standard practice in professional photography wherein each angle is photographed three times at three different exposures—one slightly underexposed, one slightly overexposed, and one at the presumed proper exposure setting—ensuring that at least one of the three images will be perfectly exposed.

Edward F. Reed. Unlike the autopsy photographs, which will not be developed until after the autopsy is completed, the X-rays, which see what the eye cannot, are developed in the hospital's fourth-floor lab and returned to the morgue a quarter of an hour later for viewing.[765]

6:40 p.m.
Assistant Dallas DA Bill Alexander pushes through the crowd in the third-floor hallway of Dallas police headquarters.

After completing the search of Oswald's Beckley room, Alexander had returned to his office and, believing there was more than enough evidence to conclude that Oswald had murdered Officer Tippit, filled in the blanks on State of Texas Form No. 141, a form denominated an "AFFIDAVIT" but referred to by all in Texas as a criminal complaint. In clear hand printing, he charged that Oswald "did . . . voluntarily and with malice aforethought kill J. D. Tippitt [*sic*] by shooting him with a gun." Gathering up some additional blank affidavits, Alexander beats a path over to police headquarters.

Now, Alexander raps lightly on Captain Fritz's private office door and steps in. Fritz is grilling Oswald as a few Dallas police officers stand against the wall, their eyes fixed on the homicide captain's prey. "What struck me about Oswald," Alexander, who did not take part in the questioning, says, "is that even under the circumstances he found himself in, he was in control of himself and acted like he was in control of the situation. It was almost as if everything he said had been pre-rehearsed by him. He was quite skillful in deflecting questions, often answering questions with other questions. He was very arrogant and defiant with Fritz. I would say his whole behavior was completely inappropriate to the situation. You ought not to be ugly to the man [Fritz] who has the option to prosecute you." Alexander said that Fritz was very courteous with Oswald, as he always was with all defendants. "I was very pissed off at Oswald because of his having killed Kennedy and Tippit, but even if he was only in there for spitting on the sidewalk, I was so infuriated with him for his insolence to Fritz [someone, Alexander says, he had feelings about almost like those he had for his father], I felt like beating the s——

out of him. Oswald didn't know this. I kept my composure. But I didn't like that little son of a bitch."[766]

Not too far into this latest round of questioning, Oswald suddenly says he doesn't want to talk any further without first talking to a lawyer. "You can have an attorney anytime you like," Fritz tells him.

"I'd like Mr. [John] Abt, in New York, to represent me," Oswald says. "He represented people who were charged with violating the Smith Act.* I don't know him personally, but that is the lawyer I want. However, I don't have any money to call him."

"That won't be a problem," Fritz replies. "Just call collect. We allow all prisoners to use the phone."

Fritz tells the two detectives present to be sure that Oswald has a chance to use the telephone.[767]†

Alexander nods to Fritz that he wants to talk to him privately. The homicide captain instructs the Dallas detectives to take Oswald out to the little holding room off Fritz's office, while Fritz and Alexander remain behind.

"I've got the complaint for Oswald on shooting Officer Tippit," Alexander says, knowing that the Dallas police have more than enough to file charges. Although he doesn't need Fritz's approval to file the complaint, he seeks his support. "I'm ready to go when you are."‡

Fritz nods in agreement. Indeed, the evidence is already substantial in

---

*Oswald was referring to an antisedition law enacted in 1940 to combat the threat of global Communism that prohibited advocating the overthrow of the U.S. government "by force or violence." Abt, himself a member of the Communist Party, won his biggest victory in 1965 when the U.S. Supreme Court held that the nation's 1950 Internal Security Act (commonly called the McCarran Act), which required that all Communists and Communist organizations register with the federal government, was unconstitutional because it violated the Fifth Amendment's right against self-incrimination. (*Albertson v. Subversive Activities Control Board*, 382 U.S. 70 [1965]; *Los Angeles Times*, August 14, 1991, p.A14)

†Despite Captain Fritz's instructions, there is no record that Oswald made any attempts to contact Attorney Abt in New York on November 22.

‡When I asked Alexander if at that time he also believed Oswald had killed Kennedy, he responded, "Yeah. We felt it was clear that the same person who killed Tippit killed Kennedy. That's why he killed Tippit, because he was stopped while in flight from Kennedy's murder. It was pretty obvious to all of us—I don't remember anyone that was thinking otherwise—that Oswald had committed both murders" (Interview of William Alexander by author on December 11, 2000).

the Tippit case. They tick it off to each other. They know Oswald took a bus to his room in Oak Cliff—they found the transfer he was issued. His landlady can testify that he came in about one o'clock, changed clothes, and left a couple of minutes later in a big hurry. He admits he picked up his pistol at the room. They have an eyewitness to the Tippit shooting, Mrs. Helen Markham, who identified Oswald in a lineup. Two other eyewitnesses—Ted Callaway and Sam Guinyard—who saw Oswald running from the scene also picked him out of a lineup. He resisted arrest at the Texas Theater, attempting to shoot the arresting officer. And the revolver he had in his possession at the time of his arrest is the same caliber as the one used to kill Officer Tippit.

"All in all, that's a lot of good evidence," Fritz says.[768] A call is put in immediately to have Justice of the Peace David Johnston come to police headquarters for the arraignment of Oswald on the Tippit murder charge.

6:50 p.m.
Across the hall from Captain Fritz's office, Lieutenant T. P. Wells answers the telephone. The caller is Barbara Davis, an eyewitness in the Tippit murder case, who says her sister-in-law, Virginia Davis, found a .38 caliber shell in their yard after police left this afternoon. "Okay, we'll be right out," the lieutenant tells her. He hangs up and instructs Detectives C. N. Dhority and C. W. Brown to drive out to Oak Cliff and retrieve the shell.[769]

Secret Service agent Forrest Sorrels informs Captain Fritz that eyewitness Howard Brennan has been located and is at police headquarters now and ready to view Oswald in a lineup. "I wish he would have been here a little sooner," Fritz tells Sorrels. "We just got through with a lineup. But we will get another one fixed up."[770] Fritz stops Detectives Brown and Dhority as they head out the door and instructs them to bring the Davis women back with them, get a statement, and arrange for them to also view Oswald in a lineup.[771]

7:00 p.m. (8:00 p.m. EST)
At Bethesda Naval Hospital, Humes and Boswell, followed by a flock of FBI, Secret Service, and navy personnel, retreat to a small alcove

within the autopsy room and snap the newly developed X-rays of the president's head up on a light box. Thirty or forty white specks can be seen scattered throughout the right hemisphere of the brain, like stars in a galaxy. These dustlike metallic particles mark the path of the missile as it passed through the right side of the skull. The largest fragment of metal, still much too small to represent any significant part of a whole bullet, lies behind the right frontal sinus. The next-largest fragment is embedded in the rear of the skull.[772] Humes figures that he can probably retrieve the two larger fragments but is beginning to wonder if it might be a good idea to have an expert in wound ballistics present during the autopsy. He and Boswell confer briefly away from the group. Humes mentions the offer of assistance made by the Armed Forces Institute of Pathology (AFIP) and suggests they take it. Boswell agrees and suggests they contact Lieutenant Colonel Pierre A. Finck, chief of the Wound Ballistics Pathology Branch of the AFIP, whom Boswell had worked with before.[773] Boswell remembers him as sharp, hard-working, and a top-notch forensic pathologist.[774] Humes is convinced and places a telephone call to Finck's home, asking the pathologist to come to the Bethesda morgue at once.[775]

7:04 p.m.

Police Chief Curry enters Captain Fritz's office and finds Fritz, Assistant DA Alexander, and Justice of the Peace Johnston. "How's the case coming?" he asks.

"We're getting ready to file on him for the shooting of the officer," Fritz replies.

"What about the assassination?" Curry asks.

"I strongly suspect that he was the assassin of the president," Fritz says. As Curry leaves, Fritz reads over and signs complaint number F-153 charging Lee Harvey Oswald with the murder of Officer J. D. Tippit. Bill Alexander also affixes his signature to the complaint and a minute later files it—not with the clerk of the court, but by merely handing it to Judge Johnston.[776]

7:10 p.m.

Detectives Sims, Boyd, and Hall march Oswald back into Captain Fritz's private office. The door closes behind them, stifling the noise of the outer office. Oswald faces Captain Fritz, Bill Alexander, David Johnston, and at least one FBI agent.[777]

"Mr. Oswald, we're here to arraign you on the charge of murder in the death of Officer J. D. Tippit," Judge Johnston says.

"Arraignment!" Oswald snarls. "This isn't a court. You can't arraign me in a police station. I can only be arraigned in a courtroom. How do I know this is a judge?"

Alexander thinks the suspect "is the most arrogant person" he has ever met and tells him, in no uncertain terms, to "shut up and listen." Oswald complies, but not before snapping back, "The way you're treating me, I'd might as well be in Russia."[778]

Johnston opens the complaint form and tells Oswald that he is charged in the complaint with having "unlawfully, voluntarily, and with malice afore-thought killed J. D. Tippit by shooting him with a gun" earlier that day.[779]

Oswald mumbles a stream of sarcastic, impudent little things.[780]

Johnston advises Oswald of his constitutional right to remain silent and warns him that any statement he makes may be used in evidence against him for the charges stated. "You'll be given the opportunity to contact an attorney," Johnston says as he completes the formalities. "Bond [bail] is denied on this capital offense. I hereby remand you to the custody of the sheriff of Dallas County, Texas."[781] In most states, the defendant pleads guilty or not guilty to the complaint at the time of the arraignment. In the few situations where he declines, the court enters a plea of not guilty for him. But in Texas, even to this day, a defendant is not even asked to plead to the complaint, and Oswald did not plead not guilty to the charge of murder against him.[782]

7:15 p.m.

Robert Oswald walks into Dallas City Hall at the Harwood Street entrance (106 South Harwood), where one enters the headquarters of the Dallas Police Department. Robert, intending to go to the third-floor

Homicide and Robbery Bureau, mistakenly takes an elevator to a different floor and approaches a police officer who is eating supper out of a paper bag at his desk.

"Could you tell me where I could find the officer in charge of the homicide division?" he asks. "I'm Robert Oswald, Lee Oswald's brother."

The officer's expression changes immediately. He jumps up, dropping his sandwich on the desk, mumbles a few words, then regains control and says, "Let me call Captain Fritz."

After leaving his office in Denton, Texas, earlier in the afternoon, Robert had driven home and told his wife Vada that he planned to drive to Dallas and that she should take their children to her parents' farm outside Fort Worth, where they would be safe. He was worried about someone retaliating against anyone who knew Lee.

Robert then called the Acme company office in Fort Worth and told them of his plans to go to Dallas, and they told him that the FBI had been out there looking for him and wanted him to contact them. He arrived at a quarter after five at the Federal Building and spent the next two hours being interviewed by Dallas FBI agents interested in finding out what he knew about his brother's recent activities. Robert couldn't help them much, he hadn't seen Lee since the previous November. When he asked to see Lee, an agent said, "We don't have any jurisdiction over your brother," and tells Robert he'll have to go to City Hall and speak to Captain Will Fritz in the Homicide and Robbery Bureau of the Dallas Police Department. Now, Robert waits to see the man in charge.

The officer finally puts the phone down. He can't get through, so he offers to take Robert up to the third floor. As they wait for an elevator, Robert reaches into his hip pocket for a handkerchief. The officer flinches. Robert senses what the officer is thinking and freezes—then slowly withdraws his hand clutching the handkerchief. Robert suddenly realizes just how tense the situation is in Dallas.[783]

District Attorney Henry Wade marvels at the amount of reporters—it seems like three hundred—who have managed to shoehorn themselves into the small, narrow third-floor corridor outside the Homicide and Robbery office. Wade was on his way to dinner with his wife and some friends when he decided to stop by police headquarters to see how the investigation was progressing. He fights his way through the press and into the homicide office, where he learns from his assistant, Bill Alexander, that they had filed on Oswald for the Tippit murder.[784] Shouldering back through the crowd, he makes his way to the administrative offices, where Chief Curry sits behind his desk.

Wade is not surprised that Curry knows so little about how the case is coming. Relations between Fritz and Curry are better than they were with Curry's predecessor, but Fritz, as usual, is determined to run his own one-man show.

Wade himself has no power at all over the police. Under the city charter, the police are responsible to the city manager, not the district attorney. All of Wade's assistant prosecutors—Bill Alexander in particular—work closely with the police, but his office has no authority over them. For the moment, Wade and Curry are equally helpless.

Chief Curry slides Jack Revill's memo (the one saying the FBI had advance knowledge that Oswald was "capable of committing the assassination") across the desk to the district attorney.

"What do you think about that?" Curry asks.

Jack Revill is, to Wade's mind, one of the brightest of the young Dallas police officers, but his memo is highly disturbing.

"What are you going to do with it?" Wade asks.

"I don't know," Curry replies.[785]

Even in the midst of the catastrophe it's a bombshell. Curry knows that the security of the president depends not just on the Secret Service, which has the primary responsibility, but on the closest possible cooperation between the Secret Service and the FBI as well as local police authorities. Revill's memo suggests that someone wasn't playing ball, and both men know that a firestorm of public recrimination between the FBI and the Dallas Police Department is not the kind of press the city fathers are going to want to see. Wade is an astute politician. He knows that the press and public will be looking around for someone to blame. Historically, relations between the FBI and local police have never been easy, and this won't make them any easier.

Although the chief of police doesn't have to stand for reelection as Wade does, his position is scarcely less political. The son of a Dallas policeman who became a Baptist preacher, Jesse E. Curry attended police school without pay to get on the force during the Depression, then worked his way up through the ranks, finally becoming chief in January 1960, less than four years ago. He played a key role in the integration of the Dallas public schools in the fall of 1961, demonstrating his talent for careful advance planning. He works long and hard and is proud of his department, constantly fretting about the lack of manpower—1,123 men covering a vast area and a population of over half a million—and adequate equipment. Most of his men, finding it tough to live on their $370-a-month base pay, are moonlighting. Even Curry's annual salary is only $17,500—after twenty-seven years with the department.[786]

Curry is reluctant to make waves, careful of his relationship with city officials. He's even more sensitive, as is Wade, to the desires of the real powers in the city, the Dallas Citizens Council—the elite group of business and social leaders who largely control the city's destiny, and who always have the city's image in mind. Perhaps that is why Curry hasn't moved forcefully to control the melee of pressmen and their din, wanting to demonstrate to the worldwide press that the Dallas Police Department is willing to cooperate to the fullest extent, even under conditions of dire emergency. There's little question that the assassination has put Curry under a tremendous amount of pressure, from all sides.

At the moment there is little Wade can do to console the police chief.

"I'll see you later," Wade tells him and heads out for dinner.

Robert Oswald follows the police officer as he leads him through the dense crowd of reporters on the third floor. No one is paying attention to either one of them, even though the officer occasionally bellows, "Where's Captain Fritz?" Finally, someone points toward the end of the corridor. The two men squeeze through the crowd until they come face-to-face with Captain Fritz. The homicide captain looks coldly at Robert after the officer whispers an introduction.

"I'm tied up right now," Fritz says, "but I do want to talk with you later. I think your mother is still here." Fritz tells the officer to take Robert down to where Mrs. Oswald is waiting.[787] (This is the only meeting Robert Oswald has with Fritz, who never gets around to questioning him.)

The two men make their way back through the crowded hallway and enter the Burglary and Theft Bureau, where Robert finds his mother along with two *Fort Worth Star-Telegram* reporters and two FBI agents. "I see you found me," Marguerite Oswald says, rising from her chair.

The FBI men have barely finished introducing themselves when Mrs. Oswald interrupts and asks to speak to her son alone. The agents show them to an empty office. As soon as they enter the room, Marguerite leans toward him and whispers, "This room is bugged. Be careful what you say." The comment annoys Robert, but doesn't surprise him. All his life Robert has heard his mother talking about conspiracies, hidden motives, and the maliciousness of others, and has long since discounted most of what she says.

"Listen," Robert says to his mother, not bothering to lower his voice, "I don't care whether the room is bugged or not. I'd be perfectly willing to say anything I've got to say right there in the doorway. If you know anything about what happened, I want to know it right now. I don't want to hear any whys, ifs, or wherefores."

His words don't seem to register. As Robert learned by the time he was four years old, Marguerite has the ability to block out whatever she doesn't want to hear. Apparently forgetting her own words of warning about the room being bugged, she sets out her belief that Lee, whatever he had done, was carrying out official orders. Ever since his defection to Russia, Marguerite has been convinced that Lee is some sort of secret agent, recruited by the U.S. government while in the Marine Corps, and thereafter sent on mysterious and dangerous missions.[788]

But there is something else about his mother now that gives Robert a sickening feeling. It is evident to him that his mother is not really crushed at all by the terrible charges against Lee. If anything, he senses she seems

actually gratified at the attention she's receiving. She has always had an
inflated sense of her own ability and importance, a trait reflected in her
son Lee. But her quarrelsome nature and limited work skills have created
instead a life of obscurity. Now, she seems to instantly recognize that she
will never again be treated as an ordinary, unimportant woman.[789]

7:28 p.m.
FBI agent Manning C. Clements steps into the homicide office and
spots fellow agent James Bookhout. Clements has been at police headquarters since one o'clock when, under instructions from his supervisor, he had offered the assistance of the FBI in the investigation of the
president's assassination. For the last several hours he has been acting
as a liaison, relaying instructions to the other agents on the premises.[790]

Clements approaches Bookhout and asks if anyone from the bureau has
gotten a detailed physical description of Oswald, and more importantly,
questioned him in depth about his background. Bookhout tells him no
(though Captain Fritz *has* obtained some background information on
Oswald), and suggests that Clements do it. Clements seeks out Captain
Fritz and asks if there is any objection to his interviewing Oswald to get
this information.

"I've got no objection," Fritz says.

Clements enters Captain Fritz's office and finds Oswald seated and
two detectives—Hall and Boyd—standing guard nearby.[791]

The FBI agent introduces himself, shows Oswald his credentials,
advises him of his right to an attorney, and explains his purpose for being
there. Oswald is slightly haughty, but cooperative. Clements proceeds to
elicit biographical information from Oswald—date and place of birth,
height, weight, and other personal data. He then turns to the obviously
fictitious Selective Service card found in Oswald's wallet.

Clements can tell the card is a fake because of the photograph
mounted on it, something not contained on an authentic Selective Service card, and the number of obvious erasures made in typing the information on it. Besides, the card is in the name of "Alek James Hidell," but
bears Oswald's photograph.[792]

Asked about the purpose of the card, Oswald refuses to answer.

Ten minutes into the interview, the door to the office opens and Detective Sims tells the agent that Oswald is needed downstairs.[793] They lead Oswald once again out into the crush of reporters. Flashbulbs pop and questions are hurled in waves at the prisoner as reporters press in. As the detectives struggle to move Oswald toward the jail elevators, Oswald seizes the moment to exploit his situation.

"These people here have given me a hearing without legal representation," Oswald, referring to his arraignment, says into a microphone shoved in his direction.

"Did you shoot the president?" a reporter asks.

"I didn't shoot anybody," Oswald replies. "No, sir."[794]

7:30 p.m. (8:30 p.m. EST)

At the Bethesda Naval Hospital, a hot white light illuminates the hands of the two pathologists huddled over the body of the late president. In the interests of time, Dr. Humes decided not to wait for Lieutenant Colonel Finck to arrive at Bethesda. Instead, he and Dr. Boswell set about the task of recovering the two largest bullet fragments seen in the X-rays of the president's skull. The hole in the right side of the head was immense (over five inches in its greatest diameter), making access to the brain relatively easy. Portions of the skull, literally shattered by the force of the bullet, fall apart in the hands of the two pathologists as they try to reach the minute fragments behind the right eye and near the back of the skull.[795] Both are recovered, placed into a glass jar with a black metal top, and turned over later in the evening to FBI agents for transport to the FBI laboratory.[796]* To remove the brain, Humes and Boswell use a scalpel to extend the lacerations of the scalp downward toward the ears. Normally, a saw would be used to cut the skullcap and remove the brain. Here, the damage is so devastating that the doctors can lift the brain out of the head without recourse to a saw.[797] The left hemisphere of the brain is intact, while the damage to the right one is massive.[798]

---

*No bullet, or significant portion thereof, was found in either Kennedy's or Connally's body.

Just as the brain is fixed in formalin for further study, Lieutenant Colonel Finck walks into the autopsy room wearing military pants and a green scrub suit.[799] The three autopsy surgeons begin an examination of the president's head wound. What is immediately obvious to all three is a small oval-shaped hole in the back of the president's scalp. Peeling the skin away from the skull, the doctors find a corresponding but larger hole in the bone beneath the scalp. From inside the skull, the area surrounding the hole is cratered. From the outside, the skull bone around the hole is smooth. The surgeons recognize the wound to the backside of the head as having all the characteristics of an entrance wound.[800]

After taking photographs of the outer layer ("table") of the skull at the entrance wound, the photographer, John Stringer, positions himself at the head of the table. It is difficult to properly illuminate the inside layer or table of the back of the skull, in order to record the cratering effect the doctors have observed, so the doctors hold the head up slightly while Stringer snaps several exposures looking down into the cranial cavity.[801]

As to the massive hole on the right side of the president's head, it is presumably the result of the bullet exiting the head, although no specific exit point in the margins of the defect is discovered.[802]

7:45 p.m.
FBI agent James Hosty pulls out of the police garage and heads back toward the Dallas FBI field office. Oswald's words still resonate in his head, "Oh, so *you're* Hosty. I've heard about you. You're the one who's been harassing my wife!" Hosty couldn't help but think of the two visits he had paid Marina Oswald, the two visits that Oswald was clearly referring to. Hosty hadn't given the visits, or Lee Oswald for that matter, a lot of thought. Oswald was, after all, only one of the forty or fifty cases that made up his normal caseload.

Hosty had remembered reading a front-page article in the Dallas newspapers in 1959 about a former marine, Lee Oswald, who had defected to the Soviet Union. The article also grabbed the attention of Fort Worth FBI agent John Fain, who opened the case file in an effort to determine if Oswald posed any national security risks. In early June 1962, the Dallas newspapers ran another article, this time reporting that

Oswald was returning to the United States with a Russian bride. Fain interviewed Oswald twice, in June and August of 1962, and the following month, after concluding that Oswald was not a security risk, closed the file on Oswald. Hosty inherited all of Fain's case files.

Because Hosty had reviewed Marina's records at the Immigration and Naturalization Service office in Dallas for Fain, he had an uneasy feeling that she could possibly be a Soviet intelligence agent, and decided to try to locate the Oswalds, particularly after learning that Lee Oswald had subscribed to a U.S. Communist paper after Fain closed the file. But they had left no forwarding address when they moved from the last address he had on them, Neely Street in Dallas. He later learned they had moved to New Orleans, and shortly after being informed months later by the New Orleans FBI office that the Oswalds had disappeared from New Orleans, Hosty's Dallas office received a communiqué that Oswald, while in Mexico City in early October 1963, had visited the Soviet embassy there and spoken to one Valeriy Kostikov, a vice counsel at the embassy.

Eventually, the FBI's New Orleans office sent Hosty what was believed to be the Oswalds' new address at Ruth Paine's home in Irving, Texas, and asked that he verify their presence before it transfers the case file back to his jurisdiction.

On Friday, November 1, 1963, Hosty stopped at the Paine residence. Ruth Paine told him that Mrs. Oswald and her two children were living with her, and that Mrs. Oswald was temporarily separated from Lee, who visited his wife and children on weekends. Paine knew Oswald was working at the Texas School Book Depository and living somewhere in the Oak Cliff section of Dallas, but she wasn't quite sure where.

While they were talking, Marina came into the room. She looked as though she had been napping. Through her body language, Hosty could see she was frightened and he didn't try to interview her that day. He did intend to later, but he needed some of the materials from the Oswald file, which he had not yet gotten from New Orleans, to do it properly. He told Marina through Ruth that he would come back to see her at a later time. Ruth Paine told Hosty that she would find out where Lee was living and let him know.

On November 5, Hosty and a fellow agent dropped by Ruth Paine's again. The two agents chatted with Mrs. Paine briefly while standing at the front door. Ruth still didn't have Lee's address, and the only new information she volunteered was that Lee had described himself to her as a Trotskyist Marxist. They had been there less than five minutes and didn't see Marina until they were about to leave. Neither of the agents said anything to her.

Having confirmed that both Marina and Lee were living in the Dallas area, Hosty was waiting for the FBI's New Orleans office to send him copies of their entire file at the time of the assassination.[803]

As he pulls into the FBI's parking area, Hosty shakes his head and wonders how it could have come to this. What could he have possibly done differently that might have prevented the assassination? His actions concerning the Oswald file might be explainable, but Hosty knows it won't do his career any good.

Hosty heads up to his office, where a secretary tells him that he is wanted in Gordon Shanklin's office, pronto. Hosty finds his supervisor, Ken Howe, waiting there with Shanklin. They tell him to shut the door.

"What the hell is this?" Shanklin asks, clutching what appears to be a letter.

Hosty takes it and immediately recognizes it as the anonymous note delivered ten days or so earlier, the note he now realized had been delivered by Oswald.

"It's no big deal," Hosty says, trying to shrug it off. "Just your typical guff."

"What do you mean, 'typical guff'? This note was written by Oswald," Shanklin screams, "the probable assassin of the president, and Oswald brought this note into *this* office just ten days ago! What the hell do you think Hoover's going to do if he finds out about this note?" Shanklin is more upset than Hosty can remember, pacing behind his desk, puffing a cigarette.

Hosty again tries to convince Shanklin that the note is not a big deal, that Oswald hadn't threatened the president. But Shanklin knows much more will be made of the note.

"If people learn that Oswald gave you guff a week before the assassination, they'll say you should have known he'd kill the president," Shanklin cries. "If Hoover finds out about this, he's going to lose it."

Howe looks on gravely, arms folded. Hosty pleads that once they explain everything, the note, the background of the case, everyone will understand that there was no way in hell anyone could have guessed that Oswald was going to kill anyone, much less the president. Shanklin rubs his neck, unconvinced. Finally, he orders Hosty to write a memo surrounding the circumstances of the note.

Hosty returns a short while later with a two-page memo and hands it to Shanklin, with the note. The agent-in-charge shoves it into his "Do Not File" desk drawer, that special place in Hoover's FBI where every special agent in charge of an FBI field office kept personal notes on all his agents. The material in the drawer never enters the official record, and gives Hoover "plausible deniability" if anything objectionable ever reaches the public eye.[804]

7:50 p.m.

The assembly room in the basement of City Hall is once again abuzz with activity, as officers prepare for the third lineup. In the holdover area, adjacent to the stage, Detectives Sims, Boyd, Hall, and H. M. Moore arrange and handcuff the men who will appear with Oswald in the lineup. This time a pair of city prisoners have been included—Richard Walter Borchgardt, held for carrying a prohibited weapon and investigation of burglary and theft, and Ellis Carl Brazel, in custody for failing to pay some long-overdue traffic tickets. Borchgardt takes the number 1 position, Oswald is 2, Brazel is 3, and Don Ables, the jail clerk who participated in the first two lineups, takes the fourth spot.[805]

Detectives C. W. Brown and C. N. Dhority accompany sisters-in-law Barbara and Virginia Davis into the darkened end of the assembly room and have them sit down. The women, who haven't seen pictures of Oswald in the evening paper or on television, are nervous.[806] In a moment or two, Secret Service agents Forrest Sorrels and Winston Lawson, who had tracked Brennan down at his home, escort Howard Brennan into the room. The construction worker is petrified that he is the only witness who saw the gunman firing from the sixth-floor window and could give a fair description of him,[*] and over the last few hours has convinced himself that he may be putting his family in danger by stepping forward and identifying him. "Howard, I'm afraid, we don't know who might be out there looking for you," his wife, Louise, had said when he returned home earlier in the day, around three o'clock, and told her, "Louise, I was there. I saw him do it. I saw the man shoot President Kennedy. It was the most terrible thing I've ever seen in my life." Brennan thinks of moving his wife, daughter, and grandson, who was living with them at the time, out of town, but Louise seems to think there is no way to really get away.[807] Brennan is looking for a way out of his predicament.

"I don't know if I can do you any good or not because I have seen the man that they have under arrest on television," Brennan told Sorrels when he first arrived at the police station. He adds, "I just don't know if I can identify him positively or not."[808]

As they walk into the assembly room, Brennan tells Sorrels that he would like to get back a ways and view the man from a distance, closer to what it was at the time of the shooting. "We will get you clear on to the back," Sorrels says, "and then we can move up forward."[809]

The signal is given and the detectives begin marching the prisoners under the bright lights of the stage. As soon as Oswald appears, and before each man has even settled under a number, the Davis women react.[810]

"That's him," Barbara says. "The second one from the left." When the officers have the men turn sideways, and Barbara sees Oswald from the same angle she saw him crossing her front yard, she is positive.[811]

Her sister-in-law, Virginia Davis, agrees. The man they saw running from the Tippit murder scene is the number 2 man in the lineup—Oswald.[812]

Howard Brennan looks over the men carefully. He will later confide that he recognized the number 2 man, Oswald, immediately, but was afraid to say so.[813] Brennan figures that the authorities don't really need his positive identification anyway. It's not as if they'll let Oswald go if he

---

[*]The young lad Amos Euins also saw a gunman firing from the window, but his description of the gunman, as we have seen, was of little value, Euins first describing the gunman as being a colored man, and later, a white man.

doesn't identify him. After all, the police are already holding the man for the murder of Officer Tippit. Brennan calculates that he can always tell police what he really thinks at a later date, when it really matters, and not risk endangering his family.[814]

Sorrels has Brennan move a little closer.

"I cannot positively say," Brennan finally says.

"Is there anyone there that looks like him?" Sorrels asks.

"The second man from the left," Brennan answers cautiously, referring to Oswald. "He looks like him. But the man I saw wasn't disheveled like this fella."[815] (Of course, Oswald hadn't yet been roughed up by the police during his arrest at that point.)

Brennan can tell that Sorrels is disappointed.

"I'm sorry," Brennan says, "but I can't do it. I was afraid seeing the television might have messed me up. I just can't be positive. I am sorry."[816]

The agent turns and makes arrangements for Brennan to be taken home.

In New Orleans, a telephone rings at the home of Abraham Plough, foreman of the mails for the U.S. Post Office at Lafayette Square Station. The caller is Postal Inspector Joseph Zarza, who wants Plough to come to Lafayette Square Station immediately to open up the premises. When Plough arrives, Inspector Zarza tells him that postal investigators in Dallas want him to retrieve the application form for post office box 30061. Plough flips on a light, walks over to the file cabinet containing the application forms, and within a few minutes locates the one in question.[817] The form shows that box 30061 was rented to "L. H. Oswald" on June 3, 1963, and Oswald showed his home address as "657 French" Street. The box had been closed on September 26, 1963, with mail forwarded to 2515 West Fifth Street, Irving, Texas. Under the entry, "Names of Persons Entitled to Receive Mail Through Box," Oswald had written the names, "A. J. Hidell" and "Marina Oswald."[818]*

---

*Inspector Zarza checks the box and finds two copies of the *Militant* that had not yet been forwarded (7 H 296, WCT Harry D. Holmes).

Inspector Zarza calls Dallas inspector Harry Holmes and notifies him of the discovery.[819]

7:55 p.m.

In the third-floor hallway at Dallas police headquarters, detectives lead Oswald off the jail elevator and back through the crowd of reporters toward Captain Fritz's office. Oswald tells newsmen that the only reason he is in custody is because of his stay in the Soviet Union, defiantly adding, "I'm just a patsy!"[820]

8:05 p.m.

With Oswald again seated in Fritz's office,[821] FBI agent Clements continues his interview of the suspect, asking Oswald to provide the names, addresses, and occupations of relatives, as well as a sequential list of his own occupations and residences.[822] Oswald answers the agent's questions readily enough, even courteously, although he doesn't volunteer any information. Finally, on a perfectly innocuous question about his present occupation, Oswald balks.

"What started out to be a short interrogation turned out to be rather lengthy," he complains. "I refused to be interviewed by other law enforcement officers before and I've got no intention of being interviewed by you. I know the tactics of the FBI. You're using the soft touch. There's a similar agency in the Soviet Union. Their approach would be different, but the tactics would be the same. I believe I've answered all the questions I'm going to answer, and I don't care to say anything else."[823]*

---

*Under the 1966 U.S. Supreme Court case of *Miranda v. Arizona*, even if a suspect or arrestee has waived his right to have a lawyer present during his interrogation, and also waived his right against self-incrimination, once he indicates, at any time during the interrogation, that he does not want to answer any further questions, "the interrogation must cease," and any statement he makes thereafter, even if apparently free and voluntary, cannot be used against him because said statement is deemed to be, as a matter of law, "the product of compulsion, subtle or otherwise" (*Miranda v. Arizona*, 86 S. Ct. 1627, 1628). Here, as we shall see, Oswald continued to be interrogated and continued to answer questions for two more days. But *Miranda* wasn't yet in existence back in 1963.

Nevertheless, when Clements ignores his complaint and asks the same question again—what his present occupation is—Oswald answers. At that, Clements terminates the interview.[824]

8:18 p.m. (9:18 p.m. EST)
Alan Belmont, at FBI headquarters in Washington, is on the phone with Dallas special agent-in-charge Gordon Shanklin. The head of the Dallas office tells Belmont that he has made arrangements with Carswell Air Force Base in Fort Worth to fly one of his agents back to Washington with the rifle, cartridge cases, and metal fragments removed from Governor Connally just as soon as police release the evidence to the FBI.

"See if the police want us to make a ballistics test on the pistol that was used to kill Officer Tippit," Belmont asks. "If so, have it forwarded for examination along with the bullets removed from Tippit's body. If they don't want to release the pistol to us, find out all you can about the make, caliber, how many bullets were fired."

"Okay," Shanklin agrees. "I also realize that it's extremely important to locate and interview Oswald's coworkers to determine his whereabouts and actions at the time of the shooting. This is being done as we speak."

"Good," Belmont says. "President Johnson has been in touch with Mr. Hoover and wants to be sure that the FBI is on top of this case and is looking to us to solve it. You understand what that means, don't you?"

"Yes," Shanklin answers.

"It is imperative that we do everything possible in this case," Belmont says firmly.

"Understood," Shanklin reaffirms.

To handle the number of leads pouring into the Dallas office and expedite the interviewing of Depository employees, Belmont tells Shanklin that he's ordering an additional twenty agents, four stenographers, and ten cars to go to Dallas immediately.[825]

8:30 p.m. (9:30 p.m. EST)
At Bethesda Naval Hospital, the three pathologists have rolled the president onto his left side and are examining the oval-shaped bullet wound

located to the right of his spine and just above the right shoulder blade. Dr. Finck can see that the edges of the wound are pushed inward and recognizes the reddish brown skin around the margins as an abrasion collar, characteristics typical of entrance wounds.[826] After taking photographs of the bullet hole,[827] Dr. Humes probes the wound with his little finger, but finds that the bullet path seems to stop less than an inch into the hole.[828] Dr. Finck attempts to explore the wound using a flexible metal probe, but after repeated attempts he can't seem to find the path of the bullet. Afraid of making a false passage, Finck removes the probe and examines the front of the body. There are no corresponding exit wounds, only a tracheotomy incision in the front of the throat. Finck, Boswell, and Humes examine the margins of the incision, but cannot find any evidence of a bullet exit.

The doctors are perplexed. Where did the bullet go? Dr. Finck asks to examine the president's clothing, hoping that it might give a clue as to what happened to the bullet, but finds that the clothing is not available.[829] Dr. Finck then suggests that a whole-body radiographic survey be conducted before proceeding any further with the autopsy. All three of the pathologists know from experience that bullets can do crazy things when they enter the human body and might end up anywhere. The only way to be sure they haven't missed it is to x-ray the entire body.[830] Finck's decision doesn't set well with Admiral Burkley, who can see his idea of a quick recovery of evidence giving way to hour after hour of difficulties and delays.* Burkley says that Mrs. Kennedy had only granted permission for a limited autopsy, and questions the feasibility of finding the bullet that entered the president's back without conducting a complete autopsy.

"Well, it's my opinion that the bullet is still in the president's body," Dr. Humes tells him. "And the only way to extract it is to do a complete autopsy, which I propose to do."

As tempers flare, Secret Service agent Roy Kellerman confers

*Some of the military men present talked of bringing in metal detectors to expedite the search for any bullets in the president's body (ARRB MD 19, Memorandum to File, Andy Purdy, August 17, 1977, p.10).

quickly with FBI agents Sibert and O'Neill. They agree that from an investigative and prosecutorial standpoint, the bullet must be recovered, no matter how long it takes. They advise Admiral Burkley of their position, but he remains resistant to furthering the probe. Admiral Calvin B. Galloway, commanding officer of the U.S. Naval Medical Center, steps up to break the deadlock and orders Dr. Humes to perform a complete autopsy.[831] Now, to Admiral Burkley's annoyance, they will have to wait more than a hour for the entire body to be x-rayed.[832]

At Dallas police headquarters, Captain Fritz ambles back to his office to face Oswald once again. The prisoner doesn't seem to be tiring as the night drags on, although the detectives around him are beginning to feel the wear of the day.

Detective Elmer Boyd never saw a man answer questions like Oswald. He never hesitates about his answers. He shoots back an answer just as soon as the questions are asked, sometimes even before the questions are finished. Though most of the time he is calm, rather frequently his attitude suddenly changes and he gets mad, especially if he is asked something he doesn't like.[833]

"Did you keep a rifle in Mrs. Paine's garage in Irving?" Captain Fritz continues with his questioning.

"No," Oswald replies, having apparently decided to answer more questions despite his earlier refusal.

"Didn't you bring one with you when you came back to Dallas from New Orleans?" Fritz asks.

"No, I didn't," Oswald says.

"Well, the people out at the Paine residence say you did have a rifle," Fritz states firmly, "and that you kept it out there wrapped in a blanket."

"That isn't true," Oswald shoots back.[834]

Fritz lets the response hang there in the silence. He circles the desk.

"You *know* you've killed the president," Fritz says bluntly. "This is a very serious charge."

"No, I haven't killed the president," Oswald responds dryly.

"He *is* dead," the captain says.

"Yeah, well, people will forget that in a few days and there will be another president," Oswald replies, as if the day's events mean nothing.[835]

8:40 p.m.

In Chief Curry's third-floor office, Dallas FBI head Gordon Shanklin informs FBI agent Vince Drain that the FBI in Washington wants their Dallas agents to acquire the rifle found on the sixth floor, the revolver used to shoot Officer Tippit, and other various items, and bring them all to Washington immediately for examination. Drain discusses it with Chief Curry, telling him that he will personally stay with the evidence the entire trip to and from Washington to keep the chain of evidence intact.[836] Personally, Curry doesn't give a hoot what the FBI wants. This is a Dallas case under Dallas jurisdiction and the responsibility is his. Wanting to appear cooperative, though, Curry promises Drain that he'll consider the FBI's request.[837]

8:52 p.m. (9:52 p.m. EST)

The FBI sends a second Teletype to its fifty-five field offices:

> The Bureau is conducting an investigation to determine who is responsible for the assassination. You are therefore instructed to follow and resolve all allegations pertaining to the assassination. This matter is of the utmost urgency and should be handled accordingly, keeping the Bureau and Dallas, the office of origin, apprised fully of all developments.[838]

8:55 p.m.

Crime-lab sergeant W. E. "Pete" Barnes makes his way through the throng gathered on the third floor outside Homicide and Robbery. The size of the mob there is unbelievable, and frankly, Barnes finds it disgusting. He can't imagine how anyone can carry on an investigation properly with this kind of commotion going on.[839] Barnes has been ordered by his boss, Lieutenant Day, to make paraffin casts of Oswald's hands to see if there is any evidence that he has fired a weapon recently. Crime-lab detectives J. B. "Johnny" Hicks and R. L. Studebaker have come along to assist him.[840]

Also called a GSR, the gun residue test involves heating paraffin, a wax substance, to about 130 degrees. It's then brushed onto the suspect's hands and reinforced with alternating layers of bandage gauze. As the wax cools, it extracts from the skin particles of nitrates (acid elements in gunpowder residue that are deposited on the skin by the gases from a fired bullet), and these nitrates become embedded in the wax casts. The casts are then cut from the hands and sent to the crime lab for testing. There, technicians apply one of two chemicals to the casts to determine the presence of nitrates. A positive result will show up as a pattern of blue or violet dots.[841]

Barnes has been known to get exceptionally good paraffin casts, much better than some of the other detectives in his division. He once quipped, "The other detectives don't get the paraffin hot enough. They are afraid they'll burn the suspect, but I don't mind if I burn the bad guys a little in order to get a good cast."[842]

Contrary to myth, the paraffin test is not conclusive for the simple reason that the two chemicals used by laboratories to test for nitrates—diphenylamine and diphenylbenzidine—will react to most oxidizing agents, including urine, tobacco, cosmetics, pharmaceuticals, soil, fertilizer, and many others. The list is so large that a positive nitrate result doesn't preclude the possibility that the cause might be due to something other than gunpowder residue.[843] Moreover, the mere handling of a weapon may leave nitrates on the skin, even without firing it.[844] Because of their unreliability, paraffin tests have fallen into increased disfavor by law enforcement agencies in the United States.

As Barnes steps inside Captain Fritz's office, Fritz tells him that in addition to Oswald's hands, he wants Barnes to make a cast of Oswald's right cheek. Barnes knows immediately how unusual a request it is. Since 1956, when he started doing paraffin tests, this is the only time anyone had ever requested a paraffin test of a suspect's cheek. In fact, common sense tells a man of Barnes's experience that anyone firing a rifle has got

very little chance of getting powder residue on his cheek. The reason is
that the cartridge is sealed into the chamber by the bolt of the rifle being
closed behind it. Upon firing, the cartridge case expands even farther
inside the chamber, completely filling it up and preventing the nitrate
gases from escaping onto the face. Barnes doesn't question Fritz's judgment though. He has an order, and that's good enough for him.[845]

The crime-lab sergeant begins unpacking his equipment as Oswald
sits nearby, watching.[846]

"I know why you're doing this," Oswald says boastfully.

"Why?" Barnes replies, in his right-to-the-point style.

"You want to find out if I fired a gun," Oswald replies.

"I'm not trying to prove anything," the sergeant replies, as the wax
begins to heat up. "We have the test to make and the people at the lab will
determine the rest."

"Yeah, well you're wasting your time," Oswald says in a self-assured
manner. "I don't know anything about these shootings."[847]

As soon as he's done, Barnes places the paraffin casts from Oswald's
right cheek and two hands into three separate manila envelopes. A couple of patrolmen assist Barnes in wending his way through the news media
to get to the elevators that'll take him to the fourth-floor Identification
Bureau. A storm of questions are thrown at him as he snakes through the
press: "What have you got in that sack? You owe it to the news media to
tell us! What have you got there?" Barnes refuses to reply to the boister-
ous horde.[848] Arriving at the Identification Bureau, Sergeant Barnes initials the casts, seals them, and locks them in the evidence room. They'll

---

*Predictably, the paraffin cast for Oswald's right cheek showed no reaction, that is, no nitrates
indicating he had fired a weapon (4 H 276, WCT J. C. Day), but the paraffin cast on his hands, also
predictably, showed a positive reaction, indicating, though not conclusively, he had recently fired
a weapon. Though, as indicated, there is no gap between the chamber and the barrel of a *rifle* through
which gases can escape (resulting in no nitrate residue being found on Oswald's right cheek from
firing his Mannlicher-Carcano), there is a gap between the barrel and the cylinder on a *revolver*
through which gases do escape; hence, nitrate residue was found on Oswald's hands, most likely
from his shooting Officer Tippit with his .38 caliber Smith & Wesson revolver (4 H 276, WCT
J. C. Day). Indeed, the gun residue test was devised only for the firing of small arms, not rifles.

be delivered to the county crime lab at Parkland Hospital in the morning for testing.[849]*

Barnes immediately returns to Captain Fritz's office, and with the assistance of Detective Hicks, takes Oswald's finger and palm prints.[850] Oswald says nothing. When they finish, Barnes asks Oswald to sign the fingerprint card on the line that says "prisoner's signature."

"I'm not signing anything until I talk to an attorney," Oswald replies.

"That's all right with me," Barnes says, and gathers up the identification kit.[851]

In New York City, the city that never sleeps, the streets are deserted, Broadway theaters are closed, Radio City is closed, and the only nightclub that is not deserted is the famed Stork Club, "but the people there," ABC's Barbara Walters observed, "are like the people there on Christmas Eve, people with no home, no place to go."[852]*

9:00 p.m.

Detectives Stovall and Rose lead Wesley Frazier, his sister, Linnie Mae Randle, and their pastor, Reverend Campble of the Irving Baptist Church, into the back room of Homicide and Robbery. Since being arrested an hour and a half ago, Frazier has been very cooperative with police, allowing officers to search his car and his home, where they confiscated a .303 caliber rifle, a full clip, and a partial box of ammunition.[853]

To confirm that firing a rifle will not leave nitrate residue on the firer's cheeks, the FBI had one of their agents, Charles L. Killion, fire three rounds in Oswald's Carcano rifle. The result of the paraffin test conducted thereafter was negative for his cheeks and hands (3 H 494, WCT Cortlandt Cunningham; WR, pp.561–562).

*Virtually all high school, college, and professional sporting events were canceled or postponed throughout the nation that coming weekend. By far the most prominent exception (for which it has received criticism by many down through the years) was the National Football League. Although the American Football League postponed all of its Sunday games, NFL Commissioner Pete Rozelle said that "it has been traditional in sports for athletes to perform in times of great personal tragedy," and announced that the NFL's schedule of seven games would be played on Sunday. CBS announced it would not televise the games. (*Dallas Morning News*, November 23, 1963, sect.2, p.1; Rozelle quote: *Sunday Press* [Binghamton, NY], November 24, 1963, sect.D, p.1)

Captain Fritz comes back and questions both Wesley Frazier and his sister. Wesley tells him about Oswald's placing a large bag in the backseat of Frazier's car on the morning of the assassination and telling Frazier the bag contained curtain rods.[854]

Rose and Stovall begin taking affidavits from Frazier and his sister as Captain Fritz makes his way down the hall to the Forgery Bureau, where he asks Marina Oswald if she saw Oswald carrying anything when he left that morning, but she says she didn't see him leave.[855] He probes both Marina and Ruth Paine further. Had Oswald mentioned putting curtain rods in his room? Neither of them know anything about it.[856]

Captain Fritz ponders this latest piece of the assassination puzzle as he makes his way back to his office. Oswald's curtain rod story is terribly suspicious to the homicide captain. If the rifle was in the package, and Fritz strongly suspects it was, then it must have been dismantled slightly to fit the bag Frazier described as twenty-six to twenty-seven inches long. At the moment, Fritz is hesitant to question Oswald about it until he finds out more.[857] Were any curtain rods found at the Depository, or in Oswald's room? Did his apartment need curtain rods? Fritz likes to play his cards close to the vest, then pounce once he is certain of the facts.

Marguerite and Robert Oswald are brought across the hall to the Forgery office, where Marina is being held. Marguerite breaks into tears and hugs her daughter-in-law. She hasn't seen her or Lee in a year. Marina hands her baby, Rachel, to Mrs. Oswald. Neither Marguerite nor Robert had been told of the child's birth. Before Robert has a chance to greet Marina, Ruth Paine bolts toward him.

"I'm Ruth Paine," she says. "I'm a friend of Marina and Lee. I'm here because I speak Russian. I'm interpreting for Marina." (But Mr. Ilya A. Mamantov, a local research geologist who is a native of Russia, has been employed by the Dallas Police Department to interpret for Marina during questioning by police, and has been doing so.)[858]

To Robert, Mrs. Paine comes across as a dominating, controlling woman. She seemed eager to tell anyone who would listen, almost boastfully, that both Lee and Marina had been to her house. Robert's impression of her estranged husband, Michael, was equally unfavorable.[859] Robert later recalled Mr. Paine's eyes as having a cold distant look, as if he wasn't really looking at you, and described his handshake as that of a "live fish." He can't quite put his finger on it, but Robert feels that the Paines are somehow involved in this affair.[860]

Ruth turns to Marguerite and says, "Oh, Mrs. Oswald, I am so glad to meet you." Marina, she tells her, wanted to get in touch with her, especially when Rachel was born, but Lee didn't want her to. The words are not very soothing to Marguerite, who takes an instant dislike to the woman.

"Mrs. Paine," Marguerite snaps angrily, "you speak English. Why didn't *you* contact me?"

Ruth tries to explain that Marina didn't know how to contact Marguerite. Also, because the couple were separated—Lee living in Dallas, Marina in Irving—Ruth didn't want to interfere.[861]

Within five minutes of the introductions, preparations are made to leave the police station. Robert Oswald says that he is going to remain there, where he hopes to talk with Captain Fritz, and will see them tomorrow. Mrs. Paine says she will take Marina and the babies back to her house for the night.[862] Marguerite expresses her desire to stay in Dallas so that she can be close to Lee and help as much as possible.[863] When Mrs. Paine offers to put Marguerite up for the night, Robert says something about not wanting to inconvenience her and Mr. Paine. Ruth immediately shoots back, "Mr. Paine and I aren't living together," adding, "It's a long story." Michael Paine shrinks behind his domineering wife, as they head out the office door.[864]

Dallas police officers attempt to clear the way as reporters descend upon the group in the corridor. Flashbulbs snap and cameras whirl as they face a barrage of questions, none of which are answered, while Marguerite pleads to the cameras about Lee, "He's really a good boy."[865]

Remaining behind, Robert Oswald takes a seat and soon strikes up a relaxed conversation with Lieutenant E. I. Cunningham, who was present at Lee's arrest. Cunningham explains the circumstances surrounding Oswald's apprehension in a calm, sympathetic tone. Robert realizes that there are police officers in Dallas with some genuine compassion. He also realizes, for the first time, just how strong a circumstantial case the police have against his brother for the shooting of Officer Tippit. Equally disturbing to Robert is the thought that it is difficult to explain Tippit's death unless it was an attempt to escape arrest for the assassination of the president.[866]

In the Homicide and Robbery office down the hall, Captain Fritz walks over to Assistant DA Bill Alexander, Jim Allen, the former assistant DA now in private practice, and Secret Service agent Forrest Sorrels. "We need to talk about the case we've developed so far," Fritz says to Alexander, who suggests they find a quieter place.

The four men push their way through the mob of reporters, walk out of City Hall, and stroll north on Harwood to the Majestic Steak House, an eatery in Dallas's theater district favored by Dallas law enforcement officials. Ordering steaks and coffee, the men marvel over the day's events, then get down to business.[867]

"Have you got enough to file on him, Captain?" Alexander asks.

Fritz reviews what they have so far. They can place Oswald on the sixth floor of the Depository a few minutes before the shooting—the same floor where they found the hulls, the rifle, and the paper bag in which the rifle was apparently carried into the building. His wife says he owned a rifle, and it is missing from the storage area where he kept it. She says the rifle they found looks like his, but she can't be sure. The crime lab has lifted good latent prints from the boxes and the bag and hope to get some from the rifle. If they turn out to be Oswald's, they'll have him. Fritz notes that Oswald is the only employee who left the Book Depository after the shooting and didn't return. More important, all of the evidence points to Oswald as being the killer of Officer Tippit.

"All in all, that's a lot of good evidence," Fritz says. "But, I'd like to wait until we develop the firearm and fingerprint evidence before proceeding with any charges in the assassination."

They decide to hold off for an hour or so before filing against Oswald in the Kennedy case.[868]

9:40 p.m.

Ruth Paine's home in Irving is a relief after the circus at City Hall. After police drop them off, Ruth sends Michael out to get hamburgers at a drive-in so she won't have to cook. Marina feeds her two small children, then sits down to eat in front of the television, which is rerunning all of the day's events. Marina even catches a glimpse of Lee being led through the third-floor corridor at police headquarters.[869]

Marguerite begins to complain to everyone present that if they were prominent people, three of the best lawyers would be at the city jail right now defending her son. But, because they are "small" people, they won't get the same kind of attention. Ruth Paine tries to tell her that this is not a small case and will get the most careful attention possible, but she is unable to penetrate the years of self-pity that Marguerite has wrapped herself in.[870]

"Don't worry," Ruth finally says. "I'm a member of the Civil Liberties Union and Lee will have an attorney, I can assure you." Marguerite can't help but wonder why Mrs. Paine hasn't already called for an attorney.[871]

The doorbell rings and two men from *Life* magazine appear unannounced, reporter Tommy Thompson and photographer Allan Grant, two of nine *Life* correspondents and photographers who had flown into Dallas that day from around the country. (Considering the day's events, Ruth is surprised that not more newsmen have been able to locate them

---

*The way Grant explained it, when he and Thompson were at Dallas police headquarters earlier in the day, there were "so many reporters and photographers pushing and shoving" in the crammed corridor on the third floor, some "standing on chairs, some on their camera cases, all trying to get in position" for a "photograph of suspect Lee Harvey Oswald" whenever he happened to appear "being led from one room to another," that he suggested to Thompson they "get out" of the madhouse and "look for a more exclusive angle to the story." With Thompson, born in Texas, "using his Texas accent and disarming demeanor" to extract information out of a deputy sheriff, they got the address of Oswald's rooming house, and Earlene Roberts, the housekeeper, then told them of the phone calls that Oswald used to make to Irving. They headed out there and after inquiring around town, finally found the Paine residence. (Allen Grant, "Life Catches Up to Marina Oswald," *Los Angeles Times*, November 22, 1988, part V, pp. 1, 8)

by now.)* She lets them in and flips on an extra light in the dimly lit room. Thompson, of course, realizing the difficulty of speaking to Marina through Mrs. Paine, immediately begins questioning Mrs. Paine, while his partner pulls out a camera and begins snapping photographs.[872]

"Mrs. Paine, tell me, are Marina and Lee separated, since Lee lives in Dallas?"

"No, they are a happy family," Ruth says, explaining that Lee works in Dallas and has no transportation to get back and forth from Irving every day. Marguerite is fuming, partly because she doesn't think her son needs this kind of publicity but more importantly because she's beginning to realize that *Life* magazine is going to do a "life story" segment and she wants to be paid. In her paranoid mind, Marguerite is beginning to suspect that Ruth Paine invited *Life* magazine to come over and that she and Marina, while speaking in Russian, have conspired to sell Lee's life story without her.[873]

After a few more questions about Oswald's family life, Thompson asks how Lee got the money to return to the United States.

"He saved the money," Ruth replies. Marguerite finally hits the roof.

"Now, Mrs. Paine, I'm sorry," Mrs. Oswald interrupts, "I appreciate that I am a guest in your home but I will not be having you make statements that I know are wrong. To begin with, I do not approve of this publicity. But if we're going to have a story in *Life* magazine I would like to get paid. After all, we're going to have to pay for lawyers to defend my son."[874]

Suddenly there are angry words between Marguerite and Ruth, who defends Marina's right to have her story told to the reporters.

"I'm his mother," Marguerite shrieks. "I'm the one who's going to speak!" Ruth translates for Marina as Marguerite tries to explain to Marina that neither of them should speak to the reporters without getting paid. Marina, confused by the whole scene, nonetheless understands one thing quite clearly. It's all about money.[875]

Thompson says he will telephone his office and see what he can do about her request, then withdraws to another room to make the call. Meanwhile, the photographer follows Marina into the bedroom, snapping photographs of her as she undresses her daughter June and puts her to bed. Marguerite hovers nearby until Thompson comes back and tells her that *Life* will not pay them for the story, but will pay their food and hotel accommodations while they stay in Dallas. The picture taking continues until Marguerite becomes indignant.

"I have had it," she complains loudly. "You're taking my picture without my consent! Now go find out what accommodations you can make for my daughter-in-law and I so that we can be in Dallas to help my son, and let me know in the morning!"[876]

Thompson and Grant leave the house, but not the area. They sit in their rented car on the dark street in front of the house. Twirling the keys to the car on his index finger as he watches the house, Thompson says, "This, my friend, is probably going to be the scoop of my career. I will kill the first newsman that approaches that house." Grant, with slightly different priorities, says, "Let's go. I want to get this film off to New York." "We're not leaving here," Thompson says, "until those lights go out."[877]

9:50 p.m.

After talking with Lieutenant Cunningham for nearly an hour, Robert Oswald gives up any hope of speaking with Captain Fritz. He leaves the ruckus of City Hall and walks back to his car seven blocks away. The reporters don't have any idea who he is, so his stroll through the cool night air is free of pesky newsmen. Getting in his car, Robert starts driving. He has no particular destination in mind. He only wants to still the turmoil in his mind. If anyone were to ask him what he feels, he would say "unspeakable horror."

Some people are already speculating that the killing of the president was not the isolated act of one man, but the result of a great conspiracy. Robert wonders if it could be true. Is it possible that Marina could have played a role in some plot? What about the Paines? Whom could Lee have possibly become involved with? As the miles click by, he tries to assemble his thoughts and fears into some coherent order, but to no avail. Robert soon finds himself out on Highway 80, approaching the western outskirts of Fort Worth, and suddenly realizes how far he has already driven. He stops for gas, turns around, and heads back to Dallas.[878]

10:00 p.m.

No sooner than Fritz and Alexander get back to City Hall from dinner than the telephone rings in the Homicide and Robbery office of Dallas police headquarters and Alexander takes the call. It's Joe Goulden, a former reporter for the *Dallas Morning News* who is now on the city desk of the *Philadelphia Inquirer*.

"What's going on down there? We're not getting anything straight. It's all garbled. Is Oswald going to be charged with killing the president?" the reporter asks.

"Yeah, we're getting ready to file on the Communist son of a bitch," Alexander tells him. When Goulden asks Alexander why he called Oswald a Communist, Alexander tells him about all the Communist literature and correspondence they found at Oswald's Beckley address. "We have the killer," Alexander says, "but we're not sure what his connections are."

Goulden wants to know exactly when the charges will be filed against Oswald. "As soon as I can draw up the complaint," Alexander replies.

Goulden says his editor won't print the part about Oswald being a Communist for fear of a libel suit. The only way he'd print that is if he could say it was part of the formal charge.

Alexander, who would later allow that "I let my mouth overload my ass," says sarcastically, "Well, how about if I charge him with being part of an international Communist conspiracy? Could you run with that?"

He knew he couldn't draw up a complaint like that, but Alexander was itching to show Oswald for what he was, a damn Communist. Goulden was more than eager to oblige.

"You got it!" the reporter says.[879]

Ever since his meeting with Vince Drain an hour and a half ago, Chief Curry has been getting calls from Washington, insisting that the police send all of the evidence up to the FBI laboratory in Washington, although nobody will tell him exactly who it is that is making the demands, always insinuating it's someone in high authority. Curry manages to get a moment with Captain Fritz and asks him if they are in a position to release some of the evidence to the FBI for testing.

"I need the evidence here," Fritz argues. "I'd like to have some of the local gun shops take a look at this rifle and pistol and see if they can identify them. How can I do that if they're in Washington?"

Curry knows he's right. This case is not under the jurisdiction of the FBI or the Secret Service. Although Curry wants to go all out and do whatever he can to allow these agencies to observe what is taking place, in the final analysis this crime happened in Dallas and would have to be tried in Dallas and therefore it was their responsibility to gather and present the evidence. If they fail, the blame will fall on him. For the moment, the Dallas police chief is unwilling to give in to the demands from Washington.[880]

In New York City, FBI agents watch employees as they rummage through the files of Crescent Firearms Company. Louis Feldsott, president of the company, has been very cooperative, keeping employees after hours to help investigators track the assassination weapon.[881] Earlier in the afternoon, Dallas FBI agents had canvassed Dallas gun dealers to determine if any of them had ever sold surplus World War II vintage Mannlicher-Carcanos. They found only one who did—H. L. Green Company on Main Street. Albert C. Yeargan Jr., manager of the sporting goods department at H. L. Green, spent the late afternoon with agents reviewing sales receipts for the past few years to determine if his company had ever handled a Mannlicher-Carcano with serial number C2766. The search proved fruitless; however, their records did identify the importer of these Italian 6.5-millimeter rifles as Crescent Firearms Company of New York.[882]

The investigation quickly switched to New York, where for the last several hours Crescent Firearm's employees have been looking for a record of serial number C2766. Suddenly, they have a break. Their records show that C2766 had been wholesaled to Klein's Sporting Goods in Chicago.[883]

Within the hour, Chicago FBI agents are pounding on the front door of the home of William J. Waldman, vice president of Klein's. Waldman agrees to accompany agents to the office to start a search, but first he'll need some help. He calls Mitchell Scibor, general operating manager of Klein's, and asks him to meet him at the office. As Waldman gets ready, he tells waiting agents that this is not a simple matter.

"Klein's purchases a lot of sporting goods," he warns them, "of which guns are but one. It could take hours to go through our purchase records."[884]

In a small alcove of the autopsy room at Bethesda Naval Hospital, the acting chief of radiology, Dr. John Ebersole, clips the last of the X-rays onto a light box. Nothing. No bullet. The president's entire body has been x-rayed and still the doctors have been unable to determine what happened to the bullet that struck his back.[885]

"Where did it go?" someone asks.

The doctors have no idea.[886] A discussion ensues about what might have happened to it. Someone suggests the possibility that a soft-nosed bullet struck the president and disintegrated. Others contemplate that the bullet could have been "plastic," and therefore not easily seen by X-rays, or that it was an "Ice" bullet, which had dissolved after contact.[887] None of the suggestions made much sense, but then neither did the absence of a bullet. FBI agent Jim Sibert decided to call the FBI laboratory and find out if anyone there knew of a bullet that would almost completely fragmentize. He managed to reach Special Agent Charles L. Killion of the Firearms Section of the lab, who said he'd never heard of such a thing. After Sibert explained the problem, Killion asked if he was aware that a bullet had been found on a stretcher at Parkland Hospital. Sibert hadn't and is nearly certain that no one else at the morgue has either. Sibert hangs up the phone, returns to the autopsy room, and informs the three pathologists that a bullet had been recovered at Parkland Hospital.[888]

"That could account for it," Humes said of the missing bullet. He suggested that in some rather inexplicable fashion the bullet might have been stopped in its path and thereafter worked its way out of the body and onto the stretcher, perhaps during cardiac massage.[889]

10:15 p.m.

Jack Ruby, by all accounts, was having one of the worst days of his life. "He cried harder when President Kennedy was killed than when Ma and Pa died," his sister Eva would later tell me.[890] But his day had started out with anger, not mourning. He had awakened to find a large advertisement in the *Dallas Morning News* in the form of a letter captioned "Welcome Mr. Kennedy" taken out by one Bernard Weissman in which Kennedy is criticized for aiding and abetting international Communism.[891] Jack is very patriotic, has been all his life. He loves America and can't tolerate anyone saying anything negative about our government.* He was even known to insist that someone he was attending a sporting event with put out his cigarette during the playing of the "Star Spangled Banner."[892] And Jack was a great admirer of President Kennedy and his wife and family, bringing them up in social conversations and praising them.[893] In fact, when someone at the Carousel Club made a disrespectful remark not too long ago about Kennedy, Jack threw him out of the club.[894]† And Jack had forbidden his comics at the club from saying anything or using any material that reflected adversely against "Negroes, Jews, or the Kennedys."[895] How could this fellow Weissman attack "our beloved President," Ruby

---

*Although Ruby was highly patriotic, he was completely apolitical, though a lifelong Democrat, "being devoid of political ideas to the point of naivete" (CE 2980, 26 H 469–470; CE 1747, 23 H 355). Carousel comic Bill Demar, who knew Ruby well, said he "never recalled ever having heard him discuss politics" (15 H 102, WCT William D. Crowe Jr. [Bill Demar]). His rabbi, Hillel Silverman, told the FBI that Ruby was a very shallow person intellectually, and he considered Ruby to be someone "who would not know the difference between a communistic philosophy and a totalitarian philosophy, in that he was not well-read and spent little time concerning himself with this type of information." The rabbi, however, appears to have missed the mark when he said that although Ruby thought the president of the United States was the greatest individual in the world, it wasn't because of the president himself, but because of Ruby's respect for the position involved and of his high respect for the American government. (CE 1485, 22 H 906–907, FBI interview of Hillel Silverman on November 27, 1963) Though that was probably a large part of Ruby's feeling for Kennedy, the consensus of others, including those who were much closer to Ruby than Silverman, is that Ruby had an extraordinary feeling for Kennedy personally.

†The fact that Barry Goldwater, who was already gearing up to run against Kennedy for president in 1964, was brought up in the discussion by the emcee at the Carousel around the same time as the remark about Kennedy, indicates the incident probably happened within months of the assassination.

thought.[896] Indeed, he thought that John F. Kennedy was possibly the greatest man who ever lived,[897] and after the assassination started carrying a small picture of the president on his person, kissing it "like a baby" in front of his sister Eva. "My brother had such a great admiration for this man, it's unbelievable," Eva would recall.[898]

After seeing the Weissman ad, Jack called Eva, he was so upset about it. He told her he had called the *News* and bawled them out. "Where the hell do you get off taking an ad like that? Are you money hungry?" It was a rotten thing for any person to question the way the president was running the country. "If this Weissman is a Jew," he told her, "they ought to whack the hell out of him." He figured Weissman might actually be a Commie himself trying to discredit the Jews, and Ruby later clips the Weissman ad from his sister Eva's copy of the *News*, even though he still has his.[899] Jack seems to almost be more upset about the audacity of Weissman dishonoring the president by addressing his letter to "Mr. Kennedy," rather than "Honorable President" or "Mr. President," than the letter itself.[900]

When Ruby heard at the *News* that Kennedy had been shot, he turned an ashen color, very pale, and sat completely dazed, a fixed stare on his face that was remarkable enough for people in the office to notice. He said nothing, very uncommon for Ruby.[901] He eventually came out of it enough to verbally grieve with those around him on the horror and tragedy of what had happened. Ruby used John Newnam's phone to call his sister Eva, and she was crying hysterically.[902] Ruby asked Newnam to listen to his sister and held the phone up to his ear. Newnam could hear that Eva sounded very upset.[903] Ruby told Newnam, "John, I will have to leave Dallas. John, I am not opening tonight."[904] He left the building and got in his car, sobbing.[905] After returning to the Carousel, he ordered that the club be closed for the night, and his employee Andrew Armstrong made the first phone call, to a stripper, Karen "Little Lynn" Carlin, at 1:45 p.m., to tell her not to come in, but he was unable to reach her.[906] Ruby's coworkers saw that he was taking the president's death harder than even they, and he called what happened an "outrageous crime that would ruin the city of Dallas."[907]

Ruby started making a flurry of phone calls from the club,[908] the first at 1:51 p.m. to his friend Ralph Paul at Paul's Bullpen Drive-In in Arlington, Texas, telling Paul "I can't believe it," and urging him to close his drive-in restaurant "in honor of the president," which Paul told him he couldn't afford to do.[909] He called his sister Eileen, in Chicago, and was crying. "Did you hear the awful news," he asked. "Yes," she said. "Oh, my God, oh, my God," Jack said. "Maybe I will fly up to be with you tonight," he suggested, but she reminded him that Eva, who had just returned home from the hospital from abdominal surgery, needed him now more than she did. "You better stay there," she told her brother.[910]

Later in the afternoon he called Billy Joe Willis, the drummer at his club. "How could any man do such a thing?" he asked Willis, crying. He also said to Willis—not trying to connect the two acts—"Remember that man making fun of President Kennedy in the club last night?," referring to a man in the audience who called Kennedy a bum when Ruby, on stage with his twistboard, said, "Even President Kennedy tells us to get more exercise." Completely broken up over the president's death, Ruby said, "This is the most horrible thing that has ever happened," and hung up. Willis was taking the president's death hard too, but he told his girlfriend later that he couldn't understand the extent that Ruby was torn up over it.[911]

Before the day was out he also called his brother, Hyman Rubenstein, in Chicago, to lament the president's death—"Can you imagine, can you imagine?" he asked Hyman.[912]

Ruby also called Al Gruber, a friend of his from Chicago now living in Los Angeles whom he has known for many years and who had stopped by the Carousel to see Jack just two weeks earlier when he was passing through town. "Did you hear what happened?" he asked Gruber. "You mean the shooting of the president?" "Yes, ain't that a terrible thing. I'm all upset and my sister is hysterical." Gruber heard Ruby crying at this point, and Ruby said, "I'm crying and can't talk to you anymore," whereupon he hung up the phone.[913]

When Ruby heard of Officer Tippit's murder, his grief was intensified, believing it's the Officer Tippit he knows, though he will later learn it's a different Tippit. Ruby knew Dallas police detective Gayle M. Tippit, who worked in the Special Services Bureau, and who on numerous occasions had stopped by the Vegas and Carousel clubs on official business.[914] After leaving the Carousel Club in midafternoon, Ruby goes to his sister Eva's apartment to lament and cry over the president's death, and talks about sending flowers to the place right off Elm Street near the spot where the president was shot. It was the first of three visits to her apartment that day, and he called her eight times on the phone.[915]

Though his financial condition was such that he could ill afford to do it, he made the decision at Eva's place to close his two clubs for not just one but three days, the first time the Carousel had ever been dark.[*] Ruby had first told Don Safran, the entertainment columnist for the city's evening paper, the *Dallas Times Herald*, that his club would be closed that evening as well as the entire weekend. He then tried to cancel his ads at the *Dallas Morning News* for the weekend, and when he was told that his space had already been reserved for him, he told the paper to just say in the ads that his Vegas and Carousel clubs would be closed for the weekend.[916] Eva had asked Jack to bring some food over when he came, but he brought enough "to feed twelve people," Eva explaining that Jack was so out of it "he didn't know what he was doing then." She said her brother was so upset over what happened that he only took one "spoonful or forkful," then started making more phone calls. At one point, he was sick in the stomach enough to go into the bathroom, but he did not vomit. "Someone tore my heart out," he told Eva, who herself was experiencing great grief, literally screaming over the telephone to a friend earlier that "the president is dead." Jack told Eva, "I didn't even feel so bad when Pops died because Papa was an old man. He was close to ninety." Eva looked at her brother sitting in front of her and got the sense that he felt life wasn't worth it anymore, "like he thought they were out to get the world, and this was part of it." "This man," Jack said to Eva about

---

[*]At some time during the afternoon, Ruby stopped in to see a friend of his, Joe Cavagnaro, the sales manager at the Statler Hilton Hotel. He told Cavagnaro about his plans to close the Carousel for three days. Cavagnaro said, "He asked me what *we* were going to do. I told him, 'Jack, you can't just close a hotel. People have to have a place to eat and sleep.' But he expected the whole city to close down." (Wills and Demaris, *Jack Ruby*, pp.38, 40)

Kennedy and his efforts with his brother Bobby toward integration in the South, was "greater than Lincoln." When Jack left her apartment in the early evening "he looked pretty bad, a broken man."[917]

At the Shearith Israel Synagogue, where he went to pray for the fallen president, arriving near the end of a two-hour service that had started at 8:00 p.m., the day's events preyed on his mind. When a friend, Leona Lane, remarked to him after the services "how terrible" the assassination of President Kennedy had been, Ruby said, "It is worse than that."[918] The rabbi, Hillel Silverman, noticed that Ruby appeared to be "in shock" and in a daze, though Ruby didn't mention the assassination to him, merely thanking him for visiting Eva at the hospital a few days earlier.[919] When he left the synagogue for the parking lot, he got his pistol, a .38 caliber Colt Cobra, out of the trunk and slipped it into his right front trouser pocket. It's a lightweight revolver with a two-inch barrel, and a shroud over the hammer makes it easy to carry in his pocket without snagging the cloth.[920] He wouldn't take it into the synagogue, but he usually carries the pistol when he has a lot of cash on him from the Carousel, which he does tonight.[921]

Now, around 10:15 in the evening, he's worried about the other Dallas clubs and whether they are properly respecting the death of the president, so he makes a point of driving by the Bali-Hai Restaurant, and notes grimly that it is open. He drives past the Gay Nineties too. It is closed.

As he goes on down Preston Road, he listens to the car radio, hungry for any new information about the assassination. He hears that the police are working overtime, and is overcome by a feeling of respect and admiration for them. He has always felt close to the police department—he doesn't even know why—and believes Dallas has the greatest police force in the world. He has many friends on the force and often visits the police at the station, encouraging them to come to his clubs when they are off duty. Jack gives them the cut rate on drinks he normally reserves for newsmen, hotel receptionists, bellboys, and others who might help to generate business.[922] And if all an officer wanted was a snack, "Jack kept coffee and sandwiches in the back for the police."[923]

On an impulse he stops at Phil's Delicatessen on Oak Lawn Avenue and tells the counterman, John Frickstad, to cut him ten corned beef sandwiches with mustard. And ten soft drinks—eight black cherries and two celery tonics. He chats a bit with the owner, Phil Miller.

He goes to the phone, calls police headquarters, and gets Detective Sims, a fifteen-year acquaintance.

"I hear you guys are still working," he says. "I want to bring you some sandwiches."

"Jack, we wound up our work already. We finished what we were doing. I'll tell the boys about your thoughtfulness. Thank you."[924]

Those sandwiches are already being made, and it's a shame to let them go to waste. Ruby remembers Gordon McLendon, and how good McLendon has always been to him, giving him a lot of free plugs for his clubs on his Dallas radio station. McLendon owns many radio stations, including KLIF in Dallas, the one Ruby had been listening to in the car. One of the disk jockeys, Joe Long, is down at the police station, phoning information to the station as it comes in, and others are working late too—the guy on the air and the engineers at the station. He tries calling KLIF, but because it's after six no one answers. He knows there is a hotline right into the control room, but he doesn't know the number.

He calls out to Frickstad, "These sandwiches are going to KLIF, and I want you to make them real good."

There's another disk jockey he knows at KLIF, Russ Knight, big with the kids in the late-afternoon hot spot, but he can't get his home number from information. He tries Gordon McLendon, who lives out near the synagogue and whose number he does know. A little girl answers. Maybe her name is Christine, Jack thinks.

"Anyone home?"

"No."

"Is your daddy or mommy home? I would like to get the number of the station, so I can get in the building at this time." The little girl leaves the phone and comes back with a number in the Riverside exchange.

Jack dials the Riverside number but it has been disconnected. He calls Eva, tells her he's at Phil's getting sandwiches and is going to the station, and if she needs him, she can reach him there, though he still doesn't have the station's number. The sandwich bill only comes to $9.50 plus tax—Frickstad made only eight sandwiches instead of the ten Jack ordered. Frickstad helps Jack with the sandwiches out to his car and receives Jack's customary tip, a free pass to the Carousel or Vegas, for his pains.[925]

It's four or five miles from Phil's to downtown, and Ruby still doesn't know how he's going to get into KLIF to bring the sandwiches to the gang on duty. He drives up McKinney Avenue to check on some more clubs, and finds more open. Jack simply can't understand how they would remain open at such a tragic time. Jack proceeds to the KLIF station, near City Hall. He knew the front door would be locked, of course, but he hopes his knocking is loud enough for them to hear him, but because of the long distance between the bottom of the flight of stairs and the studio, no one does, so he proceeds to City Hall to look for KLIF reporter Joe Long to get the control-room phone number.[926]

It's about eleven in the evening when he parks at Commerce and Harwood, leaving the sandwiches and his dog Sheba in the car, and goes to the police department, taking the elevator to the second floor. Ruby's an experienced gatecrasher, he can get in anywhere by putting on a busy, peremptory manner, "taking," as he puts it in his weirdly mangled way of talking, "a domineering part about me."

"Where is Joe Long?" he speaks assertively to the officer at the desk. "Can I go look for him?" The officer lets him in.

Emerging from the elevator on the third floor into a throng of reporters, Ruby asks everyone, cops and reporters, if they know where he can find Joe Long, determined to find Long so he can deliver his load of sandwiches out at KLIF. He even has an officer page Long, but with no luck. He knows a lot of the officers, and stops to chat with Lieutenant Leonard and Detective Cal Jones. Roy Standifer, the desk officer in the Burglary and Theft Bureau, calls out, "Hi, Jack," and Jack calls out, "Hi, Sandy"—he calls Roy that, short for Standifer. No one else, Standifer notes wryly, ever does. Standifer, who has known Jack for thirteen years, recognizes Ruby's use of a first name as one of his tricks. On Jack's frequent visits to police headquarters, Standifer has seen him ask someone for the first name of an officer he doesn't know and then greet the man by his first name like an old friend.[927]

Ruby sticks his head in the Burglary and Theft door and is delighted to spot Detective A. M. Eberhardt. The detective's work on the vice squad used to bring him to the Carousel regularly a few years back, and he even brought his wife there once on a night off. Ruby gave "Michael"—for some reason he uses Eberhardt's middle name—a couple of tips too. He reported one of his own girls when he discovered she was forging checks and using drugs, and Eberhardt busted her right there in the club. Another time Ruby heard from some parking-lot boys that a guy under indictment for white slavery was in town and staying at the Baker, half a block down the street from the Carousel, and Eberhardt went in with a squad and made the collar. Later, when Eberhardt was transferred to burglary, he managed to run down a couple of burglars Ruby surprised in the Carousel. Eberhardt always lent a sympathetic ear to Ruby's complaints about his competition, those damned Weinsteins. He knows Jack usually carries a large sum of money in his pocket and worries about Jack leaving the club at two or three in the morning with the night's take in a bag. They are old friends.

Ruby shakes hands, asks, as he always does, about Eberhardt's wife and kids, and tells him he's there as a "translator for the newspapers," brandishing a little notebook. "I'm a reporter," Jack says, tapping something in his lapel (had he purloined a press badge?) with the notebook. The only foreign language Eberhardt knows that Jack speaks is Yiddish, but the corridor outside is crammed with foreigners, shouting in languages he never heard before. Ruby tells him about the sandwiches he made up for the radio reporters, corned beef. "Nothing," Jack boasts, "but kosher stuff is all I bring."

---

*Throughout the rest of his life, Ruby rarely permitted the name "Oswald" to come from his lips, either purposefully or instinctively refraining from uttering the word. "I don't know why," he told the Warren Commission. "I don't know how to explain it." One explanation is that he unconsciously sensed that to do so would invest it with a human dignity it did not have. Authors Gary Wills and Ovid Demaris wrote that "Ruby could not bring himself to call *the thing* by name. It is the instinct that kept [Carl] Sandburg from using [John Wilkes] Booth's name in his long

Jack starts talking about how terrible it is for the assassination to have happened in the city. "It's hard to realize that a complete nothing, a zero like that,[*] could kill a man like President Kennedy was."

Eberhardt is busy. Even though he is only on standby, he's using the opportunity to catch up on his paperwork. So, after a few minutes, Ruby plunges back into the hubbub in the hall, and situates himself where the height of the activity is, right outside Captain Fritz's office door. Oswald, of course, is being interrogated inside. Ruby proceeds to put his hand on the door knob, turn it, and starts to step into the room when two officers stop him. "You can't go in there, Jack," one says. No problem. Ruby is content to be close to the action, right outside the door.

You have to shout to be heard in that corridor, but Ruby enjoys being able to provide information to the reporters, many of them bewildered out-of-towners, about everyone who was coming in or out of the door. "No, that's not Sheriff Decker, that's Chief Curry, C-u-r-r-y," or "That's Captain Fritz, Will Fritz. He's the homicide captain." He really likes to be helpful, particularly to important people like reporters. A detective who recognizes him bellows at the top of his voice over the heads of the reporters, "Hey Jack, what are you doing here?"

Ruby manages to get one arm free to wave to his friend. "I'm helping all these fellows," he shouts back, pointing to the foreigners.

Jack's activity is taking his mind off the tragedy and he is feeling a little better than he has all day. In a way, he feels he is being temporarily deputized as a reporter. He is, he realizes, "being carried away by the excitement of history."[928]

---

description of Lincoln's death. When he must refer to the assassin, he calls him 'the Outsider.'" The authors note that William Manchester, who does use Oswald's name many times in his book, is nonetheless "sickened by the need to do so." Manchester writes, "Noticing him [Oswald], and even printing his name in history books . . . seems obscene. It is an outrage. He is an outrage." (5 H 187, WCT Jack L. Ruby; Wills and Demaris, *Jack Ruby*, p.264; Manchester, *Death of a President*, pp.276–277)

In their book *Johnny, We Hardly Knew Ye*, JFK's two closest aides, Kenneth P. O'Donnell and David F. Powers, never used Oswald's name once, though they wrote about the horrors of JFK's death.

10:30 p.m.

Robert Oswald crosses the lobby of the Statler Hilton Hotel across the street from Dallas police headquarters. For a moment, he considers registering under a false name, to keep reporters at bay, but then decides he isn't going to start hiding. No matter, the desk clerk doesn't seem to pay any attention to the name on the registration card. When he arrives on the sixteenth floor, Robert finds a small, rather drab room with two chairs, a small table, and a sofa bed. Unable to face the depressing room, he returns to the hotel coffee shop and nibbles on a ham sandwich.[929]

Henry Wade is returning home after dining with his wife and some friends when he hears a report on the radio that Oswald is going to be charged with being part of an international Communist conspiracy to murder the president.[930] Wade, the Dallas DA since 1951, can barely believe his ears. There is no such law on the Texas books, and anyone familiar with Texas law knows that if you allege anything in an indictment, you have the burden of proving it.[931]

Wade barely gets in the door when the telephone rings. The caller is Waggoner Carr, attorney general for the state of Texas. He had just received a long-distance call from someone in the White House who had heard a similar report. Carr wants to know if Wade has any knowledge of it. Wade said he didn't.[932]

"You know," Carr says, "this is going to create a hell of a bad situation if you allege that he's part of a Communist conspiracy. It's going to affect international relations and a lot of things with this country."

"I don't know where the rumor got started," Wade says, "but even if we could prove he was part of an international conspiracy, I wouldn't allege it because there's no such charge in Texas."[933]

Within a few minutes, Henry Wade gets phone calls from his first assistant, Jim Bowie, and U.S. Attorney Barefoot Sanders—both of whom have gotten very concerned calls from Washington. Wade assures both of them that he will check into the rumor.[934]

Wade immediately decides to take "charge" of the matter and goes down to the police department to make sure that no such language appears in any complaint against Oswald. His man down there, Bill Alexander,[*] denies to Wade that he had anything to do with the rumor, not telling Wade that his own loose lips had given birth to it.[935]

In Richardson, Texas, Gregory Olds, editor of the local newspaper and president of the Dallas chapter of the American Civil Liberties Union (ACLU), reaches for the telephone ringing on his nightstand. The caller is one of the ACLU board members, who tells him he just got a call from the president of the Austin affiliate. Lee Oswald has been seen on television complaining that he's been denied legal representation and they think that someone should check into Oswald's complaint. Olds agrees and tells him that he will do it.

In a moment, Olds has the Dallas Police Department on the line and asks to speak to the chief of police. He's told that Chief Curry is busy. Olds then asks to speak to one of the deputy chiefs, but no one seems to know where they are. When Olds is asked if he would be willing to speak to a detective, he informs the officer on the phone that he is the president of the Dallas Civil Liberties Union and that he will speak with the man in charge of the investigation and no one else. An officer eventually comes to the phone and tells him, "Captain Fritz isn't available, but you can tell me."

"I'll wait," Olds tells them through clenched teeth. He has learned to be persistent when dealing with the police.[936]

When Captain Fritz finally comes on the line, Olds explains to him that the ACLU was deeply concerned over Oswald's apparent lack of legal counsel and stands ready to provide him with immediate assistance. Fritz blithely tells him that the suspect had been informed several times of his

---

*When I asked Alexander if Wade had immediately assigned him to the Oswald case, the tall, angular-faced Texan who speaks slowly, and sometimes sprinkles those words with salty, ranch-hand profanity, responded, "There was no *need* for any conversation between Henry and me. It was understood" (Telephone interview of William Alexander by author on December 11, 2000).

right to representation and offered opportunities to contact a lawyer, but he declined them. Olds thanks the captain and hangs up.[937]

The situation is nothing new for the ACLU chapter president. He knew that every city had prisoners who refuse the services of an attorney on the assumption they don't need one, deciding to represent themselves in court. Most of them pay for their mistake in prison. It would be easy for Olds to accept the word of the police department that Oswald's legal rights have been safeguarded. Instead, he rubs the sleepiness from his eyes and telephones a few ranking members of the ACLU, telling them to meet him at once in the lobby of the Plaza Hotel, across the street northwest from City Hall.[938]

10:40 p.m.

After having just left police headquarters about ten to fifteen minutes ago, Detectives Guy Rose and Richard Stovall park their car in the basement garage of City Hall and walk back into the basement entrance with Wesley Frazier, his sister, and the Reverend Campble in tow. After taking an affidavit from Frazier, they were driving the three of them back to Irving and were halfway there when they received a call over the radio to return to City Hall with Frazier and contact Captain Fritz. When Detective Rose telephones upstairs, Captain Fritz tells him to take Frazier to the fourth-floor Identification Bureau and give Frazier a polygraph test. Fritz wants to know if he's telling the truth about the curtain rod story. Did Oswald really tell him he was bringing curtain rods to work? Or is this some kind of cover story Frazier has cooked up?

"Okay, Cap'," Rose replies.[939]

Horace Busby, LBJ's longtime aide, speechwriter, and confidant, is waiting for President Johnson to arrive at Johnson's home, the Elms, a large brick home in the Spring Valley section of Washington, D.C., Johnson had purchased from well-known society figure and political hostess Perle Mesta. In the past sixteen years Busby had been through the highs and the lows and everything in between with LBJ, and knew him, he said,

better than he wanted to know any man. Yet he knows he is not now waiting for any man he had ever known. He was waiting for the president of
the United States. The Elms is being overrun with Secret Service agents
and telephone people installing new lines. After LBJ arrives and has a
meeting with his close aides, friends, and Mrs. Johnson, he retreats to the
sunroom with Busby. A large portrait of LBJ's mentor, former House
Speaker Sam Rayburn, looks down on the room. LBJ raises his hand to
the portrait, saying quietly, "How I wish you were here." Settling in a
chair, he asks Busby to turn on the television set, saying, "I guess I am
the only person in the United States who doesn't know what happened
today." When he hears talk out of Dallas about a possible Communist
conspiracy being behind the assassination, he says, "No, we must not have
that. We must not start making accusations without evidence."[940]

11:00 p.m.

At the Paine house in Irving, the rumblings of a long day are coming to
an end. Ruth and Marina talk quietly as they prepare for bed. Marina tells
her that just the night before Lee had said to her that he hoped they could
get an apartment together again soon. She is hurt and confused, wondering how he could say such a thing when he must have been planning
something that would inevitably cause their permanent separation. For
an instant, Mrs. Paine's politeness was overcome by her curiosity.

"Do you think he killed the president?" she asks.

"I don't know," Marina answers.

There is an awkward moment, and then Marina says that she doesn't
think she'll be able to sleep anytime soon and asks to borrow Ruth's hair
dryer. She wants to take a shower, which she has often said renews her
spirits. Mrs. Paine hands her the dryer and bids her goodnight.[941]

Alone, later, in her own bedroom, Marina runs across June's baby
book, which the police had failed to confiscate. She suddenly remembers
the pictures Lee had given her from the set he had her take of him in the
backyard when they lived on Neely Street. She peels the book open.
There they are, pasted into the album, two small snapshots of Oswald
wearing a pistol and holster strapped to his waist, a rifle in one hand, two

left-wing newspapers in the other. On the back of one he had written, "For Junie, from Papa." When he had given them to her, Marina was appalled and asked, "Why would Junie want a picture with guns?"

"To remember Papa by sometime," Oswald had said.[942]

She realizes now that they will only hurt Lee. She carefully removes them from the baby book and calls Marguerite into the bedroom. She shows them to Mrs. Oswald and tries to explain to her that Lee shot at General Edwin Walker in early 1963[*] and that he might have been shooting at the president too. But her thoughts only come out as a series of gestures and very broken English.

"Mama," she says, pointing at the photographs. "Walker . . . "

Marguerite doesn't seem to understand what she means by "Walker" but understands the significance of the guns in the photos. "You take, Mama," Marina says.

"No," Marguerite resists.

"Yes, Mama, you take," Marina says, shoving the photos at her.

"No, Marina," Marguerite whispers. "Put back in the book."

Marguerite then places a finger across her lips, points toward Ruth's room, and shakes her head, warning Marina, "Ruth, no." Marina understands that she is not to show the photos to Mrs. Paine, or anyone.[943]

After Marguerite leaves the room, Marina makes another discovery that takes her breath away. The police, in their hasty search, also overlooked a pale, translucent, blue-green china cup with violets and a golden rim that her grandmother had given her. Inside it she finds Lee's wedding ring. Lee had taken the ring off at work before, but this was the first time in their marriage that he had ever taken it off and left it at home. Marina immediately realizes that the shooting was not a spontaneous act, but that Lee had intended to do it when he left that morning. Apparently, he didn't expect to return.[944]

Marina didn't sleep that night. She knew little about American law.

---

[*]On the evening of April 10, 1963, retired Major General Edwin A. Walker, a prominent right-wing figure in Dallas, was shot at through the window of his suburban Dallas home. The bullet intended for him was deflected by the window frame and missed Walker's head.

She thought it would all be over in three days and Lee would be strapped in the electric chair and executed. Would she be found a criminal too for her knowledge of Lee's involvement in the Walker shooting? Would she find herself in prison? She lay awake wondering what would become of her children.[945]

Henry Wade plows his way through the field of reporters lined up in the corridor outside the Homicide and Robbery Bureau.[*] Inside, Assistant DA Bill Alexander, FBI agent Jim Bookhout, and Captain Fritz await him. At Wade's request, Fritz begins to outline the considerable amount of evidence the Dallas Police Department has impressively gathered so far— the gun, the witnesses, the arrest, and the fingerprints and probably false statements by Oswald during his interrogation. It all looks pretty good to Wade.[946]

For nearly the past five hours, thirty-five-year-old Richard B. Stolley, the Pacific Coast regional editor for *Life* magazine, has been ringing the home telephone of Abraham Zapruder every fifteen minutes or so without success. Stolley flew into Dallas from Los Angeles earlier in the afternoon with *Life* reporter Tommy Thompson and photographer Allan Grant. The team had set up headquarters at the Hotel Adolphus in downtown Dallas, and within hours Stolley learned from a local correspondent that Zapruder had reportedly taken amateur movies of the shooting.

---

[*]Wade would later tell the Warren Commission, "You just had to fight your way down through the hall through the press . . . To get into homicide it was a strain to get the door open enough to get into the office" (5 H 218). One problem is that the third-floor hallway was only about 113 feet long and just 7 feet wide (CE 2175; 24 H 848; WR, p.197), and this space was further reduced by all the radio and TV equipment, such as cables and tripods, in the corridor. To compound the problem of all the members of the media and Dallas Police Department mingling or moving about in the narrow hallway, throughout the three days of Oswald's detention the Dallas police were obligated to continue normal business in all five of its bureaus located along the same hallway. Therefore, many persons, such as witnesses and relatives of defendants, had occasion to visit the third floor on matters unrelated to the assassination. (WR, p.204)

Stolley dials the number again, and this time a sleepy voice answers, "Hello?"

Zapruder had been driving around the last few hours trying to shake the gruesome images from his mind. Stolley explains that he represents *Life* magazine and might be interested in Zapruder's film. Zapruder says Stolley is the first journalist to contact him and confirms that he does have a film that shows the shooting. Not wishing to lose an exclusive, and knowing others will soon be hot on the trail, Stolley tries to talk Zapruder into letting him come out to his home now to view the film and talk. Zapruder replies that he is too tired and distraught to discuss it tonight. He tells Stolley to come by his office at nine o'clock tomorrow morning, and hangs up.

Stolley decides to show up an hour early, just in case.[947]

It's just after midnight on the East Coast as the three pathologists near the end of their autopsy of the president's body at Bethesda Naval Hospital, when three skull fragments recovered from the floor of the presidential limousine during a Secret Service examination at the White House garage are brought into the morgue.[948] Interest in the three skull fragments grows when the three pathologists note a distinct crater on the outer surface of the largest fragment, characteristic of an exit wound.[949] Their suspicions are soon confirmed when X-rays of that fragment reveal minute metallic particles embedded in the margins of the crater.[950] There is no doubt about it. The fragment contains a portion of the exit wound.[951]

FBI agents Sibert and O'Neill, eager to submit a report on the autopsy findings, ask Dr. Humes what his findings will be?

"Well, the pattern is clear," Humes tells them. "Two bullets struck the president from behind. One bullet entered the president's back and probably worked its way out of the body during the external cardiac massage at Parkland Hospital. A second bullet struck the rear of the president's skull and fragmented before exiting."

"Is that then the cause of death, Doctor?"

Humes nods, affirmatively. "Gunshot wound of the head."[952]

As the autopsy team removes its equipment from around the examination table, a group of morticians from Gawler's Funeral Home move their portable embalming equipment into position to prepare the president's body for burial.[953] Secret Service agent Roy Kellerman signs for the photographs[954] and X-rays[955] taken during the autopsy, which will be delivered to Secret Service special agent-in-charge Robert I. Bouck at the White House in the early morning hours of November 23.[956]

Though most in attendance at the autopsy quietly leave the room, for the weary doctors the night is not over; they stay to assist the morticians. No one seems to know whether the coffin will be open or closed while the president lies in state. Although Mrs. Kennedy has expressed her wish that the casket be closed, the issue has been left unresolved. Neither Brigadier General Godfrey McHugh, the president's air force aide, nor Admiral George Burkley, the president's personal physician, can assure the morticians that the body will not be viewed. McHugh decides that it would be better to be on the safe side and have the body fully prepared and dressed.[957]

For the next three hours, the men from Gawler's are absorbed in the tedious task of putting as good a face as possible on death. The president's cranium is packed with a combination of cotton and plaster of Paris to provide the support necessary to reconstruct the head. After the hardening agent dries, the scalp is pulled together and sutured.[958] The organs from the thoracic and abdominal cavity, preserved in formaldehyde, are placed in a plastic bag and returned to the body cavity, which is then stitched closed.[959] The tracheotomy wound is sutured up and a small amount of dermal wax is used to seal the wound. Restorative cosmetics are used to hide some bruising and discoloration on the face.[960]

At the conclusion of the embalming process, the body is wrapped in plastic, then dressed in a blue-gray pinstripe suit, a white shirt, a blue tie with a pattern of light dots, and black shoes, which have been picked out and brought to the morgue by the president's friend and aide, Dave Powers. The president's hands are folded across his chest and a rosary laced through the fingers.[961] When they are finished, the body is lifted into a new casket—made of hand-rubbed, five-hundred-year-old African

*The total bill for the 255-pound Marsellus 710 coffin from Gawler's and its accompanying 3,000-pound Wilbert Triune/copper-lined vault is $3,160 (ARRB MD 130, Embalmers Personal Remarks; ARRB MD 134, Funeral Arrangements for John Fitzgerald Kennedy, November 22, 1963, p.1).

mahogany—lined in white rayon* that has been brought in to replace the Britannia casket damaged in Dallas.[962] Those who might look upon the president's face now will never know the brutal condition of his head just a few hours earlier.

11:15 p.m.
Robert Oswald finishes his light supper—a ham sandwich and a glass of milk. Perhaps Captain Fritz will finally be free to talk with him, he thinks. Leaving the hotel coffee shop, Robert heads back across the street to City Hall and is taken to Fritz's office, but again the captain is too busy to see him.[963]

In the lobby of the Plaza Hotel, Gregory Olds, president of the Dallas chapter of the American Civil Liberties Union, meets with three prominent members of his local organization. Olds rapidly outlines the situation to them as they try to work out a plan. A call to Mayor Cabell seems in order, but Olds comes back to them after a few moments to report that the mayor is busy. They wonder whether he is really busy or just too busy to deal with the ACLU. Olds has learned to deal with disappointment, and he will not be deterred.

"The best thing for us to do," he tells his fellow representatives, "is to go across the street and talk to the police directly."[964]

11:20 p.m.
Chief Curry enters the Homicide and Robbery office and joins District Attorney Wade, Assistant DA Alexander, Judge Johnston, and Captain Fritz in discussions about the evidence against Oswald. "Have we got enough to charge Oswald with the president's murder?" Curry asks. All are in agreement that there is sufficient evidence to file charges.[965]

Assistant DA Alexander drafts the language of complaint number F-154, charging Oswald with the assassination. The words are nearly identical to those used in the Tippit murder charge, only the name of the victim is different. When it is completed, Captain Fritz pulls out a pen and affixes his signature to the complaint, then hands the single-sheet document to District Attorney Wade, who adds his own signature. Judge Johnston takes the form, looks at his watch, then accepts the charge by scribbling his own name and title, along with the words "Filed, 11:26 pm, November 22, 1963."[966]*

There is a certain amount of satisfaction felt by all in attendance. The Dallas police have done an incredible, some would even say a near-impossible job over just the last eleven and a half hours. In that short span since the president's murder, they have apprehended the man they believe is responsible, and amassed evidence against him that is destined to withstand years of intense scrutiny. Despite the thousands of government man-hours yet to come, the basis of the case against Oswald is collected and assembled by the Dallas police in these first crucial hours. It is a feat the world would soon forget.

11:30 p.m.

Captain Fritz instructs Detectives Sims and Boyd to make out an arrest report on Oswald for the president's murder.[967] As they get to work, the discussion in the homicide office turns to evidence in the case. Once again, Chief Curry asks Fritz if they are in a position to release some of the evidence to the FBI for testing. Fritz tells him that he's got a local gun dealer coming down to look at the rifle to see if he can identify it.†

"How about after that?" Curry asks. Fritz looks at him, clearly agitated.

"How do we know, Chief, that we can get this evidence back from them when we need it?" Fritz asks. "I don't think we should let them have it."

"You know, this is a Dallas case," Alexander chimes in. "It happened

---

*"We wanted to file on him [Oswald] before midnight," Alexander would later recall. "It just would look better that we got the SOB on the same day he killed Kennedy" (Telephone interview of William Alexander by author on December 12, 2000).

†Alfred D. Hodge, the fifty-five-year-old owner of the Buckhorn Trading Post, was unable to identify the Mannlicher-Carcano rifle or .38 caliber Smith & Wesson revolver as being weapons he had sold (15 H 498, WCT, Alfred Douglas Hodge).

here and it's going to have to be tried here. It's our responsibility to gather the evidence and present it."

Chief Curry is keenly aware that the FBI and Secret Service have no jurisdiction over the case. It's Dallas's baby, and it'll be up to them to see it through to the end. He also knows that it'll be their fault if something gets screwed up. Still, this isn't your average, garden-variety murder case. This is an investigation involving the assassination of an American president. Curry feels that his department has to make every effort to cooperate with the federal agencies and let them see what Dallas is doing. Besides, the FBI laboratory in Washington is the best of its kind in the nation and its support could certainly help expedite the investigative process.[968]

"Chief, I think you ought to let them take it up to Washington and bring it back tomorrow night," Wade suggests, trying to break the deadlock. "Let them have it twenty-four hours."[969]

The group argues some more over whether that is a wise course of action. Finally, an agreement is reached. The Dallas police want two things to ensure an unbroken chain of possession—photographs of everything sent to Washington, and an accountable FBI agent, Vince Drain, to sign for and accompany all of the evidence to and from the nation's capital.[970] Chief Curry calls upstairs to the Identification Bureau and tells Captain Doughty to have Lieutenant Day stop all processing of the rifle and to prepare the rifle, and other key pieces of evidence, for release to the FBI.[971]

Agent Drain telephones the Dallas FBI office, telling Special Agent-in-Charge Shanklin that Curry has agreed to lend the FBI the evidence. Shanklin notifies FBI headquarters and within ten minutes a C-135 jet tanker and crew are waiting on the runway at Carswell Air Force Base in Fort Worth to fly the evidence to Washington.[972]

11:45 p.m.
FBI agents Vince Drain and Charles T. Brown sign for and receive the items to be transported to Washington, which include the Mannlicher-Carcano rifle, serial number C2766, found on the sixth floor;[973] two of the three spent hulls found under the sniper's nest window[974] (the third

spent hull[975] was retained by Captain Fritz and kept in a desk drawer in his private office[976]); one live 6.5 caliber cartridge found in the rifle chamber;[977] and the paper sack found near the sniper's nest window.[978]

Lieutenant Day scribbles some instructions on a corner of the paper sack found on the sixth floor: "FBI: Has been dusted [for prints] with metallic powder on outside only. Inside has not been processed. Lieut. J. C. Day."[979] The paper sack already had the words "Found next to the sixth floor window gun fired from. May have been used to carry gun. Lieutenant J. C. Day."[980] When Day hands the rifle, the weapon believed by Dallas police to have murdered Kennedy, to FBI agent Drain, he says, "There's a trace of a print here," pointing to the trigger housing. The agent says nothing as he takes possession of the rifle.[981] The rest of the items are loaded into a box and FBI agents Drain and Brown hustle them down the elevator to the basement and out to their waiting car for the short trip to Carswell.[982]

11:50 p.m.
Chief Curry, District Attorney Wade, and Captain Fritz step out of the Homicide and Robbery office into the crush of reporters gathered in the third-floor corridor and announce that charges have been filed against Oswald in the assassination of the president.

"We want to say this," Curry tells them, "that this investigation has been carried on jointly by the FBI, the Secret Service, the [Texas] Rangers, and the Dallas Police Department. Captain Fritz has been in charge."

The newsmen want to know if Oswald has confessed.

"He has not confessed," Curry says.

"Any particular thing that he said," a reporter asks, "that caused you to file the charges regarding the president's death against him?"

"No, sir," Curry answers. "Physical evidence is the main thing that we are relying on."

Asked to name the physical evidence, Curry declines.

"When will he appear before the grand jury?"

Curry doesn't know, although that would be the next step. "We will continue with the investigation. There are still many things that we need to work on."

"Mr. Wade, could you elaborate on the physical evidence?"

"Well," the district attorney tells them, "the gun is one of them."

"Can you tell us if he has engaged a lawyer?"

"We don't know that," Captain Fritz says. "His people have been here but we don't—"

The homicide captain's hoarse voice is drowned out by a flood of other questions: Are there any fingerprints on the gun? Can we get a picture of him? Can we get a press conference where he could stand against a wall and we could talk to him? Do you expect a confession from this man?

"No," Wade says, picking the last question to answer.

"Do you have a strong case?"

"I think it's sufficient," Wade replies.

"What is the evidence that links him to the gun?"

"I don't care to go into the evidence now," Wade says firmly.[983]

The three officials huddle to discuss the possibility of showing Oswald to the press. A nearby microphone picks up fragments of the conversation.

"We could take him to the show-up room," Fritz is heard saying, "and put him on the stage and let him stand up. They couldn't, of course, interview him from up there, you know, but if you want them to look at him or take his picture—I'm not sure whether we should or shouldn't."

"We've got the assembly room," Curry says. "We could go down there."[984]

"Speak up!" the reporters shout.

"We're going to get in a larger room," Wade tells them, "that's what we're talking about here."

"What about the assembly room?" a reporter shouts.

"Is that all right?" Wade says. "Let's go down there."[985]

Most of the reporters make their way downstairs to the City Hall basement, awaiting Oswald. A few continue to grill Wade as Fritz and Curry slip back into the homicide office.

"Will there be a way to take any pictures?"

"I don't see any reason to take any picture of him," Wade replies.

"Of Lee?" a reporter asks, incredulously.

"Yes," Wade replies.

"Well, the whole world's only waiting to see what he looks like [now]," the reporter says.

"Oh, is that all," Wade answers matter-of-factly, "the whole world."

"That's all," the reporter says. "Just the world."[986]

NBC national television is shutting down its live coverage on the East Coast, where it's approaching 1:00 a.m. David Brinkley sums up the feelings of a nation to his dwindling audience: "We are about to wind up, as about all that could happen has happened. It is one of the ugliest days in American history. There is seldom any time to think anymore, and today there was none. In about four hours we had gone from President Kennedy in Dallas, alive, to back in Washington, dead, and a new president in his place. There is really no more to say except that what happened has been just too much, too ugly, and too fast." The network signs off at 1:02:17 a.m.[987]

Saturday, November 23

12:05 a.m.

Gregory Olds and three ACLU representatives, wanting to know if Oswald is being denied legal assistance, are not satisfied by the statement to them of Captain Glen King, the administrative assistant to the chief of police, that as far as he knew Oswald had not requested such assistance. Two members of Olds's group locate and speak directly to Justice of the Peace David Johnston. Johnston assures them that Oswald's legal rights have already been explained to him and that he had "declined counsel." They report this back to Olds. Satisfied that Oswald, despite his earlier protests in the third-floor corridor, had probably not been deprived of his legal rights, the men from the ACLU decide to go home for the night.[988]

It's been dark for hours, and most of Dallas law enforcement would normally be in bed and sleeping by now. But not tonight. In the Homicide and Robbery Bureau, Captain Fritz and Chief Curry confer in hushed tones just outside Fritz's private office, where Oswald awaits them. Their discussion centers around how to make Oswald available to the press. If Captain Fritz had his way, he'd have cleared the third floor of all reporters a long time ago. To his way of thinking, they're nothing but a nuisance to the investigation. Dealing with them has been a thorn in his side all day, because there's only been one way to get Oswald to and from Fritz's office, and that's through the crowd of reporters in the third-floor corridor. Every time they move him, Oswald faces a verbal assault from the press. Some of the things they holler at him are provocative, some seem to please him, others aggravate him, but none of them help the interrogation process. In fact, Fritz thinks, he would have been "more apt to get a confession . . . from [Oswald] if I could have . . . quietly talked with him." The constant barrage by the press has a tendency to keep Oswald upset.[989]

What bothers Chief Curry the most is the beating the city of Dallas, and the police department in particular, is taking in the press. It especially disturbed him to hear a reporter telling a television audience, as he held up a picture of Oswald, "This is what the man who is charged with shooting President Kennedy looks like, or at least this is what he did look like. We don't know what he looks like now after being in the custody of the police."[990] Of course, Curry knew Oswald wasn't being mistreated. He himself had checked with Captain Fritz to make sure that Oswald had been given something to eat and wasn't being subjected to long, drawn-out interrogation sessions. But the comments, no matter how inaccurate, sting just the same. Curry had always maintained very good relations with the local press, and they respected him for it.[991] But this is different. The halls are overrun with reporters from all over the world, each one putting Dallas under a magnifying glass. Under the pervasive glare of the world media, Curry feels that he has to defend the city and his beloved department. In no uncertain terms, he wants the press to know that

Oswald isn't being mistreated, which, in his mind, means marching him out to within an arm's length of the mob of reporters waiting downstairs.

"I'm a little afraid something might happen to him," Fritz says. "Let me put him on the stage so nobody can get to him."

"No," Curry says. "I want him out in front of the stage."[992]

Acceding to his boss's request, Fritz steps into his office, where Oswald sits under the watchful eye of two detectives. "Take him on down to the assembly room," Fritz tells them, then orders the rest of his men to go down as part of a security detail. Oswald says nothing, sensing that this isn't going to be just another lineup.[993]

A few minutes later they bring Oswald out of homicide into the narrow, crowded corridor, and Jack Ruby, standing in the hallway right outside of Fritz's office, and with a loaded revolver in his right trouser pocket, finds himself within two to three feet of the man he now hates for killing the president, but the thought of shooting Oswald never enters his mind. Strangely, though he despises Oswald, he thinks Oswald is good-looking and resembles actor Paul Newman.[994] Learning they are taking Oswald down to the assembly room in the basement (next to the show-up room), Ruby follows. He feels perfectly free in what he is doing, with no one asking him any questions. As crowded as the assembly room is, he manages to get in and stand on top of a table to the rear, his back to the wall.[995]

An FBI agent returns to the office where Robert Oswald is being questioned by another agent.

"Robert," he says, "you might as well know now. They are charging your brother with the president's death."[996]

Robert sags in his chair and shakes his head. He realizes that there is not much more he can do tonight and starts for his hotel. For eleven hours he's managed to keep his emotions reasonably in check, but now, as he walks along the quiet streets of downtown Dallas, his body suddenly begins to tremble until he is sobbing. Not yet thirty years old, Robert feels like an aged and decrepit man. He stifles his emotions by the time he

reaches the hotel lobby and returns to his room. In the dark, he lies awake
unable to sleep.[997]

In the offices of Klein's Sporting Goods in Chicago, general operating
manager Mitchell Scibor paws through invoices with company vice president William Waldman. The FBI agents nearby wait patiently as Scibor
and Waldman search for a record of having received a Mannlicher-Carcano
rifle, serial number C2766, from Crescent Firearms Company of New
York. After a little more than an hour of searching, they uncover an invoice
dated February 7, 1963,[998] for a shipment of one hundred, six-shot, model
91TS 6.5-millimeter Mannlicher-Carcano rifles from Crescent Firearms,
packed in ten cartons, ten rifles to a carton, at a unit cost of $8.50. Attached
to the invoice are ten memo pages indicating the serial numbers of the rifles
in each case.

Waldman quickly looks over the list of serial numbers. There it is—
carton number 3376 had a rifle with serial number C2766.[999]

"There's no question about it," Waldman tells the FBI agents. "We
handled this rifle."

Klein's records show the rifle in question arrived on its loading dock
on February 21, 1963,[1000] was unpacked the following day,[1001] and assigned
control number VC-836,[1002] a number used by Klein's to track the history
of the gun while it's in their possession.

"Is there any way to tell who it was sold to?" an FBI agent asks.

"Yes," Waldman says, "the next move will be to hunt through microfilm records of our mail-order customers until we find this serial number. It's going to take some time because there is no specific order of
filing."[1003]

Waldman and Scibor move over to two microfilm reading machines
and begin the tedious task of looking through hundreds of microfilmed
mail-order receipts for the customer who ordered the Mannlicher-
Carcano rifle with serial number C2766 found on the sixth floor of the
Texas School Book Depository.[1004]

prisoner. For any newsman worth his salt, this is the center of the universe. Those at the back of the room can barely hear Chief Curry trying to explain the ground rules over the clamor. "If anything goes wrong with his being down here, if there's a rush up here, he's immediately going out and that's it. Now, do we understand each other?"[1005]

A chorus of voices answers, "Yes! Right! Yes!" until it disintegrates into a wall of incomprehensible sound. Curry shuffles his way back into the hallway as the newsmen crane their necks in the direction of the doorway. The homicide detectives in the Stetson hats appear first and then, suddenly, there is Oswald, sandwiched between them as they inch their way toward the front of the stage.[1006]

A huge, bulky, pool television camera from Dallas CBS affiliate KRLD-TV is mounted on a tripod near the doorway, its four-inch barrel lens trained on Oswald's face. A late-night national audience (only NBC has stopped coverage) holds its collective breath as it gets its first really good look at the man accused of murdering the president of the United States. A flock of flashbulbs pop from dozens of still cameras as police come to a stop near the center of the front of the stage.

"Down in front! Down in front!" the unfortunate newsmen in the back of the room shout in frustration. A crush of reporters are only inches from Oswald, a semicircle of handheld microphones thrust forward toward the suspect's face in eager anticipation of his first words. The noise level dips as Oswald responds to a question he has picked out of the din.

"I was questioned by a judge without legal representation," he says in his peculiarly dry, Texas-tinged boy's voice, before being drowned out by a torrent of frustrated voices.

"Louder! Down in front, down, down!" reporters holler.

Oswald stops for a moment and purses his lips, a habit that gives him a prissy, dogmatic air. When the noise subsides a little, he starts again.

"Well, I was questioned by a judge; however, I protested at that time that I was not allowed legal representation . . ."

"Hey! Down! Down!" a chorus of back-of-the-room voices again shouts at the men blocking their view. Several finally give up complaining and begin dragging metal chairs into position on which to stand for a better vantage point. The sound of clanking metal only helps to drown out Oswald's weak voice.

". . . during that . . . ah . . . that . . . ah . . . very short and sweet hearing. Ah, I really don't know what this situation is about. Nobody has told me anything except that I am accused of . . . ah . . . of . . . ah . . . murdering a policeman. [Oswald has not yet been arraigned for the murder of Kennedy and is unaware that he has been charged with Kennedy's murder.] I know nothing more than that and I do request . . . ah . . . someone to come forward . . . ah . . . to give me legal assistance."

"Did you kill the president?"

"No, I have not been charged with that. In fact, nobody has said that to me yet. The first thing I heard about it was when the newspaper reporters in the hall . . . ," Oswald's voice cracks nervously, ". . . asked me that question."

"You *have* been charged," a reporter in the front tells him.

"Sir?" Oswald says, somewhat confused, looking at the reporter kneeling in front of him.

"You have been charged," the reporter repeats.

Oswald purses his lips, then a look of astonishment crosses his face, but he says nothing.

"Nobody said *what*? We can't hear you back here," someone complains from the back of the room.

The jostling continues unabated and Curry decides he's seen enough.

"Okay, men," Curry says to the two detectives flanking Oswald. "Okay."

The men in the Stetson hats turn and begin pushing Oswald slowly toward the exit as reporters kneeling in the front continue their verbal assault.

"What did you do in Russia?"

Oswald ignores the first question.

"How did you hurt your eye?" another reporter asks.

Oswald moves along in silence. The reporter asks again.

"Oswald, how did you hurt your eye?"

Oswald leans toward the microphone.

"A policeman hit me," he whines.

After just six minutes, it is over. Newsmen in the back of the room plead for someone up front to fill them in on what Oswald had said during his brief moments in front of the cameras.[1007]

Exiting the assembly room, Detectives Sims and Boyd lead Oswald into the basement jail office, where they encounter Deputy Chief George L. Lumpkin and Sergeant Wilson F. Warren. Entering the jail elevator, the four men take Oswald up to the fourth-floor jail office, where he is searched once again and also booked, nearly eleven hours after his arrest.[1008] He is then taken to his fifth-floor jail cell.

The jail cell that Deputy Chief Lumpkin, who is in charge of jail security, has assigned Oswald isolates him from other prisoners. It's a maximum-security cell, number F-2, on the fifth floor. The maximum-security area is a group of three cells away from the rest of the units, with lockable doors that open into a narrow corridor, which itself has another lockable door that is controlled from a master control panel. Lumpkin orders Oswald to be placed in the middle cell, the two cells on either side kept empty. It is virtually impossible for any other prisoners to see or talk with him.

Oswald is ordered to strip to his underwear, and his belt and other potentially harmful personal effects are taken from him. His clothes and effects are shoved into a paper bag for retrieval the next time he's removed from the cell. The jail guard leads Oswald through the first heavily barred door. It bolts behind them. Four bare lightbulbs, screened in wire, hang in the small hallway. The jailer opens the middle cell, Oswald steps inside, and the door shuts behind him with a loud metal clang.

Oswald's twelve-by-twelve-foot cell has four bunk beds inside, the upper two made of metal, the lower two of wood, a stainless-steel sink, a toilet, and a water fountain. Bars that cross overhead give the cell a sense of a cage.[1009] Oswald flops onto a bunk while two guards take up residence right outside the cell as part of an around-the-clock vigil, a suicide watch. Chief Lumpkin is taking no chances with the prime suspect.[1010]

12:19 a.m.

After Oswald was taken from the assembly room, some of the press boys had run out to make deadlines. Others stuck around to interview District Attorney Henry Wade, hoping to pick up something juicy for their morning papers.

Wade's concern is to make sure he doesn't prejudice the rights of the accused to a fair trial. His real problem this night is his lack of knowledge about the investigation. He'd been briefed only once, little more than an hour ago. And then, only on the basics of the case.

Wade tells the reporters that Oswald has been "formally charged . . . with both killing Officer Tippit and John F. Kennedy. He's been taken before the judge and advised of his rights." (Oswald, in fact, had not yet at this point been taken before any judge on the Kennedy charge, arraigned, and advised of his rights.)

"Can you tell [us] any of the evidence against him so far, sir?"

"No," Wade replies. "We are still working on the evidence . . ."

"Do you have a good case?"

"I figure we have sufficient evidence to convict him," Wade answers.

"Are there any indications that this was an organized plot," a reporter inquires, "or was it just one man?"

"There's no one else but him," Wade says, adding, "so far."

Someone, again, asks a question about the evidence gathered so far.

"Well, there is a lot of physical evidence that was gathered," Wade says, "including the gun, that is on its way by air force jet to the FBI crime lab in Washington. It will be back here tomorrow. There are some other things that's going to delay this [until] probably the middle of next week before it's presented to the grand jury."

"Do you have witnesses to use against him in the killing of President Kennedy?"

"We have approximately fifteen witnesses," Wade answers.

"Who identified him as the killer of the president?"

"I didn't say that," Wade corrects.

A reporter asks to clarify whether he's talking about fifteen witnesses in the murder of the police officer or the president.

"Both," Wade replies.

The question of motive is raised.

"Well, he was a member of the movement—," Wade grapples for the word, "—the Free Cuba movement—"

"What's the make of the rifle, sir?"

"It's a Mauser, I believe," Wade answers erroneously.

"Does the suspect deny the shootings?"

"Yes," Wade says, "he denies them both."

"Are you through questioning him?" someone asks.

"No, we have further questioning to do. We will probably let him sleep and talk to him in the morning." It's very late, and Wade is wondering when the questions will end.[1011]

12:35 a.m.

Oswald has been in his cell less than ten minutes when Sergeant Warren opens the door and tells him to put on his clothes. Lieutenant Karl P. Knight of the Identification Bureau is there to see that Oswald is taken to the fourth floor to be photographed and fingerprinted.

"I *have* been fingerprinted," Oswald protests.

Knight knew that Oswald was referring to prints taken of him around 9:00 p.m. to compare with the latent prints discovered on the rifle and cardboard boxes found on the sixth floor. Now that felony charges had been filed against him, Knight needs something a little more permanent for the Dallas police files. As part of standard procedure, copies of these new prints will be sent to the FBI to find out if the prisoner is wanted elsewhere.* Sergeant Wilson F. Warren and jail assistant Tommy V. Todd take Oswald downstairs to the Identification Bureau to be processed. Knight and Captain Doughty see that another set of fingerprints is made and mug shots—front and profile—are taken. Oswald is arrogant and irritable. He drags his fingers across the inkpad, until a cop takes each digit one by one and rolls

---

*Why Oswald wasn't fingerprinted when he was booked into the jail just after midnight is not known.

and prints them properly. When they ask him to sign his name at the bottom of the fingerprint card, Oswald refuses. His thumb print is added to indicate that his fingerprints had been taken and placed in police files. They finish the formalities in about thirty-five minutes, and the sullen Oswald is taken back to his fifth-floor jail cell.[1012]

1:00 a.m.

While Bill Alexander and some police detectives were going over the names and backgrounds of Oswald's coworkers at the Book Depository Building before midnight, the name Joe Molina, the credit manager at the Depository, came up. It immediately "rang a bell" with Alexander. "He was a known, card-carrying Communist—at that time there were damn few Communists in Dallas, and they actually carried cards on them—that I knew from a big publicity murder case I had prosecuted a year or so earlier," Alexander would later recall. "Because of the publicity, the defense made a motion for a change of venue and Molina testified for the defense that the defendant couldn't get a fair trial in Dallas. We had no evidence of any connections between Molina and Oswald except the Book Depository Building and their Communist Party affiliation."

Alexander proceeds to prepare a search warrant for Molina's house, gets Judge Johnston to sign it, and "since Fritz's boys were busy" goes to serve the warrant with Captain Pat Gannaway, the head of the Special Services Bureau, and a few of his men, including Lieutenant Jack Revill, who is in charge of the criminal intelligence section that, among other things, investigates subversive activities. Molina, a short, stocky, and prematurely graying man of forty, lives in a small home close to downtown Dallas with his wife and four kids, one of whom is adopted. Alexander and his people arrive around one in the morning, and the loud knocking on the door at this hour scares Soledad, Molina's wife, half to death. The whole family, asleep in the two-bedroom home, was awakened. Joe comes to the door in his pajamas and is served with the warrant. Alexander doesn't say what this is all about but Molina assumes it has some connection with the assassination because of his employment at the Depository.

"Joe," Alexander says, "go back to bed. We won't ransack the house." "Go ahead and look around," Molina said, indicating he had nothing to hide. But before Joe can get back in bed, Gannaway and Revill have other plans and, during the search, question Molina about his acquaintance-ship with Oswald (he has seen him at work, but is not acquainted with him and has never spoken to him) and the political affiliation of members of the GI Forum, a local veterans group Molina, a navy vet, belonged to that had several other known Communist members. Molina says he doesn't know the political affiliation of the members of the group, but declines to write a statement to that effect. The search of Molina's house will continue for two hours.[1013]

1:10 a.m.

In the basement assembly room, remarkably, Henry Wade is still held cap-tive by an inquisitive collection of reporters. Judge David Johnston has joined him.

"Does he have a lawyer?"

"I don't know whether he has or not," Wade says.

"Does he appear sane to you?"

"Yes, he does," Wade replies firmly.

"Is he a member of any Communist-front organization?"

"That I couldn't tell you at the present time," Wade says.

"Any organizations that he belongs to that you know of?" a reporter hollers.

"Well," the district attorney answers, "the only one I mentioned was the Free Cuba movement or whatever that—"

Ruby, recalling what he heard on the radio earlier, shouts out a cor-rection from the back of the room, "Fair Play for Cuba Committee." Wade, surprised at getting a correction from his audience, recognizes the man in the horn-rimmed glasses and slicked black hair as someone he's seen around, but thinks he must be a journalist of some sort.

"Fair Play for Cuba, I believe it was," Wade continues, acknowledg-ing the correction.

"Why do you think he wanted to kill the president?"

"The only thing I do," Wade tells the throng, "is take the evidence, present it to a jury, and I don't pass on why he did it or anything else. We . . . we're just interested in proving that he did it, which I think we have."[1014]

"Are you planning to charge anyone else in this at all at this moment?"

"As of this moment," Wade says, "we are not."

"Are you looking for any other suspects at all now that you've got—"

"Well, we're always looking for other suspects," Wade shoots back, "but we have none at present."

"Henry, do you think this is part of [a] Communist conspiracy?"

The question cuts at the district attorney's nerves.

"I can't say that," he answers diplomatically.

"Well, do you have any reason to believe that it might be?" the reporter pursues.

"No," Wade answers, "I don't have any reason to believe either way on it."

"Has he said under questioning that he is either a Communist or a Communist sympathizer?"

"I don't know whether he has or not," Wade replies.

"Can you say whether you have a witness who says he saw the man pull the trigger?"

"No, I cannot," Wade answers carefully.

"What was the result of the paraffin test?" someone asks.

"I am not going into the evidence here," Wade says.

There is some continuing confusion over whether Oswald has been advised of the charge in the assassination. Judge David Johnston, standing behind Wade, steps forward to try to clear up any misunderstanding.

"He has not been advised," Johnston says.

"He has been charged?"

"He has not been arraigned on the second charge," Johnston says.

"No, but has he been charged?" the reporter presses.

"Yes," the judge replies, "he is formally charged."

The reporters question when the arraignment for the assassination will take place, but both Wade and Johnston seem uncertain. They imagine sometime that night, then suggest that it might be morning before Oswald is arraigned.[1015] Wade continues to answer questions for a few more minutes, but has little to add to what he has already said.

"Mr. Wade, was he under any kind of federal surveillance because of his background prior to today, today's events?"

Wade, no doubt thinking of Jack Revill's memo, prefers not to open that can of worms. "None that I know of. We didn't have any knowledge— We didn't have any information on him. When I say we, being the Dallas police or the Dallas sheriff's office."[1016]

Several questions return to the issue of whether this was an organized plot or just one man out to get the president.

"We don't know that answer," Wade replies. "He's the only one we have."

"Are you willing to say whether you think this man was inspired as a Communist or whether he is simply a nut or a middleman?"

"I'll put it this way," Wade says. "I don't think he's a nut."[1017]

1:20 a.m.
After Wade's press conference, he continues to be interviewed by individual reporters outside the basement assembly room, and Jack Ruby persists in his pursuit of Joe Long, who mysteriously remains elusive to Ruby. But Jack finally manages to get the control room number of the station from two reporters, Jerry Cunkle and Sam Pease, who worked for rival KBOX. Calling the control room, he's shuttled to Glenn Duncan in the newsroom, whom he tells, "I have sandwiches for you. I want to get over there," and then adds, "By the way, I see Henry Wade talking on the phone to someone. Do you want me to get him over here?"

"Yes, do that."

"Just a second, he's talking to someone from New York. I'll get him."

He goes over, collars the district attorney, and brings him back to the phone, not even telling him what station it is.

The newsman at KLIF is elated over scoring the brief interview, and tells Ruby he can "only leave the door open for five minutes."

On the way out, Ruby spots Russ Knight of KLIF with a tape

recorder. Glenn Duncan rushed him over from the station a few blocks away to get another interview with the district attorney—they didn't get the first one on the phone on tape, and Duncan wants something for the morning news. Ruby, only too happy to oblige, takes Knight to Wade.

"Ask him if Oswald is insane," Ruby suggests to Knight.

"Okay," Knight says. "That's a point well taken."

Ruby introduces them.

"Oh," Wade says, recognizing Knight's name, "you're the Weird Beard!"

Knight cringes a little—his on-the-air persona is great for the kids who have made him the top-rated DJ in Dallas, but it sounds just a mite foolish here.

Wade obliges Knight with an interview and tells Knight that Oswald is not insane. His brutal act was entirely premeditated. While Knight is interviewing Wade, Ruby leaves for the station three blocks away. But arranging the interview with Henry Wade for Russ Knight delayed Ruby beyond the five-minute window he'd been offered, and he finds the door to the KLIF studios locked when he gets there, so he waits, with Sheba, for Knight to get back.[1018]

1:30 a.m.

Wade and Judge Johnston finally escape the persistent journalists and make their way back to the third-floor homicide office. On the way, the district attorney tells Johnston that they should arraign Oswald on the Kennedy killing immediately. When the pair get to Captain Fritz's office, they confer with Chief Curry, Captain Fritz, and Assistant DA Maurice Harrell.[1019] It may be approaching the middle of the night but with all the activity one would never know it. Curry agrees that Oswald should be arraigned on the murder charge regarding the president's death soon. The U.S. Supreme Court recently ruled that a prisoner must be arraigned and informed of the charges against him as soon as possible. Curry doesn't want anyone saying that they haven't followed the law.

Curry picks up the phone and calls the jail supervisor, Sergeant Warren.

"Bring Oswald back down to the fourth-floor ID bureau," he says. "We'll meet you there."[1020]

Oswald has been asleep,* though not for very long, when Sergeant Warren awakens him.

"What's going on?" Oswald says angrily, half asleep.

"I've got my orders from the chief," the jail supervisor says. "He says to bring you down to ID again."

The man who would arguably become the most famous murderer in history, as well as the most consequential one, doesn't bother to protest. He swings his legs to the floor and holds his wrists out in front of him as the cuffs are snapped in place. Sergeant Warren and jailer Tommy Todd escort him toward the stairway.[1021]

1:35 a.m.

Oswald and his escorts emerge from the stairwell and enter the Identification bureau inside the fourth-floor jail office. A half-dozen police officials are standing behind the counter when Oswald arrives. He purses his lips and surveys the familiar faces.

Judge David Johnston stands squarely behind the counter, with complaint number F-154, the Kennedy murder charge, in his hand. The men grouped around him are some of the top brass of Dallas law enforcement: Captain Fritz, Chief Curry, Assistant Deputy Chief M. W. Stevenson, District Attorney Henry Wade, and Assistant District Attorney Maurice Harrell. A few Identification Bureau officers who happen to be on duty, including crime-lab lieutenant Carl Day, hover nearby.[1022]

"Well, I guess this is the trial," Oswald sneers sarcastically.

"No sir," Judge Johnston replies, "I have to arraign you on another offense."

For the second time this night, Johnston advises Oswald of his constitutional right to remain silent and warns him that any statement he makes

---

*The only source for Oswald ostensibly being asleep is author Jim Bishop. However, Bishop does not say who his source was, but the implication is that it was Sergeant Warren. (Bishop, *Day Kennedy Was Shot*, p.651) Even if it were Warren, Warren may simply have assumed that a physically still Oswald was asleep and called out to awaken him.

may be used in evidence against him. Then, Johnston reads the complaint to Oswald, that "Lee Harvey Oswald, hereinafter styled Defendant, heretofore on or about the twenty-second day of November, 1963, in the County of Dallas and State of Texas, did then and there unlawfully, voluntarily, and with malice aforethought kill John F. Kennedy by shooting him with a gun against the peace and dignity of the State."[1023]

"Oh, that's the deal, is it," Oswald says. "I don't know what you're talking about."[1024]

Johnston ignores the comment and advises Oswald of his right to an attorney.

"I want Mr. John Abt of New York," Oswald demands, spelling the name out. "A-B-T."

"You'll be given the opportunity to contact any attorney you wish," Judge Johnston answers calmly. "Bond is denied on this capital offense. I hereby remand you to the custody of the sheriff of Dallas County, Texas."[1025]

In ten minutes it is over. Lee Harvey Oswald has been formally arraigned on the charge of assassinating the president of the United States. Chief Curry, who has seen little of Oswald in the course of the evening, is not impressed by his truculence and arrogance. Curry nods to the jailers, who spin and take the prisoner back upstairs to his fifth-floor cell.[1026]

1:50 a.m.
Most of Dallas is asleep when Ruby finally enters the KLIF building after Russ Knight gets back from City Hall and opens the door. Several of the guys on duty are glad to see Jack's big paper sack full of corned beef sandwiches and soft drinks. "I figured you guys would be hungry," Jack tells them, "and I brought these up for you." Knight and DJ Danny McCurdy were intrigued by Doctor Black's celery tonic in its peculiarly shaped bottle and expensive-looking gold foil, which neither of them had ever seen before. Whoever heard of a soft drink with celery in it? Jack explains that it's something you normally get only in New York and is especially pleased when McCurdy thinks it's the best soft drink he's ever had.

Five minutes later Jack has worked his way into the control room, where he chats with McCurdy between announcements while Duncan and Knight get the two o'clock news ready.

Jack appreciates the way the station has switched from Top Forty to album music—easy listening, McCurdy calls it. Ruby is pale and keeps looking at the floor. McCurdy is feeling awfully low himself and thinks little of it.

"I'm closing my club down this weekend," Jack tells him morosely. "I'd rather lose twelve or fifteen hundred this weekend than not be able to live with myself later on." He gives McCurdy a card for the Carousel Club. McCurdy already has one Ruby gave him some time back, one with a picture of one of the strippers on it.

Ike Pappas comes in with a lot of tapes he wants to relay back to WNEW in New York, and the KLIF guys are happy to let him use their facilities. Pappas also gets one of the corned beef sandwiches, but is so busy with his work he never sees Ruby.

Though Duncan is getting ready to go with his two o'clock news bulletin, he chats a little with Ruby, who seems somewhat excited and happy that the case against Oswald is going well. He seems to get a real charge out of being close to the police and the news developments. Duncan is intrigued by Ruby's description of Oswald—that he looks a little like the movie star Paul Newman.

Ruby stays right there in the newsroom for the bulletin, and after Duncan leads to Knight, the latter says, "I have just returned from a trip to the Dallas County Courthouse [actually City Hall] and, on a tip from Jack Ruby, local night club owner . . ."

Jack is tickled pink at the mention of his name on the air. After Ruby chats with the guys for a quarter of an hour or so, Knight walks Ruby down to his car, parked right in front of the door, the little dachshund, Sheba, patiently awaiting his return. Ruby wants him to urge Gordon McClendon to devote one of his on-the-air editorials to the assassination and the turgid, right-wing political atmosphere in Dallas that he feels led to it. He's a great admirer of McClendon, a Kennedy supporter who ran unsuccessfully as a Democrat for the Senate and the only radio broadcaster in Dallas to do editorials, and outspoken ones at that. Ruby fishes a one-page flyer from the mess in his car and hands it to the disk jockey. "You look like a square guy, why don't you look this over and read it?"

Ruby's story about the flyer is complicated to Knight, but it has something to do with right-wing radicalism in Dallas, though Ruby doesn't use those exact words.

Ruby had gotten the flyer when he was selling a contrivance called a twistboard out at the Texas Products Show at the Exhibit Hall off the Stemmons Freeway a couple of weeks ago. Ruby's friend Ed Pullman, a furniture designer, had a booth there, and Ruby took some of his girls out there every night during the week the show was on to demonstrate and sell the device. One of them got her picture into the *Dallas Times Herald*. Ruby had stopped by the booth of H. L. Hunt, the right-wing Dallas oil tycoon, which was giving away free bags of groceries, and in his Ruby found the flyer, a script called "Heroism" for Hunt's radio show, *Life Line*. He was outraged by the script and steamed back to Pullman's booth on the mezzanine, George Senator in tow.

"I'm going to send this stuff to Kennedy," Jack raged breathlessly. "I want to send this stuff to Kennedy. Nobody has the right to talk like this about our government."

Pullman was philosophical. "Well, you just learned about it now, but *Life Line* has been out for some time, and that's what he does and that's how he gets his materials around."

"I'm going to do something about this, I'm going to see that this is taken up in Washington," Ruby insists. He even mentions the FBI. Pullman recalls to Ruby that Hunt had not been allowed to have a display at some New York fair because of that type of literature. "I'm sure that Kennedy knows all about this, and Washington knows about this."

"Maybe they don't. I'm going to send it in."

"Well, you do what you want," Pullman said.

It's all a bit of a mystery to Knight, but he takes the broadsheet from Ruby and goes home.

It's hard to figure out why Ruby had gotten so exercised about the flyer out at the fair. The flyer was all pretty harmless stuff, although it did contain this language:

Personal heroism is a vital part of the American character and the American dream . . . Nearly all nations, *when they do fail*, have forgotten what heroism is.

And,

A nation and a people which truly value their heroes *have no use for a paternal government which always claims to know best*. Such a nation cannot be coaxed or conned out of their fundamental liberties.

It's bylined "Gene Scudder from Washington." At the bottom of the back of the sheet is a list of two-dozen stations in the Dallas–Fort Worth area which carry the program, and a short list of "some of the other three hundred *Life Line* stations," almost all in the South.[1027]

Robert Donovan, Washington bureau chief for the *Los Angeles Times*, finally gets back to his Dallas hotel after an incredibly hectic day that went by without his eating since breakfast the previous morning in Fort Worth. He and some of his colleagues, equally famished and exhausted, were able to send out for food. They give the old black waiter, dressed in a young bellboy's outfit, some extra money to also get them "a jug" of liquor, telling him they had worked for hours, were frazzled, and needed it. But you couldn't buy liquor over the counter in Dallas, it being a "closed" city, and the waiter wasn't about to find some other way, illicit, to get the hooch. "No," he says evenly, "you couldn't do that because that would be breaking the law." He then adds in a voice that Donovan knows he will remember to his dying day, "There've been enough laws broken in Dallas today."[1028]

2:00 a.m.
Eventually, in the early hours of Saturday morning, Dallas police headquarters begins to quiet down for the night. Captain Fritz sends his troops home, with instructions to be back by ten, but remains in his office con-

ferring with Wade, Judge Johnston, and some of the other officers on the case until around 3:45 a.m., when they all go home. Deputy Chief Stevenson remains in his office on the third floor, where, with a couple of detectives, he continues to work, available for anything that might need to be investigated during the night. He doesn't get home until around 12:30 Saturday afternoon.[1029]

2:30 a.m. (3:30 a.m. EST)

At Bethesda Naval Hospital, the morticians are winding up the embalming and casketing of the president's body.[1030]

2:45 a.m.

After leaving KLIF, Jack Ruby decides to drive over to the *Times Herald* building. He rarely goes there to place his weekend ad, because once he gets the ad into the *Morning News*, which comes out first, he just calls the afternoon newspaper to have the ad "transpired," as he puts it, into the *Times Herald*, but he promised one of the boys over there on the night shift one of his twistboards. He had put off going there for some time, but since he hadn't called in his ad today, he feels this might be a good time to take out an ad in the *Herald* that his clubs will be closed Saturday and Sunday nights.

As he drives past a parking garage at the corner of Jackson and Field, he hears a horn honk and sees a police officer he knows, Harry Olsen, sitting in a car. He's sitting there with one of Jack's girls, Kathy Kay. The thing with Kathy is supposed to be a secret, but Jack knows all about it. Kathy's real name—most of the strippers use stage names—is Kay Coleman.

Harry's divorce came through last month, and Kay has been divorced for a time, but it would be difficult for a police officer to marry a woman who is working as a stripper. Kay is from England and, young as she is—just twenty-seven—has two little girls, ages seven and nine. Jack likes Kay a lot, and he has stopped over at her place with a few other people for a late-night breakfast a couple of times—it's only four or five blocks from his apartment out in Oak Cliff, on the same street, Ewing.

Jack climbs into the car with Harry and Kay. They had driven over to Dealey Plaza earlier, just to see where the president was shot, stopped in at the Sip and Nip on Commerce Street for a couple of drinks, and then went to see their friend Johnny Johnson, who works at the garage. They are drinking beer, ruminating on the day's sad events, and glad to see Jack. They think he's a great guy for closing his clubs. They are all upset about the assassination and find it hard to talk about much else. Harry's leg is in a cast so he has been on light duty for a while. He was off that day and spent most of it moonlighting, guarding the estate of an elderly lady out in Oak Cliff near Kay's place.

Earlier Kay had called Andy Armstrong at the Carousel from her house to find out whether the club would be open that night.

"What's Jack doing?" she asked.

"Oh, he is all upset and he is crying," Andy told her, adding, "We are closed tonight."

Harry and Kay have known Jack for a couple of years and can see that he's really upset. Harry used to work the downtown area and made routine checks of the Carousel. He's seen Jack so mad that he would shake, usually at his employees, but sometimes at customers too. Jack can fly off the handle about almost anything. Harry would take him aside and get him to calm down, and Jack, with his respect for police officers, listened to Harry.

Jack tells them he saw Oswald down at the police station, calls him an "SOB," and says, "It's too bad that a peon could do something like that," referring to the killing of Kennedy and Tippit. Kay thinks Jack is wild-eyed, with a sort of starey look. He is awfully tired, sits back, and stares off into space. He doesn't cry or anything, but he just keeps saying over and over how terrible it is. He also keeps mentioning Jackie Kennedy and her children, whose plight especially touches him. Harry thinks they should cut Oswald into ribbons inch by inch, and Jack recalls all the citizens who went out that morning with banners and posters stirring up hate against the president. "I just wonder how they feel about that now." The three commiserate about the death of Kennedy for over an hour.[1031]

2:56 a.m. (3:56 a.m. EST)
At Bethesda Naval Hospital, Secret Service agent Roy Kellerman telephones the seventeenth-floor suite where the Kennedy family and friends have been waiting for almost nine hours.

"We're ready," he tells them.

Secret Service agents escort the Kennedy entourage—Mrs. Kennedy, Robert and Ted Kennedy and Robert's wife, Ethel, the president's sisters, Dave Powers, Kenneth O'Donnell, Larry O'Brien, Robert McNamara, and others—down to a small room near the rear loading dock.[1032]

In the morgue, the casket team, under the leadership of First Lieutenant Samuel R. Bird, conducts a small ceremony placing the American flag on the casket.[1033] Finally, as a last sign of respect for the commander in chief, the Secret Service agents who have been present all night carry the casket out to the loading dock and toward the navy ambulance.[1034] The marines who have been guarding the Bethesda morgue this night snap to attention and salute as the casket passes.[1035] After the president's body is secured in the ambulance, the Kennedy entourage emerges from the rear of the hospital. Mrs. Kennedy and the president's brother Robert are helped into the rear of the ambulance. Jackie sits on a jump seat next to the coffin; Bobby crouches on the floor beside it. The others enter a bevy of limousines assembled near the loading dock.[1036]

Before leaving, Admiral Burkley turns to autopsy pathologist Jim Humes.

"I would like to have the [autopsy] report, if we could, by 6:00 p.m. Sunday [November 24] night," he says.[1037] Humes nods, in agreement.

Before the three pathologists leave the morgue, they confer on how to handle the task. It's obvious to them that a committee cannot write it. One person will have to take charge and the others can critique and refine the final language. Commander Humes volunteers to write the initial draft. They plan to meet again in Admiral Galloway's office on Sunday morning (November 24) to finalize the autopsy report.[1038]

In a few minutes, under very heavy security, the procession of cars makes its way at thirty miles an hour over the 9.5 miles toward the northwest gate of the White House.[1039] An impromptu escort of hundreds of cars, driven by ordinary citizens, trails the procession as it slips silently through the streets of Washington in the early-morning darkness. Those in the official cars look out the windows and see ordinary men of every color on their way to work standing at attention as they pass, caps held over their hearts.[1040]

At the White House, the six members of the casket team reassemble at the rear of the navy ambulance, which has pulled up close to the portico steps. They seem to be straining as they carry the casket into the White House foyer. Their commander, Lieutenant Bird, steps up quickly and slides his hands under the back of the heavy casket. A soldier in front of him whispers, "Good God, don't let go." They shuffle across the marble floor, past Marine honor guards, and into the East Room, where the casket is placed on a replica of the catafalque on which Abraham Lincoln's coffin rested.[*] As soon as the pallbearers step back, a Roman Catholic priest moves toward the casket and instructs an altar boy to light the candles that surround the catafalque. The priest sprinkles the coffin with holy water, kneels, and quietly reads from Psalm 130: "Out of the depths I cry to you, O Lord; Lord, hear my voice!" At the end of the brief ceremony, the honor guards are inspected and posted at parade rest, near the casket.

Air Force Brigadier General Godfrey McHugh and Secret Service agent Clint Hill stand momentarily alongside the casket in the hushed and cavernous East Room. It is so quiet they can hear each other breathe. An usher comes up to Agent Hill and informs him that Mrs. Kennedy, who had gone to her room, will come down shortly and would like the casket opened for a few minutes. The flag is removed from the coffin in anticipation of her arrival and the casket lid unsealed, though kept closed. In a moment, the First Lady appears, escorted by Bobby Kennedy. Several members of Kennedy's inner circle are also present, bunched together at one end of the room. Jackie looks exhausted, still wearing her "strawberry dress" caked with the president's dried blood. General McHugh orders the honor guards to leave the room. The men do a quick

---

[*]"Someone had neglected to pass the word that the original Lincoln catafalque had been located in the basement of the Capitol building," and based on a book on the Lincoln funeral that included steel-point engravings, White House carpenters had quickly constructed the replica (Bishop, *Day Kennedy Was Shot*, pp.486, 548; Manchester, *Death of a President*, p.437).

about-face and start to leave, when Mrs. Kennedy pleads, "No, they can stay." The guards freeze in place, their backs to the coffin. As the First Lady steps to the side of the casket, the lid is opened. She stands gazing for a moment upon her husband's face, then turns to Secret Service agent Clint Hill, the one who had sprung to her aid seconds after the shots, and asks for a pair of scissors. He gets them for her. She reaches in and snips a lock of the president's hair. She then turns away, saying "It isn't Jack."

When Jackie silently leaves the room, "the rest of us followed," presidential aide Arthur Schlesinger would later recall. As Jackie, exhausted, mounts the stairway and makes her way for the night to her second-floor room,* the group of Kennedy intimates stand awkwardly outside the East Room, waiting for Bobby Kennedy to direct their next move. Bobby, his cheeks damp with tears, turns to them and asks them to come back in and take a look at the body. He wants to settle the issue of an open casket before he retires, as he had promised the First Lady he would do when they were standing together beside the catafalque. "Jackie wants it covered," he tells them.

RFK had not been able to bear looking at his brother at that time, but now, for the first time, he does. Of the seven who view the remains, including Secretary of State Robert McNamara, Schlesinger, and Nancy Tuckerman (Jackie's social secretary), only two believe the president is presentable. The rest are appalled at the waxen figure.

"Don't do it," Bill Walton, a family friend, pleads.

*Earlier in the day, Jackie's mother, Mrs. Janet Auchincloss, had told Maud Shaw, Caroline and John Jr.'s nanny, that she and Jackie felt that Miss Shaw "should be the one to break the news to the children, at least to Caroline," who was five years old and would be six in a little less than a week. "Oh, no," Shaw said, "please don't ask me to do that." "Please, Miss Shaw," Mrs. Auchincloss said. "It is for the best. They trust you, and you know how to deal with them. I am asking you as a friend, please. It has to be you." In writing about the matter later, Shaw does not pinpoint the time she did this, merely indicating it was after she had tucked the children into bed for the night. She says she went into Caroline's room and started reading to her from one of her books. When Caroline asked her why she was crying, she told her she had "very sad news." She says, "Then I told her what had happened. It was a dreadful time for us both." Caroline eventually fell asleep, with Ms. Shaw still petting her. She said John Jr. still did not know and "was really too young [two, though he'd be three in a few days] to understand." Later, she said, it was decided that Mrs. Robert Kennedy would tell him the best she could. (Shaw, *White House Nannie*, pp.14, 20–21)

"You're right," Bobby says. "Close it."[1041]

Bobby turns away and goes upstairs to the Lincoln bedroom with Charles Spalding, a close friend of both Kennedy brothers.

"There's a sleeping pill around somewhere," Spalding says.

"God, it's so awful," Bobby says, sinking onto the bed. "Everything was really beginning to run so well." He is exhausted, but composed. Spalding finds a sleeping pill, hands it to him, and steps out of the room. As he closes the door, he hears Bobby break down.

"Why, God?" he sobs.[1042]

3:00 a.m.

Alexander and his people have just concluded their search of Joe Molina's home, and Molina had been cooperative throughout. "We really searched his home, up and down, not finishing until around three in the morning," Alexander would later recall. "We found nothing to connect him to Oswald or the assassination." But after a conference in Molina's kitchen, the searchers agree that they should interrogate Molina further, and ask him whether he'd prefer to come with them down to police headquarters at that time, or come on his own in the morning. Molina opts to go back to bed and says he'll see them in the morning.[1043]

4:00 a.m.

Mitchell Scibor, general operating manager of Klein's Sporting Goods in Chicago, looks up from one of the company's two microfilm machines at waiting FBI agents. It has taken nearly four hours, but he has found it at last—the order form for the rifle with serial number C2766.[1044]

This particular Mannlicher-Carcano was among those advertised in a number of magazines under catalog number C20-T750, which indicates that it was sold with a four-power telescopic sight,[1045] the sight purchased separately by Klein's from Martin B. Retting Company in Culver City, California, and mounted on the rifle at Klein's by gunsmith William Sharp.[1046] The rifle-scope assembly was then placed in a sixty-inch corrugated cardboard box,[1047] and readied for shipment. The retail price was $19.95, plus $1.50 for shipping and handling.[1048]

Although the original order form or coupon for the C2766 rifle was routinely destroyed, Klein's microfilmed records include a picture of the original order form or coupon clipped from the February 1963 issue of *American Rifleman* magazine and its accompanying envelope, postmarked March 12, 1963.[1049] Enclosed with the order was a U.S. Postal Money Order, number 2,202,130,462, for the total amount, $21.45.[1050] The order had been processed by Klein's on March 13, 1963, and shipped via parcel post on March 20, 1963.[1051] The customer had filled out the coupon and envelope in his own hand. The name is "A. Hidell" and the address is "P.O. Box 2915" in "Dallas, Texas."[1052]

The FBI agents look at each other knowingly. They know from bureau reports that Lee Harvey Oswald was carrying identification in that name at the time of his arrest.

Jack Ruby leaves Harry and Kay and proceeds to the *Dallas Times Herald*, where he delivers the twistboard to Arnold Clyde Gadash, a thirty-four-year-old printer whom Jack has known for years. The twistboard regularly sold for $3.98, and Jack had promised it to Gadash for $2.00, but since he kept him waiting so long for it, he gives it to Gadash. Gadash can see that Ruby, who takes out a black-bordered ad that his club will be closed that evening and Sunday evening, is very upset and emotional about the assassination, and Ruby brings up the Weissman ad with him, saying, as Gadash notices Jack's eyes watering, "The son of a bitch [Weissman] is trying to put the blame [for the assassination] on the Jews . . . Poor Mrs. Kennedy—Jackie and the kids," Ruby says emotionally. Other employees, some of whom know Ruby, are nearby and he temporarily starts to feel better by regaling them with stories of how close Oswald had come to him at City Hall and how he had corrected the district attorney, Henry Wade, at a press conference, intimating he was in good with the DA. He tells them he had seen Oswald being interviewed, that he looked like "a little weasel" and had "a smirk on his face." Gadash asks Jack to show him how the twistboard exerciser works, and though Jack really doesn't want to get into the hilarity of frolicking when he's so upset about the president's death, he gets on top of the board and gives a demonstration for Gadash and the other employees.[1053] God knows they can all use a good laugh.

At four-thirty Jack goes home and rouses George Senator from a sound sleep.

Senator has been staying at Jack's place for the past couple of months. A fifty-year-old World War II veteran, Senator has worked at more jobs than he can remember, mostly as a salesman, mostly without a lot of success. Ten years ago he was working out of Atlanta, selling women's apparel, when his boss said, "George, we are releasing a couple of men in Dallas and we want you to go to Dallas." George didn't want to, but the boss said, "George, you are going." He went. His wife didn't want to go either, and she didn't. A couple of years later they divorced. She kept the kid.

For a long time he lived mostly in motels, and for a period he shared rent with a couple of other guys who weren't doing well enough to afford places of their own. There were some long stretches when he wasn't employed at all, but the guys let him stay on because he was cooking and doing odd jobs for them. Soon after George first came to Dallas, in 1955 or 1956, a friend took him to the Vegas Club, where he met Jack Ruby, and after that they bumped into each other from time to time. In February or March of 1962 Jack sensed that George wasn't doing too well and invited him to move in with him for a while, over on Marsalis Avenue. George tried to hold up his end, cooking sometimes when Jack was home, but after five or six months he got a chance to go into the postcard business with the Texas Postcard & Novelty Company and he moved in with a fellow named Stan Corbat on Maple Avenue. He had been getting along fine with Jack, but he knew that Jack really liked to live alone. And Jack's place is too messy for George. Jack's clean in his person, but if he finishes reading a newspaper or something like that, it goes right on the floor.

At Corbat's, George had to sleep on the couch until he really started to get into selling postcards, and he and Stan were able to take a two-bedroom apartment on South Ewing. George told Jack about how great the building was, and within a week Jack moved into apartment 207, right next door to Corbat and George's 206. Then in August, Corbat got married and moved out, leaving George with all of the rent to pay on the apartment. George tried to stick it out for two months, but coming up with that much rent, at $125 a month, was too much of a struggle. Eventually, in late October, he moved in with Jack again into Jack's extra bedroom, which Jack had always kept available for anyone who needed a place to stay for a night or two, including homeless strippers at his club. They call George a "sales manager" at Texas Postcard, but his draw is only $61.45 a week, so the move was a terrific break for George because Jack didn't even ask him to share the rent. George occasionally helps Jack out at the club, running the lights or taking in the cash at the door, mostly on Fridays and Saturdays, but sometimes he will pop up during the week too.

George would be glad to cook regularly for Jack, but Jack is a funny guy about his food and George just can't cook it right for him. If George doesn't broil something just right, Jack complains. If he makes him eggs, he has to worry about the butter because Jack's always on some diet, and George finally got tired of it and said, "Make your own eggs." George doesn't even eat breakfast, just grabs a cup of coffee downtown once he's up and about. He can't get over Jack's habit of putting two grapefruits, skin and all, through the wringer in this machine he has, and then drinking the juice, his number one thing when he wakes up—sometimes in the middle of the afternoon.[1054]

Now it's the middle of the night and Jack is hollering and shaking him to wake up. He's all upset about that Weissman ad and some sign he saw saying "Impeach Earl Warren." He insists that George get up and get dressed. "You will have to get up, George. I want you to go with me."

It's a bit much at four-thirty in the morning, but George is truly grateful for Jack's many kindnesses to him, and he is always ready to do anything he can for Jack. As he is getting his clothes on, Jack calls Larry Crafard, the drifter kid Jack has been letting sleep in a backroom in front of his office at the club in return for answering the phone, helping to clean up, serving as a part-time bartender, and doing other odds and ends. There is no set salary, but any time Crafard needs a couple of bucks, he puts a draw slip in the till and takes some cash. It isn't a regular job, but Larry

Crafard isn't choosy. Since getting out of the army four years ago he has often been unemployed, and the dozens of jobs he's had, from fruit picker to poultry butcher, to carney roustabout and barker (in fact, he met Jack while working at the Texas State Fair the previous month), lasted days or weeks rather than months. He doesn't believe this job is going to last much longer either. "Larry, get up, get dressed, and get the Polaroid with the flashbulbs and meet me downstairs. I'll be right down," Ruby commands. The camera is for taking pictures of the customers when they dance with the girls, and Larry has worked it a couple of times.

Larry had just dressed and got the film and bulbs and was starting to get the camera when he gets a call from the parking garage next door telling him that Jack is already there and to hurry up.

They drive over to the corner of Hall and the North Central Expressway, and sure enough, there it is, a poster about three feet by four, pasted right up on the side of a building, with a photograph of Warren with the legend "Impeach Earl Warren."

They all get out of the car and Jack has Larry take three pictures of the sign with the Polaroid. It's all a mystery to Larry, since he's never heard of Earl Warren, and the conversation between Jack and George isn't all that enlightening. It strikes Larry as funny that Jack suddenly seems more excited about this billboard than he is about the assassination. Jack says, "I can't understand why they want to impeach Earl Warren. This must be the work of the John Birch Society or the Communist Party," two polar opposites politically.

After Larry takes the photos Jack wants, they stop for coffee at Webb's Waffle Shop on the ground floor of the Southland Hotel, located just a few blocks from the Carousel. Jack knows all the all-night places. At this predawn hour, the coffee shop is almost empty. He picks up a paper abandoned on the counter and reads the Weissman ad again. Jack is very suspicious about the coincidental appearance of the ad and the Warren billboard just when the president was coming to Dallas. He thinks there's a connection. Even the post office box numbers are close—1792 for the Weissman ad and 1757 for the billboard, though the latter is in some town in Massachusetts. Larry finds the conversation hard to follow, what with

Jack rereading aloud the Weissman ad in the *News* from a newspaper someone left behind, and breaking off to show the Polaroids to the guy at the counter. Jack wants to go to the post office to see what he can find out about the Weissman ad. To Larry's relief, they drop him back at the club first.[1055]

At the Dallas post office Jack and George find a box with the number for the Weissman ad, 1792, and there's a lot of mail in there. Jack presses the buzzer and asks the night clerk, "Who bought this box?"

"I can't give you any information," the clerk tells them. "Any information you want, there is only one man who can give it to you and that is the postmaster of Dallas."

George realizes that Jack is very, very disturbed. He has seen Jack hollering in those sudden outbursts of anger that he seems to forget about within seconds—George is well used to them—but this is completely different. "He had sort of a stare look in his eyes," George would later say. "I don't know how to describe it. I don't know how to put it in words," and it was nothing George had ever seen before in Ruby. When Jack talks about the president's family, he has tears in his eyes. George has known Jack for around eight years and it's the first time he has seen tears in his eyes. "Gee, his poor children and Mrs. Kennedy," he says over and over again. "What a terrible thing to happen." George sees that Jack is "deeply hurt" about the president's death, and although everyone George knows is grieving Kennedy's death, with Jack "it was worse."

The day is beginning to lighten by the time they get home from the post office, around 6:30 in the morning. Jack, back in the apartment, starts to cry "out loud." When he wasn't crying, Senator says "he looked like he was out in space." Jack calms down to watch a review of Friday's events on television for a while with George, but after a quarter of an hour they call it a day and turn in.[1056]

7:00 a.m.

Robert Oswald is already moving about after a sleepless night in the Statler Hilton Hotel's uncomfortable rollaway bed. After taking a shower, he waits in the lobby for the hotel drugstore to open. He hadn't brought a comb or toothbrush when he came from Denton, so he picks the personal items up and returns to his room to comb his hair. Rather than buy a razor and shaving cream, he decides to wait until the hotel barbershop opens and go there.

There are two barbers, both obviously unaware of Robert's identity. As one of them begins lathering up Robert's scruffy face, the barbers engage in a lively discussion of the assassination. One of the barbers has already made up his mind, Lee Oswald killed the president and should be executed immediately.

"Wait a minute," the barber shaving Robert says. "He may be guilty, or he may not. The only way to find out is to give him a fair trial."

Robert says nothing, but is so pleased with his barber's call for a fair trial that he tips him fifty cents. Robert skips breakfast and walks across the street to police headquarters in hopes that he might get in to see the chief of police, or even perhaps the man questioning his brother, Captain Fritz.[1057]

At the Dallas FBI office, Agent-in-Charge Gordon Shanklin calls his men together for their regular daily briefing. The agents have been arriving in virtual silence for the last half hour, whispering in hushed tones about yesterday's events. The office has the air of a funeral parlor.

Shanklin, rumpled, sleepless, and exhausted, reviews the events of the night.

"While you've been sleeping," he begins, "there have been some important developments. Last night at about 1:30 a.m., the county prosecutor filed first-degree murder charges against Oswald for the killing of the president. In addition, our agents in Chicago were able to trace the ownership of the rifle found on the sixth floor of the depository to Oswald."

Shanklin proceeds to outline the assignments for the day.

As the meeting ends, Bardwell Odum, a senior agent on the criminal squad, shows Hosty a surveillance photograph that had been flown up to Dallas in a two-seat navy jet fighter from Mexico City during the night.

It was thought to be a photograph of Lee Oswald as he walked out of the Soviet embassy. Hosty takes one look and knows immediately that it isn't Oswald. Odum asks if it might be an associate of Oswald's.

"Not so far as I know," Hosty tells him.

"Well, I've been ordered to show this to Oswald's wife," Odum says.

"Bard," Hosty replies, pointing to the background of the photograph, "you can't show that photo to people outside the bureau. Look, you can see the doorway to the Soviet embassy." Using a pair of scissors they crop out the doorway so no one will know where the photo was taken. They don't want the Soviets to learn that the Soviet embassy in Mexico City is under photographic surveillance, something, however, that the Soviets had to assume.[1058]

8:00 a.m. (9:00 a.m. EST)

Lee Oswald is roused at eight o'clock for breakfast. It was a short sleep, since it was nearly two when they finally locked him up in his solitary cell. The breakfast is no great treat either, just standard city jail fare, stewed apricots, oatmeal, plain bread, and black coffee. They won't let him handle a razor, but a jailer shaves him, making him roughly presentable for the long day ahead.[1059]

Meanwhile, in Washington at the White House, high drama is being played out. President Johnson arrives there, presumably to move into the Oval Office. Indeed, he appears at the door of the office of JFK's longtime secretary, Evelyn Lincoln, and asks her if she would come into the Oval Office with him. "Yes, Mr. President," she says. He proceeds to tell her that "because of overseas" (a presumed reference to nations abroad concerned about whether the country that led the free world in the cold war was as strong as ever), he needed "a transition," adding, "I have an appointment at 9:30 [EST]. Can I have my girls in your office by 9:30?" Remarkably, he was giving her a half hour to clear out of the office she had been in for three years. "Yes, Mr. President," she says quietly.

Lincoln had known that she would have to clear the West Wing of the corporeal evidence of her and her boss's presence, but she never imagined it was going to be so quick. Returning to her office, she saw RFK, and sobbed to him, "Do you know he asked me to be out by 9:30?" RFK was appalled at Johnson's insensitivity. "Oh, no," he said. When he encountered LBJ in the hall shortly thereafter, he told him that crating all of his brother's belongings out of the Oval Office (some had already been) was going to take time. "Can you wait" to move in? he asked LBJ. It wasn't he, Johnson replied, that wanted such a quick transition, but his advisers. RFK's body language let Johnson know he wasn't too impressed with that answer. Johnson, the most powerful man on earth, had been put in his place by one of perhaps only two people (the other being Jackie) capable of doing so at this moment in time, and he returned, with his people, to the Executive Office Building to conduct the affairs of state. It wouldn't be until after JFK was buried two days later that LBJ moved into the Oval Office.[1060] However, at LBJ's invitation, Jackie and the two Kennedy children continued to live in the upstairs presidential quarters until December 7, at which time they moved temporarily into the large and elegant Georgetown home of the aristocratic diplomat Averell Harriman, and LBJ and Lady Bird moved out of their twelve-room mansion into the White House.[1061]

9:00 a.m.

In Irving, the Paines are having breakfast with Marguerite and Marina Oswald when the two representatives from *Life* magazine, Tommy Thompson and Allan Grant, arrive unannounced with a female Russian interpreter.[1062]

As indicated, Marguerite had decided to take *Life*'s offer to put her and Marina up in a hotel room in Dallas so they could be near Lee. Marguerite was convinced that she would be besieged by reporters anxious to hear the life story of the accused assassin's mother. Why not rest in comfort in a posh hotel at their expense, she reasoned.[1063] It doesn't take long for Marina to get her children dressed and ready to go, packing enough diapers and baby bottles for the day. After all, she expects to return.[1064]* Marguerite is annoyed at the *Life* photographer, who is snapping pictures, and particularly with Mrs. Paine, who seems to be enjoying the media attention. The clear light of morning hasn't diminished the bitterness set off by the previous night's feud between Marguerite and Ruth. Each sees the other as an opportunist, eager to cash in on this unpleasant situation.[1065] Eventually Marguerite and Marina and her two children set off for town, where the *Life* people book them into Hotel Adolphus, right across the street from Jack Ruby's Carousel Club. Ruth Paine only wishes Marina had taken time to finish her breakfast. She knows it's going to be a trying day.[1066]

Life magazine representative Richard Stolley has been waiting outside Zapruder's office in his dress factory, Jennifer of Dallas, for about an hour when the short, balding man in glasses arrives carrying a projector. Stolley is glad that the men waiting with him are Secret Service agents and not his competitors.

Zapruder invites them in, sets up the projector, threads the film, darkens the room, and almost apologetically shows it to the small gathering. The tension in the room is incredible and there is no sound except the cranking of the old projector as it clicks away. There is the president's limousine rounding the corner and everyone knows something awful is about to happen. Suddenly there is a spray of red, a halo of pink mist as part of the president's head is shot off. A horrific silence envelopes the Secret Service men, whose job had been to protect the man in the film.

Additional journalists from the Associated Press, United Press International, and several other magazines begin arriving. Zapruder shows the film a few more times, each replay revealing more details. When he finishes, the Dallas dressmaker looks ill, then uneasy. The number of bidders has grown in the last few minutes.

Stolley knows that *Life* magazine *has* to have this film, and asks to speak

---

*In fact, Marina Oswald doesn't return as expected. Ruth Paine won't see her again until March 9, 1964, the beginning of an estrangement that exists to this day.

privately to Zapruder. Since Stolley had been the first one to contact him, Zapruder agrees to see him first, ushering Stolley quickly into a cluttered inner office. The press outside shouts that Zapruder shouldn't make up his mind until he's heard their offers too. Zapruder wastes no time telling Stolley how he feels. First, he wishes he had never taken the film. Second, now that the film exists, he realizes that it could help financially secure his family's future; however, he is determined not to let it fall into the hands of unscrupulous exploiters. He describes his worst fear to Stolley—the film being shown in sleazy movie theaters in Times Square, while men on the streets hawk it like some pornographic film. The look on Zapruder's face reveals his genuine disgust over the thought.

Stolley knows he has to find out if Zapruder understands just what his film is worth.

"Our magazine is just as anxious as you are to give your pictures a respectable display," Stolley says. "We may even be able to go as high as $15,000."

Zapruder smiles. He understands.

Stolley mentions a new figure, adding that he doesn't think the magazine can go higher. Zapruder hesitates, and Stolley goes higher. The negotiations follow this pattern for a few minutes, while the fearful cry of Stolley's competitors grows louder in the corridor outside.

Finally, *Life*'s reputation, the fact it was the most popular weekly magazine in America, with a circulation in excess of seven million, and Stolley's assurances that the pictures will not be sensationalized win Zapruder over. Stolley types up a crude contract at Zapruder's desk and the two men sign it. It calls for a payment of $50,000 for print rights only.*

*After viewing the copy in New York, *Life* publisher C. D. Jackson instructed Stolley to purchase all rights to the film, including television and movie rights, for $150,000 paid in six annual installments of $25,000. The agreement was consummated November 25 in the office of Zapruder's lawyer, Sam Passman. Zapruder asked Stolley not to reveal the fact of the sale because it might intensify the already existing anti-Jewish sentiment in Dallas. Stolley felt that Passman earned his legal fee by suggesting that Zapruder donate the first $25,000 he received for the film to the widow and family of Officer Tippit. Zapruder readily agreed and his donation of $25,000 two days later earned public applause. Zapruder died of cancer in 1970, two years after he received his last payment. (Trask, *National Nightmare*, pp. 146–150; Stolley, "What Happened Next . . . ," p. 262; Wrone, *Zapruder Film*, p. 36)

Stolley picks up the original film and the one remaining copy.

"Is there a back door?" he asks Zapruder.

Having orchestrated one of the journalistic coups of the century, Stolley slips out and leaves Zapruder to face the press, who are still clamoring just outside his office door for a chance to bid.[1067]

Across Dealey Plaza from Zapruder's office, Postal Inspector Harry Holmes arrives for work at the Terminal Annex Building. As Holmes walks into the lobby, the postal inspector on duty tells him that an FBI agent had phoned to inquire as to how the bureau could obtain an original postal money order, and had been told they would have to get it in Washington, D.C.[1068]

Although the FBI already has a microfilmed copy of the money order used to purchase the Carcano rifle, in preparing for trial prosecutors always want the original document. After depositing the money order into its bank account, Klein's, of course, no longer had the original money order.

9:30 a.m. (10:30 a.m. EST)

In Washington, Commander Humes returns to his office at Bethesda Naval Hospital, having gotten hardly any sleep since leaving the morgue six hours earlier. His early morning was consumed attending his son's First Communion at the family parish. However, the puzzling problems the three pathologists encountered during the autopsy, particularly the disposition of the bullet that struck the president's back, has been eating away at him.

Humes telephones Parkland Hospital and speaks to Dr. Malcolm Perry, the surgeon who performed the tracheotomy on the president. Humes explains the problems the pathologists had run into in trying to determine what happened to the bullet that struck the president in the back.

"We surmised that it worked its way out of the wound during cardiac massage," Humes says.

"Well, that seems unlikely, in my opinion," Perry replies. "Are you aware that there was a wound in the throat?"

The light flashes on for Humes when Dr. Perry tells him that he performed his surgery on an existing wound there, a small, round perforation with ragged edges.

"Of course," Humes realizes, "that explains it."[1069]

Suddenly, everything the pathologists had encountered when they explored the chest cavity made sense—the bruise over the lung, the bruised muscles surrounding the trachea. It was obvious. The bullet had exited the throat. Dr. Humes felt a great weight lift from his shoulders. He thanked Dr. Perry and hung up.

Humes figures that the bullet must have struck the president's back, slipped between the muscles without striking any major blood vessels, passed over the top of the right lung, bruising it, and exited the throat just below the Adam's apple.[1070]

His major dilemma solved, Commander Humes has only to write up the final report. He plans to get started later today, but first he needs some sleep.

10:00 a.m.

Bill Alexander didn't get home from the search of Joe Molina's house, and to bed, until around 4:15 in the morning, but by 8:00 a.m. he was down at the DA's office for a full day of work interviewing witnesses and preparing to take the case against Oswald for Kennedy's and Tippit's murders to the grand jury on Monday. At that time he would seek an indictment against Oswald on the murders that would supersede the two existing criminal complaints, and announce that his office would be seeking the death penalty against Oswald. To Alexander's absolute astonishment he receives a phone call from the Dallas police that Jimmy "Rughead" Martin, a local attorney, was at the police station saying he represented Oswald and presenting a writ of habeas corpus signed by Judge Joe B. Brown with bond set at $100,000. If Oswald could pay the 10 percent premium of $10,000 on the bond, he was entitled to be released on bail! Alexander knew that Judge Brown, being a District Court judge, had the authority to overrule Judge David Johnston, who was only a justice of the peace. "Pissed," Alexander immediately calls Judge Brown.

"Judge, what in the hell is going on here? We've already filed on Oswald for the Tippit and Kennedy murders and Judge Johnston has denied bond and we're not going to honor your writ."

Brown immediately backs down, acting as if he didn't know what had already transpired. He promises to immediately recall his writ, and that was the end of it.[1071]

Robert Oswald has been hanging around police headquarters for thirty or forty minutes, and still there doesn't seem to be any hope of talking with police officials. He figures that since his brother has been charged with the president's assassination, perhaps the district attorney will be amenable to talking to him. He goes down to the first floor of City Hall and telephones the DA's office from a pay phone. Assistant DA Jim Bowie answers and tells him that District Attorney Henry Wade isn't in yet, but is expected any moment.

"Come on down," Bowie advises him.

By the time Robert walks the many blocks down to the DA's office, located in the same building as the sheriff's office, Wade has arrived and asks Robert to come right in. They talk for an hour, mostly in generalities, but also about the likely date of Lee's trial. Henry Wade assures Robert that Lee will be tried in a state court, for a reason Robert finds really odd—something about there being no federal law prohibiting the killing of a president.

Wade wonders when Robert had last seen his brother. Robert says that it was about a year ago, at his home in Fort Worth.

"What can you tell me about him?" Wade asks.

Robert tells him a bit about his brother's defection to Russia and other general information. The district attorney decides to play cop for a moment.

"Now, let's see, you last saw Lee . . ." Wade repeats, casually, much of what Robert has just told him, but purposely gets some of the details wrong. The ruse is pretty transparent to Robert, who finds Wade's attempt at trickery to be fairly amusing. He just smiles at Wade, who grins broadly at having been caught. The DA leans back in his leather chair and chats amicably about subjects other than the assassination. Robert begins to realize that Wade is just a plain politician who, after a blundered effort to trick him, now only wants to make sure he leaves with a favorable impression.[1072]

"I was wondering, Mr. Wade," Roberts finally asks, "if you could arrange for Marina, my mother, and myself to see Lee today?"

"I don't see why not," Wade tells him, and telephones Captain Fritz, who tells him that arrangements have already been made for all of them to see Oswald at noon. Wade relays the information to Robert.[1073]

"You appear to be a good citizen," Wade tells him, "and I think you will render your country a great service if you will go up and tell Lee to tell us all about this thing. The evidence is very strong against your brother in the assassination," Wade adds cautiously. "What do you think about it?"

"Well, he is my brother," Robert says, "and I hate to think he would do this. I want to talk to him and ask him about it."

Robert is curious about the shooting of the police officer. Wade tells him that there are several eyewitnesses to the crime, and their accounts have convinced the DA of Lee's guilt on that murder too.[1074]

The two men rise and shake hands. Wade warns him that reporters are waiting outside.

"I won't have anything to say," Robert says and walks out.

Wade steps to the window and looks out front to see Robert Oswald push through the throng of pesky newsmen and walk off, without a word. The district attorney is impressed by the young man from Denton.[1075]

At the compound of the Kennedy family in Hyannis Port, Massachusetts, the family decides that as frail as the patriarch of the family, Joe Kennedy Sr., is from his massive stroke on a Palm Beach golf course in 1961, which left him partially paralyzed on the right side and no longer able to speak, they could no longer keep the truth from him. His wife, Rose, had learned the previous day over television of the shooting in Dallas even before her son Bobby had telephoned her. Tragedy was no stranger to Rose, having already lost a son and daughter in air crashes, but she quietly sank into a chair, trembling. She then went down to the lawn by the sea, where she strode back and forth for the rest of the afternoon. Now, the late president's youngest brother, Ted, tells his father that "there's been a bad accident. The president has been hurt very badly." Though the stroke had also caused aphasia in the old man—an impairment in the ability to understand the spoken or written word—his head snaps back and he stares directly into his son's eyes. "As a matter of fact," Ted says to his father, "he died." The elder Kennedy, as tough an Irishman as they come, immediately starts to sob. Ted and his sister Eunice try to comfort him, but it is unavailing. Even a sedative administered to him doesn't seem to alleviate the emotional response.

The next day, Rose, her daughter Eunice Shriver, and her son Teddy will board a plane, *The Caroline*, at the Hyannis Port airport for the trip to Washington, D.C., for Monday's funeral. Joseph Kennedy will remain behind in the care of his niece, Ann Gargan, and a trained nurse, Rita Dallas. Both have been with him since his stroke.[1076]

10:10 a.m.

Shortly before Oswald was brought down from the fifth-floor jail for interrogation, Chief Curry was stopped by reporters as he made his way down the third-floor corridor toward his office.

"What evidence has been uncovered so far, Chief?"

"I wouldn't want to elaborate on all the evidence that has been uncovered," Curry says hesitantly.

"How would you describe his mood during the questioning?"

"Very arrogant," Curry snaps back. "Has been all along."

"What does he still say, Chief?"

"He just denies everything," Curry says.

"Does he say anything else?" a reporter asks, hoping for more details.

"Not too much," Curry answers, looking for words, then admits, "I don't know. I haven't personally been interrogating him."[1077]

"Is there any doubt in your mind, Chief, that Oswald is the man who killed the president?"

"I think this is the man who killed the president, yes," Curry says firmly.

"Chief, could you tell us what you might have found in his rooming house in the way of literature or any papers connecting him—?"

"We found a great, great amount of Communist literature, Communist books," Curry replies. "I couldn't tell you just what all of it was, but it was a large box."

"Chief, we understand you've had the results of the paraffin tests which were made to determine whether Oswald had fired a weapon. Can you tell us what those tests showed?"

"I understand that it was positive," Curry tells them.

"But, what does that mean?"

"It only means that he fired a gun," Curry says.[1078]

"Chief, is there any plan for a reenactment of the crime? To take him to the scene or to do anything in that respect?"

"No."

"Is there any evidence that anyone else may have been linked with Oswald to this shooting?"

"At this time, we don't believe so," Curry answers. "We are talking to a man [Joe Molina] that works in the same building that we have in our subversive files and we are talking to him but he denies any knowledge of it."

One reporter wants to know how Oswald covered the distance between the Depository and the Tippit shooting scene in Oak Cliff. "I don't know," Curry says. "We have heard that he was picked up by a Negro in a car."*

"That is not confirmed?"

"No, it is not confirmed, as far as I know," Curry replies.

"Have you been able to trace the rifle? Do you know where it was purchased?"

---

*This is apparently a reference to the claim of Deputy Sheriff Roger Craig, who told police Friday evening that he saw a man who resembled Oswald get into a station wagon driven by a Negro. Evidence, including a bus transfer and Oswald's own admissions, proved Craig's claim to be false. The fact that Curry is still unaware that Oswald took a bus and a cab to Oak Cliff after the shooting, something homicide investigators learned Friday night, demonstrates how little Curry knew about the details of the assassination investigation.

"No," Curry says, "we are attempting to do that at this time."

"With this man's apparent subversive background, *was there any surveillance?* Were police aware of his presence in *Dallas?*"

"We in the police department here did not know he was in Dallas. I understand that the FBI did know he was in Dallas," Curry replies, the thought of Lieutenant Jack Revill's memo fresh in his mind.

"Is it normally the practice of the FBI to inform the police?"

"Yes," Curry says curtly.

"But you were not informed?"

"We had not been informed of this man," Curry reiterates.[1079]

It doesn't take long for FBI Director J. Edgar Hoover to get wind of Curry's statements to the press and become livid. Hoover calls Dallas FBI special agent-in-charge Gordon Shanklin and orders him to call Chief Curry and tell him to retract his statement about the FBI having prior knowledge of Oswald being in Dallas.

"The FBI is extremely desirous that you retract your statement to the press," Shanklin tells Curry over the phone, assuring him that what he said could suggest that the FBI had interviewed Oswald in Dallas and had him under surveillance, neither of which was true, he assured Curry.[1080]

Curry agrees to make a retraction and orders Lieutenant Jack Revill to remain silent about the matter as well.[1081]

Lieutenant T. L. Baker answers the telephone jangling at his desk in Homicide and Robbery. The caller is one of the supervisors at City Transportation Company, a taxi service. He's calling to report that one of his drivers, William W. Whaley, came in this morning and said that he had recognized Oswald's picture in the morning newspaper and believed he was the same man he drove out to North Beckley in Oak Cliff yesterday afternoon. Baker informs Captain Fritz, who instructs him to bring Whaley and the cabdriver who was a witness to the Tippit shooting, William Scoggins, to police headquarters to view Oswald in a lineup.[1082]

In the meantime, Fritz asks his detectives to bring Oswald down to his office for further questioning.

10:20 a.m. (11:20 a.m. EST)
The FBI sends another Teletype to all of its field offices:

> Lee Harvey Oswald has been developed as the principal suspect in the assassination of President Kennedy. He has been formally charged with the President's murder along with the murder of Dallas Texas patrolman J.D. Tippet [*sic*] by Texas state authorities . . . All offices should [continue] normal contacts with informants and other sources with respect to bombing suspects, hate group members and known racial extremists. Daily teletype summaries may be discontinued. All investigation bearing directly on the President's assassination should be afforded most expeditious handling and Bureau and Dallas advised.[1083]

In Washington, D.C., even the weather appears to have taken respectful cognizance of the tragedy that has befallen the nation's capital more than any other American city. Rain falls slowly from a bleak, overcast sky through most of the day. A shaken capital tries to piece together a new mosaic of national rule "to replace the one shattered by an assassin's bullet 24 hours before." President Johnson, the eighth vice president to be elevated because of the death of a president, has taken over the machinery of government amid pledges of support from leaders of both parties as well as from leaders throughout the civilized world. He holds his first cabinet meeting, with Attorney General Robert Kennedy present[*] and

---

[*]Quite apart from his unfathomable grief, RFK did not want to attend, finding it difficult to accept that anyone, particularly LBJ, whom he disliked, would be taking his brother's place, and he showed up five minutes late. As alluded to earlier, Johnson had a deep sense of illegitimacy following the assassination and "desperately needed affirmation." Though the American public and Congress gave it to him, it was clear to him RFK had not, and in Bobby's attitude, Johnson felt the rejection of his legitimacy he had feared from others. (Shesol, *Mutual Contempt*, p.119) "During all of that period," LBJ would later say, "I think [Bobby] seriously considered whether he would let me be president, whether he should really take the position [that] the vice

asks all members to continue to serve under him.* Later in the day, he receives former presidents Harry S. Truman and Dwight D. Eisenhower in the Oval Office. Though the Kennedy family has requested of the public that no flowers be sent, encouraging people to contribute instead to their favorite charity, bouquets of flowers arrive throughout the day and are accepted by the White House guard.

At midmorning in the East Room of the White House, where the fallen President and First Lady had once presided over their famous, glittering White House affairs and danced gaily with their friends, seventy-five intimates and relatives of the Kennedy family attend a private mass with Mrs. Kennedy and her two children said by the Reverend John J. Cavanaugh, the former president of the University of Notre Dame and a longtime friend of the family. It is believed to be the first Roman Catholic mass ever said in the White House. (Almost concurrently, in New York City, where the day is also bleak and overcast, twenty-five hundred mourners crowd into the twenty-three-hundred-seat Saint Patrick's Cathedral on Fifth Avenue for a pontifical requiem mass in which 250 clergymen take part.) After the mass, a procession of government leaders begins to file into and out of the East Room, where the president's body lies in a flag-draped coffin.

"The medium of television," the *New York Times* observed, "which played such a major part in the career of President Kennedy, is the instrument that is making the tragedy of his death such a deeply personal experience in millions of homes over this long weekend. In hushed living rooms everywhere, the uninterrupted coverage provided by the three

---

president didn't automatically move in. I thought that was on his mind every time I saw him in the first few days. I think he was seriously considering what steps to take" (Tape-recorded interview of LBJ by William J. Jorden, LBJ Library, Austin, Texas; Shesol, *Mutual Contempt*, p.119).

*Bobby Kennedy agreed to stay on as LBJ's attorney general, if for no other reason than he didn't have anywhere else to go, at least in government. His friend Dean Markham warned RFK that to resign could "boomerang," benefiting Johnson. "Public sentiment will be on his side," Markham told RFK, "and the feeling will be that he tried to cooperate and work with you, but you didn't want to." (Shesol, *Mutual Contempt*, p.124) After serving as attorney general until September 2, 1964, when he resigned to run for and win the U.S. Senate seat from New York, on March 16, 1968, Kennedy announced his decision to run against Johnson for the Democratic nomination that year, but fifteen days later, on March 31, 1968, Johnson told a stunned nation on national television that he would not seek reelection.

national networks and their affiliated stations is holding families indoors to share in history's grim unfolding, the home screen for the first time fulfilling the heart-rending function of giving a new dimension to grief."[*]

In countries throughout the world there is mourning.[†] "From Madrid to Manila churches filled and American embassies were thronged with people who wanted to sign memorial books." American viewers see downcast crowds gathering outside the American embassy in London, where the twelve bells of St. Paul's Cathedral announce the national memorial service there. More than ten thousand Poles line up eight abreast to sign the book of condolences at the U.S. embassy in Warsaw. In Berlin, Mayor Willy Brandt asks his people to light candles in their darkened windows. Within minutes, candles are flickering throughout the city. "We all feel somewhat left alone," Brandt said. Radio Moscow broadcasts a concert of memorial dirges. In Tokyo Bay, Japanese fishing boats, flags at half-mast, drift alongside U.S. warships. Buddhist monks offer prayers in front of black crepe–draped images of President Kennedy. In Paris, French men and women gather solemnly around outdoor radios, their tears hidden by the pouring rain. In Kenya, weeping Kipsigis warriors in ceremonial feathers and body paint listen as their leader extols the virtues of the murdered president. America learns just how many people around the world considered John F. Kennedy *their* president too.

World leaders also weigh in. England's prime minister, Sir Alec Douglas-Home, notes that John Kennedy left "an indelible mark on the entire world. There are times in life when the mind and heart stand still,

---

[*]Not all Americans were accepting of the uninterrupted coverage. All three networks received calls, in the low hundreds, from viewers complaining about the cancellation of their favorite shows and asking when regular programming would be resumed.

[†]While the rest of the world, including the Soviet Union, eulogized the slain president, Communist China, in sharp contrast, stood virtually alone, Peking not only not offering condolences and eulogies, but defiling, even ridiculing him. The Official New China News Agency did not let up in its attacks on Kennedy and his successor. The *Worker's Daily* went so far as to publish a cartoon of Kennedy sprawled face down in blood on the ground, his necktie bearing a dollar sign, with the caption "Kennedy Bites the Dust." (United Press International, November 25, 1963, p.24)

and one such is now." Premier Khrushchev appears at the American embassy in Moscow to pay his respects, lamenting the blow the president's death has dealt Soviet-American relations. Unable to travel to Washington because of illness, Italian president Antonio Segni, attending a mass in Rome, openly sobs. The words of a "profoundly saddened" Pope Paul VI to a crowd of thirty thousand gathered in St. Peter's Square in Rome are relayed around the world by satellite. The pope expresses his hope that "the death of this great statesman may not damage the cause of the American people, but rather reinforce it." Nineteen chiefs of state and three reigning monarchs let it be known that they will attend the president's funeral on Monday, among them France's General Charles de Gaulle.

Jack Kennedy's political opponents are no less sincere in their grief. The man he defeated to win the presidency, Richard Nixon, speaking from his home in New York, tells the viewers, "President Kennedy yesterday wrote the finest and greatest chapter in his *Profiles in Courage*. The greatest tribute we can pay is to reduce the hatred which drives men to do such deeds." Senator Goldwater, at a news conference in Muncie, Indiana, also speaks warmly of the president. Even the two implacably segregationist, Democratic governors of Alabama and Mississippi, George Wallace and Ross Barnett, whose fierce political opposition may have damaged Kennedy more than that of the Republican Party, publicly honor his memory.

An avalanche of mail pours into the networks, as though the viewers feel the necessity to enter into a dialogue with them. Many write poems. At CBS, Walter Cronkite realizes that people are "desperate to express themselves about this thing. And poetry seems a natural form. They seem intent either on finding a way to accept the guilt we are all feeling or laying it on someone or something else, or simply eulogizing the man."

NBC's Chet Huntley and ABC's Edward P. Morgan are also swept away by the outpouring of grief. "It is probable that when all this is over," Morgan muses prophetically, "we will find it created a more personal response than any other event in history."[1084]

Lee Harvey Oswald with the rifle he later used to kill President Kennedy and the pistol he used to kill Officer Tippit. This backyard photograph eventually came to national attention on the cover of the February 21, 1964, issue of *Life* magazine. *(© Corbis)*

Top left: Marina and Lee Harvey Oswald on the balcony of their apartment building in Minsk, in what was then the U.S.S.R. (*National Archives*)

Top right: Lee Harvey Oswald as a fifteen-year-old in New Orleans. He had an older brother and half brother, but always seemed to be the favorite of his mother, Marguerite. He gave little indication of reciprocating that love. (*National Archives*)

Bottom: Oswald, a fervent supporter of Fidel Castro's Cuban Revolution, passing out "Hands off Cuba" flyers on the streets of New Orleans in the summer of 1963. (*© Corbis*)

Top: Oswald's Mannlicher-Carcano rifle, the murder weapon. *(National Archives)*

Bottom: The same gun shown disassembled alongside the brown wrapping-paper bag found on the floor near the sniper's nest window at the Texas School Book Depository Building. The blanket was found in Ruth Paine's garage, where Oswald had stored his rifle. *(National Archives)*

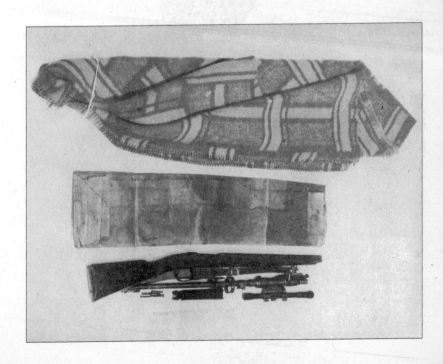

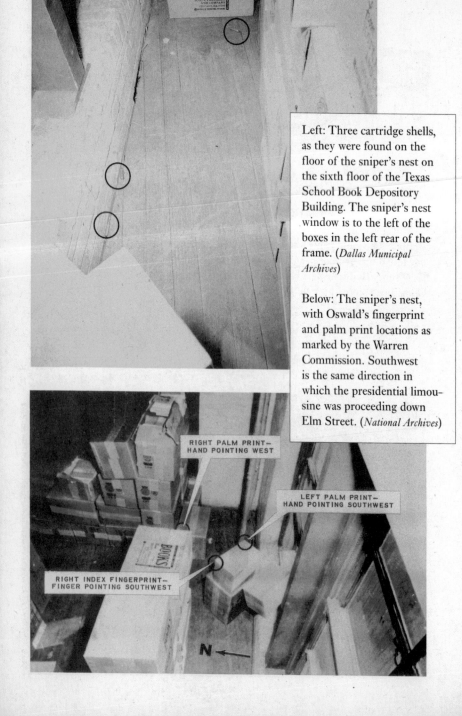

Left: Three cartridge shells, as they were found on the floor of the sniper's nest on the sixth floor of the Texas School Book Depository Building. The sniper's nest window is to the left of the boxes in the left rear of the frame. (*Dallas Municipal Archives*)

Below: The sniper's nest, with Oswald's fingerprint and palm print locations as marked by the Warren Commission. Southwest is the same direction in which the presidential limousine was proceeding down Elm Street. (*National Archives*)

RIGHT PALM PRINT—HAND POINTING WEST

LEFT PALM PRINT—HAND POINTING SOUTHWEST

RIGHT INDEX FINGERPRINT—FINGER POINTING SOUTHWEST

N

Left: While the crowds gathering near the end of the motorcade in Dealey Plaza are comparatively sparse, here in the heart of downtown Dallas the president is met by record numbers of enthusiastic well-wishers. *(Courtesy the Sixth Floor Museum at Dealey Plaza, Photographer William Beal,* Dallas Times Herald *collection)*

Below: Within seconds after the shooting in Dealey Plaza, *Dallas Morning News* photographer Tom Dillard takes this photograph of the southeasternmost windows on the fifth and sixth floors of the Texas School Book Depository Building. The top open window is the sniper's nest window. The small visible portion of a box toward the right side of the window was one of the three boxes Oswald used to construct a gun rest for his rifle. Depository employees Bonnie Ray Williams (left) and Harold Norman (right) are in the windows below. Both heard the shots being fired just above them. Norman, directly below Oswald, even heard the operation of the bolt and the three cartridge shells hitting the floor. *(Courtesy the Sixth Floor Museum at Dealey Plaza, Tom Dillard Collection,* Dallas Morning News*)*

Left: With thousands of supporters waiting to greet them, President and Mrs. Kennedy emerge from Air Force One on the gloriously bright morning of November 22, 1963. "They looked like Mr. and Mrs. America," one reporter would say. *(Cecil Stoughton, White House/John F. Kennedy Library)*

Below: Conspiracy theorists would later point out that the entry hole in the back of the president's suit was lower than, and did not match up with, the entry wound to his upper back, and hence, they argue, the Warren Commission's single bullet theory is destroyed. But this photograph, taken around two and a half seconds before the first shot that hit Kennedy, clearly shows Kennedy's suit bunched up on his back, so that fabric meant to hang below his shoulders is covering them when the bullet hits. *(Robert Croft)*

Top: Zapruder frame 133. This is the first frame of the Zapruder film that shows the presidential limousine, which has just turned onto Elm from Houston. Each frame of the film represents one-eighteenth of a second. *(Courtesy the Sixth Floor Museum at Dealey Plaza, Zapruder Collection, © 1967 [renewed 1995] the Sixth Floor Museum at Dealey Plaza, All Rights Reserved)*

Bottom: Frame 161. The consensus of most assassination researchers is that the first shot was fired around the time of this frame. Some people in Dealey Plaza thought it sounded like a firecracker or the backfire of a car. This shot missed the limousine completely. *(Courtesy the Sixth Floor Museum at Dealey Plaza, Zapruder Collection, © 1967 [renewed 1995] the Sixth Floor Museum at Dealey Plaza, All Rights Reserved)*

Top: Zapruder frame 193. As the limousine proceeds down Elm Street, the president waves to the crowd, showing no signs of physical distress. *(Courtesy the Sixth Floor Museum at Dealey Plaza, Zapruder Collection, © 1967 [renewed 1995] the Sixth Floor Museum at Dealey Plaza, All Rights Reserved)*

Bottom: Frame 204. While almost all of the limousine has disappeared from Zapruder's view behind the Stemmons Freeway sign, Kennedy, now past most of the spectators on his right, begins to lower his right arm. *(Courtesy the Sixth Floor Museum at Dealey Plaza, Zapruder Collection, © 1967 [renewed 1995] the Sixth Floor Museum at Dealey Plaza, All Rights Reserved)*

Frames 222 to 224. Connally emerges from behind the Stemmons Freeway sign. The House Select Committee on Assassinations panel of photographic experts said that he seems to be "reacting to some sort of external stimulus. He appears to be frowning, and there is a distinct stiffening of his shoulders and upper trunk." *(Courtesy the Sixth Floor Museum at Dealey Plaza, Zapruder Collection, © 1967 [renewed 1995] the Sixth Floor Museum at Dealey Plaza, All Rights Reserved)*

Above: Zapruder frames 225 and 226. As Connally shows increased distress, Kennedy comes into Zapruder's view. The president can clearly be seen reacting to a severe external stimulus, as he begins to move his elbows upward and his forearms inward. This strongly indicates, *through the film alone*, that Kennedy and Connally were struck by the same bullet. *(Courtesy the Sixth Floor Museum at Dealey Plaza, Zapruder Collection, © 1967 [renewed 1995] the Sixth Floor Museum at Dealey Plaza, All Rights Reserved)*

Top: Zapruder frame 237. This frame shows Kennedy's full reaction to being shot in the upper back. The awkward angle of his arms and elbows has mistakenly been thought by some to be the so-called "Thorburn" position, which was described in an 1887 article and sketch in a British medical journal by Dr. William Thorburn about a patient with a lesion to the cervical region of the spinal cord whose body took a similar but different posture. In a Thorburn position the elbows are elevated as Kennedy's were, but the forearms are thrust upward, not inward toward each other. Most importantly, the elbows of Thorburn's Manchester, England, patient were locked into their position for twelve days. *(Courtesy the Sixth Floor Museum at Dealey Plaza, Zapruder Collection, © 1967 [renewed 1995] the Sixth Floor Museum at Dealey Plaza, All Rights Reserved)*

Bottom: Frame 264. Kennedy's elbows are shown returning from his Thorburn position a second and a half later, which would not have happened had he been in a true Thorburn position. *(Courtesy the Sixth Floor Museum at Dealey Plaza, Zapruder Collection, © 1967 [renewed 1995] the Sixth Floor Museum at Dealey Plaza, All Rights Reserved)*

Above: Zapruder frames 312 and 313.
Right: Frames 314 to 316. This series
shows Kennedy's reaction to the fatal
shot. The bullet comes either at frame
312, as some believe, or within the next
one-eighteenth of a second, before the
explosion of the head seen at frame 313.
Note that in frame 313, the impact of
the bullet pushes the president's head
slightly *forward* (2.3 inches), indicating a shot from the rear, where Oswald is, not
from the grassy knoll, which is to the president's right front. At frame 314, his
head begins to reverse direction, now moving to the rear in what is believed to be
a neuromuscular reaction. *(Courtesy the Sixth Floor Museum at Dealey Plaza, Zapruder
Collection, © 1967 [renewed 1995] the Sixth Floor Museum at Dealey Plaza, All Rights
Reserved)*

Left: A high-contrast photo of frame 313 by the Itek Corporation. Note that the
spray of blood and tissue is to the front, again indicating a shot from the rear.
*(Courtesy the Sixth Floor Museum at Dealey Plaza, Zapruder Collection, © 1967 [renewed
1995] the Sixth Floor Museum at Dealey Plaza, All Rights Reserved/
Itek Optical Systems)*

Top: Zapruder frame 321. By this point, the backward motion of Kennedy's head, which is often referred to as the "head snap to the rear," is virtually completed. *(Courtesy the Sixth Floor Museum at Dealey Plaza, Zapruder Collection, © 1967 [renewed 1995] the Sixth Floor Museum at Dealey Plaza, All Rights Reserved)*

Bottom: Frame 328. Many conspiracy theorists, arguing that Kennedy was shot from his right front, maintain that the bullet exited explosively out of the back of his head, leaving a very large wound there. But as this Zapruder frame and all others subsequent to the head shot at frame 313 show, there is no visible damage to the back of the president's head. The entrance wound there was very small and obscured by his thick hair. *(Courtesy the Sixth Floor Museum at Dealey Plaza, Zapruder Collection, © 1967 [renewed 1995] the Sixth Floor Museum at Dealey Plaza, All Rights Reserved)*

Top: Perhaps the most famous Dealey Plaza photograph. Taken by Associated Press photographer James Altgens, this is the only photograph that shows people in the motorcade indicating, by their movement, where any of the shots came from. Here, Secret Service agents look to their right rear, where Oswald was. The photo is also famous for showing a man on the front stairs of the Depository Building who resembles Oswald (Oswald's coworker Billy Lovelady, who is just inside the columns framing the entrance). Many conspiracy theorists insist it is Oswald, proving he was not in the sniper's nest. *(AP/Wide World Photos)*

Center: Mary Moorman's Polaroid is the only known still photograph of the president at the time of the fatal head shot (about one-ninth of a second after it) and the only known photograph of the famous grassy knoll at that moment. Conspiracy theorists are convinced that the president's assassin was hidden somewhere behind the fence to the left. In various places in the foliage, some even believe they can make out figures of assassins. *(Mary Ann Moorman Krahmer)*

Bottom: Wilma Bond's photograph, taken approximately twenty seconds after the shooting, shows the full area around the grassy knoll. *(Wilma Irene Bond/Lorene Bond Prewitt)*

Above: Lyndon B. Johnson, with his wife, Lady Bird Johnson, to his right and a stricken Jacqueline Kennedy to his left, is sworn in as the nation's thirty-sixth president aboard Air Force One, two hours and eight minutes after the shooting in Dealey Plaza. The plane would transport two presidents, both LBJ and the slain Kennedy, back to the nation's capital. *(LBJ Library Photo by Cecil Stoughton)*

Left: Attorney General Robert Kennedy, who had hurried aboard the plane when it landed at Andrews Air Force Base outside Washington, D.C., stands alongside Mrs. Kennedy as the president's coffin is moved into a waiting car. *(© Wally McNamee/Corbis)*

Top: Joined by world and national leaders, Jacqueline Kennedy, her eyes straight ahead, walks between the president's brothers, Attorney General Robert Kennedy (left) and Senator Edward Kennedy, as they follow the late president's caisson from the White House to St. Matthew's Cathedral. An estimated one million people line the funeral procession route—in such silence that the clopping of the horses' hooves can be heard by a global TV and radio audience. *(© Henri Dauman / daumanpictures.com)*

Bottom left: John Kennedy Jr. salutes his father's coffin as the funeral cortege leaves St. Matthew's Cathedral for Arlington National Cemetery. *(© Bettmann / Corbis)*

Bottom right: The procession, with a three-mile line of mourners behind it, nears the president's grave. *(Time & Life Pictures / Getty Images)*

Top left: Crowds gather to mourn all over the world, as in this renamed square in Berlin. *(© Bettmann/Corbis)*

Top right: The president of Italy, Antonio Segni, who had been prevented by his health from traveling to Washington, cries at a memorial service in Rome. *(David Lees/Life)*

Bottom: The Kennedy family—Jacqueline, John Jr., John, and Caroline—dressed for mass in Palm Beach, Florida, Easter 1963. *(Cecil Stoughton, White House/John F. Kennedy Library)*

Right: Dallas police officer J. D. Tippit, whom Oswald shot and killed when Tippit pulled his squad car over to talk to Oswald just forty-five minutes after the shooting in Dealey Plaza. *(National Archives)*

Below: An aerial photograph of the neighborhood of the Tippit killing, marked by the Warren Commission with the locations of eyewitnesses to the movements of Lee Harvey Oswald. *(National Archives)*

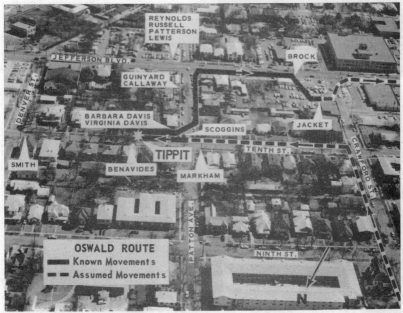

Top left: In custody of the Dallas police, Oswald raises his handcuffs and a rebellious fist. *(Courtesy the Sixth Floor Museum at Dealey Plaza, Bill Winfrey Collection,* Dallas Morning News*)*

Top right: In the chaotic corridor outside the Dallas Police Department's Homicide and Robbery office the night of the assassination, a Dallas detective thrusts the murder weapon into the air amid the press corps. *(© Bettmann/Corbis)*

Bottom left: Just after midnight on the night of the assassination, during an impromptu press conference, the media question Oswald about his role in the murder of the president. *(AP/Wide World Photos)*

Bottom right: At 11:20 a.m. on November 24, as Oswald is about to be transported from the Dallas Police Department to the county jail, Jack Ruby emerges from the crowd in the police building basement and shoots him fatally. *(Bob Jackson)*

Top left: Jack Ruby outside his strip club, the Carousel, with two of his dancers. The Carousel was always open seven days a week, but in deference to Kennedy, Ruby closed it the entire weekend following the assassination. *(Eddie Rocco)*

Top right: Ruby and dancers in his Carousel office. *(Eddie Rocco)*

Bottom: Allegations by conspiracy theorists that Ruby and Oswald were hired assassins are belied by these photographs of their rooms. The squalid conditions in which they both lived are just the opposite of what one would expect of two hit men paid well for their work. Oswald's almost closet-sized lodgings at 1026 North Beckley in Dallas, as shown by the landlady to a *Life* photographer on the afternoon of the assassination, are on the left. At right, Ruby's bedroom is shown as he left it on the morning he shot Oswald. The newspaper on the floor is open to coverage of the assassination. *(Oswald's room: Allan Grant. Ruby's room: Courtesy the Sixth Floor Museum at Dealey Plaza, Photographer William Allen, Dallas Times Herald collection)*

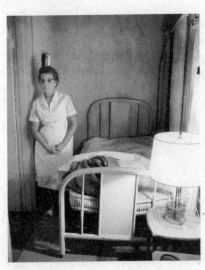

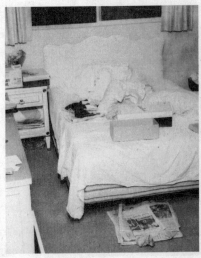

Above: The President's Commission on the Assassination of President Kennedy, led by the chief justice of the United States Supreme Court, Earl Warren, was appointed by President Lyndon B. Johnson to investigate the assassination. Although it would be difficult to come up with a group of more distinguished men, conspiracy theorists are convinced this bipartisan group deliberately conspired to keep the truth from the American people. From left, Gerald Ford, then a member of the House of Representatives; Representative Hale Boggs; Senator Richard Russell; Chief Justice Warren; Senator John Sherman Cooper; former World Bank president John J. McCloy; former CIA director Allen Dulles; and J. Lee Rankin, commission counsel. *(National Archives)*

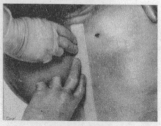

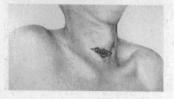

These are not photographs but drawings done for the House Select Committee on Assassinations. They were made from the photographs of the autopsy that was performed at Bethesda Naval Hospital on the night of the assassination. The Kennedy family has never authorized the public display of the actual photographs. The entire autopsy, along with the photos and X-rays taken during it, remains a major source of controversy.

Top: The back of Kennedy's head showing the entrance wound, with a portion of his scalp held in place by the hand at top. *(National Archives)*

Center: The entrance wound on Kennedy's upper back. *(National Archives)*

Bottom: The exit wound from that bullet was obscured by the incision for a tracheotomy performed on the dying president at Parkland Hospital in Dallas. *(National Archives)*

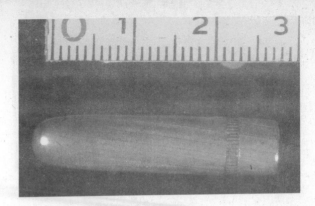

Above: The bullet that struck both Kennedy and Connally, and which conspiracy theorists have called the "magic bullet." *(National Archives)*

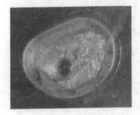

Left: One reason the theorists call it the magic bullet is that they maintain it was in "pristine" condition, but this photograph of its base, virtually never shown in a conspiracy book, proves otherwise. *(National Archives)*

Below: Lateral autopsy X-ray of President Kennedy's skull. *(National Archives)*

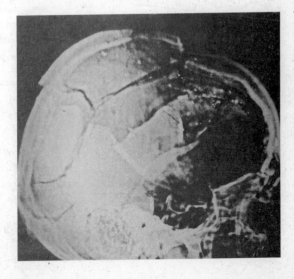

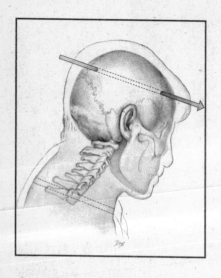

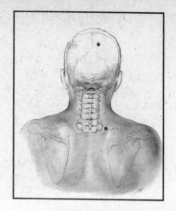

Above: This drawing documenting the two bullet entrance wounds to the president's body was made for the House Select Committee on Assassinations, as were the others on this page. (*National Archives*)

Left: These two drawings by the House Select Committee trace the path of the bullet that struck the president's head from behind (top left) and shattered his skull (bottom left). (*National Archives*)

Below: This Committee drawing shows the resulting severe damage to the upper right hemisphere of the president's brain. (*National Archives*)

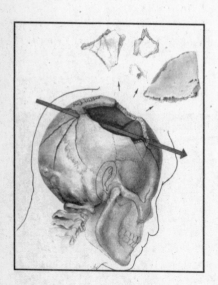

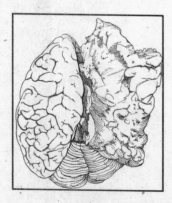

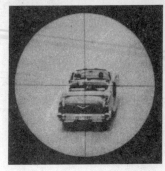

Above and right: On May 24, 1964, the FBI
conducted a reenactment of the shooting in
Dealey Plaza for the Warren Commission, with
FBI agents standing in for Kennedy and
Connally. Assuming that Oswald used his telescopic sight, these three photographs depict
the approximate view he would have had of
Kennedy and Connally from the sniper's nest
around the designated frames of the Zapruder
film at which the three shots were believed to
have been fired: top left, the first shot around
frame 161; top right, the second somewhere
around frame 210; and at right, the fatal head
shot at frame 313. The head of the FBI agent
representing Kennedy in the reenactment
photo of frame 313 seems to be farther to
the left than Kennedy's head actually was.
(*National Archives*)

Right: The three ovals drawn onto this photograph of the Texas School Book
Depository Building represent the results of
a bullet trajectory analysis by the House
Select Committee on Assassinations. The
smallest oval shows the point of the bullet's
origin if a straight line were drawn backward from Connally's back wound to
Kennedy's neck exit wound in his throat and through his back entry wound to the
oval. The middle oval traces the bullet backward from the exit wound in Kennedy's
throat to the entrance wound in his back, to the point of origin. The
largest oval runs from the exit wound in Kennedy's head to the entry wound in his
head to the point of origin. Note that whatever the margin of error in the cone cal-
culations, all trajectories lead to and encompass the sniper's
nest window on the sixth floor. (*National Archives*)

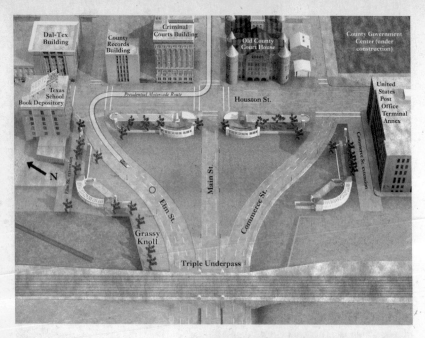

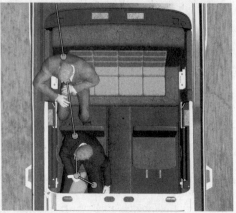

Above: An artist's rendering of Dealey Plaza on November 22, 1963. *(By Patrick Martin; 3D plaza model by Douglas Martin; Artimation of Arizona)*

Right: No one knows the exact Zapruder frame at which the president and Governor Connally were hit by Oswald's second bullet, but it was somewhere within a split second of frame 210. This is a three-dimensional overhead rendering of Kennedy and Connally as they were seated in the limousine at approximately frame 210, with the single bullet's trajectory. *(3D limo by Fred Kuentz, Artimation of Arizona; 3D plaza model by Douglas Martin; assembled by Patrick Martin)*

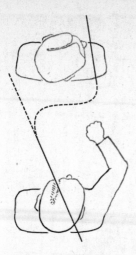

Top left: In a typical drawing seen in conspiracy books, conspiracy theorists improperly place Connally in the limousine directly in front of Kennedy. This enables them to make the argument that for the Warren Commission's single-bullet theory to work, the bullet exiting Kennedy's body would have had to make a right and then a left turn in midair before striking Connally—thus the "magic bullet," a demonstrably fraudulent conspiracy theorist creation. (*Illustration by John McAusland*)

Top right: The limousine leaving Love Field for the motorcade through downtown Dallas. Connally is actually, as can be seen here, seated substantially to the president's left and somewhat lower than the president. (*Courtesy the Sixth Floor Museum of Dealey Plaza, Tom Dillard Collection*, Dallas Morning News)

Bottom: Kennedy and Connally in the presidential limousine at approximately frame 210, from Abraham Zapruder's position (if Zapruder's camera could have seen through the Stemmons Freeway sign), with the bullet trajectory. (*Illustration by Michael McDermott; 3D limo by Fred Kuentz, Artimation of Arizona; 3D plaza model by Douglas Martin; assembled by Patrick Martin*)

Gerry Spence and Vincent Bugliosi were legal adversaries in the twenty-one-hour unscripted docu-trial of Oswald for the Kennedy assassination, held in London. This photograph shows them in 1986 in Dallas at the famous sixth-floor sniper's nest window of the Texas School Book Depository Building, from which Oswald shot President Kennedy. The two were chosen to try the case as a result of a survey of American trial lawyers. The media described them as "bitter rivals" who did not like each other, which was inaccurate. (The *London Observer* noted further that the British producers of the docu-trial "did not realize the extent of each man's desire to win the case. It soon became clear that two great egos were slugging it out.") Although there were some acrimonious exchanges during the pretrial maneuvering, the trial forged a friendship between them. Bugliosi says that Spence is "the finest trial lawyer" he has ever faced, and that he is "this generation's Clarence Darrow." Spence says that "Bugliosi knows more about the prosecution of criminals than Saint Peter himself," and, referring to the London trial, that "no other lawyer in America could have done what Vince did in this case." After a first vote of 10 to 2 for guilty, the Dallas jury returned a verdict of guilty against Lee Harvey Oswald for Kennedy's assassination. *Time* magazine called the trial, which used the original Warren Commission witnesses, "spellbinding, TV's best courtroom drama ever" and "as close to a real trial as the accused killer of John F. Kennedy will probably ever get." *(Dallas Morning News/Ken Gieger photo)*

The dark line on this map of Dallas tracks John F. Kennedy's motorcade from Love Field through Dealey Plaza to Parkland Hospital. The lighter line traces Oswald's route from the Book Depository Building to the point of his arrest. *(Sketch by Patrick Martin)*

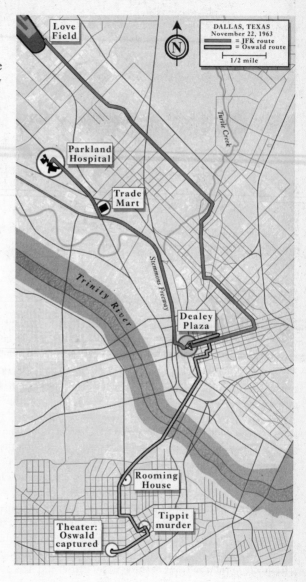

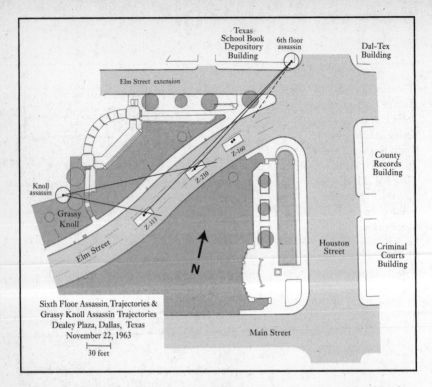

Texas
School Book
Depository
Building

6th floor
assassin

Dal-Tex
Building

Elm Street extension

Z-160

Z-210

County
Records
Building

Knoll
assassin

Grassy
Knoll

Z-313

N

Houston
Street

Criminal
Courts
Building

Elm Street

Sixth Floor Assassin, Trajectories &
Grassy Knoll Assassin Trajectories
Dealey Plaza, Dallas, Texas
November 22, 1963

30 feet

Main Street

Above: The two lines coming down from the top right show the trajectories of the two bullets that struck President Kennedy, from their common point of origin at the sniper's nest window to the presidential limousine. (The broken line represents the first bullet fired by Oswald that missed the limousine entirely.) The two lines coming from the left show theoretical grassy knoll bullet trajectories from an imaginary assassin located there. It is dogma in the conspiracy community that bullets fired from the grassy knoll (the HSCA and most conspiracy theorists pick the encircled spot behind the picket fence for the location of the assassin) struck Kennedy, one in the throat, the other on the right side of his head. But as we can see from this sketch, if this were so, both bullets would almost automatically have exited the left side of Kennedy's body. At an absolute minimum they would have penetrated into the left side of his body. Yet the autopsy revealed no exit wounds or bullet tracks on the president's left side, nor any injury there. For instance, the autopsy surgeons found that "the left cerebral hemisphere [of Kennedy's brain] is intact." Note further that, from the grassy knoll, the president would have been, because of the angles, a moving target (from left to right in front of the assassin's rifle) and hence, it would have been a more difficult shot than firing at him from the sniper's nest window, where he was on almost a straight line from the rifle's barrel. This fact, among many others, increases the unlikelihood of the grassy knoll being used by any would-be assassin. (*Sketch by Patrick Martin; based on plaza survey by Drommer & Associates, Dallas, Texas*)

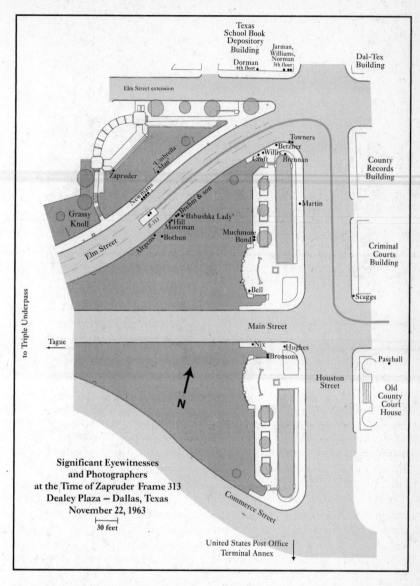

Here, dots mark the positions of significant eyewitnesses and photographers around Dealey Plaza at the time of Zapruder frame 313. *(Sketch by Patrick Martin; based on plaza survey by Drommer & Associates, Dallas, Texas)*

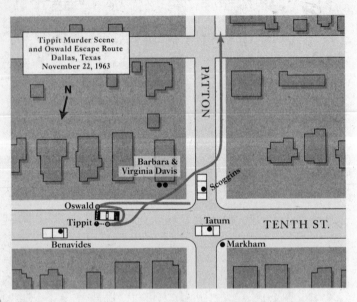

Above: A rendering of Oswald's route toward and away from the site
of the Tippit shooting. *(Sketch by Patrick Martin)*

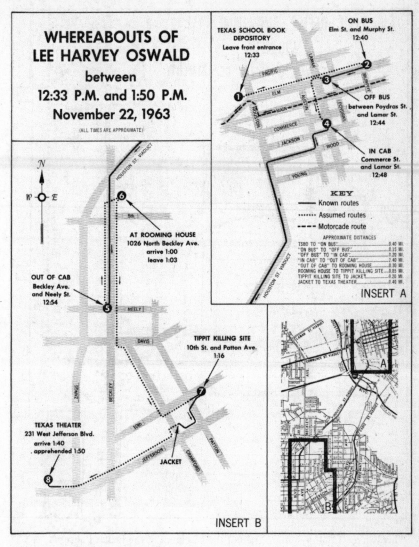

Above: These maps assembled by the Warren Commission follow Oswald's move-ments, as indicated, between 12:33 p.m. and 1:50 p.m. The times in this book vary slightly in some places from those calculated by the Commission. *(National Archives)*

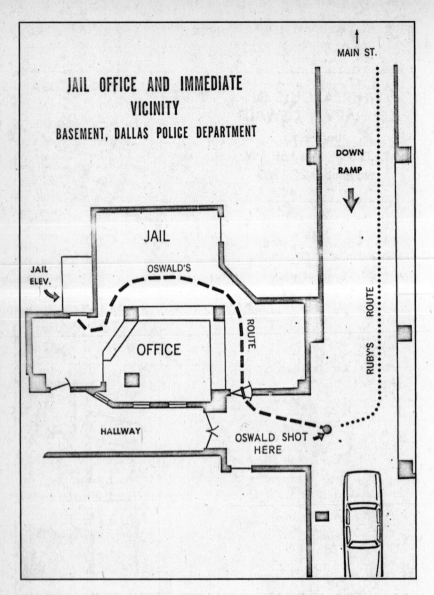

JAIL OFFICE AND IMMEDIATE
VICINITY
BASEMENT, DALLAS POLICE DEPARTMENT

MAIN ST.

DOWN
RAMP

JAIL

JAIL
ELEV.

OSWALD'S

RUBY'S ROUTE

ROUTE

OFFICE

HALLWAY

OSWALD SHOT
HERE

This Warren Commission diagram of the basement of the Dallas Police
Department indicates, with a dashed line, the route Oswald was being walked on
when he was shot. The dotted line coming down from the top right corner, from
Main Street, is Ruby's path toward him. The car at the bottom is the one that
Oswald was to ride in, which, because of the surging media, hadn't yet backed up
all the way into position. *(National Archives)*

10:25 a.m.

As the newsmen in the third-floor corridor grow anxious for Oswald's anticipated reappearance en route to Homicide and Robbery for further questioning, Deputy Chief Stevenson steps into the hubbub and in a commanding voice instructs them that there will have to be some order when Oswald is brought through the hallway.

"Gentlemen!" Stevenson shouts above the din. "Whenever this door [pointing to the jail elevator door] is open and they come through here, we don't want any of you questioning this boy. We don't want any of you pushing him. We want to cooperate with you. We want to help you every way in the world that we can but we're going to have to have room to work."

"Do you mind if we shout a question at him?" a reporter ignorantly asks.

"I don't want you shouting a question at him in no way!" Stevenson barks. "The more you upset him the more difficult it is for us to talk to him."

"We want to do whatever you want us to, so if you say no questions —" a reporter says cooperatively.

"Back up as far as you can against that wall," Stevenson orders as the reporters try to melt into the wall, but there is no place to move.

"Let's make it clear we have all agreed with the chief that we will not ask Oswald any questions," a reporter yells to fellow journalists.[1085]

A moment later, the jail elevator door opens and Oswald is led through the subdued crowd by Detectives Hall, Sims, and Boyd. The reporters follow orders and refrain from bombarding Oswald with questions. He soon disappears behind the closed doors of Captain Fritz's office.

10:35 a.m.

This morning, Oswald faces a formidable array of faces, including FBI agent Jim Bookhout, Dallas Secret Service agent-in-charge Forrest Sorrels, Secret Service inspector Thomas J. Kelley (in from Washington, D.C.), Secret Service agent David B. Grant, and Dallas U.S. marshall Robert I. Nash. Homicide detectives Boyd and Hall remain in the office as security.[1086] As usual, it is the soft-spoken, gravely voiced Captain Fritz who takes the lead.

"Lee, tell me what you did when you left work yesterday?" Fritz begins.

"I took a bus to my residence," Oswald says, self-assuredly, "and when I got off I got a transfer and used it to take another bus over to the theater where I was arrested. A policeman took the transfer out of my pocket at that time."[1087]

Fritz nods agreeably, although he knows that officers actually took the transfer out of Oswald's pocket several hours after his arrest, *not* at the theater. The fact that Oswald said he took a bus to his residence, not the cab Fritz knows he took, hasn't escaped the homicide captain.

"Lee, did you bring curtain rods to work with you yesterday morning?" Fritz asks.

"No," Oswald replies.

"You didn't bring any curtain rods with you?" Fritz asks again.

"No, I didn't," Oswald shoots back.

"Well, the fella that drove you to work yesterday morning tells us that you had a package in the backseat," Fritz tells him. "He says that package was about twenty-eight inches long, and you told him it was curtain rods."

"I didn't have any kind of package," Oswald says. "I don't know what he's talking about. I had my lunch and that's all I had."

"You didn't have a conversation with Wesley Frazier about curtain rods?" Fritz probes.

"No."

"When you left his car, did you go toward the building carrying a long package?" Fritz inquires.

"No, I didn't carry anything but my lunch," Oswald repeats.[1088]

"Didn't you tell Wesley you were in the process of fixing up your apartment . . ."

Oswald doesn't wait for the rest of the question, "No!"

". . . and that the purpose of your visit to Irving on the night of November 21st was to obtain some curtain rods from Mrs. Paine?"

"No, I never said that," Oswald replies.[1089]

Oswald's denials are meaningless to the thirty-year homicide investigator. He has learned long ago that if someone has the immorality to commit a serious crime, he certainly possesses the far lesser immorality to deny having done it. Fritz is sure, in his own mind, that Oswald carried the rifle wrapped in a long package into work Friday morning. Fritz just wants him to admit it.[1090] The homicide captain saunters over behind his desk, taking his time with his line of inquiry.

"Did you ride in a taxicab yesterday?" Fritz finally asks.

"Well," Oswald says hesitantly, "yes, I—"

"I thought you said you rode a bus home?" Fritz snaps back.

"Well, that's not exactly true," Oswald says with a smirk, like a child caught with his hand in the cookie jar. "Actually, I did board a bus at the Book Depository but after a block or two it got stalled in traffic, so I got off and took a cab back to my room. I remember a lady looking in the cab and asking the driver to call her one as I got in."

Oswald is good at volunteering details that don't amount to much.

"Did you talk to the driver during the ride home?" Fritz asks.

"Oh, I might have said something just to pass the time," Oswald answers.

"Did he say anything to you?"

"He told me the president had been shot," Oswald says.

"How much was the fare?" Fritz asks.

"It was about eighty-five cents," Oswald replies.

"This the first time you ever rode in a cab?" Fritz asks innocently.

"Yeah, but that's only because a bus is always available," Oswald answers.

"What'd you do when you got home?" Fritz asks. The question has been put to Oswald before, but Fritz is keenly aware that repetition will frequently trip up liars. They just can't keep their story straight because they don't have the truth as their framework of reference. That's why there's an expression that liars have to have very good memories—they only have their verbal lie to remember, not the full experience of the truth.

"I changed my shirt and trousers and went to the movies," Oswald says.

Fritz makes a mental note that Oswald has again changed his story. Yesterday, Oswald said he only changed his trousers.

"What did you do with your dirty clothes?" the homicide captain asks.

"I put them in the lower drawer of my dresser," Oswald says matter-of-factly.

"Lee, would you describe this clothing?"

"The shirt was a reddish color with a button-down collar and the trousers were gray."[1091]

11:00 a.m.

Robert Oswald arrives at the Hotel Adolphus and finds that room 906 is a suite. A stranger answers his knock.

"I'm Robert Oswald. Is my mother here?"

"In the next room," the man says. "Just come on through."

The suite has been transformed into the local headquarters for *Life* magazine. A Teletype machine clatters away as Robert makes his way past several reporters and photographers. In the next room he finds his mother, Marina and her children, an interpreter, and FBI agent Bardwell Odum. Not surprising to Robert, Odum is in the middle of an argument with Marguerite. The FBI agent wanted to ask Marina some questions, but the controlling Mrs. Oswald had intervened.

"I'm not going to let Marina say anything to anybody, and that's final," Marguerite says, her voice rising to a shout. Odum tries to get around Mrs. Oswald by addressing Marina's interpreter, only to be repeatedly interrupted by the shrill woman. Odum decides he might have better luck with Robert.

"Come on out here for a minute," Odum says, as he pulls Robert into the next room. "You seem to be a sensible guy. All we want is a yes or no from Marina herself, not from your mother. Could you help us?" Robert agrees to try, although he doesn't think his sister-in-law should answer any more questions without the assistance of counsel. On the other hand, he doesn't want to speak for her.

"I'll find out just what she wants to do," Robert says. The two men walk back into the room and Robert holds out his hand to stifle his mother before she can get started again.

"Now, wait a minute," he says, "let me handle this." He explains quietly to Marina through the interpreter what Odum wants. Marina's answer is short and simple, "*Nyet*."

Odum is disappointed, but Robert assures him that Marina will very probably cooperate fully once things settle down a little. Odum gives him a card with his telephone number and asks Robert to call him when Marina feels like answering some questions.[1092]

B ack at the Homicide and Robbery Bureau, Captain Fritz focuses his questions to Oswald once again on the time of the assassination.

"Did you eat lunch with anyone yesterday?" he asks.

"I ate with two colored boys I worked with," Oswald says.

"What are their names?" Fritz asks.

"One of them is called Junior," Oswald says, "and the other one is a short fellow. I don't remember his name, but I would recognize him on sight."*

"What did you have for lunch?" Fritz asks.

"I had a cheese sandwich and an apple," Oswald answers, "which I got at Mrs. Paine's house before I left."[1093]

Captain Fritz changes the subject and begins probing Oswald's relationship with the Paines. He asks Oswald to explain again the living arrangements he has for his wife, Marina.

"Mrs. Paine doesn't receive any pay for keeping my wife and children there. What she gets in return is that she's interested in the Russian language and having Marina around helps her with it."

"What do you know about Mr. Paine?" Fritz asks.

"I don't know Mr. Paine very well," Oswald says. "He usually comes by the house on Wednesday or Friday. He has his own car. Mrs. Paine has two."

*Depository employees James Jarman Jr., called "Junior" by friends (3 H 198, WCT James Jarman Jr.), and Harold Norman are believed to be the men referred to by Oswald. Both men ate lunch while on the first floor, but both said they did not have lunch with Oswald (3 H 188–189, WCT Harold Norman; Transcript of *On Trial*, July 28, 1968, p.72 [never saw Oswald after around ten in the morning]; 3 H 201, WCT James Jarman Jr.).

"Do you keep any of your belongings at the Paine residence?" Fritz asks.

"I've got some things in her garage that I brought back with me from New Orleans in September," Oswald says.

"Like what?" Fritz inquires.

"Well, let's see," Oswald says, "two sea bags, a couple of suitcases, and a few boxes of kitchen articles—dishes and such."

"That it?"

"I've got some clothes there too," Oswald adds.

"What about a rifle?" Fritz asks.

"I didn't store a rifle there," Oswald says, very perturbed. "I've already told you, I don't own a rifle."[1094]

Fritz switches gears.

"Lee, do you have any other friends or relatives living nearby?"

"My brother Robert lives in Fort Worth," Oswald replies.

"Anyone else? Any other friends?" Fritz asks.

"The Paines are close friends of mine," Oswald answers.[1095]

"Anyone ever visit you at your apartment on North Beckley?" Fritz asks.

"No," Oswald says.[1096]

"Have you ever ordered guns through the mail?" Fritz asks.

"I've never ordered guns," Oswald sighs, tiring of the game, "and I don't have any receipts for any guns."

"What about a rifle?"

"I don't own a rifle," Oswald snaps, "nor have I ever possessed a rifle. How many times do I have to tell you that?"[1097]

Captain Fritz doesn't answer him.

"Are you a member of the Communist Party?" Fritz asks instead.

"No," Oswald says. "I never joined and have never had a card."

"What about the American Civil Liberties Union?" Fritz asks.

Oswald smiles at the thought that Fritz would ask about the Communist Party and the ACLU in the same breath.

"Yes," he says, "I'm a member of the ACLU. I pay five dollars a year in dues. Does that make me a Communist?"[1098]

Oswald snickers under his breath.

"Lee, if you never ordered a gun or purchased a gun like you say," Fritz says calmly, "then where did you get the pistol you had in your possession at the time of your arrest?"

"Oh, I bought that about seven months ago," Oswald says, avoiding the obvious contradiction.

"Where?" Fritz asks.

"I'm not going to answer any more questions about the pistol or any guns until I've talked to a lawyer," Oswald fires back.[1099]

"Lee, have you ever been questioned before?" Fritz continues to ask questions of the young suspect, but for the moment, less probing questions.

"Yeah, I've been questioned a number of times by the FBI in Fort Worth after returning from the Soviet Union," Oswald says, glaring at the FBI men present in the room. "They used all the usual interrogation techniques—the hard and soft approach, the buddy system—all their standard operating procedures. Oh, I'm very familiar with all types of questioning. And I've got no intention of answering any questions concerning any shooting. I know I don't have to answer your questions, and I'm not going to answer any questions until I've been given counsel. Frankly, the FBI has overstepped their bounds!"

"What do you mean by that?" Captain Fritz asks.

"When the FBI talked to my wife, they were abusive and impolite," Oswald says angrily. "They frightened her with their intimidation. I consider their activities to be obnoxious."[1100] Oswald tells Captain Fritz that he's trying to reach the New York attorney named "Abt," but so far has been unsuccessful. "If I can't get him, then I may get the American Civil Liberties Union to get me an attorney." Captain Fritz advises Oswald that arrangements will be made so he can call Mr. Abt again.[1101]

"Where did you live in New Orleans?" Fritz asks.

"I lived at 4907 Magazine Street," Oswald says.

"Where did you work?"

"The William Riley Company," Oswald answers.

"Were you ever in trouble in New Orleans?" Fritz asks.

"Yes," Oswald replies. "I was arrested for disturbing the peace and paid a ten-dollar fine."

"How'd that happen?" Fritz asks.

"I was demonstrating on behalf of the Fair Play for Cuba Committee," Oswald explains, "and I got into a fight with some anti-Castro Cuban refugees who didn't particularly agree with me. Even though they started the fight, *they* were released and *I* was fined."[1102] Oswald shakes his head in disbelief. Like his mother, he plays the martyr well.

"What do you think of President Kennedy?" Fritz asks.

"I have no views on the president," Oswald replies. "My wife and I like the president's family. They're interesting people. Of course, I have my own views on the president's national policy. And I have a right to express my views but because of the charges, I don't think I should comment further."

"Anything about him bother you?" Fritz presses.

Oswald knows where Fritz is going with the question.

"I am not a malcontent," Oswald snaps, almost annoyed that the cops must think he's that stupid. "Nothing irritated me about the president."[1103]

"Lee," Captain Fritz asks in his grandfatherly tone, "will you submit to a polygraph examination?"

"Not without the advice of counsel," Oswald replies. "I refused to take one for the FBI in 1962, and I certainly don't intend to take one for the Dallas police."[1104]

Captain Fritz reaches into his desk and pulls out one of the two Selective Service cards Oswald had in his wallet at the time of his arrest.[1105] The card is made out in the name of Alek James Hidell, and includes a signature in that name, but bears a photograph of Lee Harvey Oswald. Even a cursory examination reveals the card to be a crude forgery.[*] Fritz shows the card to Oswald.

"Did you sign this card, 'Alex J. Hidell'?" Fritz asks.

"I don't have to answer that," Oswald says.

"This is your card, right?" Fritz asks.

---

[*]The fact that the card contains a photograph at all is evidence of forgery since a genuine Selective Service card, including the one Oswald had in his wallet at the time of his arrest in his own name, does not include a photograph of the card bearer (CE 801, 17 H 686).

"I carried it, yes," Oswald replies.

"Why did you carry it?" FBI agent James Bookhout asks.

Oswald is silent.

"What was the purpose of this card?" Fritz asks. "What did you use it for?"

"I don't have any comment to make on that," Oswald says stoically.[1106]

Captain Fritz pulls another item out of his desk drawer—an address book filled with Russian names and addresses—and asks who the people are whose names are in the book.

"Those are just the names of Russian immigrants living here in Dallas who I've visited since my return from the Soviet Union," Oswald says, half-amused.[1107]

The homicide chief looks up at the surrounding faces of law enforcement and lets them know that they can question the subject if they'd like. Secret Service inspector Thomas Kelley rises to the challenge.

"Mr. Oswald, did you view the parade yesterday?" he asks.

"No, I didn't," Oswald says.

"Did you shoot the president?"

"No, I did not," Oswald claims.

"Did you shoot the governor?" Kelley asks.

"No, I didn't know that the governor had been shot," Oswald says.[1108]

"Okay," Captain Fritz says, "that's it for now. Take him back to his cell."

As Detectives Sims, Boyd, and Hall escort Oswald from the room, Dallas Secret Service agent-in-charge Forrest Sorrels can't help but think that Oswald's defiant manner and obvious lying during this session is perhaps an attempt on his part to provoke Fritz into doing or saying something he shouldn't.[1109] Whatever Oswald had up his sleeve, it didn't work. None of Oswald's sass or lying bothered Fritz. As Dallas postal inspector Harry Holmes would later observe about a subsequent interview by Fritz of Oswald, "It was like water off a duck's back. He was too old a hand to be taken in by something like that."[1110]

11:27 a.m.

As detectives whisk him past newsmen in the crowded third-floor corridor, Oswald leans toward a microphone pointed in his direction. "I would like to contact Mr. Abt, A–B–T," Oswald says, spelling the name. "Mr. Abt in New York to defend me."

Detectives push Oswald through the doorway leading to the jail elevators.[*] The mob of reporters begins to pass the word, "Oswald wants a New York attorney named Abt to defend him." It's the first indication they've heard about whom Oswald wants to handle his case.[1111]

11:45 a.m.

Shortly after Oswald is taken back to his fifth-floor jail cell, the assistant police chief, Captain Glen D. King, is stopped by reporters as he makes his way through the third floor.

"Captain, could you detail the information you gave us a little while ago about the search for additional suspects?"

King tells a television audience about the search earlier that morning conducted by representatives of his office and the DA's office of the man (Joe Molina) who worked with Oswald at the Book Depository Building, and that the man was presently being interrogated by his office.

"Do you regard this man as a suspect in this case at this moment?" a reporter asks.

"All we regard him as right now is a person to interrogate," King says. "Certainly there's not an adequate amount of information on him to indicate he is a suspect . . ."

"Does this indicate that Oswald has said something that would lead you to believe other people were associated with him in this alleged—?"

"Not necessarily, no," King answers.

"What's the name of the man involved?" someone asks.

"I don't want to identify him, no," King says, "because there's not an adequate amount of evidence of any involvement on his part to warrant identification of him."[†]

---

[*]"Those people [press] were in our way every time we moved that man from my office to the jail and back," Captain Fritz would later tell the Warren Commission. "We had to push him and pull him through the crowd" (15 H 150).

[†]But later in the day, Chief Curry does, indeed, identify Molina by name over TV. Indeed, Molina is mentioned over national television on Saturday afternoon as someone who has been a

"Could we ask you, sir," a reporter says, "what do you know about the report that the FBI knew that Oswald was [a] priority one?"

"I know nothing about that," King says dryly.

"Did you give special consideration to the persons on your subversive list before the president came to town, know where they were, what they were doing?"

"Yes," King says.

"Then if the FBI had known about him ahead of time and had informed your office, you would have checked up on Oswald as well?"

"I'd rather not speculate on what might have happened if something else had happened," King tells him.

"We've been given information earlier today that the FBI did know he was here and had interviewed him during the last couple or three weeks," a reporter says.

"On this I have no answer," King replies.[1112]

12:00 noon

Marina, Marguerite, and Robert Oswald arrive at police headquarters for their scheduled meeting with Lee. After being escorted to the third-floor Forgery Bureau office, they are informed there will be a slight delay because they have picked up another suspect (Molina).

"Oh, Marina," Marguerite says to her daughter-in-law, "they think

---

previous subject of U.S. Department of Justice scrutiny as a possible subversive, with the vague implication that, who knows, maybe he could have been involved in the assassination in some way. FBI Director Hoover would later say that there had never been a file on Molina, and he wasn't even known to the FBI prior to November 22, 1963. Molina's wife, Soledad, had dropped him off at police headquarters at City Hall at 9:45 Saturday morning, and between then and 5:00 p.m., when the police drove him home after they were satisfied he had no connection to Oswald or the assassination, he was grilled off and on throughout the day by Dallas police detectives as well as the FBI. Though never told he was under arrest, when he once, between interviews, got up to leave, a Dallas police officer blocked his exit and told him to go sit down. Upon returning home, he learned from a horrified Soledad that he had been all over the news, and cast in a suspicious light. When his Book Depository Building employer thereafter started getting crank calls and warnings from some customers that if the company didn't let the "subversive" working for it go, they would stop doing business with the company, the employer finally let Molina go on December 30, after sixteen years of employment, telling him that automation had required his firing, but he knew better. (6 H 369–371, WCT Joe R. Molina; CE 1937, 23 H 732; CE 2036, 24 H 448–449)

another man might have shot Kennedy."[1113] Whether Marina could understand these words is not clear, but in any event, she had somehow convinced herself that maybe it was a mistake after all—that Lee may be under
suspicion because he has been to Russia and that this horrible nightmare
will all be over and they can go back to their ordinary lives.[1114]

A female officer from the Juvenile Bureau comes in and takes the two
women to another room so that Marina can nurse the infant Rachel in privacy.[1115] Meanwhile, Secret Service agent Mike Howard approaches Robert.

"We're interested in everything we can possibly find out about your
brother," Howard says. "Would you mind answering a few questions?"

"I'll do my best to answer anything I can," Robert replies.

Agent Howard wanted to know whether Robert thought that Lee had
shot at Governor Connally because of the dishonorable discharge* the
Marine Corps had handed Lee following his defection to the Soviet Union.

"I don't think that was the motive," Robert says, explaining that he never
heard Lee express any kind of resentment toward Connally and knew for a
fact that Lee had received a letter notifying him that Fred Korth had succeeded Connally as secretary of the navy and would be the one to rule on
Oswald's efforts to have his discharge changed to honorable.

As the conversation drifts toward the quirky relationship between
Marguerite and Lee, Agent Howard tells Robert that the kind of personal
details about the Oswald family that he's providing will be of interest to
Mrs. Kennedy. Robert takes the agent's comments to mean that Mrs.
Kennedy herself had requested the information and Agent Howard will
be delivering Robert's responses to her in person. Robert felt that he
should express his family's sympathy to her.

"I would like to take this opportunity to express to Mrs. Kennedy,
through you," Robert begins, and then his voice suddenly cracks. He
stops and hangs his head.

"That's all right," the agent says, "I know what you are trying to say."[1116]

---

*Actually, Oswald received an honorable discharge from the Marines following active duty,
but later received an "undesirable" discharge from the Marine Corps Reserves because of his
defection to the Soviet Union (WR, pp.386–387).

———————

Under earlier instructions from Captain Fritz, Detectives Sims, Boyd, Hall, and Dhority pull up at Oswald's rooming house on North Beckley to make absolutely sure that nothing was missed in yesterday's search, but Oswald's room has little to tell them. The detectives find a paperclip and a rubber band, which they confiscate, but nothing else. In fact, as Earlene Roberts points out, not only did the police clear all of Oswald's things out the day before, but they made off with a pillow case, two towels, and some washcloths belonging to the landlord. In less than thirty minutes, they're headed back to City Hall.[1117]

12:10 p.m.

When Chief Curry learns that reporters have been bombarding his assistant Glen King with questions about the FBI's possible prior knowledge of Oswald, he knows he'd better get out there and make a statement to the press—the retraction he had earlier promised Dallas FBI agent-in-charge Gordon Shanklin that he would make.

"There has been information that has gone out," Curry tells reporters at a press conference, with a live television audience looking in, "and I want to correct anything that might have been misinterpreted or misunderstood. And that is regarding information that the FBI might have had about this man."

Curry looks hesitant, his eyes shifting quickly from the microphones in front of him to the floor at his feet. He chooses his words very carefully as he picks his way through the political minefield he knows is enveloping his department.

"Last night someone told me, I don't even know who it was,* that the FBI did know this man was in the city and interviewed him. I wish to say this. Of my knowledge, I do not know this to be a fact, and I don't want

———

*Contrary to his statement, Curry certainly knew where he had learned that the FBI purportedly had prior contact with Oswald—Lieutenant Jack Revill. It was Revill's memo regarding FBI agent James P. Hosty Jr.'s alleged remarks in the basement of City Hall that had put Curry on alert. And Curry also may have known from Captain Fritz about Hosty's contact with Oswald's wife, which came out the previous day in Fritz's interrogation of Oswald.

anybody to get the wrong impression that I am accusing the FBI of not cooperating or of withholding information because they are under no obligation to us, but have always cooperated with us 100 percent."

The conference quickly moves on to other topics. Asked whether Oswald was asked to take a lie detector test, Curry says that it was offered to him but he refused to take it.

"Chief Curry, what are your plans now in dealing with Oswald himself?" a reporter asks. "Will he be interrogated here further or will he be transferred to the county jail to await presentment to the grand jury?"

"He will go to the county jail," Curry replies. "I don't know just when. But I am thinking probably sometime today . . . It is more convenient here to have him near us where we can talk to him when we need to, but we will probably transfer him soon."[1118]

After returning to his office, Curry calls Captain Fritz and asks if he will be ready to transfer Oswald by 4:00 p.m. Fritz says he doesn't think he will be finished questioning Oswald by then.[1119]

Under normal circumstances, an arrested person becomes the responsibility of Sheriff Bill Decker and goes to the county jail as soon as he has been booked. Details of the transfer are usually left to Decker, who has deputies from his office pick the prisoner up at the police department and transport him to the county jail. But this one may be too hot for the relatively small sheriff's department to handle. The Dallas Police Department has far more men and resources. The transfer will be from City Hall straight down Main Street to the Criminal Courts Building at Main and Houston, less than a mile away, ironically following the path of yesterday's motorcade. The problem of how and when to move Lee Oswald to the county jail will occupy much of the chief's time and attention over the next twenty-four hours.[1120]

12:35 p.m.
Captain Fritz orders Detectives Senkel and Turner to bring Oswald down from the jail for another interview. This time the questioning is perfunctory, aimed at getting a list of addresses where Oswald lived in Dallas, and in particular, where the bulk of his personal property might be stored.

The questioning lasts about a half hour, during which Oswald says that most of his belongings are stored in the garage at Mrs. Paine's house in Irving.[1121]

Captain Fritz steps outside his office and dispatches Detectives Guy Rose and Richard Stovall to Irving with instructions to pick up anything and everything in storage there. This will be the second search of the Paine residence, but the first thorough search of the Paine garage. Only the blanket that had been used to store the rifle had been recovered from the garage on Friday.[1122]

As they head out the door, Fritz orders two visitor passes for Oswald's wife and mother to see Oswald in the fourth-floor jail office.[1123]

1:07 p.m.

Robert Oswald is rather put out that three passes haven't been arranged so that he too can see his brother. Secret Service agent Mike Howard tells him that he'll see what he can do about arranging another pass for him. Robert reluctantly agrees to remain behind and let his mother and Marina use the two passes to go up and see Lee.[1124]

The policewoman from the Juvenile Bureau takes care of the babies, and the two women are led through the pack of reporters in the hallway toward the fourth-floor elevators. They are forced to wait momentarily for the next elevator car, giving the reporters a chance to descend on them like hungry vultures. The two women ignore the bushel of questions tossed at them until Marguerite finally caves in and tells them they are going up to see Lee now. The elevator doors finally open and they escape the onslaught of questions, gliding up the elevator shaft to the floor above.[1125] A gaggle of reporters turn their attention to District Attorney Henry Wade, who is leaning against a corridor wall nearby. "Mr. Wade, do you expect to call Mrs. Kennedy or Governor Connally, if he's able, in this trial as witnesses?"

"We will not, unless it's absolutely necessary," Wade tells them, "and at this point I don't think it'll be necessary."

"How soon can we expect a trial?"

"I'd say around the middle of January," Wade answers.

"Has Mr. Oswald expressed any hatred, ill will, toward President Kennedy or, for that matter, any regret over his death?" a reporter asks.

"He has expressed no regret that I know of," Wade replies.

"This man, it seems, wasn't close to anybody," a reporter interjects. "Have you discovered any close friends in Dallas?"

"No, sir," Wade replies, agreeing with the reporter that this suggests an introverted personality.

"It's rumored that perhaps this case would be tried by a military court because, of course, President Kennedy is our commander in chief," a reporter suggests.

"I don't know anything about that," Wade corrects. "We have him charged in the state court and he's a state prisoner at present."

"And you will conduct the trial?"

"Yes, sir," Wade says. "I plan to."

"And you will ask the capital verdict?"

"We'll ask the death penalty," Wade says firmly.

"In how many cases of this type have you been involved, that is, when the death penalty is involved?"

"Since I've been district attorney we've asked—I've asked the death penalty in twenty-four cases," Wade replies.

"How many times have you obtained it?"

The district attorney looks the reporter in the eye.

"Twenty-three," he says. Elected district attorney five consecutive times over the last twenty years, Wade is confident that the Oswald case will bring him a twenty-fourth death penalty verdict. Texas juries—Texans, period—are strong believers in capital punishment.[1126] In a recent Dallas murder case of Wade's, after a long and impassioned plea by the defense attorney asking the jurors to spare the life of his client, Wade rose and gave one of the shortest summations ever delivered. "Ladies and gentlemen of the jury," the DA said, "this boy belongs in the electric chair." The jury returned a verdict of death after three hours of deliberation.[1127]

1:15 p.m.

Marina and Marguerite Oswald wait nervously in the fourth-floor visiting room to meet Lee for the first time since the murders. The long, narrow room is divided in two by a heavy glass window, one side for visitors, the other for prisoners. Rounded-off plywood wings divide the partition into several cubicles. There are no chairs in the booths, just a wood shelf and a telephone—the only communication across the grimy, dusty glass barrier. It is a stale, claustrophobic room haunted by the thousands of visitors who have crossed its threshold over the years.[1128]

Although Marina has managed to convince herself of Lee's innocence, the minute she sees him caged in glass, troubled, pitiful, and alone, her confidence deserts her. They pick up the telephones on each side of the barrier.

"Why did you bring that fool with you?" Lee says in Russian, glancing over her shoulder at his mother. "I don't want to talk to her."

"She's your mother," Marina says. "Of course she came."

Marina stares at the cuts and bruises on her husband's face.

"Have they been beating you?" she asks.

"Oh no," he answers. "They treat me fine. Did you bring Junie and Rachel?"

"They're downstairs," Marina says, anxious to talk to Lee about something weighing on her mind. "Alik [Marina's Russian nickname for Lee], can we talk about anything we like?"

That morning, Marina had tucked two photographs of Lee and his rifle inside one of the shoes she was now wearing. They were there now. She desperately wants to ask him what she should do with them.

"Oh, of course," he said sarcastically. "We can speak about *absolutely* anything."

Marina could tell from his tone that he was warning her to say nothing.

"They asked me about the gun," she says.

"Oh, that's nothing," he answers, his voice rising, the words coming quickly.[1129]

Marina can't bring herself to ask him if he did it. After all, he is her husband.

"I don't believe that you did that," she finally manages to say. "Everything will turn out well."[1130]

"Oh sure," he says, "there is a lawyer in New York who will help me. You shouldn't worry. Everything will be fine."

On the surface, it is the same old Lee, full of bravado. But this time there is something different. This time, the pitch of his voice is higher. There is also fear in his eyes, betraying his guilt. He is telling her everything will turn out all right, but Marina feels that even he does not believe it. Tears start to roll down her cheek.

"Don't cry," he says tenderly. "There's nothing to cry about. Try not to think about it. And if they ask you anything, you have a right not to answer. You have the right to refuse. Do you understand?"

"Yes," Marina says, wiping the tears away. She looks him in the eye. There are tears in his eyes too, but he's working hard to hold them back.[1131]

Marguerite doesn't understand a word they're saying, since the entire conversation is in Russian. Finally, Marina hands the phone to her.

"Honey, you are so bruised up, your face," Marguerite says. "What are they doing?"

"Mother, don't worry," Lee says. "I got that in a scuffle."

Marguerite thinks that Lee is simply shielding his mother from the truth about the awful beatings behind the jail walls.

"Is there anything I can do to help you?"

"No, Mother, everything is fine," Lee replies. "I know my rights. I have already requested to get in touch with an attorney, Mr. Abt. Don't worry about a thing."[1132]

Marguerite isn't about to insult him by asking him whether he shot President Kennedy. She heard him on television saying he didn't do it and that is enough for her. Eventually she yields the phone back to Marina. Lee again tells Marina not to worry.

"You have friends," he says. "They'll help you. If it comes to that, you can ask the Red Cross for help. You mustn't worry about me. Kiss Junie and Rachel for me."

"I will," Marina promises, tears welling up in her eyes.

Two guards enter the room behind him.

"Alka," Marina says, using a variant of Alik she often used, "remember that I love you." It was her way of letting him know that he could count on her not to betray him.

"I love you very much," he says. "Make sure you buy shoes for June."[1133]

Oswald backs out of the room so that he can look at her until the very last second.

Marina now knows Lee is guilty. She knows that if he were truly innocent, he would be raising the roof about his persecution, the denial of his rights, and the evils of the system, just as he had always done over the slightest perceived transgressions by others. His very docility in his predicament tells her more than he could ever say in words. There is also a certain tranquility about his personality. She remembers how tense he was after the failed attempt to shoot General Walker. Now he is altogether different. There seems to almost be a certain glow of satisfaction. As she watches him leave, it seems he is saying good-bye with his eyes.

The door shuts behind him and Marina starts crying.

Downstairs, the women are forced once again to run the gauntlet of reporters, some of them shouting questions in Russian.

"What did he say? What did your husband say?"

"Leave me alone, it is hard for me now," Marina wants to cry out. Instead, she maintains a stoical silence.[1134]

1:40 p.m.

Lee Oswald has just been returned to his cell when word comes from the Homicide and Robbery office to let him make any telephone calls he wishes. Assistant jailer Arthur E. Eaves and the patrolman assigned to the suicide watch, Buel T. Beddingfield, take Lee from his cell and lead him over to the telephone, which is in a booth.

"Who do you want to call?" the assistant jailer asks.

"New York City, collect," Oswald replies.

The jailer gets the City Hall operator on the line and tells her that the prisoner would like to call New York City collect. The jailer hands Oswald the phone and overhears Oswald call New York City, then place a local call, after which he is returned to his cell.[1135]

———————

In Irving, Ruth Paine is out in the front yard with her children. She's thinking about doing some grocery shopping so that she'll be prepared to stay home and deal with the press and the police, who'll no doubt want to ask her questions. She's about to go inside when Dallas police detectives Rose, Stovall, Adamcik, and Moore arrive with Detective McCabe of the Irving Police Department. The men have a warrant signed by Judge Joe Brown Jr. and want to search the premises again.[1136]

She has no objection to the search but doesn't want to wait for them. They assure her that this time they are looking for something specific—the items Oswald keeps stored in the garage. Mrs. Paine takes them to the garage and shows them where the Oswalds kept their things.[1137]

"I want to go to the grocery store," she says. "I'll just go and you go ahead and do your searching."

As Mrs. Paine leaves, the detectives begin pawing through the Oswalds' effects that they missed in their first search the day before—two seabags, three suitcases, and two cardboard boxes of odds and ends. It doesn't take long before Detective Rose finds some things Marina would have surely destroyed or hidden had she known they existed.

"Look at this!" he says to the others, waving two negatives and a snapshot showing Oswald, dressed in black, holding a rifle that looks very much like the weapon found on the sixth floor of the Texas School Book Depository, the same photo Marina had been hiding from the authorities and trying to give to Marguerite. On Oswald's hip, a holstered pistol—probably, they assume, the gun he used to shoot Officer Tippit. A moment later, Detective McCabe finds the second snapshot that matches the other negative.[1138]

In the same cardboard carton Stovall finds a page torn from a magazine advertising weapons available from Klein's Sporting Goods in Chicago. One of the offerings is circled. It is for a Mannlicher-Carcano rifle.[1139]

That's not all the detectives find. They turn up some more interesting negatives, shots of a Selective Service card with something on the back of the negative to block out the space where the name would be typed in. Several prints made from the negatives were bundled with them. The resulting prints were, in effect, blank Selective Service cards. The detectives immediately recognized them as identical to the false Selective Service card that Oswald had in his wallet in the name of "Alek James Hidell."[1140]

The detectives take their time combing through the rest of the inventory, careful not to overlook anything. It takes two and a half hours to complete the task. When they're finished, they cart everything off to their car. Mrs. Paine hasn't returned from her shopping trip, so they flip the latch, lock the front door, and head back toward Dallas City Hall.[1141]

2:05 p.m.

Captain Fritz emerges from the Homicide and Robbery office and wades into the newsmen, Chief Curry at his side. "Captain, can you give us a résumé of what you now know concerning the assassination of the president and Mr. Oswald's role in it?" a television reporter asks.

"There is only one thing that I can tell you," Fritz replies in his gravely voice, "without going into the evidence before first talking to the district attorney. I can tell you that this case is cinched—that this man killed the president. There's no question in my mind about it."

"Well, what is the basis for that statement?" the reporter asks.

"I don't want to go into the basis," Fritz says. "In fact, I don't want to get into the evidence. I just want to tell you that we are convinced beyond any doubt that he did the killing."

"Was it spur-of-the-moment or a well-planned, long-thought-out plot?"

"I'd rather not discuss that," Fritz answers, "if you don't mind, please, thank you."

The homicide captain brushes the reporters aside and begins making his way toward the stairwell, near the elevators. A trail of reporters follow.

"Will you be moving him today, Captain? Is he going to remain here?"

"He'll be here today," Fritz finally answers, "yes, sir."[1142]

2:14 p.m.

Detective Jim Leavelle leads cabdrivers William Whaley and William Scoggins into the show-up room to view Oswald in a lineup. Whaley drove

Oswald to his Oak Cliff apartment after the assassination, and Scoggins witnessed the shooting of Officer J. D. Tippit. In a moment they are joined by Detective C. N. Dhority and Assistant District Attorney Bill Alexander.[1143]

In the hallway just outside, Detectives Hall, Senkel, Potts, and Brown meet the fifth-floor jailers, who have brought Oswald and three other prisoners down in handcuffs. This time, Oswald is in the number 3 position.[1144] Oswald is complaining bitterly about not being allowed to put on a shirt over his T-shirt. A nearby NBC cameraman captures a snippet of Oswald badgering the jailers.

"I've been photographed in a T-shirt," Oswald is heard to say, "now they're taking me to a lineup among these men. Naturally, I will be picked out. Right?"[1145]

The detectives tug Oswald toward the stage entrance.

Inside the show-up room, the lights are dimmed as Detective Leavelle instructs Whaley and Scoggins to look over each man carefully. "If you recognize any of these men as the one you saw yesterday," Leavelle tells them, "just hold up the number of fingers that match the number over the man in the lineup."[1146] Oswald is belligerent, complaining in a loud voice as the prisoners are led out under the bright lights of the stage.

"It's not right to put me in line with these teenagers,"* Oswald cries. "I know what you're doing. You're trying to railroad me! I want my lawyer!"[1147]

Oswald shows no respect for the detectives around him, and tells them what he thinks of them. It matters little to Whaley, though. As soon as he sees Oswald, he knows he is the man he drove to Oak Cliff yesterday. When you drive a cab as long as Whaley has—thirty-seven years—you learn to judge people by looking them over very carefully. It's the way he's learned to determine whether he can trust them or not.

---

*The three other young men in the lineup with Oswald, age twenty-four, were John Thurman Horne, seventeen; David Edmond Knapp, eighteen; and Daniel Gutierrez Lujan, twenty-six (7 H 200, WCT Walter Eugene Potts).

When Whaley saw Oswald's picture in the newspaper this morning, he recognized him immediately. Now, in the flesh, there is no doubt that Oswald is the man who got in his cab.[1148]

Leavelle asks each of the prisoners a question so that the witnesses can hear them speak, although Oswald is spared the procedure.[1149]

"Anybody up there look like the man you saw?" Leavelle asks Whaley.

"Yes, number 3, the man in the T-shirt," Whaley says. "That's him all right."[1150]

Detective Leavelle turns to Scoggins, who is holding up three fingers at his waist.[1151]

"Are you sure?" Leavelle asks.

"Well, he can bitch and holler all he wants," Scoggins says to Detective Leavelle, "but that's the man I saw running from the scene. Number 3."[1152]

The prisoners are taken away as Detectives Dhority and Assistant DA Alexander lead Whaley and Scoggins up to the third-floor Auto Theft office to take affidavits.[1153] Shortly after Oswald is returned to his cell, Bobby Brown of the Crime Scene Search Section of the Identification Bureau and Officer Jack Donahue come up to the fifth-floor jail. With Oswald's consent they obtain scrapings from under the fingernails of both of his hands and specimens of hair from his head, right armpit, chest, right forearm, pubic area, and right leg. The specimens are turned over to FBI special agent C. Ray Hall for comparison tests to be conducted at the FBI's Washington, D.C., crime lab.[1154]

2:25 p.m.

After their visit with Lee,[1155] Marguerite and Marina and her children climb into a squad car, which circles the city for twenty minutes to shake any members of the press who might be following them on their way back to the Hotel Adolphus. At the eleventh floor in the hotel, the police ask Tommy Thompson of *Life* for his credentials—something Marguerite realizes she hasn't thought to check herself. Satisfied of Thompson's bona fides, the police officers leave the Oswalds in his care. Thompson opens the door and lets Marguerite, Marina, and her children into the suite.

"Mrs. Oswald, what do you plan to do now?" Thompson says, turning to Marguerite.

Marguerite fears he is about to renege on his promise.

"Well," she reminds him, "the arrangement was that we are going to stay here in the hotel for a few days, and you are going to pay expenses."

"But you haven't given us any facts," Thompson shoots back.

Marguerite finds it strange that Thompson doesn't ask about her visit with Lee, even though he knew they left that morning to talk to him.

"Mrs. Oswald," Thompson continues, "reporters will be coming here in flocks. They know where you are . . . Just a minute."

Thompson gets on the telephone and calls the ninth-floor room where the rest of *Life*'s representatives are staying.

"Come up here," he says into the phone.

In a few minutes, Allan Grant and another *Life* rep show up. Marguerite helps Marina change the baby's diaper while the men converse with Thompson in hushed tones. Thompson then tells Marguerite that they intend to move her and Marina to the outskirts of town, so reporters won't know where they are. "Here is some money," he tells her, "for your expenses in case you need anything." He gives her a fifty-dollar bill for expenses. She stuffs it into the pocket of her nurse's uniform without even looking at it. A few minutes later, Grant drives Marguerite, Marina, and the kids out to the Executive Inn, a hotel not far from Love Field.

"Mrs. Oswald," he says, "I've arranged for you to stay here for two or three days. I have to be back in San Francisco. Anything you want, you have the cash that Mr. Thompson gave you. He'll be in touch with you."

Grant and a porter escort the women and children up to the rooms—two very nice adjoining suites. Marguerite is pleased with the arrangements. It is only after Grant leaves that she begins to have misgivings about her predicament, stranded with a Russian daughter-in-law she barely understands and two small children. Marguerite orders room service and shoos Marina out of sight when the food comes, to avoid being recognized—they had, after all, been paraded in front of those television cameras up at City Hall.

Marguerite sees Marina hunched over an ashtray on the dressing table. Marina has torn up the photographs of Lee and his rifle that she's kept hidden in her shoe and thrown them into the ashtray. She strikes a match and sets the pieces on fire. But the heavy photographic paper doesn't burn very well. Marguerite decides to help and empties the remains into the toilet, flushing them away.[1156]

3:00 p.m.

With the help of Secret Service agent Mike Howard and his partner, Charley Kunkel, Robert Oswald has been trying to wrangle a visitor's pass to see his brother for the better part of two and a half hours, with little success. Agent Kunkel heads down the hall again to see what he can do.

Secret Service inspector Thomas J. Kelley comes into the Forgery Bureau a moment later and introduces himself. Howard explains to Kelley that Robert is being cooperative and answering any questions he can. The three men speculate as to whether Lee Oswald will admit anything to his brother when he sees him.

"I'm just as anxious as anyone to learn the reason behind the assassination," Robert tells them, "and to discover whether anyone else is involved."

Kelley sends Mike Howard down the hall to help Kunkel arrange the pass, then fights his way through the mob of reporters to retrieve some peanut-butter cookies and a soft drink for Robert from the machine at the end of the hall. It's thirty minutes before Kelley returns. He picks up the telephone and checks on the pass several times. Finally, he turns to Robert, "Okay, we've got it."[1157]

3:37 p.m.

Inspector Kelley, holding the pass signed by Captain Fritz, and a Dallas police officer take Robert Oswald upstairs in the elevator to the visiting room.[1158]

Inspector Kelley and the officer wait outside. For a moment Robert is alone in the stifling atmosphere of the room, the only sound that of the portable camera in the hands of a cameraman who plants himself in the doorway and, without saying a word to Robert, grinds away, collecting footage to sell to television.

Robert doesn't even hear the clank of the steel door, and Lee is almost at the smudged glass before Robert realizes he has come in. Lee points to the telephone on Robert's side of the transparent partition, as he picks up the one on his side. His voice is calm as he says, "This is taped."[*]

Robert realizes that Lee is warning him to be careful of what he says.

"Well, it may or may not be," Robert answers.

"How are you?" Lee asks evenly.

"I'm fine," Robert replies. "How are you?"

Robert is surprised at his brother's physical appearance. He knew about the scuffle in the theater but didn't know that Lee had sustained cuts and bruises. The liberally applied Mercurochrome makes it look worse than it is.

"What have they been doing to you?" Robert asks. "Were they roughing you up?"

"I got this at the theater," Lee says. "They haven't bothered me since. They're treating me all right."

Robert is astonished at how completely relaxed Lee is, as though the world's frenzied consternation over yesterday's events had nothing to do with him. Lee talks as if they're discussing a minor incident at the Depository. Robert doesn't know how long he's got to talk with Lee, but resists the temptation to ask the one question he wanted to ask most. Instead, they talk casually for a few minutes.

"Mother and Marina were up earlier," Lee says.

"Yes, I know," Robert replies.

"What did you think of the baby?" Lee asks with a grin.

"Yeah," Robert says, "thanks a lot for telling me. I didn't even know you had another one."

---

[*]Oswald's warning was unnecessary. Truth is, the visitors' telephones were not tape-recorded by the police (4 H 154, WCT Jesse E. Curry).

"Well, it was a girl," Lee says, "and I wanted a boy, but you know how that goes."

Finally, Robert can't resist anymore.

"Lee, what the Sam Hill is going on?" he asks bluntly.

"I don't know," Lee answers.

"You don't know?" Robert says, disbelieving. "Look, they've got your pistol, they've got your rifle, they've got you charged with shooting the president and a police officer. And you tell me you don't know? Now, I want to know just what's going on."

Lee stiffens, his facial expression suddenly becoming tight.

"Don't believe all this so-called evidence," he says firmly.

Robert studies his face, then his eyes, looking for some expression of the truth. Lee realizes what his brother wants.

"Brother, you won't find anything there," he says.

After an awkward silence, Lee, now more relaxed, mentions Marina again.

"Well, what about Marina?" Robert interrupts. "What do you think she's going to do now, with those two kids?"

"My friends will take care of them," he answers.

"You mean the Paines?"

"Yes," Lee replies, obviously surprised that his brother knew of them.

"I don't think they're any friends of yours," Robert tells him, revealing his distrust and suspicion.

"Yes, they are," Lee snaps back.

Another awkward silence.

"Junie needs a new pair of shoes," Lee finally says.

Robert had noticed yesterday that one of the little girl's shoes was practically worn through.

"Don't worry about that," Robert says sympathetically. "I'll take care of that."

Robert asks about the attorney, Mr. Abt, that Lee has been asking for.

"He's just an attorney I want to handle my case," Lee says.

"I'll get you an attorney down here," Robert answers.

"No, you stay out of it," Lee commands.

"Stay out of it?" Robert says, incredulously. "It looks like I've been dragged into it."

"Well, I'm not going to have anyone from down here," Lee says firmly. "I want this one."

"All right," Robert concedes.

A police officer suddenly enters the room behind Lee, taps him on the shoulder, then steps back and waits for them to finish. Robert is surprised and disappointed at the interruption. He feels that they were just beginning to talk easily with each other.

Robert hadn't expected his brother to flat-out admit his guilt. But he felt it was conceivable that Lee had made up his mind that the assassination was necessary for some reason that was sufficient to him, and that he would have wanted to make that motive clear to someone, and Robert felt that he was closer to Lee than anyone else in a lot of ways. He had hoped he would tell him. But he hasn't.

"I'll see you in a day or two," Robert says.

"You've got your job and everything," Lee replies. "Don't be running back and forth all the time and getting yourself in trouble with your boss."

"Don't worry about that," Robert tells him. "I'll be back."

"All right," Lee says. "I'll see you."

They are the last words Robert ever hears him say.[1159] Secret Service inspector Kelley is still waiting for Robert outside the visiting room.

"What did he say?" the inspector asks.

"Let's wait until we're downstairs," Robert replies, miffed that the persistent cameraman is still grinding away. It makes him feel like a zoo specimen. Back in the Forgery Bureau, and away from the prying ears of the news media, Robert tells Mike Howard and Inspector Kelley, "He didn't say anything because he said the line was tapped."

"If that were true," Kelley replies, "I wouldn't be asking you, would I?"

Robert can only shrug. Inspector Kelley asks Robert to reconstruct their conversation as carefully as he can, and Robert does exactly that. He is deeply unsatisfied by his brother's demeanor, which he found disturbingly machine-like, with an uncanny lack of emotion for a man in

Lee's predicament, innocent or guilty. Robert was not talking to the brother he knew. The man in jail was a stranger to him.[1160]

3:51 p.m. (4:51 p.m. EST)

President Johnson, from the White House, issues a "Proclamation" which is "to the People of the United States," in which he calls John F. Kennedy "a man of wisdom, strength and peace" who "molded and moved the power of our nation in the service of a world of growing liberty and order. All who love freedom will mourn his death." Johnson proceeds to "appoint Monday next, November 25, the day of the funeral service of President Kennedy, to be a day of national mourning throughout the United States," urging Americans to "assemble on that day in their respective places of divine worship."[1161] Other than an exhortation to go to one's place of worship, the proclamation, of course, is unnecessary, as the shock, grief, and tears of millions of Americans had not even begun to subside.

4:00 p.m.

Dallas police lieutenant Thurber Lord is the jail lieutenant in charge on the 2:30 p.m. to 10:30 p.m. shift on November 23. Around 4:00 p.m. he gets a call from Detective M. G. Hall of the Homicide and Robbery Bureau telling him that Oswald had requested permission to use the telephone again and that it would be okay for him to do so. Lord telephones Officer J. L. Popplewell on the fifth floor, where he had been assigned to guard the area in front of Oswald's cell.

Popplewell takes Oswald to the phone and Oswald tells the operator he wants to call Mr. John Abt, an attorney in New York. Oswald apparently didn't keep the number he had used earlier to call Abt because the operator looks up the number and gives it to him. Oswald hangs up, but can't remember the number he was just given. He asks Popplewell for a pencil and a piece of paper to write on. The officer tears a corner from a telephone contact slip and gives it to Oswald, along with a pencil. Oswald calls the operator again and this time writes down the number she gives him. He then tries to place the call collect, but there is no answer.[1162]

4:22 p.m.

After Oswald unsuccessfully attempts to reach attorney John Abt in New York City from the phone booth on the fifth floor of the jail, he places a local call. In Irving, the telephone rings at the home of Ruth Paine. She answers it.

"This is Lee," a voice says. She knows who it is—Lee Oswald.

"Well, hi!" she says, unable to hide the surprise in her voice that he would telephone her at all.

"I would like you to call Mr. John Abt in New York for me after six o'clock this evening," Oswald says. "I've got two numbers for you." Mrs. Paine grabs a nearby pencil and notepad. He gives her two telephone numbers—an office and a home number. Mrs. Paine quickly scribbles the numbers down.

"He's an attorney I would like to have represent me," Oswald tells her. "I would be grateful if you would call him for me."

She is very irritated by the fact that he sounds as if nothing out of the ordinary has happened. It seems to him, she feels, that this is a call like any other call, a favor like any other favor. He doesn't mention the assassination, the fact that he is in jail, or the reason he needs a lawyer. He seems so apart from the situation. Still, she agrees to make the call.

"Okay," Mrs. Paine manages to say.

Oswald thanks her and hangs up. The receiver is barely back in the cradle when the telephone rings again. Ruth answers it.

"Hi, this is Lee."

It's Oswald, calling back again. Mrs. Paine is stunned to hear Oswald repeat his request, nearly word for word. It all seems so strange to her.[1163]*

5:45 p.m.

H. Louis Nichols, president of the Dallas Bar Association, trots up the concrete steps leading to City Hall. Nichols, a member of the American

---

*Mrs. Paine attempted to reach attorney John Abt after six o'clock, as Oswald requested, but was unable to get an answer at either number. She testified that she could not recall if she conveyed the results of her efforts to Oswald during a subsequent conversation at 8:00 p.m. Saturday evening. Mrs. Paine made another attempt to reach Mr. Abt at home on Sunday morning, again without success. (3 H 88–89, WCT Ruth Hyde Paine)

Bar Association since 1949, has been on and off the telephone since two o'clock this afternoon. He had gotten a call from the dean of an eastern law school who said that the media back there were reporting that Lee Oswald couldn't get a lawyer to represent him in Dallas and he wanted to know if Nichols was doing anything about the situation. Nichols acknowledged that he hadn't, but promised he would look into it. Under Texas law at the time, an attorney had to be appointed for an accused (if he didn't already have one) only after he had been indicted by a grand jury, which Oswald hadn't been yet. But if any defendant needed a lawyer immediately to make sure his rights were being protected, it was Oswald.

Nichols had worked in the city attorney's office, still represented the city's credit union, and has a brother on the police force, so he knows many of the top men there. He telephones the assistant police chief, Captain Glen King, who tells him that so far as he knows, Oswald hasn't asked for a lawyer.

"Well, Glen," Nichols says, "if you know at any time that he asks for a lawyer, or wants a lawyer, or needs a lawyer, will you tell him that you have talked to me? And that as president of the Bar Association, I have offered to get him a lawyer if he wants one?"

"Why don't you come down here and talk to him," King says.

"I don't know whether I want to do that at this point or not," Nichols replies.

Within an hour, Nichols got a call from another law school dean, questioning whether the Dallas Bar was doing anything about Oswald's right to an attorney. That was enough for Nichols, who decides he might as well go down and talk to Oswald directly.

The Dallas Bar Association president takes an elevator to the third floor, where he knows he'll find the Dallas police administrative offices. When the doors open, Nichols is flabbergasted to find an ocean of reporters and photographers stepping over and around a tangle of television cameras, cables, and electrical cords stretched out across the corridor. He pushes his way through the jam to the eastern end of the building and into Chief Curry's outer office. Nichols can see Chief Curry in his office talking with three or four men.

"Is Captain King in?" Nichols asks an officer standing nearby.

"I don't think so," the officer replies.

Just then, Chief Curry looks up, recognizes Nichols, and motions for him to come in. Nichols tells Curry why he is there.

"Well, I'm glad to see you," Curry says. "I'll take you up to see Oswald myself." They walk out into the hallway and take an elevator to the fifth floor.

The jailer opens the outer door of the maximum-security area of the fifth-floor jail and Nichols and Chief Curry step inside the narrow corridor. Oswald, in trousers and a T-shirt, is lying on his bunk. Oswald gets up as Curry asks the officer seated in the corridor to open Oswald's cell.

"Mr. Oswald," Curry says, "this is Louis Nichols, president of the Dallas Bar Association. He's come here to see whether or not you need or want a lawyer."

With that short introduction, Chief Curry steps back into the outer hallway, so that they can talk freely, without interference. Curry is far enough away that neither Nichols nor Oswald can see him from inside the cell.

Oswald sits back down on the edge of the bunk. Nichols takes a seat on the bunk across from him, three or four feet away.

"Do you have a lawyer?" Nichols begins.

"Well, I really don't know what this is all about," Oswald says. "I've been incarcerated and held incommunicado."

"It's my understanding that you're under arrest for the shooting of President Kennedy," Nichols tells him. "I'm here to see if you need or want a lawyer."

"Do you know a lawyer in New York named John Abt?" Oswald asks.

"No, I don't," Nichols says.

"Well, I would like to have him represent me," Oswald says in a calm and clear voice. "Do you know any lawyers who are members of the American Civil Liberties Union?"

"I'm sorry," Nichols says, "I don't know anybody who is a member of that organization."

"Well, I'm a member of that organization," Oswald says, "and if I can't get Mr. Abt, I would like to have somebody from that organization represent me."

Nichols can see that Oswald is in full control of his faculties. He is neither belligerent nor does he appear to be frightened or subdued.

"If I can't get either one of those to represent me," Oswald adds, "and if I can find a lawyer here who believes in my innocence . . ."

Oswald hesitates for a moment, then continues.

". . . as much as he can, I might let him represent me."

"What I am interested in knowing, Mr. Oswald," Nichols responds, "is do you want me or the Dallas Bar Association to try to get you a lawyer right now?"

"No, not now," Oswald replies. "I talked with members of my family this afternoon and they're trying to get in touch with Mr. Abt." Oswald adds, "You might come back next week and if I don't get some of these other people, I might ask you to get somebody to represent me."

Satisfied that Oswald knows what he is doing and is aware of his right to counsel, Nichols leaves the cell. As he and Curry climb back into the elevator for the ride back to the third floor, Curry asks if he wants to make a statement to the press.

"I don't know," Nichols says. "I don't know whether it's the thing to do or not."

"Well, they are going to be right outside the door here," Chief Curry warns him, "and if you want to say anything this would be an opportunity to do it." Curry adds, "Incidentally, I am very glad you came up here. We don't want any question coming up about us refusing to let him have a lawyer. That takes the burden off us."[1164]

6:15 p.m.

The elevator doors open and they step into a swarm of photographers and cameramen. When the media see who it is, they pack in closer. Chief Curry raises his voice above the ruckus.

"This is Mr. Nichols, president of the Dallas Bar Association," Curry announces. "He has been talking to Mr. Oswald and he will make a statement for you if he desires."

Flashbulbs pop and microphones are pushed toward Nichols's face as he suddenly finds himself on live television, wholly unprepared.

Nichols explains what has just transpired.

"Did he seem to be in possession of all his faculties? Did he deny the shooting to you?"

More questions follow until little can be understood. Nichols picks one out of the noise and answers.

"He appeared to be perfectly rational and I could observe no abnormalities about him at all in the short time that I visited with him," Nichols says.

"Do you know anything about John Abt?" someone asks.

"I don't know anything about him," Nichols says.

"How long did you talk with him?"

"About three minutes," Nichols replies.

"Do you think he can get a fair trial in Dallas?" a reporter asks skeptically.

"I think he can get a fair trial in Dallas," Nichols says with assurance.

"Would you be willing to represent him?" someone asks.

Nichols's answer is quick and direct.

"I do not practice criminal law," he says, "and I've never tried a criminal case so I don't know the answer to that."[1165]

Lieutenant Robert E. McKinney of the Forgery Bureau appears at the office of Justice of the Peace David Johnston in Richardson, Texas, with a criminal complaint ("Affidavit" number F-155) he's prepared and signed as an affiant charging Oswald with assault with intent to murder Governor John Connally. Johnston affixes his signature to the complaint and it is officially filed at 6:15 p.m.[1166] Oswald will never be arraigned on this charge.[1167]

Back in Homicide and Robbery, Captain Fritz picks up the telephone and calls the Identification Bureau on the fourth floor. "Have them bring those pictures down to my office," he orders.

They know what pictures he's talking about—the photographs of Oswald holding a rifle.

6:24 p.m.

Under orders from Captain Fritz, Detectives Sims, Hall, and Graves escort Oswald down from his jail cell to the Homicide and Robbery office for another interrogation session. Once again, Oswald is marched through the third-floor corridor. He's getting good at playing to the crowd of reporters, using their microphones to take jabs at the police department and build sympathy. This time he complains about being denied "the basic fundamental hygienic rights like a shower."[1168]

The smirk quickly evaporates from Oswald's face as he's brought into the homicide captain's office. Three homicide detectives in white Stetson hats stand guard, silently.[1169] Fritz walks in, followed by Secret Service inspector Thomas Kelley, FBI agent James Bookhout, and homicide detective Guy Rose, who is carrying an envelope.

Oswald immediately complains about not being allowed in the last lineup to put on clothing similar to that worn by some of the other individuals in previous lineups.[1170] No one says anything. The hostile prisoner braces himself for another onslaught of questions, but Fritz begins slowly with a methodical list of mundane questions designed to relax and settle Oswald down. Oswald is eager to talk about anything that doesn't pertain to the assassination investigation and eventually softens with the gentle banter. Soon, Oswald is rambling on about how life is better for the colored people in Russia than it is in the United States.[1171] Finally, Fritz turns to the business at hand.

"Now, you told me yesterday that you'd never owned a gun," Fritz says innocently.

"That's right," Oswald replies. "I never owned a gun."

"Okay," Fritz says, reaching for the envelope Detective Rose has laid on his desk. "I want to show you something."

Oswald purses his lips and eyes the envelope the captain is reaching into. Like Houdini pulling a rabbit out of a hat, Fritz suddenly produces an eight-by-ten-inch black-and-white photograph and holds it out in front of Oswald.

"How do you explain this?" he says.

The photograph is an enlargement of one found earlier in the afternoon among Oswald's possessions stored in Mrs. Paine's garage. After returning to City Hall, and showing it to Captain Fritz, Detective Rose has been working with officers in the Identification Bureau to produce this slightly cropped blowup.[1172] Everyone present can see that Oswald is flustered.

"I'm not going to make any comment about that without the advice of an attorney," Oswald replies smugly.[1173]

"Well, is that your face in the picture?" Fritz asks, pointing at the image.

"I won't even admit that," he sneers.[1174]

"That's not your face?" Fritz asks, scarcely believing that Oswald would deny what is so obvious.

"No," Oswald says. "*That's not even my face*. That's a fake. I've been photographed a number of times since I got here—first by the police, and now every time I get dragged through that hallway. Someone has taken *my picture* and put *my face* on a different body."

"So that *is* your face?" Fritz asks.

Oswald answers quickly to cover his own contradiction.

"Yes, that's my face," he says, "but that's not my body. I know all about photography, I've worked with photography a long time. Someone has photographed me and then superimposed a rifle in my hand and a gun in my pocket. That's a picture that someone has made. I've never seen that picture before in my life."[1175]

Fritz lays the photograph on his desk.

"We found this photo in Mrs. Paine's garage, among your effects," Fritz tells him.

Oswald rolls his eyes toward the ceiling.

"*That* picture has never been in my possession," he snaps.

"Wait a minute," Fritz shoots back, "I'll show you one you probably have seen."

The captain reaches back into the envelope and pulls out a small snapshot, the original photograph used to produce the enlargement. He shows it to Oswald, who squirms.

"I never have seen that picture either," he says, defiantly. "That picture's been reduced from the big one."[1176]

Fritz asks him how that's so, and Oswald gets into a long argument with Fritz about his knowledge of photography, asking Fritz a number of times whether the smaller photograph was made from the larger or whether the larger was made from the smaller.

"We made this enlargement from the snapshot we found in the search," Fritz finally acknowledges.

"Well, I understand photography real well," Oswald says arrogantly, "and at the proper time I will show that they're fakes. Right now, I have nothing more to say about them."[1177]

7:00 p.m.

In the third-floor corridor outside, reporters scramble toward Chief Curry, who is about to make a statement. He waits for everyone to settle down.

"The FBI has just informed us," Chief Curry begins, "that they have the order letter for the rifle that we have sent to the laboratory. They . . . received it from a mail-order house in Chicago. This order letter has been to the laboratory in Washington, D.C., and compared with known handwriting of our suspect, Oswald, and the handwriting is the same on the order letter as Oswald's handwriting. The return address on this order letter was to the post office box in Dallas, Texas, of our suspect, Oswald, and it was returned under another name. But it has definitely been established by the FBI that the handwriting is the handwriting of Oswald."

The reporters shout questions at once. One can be heard clearly above the others.

"Was it a recent purchase?"

"This purchase was made on March the twentieth of this year," Curry tells them.

"What about the ballistics test, Chief?"

"The ballistic test—we haven't had a final report, but it is—I understand [it] will be favorable," Curry replies.

"Is this the development you referred to today as making this case ironclad in your opinion?"

"This was not what I had reference to earlier," Curry says.

"Will you give us an indication of what that is?" a reporter shouts. "Were you referring to the photograph earlier?"

The media are already aware of the photographs of Oswald holding a rifle found by police in Mrs. Paine's garage. Curry doesn't have time to answer the question before another is shouted out.

"Where did these photographs come from, Chief?" a newsman asks.

"The photographs were found in his—out at Irving, where he had been staying and where his wife had been staying," Curry says.

"Does [the rifle in the photograph] look like the one that you have, that you think is the murder weapon, sir?"

"It does," Curry responds.

"How is he taking this information as it builds up?" someone asks.

"I don't know," Curry says.

"Chief, just a moment ago he came out . . . bitterly complaining about being deprived of his citizenship rights because he can't take a shower. Do you have any comment on that?"

"I didn't know he had asked to take a shower," Curry says. "We have a shower up there where he could take a shower if he wants one."

"What was the name under which he ordered the rifle?" a reporter asks.

"The name—the return—the name on the return address was A. Hidell," Curry tells them.

"Do you consider the case shut tight now, Chief?"

"We will continue to work on it," Curry replies, "and try to get every shred of evidence that's possible."[1178]

The chief's statements set off alarm bells at FBI headquarters. FBI Director J. Edgar Hoover can't believe that Curry is willing to give the press details about the evidence against Oswald. Curry's comments are being broadcast nationally, and Hoover doesn't think that cases should be tried in the newspapers. The bureau has a policy of "no comment" until it has a warrant and makes an arrest. Then a release is prepared, briefly stating the facts of the case and the charges. The details of the evidence are kept secret until the case goes to trial. The kind of information Curry is blabbing about would never, under any circumstances, be given out to the press by the FBI. Hoover is particularly incensed that Curry is talking about evidence that is being developed in the FBI's Washington, D.C., crime lab. Hoover gets Gordon Shanklin, agent-in-charge in Dallas, on the phone.

"Talk to Chief Curry," Hoover tells Shanklin, "and tell him that I insist that he not go on the air any more and discuss the progress of the investigation."

Hoover has little direct authority over the Dallas police chief. The FBI crime lab furnishes free service to all law enforcement agencies throughout the country. What they do with the FBI's lab reports, once they've received them, is their business. But because of the fact that President Lyndon Johnson has asked Hoover to take charge of the case, Hoover feels justified in asking Curry to abide by his wishes.

"You tell him," Hoover adds, "that I insist that he and all members of his department refrain from public statements!"[1179]

The IBM computers at the U.S. Postal Records Center in Alexandria, Virginia, have been humming for nearly seven hours now (though state-of-the-art at the time, these computers are a far cry from today's technology) searching for the original money order used to purchase the assassination weapon. There's no telling how many man-hours it might take to do a manual search.

Suddenly, a match is found, and the money order is located.

The center rushes the original money order by special courier to the chief of the Secret Service in Washington. A handwriting analysis by a questioned-documents expert for the Department of the Treasury shows that the handwriting on the money order is that of Lee Harvey Oswald.[1180]

If there is one thing that is now unquestionably certain, it is that Lee Harvey Oswald ordered and paid for the Mannlicher-Carcano rifle that was found on the sixth floor of the Texas School Book Depository Building shortly after the assassination.

7:10 p.m.

Secret Service inspector Thomas Kelley is very impressed by Captain Fritz, who has shown great patience and tenacity in his efforts to uncover the truth from Oswald about the rifle photographs. But Oswald remains arrogant and uncooperative. Fritz asks Oswald about some of the places where he's lived, trying to get him to admit where the pictures were taken. Oswald tells him about one of the places he lived in Dallas, but is very evasive when Fritz questions him about living on Neely Street.[1181]

"You never lived there?" Fritz asks.

"No!" Oswald says, defiantly.

"You didn't take any photographs there?" Fritz persists.

"No!" Oswald snaps back.

"I've got statements from people* who say they visited you when you lived there," Fritz tells him.

"They must be mistaken," Oswald answers.[1182]

Fritz can only shake his head in frustration. It is apparent to everyone that Oswald, though shaken by the photographic evidence, has no intention of furnishing any more information about the rifle pictures. After forty-five minutes of trying to pull impacted teeth to get answers, Captain Fritz orders Oswald returned to his cell.[1183]

7:15 p.m.

Detectives Hall, Sims, Graves, and Boyd lead a very hostile Oswald into the bright news lights basking the third-floor hallway.[1184] A reporter yells, "Here he comes!" to his colleagues as a live television camera swings around and zooms in on the T-shirt–clad Oswald. Newsmen rush toward him, arms outstretched, microphones searching for a brief statement.

"Did you fire that rifle?" a reporter shouts.

---

*Michael Paine had told Fritz that he and Ruth had visited the Oswalds when they lived on Neely Street. Fritz later determined that the photographs were taken in the backyard at Neely. (CE 2003, 24 H 268)

Oswald is smoldering, his voice finally exploding in anger.

"I don't know what dispatches you people have been given," he roars, "but I emphatically deny these charges!"

The officers pull him sharply through a doorway into the vestibule of the jail elevator, and out of sight of the live television audience.

"What about Connally?" a newsman hollers, shoving his microphone into the doorway.

Like Dr. Jekyll and Mr. Hyde, another persona seems to slip under Oswald's skin as his anger suddenly gives way to a gentler side.

"I have nothing against anybody," he says, his voice returning to its usual calm state. "I have not committed any acts of violence."[1185]

7:20 p.m.

Marguerite Oswald is in her robe and slippers when there is a knock on the door of the suite at the Executive Inn, where she and Marina are staying.

"Who is it?" Marguerite says, moving toward the door.

"This is Mr. Odum," a voice responds.

She opens the door a crack to see two FBI agents. They are wet from the pouring rain.

"Mrs. Oswald," Agent Bardwell Odum says, "I would like to see Marina."

She peers at him through her heavy, black-framed glasses, the door barely open.

"Mr. Odum, we're awfully tired," she says.

"I just want to show her a photograph," Odum replies.

"She's completely exhausted," Marguerite pleads. "I am not calling my daughter-in-law to the door. As a matter of fact, she's taking a bath."

Marina isn't really in the bathtub. Marguerite will say anything right now to get rid of the FBI men.

"Mrs. Oswald," Odum says, "let me ask you a question then."

"Yes, sir."

Odum holds up his hand to the crack in the door. Cupped in his palm is a glossy black-and-white photograph, its corners carefully trimmed with a pair of shears. It's the image of an unknown individual, originally thought to be Oswald, leaving the Soviet embassy in Mexico City in early October 1963. Only the head and shoulders of the man are visible in the photo. The FBI knows that it's not Oswald, but they wonder if it could be an accomplice.

"Do you recognize this individual?" he asks.

Marguerite looks at the photo briefly through the crack in the door.

"No, sir, believe me," she says.

The rain pelts the ground around the two men. Odum lowers his hand.

"Thank you," he says, as she closes the door.[1186]

7:46 p.m. (8:46 p.m. EST)

NBC commentator Chet Huntley announces that "all the personal effects of the late president have now been removed from the White House."[1187]

8:00 p.m.

In Irving, Ruth Paine answers the phone and hears Lee Oswald say in Russian, "Marina, please." That's the opening phrase he normally uses when he wants to speak to his wife, and he's used it on many occasions.

"She's not here," Mrs. Paine replies, in English.

Oswald is clearly irritated that his wife is not available to speak with him.

"Where is she?" he asks, an edge to his voice.

"I've got an idea where she might be, but I'm not at all certain," Ruth answers. "I'll try to find out." She doesn't tell Lee, but earlier today, while FBI agent Bardwell Odum was at her home, she overheard Odum talking on the telephone to the *Life* magazine people staying at the Hotel Adolphus. He was trying to find out where Marina was staying and she heard him say, "Executive Inn," and saw him jot it down. She thinks that Marina may be there.

"Tell her she should be at your house," Oswald says tersely.

"I'll try to reach her and give her your message," Mrs. Paine answers.

Oswald hangs up. Mrs. Paine had been waiting to hear from Marina since she left that morning. She had no intention of attempting to reach her. She felt that if Marina wanted to talk to her, she would call. Of course, she was hurt that Marina hadn't called or made any attempt to contact her. But now that Lee is trying to reach Marina, Ruth Paine decides to make the first move. She telephones the Executive Inn and asks the hotel operator to speak to Tommy Thompson, the *Life* representative. There is a short pause, then a female voice answers, "Hello?" It's Marguerite Oswald.

"Hello, this is Ruth Paine. I'd like to talk to Marina."

There is no love lost between Mrs. Paine and Oswald's mother, who is suspicious of Ruth and her husband.

"Marina's in the bathroom," Marguerite tells her.

"Lee called me," Mrs. Paine tells her, "and he wanted me to deliver a message to Marina."

"Yes?"

"He wants me to contact an attorney for him," Ruth says, "and he was very upset that Marina was not at my house."

"Well, he is in prison," Marguerite replies callously. "He don't know the things we are up against, the things that we have to face. What he wants doesn't really matter."

Ruth is shocked that Marguerite doesn't have any respect for Lee's wishes.

"Please let me speak to Marina," Ruth asks.

Marguerite finally relinquishes control of the telephone to her daughter-in-law. Mrs. Paine repeats Lee's message to her, in Russian. Marina only says that she is very tired and wants to get to bed. Ruth agrees that it's best that she stay at the hotel tonight. Ruth is disappointed that Marina doesn't tell her what she plans to do tomorrow.

"Did you see Lee today?" Ruth asks.

"Yes, around noon," Marina says.

It's obvious she doesn't want to talk, so Mrs. Paine says good-bye and hangs up.[1188]

Marguerite asks Marina what Mrs. Paine said, but Marina doesn't answer her. Marguerite's suspicions escalate and she begins to imagine that everyone is working against her. She begins to wonder how Mrs. Paine knew where they were staying? What did she say to Marina that caused Marina to withdraw and not want to tell her what Mrs. Paine said? In her conspiratorial mindset, FBI agent Odum's earlier visit and insistence on seeing Marina, and Mrs. Paine's call are somehow tied together. And whatever these people are up to, it's no good.[1189]

On the third floor of City Hall, reporters approach Assistant Police Chief Charles Batchelor outside the administrative offices. They are hungry and want to go out to dinner, but they don't want to miss anything if the Dallas police decide to move the prisoner to the county jail. Just then, Chief Curry walks up.

"How about it, Chief?" they ask. "Are you going to move Oswald tonight?"

"No," he tells them. "It probably will be in the morning."

"When?" they want to know.

"I think if you fellows are back here by ten o'clock in the morning you won't miss anything," Curry says.

With that, the newsmen head out for dinner. Curry decides he'd better double-check with Captain Fritz to see when he plans to transfer Oswald. He walks down the hall to Fritz's office.[1190]

Fritz doesn't think it's a good idea to transfer Oswald at night. An attacker could use the cover of darkness to his benefit and hinder the police from preventing trouble. Fritz suggests they wait until daylight. Besides, Fritz would like to question Oswald again in the morning.

"Okay," Curry says. "What time do you think you will be ready tomorrow then?"

"I don't know exactly when, Chief," Fritz answers.

"Do you think about ten o'clock?" Curry suggests. "I need to tell these people something definite."

Fritz nods his head.

"I believe so," he replies.[1191]

Curry returns to his office and tells Assistant Chief Batchelor of the plans. Then Curry decides that he might as well make an announcement to the press in the corridor. Otherwise, they'll be there all night.[1192] Once again, Chief Curry steps into the crowd of reporters gathered in the third-floor hallway and tells them that Oswald will be transferred to the sheriff's office tomorrow. "If you men would be here by no later than ten o'clock in the morning . . . that will be early enough."

"Are you through with him for the night, sir?" someone asks.

"Captain Fritz says he is finished with him unless possibly some witness might show up that we needed to bring him out for a show-up," Curry says. "But, I think—I don't believe there will be any more questioning tonight."

Someone wants to know what progress has been made toward a confession in the assassination.

"I don't think we've made any progress toward a confession," Curry replies.

"You don't think so?"

"No," Curry answers firmly.

"Why are you so pessimistic about a confession?"

"Well," Curry says with a smile, "you know we've been in the business a good while—"

Laughter ripples through the crowd of reporters.

"—and sometimes," Curry continues, "you can sort of draw your own conclusions after talking to a man over a period of time. Of course he might have a change of heart but I'd be rather surprised if he did."

Someone asks why Oswald's mother and wife were at police headquarters today. The chief says they visited Oswald and are attempting to get in contact with his attorney, John Abt, out of New York.

"Has anyone heard anything from Abt?" a reporter asks.

"Well, it's hearsay with me," Curry responds, "and I don't know who said this but somewhere back in the office someone said that they understood John Abt did not want to handle the case."*

"Chief, will you transfer him under heavy guard?"

---

*Abt testified that he told reporters who called him at his cabin in the Connecticut woods, where he had gone to spend the weekend, that "if I were requested to represent him, it would probably be difficult, if not impossible, for me to do so because of my commitments to other clients." Abt said he was never contacted directly by Oswald or any member of his family. (10 H 116)

"I'll leave that up to Sheriff Decker," Curry says. "That's his responsibility."

"The sheriff takes custody of him here?" someone asks.

"Yes," Curry answers.* "That's all I have, gentlemen, thank you."

A chorus of thank-yous follows the chief as he retreats down the hall
for the night.[1193]

Sunday, November 24

12:00 midnight

The press having been told they could go home for the night without
missing anything, the pressroom at Dallas City Hall has been nearly
deserted for two hours.[1194] Only two reporters—*Dallas Times Herald*
reporter Darwin Payne and the longtime police beat reporter for the *Dallas Morning News*, Johnny Rutledge—remain to cover the late shift, their
normal assignment.

The telephone rings. It's the *Times Herald* news editor Charles F.
Dameron asking for Payne, who takes the phone. Dameron has heard that
Dan Rather was on WCBS radio saying that the Dallas Police Department had an eyewitness in protective custody who could identify Oswald
as the one who pulled the trigger in the Book Depository. Dameron wants
to know if there's any truth to the vague report.

"I'm not sure," Payne says in a whisper, afraid his competition might
overhear him.

"Find out," Dameron commands.

Payne hangs up and eyes Rutledge sitting quietly across the room.
Payne can't help but think that the *Dallas Morning News* already has the
story wrapped up and is going to run it as a big banner in the morning
paper. How would that make the *Times* look? Darwin Payne has only been

---

*Normally, except in rare instances, men from Sheriff Decker's office handle the transfer of
prisoners between the city and county jails. Decker testified that the city police handle "maybe
one-tenth of maybe 1 percent" of the transfers (12 H 45).

at the newspaper three months, but he knows one thing. He *has* to get that story.

Payne slips out of the pressroom and runs down the night-watch commander. He says it might be true, but he doesn't know anything about it. Payne scrounges around a bit more, but comes up empty-handed.[1195]

1:00 a.m.

With the deadline for the final edition rapidly approaching, Darwin Payne, desperate, calls his office. He has no details to report to Dameron. They confer briefly and decide that Payne should call Chief Curry at home. Payne hates the thought of waking the chief, who surely is in bed at this hour. Dameron gives Payne the police chief's home telephone number anyway.

"Call him," Dameron says.

When the telephone rings, Curry's wife answers, obviously awakened from a sound sleep.

"Yes," she mumbles, "I'll give you the chief."

In a second or two, Curry comes on the line, half-asleep. Payne tries to explain to him the information he has and asks if the story is true or not? Curry is nearly incoherent, mumbling softly as if he's in a dream. The reporter frantically scribbles down notes, hoping to make sense of them later. Finally, he gives up trying to make Curry understand and hangs up. Payne's notes are useless. The frustrated reporter is forced to telephone his boss and report that he is unable to confirm the story.[1196]*

The chief of police rolls over and drifts back into a deep sleep. His wife knows just how exhausted he feels. There's been a constant barrage of phone calls since he came home. She reaches over and takes the telephone off the hook so that she and her husband can get a much-needed night of uninterrupted sleep.[1197]

---

*There actually was no person in protective custody as described in the story. Darwin Payne later stated that the report may have been a distorted reference to Howard Brennan, who had been assured by police that he and his home would be under surveillance by law enforcement. (Hlavach and Payne, *Reporting the Kennedy Assassination*, p.94)

2:30 a.m.

FBI security patrol clerk Vernon R. Glossup receives a telephone call while working the night desk at the Dallas FBI office.

"I would like to talk to the man in charge," a male voice says calmly.

"The special agent-in-charge is not in at the present time," Glossup answers. "Is there someone else that could help you?"

"Just a minute," the anonymous caller says. There is a brief pause, and Glossup is under the impression, though he can't be sure, that the caller hands the telephone to someone else. A second, more mature-sounding voice speaks next.

"I represent a committee that is neither right nor left wing," the man says, "and tonight, tomorrow morning, or tomorrow night we are going to kill the man that killed the president. There will be no excitement and we will kill him. We wanted to be sure to tell the FBI, police department, and sheriff's office. We will be there and we will kill him."

The caller hangs up.

Glossup immediately notifies FBI special agent Milton L. Newsom and quickly prepares a memorandum on the call.[1198]

3:00 a.m.

FBI agent Newsom telephones the Dallas County sheriff's office to advise them of the call, only to learn from Deputy Sheriff C. C. McCoy that he too got such a call. The message was nearly identical except that the anonymous caller said that he represented a group of around one hundred people "who have voted to kill the man who killed the president." The caller said they were advising the sheriff's office because they didn't want any of the deputies to get hurt, but that they were going to kill Oswald anyway. The two lawmen shift into action. Newsom tells McCoy that he'll contact the Dallas police and let them know what's going on. Meanwhile, McCoy calls Sheriff Decker at his home and informs him of the threats they've received.

"Call in a pair of our supervisory personnel," Decker orders, "and have them stand by at the office in case the Dallas police decide to transfer Oswald tonight."[1199]

3:20 a.m.

Captain William B. Frazier, the senior man on duty at the Dallas Police Department, takes the call from FBI agent Newsom.[1200] Informed of the threats, Frazier tells Newsom that the Dallas police haven't received any threatening calls at the department. He will, however, notify his superiors and the FBI will be advised of any change in the transfer plans.[1201]

5:15 a.m.

Nearly two hours later, Frazier calls the apartment of homicide captain Will Fritz, a notorious early riser. Frazier relates the threatening calls, but Fritz reminds him that Chief Curry is handling the particulars of the transfer and that he should be contacted directly.[1202]

A few minutes later, Deputy Sheriff McCoy telephones the Dallas Police Department and tells Captain Frazier that Sheriff Decker would like Chief Curry to call him as soon as possible about the transfer plans, adding that Decker thinks the police should transfer Oswald immediately to the county jail.[1203]

6:00 a.m.

Frazier telephones Chief Curry's residence but is unable to get through. He continues to ring the line for the next fifteen minutes, with no success. Finally, Frazier calls the telephone operator and asks her to check the phone to see if a conversation is in progress or if the line is out of order. The operator calls back in a few minutes and tells him that the telephone is out of order.[1204]

6:15 a.m.

By now, the second shift is beginning to arrive at City Hall, including Platoon Captain C. E. Talbert, who is scheduled to relieve Captain Frazier. Before going off duty, Frazier tells Talbert of the overnight threats and his repeated attempts to contact Chief Curry. Talbert immediately calls the assistant chief of police, Charles Batchelor, and informs him of the threat and the fact that they can't raise Curry on the telephone. Batchelor instructs Talbert to send a squad car over to Curry's house and wake him.

Not long thereafter, officers are pounding on the chief's front door to tell him of the death threats against Oswald.[1205]

6:30 a.m.

Captain Fritz's homicide team, the big, taciturn Texans in sober, off-the-rack suits and obligatory Stetsons who are the top drawer on the force and operate on their own time schedule, are also on the job early. Detective E. R. Beck arrives at 6:30, getting there even before the indefatigable and early-rising Captain Fritz. C. W. Brown gets in at seven. Most of the crew is in well before nine.[1206]

7:28 a.m.

Captain Talbert telephones the Dallas FBI office and informs Special Agent Newsom that the police chief has been advised of the threat against Oswald and that Curry expects to be in the office sometime between eight and nine o'clock this morning.

"What about the transfer plans?" the FBI agent asks.

"Well, I don't know," Talbert tells him. "But personally I don't think there'll be any effort to sneak Oswald out of the city jail. We want to maintain good relations with the press and right now extensive coverage has been set up to cover the transfer. I don't think that Chief Curry will want to cross the media."[1207]

8:00 a.m.

Marguerite Oswald is up early at the Executive Inn near Love Field. She has been worried all night. She and Marina haven't heard from the *Life* representatives since they arranged their suite at the inn. Marguerite feels stranded, alone in a strange motel with a Russian daughter-in-law and two babies. She wonders whom she can call for help. She doesn't want to call Mrs. Paine, a woman she has no use for. Nor does she want to telephone Robert, who is clear out in Boyd, Texas, at his farm.[1208] Instead, she remembers Peter Gregory, a Fort Worth petroleum engineer who taught Russian language classes at the library. Gregory was a Russian émigré who came to the United States in 1923 to attend the University of California.[1209]

About three weeks ago Marguerite read an advertisement in the Fort Worth newspaper announcing that free Russian classes were being offered at the public library beginning November 12. Although she had not heard from either Lee or Marina for nearly a year, she hoped in her heart that they would contact her some day, and she thought the instruction might help her communicate with her daughter-in-law. As it turned out, her car broke down just one block from the library before the second class started—just three days ago—and had to be towed. She walked to the class, and Gregory, when he found out that she lived only about ten blocks from his house, kindly drove her home.[1210]

Marguerite approaches Marina, who is up with the babies.

"Marina," Marguerite says, "we need help, honey. I am going to call Mr. Gregory."

She tells Marina about taking Russian language lessons.

"Oh, Mama," Marina exclaims, "I know Mr. Gregory. Lee know Mr. Gregory."[1211]

Marguerite had no idea that Lee and Marina had already met Peter Gregory, Lee having gone to Gregory's office in June of 1962 seeking his help in getting a job as a Russian translator or interpreter. She thinks it's a terribly odd coincidence that they already know him, but feels that somehow her guardian angel is guiding her actions.[1212] She picks up the telephone, gives a fictitious name to the hotel operator, and has her dial Mr. Gregory's residence.

"Mr. Gregory, I can't say who I am," she tells him when he answers, "but you know my son and you know my daughter-in-law, and I am in trouble, sir."

"I'm sorry," Mr. Gregory says, "but I won't talk to anybody I don't know."

"I would rather not tell you who I am," she replies, "but I shall identify myself by saying I am one of the students in the Russian class in the library."[1213]

Mr. Gregory recognizes the voice of Mrs. Oswald.

"You know my son real well," she adds.

Gregory realizes for the first time who the woman caller is.

"Oh, you are Mrs. Oswald," he says, sitting up in bed.

"Mr. Gregory, I need your help," she confesses. "The reporters, the news media are badgering me."

This is a lie, of course. But Marguerite has learned to twist the truth to suit her own ends.

"My daughter-in-law Marina and I are at the Executive Inn in Dallas, stranded," she continues. "I wonder if some of your friends, or you, could provide a place for me to hide from them."

To Peter Gregory, it sounds as if Marguerite is crying on the telephone, although he finds it hard to believe that Mrs. Oswald cries easily. Still, he's not entirely unsympathetic.

"I'll tell you what I will do, Mrs. Oswald," Gregory says. "You stay where you are and I promise you that I will come to see you sometime today."[1214]

In fact, Peter Gregory already knows where Marina and Marguerite Oswald are. Secret Service agent Mike Howard had called him on Saturday and asked him to come out to the Executive Inn and translate an interview with Marina. He hadn't done it because it turned out that his services weren't necessary—the interview didn't take place.

As soon as Gregory hangs up the telephone, he calls Agent Howard, who lives just north of Fort Worth, and reports his conversation with Mrs. Oswald.

"Well, that's fine," Howard tells Gregory, "we'll find a hiding place for Marguerite and Marina Oswald and the babies." He offers to come by Gregory's house in forty-five minutes to an hour or so and they can go over to the Executive Inn together.[1215]

8:05 a.m.
Chief Curry pulls his car into the basement garage at City Hall, parks, and heads for the elevators that'll take him upstairs to his office, where he meets Assistant Police Chief Charles Batchelor and the assistant police chief in charge of investigations, M. W. Stevenson, to discuss the Oswald death threats, the word of which had spread quickly through the police department. The men discuss security precautions that might

thwart such an attempt. They even discuss the possibility that a detective or some police officer might be so emotionally charged that he tries to make some move against Oswald. They agree that the men assigned to the basement security detail should be men they know to be emotionally stable.[1216]

8:17 a.m. (9:17 a.m. EST)

Cardinal Cushing, presiding over a pontifical mass in Boston, says, "The world stands helpless at the [president's] death." He speaks of the "unprecedented sorrow" and that "millions lament in a silence which will never be broken."[1217]

9:00 a.m.

Detective Jim Leavelle, along with Detectives Dhority and Brown, has already run over to the Statler Hilton Hotel after receiving a tip from the hotel security officer that a man who said he represented a California munitions company had checked in. The detectives determine very quickly that there is nothing to be concerned with. Such is the tension and concern in Dallas this Sunday morning.[1218]

The Dallas police may believe Oswald is the ultimate scum, but they have to make sure he is protected so he can stand trial for murdering the nation's president.

Across town, Postal Inspector Harry Holmes pulls up in front of a church with his wife and daughter. All the way there, Holmes has been thinking about the whirlwind of events that have driven him to near exhaustion. On the seat next to him is a folder with the postal documents he's been busy gathering on Oswald all weekend. He figures on running them over to Captain Fritz later that day. As his wife and daughter climb from the car, Holmes suddenly has a change of heart.

"You know, I think I'll run down and see if I can help Captain Fritz with anything," he tells his wife. She knows that look in his eye, and she knows there's no use talking to him about why he should spend Sunday with his family at church services. She agrees to find a ride home with friends. Holmes spins the family car around and heads downtown.[1219]

9:10 a.m.

At Dallas police headquarters, Chief Curry calls Captain Fritz's office and asks when he'll be ready to have Oswald transferred.

"We'll be talking to him shortly," Fritz says. "I suppose we'll be ready around ten o'clock."[1220]

"Fine," Curry says. He hangs up and dials Sheriff Decker. The two decide that since the Dallas Police Department is investigating the case and also has a lot more manpower, it would be better to depart from protocol and have the police, rather than Decker's boys, transport Oswald to the county jail.[1221]

Curry hangs up the telephone, tells Deputy Chief Stevenson and Assistant Chief Batchelor that their office will be moving Oswald, and asks, "What do you think about getting an armored truck?"

"I think I know where I can get one," Batchelor replies, telling Curry that he knows the vice president of Armored Motor Car Service, an outfit that serves the Fort Worth–Dallas area. Curry nods his approval. The three discuss a possible route and settle on leaving the jail office in the basement* via the Commerce Street exit ramp, taking Commerce to the Central Expressway, north on Central to Elm, west on Elm to Houston, and south on Houston to the entrance to the county jail. It's decided that Chief Curry's car will lead the caravan, followed by a car of detectives, the armored car, another car of detectives, and Batchelor and Stevenson in the rear car.[1222]

Batchelor returns to his third-floor office and looks up the home number of the armored car company's vice president, Harold Fleming, in the city directory. When the phone rings, Fleming is shaving, getting ready for church. Batchelor makes a pitch for the use of an armored truck.[1223] Fleming replies that he has two that he can send down—one large, one small—and the police can take their pick once they see them.

"I'll need them here about ten o'clock," Batchelor says.

---

*There are two jail offices in the police building, one in the basement next to the parking area, the other on the fourth floor.

"I'll call you as soon as I can arrange a couple of drivers," Fleming responds.[1224]

Downstairs, in the police garage, Captain Cecil Talbert notices a crowd beginning to build just outside the Commerce Street exit, apparently in anticipation of the transfer. To avoid the chaos of a last-minute security check, Talbert, who is a captain of a patrol division and not assigned to any security detail for Oswald's transfer, takes the initiative to begin securing the basement area of City Hall against anyone or anything that could pose a threat to Oswald. He orders Lieutenant Rio S. Pierce to pull three squads from each of the three outlying police substations and four from the central station; then, using two-man squads, they are to search the basement area, clear it, and keep it cleared of everyone but authorized personnel. He also moves three tear gas grenade kits into the basement, just in case a large threatening crowd storms the jail entrance for a good old-fashion lynching.[1225]

Lieutenant Pierce assigns Sergeant Patrick T. Dean to be in charge of the security detail in the basement garage, to be assisted by Sergeant James A. Putnam. Pierce, apparently, didn't tell Dean who was supposed to conduct the search, but Dean commandeers thirteen reserve officers (including their captain, Charles Arnett) who were congregated in the police assembly room, and together with himself, Putnam, Officers L. E. Jez and Alvin R. Brock, they proceed to empty everyone out of the basement garage, including other officers and members of the media who had already started to wait there.[1226] Dean's group searches the entire garage basement, including the air-conditioning and heating ducts, even the trunks of the cars that are in the basement.[1227] Other than four hunting rifles in the squad cars of officers who were going deer hunting, nothing is found.[1228] Two doors that would give ingress into the basement garage, one just east of the Commerce Street exit ramp, the other in the interior parking area of the garage just north of the adjacent elevators (a service elevator is nearby), are also checked and seen to be locked. In addition to Dean's assigning officers to cover every door or other possible entryway into the basement garage, Dean assigns Officer R. E. Vaughn to the Main Street entrance ramp leading down to the basement garage and Officer

B. G. Patterson to the Commerce Street exit ramp.[1229] Sergeant Putnam
assigns Officer A. R. Brock to cover the elevator area.[1230] Dean then lets
the press and any other authorized personnel back into the garage.[1231]

On the third floor, Captain Fritz turns to Detectives Leavelle, Graves,
and Dhority and orders them to bring Oswald down for further questioning.[1232]

9:30 a.m.

George Senator doesn't even know what time it is when he hears Jack Ruby
get up and go to the bathroom, always his first stop when he awakens for the
day, but it's probably around 9:30. George himself has been up since eight
or so. He notices that Jack looks a little worse than the day before and was
"even mumbling, which I didn't understand." Jack turns on the TV, which
is carrying the preparation for the elaborate state funeral of the president.
Over Jack's breakfast of scrambled eggs and coffee (George only had a cup
of coffee) George notices that Jack had "this look about him that didn't look
good." It was almost as if he was "in shock."[1233]

The previous day, Saturday, was almost a carbon-copy extension of the
day before for Ruby, who continues in his grief over the assassination and
in his impulsive, frenetic activity with respect to it. The morning got off
to a bad start when around 8:30 a.m. Crafard awakens Ruby with a phone
call from the club to say he needs dog food for Ruby's dogs he's taking
care of for Ruby at the club. Jack chews Crafard out royally for wakening
him after only two hours' sleep, but he doesn't go back to bed again. (Crafard, not appreciating Jack's vitriol, gathers his meager belongings, takes
from the till the five dollars Ruby owes him, and begins hitchhiking to
Michigan to visit his sister.)[1234]

Ruby turns on the TV to hear a rabbi eulogizing about Kennedy that
here was a man who fought in the war, went to every country, and had to
come back to his own country to be shot in the back.[1235] When a stripper
calls Ruby around noon to find out if the club will be open that night, he
tells her no. She notices his voice is shaking, as he talks about the "terrible" events of yesterday.[1236] With Ruby leaving his apartment shortly after
1:00 p.m., there is irreconcilable confusion as to the chronology of his

movements that Saturday afternoon, irreconcilable to the point where no one, at this late date, will ever know for sure what the chronology was. But the conflict is only as to the sequence. With one exception, everyone agrees that Ruby went to all the places mentioned. Each separate view has its advocates, but the confusion is so great that each view is itself internally inconsistent. The following is one view.

After leaving home, Ruby drives downtown to his club, the Carousel. Stopping by the Nichols garage next door to the club, where he and Carousel customers park their cars, he uses the garage phone to call someone and advises that person, in the presence of the garage attendant, Tom Brown, where he could find Chief of Police Jesse Curry. He then tells Brown that two men would probably be coming to the club to see him and to inform them that the club would not be open that night.[1237] Garnett "Claud" Hallmark, the parking-lot manager, overhears Ruby in a separate call talking to a newsman about having heard that Oswald was going to be transferred to the county jail that afternoon and telling the newsman that he'd be there. Ruby tells Hallmark, "I am acting like a reporter."[1238]

On the other end of the line is Dallas radio station (KLIF) announcer Ken Dowe. Dowe hardly knows Ruby, but Ruby says, "I understand they are moving Oswald over to the county jail. Would you like me to cover it, because I am a pretty good friend of Henry Wade's and I believe I can get some good news stories." Dowe, who needs all the help he can get, says "Okay."[1239] The word, incorrect, had gone out to some that Oswald was going to be transferred at 4:00 p.m.[1240]

Ruby then proceeds to Sol's Turf Bar and Delicatessen a few blocks away at 1515 Commerce Street. It is around 2:00 p.m. when Frank Bellocchio, a self-employed jeweler who had known Ruby casually for seven or eight years, sees Ruby near the back of Sol's. Bellocchio had been seated at the bar with a friend, Tom Apple, discussing the assassination. It is Bellocchio's position that the city of Dallas is responsible for the assassination, but his friend, Apple, disagrees. Bellocchio leaves his seat at the bar and approaches Ruby and they get into it on the cause of the assassination, Bellocchio taking from his pocket a folded copy of the full-page ad taken out in the *Dallas Morning News* the previous day by Bernard Weissman. Bellocchio was confused by Ruby's response. On one hand, Bellocchio said, Ruby, who was very upset about the ad, said he had learned that there was no person named Bernard Weissman, and that the ad was probably taken out by a group trying to stir up racial problems. Bellocchio "assumed" that Ruby meant arousing feelings against the Jews, and it was this group, not Dallas, that was responsible for the assassination. But then Ruby takes two of his "Impeach Earl Warren" photos out of his pocket to show Bellocchio, from which Bellocchio felt that Ruby was taking the contrary position that Dallas was responsible. "He seemed to be vacillating between the two sides . . . He seemed to be very incoherent," Bellocchio said. Bellocchio asks Ruby for one of the two copies of the Earl Warren impeachment photo but Ruby refuses to give him one, Bellocchio saying he "believed" Ruby said something about the photos being "some sort of a scoop" for him and he wanted to see that the right persons got the photos.[1241]

After leaving Sol's Turf Bar around three o'clock, Ruby drives over to Dealey Plaza, where he looks at all the wreaths there for the president and talks to a police officer he knows, James Chaney, about the "tragedy" of what had happened. Ruby walks off because he starts to choke up and doesn't want Chaney to see him crying. When Ruby sees Wes Wise, a newsman at KRLD in town whom he also knows, parked in his car near the Book Depository Building (Wise was calling back to his station that he couldn't gain entrance into the building), he knocks on the window of Wise's car, and when Wise rolls it down, they talk for around ten minutes about the tragedy. When Wise tells Ruby that he had been at the Trade Mart waiting for the president's arrival the previous day and had seen in the president's waiting room two large presents meant for Caroline and John Jr.—western saddles—that were going to be given to the president to give to his children, Wise notices tears in Ruby's eyes, and Ruby walks away. But he returns to Wise's car shortly thereafter to give him a tip, that Captain Fritz and Chief Curry were "over there looking at the flowers" for the president and hints that Wise should go and take their picture. Wise is grateful to Jack and he does just that.

Ruby then walks the short distance over to the entrance to the county jail on Houston between Elm and Main, where a large crowd has gathered in anticipation of Oswald's arrival at four o'clock, but the transfer doesn't take place and Ruby drives off for his home, leaving shortly thereafter for his sister Eva's apartment.[1242]

Ruby stays at his sister Eva Grant's apartment "for a good four hours." Eva, who herself feels like "the world was coming to an end" with the president's murder, feels for her brother, "sitting like a broken man crying." Jack starts up again on the Weissman ad, and Eva senses that Jack feels that "Bernard Weissman" may very well be a gentile using a Jewish name trying to get Jews in trouble. He's also still upset about the Earl Warren sign, and he calls Russ Knight over at KLIF and asks him, "Who is Earl Warren?"[1243] reflecting that Ruby had only known that the billboard words were an attack on a high official of the U.S. government, a government Ruby honored and was protective of. In the late afternoon at his sister's apartment Ruby calls Stanley Kaufman, a lawyer friend of his, brings up the Weissman ad with which he has become obsessed, and suggests to Kaufman that the black border of the ad was a tipoff that Weissman knew the president was going to be assassinated. He asks Kaufman if Kaufman knows how he, Ruby, could locate Weissman, but Kaufman has no idea. He tells Kaufman that he "doesn't know why" he wants to "connect" the ad and the Warren sign "with Oswald, but I do." He leaves no doubt in Kaufman's mind that he sees a connection between the ad and the assassination. Though Kaufman has known Ruby for almost ten years, and knows how very quick-tempered he is, Kaufman has never seen Jack so upset.[1244]

Jack asks Eva if she feels up to going to Officer Tippit's funeral with him. It doesn't surprise her. Other than the wife of an officer, she feels that no one in Dallas loves the police more than her brother Jack. He goes to the funerals of all Dallas police officers who die in the line of duty, and if he knows an officer personally, even to the funerals of their loved ones. In fact, when one officer, Johnny Sides, was killed in the line of duty a while back, Ruby held a benefit at his club and turned the proceeds over to Sides's family. But Eva is still weak and sick from her recent surgery and tells him she won't be up to it.[1245]

Ruby leaves Eva's apartment and returns home to his apartment five miles away around 8:30 p.m. Around 9:30 he receives a call from one of his strippers, Karen Bennett "Little Lynn" Carlin. Little Lynn and her husband, not getting the message that the Carousel was closed, find it locked when they arrive. She calls Jack from the Colony Club next door to find out if he's going to open the club, and Jack erupts. "Don't you have any respect for the president?" he barks at her. "Don't you know he's dead?" He adds, "I don't know when I will open. I don't know if I will ever open." Little Lynn feels Jack is "very hateful" to her, but since she and her out-of-work husband only have forty to fifty cents on their person together, she still asks him if he could pay her an advance on her salary so they can get back home to Fort Worth. He tells her he'll be down to the club in an hour to help her, but he doesn't show up, so her husband calls back from the garage next to the Carousel. Jack gets the garage attendant on the phone and gets him to give Little Lynn five dollars, which he'll reimburse him for, and when Lynn gets back on the phone and tells him she'll need rent money tomorrow, he tells her to call him.[1246]

Ruby places a few calls from his apartment that night, including to a friend from Chicago, Lawrence Meyers, who is in town. Ruby talks of the "terrible, terrible thing" that has happened and is very critical of his main competitors, Abe and Barney Weinstein, whom he refers to as "money-hungry Jews," for keeping their clubs (the Theatre Lounge and the Colony Club) open, and tells Meyers he's "going to do something" about it. Meyers, also Jewish, feels there are just as many "money-hungry Christians," but now was not the time to argue with his old friend, who kept repeating, to the point of almost being incoherent, "these poor people, these poor people, I feel so sorry for them," referring to Jackie and her two children. Meyers has never seen his old friend anywhere near like this before, and feels like Jack has "flipped his lid." When Ruby invites Meyers to join him for a cup of coffee, Meyers declines, saying he didn't want to get up and get dressed, but tells Jack that if he wants to talk, to come over to his motel for a cup of coffee, but Jack also declines, and they agree to meet the following evening for dinner.[1247]

Shortly after 11:00 p.m., after repaying the five dollars the garage attendant had given Little Lynn,[1248] he goes to his office at the Carousel and makes some more calls, among them to his friend Ralph Paul in Fort Worth, and Breck Wall, an entertainer friend of Jack's who had gone to Galveston to visit a friend when his show in Dallas suspended its performance out of respect for the president. Wall had just been elected president of the Dallas branch of the American Guild of Variety Artists (AGVA), and Ruby wants to know if AGVA, which includes among its members striptease dancers, had met to discuss his beef with the union— their failure to enforce AGVA's ban on "striptease contests" and performances by "amateurs," both of which the Weinsteins were guilty of—but AGVA hadn't met yet on the issue. Ruby, Wall can tell, is "very upset" about the assassination and curses the Weinsteins for not having the decency to close their two clubs out of respect for the dead president.[1249]

Ruby caps his evening around midnight at the Pago Club, about ten minutes from the Carousel, where he orders a Coke (Ruby rarely drinks alcohol) and asks the waitress in a very disapproving tone, "Why are you open?" "Ask my employer," she says, and leaves Ruby's table. The manager of the club, Robert Norton, knows Jack, and when he sees him sitting alone he joins him to chat. He tells Jack he doesn't know whether he should keep his club open and Ruby tells him he has closed his. During their short visit Norton brought up the assassination, saying "it was terrible" and "an insult to our country," adding that "we couldn't do enough to the person that had done this sort of thing." For once, Ruby, apparently already all talked out for the day about the assassination, shows no emotion and says nothing except he was "tired" and was "going home."[1250] Ruby then heads home and goes to bed around 1:30 a.m.[1251]

Jack's ugly mood when he awakens worsens when he sees in the Sunday morning's *Times Herald* a heartbreaking letter to "My Dear Caroline" dated two days earlier from a Dallas resident who tells her that "even as I write, you probably have not yet received" the news of her father's death. "This news is now being transmitted to all parts of the world . . . In all of this, my thoughts turn to you." Saying that though she was "old enough to feel the awful pain" but not yet "mature enough to understand this sorrow," he tells her he is a man of forty with two young daughters whom he had taken out of school "in order that they might get to see your mother and daddy" when they visited Dallas. From a position on the street not too far from Love Field, he said Caroline's mother and father looked "so very nice and appeared so happy." He said when the limousine passed by, "your daddy . . . did something that made me love him very much. It seemed like such a little thing, but it made me appreciate him the more for it. He looked at the grownups for just a second, and then he looked squarely at my youngest and then my eldest daughter. He smiled broadly and waved just to them in his warm way. Caroline, it was then I first thought of you. I thought your daddy must love little boys and little girls very much. Only one who loves and understands little children would realize just how much it would mean to them to be noticed in the presence of so many adults. I thought then how much he must love you."

He goes on to conclude, "No one can erase this day . . . You will cry. (My children did, my wife did, and I did). You will miss him. (We will). You will be lonely for him . . . You will want to know why anyone would do a thing like this to your father." Telling her he wished there was something he could do to help her, he says that she would be given strength and help and love by her mother and friends. "Most of all, God will help you. You see, God loves little girls, too," and closes by praying that Caroline would "be cradled in God's love."[1252]*

The letter has a devastating effect on Ruby. He also reads in another article in the *Times Herald*, captioned "State's Biggest Trial Expected," that when asked about "the possibility of Jacqueline Kennedy" being used as a witness at the trial of Oswald, DA Henry Wade said, "We will try to avoid [issuing a] subpoena" for Mrs. Kennedy, that she wouldn't "necessarily" have to come to Dallas to testify.[1253] Ruby seethes. If something

---

*See photo section for photo of November 24, 1963, *Dallas Times Herald* found on the floor at the foot of Ruby's bed after he shot Oswald. The paper is opened to page A3, the facing page, A2, being the "My Dear Caroline" letter. (CE 2426, 25 H 525; WR, p.355)

happened to the president's killer, his jumbled mind thinks, then Mrs. Kennedy won't have to come back for the trial. He decides that he just *has* to kill Oswald. He suddenly gets this tremendously emotional feeling that someone owes a debt to the slain president to spare his wife the ordeal of coming back to Dallas. He doesn't know what the connection is, but he also has this feeling about wanting to show his love for his Jewish faith and demonstrate to the world that a Jew has guts. In the welter of emotions is his hatred for the SOB who had killed his president. If he had confessed, then Jack could know he'd get what was coming to him. But he hasn't and there apparently is going to be a trial. Jack recalls that hotel guy who killed a Dallas police officer a while back and he beat the rap and got away with the killing. It's possible Oswald could get turned loose too.[1254]*

He knows there are people going about their regular activities, out dancing at the clubs and having a good time, not suffering the way he is. The civic leaders of Dallas are probably sincere in their sorrow, but they're helpless to overcome the everlasting stain on the reputation of Dallas, a city he loves and is proud of. The officers of the Dallas Police Department are helpless to do anything to Oswald for killing the president and one of their own. He saw Bobby Kennedy on television, saw how much he loved his brother, and thought how much Bobby would like to do something to Oswald, but of course he can't do anything either. Somebody ought to do something, something that no one else can apparently do. Though Jack is not insane, most people know he's not all there either, and his limited intellect gets carried away emotionally by the power of his thought to kill Oswald, though he has no idea exactly when or where he will attempt to do this.[1255]

Jack is in another world when Elnora Pitts, the aging, colored maid,

*A Dallas police detective, Leonard Mullenax, was shot to death the previous year in a hotel room while working undercover on a drug case. Though Ruby didn't know Mullenax well, he was sufficiently depressed over it to contribute two hundred dollars to his widow, close his club, and take his strippers with him to the funeral. Because of lack of sufficient evidence, Mullenax's alleged killer was never prosecuted. (Kaplan and Waltz, *Trial of Jack Ruby*, pp.66–67; Hall [C. Ray] Exhibit No. 2, 20 H 43)

calls to see whether Jack wants her to come clean the apartment, as she has for the past eight months or so. He paid her $7.50 the first time she came, because it was pretty dirty. The next time it was $4.00 and bus fare, and then one day he said, "Well, it's getting pretty dirty, I'm going to give you a little raise today," and from then on he paid her $5.50 for a half day's work. She came Tuesdays first, then on Saturday, but eventually they settled on Sunday, because Jack liked to have it clean in case he had guests that day.

Jack sounds very strange to Elnora on the phone. "What do you want?" he asks.

"This is Elnora."

"Yes, well, what? You need some money?"

"No," Elnora says, puzzled. "I was coming to clean today."

"Well, what do you want?" Jack kind of hollers.

"I was coming to clean today." She doesn't think she should have to tell him that, much less repeat it.

"You coming now?"

"No."

"When?"

She says she'll try to be there before two.

"Why so late?"

"I have to go to the store, and I have got some things to do. You seem so funny to me," Elnora says. "Do you want me to come today?"

"Well, yes, you can come," Jack says, "but you call me."

"That's what I'm doing now, calling you so I won't have to call you again."

"Are you coming to clean today?"

"Who am I talking to? Is this Mr. Jack Ruby?"

"Yes. Why?"

"Oh, nothing," she says. Jack is sounding terribly strange to Elnora, doesn't sound like himself, so she says, "Well, I'll call you."

"Yes, so I can tell you where the key will be and the money," he says.

"Okay," Elnora says, completely bewildered, and she hangs up.

Elnora thinks there is something wrong with Jack, wrong enough to scare her, wrong enough for her to call her daughter, who asks, "Well, are you going over there now?"

"No, he don't sound right to me over the phone," Elnora tells her daughter. "I am going to wait."[1256]

Postal Inspector Holmes hurries up the steps at City Hall and takes the elevator to the third floor. Holmes spots Captain Fritz standing in the corridor just outside the Homicide and Robbery Bureau. Fritz motions to him.

"We're getting ready to talk with Oswald one more time before we transfer him to the county jail," Fritz says. "Would you like to join us?"

"I sure would," Holmes replies.

"Well, come on in," Fritz says, pushing the door open. "I'm waiting here now for them to bring him downstairs from the holdover."[1257] Fritz leads Holmes into his office and closes the door. Secret Service agent Forrest Sorrels and Dallas police detective L. D. Montgomery are already there. So is Chief Curry, who has stopped by briefly to talk with Captain Fritz.[1258]

In a moment, Detectives Leavelle, Graves, and Dhority bring Oswald into the office, his hands cuffed in front of him. Oswald slouches into the wooden chair next to Fritz's desk. Oswald appears in a particularly arrogant mood.

"Are there any FBI men in here?" Oswald asks, looking at the faces around him.

"No," Fritz says, "no FBI men."

"Well, who is that man?" Oswald snaps back, motioning toward Holmes.

"He's a postal inspector and he has a few questions for you," Fritz says calmly.

Oswald seems to relax at the answer.

"Okay," he says.[1259]

Captain Fritz hands Oswald a telegram from an East Coast attorney who is volunteering to represent Oswald. Oswald reads it.

"Maybe you should call him," Fritz says.

"I'll call him later, if I can't reach Mr. Abt," Oswald replies, predictably.[1260]

There is a light knock at the door. It opens a crack and Secret Service inspector Thomas Kelley comes in, slightly out of breath, and takes a seat next to Agent Sorrels. Captain Fritz circles his desk, reaches into a drawer, pulls out the photograph of Oswald holding the rifle, and lays it on the desk next to the prisoner. Oswald purses his lips.

"Lee, why don't you tell us where this picture was taken?" Fritz asks.

Oswald is silent.

"You know, you'll save us a lot of time if you'll just tell us," Fritz continues, slow and methodical. "We'll find the location sooner or later."

"I don't have anything to say about it," Oswald answers defiantly.[1261]

"Did you shoot the president?" Fritz suddenly asks.

"No," Oswald says.

"Do you have any knowledge of the shooting?"

"No," Oswald replies.

"What about the shooting of Officer Tippit?" Fritz asks.

"Look, I don't know why you're asking me these questions," Oswald says, shaking his head negatively. "The only reason I'm here is because I popped a policeman in the nose at the theater on Jefferson Avenue. Okay, I admit it. But the reason I hit him was because I was protecting myself. As far as the rest of it, I emphatically deny having anything to do with shooting an officer or killing the president."[1262]

Chief Curry has had enough of Oswald's arrogance. Besides, he has transfer arrangements to see to. The police chief silently pulls open the office door and slips out.[1263]

9:45 a.m.

Curry hooks up with Batchelor and Stevenson and the three descend in the elevator to the basement garage to survey the security requirements for the forthcoming transfer.[1264]

The press has been arriving in force since nine and have nearly taken over the basement jail office. Cameramen, reporters, and all of their equipment are everywhere, including on top of the booking desk. The media have been insisting all morning that Chief Curry gave them permission to be there. When Curry comes down, they learn otherwise.[1265]

"Let's clear this area out," Curry tells jail lieutenant Woodrow Wiggins. "Move the patrol car and paddy wagon from those first two parking spaces and have the television cameras set up there. If the media want to be down here, put them over behind the rail." Curry is pointing to an area across the ramp from the jail office.[1266]

The top brass are pleased to learn that Captain Talbert has already begun, on his own, making security arrangements for the transfer.[1267]

Back up in Homicide and Robbery, Captain Fritz motions to Inspector Holmes to go ahead and question Oswald. Holmes introduces himself and opens the folder he brought.

"Did you have a post office box here in Dallas?" Holmes asks.

"Yeah."

"What number?"

"Box 2915," Oswald answers. "I rented it at the main post office for a few months before moving to New Orleans."

"Did you rent it in your own name?" Holmes asks.

"Yes."

"How many keys did you have?"

"Two," Oswald says. "When they closed the box I had them forward my mail to my new address in New Orleans."[1268]

Holmes glances at the forms in his folder as Oswald answers. Everything he offers is correct, although Holmes is surprised that Oswald is willing to volunteer so much information about the post office box that the assassination rifle was shipped to. Of course, Oswald isn't telling him anything that he doesn't already know. Holmes quickly learns that this is Oswald's game.

"Did anyone else receive mail in that box, other than yourself?" Holmes asks.

"No."

"Did anyone have access to the box, other than yourself?" Holmes asks.

"No," Oswald says again.

"Did you permit anyone else to use the box?"

"Well, it's possible that I may have given my wife one of the keys to go get my mail," Oswald replies, "but that was rare. Certainly, no one else used it."

"Did you ever receive a package in that box?" Holmes asks.

"What kind of package?" Oswald asks innocently.

"Did you ever have a rifle shipped there?"

"No," Oswald says, testily. "I did not order any rifle!"

"Ever order a rifle under another name?" Holmes asks.

Oswald emphatically denies that he ever ordered a rifle under his name or any other name, nor permitted anyone else to order a rifle to be received in his post office box.[1269]

"In fact," Oswald says, "I've never owned a rifle. I haven't practiced or shot a rifle since I was in the Marine Corps."

"You've never shot a rifle since your discharge?" Fritz asks, disbelievingly.

"No," Oswald says, then backs up. "Well, maybe a small-bore .22 or something."

"You don't own a rifle?" Fritz questions.

"Absolutely not!" Oswald insists. "How can I afford a rifle on my salary? I make $1.25 an hour. I can hardly feed myself on what I make."

"What about this?" Fritz asks, pointing to the photograph of Oswald and the rifle.

"I don't know what you're talking about," Oswald sneers.[1270]

"You mentioned that when you moved to New Orleans you had your mail forwarded to your new street address," Holmes says. "Did you rent a post office box while you were in New Orleans?"

"Yes," Oswald says. "Box 30061."

"Why did you have a post office box if you were getting mail at your residence?" the postal inspector asks.

Oswald explains that he subscribed to several publications, at least two of which are published in Russia, one being the hometown paper published in Minsk where he met his wife at a dance.[1271] "I took the two newspapers for her benefit, because it was local news to her," Oswald says. "She enjoyed reading about the hometown folks."[1272] He explains that he moved around so much that it was more practical to simply rent post office boxes and have his mail forwarded from one box to the next rather than going through the process of furnishing changes of address to the Russian publishers.[1273]

"Did you permit anyone other than yourself to get mail in the post office box in New Orleans?" Holmes asks.

"No," Oswald answers.

Holmes looks at the original application for Oswald's New Orleans post office box, which Oswald filled out in his own hand. Under the entry, "Persons entitled to receive mail through box," Oswald has written "Marina Oswald" and "A. J. Hidell."*

"Your application here lists Marina Oswald as a person entitled to receive mail in the box," Holmes reminds Oswald.

"Well, so what?" Oswald says mockingly. "She was my wife. I don't see anything wrong with that. It could very well be I did put her name on the application."

"Your application also shows the name A. J. Hidell as another person entitled to receive mail in the box."[1274]

Oswald simply shrugs his shoulders.

"I don't recall anything about that," he says.[1275]

Secret Service inspector Thomas Kelley jumps into the fray.

"Well, isn't it a fact that when you were arrested you had an identification card with the name Hidell on it in your possession?"

"Yes, that's right," Oswald grunts.

"How do you explain that?" Kelley asks.

"I don't explain it," Oswald says flatly.[1276]

Holmes refocuses on the Dallas post office box.

---

*In accordance with postal regulations, the portion of Oswald's application for his post office box in Dallas that listed names of persons other than the applicant who were entitled to receive mail was thrown away after Oswald closed his box on May 14, 1963 (7 H 527, WCT Harry D. Holmes; Cadigan Exhibit No. 13, 19 H 286). But the New Orleans post office did not comply with this regulation, and that portion of Oswald's application for his New Orleans post office box still existed (7 H 527, WCT Harry D. Holmes).

"Did you receive mail through box 2915 under any name other than Lee Oswald?"

"Absolutely not," Oswald says.

"What about a package to an A. J. Hidell?"

"No!" Oswald snaps.

"Did you order a gun in that name to come there?" Holmes asks.

"No, absolutely not."

"If one had come under that name, could this fellow Hidell have gotten it?" Holmes presses.

"Nobody got mail out of that box but me," Oswald retorts.[1277]

Holmes has the impression that Oswald has disciplined his mind and reflexes to the point that the inspector personally doubts he will ever confess.[1278]

10:15 a.m.

Lieutenant Rio S. Pierce walks through the City Hall basement garage and checks security arrangements. Pierce can see that Sergeant Dean and his men have done a fine job. He deems the basement secure and returns to the third-floor homicide office to await further instructions.[1279]

In Washington, Commander Humes arrives at Bethesda Naval Hospital for a conference in Admiral Calvin B. Galloway's office with his colleagues from the autopsy, Drs. Boswell and Finck. Dr. Humes has been up half the night[*] working on a longhand draft of the autopsy report, incorporating notes made during the autopsy with the information he had obtained from Dr. Perry on Saturday morning. The result is the fifteen-page draft he now has in his hands. Humes, Boswell, and Finck carefully review the language of the handwritten draft, making minor corrections and clarifications.[1280] Although the details are extensive, the conclusion is short and to the point:

---

[*]Humes completed the autopsy report between 3:00 and 4:00 a.m. EST (1 HSCA 330; ARRB Transcript of Proceedings, Deposition of Dr. James Joseph Humes, February 13, 1996, p.135).

It is our opinion that the deceased died as a result of *two* perforating gunshot wounds inflicted by high-velocity projectiles fired by a person or persons unknown. The projectiles were fired from a point *behind* and somewhat *above* the level of the deceased. The observations and available information do not permit a satisfactory estimate as to the sequence of the two wounds.

The fatal missile entered the skull above and to the right of the external occipital protuberance. A portion of the projectile traversed the cranial cavity in a posterior-anterior direction (see later skull roentgenograms), depositing minute particles along its path. A portion of the projectile made its exit through the parietal bone on the right, carrying with it portions of cerebrum, skull, and scalp. The two wounds of the skull combined with the force of the missile produced extensive fragmentation of the skull, laceration of the superior sagittal sinus, and of the right cerebral hemisphere.

The other missile entered the right superior posterior thorax above the scapula and traversed the soft tissues of the suprascapular and supra-clavicular portions of the base of the right side of the neck. This missile produced contusions of the right apical parietal pleura and of the apical portion of the right upper lobe of the lung. The missile contused the strap muscles of the right side of the neck, damaged the trachea, and made its exit through the anterior surface of the neck. As far as can be ascertained, this missile struck no bony structures in its path through the body.

In addition, it is our opinion that the wound of the skull produced such extensive damage to the brain as to preclude the possibility of the deceased surviving this injury.

A supplementary report will be submitted following more detailed examinations of the brain and of microscopic sections. However, it is not anticipated that these examinations will materially alter the findings.[1281]

It will take some time to type up the final draft, but Commander Humes is confident that he can deliver it to Admiral George Burkley at the White House by Sunday evening as promised.

10:19 a.m.
Jack Ruby and his roommate George Senator are still in their underwear when the phone rings, and George can tell from Jack's end of the conversation that it's Little Lynn.

She says she is calling "to try to get some money, because the rent is due and I need some money for groceries, and you told me to call."

"How much will you need?"

She confers with her husband Bruce and asks for twenty-five dollars.

"I have to go downtown anyway," Jack says, "so I'll send it to you by Western Union."

She asks him to use her real name, Karen Bennett, and wonders what time she should expect it to arrive at the Western Union office in downtown Fort Worth, but he can't say. He's not dressed yet and he has to do something about the dog, but he promises to take care of it this morning.

"I sure would appreciate it," she says.

He still seems sort of hateful and short with her, but not as much as last night, and she's grateful that he doesn't give her any problem about the money.

Jack finally gets it together enough to shower, shave, and get dressed —an elaborate process that never takes him less than half an hour—but his mood doesn't change. Even after he's fully dressed and ready to go out, he paces nervously from bedroom to living room and back for another ten minutes or so, mumbling to himself, too low for George to catch any of it, and George is too wrapped up in his newspaper to pay much attention in any case.[1282]

10:20 a.m.
In the anteroom of Chief Curry's office, a dozen or so members of the news media have come up from the basement and lay in ambush for the chief, hoping to get some advance word on Oswald's transfer. Comfortable with the security arrangements, Curry steps out of his office and holds an impromptu news conference while he waits for Captain Fritz to finish this morning's interrogation.

"Chief, you say you're going to take him to the county jail in an armored car," a reporter asks. "Have you ever had to do this with another prisoner?"

"Not to my knowledge," Curry says.

"Is it a commercial-type truck, the kind that banks use?"

"Yes, sir."

"Did [the] threats on the prisoner's life . . . did they come in right through the police switchboard?"

"Yes," Curry replies.

"Do you have any details at all on them?'" someone asks.

"No."

"Is there any way we can get some [details] on [the calls], sir?"

"I don't know who took the calls or what was said," Curry says, feigning ignorance.

Someone asks again about the possibility that Oswald might have had accomplices.

"This is the man, we are sure, that murdered the patrolman and murdered . . . assassinated the president," Curry says confidently. "But to say that there was no other person that had knowledge of what this man might do, I wouldn't make that statement because there is a possibility that there are people who might have known this man's thoughts and what he could do, or what he might do."

"Does he show any signs of breaking—to make a clean breast of this, [and] tell the truth about what happened?"

"No, sir," Curry answers, "there is no indication that he is close to telling us anything . . ."

The press questions Curry about Oswald's relationship with his wife, whether Oswald has any friends, about the backyard photographs showing Oswald holding a rifle, and other topics, but Curry isn't really telling them anything they don't already know.[1283]

Jerry O'Leary of the *Washington Star* is less interested in what Curry has to say and more interested in coming up with a plan to cover Oswald's descent to the basement. O'Leary wants to be on the third floor when Oswald is led to the elevator, in case Oswald makes a statement, and also wants to be in the basement when Oswald is put in the armored truck. He figures the only way he'll be able to cover both events is to race down the stairwell once Oswald is safely on his way down in the jail elevator. O'Leary and New York radio reporter Icarus "Ike" Pappas set up a test race to see if it can be done, with O'Leary and Pappas starting to run down the stairway at the same time the public elevator starts down. When O'Leary and Pappas reach the bottom, they can dash out of the stairwell just ahead of the elevator. The reporters can only hope the jail elevator will be as slow as the public elevator when the time comes. Neither thinks about it until later, but curiously no one questions or asks them for their credentials while running up and down the stairwell.[1284]

In Captain Fritz's third-floor office, Holmes grills Oswald about his current post office box rentals. Oswald says that after he came back to Dallas from New Orleans and shortly after he went to work at the Book Depository, he rented a new post office box in Dallas, number 6225.

"Rented it in your own name?" Holmes asks.

"Yes," Oswald says. "I checked out one key."

All of this was true. The police confiscated the key, which they found in Oswald's pocket after his arrest. Holmes has already compared it to the master key for box 6225 and found them identical.[1285]

"Did you show [in your application for the box] that anyone else was entitled to get mail in the box?" Holmes asks.

"No."

"What did you show as your business?"

"I didn't show anything," Oswald replies.

"Well, your box rental application here says Fair Play for Cuba Committee and the American Civil Liberties Union," Holmes tells him.

"Maybe that's right," Oswald admits.

Holmes wants to know if he rented the box for these groups, but Oswald denies it. "I paid for it out of my own personal money," he says.

Asked why he put them on the application, Oswald only says, "I don't know why."[1286]

"How did you get involved with the Fair Play for Cuba Committee?" Captain Fritz interrupts.

"Well, I first became interested when I went to New Orleans," Oswald says. "It started out as simply a group of individuals who thought and had political opinions like my own. We decided to organize, and did after a while."

"Who is the head of the organization?" Fritz asks.

"We don't have any elected officers," Oswald replies.

The homicide captain presses Oswald, trying to get him to admit that he is the head man of the New Orleans chapter, but Oswald is very evasive.

"Well, I could probably be considered the secretary," Oswald finally admits, "since I wrote some letters on their behalf and tried to collect dues."

"How much were the dues?" Fritz asks.

"A dollar a month," Oswald shoots back.

"Isn't there a Fair Play for Cuba Committee in New York?" Fritz asks.

Oswald smiles. "Yes, but they're much better organized than we are."[1287]

"Did you contact them?" Fritz asks.

"Yes, I wrote to them," Oswald replies, "and they sent me some Communist literature and a letter signed by Alex Hidell."[*][1288]

Oswald's statement about Hidell, someone he previously claimed he knew nothing about, doesn't escape the lawmen, but for the moment they let him go on.

"I distributed the literature in New Orleans," Oswald tells them, "and it was at that time that I got into an altercation with a group of Cuban exiles and was arrested. I appeared on Bill Stuckey's television program in New Orleans on a number of occasions and was interviewed by the local press often.[†] So you see my opinions on the Fair Play for Cuba Committee are well known."

---

[*]There is no evidence that the Fair Play for Cuba Committee in New York ever sent Oswald a letter signed by Alex Hidell.

[†]In fact, Oswald appeared on Stuckey's television program once, a related radio program once, and was interviewed once by the press in relation to his court appearance.

"Did you know Hidell in New Orleans?" Secret Service inspector Kelley asks.

"I never knew him or ever saw him in New Orleans," Oswald replies.

"Do you believe in what the Fair Play for Cuba Committee stands for?" Kelley asks.

"Yes," Oswald says. "Cuba should have full diplomatic relations with the United States. There should be free trade with Cuba and freedom for tourists from both countries to travel within each other's borders."

"Is that why you came to Dallas," Postal Inspector Holmes asks, "to organize a cell of the Fair Play for Cuba Committee in Dallas?"

"No, not at all," Oswald says.

"Did you work on it or intend to organize here in Dallas?"

"No, I didn't," Oswald chuckles. "I was too busy trying to get a job."[1289]

"Do you think that the attitude of the U.S. government toward Cuba will change since the president has been assassinated?" Kelley asks.

Oswald turns to Fritz. "I'm filed on for the president's murder, right?"

"Yes," Fritz says.

"Under the circumstances," Oswald says to Kelley, "I don't believe I will answer the question because whatever I say might be misconstrued."

Despite his declaration, Oswald answers the question anyway. "When the head of any government dies," he says, "there is always a second in command who takes over and in this particular case it will be Johnson. So far as I know, Johnson's views and President Kennedy's views are the same, so I don't think the attitude of the U.S. government will change toward Cuba."[1290]

"Are you a Communist?" Captain Fritz asks.

It's the kind of question Oswald likes. "No, I am not a Communist," Oswald says. "I am a Marxist, but not a Marxist-Leninist."

"What's the difference?" Fritz asks.

"It would take too long to explain," Oswald replies, enjoying the fact that he knows more about the subject than the homicide captain.

"Try me," Fritz shoots back.

"Well, a Communist is a Leninist-Marxist," Oswald explains, "while

I am a true Karl Marxist. I've read just about everything by or about Karl Marx."[1291]

"Do you read a lot of Communist publications?" Fritz asks.

"I'm an avid reader of Russian literature," Oswald says, "whether it's Communist or not."

"Do you subscribe to any Russian magazines or newspapers?" Agent Kelley inquires.

"Yes, I subscribe to the *Militant*," Oswald replies. "That's the weekly of the Socialist Party in the United States."

Oswald is suddenly intrigued by Agent Kelley.

"Are you an FBI agent?" he asks.

"No, I'm not," Kelley tells him. "I'm a member of the Secret Service."

"Oh, I see," Oswald says, nodding his head. "When I was standing in front of the Depository, about to leave, a young crew-cut man rushed up and said he was from the Secret Service, showed me a book of identification, and asked where the phone was."

"Did you show him?" Kelley asks.

"Well, I pointed toward the pay phone in the building," Oswald says, "and he started toward it, and then I left."[1292]*

10:45 a.m.
The vice president of the Armored Motor Car Service, Harold Fleming, calls Assistant Chief Batchelor and tells him he has two armored trucks, a smaller and a larger one, with drivers ready and waiting for instructions.

"Send them down to the Commerce Street ramp," Batchelor tells him, adding that after picking the one they want, "we're going to back the truck into the ramp so they'll be leaving the ramp in the right direction when they pull out." They already know that the low ceiling in the basement

*Later investigation revealed that Oswald's encounter was probably with a young, crew-cut WFAA radio newsman named Pierce Allman, who ran into the Depository to telephone the radio station about the shooting. Allman reported encountering a young man on the front steps who pointed toward the telephone inside, although Allman told the Secret Service he couldn't say for sure whether the man was Oswald or not (CD 354, p.2, Secret Service interview of Pierce Allman on January 29, 1964).

garage will prevent the driver from backing the truck all the way down into the basement. They're simply hopeful that they can get the truck backed down far enough so that they can get Oswald into it without exposing him to the street traffic.[1293]

Deputy Chief Stevenson approaches Captain Orville A. Jones of the Forgery Bureau and directs him to take any remaining detectives who are available on the third floor down to the basement to assist the officers already stationed there. Stevenson and Assistant Chief Batchelor then head down to the basement to meet the armored trucks and check the security arrangements again.

Captain Jones makes his way down the hall and tells the duty officers in the Juvenile, Forgery, and Burglary and Theft Bureaus to have all available officers report to the basement jail office for security detail. Two or three detectives accompany him at that time to the basement, where he stations them at the jail office.

Jones then walks to the head of the Commerce Street ramp. He instructs the two officers there to clear the way and assist the armored truck that will be arriving at any moment.[1294] Nearby, Batchelor and Stevenson are going over the proposed route of the caravan with Captain Talbert.

"Are you planning to use sirens to stop traffic at each intersection?" Talbert asks.

"I don't want to attract any more attention to the transfer than we already have," Stevenson says. "Do you have enough men available to cover each of the intersections along Elm Street?"

"I'm sure we can get them," Talbert replies, calling Sergeants Patrick T. Dean and Don F. Steele over and instructing them to get some officers and station them along the Elm Street route to cut cross traffic at all the intersections as the convoy comes through. When Sergeant Steele says he doesn't have enough men available, Talbert orders him to get any additional forces he needs from Captain Perdue Lawrence of the Traffic Division.

"Instruct the men stationed along Elm," Talbert tells Steele, "to fall in line behind the convoy as they come past and be prepared to handle any trouble that develops down at the county jail," where a crowd of around six hundred people has gathered.[1295]

Batchelor and Stevenson can see officers stationed at the top of the Main and Commerce Street ramps. The two men walk up the Commerce Street ramp and survey the crowd that is gathered across the street. A police supervisor advises the deputy chiefs that no one but police officers are allowed on the side of the street next to City Hall. Batchelor can see a few officers stationed across the street, helping to control the crowd. Everything seems to be in order.[1296]

In the third-floor homicide office, Secret Service inspector Kelley can sense, like many others before him, that Oswald likes to talk about himself and express his opinions. Perhaps this is the key to cutting through his denials.

"What do you think about religion?" Kelley asks Oswald.

"Karl Marx is my religion," Oswald replies.

"What I mean is, what faith are you?" Kelley inquires.

"I have no faith," the prisoner answers, then a moment later, "I suppose you mean the Bible?"

"Yes, that's right," Kelley says.

"Well, I've read the Bible," Oswald begins. "Some people might find it interesting reading, but not me. As a matter of fact, I'm a student of philosophy and I don't consider the Bible to be even a reasonable or an intelligent philosophy."

"You don't think much of it?" Kelley sums up.

"You could say that."[1297]

"As a Marxist, do you believe that religion is an opiate of the people?" Agent Kelley asks.

Oswald is in his element, and lights up at the chance to talk about ideology.

"Most definitely so," Oswald says. "All religions tend to become monopolistic and are the causes of a great deal of class warfare."

"Do you consider the Catholic Church to be an enemy of the Communist philosophy?" Kelley probes.

"Well, there is no Catholicism in Russia," Oswald answers. "The closest thing to it are the Orthodox Churches. But, I'm not going to discuss my opinions about religion any further since this is an attempt to get me to say something which could be construed as antireligious or anti-Catholic."[1298]

"Do you believe in a deity?" Fritz interjects, trying to pick up the ball. But Oswald will have none of it.

"I don't care to discuss that with you," Oswald replies sharply.[1299]

The homicide captain turns back to the issues of evidence.

"I understand you were dishonorably discharged from the Marine Corps—"

Oswald bristles noticeably and cuts him off.

"I was discharged *honorably*," Oswald snaps. "They later changed it because I attempted to renounce my American citizenship while living in Russia. Since my change in citizenship did not come to pass, I wrote a letter to Mr. Connally, who was then secretary of the navy, to have this discharge reversed, and after a considerable delay, I received a very respectful reply in which Mr. Connally stated that he had resigned to run for governor of Texas, and that my letter was being referred to the new secretary. I'm still waiting."

Some reporters had been speculating that Oswald's intended target was Governor Connally, rather than the president. But Captain Fritz doesn't detect any animosity toward the governor in Oswald's voice.[1300]

"Lee, we found a map in your room with some marks on it," Fritz says, shifting subjects. "What can you tell me about those marks? Did you put them on there?"

"Oh, God!" Oswald says, rolling his eyes. "Don't tell me there's a mark where this thing happened?"

No one says anything.

"What about the other marks?" Oswald says. "I put a lot of marks on that map. I was looking for a job and marked the places where they were interviewing."

Oswald explains that he has no transportation and either walks or rides a bus and that he was constantly looking for work. He says that as he got leads he would chart them on the map to save time in traveling.

"Why was there an X at the location of the Book Depository?" Fritz asks.

"Well, I interviewed there for a job," Oswald replies. "In fact, I got the job. That's all that map amounts to."[1301]

11:00 a.m.

In the basement jail office, Captain Frank Martin and a posse of detectives walk up to assist in the security measures, having just come down from the third-floor Juvenile Bureau.[1302] They're there only a moment when someone hollers, "The armored trucks are here!"

Assistant Chief Batchelor heads up the Commerce Street exit ramp and after a quick inspection of the vehicles, he decides that the larger truck, with room for two guards, is better suited for the mission. There wasn't sufficient clearance for the truck to be taken to the bottom of the ramp, and the driver believed that because of the truck's weight, if he parked the truck on the incline, when he started to pull out he might stall the truck on the ramp. It was decided to leave the truck at the top of the ramp, the front wheels on the sidewalk on Commerce Street, and the rear wheels on the incline of the ramp.

"That's fine," Batchelor tells the driver, and points out the car that he will be following when they get ready to leave. There is very little room for anyone to squeeze by the truck—a foot to two feet on either side is all. It's effectively plugging the ramp.[1303] Batchelor then opens the back of the truck to make sure it's clean. An empty Nehi soft-drink bottle rolls out and pops as it shatters on the concrete. The sound causes a commotion among the reporters at the bottom of the ramp. What was that? A shot? A group of them break toward the armored truck to see what happened.[1304]

On the third floor, time is growing short, and Captain Fritz makes one more attempt to shake Oswald's story.

"Lee, why did you go to Irving to visit your wife on Thursday night instead of Friday, like you normally did?" the homicide chief asks.

"I learned that my wife and Mrs. Paine were giving a party for the kids," Oswald tells him, "and that they were going to have a house full of neighborhood kids there. I just didn't want to be around then. So, I went out Thursday night."

"Did you bring a sack with you the next morning?"

"I did," Oswald says.

"What was in the sack?" Fritz asks.

"My lunch."

"How big of a sack was it?" Fritz asks. "What was its shape?"

"Oh, I don't recall," Oswald replies, tiring of the cat-and-mouse game. "It may have been a small sack or a large sack, I don't know. You don't always find one that fits your sandwiches just right."

"Where did you put the sack when you got in Wesley's car?" Fritz questions.

"In my lap," Oswald says, "or possibly on the front seat next to me. That's where I always put it because I don't want it to get crushed."

"You didn't put it in the backseat?" Fritz asks.

"I didn't put any package in the backseat," Oswald says vehemently.

"Wesley Frazier says that you brought a long parcel over to his house and put it in the backseat of his car," Fritz tells him. "Do you deny that?"

"Oh, he must be mistaken," Oswald claims, "or else thinking about some other time when he picked me up."

"Didn't you tell him you had curtain rods?" Fritz asks.

"Absolutely not!" Oswald snaps. "I *never* said such a thing."[1305]

Captain Fritz asks Oswald again where he was at the time of the shooting.

"When lunchtime came," Oswald says, "one of the Negro employees invited me to eat lunch with him, and I said, 'You go on down and *send the elevator back up* and I will join you in a few minutes.'" He said that before he could finish what he was doing, all the commotion surrounding the assassination took place, so he said, "I just went on downstairs" to "see what it was all about." On the way, he says, he stopped to get a Coke, and before he could proceed on his way out of the building, "a police officer stopped me" to ask some questions, but "my superintendent stepped up and told the officer that I am one of the employees of the building. So, he told me to step aside for a little bit and we will get to you later. Then I just went out the front door and into the crowd to see what it was all about."[1306]

Postal Inspector Holmes notices that Oswald didn't say what floor he was on at the time of the shooting, or whether he had taken the elevator or stairs down.* He also wonders why Oswald left the scene and how he got away, but figures that Fritz had covered these areas in a previous session.[1307] What Holmes doesn't realize is that Oswald, like thousands of guilty people before him who incriminate themselves by telling inconsistent stories, has changed his story significantly.

Shortly after his arrest, Oswald told Fritz that at the time of the shooting he was eating lunch on the first floor. Also, that he *had gone up* to the second-floor lunchroom to get a Coke when he was stopped by Officer Baker and the building superintendent, Roy Truly. Now, Oswald was *admitting that he was on an upper floor of the Depository when the shooting occurred* and was on his way down to the front door when he was stopped.

Through the venetian blinds, Captain Fritz can see Chief Curry milling about impatiently in the outer office. Finally, the chief raps lightly on the door and opens it a crack.

"We'll be through in a few minutes," Fritz tells him.[1308]

Curry closes the door and the questioning continues, with Dallas Secret Service agent-in-charge Forrest Sorrels and Fritz returning one final time to Oswald's use of the name A. Hidell at his post office box in New Orleans and elsewhere.

"Now, you say that you have not used the name A. Hidell," Sorrels says, "but you show the name on this change-of-address card† as a person entitled to receive mail at this address. If you don't know anyone by the name Hidell, why would you have that name on this card?"

---

*But Holmes testified that Oswald made it clear that "he was still up in the building" when the shooting started and had "rushed downstairs to go out to see what was going on" (7 H 302, 306).

†Sorrels probably misspoke here since the Warren Commission investigation never came up with a change-of-address card, if there ever was one, for Oswald in New Orleans. Sorrels probably was referring to the portion of the application for Oswald's post office box in New Orleans that listed "A. J. Hidell" as someone entitled to receive mail through the box.

"I never used the name of Hidell," Oswald says, dodging the issue.[1309]

The door to Fritz's office opens again, and this time Chief Curry steps inside.[1310] Although no words are spoken, it's clear that he wants the interrogation to come to an end. But Captain Fitz, following up on Sorrels's question, once again asks Oswald, "Lee, do you know anyone by the name of A. J. Hidell?"

"No," Oswald says.

"Have you ever used that name as an alias?" Fritz presses.

"No!" Oswald insists. "I never used the name and I don't know anyone by that name."

"What about the draft registration [Selective Service] card we got out of your wallet showing the name A. J. Hidell?" Fritz fires back.

Oswald boils over.

"I've told you all I'm going to about that card!" Oswald flares. "You took notes! Just read them for yourself, if you want to refresh your memory. You know as much about it as I do."[1311]

That's it. There'll be no more from Oswald, at least until after the transfer. Both Fritz and Sorrels plan to question Oswald further in the days ahead. Captain Fritz and Chief Curry huddle briefly, whispering in hushed tones, then step out into the outer office to confer in private.[1312]

Secret Service inspector Kelley tells Oswald that the Secret Service is responsible for the safety of the president, and that as soon as he has secured counsel, the Secret Service is very anxious to talk with him to make sure that the correct facts are being developed regarding the assassination.

"I would be glad to discuss your proposition with my attorney," Oswald says, "and after I have talked with one, you can discuss it with me or my attorney, if my attorney thinks that it is a wise thing to do. But, at the present time, I have nothing more to say."[1313]

It's around eleven by the time Jack Ruby starts to leave his apartment to send Little Lynn her money. He tells George he's also going to take Sheba down to the club, and he puts his revolver in his right coat pocket. He normally carries it in his right trouser pocket because he doesn't want to get his coat out of shape.[1314] In the fifteen-minute-or-so drive downtown on the Thornton Expressway, Ruby listens to his car radio but doesn't hear anything that informs him Oswald hasn't yet been moved. He decides to go by Dealey Plaza once again to see the wreaths there, and takes the Industrial Street turnoff to Main, where he takes a right and proceeds past the Criminal Courts Building. He is surprised to see a crowd gathered outside the county jail on the other side of rope barricades since he had heard Oswald was going to be moved to the county jail at ten, and it's now well past eleven. But as he passes City Hall, he notices quite a crowd there too, so he figures maybe they haven't moved Oswald yet and he makes an illegal left turn into a parking lot across the street from the Western Union office on Main, just one block away (at the end of the same block and on the same side of the street) from police headquarters. Leaving Sheba in the car, he takes his keys and locks the trunk—there's over eight hundred bucks in cash in a grocery bag in there, half of it in five-dollar bills. He then puts the trunk key and, oddly, his billfold, with all of his identification in it, in the glove compartment of his car, a 1960s Oldsmobile. Leaving the car itself unlocked, he walks across the street to Western Union. In addition to the gun, he's carrying more than two thousand dollars in cash, wads of it, bundled in rubber bands, stashed in every pocket. He often carries the cash from the Carousel around with him for a couple of days, sometimes as long as a week, and there's almost always money in the trunk of the car, particularly by Sunday night, when he has to make the payroll.[1315]

11:05 a.m.
With the armored truck in place, Captain Jones walks back down the ramp to the basement jail office, where he meets the men who have come down from the Juvenile and Forgery Bureaus, as well as the Burglary and Theft Bureaus. He instructs them to form a line on each side of the passageway leading from the jail office to the ramp and parking area so that Oswald and his escorts will have a protective lane to pass through on their way to the armored car once they emerge from the jail office. Altogether, there are around seventy members of the Dallas Police Department in the basement to make sure there are no problems.

"Don't allow anyone into this area," Captain Jones barks over the noise of the basement garage. "Do not allow the press to approach or even attempt to converse with the prisoner. And don't allow anyone to follow the caravan until after it's left the basement. Is that clear?"

"Yes, sir," a chorus of officers answers. Jones than commands the media horde, "Do not speak to the prisoner as he is led from the building."[1316]*

Of course, few newsmen plan to heed the captain's order.

"I'll go let them know we're ready," Chief Stevenson says to Batchelor as he heads for the elevators.[1317]

On the third floor, Captain Fritz and Chief Curry are discussing the transfer plans in the outer office of the Homicide and Robbery Bureau. A small group of investigators surrounds them—Postal Inspector Harry Holmes, Secret Service agent-in-charge Forrest Sorrels, Lieutenants Rio S. Pierce and Richard E. Swain, and Detective Jim Leavelle.[1318]

"Are you ready for the transfer?" Curry asks.

"When the security downstairs is ready, we're ready," Fritz replies.[1319]

Curry tells Captain Fritz that everything is ready, that an armored truck is in position at the Commerce Street ramp and will transport the prisoner to the county jail. But Fritz suddenly shakes his head.

"Chief, I don't think it's a good thing to try to move him in that money wagon," he tells Curry. "I don't think it's a good idea at all. For one thing, we don't know the driver or anything about that wagon, and if someone tries to take our prisoner, we should be in a position to be able to cut out

---

*As can be seen in the sketch of the layout of the basement in the photo section of this book, looking out from the jail office to the garage basement ahead, there is a traffic lane that starts at the top of the Main Street entrance ramp on the left. The lane descends into the garage basement and continues past the jail office until it exits the basement by way of the Commerce Street ramp on the right. Most of the media are on the far side of the lane behind a railing that runs alongside the lane, their backs to the parking lot behind them, their eyes facing the jail office. To enable those reporters craning their necks behind others to have a better view, Assistant Chief Batchelor has given permission for them to stand in a semicircle extending from the end of the railing across the bottom of the Main Street ramp. However, on their own, many have also spilled over beyond the railing on the Commerce Street side and are on the jail side of the railing close to the armored truck. (15 H 119–120, 12, H 17–18, WCT Charles Batchelor; 12 H 101–102, WCT M. W. Stevenson; Batchelor Exhibit No. 5001, 19 H 116; 12 H 119, WCT Cecil E. Talbert; CE 2179, 24 H 851; Talbert Exhibit No. 5070, 21 H 668; 15 H 150, WCT John Will Fritz)

of the caravan, or to take off, or do whatever is necessary to protect him. That heavy money wagon will be too awkward in that kind of a situation. I would prefer to transfer him in an unmarked car."[1320]

Curry can see the merit to his plan and isn't about to argue with Fritz.

"Well, okay," Curry says, "but we'll still use the armored car as a decoy and let it go right on down Elm just as we planned and if anyone tries to take the prisoner away from us, they'll find themselves attacking an empty armored car."[1321]

"I'll transport him in one car, with myself and two detectives," Fritz says, "and we'll have another carload of detectives as backup. We can cut out of the caravan at Main Street and head straight west on Main Street to Houston, then make a right turn to the county jail. The rest of the convoy can go on to Elm Street to Houston, turn left, but not enter the jail. We'll be in the county jail before they even get there."[1322]

Curry nods his approval, "Okay."

The door to the homicide office opens and Deputy Chief Stevenson comes in and tells Chief Curry that the armored truck is in place. Chief Curry tells him there has been a change in plans and that they're going to move Oswald in an unmarked police car.

"You know, Chief," Fritz says, "we ought to get rid of the television lights and cameramen so they don't interfere with our getting to the car."[1323]

Curry knows that Fritz is suggesting he get rid of the press entirely.

"The lights have already been moved back," Curry replies, "and the media have been moved back in the basement, back of the rail, and the spectators have been moved across the street. You won't have any trouble."[1324]

Detective Leavelle takes Fritz aside. "Why don't we take him out on the first floor and put him in a car on Main Street," Leavelle says to Fritz. "We could be in the county jail before they even know we've left the jail."[1325]

"Well, we wouldn't have much protection getting off on another floor," Fritz replies. "You can only get so many men on the elevator." Fritz adds that he didn't think Curry would go for it because the chief had given his word to the press that they would be able to witness Oswald's transfer.[1326]

11:10 a.m.

There is a flurry of activity now as the police brass make last-minute changes to the transfer plan. Captain Fritz instructs Detectives C. N. Dhority, C. W. Brown, and E. R. Beck to go to the basement and get two cars set up for the transfer. Dhority will drive the car transporting Oswald. Fritz tells him to park it near the entrance to the jail office, the door Oswald will emerge from in the basement. (The car will be between Oswald and the media behind the railing on the other side of the ramp.) Beck will drive a posse of detectives in the lead car,* parked directly ahead of Oswald's car. When both cars pull out of the Commerce Street exit behind the armored car, they will turn left two blocks to Central, turn left one block to Main, turn left and go west on Main to Houston, then right a half block to the county jail. Beck will drive past the entrance, and Dhority and Fritz, behind them, will pull right in to the jail entrance.[1327] Someone is already on the telephone to Sheriff Decker, making arrangements to have the steel gate at the county jail entrance open when they arrive.[1328]

"Get going," Fritz tells the detectives, who head downstairs.

Curry turns to Lieutenant Rio S. Pierce and instructs him to get a third car, to be used as a decoy, park it in front of the armored truck, and when the signal is given, lead the caravan left two blocks to Central, turn left up to Elm (while the Oswald vehicle breaks away from the caravan by turning left a block earlier on Main), turn left on Elm to Houston, then left past the jail.[1329]

Captain Fritz is so intent on preventing anyone from harming Oswald or allowing him the opportunity to escape that he pulls Leavelle aside and orders him to handcuff himself to the prisoner.[1330]

"Lee, I want you to follow Detective Leavelle when we get downstairs," Fritz says, "and stay close to him."

Fritz realizes that Oswald is clad only in a T-shirt.

"Do you want something to put over your T-shirt?" he asks.

"Yes," Oswald says.

---

*For whatever reason, Brown, not Beck, will end up being behind the wheel of this car (CE 2003, 24 H 295; 12 H 19, WCT Charles Batchelor).

Fritz orders a detective to go and get some of the clothing police confiscated from Oswald's room. No more than a minute later, they bring in some clothes on hangers and hand Oswald one of the better-looking items, a light-colored shirt.

"If it's all the same to you," Oswald says, "I'd rather wear that black sweater. That might be a little warmer."

Oswald points at a black, Ivy League–type, slip-over sweater that has some ragged holes near the right shoulder. Someone makes a remark that the other shirt looks better, but Oswald insists on the black sweater. They hand it to him as Detective Leavelle releases one of the handcuffs from Oswald's wrists. Detective Graves helps him pull it over his head.[1331] In his black trousers and black sweater, Oswald looks very much the way he did in the backyard photographs, the snapshots where he posed proudly with a rifle and pistol. Captain Fritz asks whether Oswald would like to wear a hat to camouflage his appearance during the transfer, but Oswald doesn't want to do that.[1332]

11:15 a.m.
In the City Hall basement, Deputy Chief Stevenson corrals Chief Batchelor and Captain Jones.

"There's been a change in plans," he advises them. "We are going to put two cars on the driveway and transfer him in one of them." Stevenson quickly outlines how the armored truck will now be used as a decoy.

"Why?" Batchelor wants to know.

"Curry and the others in homicide have decided using the decoy would be a wise move in case anyone attacks the caravan," Stevenson says.[1333]

By the time Ruby fills out the money order in the Western Union office, there's only one client ahead of him in line. Doyle Lane, the thirty-five-year-old senior delivery clerk on duty, recognizes Ruby as a fairly frequent customer. Ruby has already filled out the order in large printing, "$25.00, to KAREN BENNETT, WILL CALL, FTH WORTH," but Lane crosses out "FTH WORTH" and, according to the company regulation, which requires the full destination on the body of a money order, writes "Fort Worth, Texas" in the space provided. He asks Ruby for his own name and address and fills in Ruby's reply: "Jack Ruby, 1312½ Commerce." Doyle writes "Mod FTW," for "Money Order Department Fort Worth" and "rates" the order, adding a charge of $.55, a toll charge of $1.20, and the tax of $.12, for a total of $26.87. He makes change from $30.00 in bills Ruby gives him, stamps the money order and the receipt with the time clock, which rotates on the counter on a minute-to-minute basis, and hands a copy of the receipt and the change back to Ruby. The time, signifying the end of the transaction and synchronized to the U.S. Naval Observatory time in Washington, D.C., as are all Western Union clocks at eleven every morning, reads 11:17.

As Doyle puts the money order into the pneumatic tube that blows it upstairs for transmission, he sees Ruby turn from the counter, walk out the door and turn left, toward City Hall at the other end of the block, walking at an ordinary gait.[1334]

It will be more than an hour before the money order is wired to Fort Worth. Normally it takes no more than about twenty minutes for a transmission to Fort Worth, but the office has had a lot of reporters running in with their scribbled notes, and the extra traffic has slowed the wire way down.[1335]

11:18 a.m.

In the third-floor Homicide and Robbery Bureau, Captain Fritz steps out into the outer office, where Chief Curry waits.

"Is everything ready?" Fritz asks.

"Yes, as far as I know," Curry replies. "Everything is ready to go. I'll go on down to the basement. Chief Stevenson and I will meet you at the county jail."[1336]

As Curry leaves, Secret Service agent Sorrels approaches Fritz.

"If I were you, I would not move Oswald to the county jail at an announced time like this," Sorrels says. "I would take him out at three or four in the morning when there's no one around."

Personally, Fritz couldn't agree more. But this is not his show.

"Chief Curry wants to go along with the press and not try to put anything over on them," Fritz tells him.[1337]

Curry has just exited the Homicide and Robbery Bureau when an officer walks up to him.

"Mayor Cabell is on the phone for you, Chief."

Curry heads to his office down the hall, where he takes the call. Cabell wants to know how everything is progressing, and when Curry plans to transfer Oswald to the county jail.

"We're getting set to transfer him now," Curry says, and quickly brings the mayor up to speed on the transfer.[1338]

Four floors below, the public elevator opens onto the basement corridor just outside the jail office, and a crowd of detectives piles out followed by two WBAP cameramen, struggling to push a rolling tripod with a large TV camera perched atop it. When it nearly topples over, a third crewman from the WBAP basement team rushes over and helps them roll it out to the ramp. The word from the two crewmen who have just come from the third floor is that Oswald could be brought down at any moment.[1339]

11:19 a.m.

In Captain Fritz's office, Oswald stands quietly, his hands manacled in front. Detective Leavelle snaps one end of a second pair of handcuffs on Oswald's right wrist, the other end on his own left wrist.

"Lee, if anybody shoots at you, I hope they're as good a shot as you are," Leavelle says half-jokingly, not only meaning that he hopes Oswald gets hit and not him, but that he knows Oswald killed Kennedy.

"Aw, there ain't going to be anybody shooting at me," Oswald replies with a laugh, one of the few jovial moments he's had since his arrest, "you're just being melodramatic."

"Well, if there's any trouble, you know what to do?" Leavelle says. "Hit the floor."

"Captain Fritz told me to follow you," Oswald answers. "I'll do whatever you do."

"In that case," Leavelle tells him, "you'll be on the floor."[1340]

With the Commerce Street exit blocked by the armored truck, Lieu-

tenant Rio S. Pierce, who has been assigned to drive a car with two
detectives in front of the armored truck, decides to exit the basement
with his squad car via the Main Street ramp (which is actually the
entrance into the basement), circle the block, and back up in front of
the armored truck. It will mean he'll have to travel the wrong way on
what is normally a one-way ramp, but he has little choice. With Sergeant James Putnam in the passenger seat and Sergeant Billy Joe Maxey
in the left backseat, Pierce flips on the flashing red lights, cranks the
steering wheel to the right, and inches toward the newsmen lined up
across the bottom of the ramp. Captain Talbert splits the group apart so
Pierce can get through. As soon as the squad car moves through the line
of reporters, the line closes up like water behind a boat.[1341] Two more
cars, driven by Detectives C. N. Dhority and C. W. Brown, one of
which will transport Oswald, begin to move into position at the base of
the Commerce Street ramp behind the armored truck.[1342]

In the third-floor hallway outside Homicide and Robbery, uniformed
officers and plainclothes detectives have begun moving the dozen or so
reporters still on the third floor against the far wall of the corridor.
They're told not to move toward Oswald when he comes out, or ask any
questions or shout at him. In the basement, two lines of Dallas detectives
form to protect Oswald from the jail office door to where the vehicle to
be used for the transfer of Oswald will soon appear. They have instructions to close in behind the prisoner as he walks past them.

Inside the homicide office, Captain Fritz turns to Lieutenant T. L.
Baker.

"Call down and tell them we're on our way," he orders.

The door opens into the third-floor hallway and Lieutenant Swain
leads the way out, followed by Captain Fritz. As reporters jostle for position, Detective Leavelle steps out the door with Oswald's right wrist
cuffed to Leavelle's left wrist. Detective L. C. Graves is close behind,
holding Oswald's left arm. Detective L. D. Montgomery follows, covering the rear.[1343] As soon as Oswald emerges, several reporters ignore

police orders and begin shouting questions at him. A microphone picks up part of Oswald's response to one question.

"I'd like to contact a member . . . representative of the American Civil Liberties Union . . ."

Oswald's words are broken off as he is pulled into the anteroom of the jail elevator. As soon as he disappears, reporters Jerry O'Leary of the *Washington Evening Star* and Ike Pappas, from New York's WNEW radio, accompanied by Maurice "Mickey" Carroll of the *New York Herald Tribune*, bolt for the stairway in their planned bid to get to the basement before Oswald does.[1344]

11:20 a.m.
The telephone in the jail office rings and Lieutenant Woodrow Wiggins, standing at the booking desk, answers it.

"They're on their way down," Lieutenant Baker says. "Is everything ready?"

"All clear," Wiggins replies. He hangs up the phone and sees the jail elevator lights cascading downward as the elevator makes its descent.[1345]

Patrolman Roy E. Vaughn, assigned to guard the entrance to the Main Street ramp, is surprised to see the squad car driven by Lieutenant Pierce exiting from the entranceway. As the squad car approaches the top of the ramp, Vaughn, who was not standing at the top of the ramp but inside a few feet (apparently to see as much of what was going on below as he could), is forced to step to his right to get out of the way of the car, all the while backing up to the top of the ramp that faces the sidewalk. There are small groups of people on each side of the ramp exit on the sidewalk. He clears them, steps out into the sidewalk, checks for traffic on Main, and waves the car through. Pierce turns left onto Main Street and heads for the top of the Commerce Street exit ramp to position himself in front of the armored truck.[1346]

As Ruby, who has walked the long block on Main from the Western Union office to City Hall, approaches the top of the Main Street ramp, he sees, with a quick glance, the officer at the entrance (Vaughn) backing up and stepping to his right, his back toward Ruby. By the time Ruby reaches the entrance to the ramp, Pierce's car has temporarily stopped at the sidewalk outside the ramp, and Ruby recognizes Pierce. Jack is one of many who call the detective by his middle name, Sam, rather than his first, Rio. Ruby sees Vaughn stoop down to acknowledge the officers in the car. Without breaking his stride, Ruby turns left toward the ramp, slips past the car, and hurries down the ramp, not sure whether Vaughn has seen him or not. He knows from a lifetime of gatecrashing that the best way to get in is to look as though you belong there. Halfway down the ramp he hears someone shout something like, "Hey, you," but he pays no attention, just keeps walking down the ramp into the basement.[1347]

At the bottom of the ramp, there is considerable excitement as the reporters know it's just a matter of moments before Oswald appears. Adjacent to them, in the level area between the Main Street entrance ramp and the Commerce Street exit ramp, the two unmarked police cars driven by Detectives Dhority and Brown are having a difficult time maneuvering in the tight quarters behind the armored truck.

Detective Brown swings a pea-green Ford up behind the armored truck, his partner, Detective Dhority, right behind him in an unmarked white sedan. But Brown doesn't pull far enough forward for Dhority to get his vehicle in line behind it.

Captain Talbert can see the predicament and hollers to Brown, "Pull forward!"

When he does, Dhority drives the white sedan onto the Commerce Street ramp, then puts the car into reverse and begins backing up toward the jail entrance to wait for Oswald, but a mass of reporters, who have defied instructions and come out from behind the railing, is blocking his path.

Chief Stevenson and Captain Jones shout out to them, "Get out of the way."

Captain Talbert, along the sedan's left side, pushes at the newsmen, who do not respond instantly because their attention is fixated on the door where Oswald is expected to emerge.

"Get back, get back," he repeats, tugging on their shoulders.

Detective Dhority finally resorts to blowing the horn at the reporters as he rolls the car back toward the door of the jail office.

Suddenly, someone shouts, "Here they come!"

Television floodlights flip on, bathing the garage in a blinding white light as newsmen start rushing as close as they can get to the jail office entrance, craning their necks over the cordon of detectives who are in place to shield Oswald, trying to get a glimpse of him. Stevenson, Jones, Talbert, and other officers hopelessly shout at the wave of humanity, their commands falling on deaf ears, "Get back! Get back!"[1348]

Reporters Jerry O'Leary, Ike Pappas, and Mickey Carroll burst out of the basement stairwell as planned, arriving just before the jail elevator. As they rush through the public corridor and out into the garage, a police officer asks O'Leary and Carroll to show identification. They flash their press credentials and Ike Pappas manages to squeeze in close to the door-way where Oswald will emerge from the jail office.[1349]

The jail elevator doors open and Lieutenant Swain and Detective Montgomery step off into the jail office, then move aside as Captain Fritz emerges. Fritz turns back and grabs Swain by the arm.

"I want you to lead the way," Fritz tells him and motions for him to take the point position.

As Swain begins making his way around the booking desk toward the exit door, Detectives Leavelle and Graves cautiously step out of the elevator with Oswald between them.

Multiple voices ripple through the crowd of reporters: "Here he is. Here he comes."[1350]

Two of the three national television networks are on hand to broadcast Oswald's departure from the City Hall basement. (ABC television opted to cover Oswald's arrival at the county jail and consequently had no live camera coverage in the basement.)[1351] The NBC television network is just concluding a two-minute report from the Kennedy family compound at Hyannis Port when Frank McGee, the anchor in New York,

hears through his earphone correspondent Tom Pettit in Dallas shouting, "Give me air! Give me air!" A switch is flipped in New York and the
live camera feed from the basement of City Hall comes up on the screens
of millions of viewers.[1352]

CBS correspondent Nelson Benton is also shouting into his microphone, "Take it, take it, take it! They're at the door!" CBS cameras are
picking up the scene, but the program controllers in New York refuse to
cut away from the preparations in Washington, D.C., to move the president's body from the White House to the Capitol rotunda. Dan Rather,
in the local CBS affiliate control room in Dallas, leans on the guys in New
York, "You've *got* to come to us now!"

"Hold on just a minute," New York says. "We have to get through this
Roger Mudd piece, then Harry Reasoner has a one-minute essay."
Rather can't believe it. It is clear to him that by the time New York
switches over, the transfer will be over.[*] Only NBC is broadcasting live
to the nation.[†]

---

[*]Roger Mudd was still ten seconds from the end of his piece when the shot was fired. Since
CBS television was taping Mudd, it missed the live broadcast from the Dallas basement. Dan
Rather partially redeemed CBS's blunder by coming up with the idea of a televised slow-motion
playback of the shooting with freeze frames and analysis. This was a national television first, but
Dallas's KRLD-TV had been using the technique occasionally for local sporting events. Unbe-
knownst to Rather and the technicians working with him at KRLD-TV, in New York, Don Hewitt,
one of two executive editors of CBS News, was on the telephone trying to reach Rather to suggest the same idea. An hour and a half after the shooting, Rather was on the air with a slow-motion
version of the shooting, using a pointer to draw the audience's attention to the critical frames and
movements. (However, it was not the first slow-motion showing of the shooting of Oswald [with-
out freeze-frame analysis] on national television. At 12:42 EST, NBC television commentator
Frank McGee at NBC headquarters in New York tells his national audience, "We will replay the
tape of this bizarre shooting in slow motion.") (Rather with Herskowitz, *Camera Never Blinks*,
pp.120, 139–140; NBC News, *Seventy Hours and Thirty Minutes*, p.93) In *Air Time: The Inside
Story of CBS News*, author Gary Paul Gates writes, "November 22, 1963, was, in career terms,
the most important day in Dan Rather's life. His swift and accurate reporting on the Kennedy
assassination and its aftermath that weekend transformed him from a regional journalist into a
national correspondent. A few days after the assassination, he received a call from [CBS headquarters in New York] informing him that he was being transferred to Washington to cover the
White House" (Gates, *Air Time*, p.293).

[†]However, less than a minute later, CBS headquarters in New York, upon seeing the tape of
the shooting from its local affiliate's live coverage in Dallas, which was received over closed cir-
cuit in New York, puts the tape on over the network to a national audience (*New York Times*,
November 25, 1963, p.1).

Detectives Leavelle and Graves fall in behind Swain and Captain Fritz as they escort Oswald through the jail office and toward the doorway leading out into the basement garage. Detective Montgomery is right behind them. Fritz looks toward the booking desk, where Lieutenant Wiggins stands.

"Are they ready?" Fritz asks.

Wiggins indicates that everything is in place, walks out from behind the desk, and steps through the doorway to the garage just ahead of Swain.[1353]

WNEW radio reporter Ike Pappas, just six feet from the doorway, speaks into his microphone, "Now the prisoner, wearing a black sweater, is being moved out toward an armored car. Being led out by Captain Fritz."

Lieutenant Swain steps through the doorway of the jail office and into the bright television floodlights. Captain Fritz is a few feet behind him. Swain walks toward the sedan that will carry Oswald as it continues to roll back into position. The driver, Detective Dhority, hits the car horn again to clear the media away.

Leavelle and Graves hesitate momentarily at the doorway, holding Oswald just inside the jail office. "Is it okay?" Leavelle asks. Detective Wilbur J. Cutchshaw, standing just outside the doorway, answers Leavelle, "Okay, come on out, Jim."[1354]

Detectives Leavelle and Graves march out, Oswald firmly between them, but manacled only to Leavelle. For a moment Leavelle and Graves are blinded by their first exposure to the lights, making it impossible for them to observe any movements originating from their left front. But they soon regain their vision and are surprised that nothing is ready. The white sedan that is supposed to be parked about thirteen to fourteen feet just outside the door is still rolling back, struggling to get into position against the tide of reporters who have come around or over the railing they had been ordered to remain behind and are now surging toward Oswald.[1355] The driver blasts the horn again as Captain Fritz reaches for the back-door handle.[1356] Oswald and his police escorts nearly come to a halt as the protective lane around Oswald begins to collapse. Detective Graves finds himself rubbing elbows with reporter Ike Pappas on his left.[1357]

Pappas thrusts his microphone forward and shouts a question as Oswald turns slightly toward him.

"Do you have anything to say in your defense?" Pappas asks Oswald.

Suddenly, a man with a hat lunges from the crowd to Oswald's left front, his arm outstretched with a gun in his right hand. Detective Don Ray Archer, to the man's left, thinks it's someone who has jumped out of the crowd to "take a sock" at Oswald.[1358] The man's face is familiar to Leavelle, and in a split second he realizes the man is Jack Ruby.[1359]

Detective Billy H. Combest, who is part of the line of officers forming a protective lane on each side of Oswald and his escorts, also recognizes Ruby and shouts, "Jack, you son of a bitch, don't!"[1360]

11:21 a.m.

BANG! The shot reverberates through the basement garage.* Several police officers jump at the sound. There is a cold moment of silence, a split second, then Oswald lets out a loud cry, "Ohhh!" and grabs his stomach, his face contorting in pain. No one can believe it. The unthinkable has happened.† Tom Pettit, the NBC News correspondent broadcasting

---

*An FBI examination of Pappas's tape at the FBI laboratory "revealed that no identifiable utterances were made by Ruby at the time he shot Oswald . . . Two groans are heard on the tape immediately following the shot. However, it cannot be said whether any utterance by Ruby would have been picked up by the microphone at this time" (FBI Record 124-10072-10368, July 17, 1964, Letter from J. Edgar Hoover to J. Lee Rankin; see also CD 1314, July 29, 1964). The Ike Pappas tape recording (CD 1314a) is available at the National Archives and reveals that the shot was fired one minute and fifty-eight seconds after Oswald left the third-floor Homicide and Robbery office (see also 15 H 368–369, WCT Icarus M. Pappas).

The famous photo of Ruby shooting Oswald (see photo section) was snapped by *Dallas Times Herald* photographer Robert Jackson. It won Jackson a Pulitzer Prize. Another photo, taken six-tenths of a second before by rival *Dallas Morning News* photographer Jack Beers, did not. Beers's daughter said that this six-tenths of a second bothered her late father to the day he died, her father feeling he had been cheated by fate. He had a "depression that went untreated" and it was "all due to that picture." Bitter and despondent, Beers died of a heart attack in 1975 at the age of fifty-one. (Michael Granberry, "Six Tenths of a Second, Two Lives Forever Changed," *Dallas Morning News*, June 30, 2002, pp. 1A, 33A)

†The Dallas Police Department had failed to protect the accused presidential assassin, and hence he would never be brought to trial for a jury to decide whether he was guilty, a fact that will reverberate, to the benefit of those who question the official position of the Warren Commission, down through the centuries. "If we had had jurisdiction," J. Edgar Hoover would later say, "we would have taken custody of him and I do not believe he would have been killed by Rubenstein [Ruby]" (5 H 115).

television's first live murder, instantly utters into his NBC microphone what would become the most famous and replayed live words in the entire Kennedy assassination saga: "He's been *shot*," Pettit exclaims. "He's been *shot*. Lee Oswald's been *shot*," he repeats in a tone more declaratory than incredulous. "There's been a shot," Ike Pappas shouts out almost simultaneously, his astonishment captured on his personal audiotape. "Lee Oswald has been shot." The police spring into action as Oswald's knees crumple and he falls to the garage floor.

Leavelle pushes back on the gunman's shoulder as Graves grabs the pistol. He can feel the man trying to squeeze the trigger again.

"Turn it loose! Turn it loose!" Graves yells, wrenching the revolver from the gunman's hand with a twisting motion.[1361] A platoon of detectives pile on the gunman, knocking him to the concrete, his hat tumbling under their feet. "I hope I killed the son of a bitch," Ruby manages to say while being held down on the floor of the basement.[1362]

Chaos breaks out as the crowd of reporters push madly toward the scuffle. NBC's live national audience hears correspondent Tom Pettit shouting above the din, "There's absolute panic, absolute panic here in the basement of the Dallas Police Headquarters . . . pandemonium has broken loose here!" The appalled anchormen at NBC headquarters in New York cannot contain their shock and outrage. While none of them are sure of what just happened, they know they have witnessed a disaster.[1363]

Captain Talbert vaults over the trunk of an unmarked squad car, throwing himself between the reporters and the melee on the floor.

"Get back! Get back!" and "nobody out," he shouts, shoving the newsmen back hard against the railing.[1364] Several officers draw their pistols and Dick Swain, a burly detective, jumps in with his arms outstretched, fists tight. "I'll knock you on your ass!" he yells at reporters.[1365]

Bob Huffaker, reporting live for CBS through its local channel, KRLD, reports excitedly into his microphone that "police have ringed the inside." He gets only four words into a sentence, "And no one is . . . ," when he falters, buckling under the weight of reporters who are moving and pressing in on him. He holds on tight to his mike cord as they step on it, pulling him farther down. Still not uttering another word into his mike, he manages to regain his footing, but only at a low crouch as he thrusts upward as hard as he can, shoving men off his shoulders on the way up through the brawl.[1366]

Someone shouts, "Get a doctor!" as Detective Combest helps Jim Leavelle drag Oswald back into the jail office. Oswald is moaning as they take the handcuffs off him, his sweater ripped open by the gun blast.[1367]

Police detectives bring the gunman to his feet and rush him back into the jail office. Captain Jones spots some people running up the ramp out to the street. A number of reporters are trying to escape with the news.[1368]

"Block the exits! Don't let anybody out!" Jones yells.[1369]

Fellow officers join in.

"Nobody out! Nobody out!"[1370]

An officer at the top of the ramp pulls his gun, "Get back down!" The reporters quickly retreat, a few managing to escape through the corridor near the jail office to the floors above, where they telephone their newspapers.[1371]

One of them is *Washington Star* reporter Jerry O'Leary, who rockets up the public elevator to the third floor in search of a phone. He notices Chief Curry in his office, apparently unaware of what has happened. He pokes his head in.

"Oswald's been shot," O'Leary says.[1372]

Curry's face turns ashen as the phone in the next office begins ringing. A police officer comes in and confirms the news.[1373]

Secret Service agents Sorrels and Kelley are standing just outside Deputy Chief Batchelor's office when they hear of the shooting. They both run for the basement.[1374]

Captain Talbert pushes his way into the basement jail office and over to the group of detectives who have the gunman on the floor. One of them has his knees on the man as they slap a pair of handcuffs on him. Everyone is talking all at once.

"Who is this son of a bitch?" Talbert asks.

"Oh, hell! You guys all know me, I'm Jack Ruby!" the gunman says.

Indeed, many of them do.

"He operates the Carousel Club," an officer chimes in. Talbert, his mind swirling, manages to remember being introduced to Ruby by Lieutenant Pierce a while ago at a restaurant in Dallas.[1375]

A few feet away, Detective Combest bends down over Oswald as Leavelle unleashes the two pairs of handcuffs. Combest pulls Oswald's sweater up and sees a bullet hole in the lower left part of his chest, the flesh around it bruised and purple. There doesn't seem to be a lot of blood. Combest thinks that maybe the point of entry has been seared by the gun blast, or that perhaps the wound is not too serious. He reaches around Oswald's right side and feels a lump. The bullet is just below the skin. It has almost passed completely through him. Oswald continues to moan and seems conscious.

"Is there anything you want to tell me?" Combest asks him. "Is there anything you want to say right now before it's too late?"

Oswald's eyes are open. He seems to recognize that Combest is speaking to him.

"Do you have anything you want to tell us now?" Combest asks again. Oswald only shakes his head slightly, as if to say, "No."[*]

Combest goes on appealing to him, but Oswald is fading before his eyes. Finally, the detective is no longer sure that Oswald even hears him.[1376]

At the booking desk a few feet away, Patrolman Willie Slack, who was telephoning the dispatcher's office at the time of the shooting to tell them that Oswald was on his way to the county jail, instead tells the dispatch

---

[*]There's a rather interesting addendum to this. Although Combest never mentioned this in his testimony before the Warren Commission, he told author Anthony Summers in August of 1978 that Oswald accompanied his shaking of his head with "a definite clenched-fist salute" (Summers, *Not in Your Lifetime*, p.407 note 85). Anti-conspiracy author Joan Davison wrote in 1983, "When Combest testified [before the Warren Commission] in 1964 he probably didn't know what a clenched-fist salute was. Although the gesture had been a socialist salute in Spain in the 1930's, it didn't become a widely recognized symbol of political militancy in this country until the late 1960's. It was probably then that Combest reinterpreted Oswald's gesture as a political statement. Second, a news photograph taken of Oswald after his arrest [see photo section of this book] shows him raising his right manacled arm in what very clearly appears to be a clenched-fist salute. In any event, a raised fist was Oswald's last comment" (Davison, *Oswald's Game*, p.254).

Davison limits the salute to Spanish socialists in the 1930s, but no one was watching the Communists more in 1963 than the John Birch Society, and in a February 1964 article in its publication, *American Opinion*, a contributor wrote that what Oswald gave was "the Communists' clenched-fist salute" (Oliver, "Marksmanship in Dallas," p.14; Oliver Exhibit No. 2, 20 H 721).

operator, "This is Slack at the jail office. Somebody just shot Oswald. We need a doctor."[1377]

The operator picks up the hotline to O'Neal's Funeral Home, a direct connection to its ambulance service, and tells the man on the other end that Oswald has been shot, they need an ambulance at City Hall as fast as possible. He tells her that an ambulance is on its way. The operator then immediately informs police dispatcher Clifford E. Hulse.[1378]

Dispatcher Hulse recalls that Michael Hardin and Harold Wolfe, another ambulance team from O'Neal's, have just become available a short distance from downtown. The dispatcher contacts them via radio and orders them to report to the City Hall basement, Code 3. The ambulance driver switches on his red lights and siren and races toward Main Street.[1379]

11:22 a.m.

Frederick A. Bieberdorf, a twenty-five-year-old medical student at Southwestern Medical School and the on-duty first-aid attendant for inmates at the city jail, frantically bangs on the door leading into the basement jail office, but the man standing guard, Detective Wilbur J. Cutchshaw, won't let him in.

"I'm a doctor! Someone called me!" Bieberdorf cries.

Cutchshaw finally opens the door and quickly runs his hands down the young man's coat. He discovers a stethoscope in his right coat pocket and lets him through.[1380]

Bieberdorf dashes around the booking counter, and drops to his knees. Oswald's pupils are slightly dilated. The young medical student is unable to detect a pulse, heartbeat, or any signs of breathing, although there is so much noise and confusion he's not sure whether he'd be able to hear one anyway. Bieberdorf reaches around and feels the bullet bulging between the ribs on Oswald's right side. He starts to massage Oswald's sternum in an effort to get a heartbeat.[1381]

Assistant Chief Batchelor makes his way over to where officers have Jack Ruby on the floor. Captain Talbert asks Batchelor for permission to put all the media in the assembly room for an immediate search when someone says, "Graves has the gun."[1382]

"Let's get him onto the elevator and take him to the fifth-floor jail," Captain Glen King roars. The detectives assist Ruby to his feet and march him past Oswald's body toward the jail elevator.

"I hope I killed the son of a bitch," Ruby hollers out again. "It'll save everybody a lot of trouble."[1383]

As they crowd him into the elevator for the ride to the fifth floor, Ruby adds, "Do you think I'm going to let the man who shot our president get away with it?"[1384]

Captain Talbert grabs a batch of memo pads from the jail office and begins passing them out telling officers to get the names, identification, and location of each person in the basement at the time of the shooting.[1385]

Chief Batchelor checks with Lieutenant Wiggins to make sure an ambulance has been called,[1386] then orders Captain Talbert to go to Parkland Hospital immediately and secure it for Oswald's arrival.[1387]

Secret Service agent Forrest Sorrels enters the jail office and sees Oswald on the floor, being attended to. Sorrels uses the Signal Corps security telephone mounted on the wall to call Secret Service deputy chief Paul Paterni in Washington and tell him of the shooting. Sorrels believes the assailant's name is "Jack Rubin."[1388] Paterni instructs him to get as much background information on the man as possible and report back immediately. Sorrels hangs up and takes the elevator back to the third floor, believing that "Rubin" has been taken to Captain Fritz's office.[1389]

Outside the basement jail office, the newsmen, desperate for any information at all, begin interviewing each other. Almost none of them actually saw what happened—all eyes were focused only on Oswald. They cluster around Francois Pelou, a French journalist, who excitedly tells them he saw the blue muzzle flash against the background of Oswald's black sweater. Ike Pappas recalls seeing the flash too.[1390]

Immediately after the shot, someone came running from the left of KRLD film cameraman-reporter George Phenix and nearly knocked him down. His eye came away from the eyepiece as his unipod slipped to a lower level, but he just kept shooting, not knowing whether he captured anything on film or not. He later learned he got it all—the shooting and the struggle for Ruby's gun.[1391]

John McCullough of the *Philadelphia Bulletin* was on the other side of the ramp from the action, but high enough to see Ruby's sudden lunge toward Oswald. At first he thought it was just a photographer disobeying the instructions not to move toward Oswald when he came out. When Ruby's right hand came up, he wondered for a fraction of a second whether he was going to shake hands with him. Only at the last instant did he see the gleam of metal in Ruby's hand and the muzzle flash against Oswald's sweater.[1392]

The millions of viewers who were watching the event on television hardly fared better. Although the tape of the incident is already being rebroadcast over and over, the shooting lasts just a fraction of a second and all anyone can really see is Oswald's grimace as the shot rings out.[1393]

11:23 a.m.

Up on the fifth floor of the jail, Detectives Archer, McMillon, and Clardy push Ruby against the wall and tell him to "spread-eagle." With help from the jail officer, they frisk him, tossing the items they find into Ruby's hat, including a sizable roll of money. They remove the handcuffs and have Ruby strip down to his shorts, searching his clothes completely for weapons. In his underwear, Ruby no longer seems all that threatening.[1394]

"Jack, I think you killed him," Archer says, recalling the look on Oswald's face as he lay on the jail office floor.[1395]

"Somebody had to do it," Ruby says. "You all couldn't."[1396]

"Did you think you could kill the man with one shot?" someone says.

"Well, I intended to shoot him three times," Ruby replies. "I didn't think that I could be stopped before I got off three shots."[1397]

"How'd you get into the basement?" Detective Barnard Clardy asks.

"Rio Pierce drove out in the car," Ruby says, referring to the Main Street ramp, "and the officer stepped out from the ramp momentarily to talk to Pierce, or said something to him, and I came in behind him right on down the ramp. When I got approximately halfway down the ramp I heard somebody holler, 'Hey, you,' but I don't know whether he was hollering at me or not, but I just ducked my head and kept coming . . . It was one chance in a million . . . If I had planned this, I couldn't have had my timing any better."[1398]

Down in the basement, reporters wander about like sleepwalkers among the noise and chaos, trying to get some information, any information, that might make sense out of the past few minutes.

"How would it have been possible for him to slip in?" NBC's Tom Pettit asks Sergeant Dean above the din. Dean, whose job it was to make sure that no one like Ruby could slip in, is wondering the same thing, but he isn't about to discuss it on television. "Sir, I can't answer that question." Although Dean knows Ruby, he refuses to name him.[1399]

Pettit manages to corner Captain Fritz next. "Do you have the man who fired the shot?"

"We have a man, yes," Fritz replies tersely.[1400]

Although the Dallas Police Department has just sustained the greatest blemish on its record ever in not protecting a presidential assassin for his historic trial, and the officers are visibly upset and humiliated, others aren't upset at all. Outside the entrance to the Dallas county jail on Houston Street, several hundred people had congregated in a roped-off area across the street awaiting Oswald's expected arrival. When Dallas sheriff Bill Decker walks out into the middle of the street and announces, "Ladies and gentlemen, Lee Harvey Oswald has been shot and is on his way to Parkland Hospital," very loud cheers and applause immediately erupt from the crowd of smiling faces.[1401]

11:25 a.m.

It doesn't take long for the ambulance to get to City Hall, arriving just four minutes after the shooting.[1402] Newsmen jump out of the way as the ambulance comes down the Main Street ramp into the basement garage, its flashing red lights sweeping over the concrete walls. Police scramble to move the two unmarked sedans still parked at the foot of the ramp.

Twenty-three-year-old ambulance driver Michael Hardin leaps from the station wagon and scurries toward the back of the wagon. A police officer shoves him back into the crowd of reporters, before realizing that he's the driver. Hardin and assistant Harold Wolfe flop open the back hatch and roll the stretcher into the jail office. They find

Oswald on the floor surrounded by officers. There is little they can do at the scene. It is long before the days of trained paramedics, and attendants Hardin and Wolfe are simply there to get the victim to a hospital as fast as possible, their ambulance being equipped with little more than an oxygen tank and a resuscitator cup. They pick up Oswald's limp body and put him on the stretcher and within seconds are wheeling him out toward the ambulance, his left arm dragging along the floor.

Ike Pappas breathlessly describes the scene, his tape recorder capturing the chaos of the moment for posterity.

"Here is young Oswald now," Pappas says in a rush of words. "He is being hustled in, he is lying flat, to me he appears dead. There is a gunshot wound in his lower abdomen. He is white."

The attendants lift the stretcher and slide it into the back of the station wagon.

"Pull the truck out! Pull the truck out!" several anxious policemen yell, suddenly realizing that the armored truck is still blocking the Commerce Street exit.

"Let the driver by," someone pleads to newsmen crowding around the ambulance. Detectives Graves and Leavelle, along with first-aid attendant Fred Bieberdorf, pack into the back of the wagon alongside the stretcher. The tail gate is slammed shut as an officer hollers again, "Get the truck out of the way!"

"Oswald—white, lying in the ambulance," Pappas says into his microphone, now nearly shouting over the noise. "His head is back. He is out—unconscious! Dangling—his hand is dangling over the edge of the stretcher."[1403]

The armored truck crawls out onto Commerce Street as the ambulance slips up the ramp, turns left, passes the armored truck, and screams off to Parkland Hospital, sirens wailing.[1404] Captain Fritz, along with Detectives Beck, Montgomery, and Brown, follow in Beck's car.[1405] The detectives are all talking about Jack Ruby.

"Who is Jack Ruby?" Fritz asks.

"He's a man that runs the Vegas Club out in Oak Lawn," Montgomery tells him.

"Do you know him?" Fritz wants to know.

"Yes," Montgomery says, "I used to have a district for about four years out there."[1406]

11:27 a.m.

At the foot of the ramp, newsmen plead with police officials to allow them to leave the basement so they can file their stories.

"Who is he?" Pappas asks, as he slips his microphone into the group.

"Jack Ruby is the name," a police official replies. "He runs the Carousel Club."

"He runs the Carousel Club," Pappas repeats into his mike.

The name rings a bell with several of the newsmen gathered there.

"He handed me a card the other day," a reporter says.[1407] Suddenly, Pappas remembers a curious little man he met Friday night in the third-floor hallway of police headquarters.

Pappas was standing at a telephone, waiting for District Attorney Henry Wade to join him for an interview he had arranged with WNEW in New York. The line was open and Pappas was frustrated because Wade was tied up on another telephone interview a short distance down the hall. Just then a nattily dressed man in a gray fedora hat, who Pappas first thought was a detective, walked up and asked, "Where are you from?" Pappas told him he was a reporter from New York and was in town to cover the story. The man reached into his pocket and handed him a business card with the words, "Carousel Club, Jack Ruby your host" on it. Pappas asked if he was Jack Ruby and Ruby said, "Yes, come on over to the club if you get a chance and have some drinks. There are girls there." Pappas slipped the card into his pocket and Ruby disappeared into the crowd. A short time later, Ruby passed him again, Pappas still waiting for Wade. The reporter must have looked cross because Ruby asked, "What's the matter?" Pappas explained that he was trying to get Wade over to the phone. Ruby asked, "Do you want me to get him?" Pappas said, "Sure," grateful for any kind of help. He watched as Ruby pushed through the crowd, said something to Wade, who was on another phone, pointed over at Pappas, and disappeared again into the crowd. Whatever he said worked, because a short time later, Wade finished his call and came over to be interviewed by Pappas.[1408]

Now, Pappas reaches into his pocket and thumbs through a stack of business cards he's been collecting all weekend.

"I know him," Pappas announces. "Here it is."

"I got a card from him the other day," another reporter says. Apparently Pappas isn't the only one Ruby gave a card to.

"Here he is," Pappas says, fishing the Carousel Club card out and showing it to police officials. "Jack Ruby. Is this him? Carousel Club?"

"That's him!" a reporter says.

"Yeah, yeah," police officials agree.

"Jack Ruby," another reporter says, "I seen him around several times."

"Who's going to give a complete briefing on this?" someone calls out.

"Chief Curry, at his office on the third floor as soon as we can get one set up," a police official says with a thick Texas drawl.

Excited reporters repeat the name, Jack Ruby.

"Jack Ruby," Pappas sputters into his microphone, "who we noticed the other day, he was hanging around police headquarters. Apparently he's very well known here. And he was in the offices and mingling around and now, so we understand, he has shot Oswald."

Pappas turns and starts sprinting up the basement ramp.

"Holy mackerel!" he says into his mike between breaths. "One of the most sensational developments in this already fantastic case."[1409]

11:28 a.m.

At the Executive Inn near Love Field in Dallas, Robert Oswald and Mr. Paul Gregory, the Russian language instructor, are trying hard to get Marguerite and Marina Oswald packed and into the car outside, where Secret Service agents Mike Howard and Charley Kunkel wait.

Marguerite is having kittens over the state of her and Marina's clothes, the lack of clean diapers, and last night's visit by FBI agent Bardwell Odum, who had shown Marguerite a photograph of an unknown individual. Robert doesn't want to hear it.

"Mother," he says, "will you stop talking and hurry up. We have to get you out of here."[1410]

Robert simply wants to get them out to his in-laws' farm in Boyd, Texas, about forty-five miles from Dallas, with as little fuss as possible.[1411] None of them has any idea what has happened. But his mother won't listen.

"What's your hurry?" she asks. "All we have been doing is running from one place to the other. The diapers are wet. And I want you to know how we got here. Mrs. Paine called last night and said that Lee called, and then I was shown a picture of this man—"

"Mother," Robert says again, his patience wearing thin, "*stop talking*. We have got to get you out of here."

Robert tells her he is going down to the desk to take care of the bill while they finish packing. Marguerite hands him the fifty-dollar bill given to her by the *Life* representatives. It is just enough to cover the charges.[1412]

Robert walks back out to the car, where the two agents have been listening to a Dallas police radio channel. Agent Mike Howard comes over to him.

"Now, don't get excited, Robert," he says, "but we've just gotten word that Lee's been shot. It isn't serious, and they've captured the man who shot him."

The weight of the news pushes Robert up against the side of the car. The only thing that seems reassuring about the news of his brother's shooting is the calmness in Mike Howard's voice.

"Where are they taking him?" Robert finally manages to ask.

"Parkland Hospital."

Robert stares into space a moment, lost in thought.

"What do you want to do now?" Agent Kunkel asks.

"I believe I'll go to Parkland," Robert replies. "But I wish you'd take Mother and Marina and the children on to the farm."

Kunkel suggests that Marina go with him to Parkland, but Robert doesn't think that will be best. "I'll find out how serious it is and let you know then," he says firmly. Robert asks the two agents not to tell his mother or Marina what has happened.

"If they knew," he says, "I'm sure they'd insist on going to the hospital with me."[1413]

Marguerite and Marina and the children come down to the cars and climb into one with Mr. Gregory and the two agents. Robert gets into his car and heads off for Parkland Hospital. Marguerite demands to know where they are going. "We're taking you to Robert's in-laws' house," Mr. Gregory tells her.

"No!" Marguerite complains. "You are not taking me out in the sticks. I want to be in Dallas where I can help Lee."

The Secret Service agents explain that it's for security reasons, but Marguerite won't hear of it.

"You can give me security in a hotel room in town," she whines.

Mr. Gregory has finally had enough of this self-centered woman.

"Mrs. Oswald," he snaps, "you called me at my home and asked me to come and help you, to provide a place for you to stay, and here I am. Now, if you don't like it, then I am through with you!"[1414]

Marguerite is momentarily stunned by Mr. Gregory's forthrightness. The agents start the car and pull away from the Executive Inn. It isn't long before Marguerite insists that they need clothes and diapers for the babies. She suggests that they stop in Irving at Mrs. Paine's house and pick up some of the necessities. The agents radio the FBI dispatcher and learn that a cluster of reporters is staked out in front of the Paine residence. The dispatcher suggests they avoid the media and go to the nearby home of the chief of police of Irving. From there they can telephone Mrs. Paine and have some things brought over. The agents agree and for the moment don't tell the women why they are making the detour.[1415]

11:30 a.m.

The ambulance carrying Oswald speeds down Harry Hines Boulevard toward Parkland Hospital.[1416] First-aid attendant Fred Bieberdorf has placed an oxygen resuscitator cup over Oswald's mouth and continues to massage his sternum in the cramped rear bed of the station wagon. Oswald has been unconscious the entire trip and quite still. Beiberdorf thinks he may already be dead. Five blocks from the hospital, Oswald suddenly starts thrashing about, resisting Beiberdorf's efforts to massage his chest and pulling at the resuscitator cup over his mouth.[1417]

The ambulance swings around to the hospital's emergency entrance, the same one President Kennedy was brought to less than two days earlier. A police contingent is already in place and assists the ambulance driver as he backs up to the entrance. A crowd of citizens, reporters, and cameramen are also on hand as Oswald is quickly unloaded and wheeled into the hospital.[1418]

To Parkland's assistant administrator, Peter N. Geilich, it looks as though a wave of humanity is coming through the door with the stretcher. Flashbulbs seem to be popping everywhere. He gets a good look at Oswald, dressed in black, his face ashen. The police, besieged by reporters and photographers, set about clearing the emergency area and closing off the hallway.[1419]

At the suggestion of a Parkland doctor who felt that it would be tantamount to a sacrilege to treat Oswald in Trauma Room One, Oswald is rushed into Trauma Room Two, across the hall from where President Kennedy had been treated.[1420] Orders are given to clear Trauma Room Two of all unnecessary personnel. An enterprising reporter, Bill Burrus of the *Dallas Times Herald*, evades the sweep for a time by hiding behind a curtain in Trauma Room One across the hall but is eventually discovered and ejected.[1421]

Drs. Malcolm Perry and Ronald Jones, who had both worked to save the president's life on Friday, rush down from the surgical suite and meet the stretcher as it's wheeled into Trauma Room Two. A battery of doctors and nurses, many of the same faces from Friday's ordeal, are already there. Dr. Perry makes a rapid assessment of Lee Oswald's condition. Unconscious and very blue, due to a lack of oxygen, Oswald has no blood pressure. An infrequent, barely audible heartbeat is accompanied by agonal attempts at respiration. Dr. Marion T. Jenkins, an anesthesiologist, immediately inserts an endotracheal tube down Oswald's throat to facilitate breathing, while Dr. Perry quickly examines his chest. Noting the bullet wound in the lower left part of the chest, Dr.

Perry reaches around and feels for an exit wound. He encounters a lump on the right side. The bullet is just under the skin at the margin of the rib. Perry knew at a glance that the bullet had likely traversed every major organ in the abdomen. Detective Leavelle, who is in the room, wants the bullet as evidence and he says that someone, maybe Perry, "pinched the skin and the bullet just popped out in a tray, like a grape seed." Leavelle realizes that if the bullet hadn't been stopped by a rib on the right side, it would have automatically gone on to exit Oswald's body and hit him.[1422]

The emergency team swings into action, starting resuscitation routines designed to stabilize the patient. Three small venous incisions are performed on each of Oswald's legs, as well as his left forearm, to introduce fluids. A chest tube is inserted to prevent the left lung from collapsing, and the front of the gurney is lowered to help get blood to Oswald's heart and brain. The irony is not lost on some that every effort is now being made to save the life of someone who virtually everyone believes extinguished the life of President Kennedy just two days earlier.

Dr. Tom Shires, the chief of surgery at Parkland, and Dr. Robert McClelland enter the room just as Dr. Perry orders Oswald taken to the second floor and prepped for surgery. Perry quickly fills in the chief surgeon.[1423]

Dr. Shires knows that it will be virtually impossible to save Oswald's life. Had the shooting happened right outside the operating room, they might have some chance, but Oswald has lost too much blood during the twenty minutes that have elapsed since the shooting. There are no doubt multiple internal bleeding points that will take considerable time to get under control. The tremendous blood loss will result in anoxia, the state of being deprived too long of blood-supplied oxygen, a fatal condition.[1424]

Hospital administrator Steve Landregan manages to get a word with Dr. Shires as he and the other surgeons come out of Trauma Room Two, and he immediately passes it on to the press—Oswald has a gunshot wound in his left side with no exit. He is in extremely critical condition and is being taken immediately to surgery. For the moment, that's all anyone is willing to say.[1425]

11:34 a.m. (12:34 p.m. EST)

Jackie Kennedy, her two children, and RFK enter the East Room of the White House, where the president's body lies in state for a private viewing. Jackie had earlier written a letter to her lost husband, and minutes earlier upstairs in the family quarters, she had Caroline, soon to be six years old, write a letter to her father in which she said, "Dear Daddy. We're all going to miss you. Daddy I love you very much. Caroline." Then Caroline, holding John-John's hand, had him scribble up and down something illegible on a separate sheet of paper. Now at the casket, it is opened. "It isn't Jack, it isn't Jack," Jackie thinks, repeating her observation of several hours earlier as she looks at the grotesquely familiar figure before her, happy that the casket had been closed for the rest of the world. She places the three letters, from herself, Caroline, and John-John, along with a scrimshaw (a decorative article carved from whale ivory) and a pair of cufflinks she had given JFK, in the coffin. Bobby, kneeling beside Jackie at the coffin, places a silver rosary his wife, Ethel, had given him at their wedding, and the PT-109 tie clip his brother had given him, next to his brother's body in the coffin. The coffin is closed, and Jackie and Bobby quietly and slowly leave the room, their minds and souls racked with inconsolable pain.[1426]

11:38 a.m.

At Dallas police headquarters, the public elevator opens onto the third floor and Sergeant Patrick Dean steps off. He's hoping to find someone in Captain Fritz's office who can tell him if it's all right to release to the press the name of the man who shot Oswald. Dean is unaware that the name "Ruby" is already spreading like wildfire through the press corps in the basement below. As soon as Dean steps off the elevator, he encounters Chief Curry and a Secret Service agent.[1427]

"This is Mr. Forrest V. Sorrels, head of the Secret Service in Dallas," Curry says. "Here's my keys. Take him to the fifth floor to interview Ruby."[1428]

Curry hands Dean a packed key ring, including the one Dean will need to operate the third-floor jail elevator.[1429] As the two men ascend to the fifth floor, Agent Sorrels wrestles with a dilemma. He knows that before questioning Ruby he should advise him of his constitutional right to remain silent under the Fifth Amendment.* However, Sorrels also knows that it is paramount that he find out if Ruby is involved with Oswald in the assassination, or if Ruby has accomplices. Sorrels figures that if he warns Ruby of his right to remain silent, Ruby might not tell him what he wants to know. By the time Dean and Sorrels reach the fifth floor, Sorrels decides not to warn Ruby, believing that at the moment it's far more important to the Secret Service to determine whether or not Ruby has accomplices, and of critical interest to determine whether or not Oswald and Ruby know each other.[1430]

The elevator doors open onto the fifth floor of the jail and Sergeant Dean and Secret Service agent Sorrels step off. Sorrels surrenders his sidearm to the officer just outside, and they walk over to where three detectives are standing with Jack Ruby, stripped to his shorts.

"This is Mr. Forrest V. Sorrels," Dean says, introducing the two men. Ruby stops him.

"I know who he is," Ruby says. "He's with the FBI."

"No, I am not with the FBI," Sorrels replies. "I'm with the Secret Service."

"Well, I knew that you were working for the government," Ruby answers.

"I want to ask you some questions," the Secret Service man says.

"Is this for the magazines or press?" Ruby asks.

"No, it's for myself," Sorrels tells him.[1431]

Ruby seems to be mulling over whether he's going to answer any of Sorrels's questions. The agent tries to think of a way to make Ruby feel comfortable talking to him. He remembers looking out Assistant Chief Batchelor's window just before the shooting and seeing Honest Joe Goldstein, a pawnbroker and one of the town's more colorful characters, across

---

*Prior to the *Escobedo* case in 1964, federal law enforcement agencies had a *policy* of doing this, but as indicated earlier, there was no *legal requirement* that they advise suspects of this constitutional right, and if they didn't, any statement made by the defendant thereafter would be inadmissible at the defendant's trial.

the street. It's not easy to overlook Goldstein, who's often seen in his gar-
ishly painted Edsel with its plugged .50 caliber machine gun mounted on
the top. Honest Joe is well off and generous, always willing to cut prices for
a police officer, and a publicity hound to boot. He likes to lend money on
oddities, like artificial limbs, just to get his name in the paper—"Honest
Joe Goldstein, the Loan Ranger."

"I just saw Honest Joe on the street," Sorrels says. "I know a number
of Jewish merchants here that you know." It seems to break the ice.

"That's good enough for me," Ruby says. "What is it you want to
know?"[1432]

"Are you Jack Rubin?" Sorrels asks.

"No, it's Jack Ruby," the fifty-two-year-old nightclub owner says. "I
was born Jack Rubenstein, but had my name changed legally when I came
to Dallas."

In answer to a series of questions, Ruby says he is in the entertainment
business, operating the Carousel Club on Commerce Street and the Vegas
Club on Oak Lawn. He has an apartment on South Ewing Street in Dallas.

"Jack—why?" Sorrels finally asks.

Ruby is longing to talk, and it all comes tumbling out.

"When this thing happened," Ruby says, "I was in a newspaper office
placing an ad for my business. When I heard about the assassination, I
canceled my ad and closed my business and have not done any business
for the last three days. I have been grieving about this thing. On Friday
night, I went to the synagogue and heard a eulogy on the president. I
thought very highly of him."

Tears come to Ruby's eyes.[1433]

"My sister," he continues, "who has recently had an operation, has
been hysterical. When I saw that Mrs. Kennedy was going to have to
appear for a trial, I thought to myself, why should she have to go through
this ordeal for this no good son of a bitch. I had read about a letter to little Caroline. I had been to the Western Union office to send a telegram.
I guess I had worked myself into a state of insanity to where I had to do
it. I was afraid he might not get his just punishment. Sometimes they
don't, you know?"

Jack looks up at Sorrels.

"I guess I just had to show the world that a Jew has guts," he says.[1434]

Sorrels asks him if he was ever politically active and Ruby tells him that he was a labor organizer years ago. Asked if he ever was convicted of a felony, Ruby says he was not.

"I was arrested and taken before a justice of the peace in 1954," Ruby says, "but I was released."

"What for?" Sorrels asks.

"Investigation of violation of state liquor laws," Ruby replies.

"Why were you carrying a gun today?" Sorrels asks.

"I often have a large amount of money on me from my business," Ruby tells him.

Now, Sorrels gets to what he really wants to know. "Was anyone involved with you in the shooting of Oswald?"

"No."

"Did you know Oswald before?"

"No," Ruby says again, "there is no acquaintance or connection between Oswald and myself."[1435]

Before it's all over, Ruby says that he has the highest regard for the Dallas police and that they all know him. After getting the answers to a few more questions about Ruby's background and family, Sorrels excuses himself and leaves.[1436]

The interview has lasted less than seven minutes, but Sorrels has all the information he needs to get an investigation rolling and needs to find a telephone to call Washington immediately. He retrieves his sidearm, steps into the jail elevator, and is whisked back to the third floor.[1437]

Now, Sergeant Dean turns to face the prisoner.

"Jack, I want to ask you a couple of questions myself," he says.

Dean has known Ruby since about 1960 when he commanded a downtown patrol and routinely checked out the Carousel Club. He had even gone there three or four times with friends when he was off duty. Occasionally he would run into Ruby on the street, and Jack was always very friendly, inviting him up to the club to see the latest show. However, Dean didn't want to get cozy with Jack, and kept his contacts on an impersonal basis.[1438]

"How did you get in the basement?" the sergeant asks.

"I walked in the Main Street ramp," Ruby says calmly, repeating what he's already told Detective Clardy. "I had just been to the Western Union to mail a money order to Fort Worth. I walked from the Western Union to the ramp and saw [Rio] Sam Pierce drive out of the basement. At the time the car drove out is when I walked in."[1439]

"How long had you been in the basement before Oswald came out?" Dean asks.

"I just walked in," Ruby replies. "I just walked to the bottom of the ramp when he came out."[1440]

11:40 a.m.

In the Dallas FBI office, Agent Jim Hosty heads down the stairs to the eleventh floor, having just finished an interview with Katya Ford, a Russian-born refugee who had befriended Marina Oswald and knew Lee as an abusive husband. Just as Hosty reaches the bottom step, his supervisor, Ken Howe, scrambles toward him, dodging desks and chairs.

"Goddamn it, Jim, they've just killed Oswald!" he shouts.

Hosty is stunned. His mouth opens but nothing comes out. Howe pushes him aside and dashes up the stairs. Hosty can't believe it. The police had been warned of the threats against Oswald. Why had they not taken them seriously?

Hosty's desk phone rings and he answers. It's W. P. "Pat" Gannaway, captain of the Dallas police intelligence unit. "What do you guys have on a Jack Rubenstein, alias Jack Ruby?" Gannaway asks. "We've arrested him for shooting Oswald."

"Let me check," Hosty says. "I'll get back to you, okay?"

"Sure. As soon as you can," Gannaway says, and hangs up.

Hosty quickly locates the FBI file on Jack Ruby, which shows that Ruby was classified as a PCI—potential criminal informant. There are four pages in it. The first is a memo from Agent Charles Flynn saying he is opening the file. The second is a "contact" page, showing that Flynn had several contacts with Ruby but no information had been developed. The third page was a memo saying the Ruby file was closed because Agent

Flynn had been routinely transferred to another city. The final page was a misfiled item that had nothing to do with Ruby.

Hosty knew Flynn as a young, new agent in the Dallas office who, like most new agents, aggressively sought out new potential informants. It was department policy and an easy way to keep bureau authorities off a new agent's back. Hosty ran the file over to Ken Howe's desk.

"Gannaway just called and said they've arrested a guy named Jack Ruby for shooting Oswald," Hosty tells him. "He wants to know what we have on Ruby. Here it is."

Hosty hands Howe the file. "Ruby was one of our PCIs."

Howe grabs the folder and scans the contents a moment.

"Don't call Gannaway back," Howe orders. "I'll take care of it."

Obviously, Howe was worried about how Ruby's PCI status would be viewed if it were ever made public that the gunman in the Oswald shooting was also one of the FBI's potential criminal informants. He knew the press would eat it up. The FBI ultimately decides to handle it the easy way. They bury it—for thirteen years.[1441]

11:42 a.m.

On a second-floor operating table at Parkland Hospital, Dr. Malcolm Perry, under the supervision of chief surgeon Tom Shires, quickly lays open Oswald's abdomen in an operation called a laparotomy. The damage is, much as they suspected, massive. Both of the major vessels leading to and from the heart, the aorta and the inferior vena cava, have been ripped open, with catastrophic loss of blood and circulation. The abdomen is swamped with an excess of three quarts of blood, both liquid and in clots. The whole team—Shires, Perry, McClelland, and Jones—assisted by three anesthesiologists and five nurses, work quickly to remove the blood by suction, lap packs, and their own latex glove—covered hands. Sixteen 500-milliliter bottles of whole blood, along with huge quantities of lactated Ringer's solution, are given to Oswald as the doctors feverishly work to stop the bleeding points one by one. The bullet has shattered the top of the spleen, damaged the area around the pancreas, and torn off the top of the right kidney and the right lobe of the liver before lodging in the right lateral body wall. Along the way the bullet has also injured the stomach. The doctors first concentrate on the right side, using packing to control the bleeding around the kidney, then turn to focus on the left where the bleeding is massive. A multitude of organs and tissues are dissected free, then clamped, only to reveal more damage. Dr. Perry finds the source of most of the bleeding, a ruptured aorta, and uses his fingers to clamp it while Dr. Shires tries to stop the bleeding from another main artery that has been sheared away. Working at a breakneck pace for the next hour, the surgical team manages to stop all the major bleeding and restore Oswald's blood pressure to 100 over 85. They begin to think that they may be able to save Oswald after all.[1442]

In New York, CBS anchor Walter Cronkite calls a cousin of his in Dallas whom he grew up with and was like a brother to him. The cousin was the vice president of the local branch of the National Distillers. As such, he knew all the bars in Dallas. "Do you know anything about Jack Ruby?" Cronkite asks. "Oh, Jack Ruby, he's a nut. Why are you calling me [about him]?" It hadn't been on the air yet but Cronkite said it is believed he's the person who shot Oswald. "No kidding," the cousin says. "Tell me more about him," Cronkite says. "Well, he's kind of a nut. He's been around town a long time. He's owned several bars. He has always been a strange sort of character. I can't imagine why he'd be shooting Oswald. He didn't strike me as the kind of patriot who would want to get rid of this assassin."[1443]

11:45 a.m. (12:45 p.m. EST)
On all three networks, most of America is watching the televised proceedings in Washington, where the weather is crisp and sunny.

Jackie Kennedy, in black, her eyes swollen from hours of crying, holds the hands of her two children as she watches the president's coffin being carried by military pallbearers from the North Portico of the White House and placed in an artillery caisson, a gun carriage without its gun. Six magnificent white horses (which equestrians always call, no matter

how white they may be, "grays") will pull it up Pennsylvania Avenue to
the Capitol. Immediately behind the caisson is Sardar, a riderless bay gelding given to Mrs. Kennedy by the president of Pakistan, and a ten-car
procession—with Mrs. Kennedy and her two children, Robert Kennedy,
and Lady Bird Johnson in the first car. An estimated three hundred thousand people line the procession route on Pennsylvania Avenue. Seldom
have so many people made so little noise. The crowd's silence is
uncanny—loud to the senses. The sound of muffled drums—sticks beating slowly on slackened drumheads—from the corps of military drum-
mers following the caisson increases the emotion of the moment for the
hushed throngs. Many have never heard the oppressive and ominous
sound before, but few will ever forget its monotonous expression of
unremitting and unrelievable grief.

Upon the arrival of the caisson, the same one that bore Franklin D.
Roosevelt, at the Capitol steps, and with the Kennedy entourage now
standing nearby, a military officer shouts, "Pre-sent! Arms!" the words
echoing across the square. In nearby Union Station Park an artillery
battalion commences firing a twenty-one-gun salute, after which the
navy band breaks into a dramatically melancholy version of "Hail to the
Chief." As the notes ring out, Jackie Kennedy's heretofore incredible
public poise crumbles, her head bows and beneath the mantilla of black
lace, she sobs openly. It is a scene that brings a nation to its knees.

When the last measure has been played, the nine-man casket team from
the United States Army, Navy, Marines, Air Force, and Coast Guard
unbuckles the coffin and carries it slowly up the thirty-seven steps of the
Capitol, the widow and her two children following behind. Inside the
rotunda, they ease the coffin onto the catafalque, the honor guards take
their positions, and the circle of mourners closes in around them.

They endure a few brief eulogies, starting at 2:02 p.m. (EST), by Senate Majority Leader Mike Mansfield, Speaker of the House John McCormack, and Chief Justice Earl Warren. The rotunda, with its vast spaces
and hard reflective surfaces, is a very poor sound studio, and Mansfield's
voice is faint, often buried under the barrage of nervous coughing from
the onlookers.

"He gave us of a good heart," Mansfield says, "from which the laughter came . . . Of a profound wit, from which a great leadership emerged. He gave us of a kindness and a strength fused into a human courage to seek peace without fear."

Chief Justice Warren speaks of a man who was a "believer in the dignity and equality of all human beings, a fighter for justice and apostle of peace," and that he had "been snatched from our midst by the bullet of an assassin . . . The whole world is poorer because of his loss."

It is not the words, though, but the images that are seared into the collective consciousness—Jackie Kennedy once again poised and collected, little Caroline by her side,[*] unable to understand fully what the chief justice is saying.

The president's brother looks drained, deaf to the words of Speaker McCormack, who says, "Thank God that we were privileged, however briefly, to have had this great man for our president. For he has now taken his place among the great figures of world history."

President Johnson follows a soldier bearing a wreath of red and white carnations to the catafalque. Johnson pauses in momentary prayer, then retreats to his place. The rotunda falls silent. The ceremony has ended, but no one seems to want to leave. Mrs. Kennedy suddenly realizes that everyone is waiting for her. She turns to Robert Kennedy and whispers, "Can I say good-bye?" He nods once.

"We're going to say good-bye to daddy," the First Lady says quietly, turning to her daughter, "and we're going to kiss him good-bye, and tell daddy how much we love him and how much we'll always miss him."

They step forward solemnly toward the casket, Caroline keeping her eyes on her mother to see what to do. Mrs. Kennedy kneels at the coffin, then Caroline, as the whole world watches.

"You know, you just kiss," whispers Jacqueline.

She leans forward to brush her lips against the flag, and Caroline does the same, her small white-gloved hand slipping beneath to touch the closed casket. The microphones are too distant to capture the whispers,

[*]During the ceremony, John-John, age three, was kept busy in a room off the rotunda.

but the image strikes a deep chord in the hearts of the world. A cutaway
to the faces of the Joint Chiefs of Staff shows them standing at attention
with tears streaming down their faces. It is one of the most moving
moments of the entire four days of television broadcasting.

As the family emerges from the rotunda, squinting in the stabbing
sunlight, they see the immensity of the crowd that has gathered and is
still growing—people as far as the eye can see waiting to walk past the
president's coffin in the rotunda. The streets leading from the Capitol
are filled, an ocean of people everywhere, between the congressional
office buildings, around the Supreme Court, the Library of Congress,
and the Folger Library, from the Botanic Gardens to the Taft tower. The
fact that the rotunda would remain open was announced on television,
and people are already flowing toward it in a tide that cannot be
stemmed. Cars on New York Avenue are bumper to bumper and by
dusk will stretch all the way back to Baltimore, thirty miles away.[1444]

12:35 p.m.
FBI agent C. Ray Hall is in Chief Curry's office when a call comes in from
the man in charge of the Dallas FBI office, Gordon Shanklin. Hall walks
out and picks up a phone just outside Curry's office.

"Get in and interview Ruby," Shanklin orders.

Hall slips the phone back into the cradle, returns to the police chief's
office, and requests permission to interview Jack Ruby.

"Of course," Curry replies, and asks a uniformed officer to take Agent
Hall up to Ruby's fifth-floor jail cell, immediately. When he arrives, Hall
finds Ruby in the same block of maximum-security cells where Oswald
had been imprisoned. The jailer, K. H. Haake, opens the outer door that
leads into a small corridor in front of the three cells. There is a table and
some chairs there. Detective T. D. McMillon is seated on one of them. A
few minutes later, Detective Barnard Clardy joins him. Agent Hall enters
the maximum-security block and sees Ruby sitting alone in the center
cell, clad only in shorts. Like Oswald, the cells on either side are empty.

Ruby is led out of the cell and told to sit down at the table. Agent Hall
sits across from him and introduces himself.

"Be advised, Mr. Ruby," Hall tells him, "that you do not have to make any statement. You have the right to talk with an attorney before making any statement. Any statement you do make could be used against you in a court of law."[1445]

Ruby tells him he understands. With that, Agent Hall begins to question the prisoner in his search for answers as to why Ruby shot Oswald.

"When were you born?" Hall asks.

"March 25, 1911," Ruby says. "In Chicago."

Under a string of questions during a long interview, Ruby tells the FBI man of his childhood in Chicago, how he grew up on the west side, how he was hustling refreshments at rodeos and sporting events and scalping tickets as soon as he was old enough. He says he drifted to California in the mid-1930s and sold tip sheets at the race track and subscriptions to the Hearst newspapers to get by. A year later he returned to Chicago and, with the help of attorney Leon Cooke, became secretary/treasurer of the Scrap Iron and Junk Handlers Union. Two years later, his life came crashing down when Cooke was shot and killed during an argument at a union meeting. Ruby says he often uses "Leon" as his middle name, as a tribute to the man he admired so much.

In early 1940, he quit the union and drifted east, where he hawked punch boards at area factories until he was drafted in 1943. He served state side in the Army Air Corps as a mechanic and was honorably discharged three years later at the rank of private first class. He returned to Chicago and helped his brother Earl with a mail-order business and then moved to Dallas in 1947 to help his sister open the Singapore Club, a nightclub. After a brief return to Chicago, Ruby says he eventually settled in Dallas and struggled to stay in the nightclub business. By the late 1950s, Ruby had owned or had an interest in several nightclubs, all failures except one, the struggling Vegas Club, which his sister Eva still operates. In 1960, with financial help from his brother Earl, and Bull Pen restaurant owner Ralph Paul, Ruby bought the Carousel Club on Commerce Street in Dallas.

Ruby says that through the years he has become personally acquainted with many Dallas police officers.[1446]

12:50 p.m.

Robert Oswald's head is a dull, numbed mass of confusion. He has learned little about his brother's condition since arriving at Parkland twenty minutes ago. It took ten minutes just to get past two Secret Service agents, who, for whatever reason, wouldn't let him inside. Eventually, they escorted him to the hospital's volunteer office, but only after frisking him for a concealed weapon. How ironic, Robert later thought. If only they had done this to the man who had slipped into the City Hall basement.

The hospital is swarming with police officers and Robert waits to be told where to go to get a report on Lee's condition. A Secret Service agent comes into the room and says, "Robert, he's going to be all right. Don't worry about it." It's not much, but it's the first clear report he's heard since the shooting and it sounds reassuring. Robert finally begins to relax and starts chatting with Secret Service agent John Howlett, who seems willing to help him pass the time.[1447]

Upstairs, Dr. Shires's operating team has managed to stop the massive bleeding in Oswald's abdomen. The doctors take a moment to determine how to best go about repairing the damage done by Jack Ruby's bullet. They realize that clamping the aorta has stopped the bleeding, but it's also preventing blood from flowing to the kidneys, a hazardous situation if prolonged. They decide that this major artery must be repaired immediately in order to restore blood to the kidneys and the lower portion of Oswald's body.

Suddenly, Dr. Jenkins reports that Oswald's heart is weakening. The pulse rate abruptly drops from 85 to 40, then seconds later, to zero. Dr. Perry reaches in and feels the aorta. No pulse. The tremendous blood loss has set the stage for irreversible shock and cardiac arrest. Dr. Perry grabs a knife, opens the left side of the chest, and reaches in to massage the heart. It is flabby, dilated, and apparently contains little blood. Perry vigorously massages the organ and manages to obtain a palpable pulse in the blood vessels feeding the neck and head, but he's unable to get the heart to pump on its own. Calcium chloride and then epinephrine-Xylocaine are injected directly into the left ventricle of the heart, causing fibrillation, an uncontrolled twitching of the heart muscles, but no heartbeat. They hit Oswald with 240, 360, 500, and finally 700 volts of electricity, but still no heartbeat. A thoracic surgery resident hands Dr. Perry a cardiac pacemaker, which he quickly sews into the right ventricle of the heart, hoping to artificially induce the heart to pump. The pacemaker creates a small, feeble, localized muscle reaction but no effective heartbeat. After a frenzied, almost instinctual struggle, Dr. Jenkins calls a halt. Oswald's pupils are fixed and dilated, there is no retinal blood flow, no respiratory effort, and no effective pulse. They have done everything they know how to do and it isn't enough. Oswald is dead. It is seven minutes after one o'clock, almost exactly two days after Kennedy expired.[1448]

1:00 p.m.
Dallas detectives Guy Rose, H. M. Moore, and J. P. Adamcik arrive at the Marsala Place Apartments, where Ruby lives, to search his unit, but the search warrant has an apartment number on it other than number 207, Ruby's apartment, and the manager won't open the door to 207 until after Rose calls Joe B. Brown Jr., the Oak Cliff judge who had the original warrant, and Brown comes out to correct the error. The detectives examine everything in the apartment, find nothing of evidentiary value, and leave Ruby's apartment around 2:00 p.m. without taking anything with them.[1449]

1:16 p.m.
Parkland's assistant administrator, Peter Geilich, dashes up the stairs to the second-floor operating room to get more news for the press he has corralled into the hospital's makeshift pressroom. As he gets there, Dr. Shires and the other members of the surgery team are coming out the door and tell him the news. Geilich sees Dr. Malcolm Perry among the group and can't help thinking that Perry has certainly been in the thick of things over the last few days. Geilich grabs Dr. Shires by the arm.

"The press wants to talk to you," he says. "We have promised them that you would make a statement as soon as you came out of surgery."

Dr. Shires looks down and sees that he is covered in blood. He slips into the doctors' locker room and puts on a clean lab coat. Then, he and Mr. Geilich make their way down to the classroom-turned-pressroom to face the live television cameras.[1450]

"Is he alive, Doctor?" a voice asks from the battery of reporters and cameramen crowding around.

Dr. Shires shakes his head, "No, he has died."

"Let Dr. Shires make his statement, please," hospital administrator Steve Landregan pleads.

"When did he die, Doctor?"

"He died at 1:07 p.m.," Dr. Shires replies, "of his gunshot wounds he had received."

Shires fields dozens of questions regarding Oswald's final moments, his condition when he arrived at the hospital, the damage caused by the bullet, and the names of the other doctors in attendance during surgery.

"Did you first inform his relatives of the death before you came here?" one reporter asks.

"No, I came right here from the operating room," Shires tells him.[1451]

In the volunteer office down the hall, Secret Service agent John Howlett picks up the telephone and listens intently as Robert Oswald looks on. After thirty seconds or so, Howlett says, "Would you repeat that?"

His tone of voice fills Robert with dread.

Howlett hangs up and starts around the desk toward him.

"Robert," he says, "I'm sorry, but he's dead."

Robert slumps in his chair, crushed by the intolerable weight of the news. His hand rises to his face, but it can't cover the sobs that follow.[1452]

Agent Howlett is trying to locate the other Oswalds by telephone through the Dallas police radio system when Geilich comes in and asks Robert whether he wants to talk to the press.

"No, no, not at this time," Robert sobs. "Can I see my brother?"

Geilich calls Jack Price, the county hospital administrator, to see if he can arrange for Robert to see his brother's body.

"Most certainly," Price tells Geilich, "let them have whatever we give any other patient's family."

Geilich checks with the operating room supervisor, Audrey Bell, who says it's not a good idea to bring Robert up to the operating room, which is a mess. The body, she says, will be taken to the morgue within ten or fifteen minutes. Geilich hangs up the phone.

"It'll be a few minutes, Mr. Oswald," Geilich tells him. "The hospital chaplain is in the next room. Would you like to see him?"

Robert nods. Geilich leaves for a moment and returns with one Chaplain Pepper. He and Robert speak quietly for a moment, then pray together.[1453]

The office door opens and Secret Service inspector Thomas Kelley barges in with several other agents. Kelley looks at Robert's tear-stained face.

"Well, what do you expect?" Kelley says. "Violence breeds violence."

The coldness of his remark cuts to the bone.

"Inspector," Robert replies, "does that justify anything?"

Kelley leaves the room without answering.[1454]

1:20 p.m.

En route with the Secret Service to the farm of Robert Oswald's in-laws, Marguerite mentions that Marina's two little babies are all wet, that there are no clean diapers for them, that she and Marina have no change of clothing for themselves, and so forth. Marguerite insists that they turn the car around and go by Ruth Paine's house to pick up what they need. Since the Secret Service learned there were many reporters and people at the Paine residence, they stop at the home of the Irving chief of police. Outside the chief's home now, Marguerite waits in the car with Marina's children and Secret Service agent Mike Howard. Marina is inside with Agent Kunkel and Peter Gregory, making arrangements on the phone with Ruth Paine to have some clothes and diapers picked up and brought over from Ruth's house nearby.[1455] (Irving police are already at Mrs. Paine's home to ferry the items from her house to the police chief's house at the time Marina called.)[1456]

The Secret Service men hid the fact that Lee had been shot until they arrived at the police chief's house several minutes ago. They realized then that the chief's wife was sure to have the television on and that the

Oswalds would find out soon enough. When the car rolled to a stop in front of the house, Agent Howard turned around and bluntly told Marguerite, "Your son has been shot."

"How badly?" Marguerite asked, stunned.

"In the shoulder," the agent told her.

Now, the radio on the front dash crackles to life. Agent Howard picks up the microphone. "Go ahead," he says. Marguerite can't quite make out what is being said.

The agent mashes the radio microphone button. "Do not repeat. Do not repeat."

Marguerite can tell that something has happened.

"My son is gone, isn't he?" she asks.

Howard doesn't answer.

"Answer me!" Marguerite demands. "I want to know. If my son is gone, I want to meditate."

"Yes, Mrs. Oswald," Agent Howard tells her, "your son has just expired."

Howard can't keep Marguerite from getting out and going into the chief's house.

"Marina," she cries out, "our boy is gone."

Marina already knows. Peter Gregory had told her moments before.[1457]

The two women weep as the agents watch replays of the shooting on the television, which has been turned around so the women can't see it. The chief's wife brings the women coffee as they sit on the sofa.

"I want to see Lee," Marguerite insists.

Marina joins in, "Me, too, me want to see Lee."

The chief and Peter Gregory both tell her, "It would be better to wait until he is at the funeral home and ready to view."

"No," Marguerite persists, "I want to see Lee now."

Marina is equally stubborn, but the agents have real concerns for their safety. To pacify them, Agents Howard and Kunkel take them back to the car and start for the hospital, all the while trying to convince them to turn back.

"Mrs. Oswald," Mike Howard says as he drives, "for security reasons it would be much better if you would wait until later on to see Lee, because this is a big thing."

"For security reasons," Marguerite retorts, "I want you to know that I am an American citizen, and even though I am poor I have as much right as any other human being. Mrs. Kennedy was escorted to the hospital to see her husband. And I insist on being escorted and given enough security so that I may see my son too."

Agent Howard doesn't bother to argue with her anymore.

"All right, we'll take you to the hospital," he says. "But I want you to know that when we get there we will not be able to protect you. Our security measures end right there. The police will be in charge of your protection. We cannot protect you."

"That's fine," Marguerite replies. "If I'm to die, I will die that way. But I am going to see my son."

Gregory turns and glares at Marguerite sitting in the backseat.

"Mrs. Oswald, you are being so selfish," he snaps. "You are endangering this girl's life, and the life of these two children."

Marguerite is appalled that he would speak to her, a mother who has just lost a son, in that tone. It also ruffles her feathers that he is thinking of Marina's well-being, and not hers. She sees Mr. Gregory as another "Russian" sticking up for her Russian daughter-in-law, and it bothers her. "These Russian people are always considering this Russian girl," she thinks. "What about me?"

"Mr. Gregory, I am not talking for my daughter-in-law," she finally says. "She can do what she wants. I am saying, I want to see my son."

"I, too, want to see Lee," Marina says, somewhat diffusing the tension in the car.[1458]

Inside the rotunda, cameras rove over the statue of Abraham Lincoln as television commentator Edward P. Morgan puts into words what millions of Americans are feeling as they watch Jack Kennedy's family pay their last respects: "It is not the great solemn grandeur but the little human things that are almost too hard to bear . . ."

Suddenly, the network abruptly cuts into the flow of images with a bulletin: FLASH . . . LEE HARVEY OSWALD IS DEAD.

Morgan comments to his colleague, Howard K. Smith, "You keep thinking, Howard, that this is a dream from which you will awake—but you won't."[1459]

1:29 p.m.
The third-floor hallway at Dallas police headquarters has been packed with reporters for nearly two hours, awaiting a statement from Chief Curry. Unlike the previous two days, the corridor leading to the administrative offices is blocked by three uniformed police officers standing shoulder to shoulder.

When Chief Curry finally emerges from his office, he passes through the crowd without a word. The look on his face says everything. The press follows him down to the assembly room, where Curry takes a position at the front of the room. There is a scramble and a slight delay as cameramen and television crews get their equipment set up. Curry stands waiting, the very picture of dejection.

When the press is ready, Curry steps to the battery of microphones assembled before him.

"My statement will be very brief," he says. "Oswald expired at 1:07 p.m."

"He died?" one addled reporter in the back of the room asks.

"He died," Curry repeats, "at 1:07 p.m. We have arrested the man. The man will be charged with murder."

Curry then identifies the man as Jack Rubenstein and tells the media he goes by the name of Jack Ruby.

When the press start asking questions about Ruby, Curry responds firmly, "I have no other statements to make at this time," and promptly leaves the room.[1460]

Seth Kantor, a Scripps-Howard reporter in the assembly room, later writes, from his tape-recorded impression of what has transpired, "The boner of the Dallas Police Department [in failing to protect Oswald] would rank now with the building of the Maginot Line by the French to keep the Germans from marching into their country during World War II, when the Germans merely went around the thing. Remember the picture of the Frenchmen crying in the streets of Paris then? Only the tears were missing from the tragedy on Curry's face."[1461]

"Up until Oswald was shot," Dallas police sergeant Gerald L. Hill said, "we were smelling like a rose. Within a short period of time, street cops, sergeants, detectives, patrolmen, and motorcycle officers had caught the man who had killed the President of the United States, had lost an officer in the process, and had managed to do so without the FBI, Secret Service, or any of the other glory boys. Nobody could have faulted us for anything at that point."[1462]

1:58 p.m.

The metal door clangs open as a uniformed jail guard steps into the narrow corridor of the fifth-floor maximum-security block where FBI agent C. Ray Hall is interviewing Jack Ruby. "There's an attorney downstairs who wants to talk with Mr. Ruby whenever he's available," the jailer says.

"He's available right now," Hall says, then turns back to face Ruby. "Jack, why don't you go down and talk with him and we'll continue this when you get back."

The police give Ruby his clothes back and he gets dressed.

With Agent Hall and Detectives McMillon and Clardy in tow, Ruby is led down to the fourth-floor jail office and into a room where he confers privately with attorney Tom Howard, an old acquaintance who had represented him in the past. Their meeting lasts four minutes.[1463]

When Ruby comes out, Detective McMillon asks Dr. Fred Bieberdorf, who had returned from Parkland Hospital, to take a look at Ruby to see if he had any complaints or injuries as a result of the scuffle in the basement garage.

"I'm okay," Ruby says, taking off his suit coat. He shows Dr. Bieberdorf a few bruises on his right arm and wrist and assures him that they aren't bothering him.

"I have a great deal of admiration for the Dallas police," Ruby says. "They only did what they had to do. They didn't hurt me more than was necessary, no more than what I would expect. They were just doing their job and doing it very well."

In a few minutes, the doctor finishes the examination and Ruby is returned to his fifth-floor cell, where he is again stripped to his shorts, and FBI agent Hall resumes his questioning.[1464]

2:11 p.m. (3:11 p.m. EST)
Less than an hour after the eulogies ended in the rotunda of the Capitol on Sunday afternoon, the District of Columbia police reported that a serious problem was developing as people surged toward the Capitol building. The original plan called for closing the rotunda to the public at nine Sunday evening, but no one dreamed there would be such an incredible multitude of people who would show up for the opportunity to pay their final respects to the president, each allowed a maximum of thirty seconds of meditation at the president's casket. The decision is ultimately made to keep the rotunda open all night to accommodate the crowds.[1465]*

For the millions watching television at home, both in America and around the world via satellite, there is little relief from the images of people streaming into the rotunda. As has been the situation with all three networks since the assassination, there are no breaks for commercials or indeed for any of television's routine news, weather, or sports reports. To relieve the monotony there is little but endless replays of earlier events, although by now many viewers have seen the clips several times. With the constant regressions and recyclings of black-and-white footage, time seems to loop back on itself, becoming both fluid and petrified. Saturday afternoon exists in the same frame with Friday morning and Sunday evening. When time does advance, it does so in tiny, almost imperceptible increments. Early this morning the cameras caught a glimpse of the president's mother, Rose Kennedy, emerging from a church in Hyannis Port. At half past three in the afternoon she was briefly seen again, this time

---

*At midnight, police begin warning those at the rear of the line that extends for miles from the Capitol, that they might as well go home—the rotunda would be closed at nine in the morning in preparation for the burial later that day. Most paid no heed. (*New York Times*, November 26, 1963, p.10)

with her daughter Eunice Shriver and son Ted as they left Hyannis Port for Washington and tomorrow's funeral. An hour later the cameras' view shifted to Dulles International Airport to cover the arrival of France's head of state, General Charles de Gaulle, where he was met by Secretary of State Dean Rusk and a crew of State Department officers who will be on hand all evening to receive an unprecedented inflow of dignitaries—King Baudouin of Belgium, Chancellor Erhard of West Germany, Emperor Haile Selassie of Ethiopia, President Eamon De Valera of Ireland, and an English delegation including Prince Philip, Sir Alec and Lady Douglas-Home, the Duke and Duchess of Devonshire, and Harold Wilson and Jo Grimond, heads of the British Labour and Liberal parties.[1466]

Nearly a hundred nations have sent representatives—usually several—to form the largest assembly of ruling statesmen ever gathered in the United States, probably anywhere, for any event. Even the Soviet Union, which plans to broadcast the funeral in its entirety on state-run television, sends its first deputy premier, Anastas I. Mikoyan. The UN contingent includes Secretary-General U Thant, Dr. Ralph Bunche, and seven others. The European Coal and Steel Community sends two, the European Economic Community and Euratom one each, while the Vatican is represented by the Most Reverend Egidio Vagnozzi, archbishop of Myra and an apostolic delegate. Thirty state governors, twenty Harvard professors, and three Roman Catholic prelates arrive and scatter to their various destinations without any notice from television at all.[1467]

Among the televised arrivals there are a sprinkling of special programs. A memorial concert by the New York Philharmonic Orchestra, quickly organized and conducted by Leonard Bernstein, is broadcast, as well as "Largo" and "Requiem" performed by the Los Angeles Philharmonic Orchestra.[1468]

No one really knows how much the television coverage is costing the networks and local radio and television stations. The three networks normally earn a total of about fourteen million dollars each night alone from the sale of advertising during prime time, but when the revenues lost to hundreds of local stations is added in, the cost to the industry altogether could run to one hundred million dollars.[1469]

Although the waning day had been almost cloudless, it was cold and windy, the temperature dipping to thirty-nine degrees at midnight, but neither the cold nor the prospect of the long ordeal ahead daunt very many. As late as eleven o'clock, the line of people, several abreast, is still nine miles long.[1470] Everyone is there, toddlers as well as the elderly and infirm. Men and women on crutches and in wheelchairs wait as long as fourteen hours in the bitter cold. People accustomed to being driven to the Capitol entrance in limousines rub shoulders with those who have come by city bus, but they seem united in a single outpouring of grief. However controversial the young president had been to some just two days before, everyone is equally grieved at his passing and draws sustenance from being so tangibly a part of the vast multitude sharing their feelings. Here and there guitarists keep spirits up with folk songs, including the president's favorite, "Won't You Come Home, Bill Bailey?" There are spirituals like "Swing Low, Sweet Chariot" and songs from the burgeoning civil rights movement like "We Shall Not Be Moved." Some weep, some pray, almost all ask themselves and others, "Why?" The sheer senselessness of it all remains incomprehensible, indigestible, unbearable.[1471] In a way, not really believable.

As the evening wears on, the ropes around the coffin are moved inward to allow more people to circle it at the same time. The flow of humanity widens into a river, seemingly endless. Edward P. Morgan describes the atmosphere as a "mood of mutinous, somber sadness."[1472]

2:25 p.m.

Secret Service agent Mike Howard delivers the two Oswald women to a rear entrance at Parkland Hospital. All his attempts to dissuade them from going there have been stubbornly rejected by the voluble Marguerite. The agents escort the Oswald women and children into the freight entrance, where they are met by Nurse Doris Nelson and taken to the Minor Medicine and Surgery room near the emergency entrance.

"I'll have the doctor come in and talk to you," she tells them, and leaves to inform the medical examiner, Dr. Earl F. Rose, that they are there.

The hospital staff has already cleared and prepped the X-ray Department down the hall so that the family can view the body there. Under Dr. Rose's supervision, Oswald's body is placed on a hospital gurney and wheeled down from the second-floor operating room to the X-ray Department under heavy police guard. Nurse Nelson and several police officers help drape the body with sheets for viewing, while Dr. Rose heads down the hall to talk with the family.[1473]

Two nurse's aides attend to the babies while Marina and Marguerite, and their Secret Service escorts, follow Dr. Rose into the room near emergency.[1474] For some reason, no one thinks to go to the volunteer office and get Robert Oswald, or even inform him that his mother and sister-in-law are in the hospital.

"Now, you know," Dr. Rose warns them, "that Texas law says that we have to have an autopsy on the body."

"Yes, I understand," Marguerite says. She is sure that Marina, who was a pharmacist in the Soviet Union, understands as well.

"I understand that you wish to see the body," Rose continues. "Now, I will do whatever you ladies wish. However, I will say this. It will not be pleasant. All the blood has drained from him, and it would be much better if you would see him after he is fixed up."

"I am a nurse," Marguerite says. "I have seen death before. I want to see my son now."

"I want to see Lee too," Marina cries.

With that, Dr. Rose leads them down the hall into the X-ray Department and closes the door. Lee Oswald's body is lying under a sheet, his face visible. Several Dallas police officers are standing nearby.

Marina approaches the body and, to Marguerite's astonishment, pulls open his eyelids.

"He cry," Marina whimpers in broken English. "He eye wet."

"Yes," Dr. Rose replies softly.[1475]

Marina wants to see the wound that had killed him. She *has* to see it. She reaches out to lift the sheet away and someone grabs her arm and stops her. She leans down and kisses her husband. His flesh is cold. "In Russia," she thinks to herself, "it wouldn't have happened. They would have taken better care of him."[1476]

Marguerite doesn't touch the body, but sees enough to know beyond a shadow of a doubt that it is her son. She leaves the room with a parting shot for the police officers.

"I think some day you'll hang your heads in shame," she says. "I happen to know, and know some facts, that maybe my son is the unsung hero of this episode. And I, as his mother, intend to prove this if I can."[1477]

Down the hall, Robert Oswald waits in the purchasing agents' office, where the Secret Service has moved him in anticipation of seeing Lee's body.[1478] Soon, Marguerite, who is quite upset, and Marina, who has a look of shock about her, are brought down to join Robert.[1479] Marguerite, who believes Lee was an agent of the U.S. government, suggests to Robert that he should be buried at Arlington National Cemetery in Washington.

"Oh, Mother, forget it," he tells her.[1480]

The Oswald children are brought in and reunited with Marina. Chaplain Pepper asks that the hospital staff bring something for Marina to drink as she has had nothing all day and is trying to nurse the baby. The staff complies and brings in a tray of coffee.

Secret Service agents announce that they are leaving the case and that the Dallas police will be in charge of protecting the Oswald family. However, a few minutes later, after receiving orders to stay with the Oswalds until further notice, the agents tell them that they will continue to provide protection services.[1481]

Marguerite asks to speak to Chaplain Pepper in private. They adjourn to a side room and she tells him that she believes her son was an agent of the U.S. government and wants to have him buried in Arlington Cemetery.

"I would like you to talk to my son Robert," she says. "He does not listen to me, never has, ever since he joined the Marines. I don't know how the public will take the news that the FBI helped a Marxist, but I think my son should be buried in Arlington. Will you talk to Robert about it?" Marguerite rambles on in some detail about it, although she never really explains why she thinks Lee is an agent. She tells Pepper that financially she is in very poor straits and that she wants him to speak to Robert about having Lee buried in the national cemetery.[1482]

2:45 p.m.

Meanwhile, Mr. Geilich, Parkland's assistant administrator, is at the morgue entrance trying to get permission for Robert to view his brother's body. Rebuffed by the police, Geilich tells the Secret Service agents, who insist that Geilich return to the morgue and ask the medical examiner directly. "Under no circumstances can anyone else view the body," Dr. Rose tells him, after being called to the morgue entrance. "The legal requirements of family identification have been met and I'm not going to let anyone else in to view the body."

In fact, Dr. Rose has already begun taking a series of postmortem photographs of the corpse. Mr. Geilich returns and tells the Secret Service agents, who ask him to break the news to Robert since they would have to be with the family for the next several days and don't want to increase tensions. Geilich is relieved to find Chaplain Pepper in an adjoining room already telling Robert the medical examiner's decision. In a few minutes, Robert emerges and seems composed for the first time since hearing of his brother's death.[1483]

The Secret Service agents have two cars brought around to the freight entrance, but two-dozen photographers and reporters guessed right and are waiting for them.

"Do you have any comments?" they shout at the family as the agents hustle them into the cars. "Do you have anything to say?"

One of the photographers is nearly run over as the cars pull out at top speed.[1484] Several reporters jump into two waiting taxicabs and try to catch up. They nearly do, even though the two Secret Service cars are traveling at high speed. The agents with Robert Oswald radio the Dallas police and ask for assistance. Within minutes, four Dallas police cars appear, roar up behind the taxicabs, and force them to the side of the road. The two Secret Service cars bearing the Oswalds quickly disappear out of sight.[1485]

2:50 p.m.

On the fifth floor of Dallas police headquarters, following a meeting with attorney Tom Howard, FBI agent C. Ray Hall and Jack Ruby once again face each other across a table set up in the maximum-security cell block.

"Tell me about this morning, Jack," Hall says. "What did you do?"

"I left my apartment at about ten o'clock," Ruby replies, "and drove to the Western Union office at the corner of Main Street and the North Central Expressway. Before I left home, I put my revolver, a .38 caliber Colt, in my right coat pocket. After parking my car, I went into the Western Union office and sent a twenty-five-dollar money order to one of my employees, Karen Bennett. She had requested it. Sometime after sending the telegram, I entered the basement of City Hall."

"From which side?" Hall asks.

"From the Main Street side," Ruby replies.

"Did you use a press badge?" Hall asks.

"No," Ruby says.

"Did you help bring in a camera or press equipment?"

"No," Ruby says again. "I really don't want to say exactly how I got in, what time, or anything like that, but I will say that no one helped me in any way to get into the building."[1486]

"Then what happened?" Hall asks.

"When Oswald was brought out through the door," Ruby says, "I pulled my revolver and shot him. Believe me, I didn't plan to shoot him when I went into the basement."[1487]

"Then why did you bring your revolver with you?" Hall asks.

Ruby refuses to say.[1488]

"Did you talk to anyone about shooting Oswald?"

"No, I didn't," Ruby answers.

"Did you make any telephone calls to anyone about it?" Hall persists.

"No."

"Did you tell anyone directly or indirectly that you intended to shoot Oswald?" Hall asks.

"No," Ruby says again, "I made no plans to shoot Oswald. If he had confessed to shooting the president, I probably would never have even shot him."

"Why is that?" Hall asks.

"Because I think he would have been convicted in court," Ruby says, "but since he hadn't confessed, I was afraid he might be turned loose."

After a moment, Ruby says, "You know, hundreds of people probably had thought about doing what I did, but I knew that no one would do anything about it. Although, I must say, after I shot him, I wondered if I'd been a sucker."

"You acted alone then?" Hall asks.

"I was not involved in any conspiracy with anyone," Ruby replies. "No one asked me or suggested to me that I shoot Oswald."

"It was simply a compulsive act?" Hall asks.

"That's right," Ruby says.[1489]

3:15 p.m.

Amid a crush of reporters, Jack Ruby is escorted by detectives through the third-floor corridor to the Homicide and Robbery Bureau in a scene eerily reminiscent of those played out by Oswald over the past two days.[1490]

Captain Fritz, Secret Service agent-in-charge Forrest Sorrels, and Judge Pierce McBride await Ruby in Fritz's office. McBride reads a complaint signed by Captain Fritz to Ruby advising him that he is charged with shooting and killing Lee Harvey Oswald with "malice aforethought." A capital offense, no bond is set. Ruby is to remain a prisoner.[1491]

As Judge McBride leaves the room, Captain Fritz tells Ruby he would like to ask him some questions.

"I don't want to talk to you," Ruby answers. "I want to talk to my lawyers."

"Do you have an attorney?" Fritz asks.

Ruby says that he might get Tom Howard, Fred Bruner, Stanley Kaufman, Jim Arnton, or C. A. Droby to represent him[1492] and that he's already been advised by Mr. Howard.[1493] Captain Fritz asks a couple of questions about Ruby's legal name change and the prisoner begins to relax.

"If you'll level with me," Ruby tells him, "and you won't make me look like a fool in front of my lawyers, I'll talk to you."[1494]

In answers to Fritz's questions, Ruby says he bought his Colt revolver at Ray's Hardware and Sporting Goods store in Dallas, and that his roommate was George Senator. When the subject gets to Oswald, Ruby calls him a "Red."

"Do you think the Communists were behind the assassination?" Fritz asks.

"No, I think Oswald was alone in what he did," Ruby replies.

"How did you know who to shoot?" Fritz asks.

"I saw Oswald in the show-up room Friday night," Ruby tells him. "I knew who I was going for." Then Fritz asks Ruby point-blank, "Why did you shoot him?"

"I was all tore up over the president's killing," he says. "I built up a grief, and I just felt terribly sorry for Mrs. Kennedy and I didn't want to see her have to come back to Dallas for a trial."[1495]

The answers are coming quicker now. Secret Service agent Sorrels notices that Ruby is considerably more composed than he was when Sorrels questioned him shortly after the shooting.

"How did you get down in the basement?" Fritz asks.

"I came down the Main Street ramp, from outside," Ruby answers.

"No, you couldn't have come down that ramp," Fritz argues, "because there was an officer at the top and an officer at the bottom,* so you couldn't have come down that ramp."

Ruby senses a trap of some kind.

"I am not going to talk to you any more," he says. "I'm not going to get into trouble."[1496]†

Ruby doesn't say any more about how he got into the basement, but he does continue to talk to Captain Fritz, covering much of the same ground he did in previous interviews with the Secret Service and FBI agents. Ruby reiterates that the shooting of Oswald was due to a buildup of grief; that Saturday night he had driven around and that people were in nightclubs laughing and no one seemed to be in mourning; that he

---

*Fritz may have misspoken here, as there is no evidence that any Dallas officer was stationed at the bottom of the ramp.

†In a December 6, 1963, meeting between Captain Fritz and Tom Howard, attorney for Jack Ruby, Fritz asked Howard if Ruby knew the officer at the top of the ramp, to which Howard replied no. Fritz asked why, then, did Ruby refuse to discuss this point with him during questioning, and Howard stated that "the reason was because Ruby did not want to get the officer in trouble." (CE 2025, 24 H 438–439)

saw eulogies for the president on television and saw his brother Bobby Kennedy; that he had read about a letter that someone had written to "Little Caroline"; and that all of this had created a moment of insanity.

Ruby tells Fritz that he has a fondness for the police department, that he knows the Dallas Police Department is wonderful and that his heart is with them and that he had hopes that if ever there was an opportunity for participation in a police battle that he could be part of it with them. At one point he looks at Captain Fritz and says, "I don't want you to hate me."[1497]

For the most part, Ruby is cooperative. Some of Fritz's questions, however, are either met by a quick "I will not answer that," or ignored altogether. When Fritz asks him when he first decided to kill Oswald, Ruby simply talks about something else.[1498]

It doesn't take long for the interrogators to figure out that Jack Ruby is a colorful character. Agent Sorrels later wrote that at one time during the interrogation, Ruby asked Fritz, "I would make a good actor, wouldn't I?"[1499]

4:00 p.m.
Homicide detectives escort Jack Ruby past reporters and back to the jail elevator, where he is returned to his fifth-floor jail cell to face additional questioning from FBI agent C. Ray Hall.[1500] A few minutes later, Captain Fritz steps through the homicide office door and faces the press.

"Captain, is there any doubt in your mind that Oswald was the man who killed President Kennedy?" a reporter asks.

"No, sir," Fritz says, "there is no doubt in my mind about Oswald being the man. Of course, we'll continue to investigate and gather more and more evidence, but there is no question about it."

"Is the case closed or not, then, Captain?"

"The case is cleared," Fritz says, "but we'll be anxious to find out more about it—all we can find out."

"Captain, was anyone else connected with Oswald in the matter?"

"Well, now, not that I know of," Fritz replies.

"Did Jack Ruby say why [he shot Oswald], Captain?"

"Some of those things I can't answer for you," Fritz says. "And he, of course, has talked to his attorney, and there are certain things he didn't want to tell me. He did tell me that he had built up a grief. Those are his words, 'built up a grief.'"

"Captain, what excuse [is there for] letting him get that close?" someone finally asks.

"What excuse did *he* use?" Fritz asks back.

"No, what excuse do *you* all have, you know, that he got that close?"

Fritz can't believe the nerve of some people.

"I don't have an excuse," he snaps.[1501]

4:30 p.m.

FBI agent C. Ray Hall resumes his questioning of Ruby in Ruby's fifth-floor jail cell. Agent Hall asks Ruby to relate the events leading up to his shooting of Oswald.

"After I heard that the president had been assassinated," Ruby says, "I put signs in both my clubs, saying that they'd be closed until after the funeral on Monday. I didn't think anyone would be dancing until then." But as it turned out, they did, Ruby notes, clearly at a loss to understand how.

"That night," Ruby continues, "I went to the synagogue and heard Rabbi Silverman tell the assembly there that the assassination should make them better people. After services, I went to a delicatessen and had some sandwiches made up to take over to the Dallas Police Department. I called homicide detective Richard Sims and told him I knew how hard the police were working and that I wanted to bring some sandwiches down, but Sims said they had already eaten. So, I called radio station KLIF to see if they wanted them but I couldn't raise anyone on the phone."

Ruby explains that he went to the police station to see if he could get the control booth phone number from one of the KLIF reporters there. Ruby says he was in the hall when Oswald was taken to the assembly room late that night. He remembers that Oswald mumbled something as he went past him. After the midnight press conference, Ruby says he returned home, where he watched coverage of the assassination on television and read the newspapers.

Ruby tells Hall that on Saturday morning, November 23, he went down to Dealey Plaza and talked with Dallas police officer Jim Chaney, who was on duty there. Chaney had been one of the motorcycle escorts riding alongside the presidential limousine when the shots were fired.

"Then, what did you do?" Hall asks.

"I went home, watched television, and cried a great deal," Ruby tells him.

"Why?" Agent Hall asks.

"Because President Kennedy was my idol," Ruby says, his voice straining, "and it grieved me that this nut Oswald had done such a thing that brought so much grief to the people of Dallas and people all over the world."

Ruby says that on Saturday night he called Tom O'Grady, a friend and former member of the Dallas Police Department, and talked with him about the president's death.

"Did you talk about shooting Oswald?" Hall asks.

"No," Ruby says, "such a thought hadn't occurred to me at that time."[1502]

Agent Hall asks Ruby for a more detailed account of his activities, and the names of any other persons he has been in contact with during the past few days, but Ruby declines to do so.[1503]

Ruby does say that many grievances built up inside him until he reached the point of insanity. He says he was upset over the advertisement placed by Bernard Weissman that appeared in the *Dallas Morning News* the day of the assassination.

"I am proud that I'm a Jew," Ruby says, "and ashamed that anyone named Weissman would criticize the president."[1504]

Ruby says that he also read in the newspapers about Oswald's forthcoming trial and he thought that Jackie Kennedy would have to return to Dallas for the trial and he did not think she should have to undergo that ordeal.

"I saw Bobby Kennedy on television," Ruby says, "and I thought about how much he must have loved his brother. I read articles about the president's children and thought of the sorrow that had been brought upon them. I thought about how Bobby Kennedy would like to do something to Oswald but couldn't. I knew the Dallas police were also helpless to do anything to Oswald."[1505]

Ruby tells the FBI agent that he entered the basement from the Main Street side, but says he did not wish to say how he got into the basement (which he had already told Detective Clardy and Sergeant Dean).

Ruby says he's proud of the city of Dallas, thinks it is the greatest city in the world, particularly the way it's handled racial problems.

"I wanted to be something," Ruby says, "something better than anyone else."[1506]

5:00 p.m.

With the murder of Oswald, the Secret Service knew that it needed a more secure place for the Oswald family (Marguerite, Marina, Lee and Marina's two children, and Robert) to stay, and the Service chooses the Inn of the Six Flags, a large modern motel in Arlington, Texas. It becomes like an armed camp. Secret Service men, carrying M-1 carbines, and Arlington police officers patrol the perimeter around two adjoining rooms, 423 and 424, in the most isolated part of the inn. A few months out of the year the inn is overrun with people eager to see the "Six Flags over Texas" exhibition, but at this time of the year the place is nearly deserted. It becomes the perfect spot to keep the Oswalds under Secret Service protection. More Secret Service men turn up at the motel every few minutes, flying in from Washington, D.C., California, and other parts of the United States. It seems that the motel is serving as some sort of regional headquarters.

"All we need is to have one more of you killed," an agent tells Robert Oswald.

Although at least some of the agents have been thinking they would be turning the operation over to the FBI at any moment, it doesn't turn out that way. After a telephone call from Secret Service inspector Kelley, Agent Howard tells Robert Oswald, "It looks like we are going to take care of

Marina and your mother." But Howard adds that "it seems to me that they're overlooking you." Mike Howard checks back with Inspector Kelley, who apparently consults with a higher authority in Washington. Later, Howard tells Robert, "They've talked to the president and he has expressed concern for you and the entire family. So has the attorney general."

Robert is struck by the reference to Robert Kennedy. Is the attorney general concerned simply because he is the nation's top law enforcement official, or can Kennedy, out of the depths of his own grief, have fashioned some genuine personal concern for the mother, wife, brother, and children of the man accused of assassinating his brother?[1507]

6:00 p.m.

The eleventh-floor offices at the Dallas headquarters of the FBI in the Santa Fe Building at 1114 Commerce Street (just two blocks west of Jack Ruby's Carousel Club) are quiet. Most of the stenographers and clerks, having worked late on Friday and Saturday, are off duty. Jim Hosty is filled with foreboding when Ken Howe, his supervisor, stops at his desk to tell him that both of them have been summoned by the special agent-in-charge, Gordon Shanklin. They make their way to the twelfth floor together.

Shanklin, it seems to Hosty, is not bearing up well under the strain. Working on as little sleep as his men and under far more pressure, Shanklin is additionally fielding repeated calls from Hoover and other top bureau officials in Washington. Hosty knows that every aspect of the bureau's conduct concerning the Oswald file is under intense scrutiny and that both he and Agent John Fain, who handled parts of the case earlier, are in the hot seat.

Now, to make things worse, the bureau has turned up some newspaper articles from a couple of years ago, interviews with Marguerite Oswald when she visited Washington, D.C., to buttonhole lawmakers about her son, then living in Russia. Even then, she was telling anyone who would listen that Lee was an FBI agent. There isn't a scrap of evidence in the files that points to any FBI involvement with the defector, but that will hardly mollify J. Edgar Hoover, whose jealous guardianship of the bureau's reputation is a watchword in the FBI.

The interview is short, tense, and unpleasant. Shanklin, standing behind his desk, does not invite Hosty to be seated. Looking over his shoulder, Hosty sees that Howe is standing in the doorway, watching. Shanklin reaches down into a desk drawer and comes up with Oswald's scrawled threat and the memorandum Hosty filed on it.

"Jim, now that Oswald is dead, there clearly isn't going to be a trial," Shanklin says, handing the note and memorandum to Hosty. "Here, take these. I don't ever want to see them again."

Hosty looks perplexed and Shanklin can read it in an instant.

"Look, I know this note proves nothing," Shanklin says, cigarette smoke billowing from his nostrils, "but you know how people will second-guess us."

Hosty knows that those "people" are Hoover and his assistants, whose Monday-morning quarterbacking is legendary within the bureau. Hosty begins tearing up the Oswald note on the spot.

"No! Not here!" Shanklin practically screams. "I told you, I don't want to see them again. Now get them out of here."

Hosty walks back to his desk. There's a shredder in the office, but Hosty realizes he can't do it there—he has to be alone. He walks out to the stairwell, down a half flight of stairs, and into an empty men's room. He continues tearing up the note, and his accompanying memorandum, into tiny bits and tosses them into the toilet.

Two short paragraphs, poorly written by a half-wit no one could have taken seriously, have become dynamite. To some, they might prove that the FBI knew, or should have known, two weeks before the president's visit, that Lee Harvey Oswald was potentially dangerous, and should have notified the Secret Service so Oswald could have been put on the Secret Service's "risk list," or security index, of the loonies who are detained or watched when the nation's chief executive comes to town. Worse yet, someone might even conclude that it was Oswald's rage at the FBI that tipped him over the edge and sent him off to murder the president.

Hosty flushes the toilet and watches the swirling water suck the fragments of paper into the oblivion of the Dallas sewer system. He fears his career with the Federal Bureau of Investigation is going down with them.[1508]

7:30 p.m.

Robert Oswald gets a call from Parkland Hospital from somebody who wants to know what is to be done with his brother's body. In the rush of the afternoon, Robert hasn't even thought about funeral arrangements. He turns to Secret Service agent Mike Howard for help. Howard puts in a call to a friend, Paul J. Groody, the director of the Miller Funeral Home. In a moment, Groody is on the line and asks Robert, "What kind of casket do you want?"

Robert isn't interested in an elaborate casket, but he does want an outer vault that will be safe from vandals. The funeral director promises to take care of everything as soon as the hospital releases the body to him.[1509]

Official Washington is increasingly concerned about the wave of paranoia building up in the country as the inevitable result of the fragmentary and halting flow of information from Dallas about the assassination. The media in the United States have been remarkably reluctant to speculate about the possibility of involvement of others in an assassination plot, but the Europeans have not been so circumspect. Speculation in the foreign press is running wild, partly because unlike the United States, European leaders are rarely assassinated by lone gunmen, conspiracies being the norm.

Communist Party newspapers in France, unable to cope with the idea that the killing of Oswald by Ruby is without broader political significance, are convinced that Oswald was eliminated in the execution of a plot. Even the staid *Le Monde*, France's journal of record, hit the streets in the early afternoon with an entire page devoted to "serious doubts" about the Dallas police and to what the two killings appear to reveal about American society. That question is of peculiar interest to Europeans, who, although they rarely question America's assumed right to lead the world, are often uneasy about it.

"What's happening, what's going on?" a bewildered diplomat asks as he leaves the requiem mass for the president in the cathedral of Notre Dame in Paris. "This isn't the America we look to for leadership. How do we answer our anti-American radicals now?"

The state of Texas and the Dallas police have already emerged as the villains. *Le Monde* notes that Texas, "rich and conservative," is a state that largely financed the late Senator Joe McCarthy. Reporting on the pamphlets distributed in Dallas accusing the president of treason, the paper says this indicates "the enormous publicity Americans give to the most fantastic accusations." The French want to know how Jack Ruby ever got close enough to kill Lee Oswald, and they frankly do not believe the story given by the Dallas police.

The English are putting the same questions to the American press: Is there a plot in which the Dallas police are involved, and is lawlessness taking over in the United States? Americans in London—or anywhere else, for that matter—have no easy answers, but there is a general feeling that the evidence against Oswald must be brought out fully and very quickly.

The Justice Department is moving swiftly to do just that, insofar as it is able. Although there is "strong evidence" for Oswald's guilt, a department spokesman assures the press that "the case will not be closed until all the facts are in and every lead followed up."[1510]

Premier Fidel Castro, one head of state who was conspicuously not invited to the funeral, airs his views on the assassination in a two-hour televised address to the Cuban people. He calls Kennedy's murder "grave and bad news from the political point of view." He notes that it could change U.S. foreign policy regarding Cuba from bad to worse.

"As Marxist-Leninists," he says, "we recognize that the role of a man is small and relative in society. The disappearance of a system would always cause us joy. But the death of a man, although this man is an enemy, does not have to cause us joy. We always bow with respect in front of death. The death of President Kennedy can have very negative repercussions for the interests of our country, but in this case it is not the question of our interest, but of the interest of the whole world." Noting that President Johnson has assumed office without the moral authority of having been elected, Castro fears the ascendancy of reactionary forces.[1511]

9:25 p.m.
Around five o'clock, Dallas district attorney Henry Wade awakened from a brief nap and heard a national television commentator accuse the Dal-

las police of letting Oswald be killed, and giving Wade hell for saying the "case was closed," even though Wade knows he never made any public statement to this effect. Three hours later, Wade makes his way to police headquarters on the third floor and meets with the police brass; everyone except Chief Curry, who is not available.

"People are saying that you had the wrong man and you led Oswald out there to have him killed, intentionally," Wade tells them. "Somebody ought to go out on television and lay out the evidence that you have on Oswald and tell them everything." Wade is told that Curry would have to approve. Meanwhile, determined to see that it is done, the district attorney walks down the hall to Captain Fritz's office, grabs a notepad and pencil, and begins listing from memory the crucial pieces of evidence against Oswald. It isn't long before the police brass get hold of Curry and he tells them no statement will be made like this by the Dallas police, that he had given his word to the FBI that he would no longer speak out on the evidence.

"Look, you're the ones that know about this," Wade pleads. "If you've got the right man, the American people ought to know. You can't use the evidence anyway, he's dead. You can't try him. Tell the public what you have on Oswald. I think you've got a good case."

Wade's pleas have no effect on Curry's decision; the police will not make a statement and that's final. When Wade asks police to give him details about the evidence so he can present it to the press, they refuse to cooperate. Stubbornly, and foolishly, Wade decides to face the press anyway.[1512]

"The purpose of this news conference," Wade tells an assembly room full of reporters and cameramen, "is to detail some of the evidence against Oswald for the assassination of the president."

Pulling from his memory and a page of hastily jotted notes, the district attorney offers a hodge-podge of fact and misinformation that ultimately causes more harm than any good he intended.

"As all of you know," he says, "we have a number of witnesses that saw the person with the gun on the sixth floor of the Book Store Building." (Many took Wade to mean that Oswald was seen by a number of witnesses; however, the only eyewitness who claimed to have seen Oswald, specifically, was Howard Brennan.) Among many accurate statements in his recitation of the evidence against Oswald, Wade went on to make about nine or ten misstatements, including, for example, telling the press that right after the shooting in Dealey Plaza, Oswald's name and description had gone out over the police radio (only his description had); that Oswald told the bus driver the president had been shot (he didn't); that the Tippit killing took place a block or two from Oswald's rooming house (the distance was nine-tenths of a mile); and that three witnesses saw Oswald shoot Tippit three times (the evidence thus far is that Tippit was shot four times, and only one witness, at that time, was known to have actually seen Oswald kill Tippit).

After running through the list of evidence, Wade fields questions from the reporters.

"Do you know whether Oswald's been recognized as a patron of Ruby's nightclub here?" a reporter asks.

"I don't know that," Wade replies.

"Do you know of any connection between Mr. Ruby and—?"

"I know of none," Wade shoots back.

"Are you investigating reports that [Oswald] might have been slain because Ruby might have feared he would implicate him in something?"

"The police are making an investigation of that murder," Wade says. "I don't know anything about that. Although charges have been filed, it will be presented to the grand jury on Ruby immediately within the next week and it'll probably be tried around the middle of January."

"Has the district attorney's office closed its investigation of the assassination of the president?"

"No, sir," Wade replies. "The investigation will continue on . . . with reference to any possible accomplice or—that assisted him in it."

"Do you have any suspicions now that there were?" someone asks.

"I have no concrete evidence nor suspicions at present," Wade says.

"Would you be willing to say in view of all this evidence that it is now beyond a reasonable doubt at all that Oswald was the killer of President Kennedy?"

"I would say that without any doubt he's the killer," Wade answers firmly.

"That case is closed in your mind?" a reporter asks.

"As far as Oswald is concerned, yes," Wade tells them, asserting the very thing that angered Wade when a national television commentator accused Wade of saying it.

"What do you think Oswald's motive was?" someone asks.

"Don't—can't answer that," Wade says.

"How would you evaluate the work of the Dallas police in investigating the death of the president?" a reporter asks.

"I think the Dallas police did an excellent job on this," Wade replies, "and before midnight on [the day Kennedy] was killed had the man in custody and had sufficient evidence to convict him."

"Is there any doubt in your mind that if Oswald was tried that you would have him convicted by a jury? With the evidence you have?"

"I don't think there's any doubt in my mind that we would have convicted him," Wade replies. "But, of course, you never know what—we've had lots of people we thought—but somebody might hang the jury or something, but there's no question in my—"

"As far as you are concerned," a reporter interrupts, "the evidence you gave us, you could have convicted him?"

"I've sent people to the electric chair on less," Wade replies.

Speaking of the electric chair, a reporter wants to know if Wade will also seek the death penalty against Ruby. Wade says, "Yes."[1513]

By the time the district attorney gets back to the third-floor police administrative offices, there is a phone call from an FBI inspector, asking him, "Please don't say anything more about the case."[1514]

9:45 p.m.

Robert Oswald finds that getting his brother's body released from the morgue for burial turns out to be more difficult than it sounds. Parkland Hospital refuses to release the body merely on the basis of a phone call, even from a Secret Service agent. Eventually a procedure is worked out. Parkland will give a message to the Dallas police with a secret password. The police will pass it on to the Secret Service at the Six Flags motel. They will tell Robert, and Robert will call the hospital, saying only the password to the person who answers. When the time comes, Robert places the call to Parkland. Administrator Bob Struwe answers the phone.

"Malcolm," Robert says.

"All right," Struwe replies and hangs up.

The password was the first name of one of the emergency room surgeons, Malcolm Perry, who tried so hard to save the lives of both Jack Kennedy and Lee Oswald.[1515]

All through the night, the three national TV networks silently cover the endless procession of mourners past the president's bier, only making periodic observations, such as that the music in the background in the rotunda is Beethoven's Seventh Symphony, second movement—a dirge; of the changing of the guard every half hour; of Washington police announcing that mourners were still lined up for three miles, five abreast; the temperature dipping to thirty-two degrees, freezing, at 3:15 a.m. EST; Jersey Joe Wolcott, former heavyweight champion of the world, filing past the coffin; and so on.[1516] The president's body would lie in state for eighteen hours. By the time the viewing in the rotunda is over at nine Monday morning, a quarter of a million mourners have filed silently past the body of the fallen president, and five thousand have been turned away. At the tail end of the line allowed in before the rotunda was closed were a group of nuns, who had been waiting since 1:00 a.m.[1517]

Monday, November 25

8:30 a.m.

Robert Oswald has been up for two hours in his two-room suite at the Inn of the Six Flags. He telephones Paul J. Groody, funeral director at the Miller Funeral Home, and learns that Laurel Land Cemetery on Old Crowley Road in Fort Worth will hold the burial service. Groody admits, though, that he is having a hard time locating a minister to give the service. Robert can only shake his head in disgust and says he'll start telephoning ministers in the Dallas–Fort Worth area to find one to conduct the burial services. They both agree to set the funeral for four o'clock that afternoon.

Marguerite Oswald pounces on the photograph of Jack Ruby in the morning newspaper, her first glimpse of the man who killed her son. She brings it to Robert. "This," she whispers to him dramatically, "is the same man the FBI showed me a picture of Saturday night" (referring to the man outside the Russian embassy in Mexico City).

"All right, Mother," he barks. "If that's so, don't tell me. Tell the Secret Service man right over there."

Robert is offended, impatient. He has had a lifetime of his mother's cunning conspiracies, all of them somehow designed to prevent Marguerite from being recognized as the pivotal figure she has always imagined herself to be. If the FBI had really showed Marguerite a photo of Jack Ruby before Ruby shot Lee, Robert is certain that the Secret Service agents will report the episode to the proper authorities. Right now, he doesn't want to hear any more about it.

Robert begins telephoning ministers in the Dallas–Fort Worth area. He is absolutely astonished at the reactions of the ministers he speaks to. One after another flatly refuses to even consider his request to have someone officiate at his brother's funeral. One minister, a prominent member of the Greater Dallas Council of Churches, says sharply, "No, we just can't do that."

"Why not?" Robert asks.

"We just can't go along with what you have in mind."

Robert has only the simplest possible funeral service in mind and can't understand what the minister means. Then he hears the minister say, "Your brother was a sinner."

Robert hangs up and breaks down.

Robert Oswald is still making phone call after phone call into the late morning to find a clergyman when Marina tells him she wants to watch the funeral service for President Kennedy. Robert switches the television on. As they wait for the sound to come on, one of the Secret Service agents says, "Robert, I don't think you all should watch this." He leans down to switch it off.

"No," Marina says firmly. "I watch."

As they watch the funeral services in Washington, a call comes in for Robert. It is Chaplain Pepper, from Parkland Hospital, asking whether all the funeral arrangements have been taken care of. Robert tells him about the reactions he's been getting from the ministers in the area.

"It seems to me that there are a lot of hypocrites around," Robert tells him. "After all, can the assassination be the act of a sane man?"

"Maybe I can convince some of the ministers by raising that question," the chaplain says. "They surely would agree that you can't hold an insane person responsible for his acts."[1518]

9:23 a.m. (10:23 a.m. EST)

In Washington, D.C., the weather, milder than yesterday, is still raw and wintry with whipping winds. But the day is crystal clear, with deep and hard-edged shadows. Six limousines wait in the White House driveway to convey the Kennedy family to the Capitol rotunda. Jackie Kennedy appears first, quickly followed by Pat Lawford, Bobby, Teddy, Eunice Shriver, and other Kennedy in-laws and children. The late president's children, Caroline and John-John, are notably absent—their mother is sending them on ahead to St. Matthew's Cathedral, where she will meet them for the Low Pontifical Mass. She has planned to spare the children the trip to the cemetery as well.

It takes thirteen minutes for the motorcade procession to reach the Capitol plaza, where Jackie and the president's brothers once again climb the broad, imposing flight of steps to the rotunda. They kneel briefly at the coffin, back away, and leave, reentering their limousine for the trip back to the White House.

It takes another seven minutes for the military pallbearers to remove the flag-draped casket from the rotunda and place it on the caisson that will bear it down Constitution Avenue and then Pennsylvania Avenue to the White House and then to St. Matthew's on Rhode Island Avenue, N.W. The huge crowds lining the streets are so quiet that the clop of hooves, the grating of the caisson's iron tires on the pavement, and the mournful tolling of the bell at nearby St. John's Episcopal Church are easily heard on the radio and television broadcasts being listened to and seen by a global audience.

It is now a full military funeral procession, including the Marine Band—called "the President's Own"—and crack drill units from all four academies, army, naval, air force, and coast guard, and it takes about three-quarters of an hour for the slow-moving cortege to reach the front of the White House.[1519] The funeral procession stops in front of the White House around 11:35 a.m. EST, where the Kennedy family leaves its limousines and joins the ranks of foreign heads of state, reigning monarchs, and dignitaries who had gathered in front of the White House. After several minutes, the procession sets out on foot, with Mrs. Kennedy, the first First Lady ever to walk in her husband's funeral procession, and the slain president's two brothers on each side of her, leading the way on the long eight-block march to St. Matthew's Cathedral.

It's a bodyguard's nightmare. Walking bareheaded, in plain view of any potential sniper, are twenty-two presidents, ten prime ministers, and much of the world's remaining royalty—kings, queens, princes, and emperors. There are more than two hundred officials from a hundred countries, the United Nations, other international organizations, and the Roman Catholic Church. An estimated one million people line the funeral procession route.[1520] The Secret Service, seeing the obvious danger, urges the president to ride to the funeral in a bulletproof car, and Johnson considers it for a moment, but refuses. He and Lady Bird walk along right behind the Kennedys, trailed by the color guard with the presidential flag.[1521]

The great phalanx of luminaries marches straight into the lens of the television camera, the front line dominated by the towering figure of General Charles de Gaulle.* Queen Frederika of Greece is remarkable as the

---

*Murray Kempton and James Ridgeway would write in the *New Republic*, "It had been less than three years since Mr. Kennedy had announced that a new generation was taking up the torch. Now, old General de Gaulle and old Mr. Mikoyan were coming to see him buried" (Kempton and Ridgeway, "Romans," p.10).

only woman dignitary visible.[1522] They set out to the skirl of pipes played by the band of the Royal Highland Black Watch Regiment, which interrupted an American concert tour to appear at the funeral, at Jackie's behest. Just twelve days earlier the renowned pipers had played on the White House south lawn for the Kennedy children and seventeen hundred other children, and the president put aside his own duties to view their performance. It would be the last public appearance of the presidential family together.[1523]

Shoulders erect and her eyes straight ahead, Jackie Kennedy, as one observer noted, bearing her grief "like a brave flag," walked with a poise and grace as regal as any king or queen who followed her. Indeed, the *London Evening Standard* was moved to say extravagantly, "Jacqueline Kennedy has given the American people from this day on the one thing they have always lacked—majesty." UPI's Helen Thomas said, more soberly, that Mrs. Kennedy had "hidden tears and kept a decorum that few women could under such circumstances."[1524]

Arriving at the cathedral just before noon (EST) the family is greeted by Richard Cardinal Cushing, an old and beloved friend, who comes out to meet them. Cushing, the archbishop of Boston, had married John and Jacqueline, christened their two children, and only last August buried their infant son, Patrick Bouvier Kennedy, who died thirty-nine hours after his birth. He bends to the two children, kissing Caroline and patting John-John on the head, then puts a comforting arm around Mrs. Kennedy's shoulder.[1525]

As the military pallbearers, who seem to be carrying the weight of the world, struggle up the steps of St. Matthew's, the familiar voices of the television commentators are drenched in emotion.[1526] By far the largest television audience in history, perhaps even to this day, had been watching the historic events unfold. In America alone, an estimated 93 percent of all sets, and 175 million people, were transfixed by the images on the screen, and Relay, a U.S. communications satellite orbiting the globe, brought segments of the events into the homes of twenty-three other countries; for the citizens of Russia, it was the first time they had ever been permitted to watch live television from abroad. The apex of the viewing audience seemed to be the funeral. *National Geographic* magazine, with representation worldwide, captioned a portion of their 1964 article, "World Stops at Moment of Funeral." The magazine reported that "for the next few minutes [referring to the casket being brought from the limousine to the cathedral portico], whatever the hour in other lands, countless millions of the earth's people paused to honor the dead President . . . Across our nation trains stopped. Jets halted on airport runways. The Panama Canal suspended operations. Motorists paused in New York's Times Square. Evening traffic halted in Athens, Greece. Around the world flags stood at half-mast."[1527]

11:00 a.m.

At police headquarters, Jim Leavelle, the lead detective in the Tippit murder case, is sipping coffee in the squad room with a couple other detectives, waiting for Captain Fritz when Fritz calls.

"Are you in a position to talk?" Fritz asks.

"No, not really," Leavelle says.

"Well, go into my office and pick up the phone in there," Fritz tells him.

Leavelle quietly saunters to the privacy of Fritz's office.

"What's up?" he asks.

"I'm down here at the Greyhound bus station with Graves and Montgomery," Fritz says. "We've cased the county jail and it looks clear. I'm going to make a suggestion to you, and if you don't think it will work, I want you to tell me."

"Okay," Leavelle replies, wondering just what Fritz has up his sleeve.

"Go get Ruby out of jail any way you want to, and bring him down in the elevator to the basement," Fritz says. "We'll pull through the basement at a prearranged time, load him up, and whisk him right on down to the county jail with another squad car following us. Do you think it will work?"

"Yes," Leavelle agrees. "I think it will the way you've got it set up."

"I haven't called [Sheriff Bill] Decker or asked the chief about it," Fritz admits.

"Well, all you can do is get bawled out," Leavelle says, "but a bawling out is better than losing a prisoner."

The two homicide men set about conspiring to move Ruby in secret.

"How many men you got there to help you with him?" Fritz asks.

"Three or four," Leavelle answers.

"Okay. Don't tell anybody where you're going," Fritz orders. "Just get them like you're going after coffee and get downstairs or somewhere and tell them what you're going to do. I'll meet you in the basement at exactly eleven-fifteen."

The two men synchronize their watches.

"Okay, Captain," Leavelle says, and hangs up. He walks out into the squad room and without a word motions to Detectives Brown, Dhority, and Beck to follow him. The men follow, their curiosity piqued.

A reporter squares off with Leavelle the minute the detectives step into the third-floor hallway.

"When are you going to transfer Ruby?" the newsman asks.

"Oh, I don't know," Leavelle says coyly, and keeps walking.

When they get downstairs, Leavelle outlines the plan. He tells Brown and Beck to get another car out of the garage and get it in position to go out the ramp. He and Dhority go up to the fifth floor and check Ruby out of jail. They bring him down to the basement in the jail elevator, the same elevator Oswald rode on his fateful journey. Leavelle, who has known Ruby and been friendly with him (though not friends) since 1951, says to Ruby on the way down, "Jack, in all the years I've known you, you've never deliberately caused any police officer any trouble that I know of [but] you didn't do us any favor when you shot Oswald. You've really put the pressure on us." Ruby replied, "That's the last thing in the world I wanted to do. I just wanted to be a damned hero and all I've done is foul things up."

"Wait here," Leavelle tells Dhority, who has a tight grip on Ruby's arm, as they reach the basement.

Leavelle slips out of the elevator, letting the door close behind him. He looks at his watch. They're only two minutes early.

"Don't let anybody ring for this elevator," he tells the unaware lieutenant standing behind the booking desk. "We're going to have it tied up."

Detective Brown talks casually with one of the jail officers just outside the jail office door, his eyes glancing at the top of the Main Street ramp every now and then. A few feet away, Detective Beck sits behind the wheel of an unmarked squad car, its motor running.

Brown spots Captain Fritz's car, with Detective L. D. Montgomery driving and Fritz in the passenger's seat, pulling into the Main Street ramp. Brown turns and nods toward Leavelle, who opens the elevator door so Dhority and Ruby can step out.

"I don't want to have to push or shove you," Leavelle tells Ruby, whom he hasn't bothered to shackle himself to. "But I want you to move."

Ruby is shaking, afraid another vigilante is lying in wait for *him*. Captain Fritz's car glides to the bottom of the ramp and stops. Detective Graves, in the rear seat on the far side, leans over to open the rear door and when he does, Ruby dashes away from Leavelle and Dhority, as astonished jail officers look on, running to the open door where he crawls on his hands and knees onto the floorboard in the backseat and lies on his stomach.* Leavelle follows Ruby into the backseat and places his feet on Ruby's back. "Jack was frightened and that's where he wanted to stay," Leavelle said, referring to Ruby's prone position on the car floorboard, which he would stay in all the way to the county jail. The car leaves the basement garage with Dhority, Brown, and Beck in the backup car. The two-car caravan catches every green light en route to the county jail. When they arrive, the detectives in the lead car get out and cover the jail entrance. In a matter of seconds, Jack Ruby is safely inside the county jail.[1528]

11:18 a.m. (12:18 p.m. EST)
At St. Matthew's Cathedral in Washington, the cameras inside pick up the last of the mourners as they crowd into the church. Admission is by invitation only, but in spite of the planners' best efforts, the green-domed

---

*"How come you weren't handcuffed to Ruby?" I asked Leavelle. "No need to," Leavelle said. "Jack wasn't going anywhere I didn't want him to. If he did, I'd know where to find him," he added in the special dry wit of Texans. (Telephone interview of James Leavelle by author on November 19, 2004)

edifice is overflowing with a thousand people, many uninvited. The casket rests at the foot of the altar as Cardinal Cushing, in the Pontifical Low Requiem Mass, prays "for John Fitzgerald Kennedy and also for the redemption of all men . . . May the angels, dear Jack, lead you into paradise." First Mrs. Kennedy, then Robert and Ted Kennedy and hundreds in attendance receive Holy Communion from the cardinal, and Bishop Philip Hannan gives an eleven-minute sermon in which he quotes liberally from the late president's speeches.[1529]

New York Times reporter R. W. Apple describes his city as being "like a vast church," where schools and businesses are closed and four thousand people stand silently in Grand Central Station to watch the funeral rites on a huge television screen, some of them genuflecting or making the sign of the cross. At anchor at Bayonne, New Jersey, the aircraft carrier *Franklin D. Roosevelt* fires its deck guns twenty-one times, once a minute from 12:00 noon to 12:21.[1530]

"For those who are faithful to You, Oh Lord, life is not taken away; it is transformed," Cardinal Cushing says solemnly. He blesses the casket with holy water.[1531]

Outside the cathedral, after the one-hour funeral service, John-John stands hard by his mother as the casket is brought out, still clasping a pamphlet he was given as a distraction while sitting out the main body of the mass with a Secret Service agent in a cathedral anteroom. As the coffin is returned to the caisson, Jackie bends to her young son, takes the pamphlet from his tiny hand, and whispers something. In a heartbreaking gesture, the president's son, who turned three today, cocks his elbow and salutes his father's casket. Spectators standing across the street almost buckle at the sight. Of all the images burned into the consciousness of America, nothing comes close to the power of that tiny salute.[1532]

As the caisson starts to roll, the heads of state and other dignitaries stand about waiting for their cars—the distance to Arlington National Cemetery is much too far to walk. Two former presidents, Dwight Eisenhower and Harry Truman, passionate political enemies only a few years earlier, walk to their car together. The muffled drums begin again, a constant rumble that nonetheless fails to drown out the spirited clack of the hooves of Black

Jack, the magnificent sixteen-year-old riderless horse with a sword strapped to the empty saddle and stirrups holding empty boots pointed backward, a part of an ancient tradition in the funeral procession of a fallen leader, symbolizing that he will never ride again. The family cars roll slowly in behind the honor guards, followed by President Johnson's automobile and the ever-present Secret Service. One by one the other vehicles fall into position in the one-hour, three-mile-long procession, which snakes along Connecticut Avenue to Seventeenth, and then Constitution to the Lincoln Memorial, where it crosses the Potomac River on the Memorial Bridge to Arlington National Cemetery, where only one other president is buried, William Howard Taft. David Brinkley muses that the first cars are quite likely to arrive at Arlington before the last cars depart St. Matthew's Cathedral. The cameras mark time by showing faces from the crowd of ordinary Americans: a young priest, a soldier in dark glasses, a college boy holding a radio to his ear, an older woman clutching a large purse, and a family eating their lunch on the curb.[1533]

As the cortege starts across the bridge, the cameras catch stunning shots from the heights on the Virginia side, the Lincoln Memorial perched majestically in the background. Waiting at attention at the bridgehead, facing the memorial in the far distance, are members of the army's ceremonial Old Guard Fife and Drum Corps in their blazing red tunics and tricorn hats, a colorful reminder of the country's revolutionary origins.[1534]

The matched gray horses begin to labor as they pull the caisson up the winding roadway that leads to the 420-acre, one-hundred-year-old cemetery situated on land once owned by Confederate general Robert E. Lee. Last spring President Kennedy stopped here to relax and enjoy the view of the sparkling city across the river. "I could stay up here forever," he remarked.[1535] Just fourteen days ago, November 11, the president, himself a decorated navy veteran of World War II, had driven here with his son John Jr. to lay a Veterans' Day wreath on the Tomb of the Unknown Soldier, which is close to his grave site.[1536]

As the procession nears the site of the open grave on a sloping hillside, the Irish Guard, a crack drill unit President Kennedy admired on his

recent trip to Ireland, stands at parade rest. The casket advances slowly to
the wail of bagpipes. As it reaches the grave site, a flight of fifty jet fight-
ers, one for each state, thunders overhead at a speed so fast they precede
their own sound. One position, in the otherwise perfect V-formation, is
left empty, in accordance with air force tradition. The last plane to fly
over, at a terrifying altitude of just five hundred feet, is the president's
personal jet, Air Force One, dramatically dipping its wings in tribute.[1537]

The roar of the jet engines soon gives way to the silence of a hillside of
somber faces. Cardinal Cushing intones the final prayer: "Oh God,
through Whose mercy [the] souls of the faithful find rest, be pleased to
bless this grave and . . . the body we bury herein, that of our beloved Jack
Kennedy, the thirty-fifth President of the United States, that his soul may
rejoice in Thee with all the saints, through Christ our Lord. Amen."[1538]

The network pool camera sweeps over the line of military graves to
the Custis-Lee Mansion on the hill above the ceremony, then cuts to Mrs.
Kennedy. As each fusillade of the twenty-one-gun salute from three 76-
millimeter canons is fired over the grave by the riflemen of the Old Guard,
she shudders.

Cardinal Cushing asks the Holy Father to grant John Fitzgerald
Kennedy eternal rest, and bugler Sergeant Keith Clark steps forward to
play taps. His lips are chilled blue—he has been waiting in the cold wind
on the exposed hillside for three hours—and one note cracks, adding an
unexpected poignancy to the mournful air.[1539]

The flag folding begins. The camera moves in for close-ups of the white-
gloved hands rapidly creating the traditional triangular bundle of the great
flag, which has until now draped the casket. The flag is rapidly passed
through the honor guards from hand to hand until it reaches John C. Metzler, superintendent of the cemetery, who turns and places it in the hands
of the young widow, whose lips, for the first time in public, visibly tremble. The Cardinal sprinkles holy water on the coffin, and Mrs. Kennedy,
touching a torch to a jet of gas, lights the eternal flame.* Their hands locked
in embrace, Bobby Kennedy then leads Jackie from the grave.[1540]

---

*The idea of the eternal flame at Kennedy's grave site, one that would glow forever, was
Jackie's. She had seen one under the Arc de Triomphe in Paris (one of only two in the world, the

Although the rites are concluded at 3:15 p.m. EST,[1541]* television lingers at the scene, giving the commentators a chance to recall special moments from the four-day ordeal. Somehow television itself, improvising blindly to cover a unique event in the history of the medium, has become a major component of the larger historical event, and those who constructed that effort are already beginning to realize that some of them are inextricably woven into the texture of the experience—the sad eyes of Walter Cronkite, the poetic irony of Edward P. Morgan, the righteous anger of Chet Huntley. The television images have also conveyed the feelings of a nation, something that was impossible to adequately express in words.

Jacqueline Kennedy has one further official duty to attend to, and despite her mental state, it is of her own choosing. She will receive the foreign dignitaries who had come to the funeral from more than one hundred countries at the White House. "It would be most ungracious of me not to have all those people in our house," she says, and manages a smile and thank you for each of them. JFK had once said of Jacqueline, "My wife is a shy, quiet girl, but when things get rough, she can handle herself pretty well."[1542]

Approaching midnight, Bobby Kennedy, alone with Jacqueline on the second floor of the White House, says quietly, "Should we go visit our friend?" After gathering up lilies of the valley she had kept in a gold cup

---

other at Gettysburg), and insisted on one for her husband, saying she didn't want the country to ever forget him. Her request threw those around her, as well as those in charge of the funeral, into a tizzy, no one knowing how to produce such a device—at one point prompting Richard Goodwin, a JFK assistant and writer, to bark into the phone at an officer at nearby Fort Myers, "If you can design an atomic bomb, you can put a little flame [one that wouldn't die] on the side of that hill." The military ended up passing, resorting instead to the yellow pages of the telephone directory under "Gas Companies," and securing a modified road torch supplied by the Washington Gas & Light Company. (Manchester, *Death of a President*, pp.550–552)

*A quarter hour after the Kennedy family had left the cemetery, the president's coffin was lowered into the grave under the vigilant eyes of the network television cameras. It's 3:32 p.m. Three minutes later, under orders from John C. Metzler, Arlington Cemetery's superintendent, the power to the network cameras was cut to allow the final stages of the burial to be carried out in private. Shortly thereafter, the burial vault was sealed, the grave filled with dirt, a picket fence erected around the plot, and the surrounding ground dressed with evergreen boughs and flowers. (Manchester, *Death of a President*, p.604; 3:32 p.m.: ARRB MD 134, Funeral Arrangements for John Fitzgerald Kennedy, November 25, 1963, p.3, "at precisely 3:32 p.m., the casket was slowly lowered into the ground"; see also *New York Times*, November 26, 1963, pp.2, 4)

on a table in the hall, they arrive at the cemetery at 11:53 p.m. in their black Mercury, followed by a car with two Secret Service agents. In the presence of only Secret Service agent Clint Hill, two military policemen, and the cemetery superintendent standing at a distance, and the only light being that from the flickering eternal flame, blue in the night, the attorney general and former First Lady drop to their knees and pray silently. Rising, Jackie places the spray of lilies on the grave. Together, they turn and walk down into darkness and into lives that would never be the same.[1543]

1:30 p.m.

Earlier in the day Robert Oswald had gotten a call from Miller Funeral Home director Paul Groody and learned, to his horror, that Laurel Land Cemetery was refusing to accept his brother's remains for burial. Groody had also called other area cemeteries, but everyone had refused, staying away from Oswald's body the way the devil stays away from holy water.

"What do they say?" Robert asked.

"The one in Fort Worth is associated with Laurel Land Memorial in Dallas," Groody explained, "which is where Officer Tippit will be buried."

That, Robert can understand.

"The rest offer vague reasons," Groody continued.

Robert and the funeral director agreed that the rest of the cemeteries are acting out of nothing short of prejudice. Christian charity, it seems, doesn't extend to the presumed assassin of President Kennedy. Groody promised to make arrangements elsewhere as soon as possible.[1544]

Groody now finally calls back and tells Robert, to his great relief, that arrangements for Lee's burial have been secured with Rose Hill Cemetery in Fort Worth, and he is continuing in his search for a minister. The burial will take place at four o'clock and Robert knows he has just three and a half hours to find a minister. He thanks Groody for his help and hangs up.

Shortly thereafter, two Lutheran ministers show up at the Inn of the Six Flags. While one waits in the lobby, the other, Reverend French, is escorted to meet with Robert and his family. The minister takes a seat on the sofa, with Robert and Marguerite on each side of him. It is obvious from the start that Reverend French is not eager to officiate at any services for Lee Oswald, and refuses, despite Robert's request, to hold any kind of service in a church. Robert begins crying, trying to get the minister to agree to his wishes, but the reverend only quotes scriptures, referring to Lee as a "lost sheep."

"If Lee is a lost sheep," Marguerite snaps, "then he is the one who should go to church! The good people do not need to go to church. If he is a murderer, then it is he we should be concerned with."

A Secret Service agent steps over to them.

"Mrs. Oswald, please be quiet. You are making matters worse," he says, rankling Marguerite.

Reverend French reluctantly gives in, agreeing to officiate at the services as long as they are held in a cemetery chapel, not a church. Two Secret Service men who are in the room confirm with the minister the time for the service—4:00 p.m.—and make sure he knows how to get to Rose Hill.[1545]

1:50 p.m.

At the Dallas county jail, Jack Ruby is interrogated once again, this time by FBI agents C. Ray Hall and Manning C. Clements. In the presence of his lawyers, Melvin Belli, Joe Tonahill, Sam Brody, and William Choulous, he talks about seeing Oswald coming out of the jail office just as he got to the bottom of the Main Street ramp. "To me," he says, "he had this smirky, smug, vindictive attitude. I can't explain what impression he gave me, but that is all I can . . . well, I just lost my senses. The next I know I was on the ground and five or six people were on top of me." He said that when Oswald killed Kennedy, "something in my insides tore out."[1546]

2:00 p.m.

In Dallas seven hundred uniformed policemen from throughout the state of Texas congregate at the Beckley Hills Baptist Church to honor the other victim of Friday, Officer J. D. Tippit, gunned down by Lee Oswald on a quiet back street of Oak Cliff. Largely overlooked by the millions absorbed in the grand spectacle in Washington, the funeral of Tippit nonetheless attracts around fifteen hundred citizens of Dallas, over a thousand of whom, unable to find room inside the 450-seat red-brick church, mill around outside, while many others watch the ceremony on local and closed-circuit television. An organist, nearly hidden by a bank of flowers five feet high, plays "The Old Rugged Cross," and the choir, perhaps overly conscious of the cameras trained on them, sing with unusual stiffness.

In the front row, Tippit's widow, Marie, is flanked by her brother Dwight and J. D.'s neighbor and fellow officer, Bill Anglin, while Marie's other brother, Norvell, looks after two of the thirty-nine-year-old fallen officer's three children, Brenda, ten, and Curtis, four. His oldest son, Allen, thirteen, sits next to them. The pews behind them are filled with J. D.'s mother and father, brothers, sisters, nieces, nephews, cousins, and close friends; their faces stained with tears as they bid farewell to the man that they, and many others, considered "a lovable guy."[1547]

Others, some from far beyond the southern suburbs of Dallas where J. D. was a familiar and reassuring figure, have not forgotten the fallen hero. Contributions to the bereft family's welfare have been flowing into the police department ever since the nation learned that the policeman's $7,500 life insurance policy wouldn't take his family very far. Donations have been arriving from all over the country—Boy Scout troops, police departments, church groups, mothers, fathers, and even children have been reaching out from every state. In a child's handwriting, one letter contained the simple words, "This money is yours because your daddy was brave." Enclosed was a dollar bill. Each member of the Detroit Lions football team contributed $50 for a total of $2,000, two brokers collected $5,000 on the floor of the New York Stock Exchange, and Walter H. Annenberg, the publisher of the *Philadelphia Inquirer*, paid off the $12,217 mortgage on the Tippit home. Newspapers even report that two prisoners serving life terms raised $200 for the Tippit fund from the inmates of a Texas prison.[1548]

Within months, forty thousand pieces of mail containing close to $650,000 in donations are given to the Tippit family, the largeness of the amount perhaps being partially attributable to NBC commentators Chet

Huntley and David Brinkley, each telling a national television audience that calls were coming in to the network urging that in lieu of flowers for the late president, money should be sent to J. D. Tippit's family, care of the Dallas Police Department.* Marie Tippit is grateful for the nation's kindness, and treasures forever a gold-framed photograph of the president's family inscribed by his widow: "There is another bond we share. We must remind our children all the time what brave men their fathers were." And the president's brother, Attorney General Robert F. Kennedy, and President Johnson personally call the thirty-nine-year-old widow to express their sympathies.[1549] President Johnson wanted her to know, Marie Tippit said, that her husband "gave his life for a good cause"—that Oswald may not have been caught "had he not given his life."[1550]

"Today we are mourning the passing of a devoted public servant," the Reverend C. D. Tipps Jr. says. "He was doing his duty when he was taken by the lethal bullet of a poor, confused, misguided, ungodly assassin—as was our President."[1551]

After the eulogy, Mrs. Tippit is helped forward. She weeps softly as she takes a long, last look at her husband in the open casket. Then, she turns away, dabbing her eyes with a handkerchief, and is helped from the church. Six police pallbearers carry Tippit's gray casket to the waiting hearse.[1552]

A fifteen-man motorcycle escort then leads the cortege to the rolling hills of Laurel Land Memorial Park where J. D. Tippit will be laid to rest in a special plot set aside for Dallas's honored dead.

*In a court distribution on October 21, 1964, Mrs. Tippit received $312,916 in cash, and a trust fund for $330,946 was set up for the Tippit children. Also, $3,716 went to policemen's and firemen's funds. ("$650,000 for Family of Man Killed by Oswald," p.9)

At least financially, Mrs. Tippit would now have no worries. In an AP interview during the weekend after her husband's death, Marie Tippit said, "We always kept thinking we'd put money [aside], but with three kids it just never worked out. It was one payday to the next." Tippit's police salary when he died was $490 per month. She said that to get by, her husband "worked at Austin Barbecue Friday and Saturday nights and at the Stevens Park Theater Sundays." Her eyes swollen with tears as she sat in her neat, three-bedroom, pink-brick home, she spoke lovingly of her husband. "He was very quiet, likeable—almost a lovable guy . . . He was a good father. He always told the kids, 'If you're going to do a job, do it right or not at all.' There was no hollering around here. He wanted me to stay at home and take care of the children." (*Pittsburgh Post-Gazette*, November 25, 1963, p.2)

At the grave site, three-dozen red roses are laid across the casket as family and friends gather under the green awning that brings a bit of relief from the hot Texas sun. Tippit's slender, blue-eyed widow is unconsolable as the minister says a final prayer. Tears can be seen on many of the faces of the stiff-backed policemen standing at attention nearby.[1553]

Marie Tippit and her three children turn away at last.

"Oh God, oh God," she sobs.[1554]

4:00 p.m.

Just outside Fort Worth, two unmarked cars hurry along a back road toward Rose Hill Cemetery. Secret Service agents Mike Howard and Charley Kunkel are riding with Marguerite, Marina, and the children in one of them; Secret Service agent Roger Warner, Arlington police officer Bob Parsons, and a Tarrant County sheriff's deputy accompany Robert in another. Robert Oswald finds the long ride unusually depressing, largely because of the attitudes of the people he has encountered while making the arrangements for his brother's funeral. As they near the cemetery, the driver breaks the gloomy silence.

"What about that car behind us?"

Bob Parsons, cradling an M-1 carbine in the backseat next to Robert, turns around.

"It's just two old ladies," Parsons says, "but one of them has a burp gun."

Everyone laughs, even Robert, who hasn't laughed in three days. He knows that Parsons is trying to shake him from his depression, and he's grateful.

The Secret Service and the Fort Worth police have set up a heavy guard at Rose Hill, with uniformed officers posted every few yards along the fence surrounding the cemetery.

All cars are stopped and thoroughly searched at the main gate.

They drive to the chapel perched on a low hill. A number of people are standing quietly at the fence line, staring at the grave at the bottom of the hill. They enter the chapel and find it completely empty. There is no sign of any preparation for a funeral service.

"I don't understand," Robert says to Mike Howard and Charley Kunkel. The two agents are equally puzzled. Two or three minutes later one of them comes back with the story.

"We were a few minutes late," he says. "There's been some misunderstanding and they've already carried the casket down to the grave site. We'll have a graveside service down there."

It is the final emotional straw. Robert hits the wall with his fist. "Damn it!" he says loudly.

The agent decides that it's probably better not to tell Robert the rest of the story just now. In the absence of pallbearers—the accused assassin has no close friends—Lee's coffin, an inexpensive, cloth-covered wooden box, had to be carried down to the grave from the chapel by six of the reporters assigned to the story, three from the *Fort Worth Star-Telegram*.

On the way out of the chapel, as Robert hurries back to the car, a photographer walks backward in front of him, snapping off pictures. Robert wants to punch him, but manages to control himself, and climb into the car. Bob Parsons, ordered to stay in the car with the carbine, is waiting for him.

"You're doing all right now," Bob says soothingly. "Just hold on."

They drive down a curving road to the grave site. One of the Secret Service men turns to Parsons and says, "All right now, you stay in the car with the carbine. If anything happens, come out shooting."

"Nothing would give me greater pleasure than to mow down fifteen or twenty reporters," Parsons quips.

The funeral director, Paul Groody, introduces the caretaker of Rose Hill to Robert, explaining that the man agreed without hesitation, though at some risk to his own job, to sell the plot to the family. Groody tactfully suggests that the man's risk might be lessened if Robert, in speaking of the plot, were to create the impression that the plot has been in the family for some time—as though the cemetery itself had no choice in the matter. Robert, moved by the caretaker's warmth and compassion, readily agrees.

The Lutheran minister who had promised to officiate over the services is not there. The Secret Service learn that he won't be coming out at all. Fortunately, Reverend Louis Saunders, executive secretary of the Fort

510

Vincent Bugliosi

Worth Council of Churches, is willing to step in. Hastily summoned by Fort Worth police chief Cato Hightower, Saunders drove out to Rose Hill to do what he can. He hasn't presided at a burial in over eight years, but felt that "someone had to help this family."

The Oswalds take their seats on several of the five battered aluminum chairs placed at the grave site under a faded green canopy. Marina, dressed in a simple black dress and beige coat, holds June while Marguerite cradles the baby, Rachel, in her arms. Inexplicably, there are two floral arrangements, a white blanket of carnations and a spray of red carnations, from someone named Virginia Leach.

Marguerite is annoyed at the crowd of police, Secret Service men, reporters, and Rose Hill employees gathered there. "Privacy at the grave," she pleads, "privacy at the grave."[1555]

When a French reporter whispers something to Marina in Russian, Robert tries to shoo him away. When the reporter persists, Robert stands up and starts to move on him, but Marina quickly turns to her brother-in-law and says in broken English, "He says sorrow."

Robert turns to Secret Service agent Mike Howard and tells him he plans to have the coffin opened and would like to have all reporters and spectators moved back. The agent nods and in the late-autumn afternoon a dozen plainclothes officers move the seventy-five or so newsmen back from the grave, forming a protective, semicircular barrier. Beyond the cemetery fence there is a scattering of onlookers, who have guessed what is going on at the grave.[1556]

The undertaker opens the coffin to give the family one final look at Lee Oswald. Marina kisses her husband, dressed for burial in a dark brown suit, white shirt, brown tie, and brown socks. She slips two rings on his finger. Her stoic, almost distant composure dissolves into bitter sobs. The two infants, hearing Marina, cry loudly as Robert and Marguerite take a long, last look at Lee's face. As they return to their chairs, the gaunt Reverend Saunders steps up to conclude the stark service.

"God of the open sky and of the infinite universe, we pray and petition for this family who are heartbroken. Those who suffer and who have tears in their hearts will pray for them . . . Their need is great."

For Lee Harvey Oswald he reserves the final words: "May God have mercy on his soul."

It's over in twenty minutes. After the service, Marguerite, Marina, and the children are escorted back to the car to return to the Inn of the Six Flags. Robert lingers for a moment to watch his brother's coffin lowered into the steel-reinforced concrete vault. He finally returns to his waiting family and the two-car caravan drives off.

The grave diggers work hard to get the grave filled before dark, watched by a sprinkling of reporters and a few spectators. Finally, a light bulldozer moves in to help. The two floral arrangements are tossed onto the mound of raw earth. Two policemen are ordered to start an around-the-clock watch on the grave.

"We like to think Fort Worth folks are even-tempered," Chief High-tower explains, "but we can't take any chances. We don't want this grave bothered."

As the crowd melts away, a few more of the onlookers beyond the fence slip over and come down to collect a few souvenir clods of dirt from the assassin's grave.[1557]

Four of the darkest days in American history are finally over.

In an address to a joint session of Congress two days later, President Johnson says:

> All I have I would have given gladly not to be standing here today.
>
> The greatest leader of our time has been struck down by the foulest deed of our time. Today John Fitzgerald Kennedy lives on in the immortal words and works that he left behind. He lives on in the mind and memories of mankind. He lives on in the hearts of his countrymen.
>
> No words are sad enough to express our sense of loss. No words are strong enough to express our determination to continue the forward thrust of America that he began.
>
> The dream of conquering the vastness of space, the dream of

partnership across the Atlantic—and across the Pacific as well—
the dream of a Peace Corps in less-developed nations, the dream of
education for all of our children, the dream of jobs for all who seek
them and need them, the dream of care for our elderly, the dream
of an all-out attack on mental illness, and above all, the dream of
equal rights for all Americans, whatever their race or color—these
and other American dreams have been vitalized by his drive and by
his dedication. And now, the ideas and ideals which he so nobly represented must and will be translated into effective action . . . No
memorial or oration or eulogy could more eloquently honor President Kennedy's memory than the earliest possible passage of the
civil rights bill for which he fought for so long. We have talked long
enough about equal rights in this country. It is time now to write
the next chapter and write it in the books of law.

The landmark Civil Rights Act of 1964 quickly followed.

Abbreviations Used for Citations

AFIP, Armed Forces Institute of Pathology
ARRB, Assassination Records Review Board
ARRB MD, Assassination Records Review Board, Medical Deposition
ASAIC, assistant special agent-in-charge (Secret Service)
CD, Warren Commission document
CE, Warren Commission exhibit
DA, district attorney
DMA, Dallas Municipal Archives (formerly the Dallas Municipal Archives and Records
    Center)
DOJ, Department of Justice
DOJCD, Department of Justice, Criminal Division
DPD, Dallas Police Department
FOIA, Freedom of Information Act
H, Warren Commission hearings and exhibits (volumes 1–15 are testimony; volumes 16–26
    are exhibits)
HPSCI, House Permanent Subcommittee on Intelligence
HSCA, House Select Committee on Assassinations (12 volumes)
JCS, Joint Chiefs of Staff
KISS-SCOW, Kissinger-Scowcroft
LBJ, Lyndon Baines Johnson
NARA, National Archives and Records Administration
NAS-CBA, National Academy of Science's Committee on Ballistic Acoustics
NSA, National Security Agency
ONI, Office of Naval Intelligence
SA, special agent
SAC, special agent-in-charge (FBI)
SAIC, special agent-in-charge (Secret Service)
SSCIA, Senate Select Committee on the CIA
WC, Warren Commission
WCT, Warren Commission testimony
WR, Warren Report
Z, Zapruder film

Source Notes

1. 1 H 65–66, 69, 72, 121–122, WCT Marina N. Oswald; 3 H 68, WCT Ruth Hyde Paine; McMillan, *Marina and Lee*, pp.524–525; Manchester, *Death of a President*, p.111.
2. McMillan, *Marina and Lee*, p.73.
3. 1 H 22, 46, 52, 64–66, WCT Marina N. Oswald; 2 H 515–516, 3 H 41, 44–47, WCT Ruth Hyde Paine; height and weight of Oswald: CE 1981, 24 H 7; McMillan, *Marina and Lee*, pp.515–517.
4. 2 H 508, 3 H 46, 56–57, 9 H 414–415, WCT Ruth Hyde Paine; 1 H 65, WCT Marina N. Oswald; lonesome for girls: McMillan, *Marina and Lee*, p.521.
5. 1 H 65–67, 69, WCT Marina N. Oswald; McMillan, *Marina and Lee*, pp.524–525; teaches part-time: 4 H 448, WCT James Patrick Hosty.
6. McMillan, *Marina and Lee*, p.525; 1 H 70, 72, WCT Marina N. Oswald; 3 H 112–113, WCT Ruth Hyde Paine.
7. 1 H 72, WCT Marina N. Oswald; 3 H 112, WCT Ruth Hyde Paine; McMillan, *Marina and Lee*, pp.525, 544; Manchester, *Death of a President*, p.111.
8. 2 H 225–226, WCT Buell Wesley Frazier.
9. 2 H 248–250, WCT Linnie Mae Randle.
10. 2 H 241, 245–246, WCT Linnie Mae Randle.
11. 3 H 34, WCT Ruth Hyde Paine.
12. 2 H 248, WCT Linnie Mae Randle; 2 H 224, WCT Buell Wesley Frazier.
13. 2 H 220, WCT Buell Wesley Frazier.
14. 2 H 220, 228, WCT Buell Wesley Frazier.
15. 2 H 226, WCT Buell Wesley Frazier; CD 87, p.491, Secret Service interview of Buell Wesley Frazier on December 7, 1963.
16. 2 H 216, WCT Buell Wesley Frazier.
17. 2 H 216, 220, WCT Buell Wesley Frazier.
18. Wills and Demaris, *Jack Ruby*, pp.22–23; Hunter and Anderson, *Jack Ruby's Girls*, pp.11, 16–17; live on their tips: see CE 1322, 22 H 506–507, where there is no reference to salaries for waitresses and cocktail girls.
19. Hunter and Anderson, *Jack Ruby's Girls*, pp.11–15; Wills and Demaris, *Jack Ruby*, p.23.
20. 14 H 177, WCT George Senator; CE 1477, 22 H 897.
21. Crafard Exhibit No. 5226, 19 H 353–354.

22. Hall (C. Ray) Exhibit No. 3, 20 H 47.

23. 13 H 204, WCT Bruce Ray Carlin; 13 H 206, 210, WCT Karen Bennett Carlin.

24. Sneed, *No More Silence*, pp.490–491; CE 1561, 23 H 49–51, FBI interview of Janet Adams Conforto on December 4, 1963. From *No More Silence: An Oral History of the Assassination of President Kennedy*, © 1998 Larry A. Sneed. Published by University of North Texas Press.

25. 15 H 210–211, WCT Thomas Stewart Palmer; CE 2265, 25 H 190, FBI interview of Max Rudberg.

26. CE 2251, 25 H 176.

27. 15 H 248–249, WCT Norman Earl Wright.

28. CE 2399, 25 H 380–381.

29. Holloway, *Dallas and the Jack Ruby Trial*, p.21; Kantor, *Ruby Cover-Up*, p.332; 14 H 316, WCT George Senator; CE 2411, 25 H 482.

30. Manchester, *Death of a President*, pp.29, 112; Bishop, *Day Kennedy Was Shot*, p.5.

31. Manchester, *Death of a President*, p.112.

32. Manchester, *Death of a President*, pp.61, 63; Crown: Beschloss, *Taking Charge*, p.17.

33. Manchester, *Death of a President*, p.62; Bishop, *Day Kennedy Was Shot*, p.6.

34. CE 2647, 25 H 917; 2 H 227, WCT Buell Wesley Frazier.

35. 2 H 227–229, WCT Buell Wesley Frazier; 3 H 214, WCT Roy Sansom Truly; CD 897, p.148, FBI interview of Buell Wesley Frazier on March 11, 1964, p.1; CE 361, 16 H 957; CD 87, p.2; CD 5, p.318; FBI Record 124-10062-10262, FBI Briefing Book, "Texas School Book Depository: Photographs, Floor Plans, Parking Lots," photographs 38 and 39, parking lot diagram; see also CD 496.

36. 2 H 227–228, 239, WCT Buell Wesley Frazier.

37. 2 H 228, WCT Buell Wesley Frazier.

38. 2 H 213, 228–229, 232, WCT Buell Wesley Frazier; CD 5, pp.317–318.

39. Collier and Horowitz, *Kennedys*, pp.201–202; Nichols, "President Kennedy's Adrenals," p.129; Reeves, *President Kennedy*, p.43; O'Brien, *John F. Kennedy*, pp.25–26; "sick all the time": Dallek, *Unfinished Life*, p.37.

40. Reeves, *President Kennedy*, pp.43, 146–147; Baden with Hennessee, *Unnatural Death*, p.14.

41. Reeves, *President Kennedy*, pp.42–43.

42. Manchester, *Death of a President*, pp.55, 63; Dallek, *Unfinished Life*, p.196.

43. Collier and Horowitz, *Kennedys*, p.210 footnote.

44. 2 H 125, WCT William Robert Greer.

45. Manchester, *Death of a President*, pp.106, 112; Bishop, *Day Kennedy Was Shot*, pp.21, 43.

46. O'Donnell and Powers with McCarthy, *Johnny, We Hardly Knew Ye*, pp.429–430; Manchester, *Death of a President*, p.8.

47. WR, pp.1, 12; Connally and Herskowitz, *From Love Field*, pp.65–68, 142; Jackie Kennedy enjoying herself: 7 H 456, WCT Kenneth P. O'Donnell.

48. Newseum with Trost and Bennett, *President Kennedy Has Been Shot*, p.7.

49. Manchester, *Death of a President*, pp.112, 117.

50. Manchester, *Death of a President*, p.113.

51. Manchester, *Death of a President*, pp.89, 113.

52. 7 H 441–442, 444, WCT Kenneth P. O'Donnell.

53. *Dallas Morning News*, November 22, 1963.

54. *Dallas Times Herald*, November 21, 1963.

55. CE 996, 18 H 646.

56. WR, pp.292, 298; CE 1365, 22 H 617.

57. Curry, *JFK Assassination File*, p.7; CE 1378, 22 H 630; *Dallas Morning News*, November 21, 1969.

58. *New York Times*, October 25, 1963, pp.1, 6; McKeever, *Adlai Stevenson*, pp.538–539.

59. *New York Times*, October 26, 1963, p.1; *Dallas Morning News*, October 27, 1963, pp.A1, A22.

60. *Dallas Morning News*, October 27, 1963, p.A1.

61. HSCA Report, p.36; Schlesinger, *Thousand Days*, pp.1020–1021; Manchester, *Death of a President*, pp.38, 41, 44.

62. *Dallas Morning News*, November 22, 1963; Manchester, *Death of a President*, p.113; HSCA Report, p.35.

63. *New York Times*, November 25, 1966, p.30.

64. HSCA Report, p.36.

65. Connally, "Why Kennedy Went to Texas," p.86B; Manchester, *Death of a President*, p.3; only city: Holland, *Kennedy Assassination Tapes*, p.3.

66. 1 HSCA 11–15; Connally, "Why Kennedy Went to Texas," p.86A.

67. Hlavach and Payne, *Reporting the Kennedy Assassination*, pp.44–45.

68. Connally and Herskowitz, *From Love Field*, p.62.

69. O'Donnell and Powers with McCarthy, *Johnny, We Hardly Knew Ye*, p.viii; most powerful member: "Fateful Two Hours without a President," p.69.

70. Collier and Horowitz, *Kennedys*, p.180.

71. Collier and Horowitz, *Kennedys*, pp.223–224.

72. CE 1362–1377, 22 H 614–629; CE 2646–2647, 25 H 916–918.

73. Kantor Exhibit No. 4, 20 H 406.

74. MacNeil, *Right Place at the Right Time*, p.202.

75. Kantor Exhibit No. 4, 20 H 406.

76. Audio recordings of the president's address, November 22, 1963, Sixth Floor Museum at Dealey Plaza, Dallas, Texas; Manchester, *Death of a President*, p.114.

77. Manchester, *Death of a President*, p.114.

78. Manchester, *Death of a President*, pp.116–117.

79. Manchester, *Death of a President*, p.117.

80. *New York Times*, November 24, 1963, p.12; Manchester, *Death of a President*, pp.117–118.

81. WFAA-TV Collection, November 22, 1963, PKT-1; KRLD-TV Collection, November 22, 1963, reels 1 and 1A, Sixth Floor Museum at Dealey Plaza; *New York Times*, November 24, 1963, p.12; Manchester, *Death of a President*, p.117; Bishop, *Day Kennedy Was Shot*, p.78; dreaded idea of looking ridiculous: Vanocur, "Kennedy's Voyage of Discovery," p.42.

82. 3 H 165–166, WCT Bonnie Ray Williams; 3 H 215, WCT Roy Sansom Truly.

83. 3 H 200, WCT James Jarman Jr.

84. Since January of 1962: File CO-2-34030, Secret Service Report, December 7, 1963.

85. 3 H 215–216, WCT Roy Sansom Truly.

86. 3 H 213–214, 217–218, WCT Roy Sansom Truly.

87. 3 H 199–200, WCT James Jarman Jr.

88. 3 H 201, WCT James Jarman Jr.; see also Transcript of *CBS News Inquiry: The Warren Report*, part I, June 25, 1967, p.6, CBS Television Archives.

89. Manchester, *Death of a President*, pp.120–121.

90. CE 1031, 18 H 835.

91. O'Donnell and Powers with McCarthy, *Johnny, We Hardly Knew Ye*, pp.25–26; Manchester, *Death of a President*, p.121.

92. Manchester, *Death of a President*, pp.14, 35.

93. 7 H 456, WCT Kenneth P. O'Donnell.

94. Manchester, *Death of a President*, p.122.

95. Manchester, *Death of a President*, pp.121–124; Bishop, *Day Kennedy Was Shot*, pp.101–104.

96. 14 H 177, 288–289, WCT George Senator; CE 1478, 22 H 897; Wills and Demaris, *Jack Ruby*, p.3.

97. CE 1499, 22 H 900; CE 2321, 25 H 281; Hall (C. Ray) Exhibit No. 3, 20 H 49.

98. WR, p.334.

99. CE 2405, 25 H 388.

100. 5 H 183, WCT Jack L. Ruby; Wills and Demaris, *Jack Ruby*, p.12.

101. CE 2321, 25 H 281–282; recently dated: CE 1479, 22 H 900.

102. CE 2436, 25 H 563; Aynesworth with Michaud, *JFK: Breaking the News*, p.16; cafeteria on second floor: Telephone interview of Bob Miller, longtime *Dallas Morning News* employee, by author on September 13, 2005.

103. 15 H 535, 538–539, WCT John Newnam; CE 2263, 25 H 189; preparing his ad: CE 1479, 22 H 900.

104. On the third floor: Telephone interview of Bob Miller by author on September 13, 2005.

105. Hlavach and Payne, *Reporting the Kennedy Assassination*, pp.106–107.

106. 5 H 183–184, WCT Jack L. Ruby; CE 2405–2406, 25 H 386–390, 392, Campbell's testimony at Ruby's trial; WR, p.334; (in Hall [C. Ray] Exhibit No. 3, 20 H 48, Campbell's name is mistakenly written as "Connors"); CE 2436, 25 H 563; 15 H 539, WCT John Newnam; WR, p.335; trouble with Jada: 15 H 410–412, WCT Nancy Monnell Powell ("Tammi True").

107. O'Donnell and Powers with McCarthy, *Johnny, We Hardly Knew Ye*, p.27; Manchester, *Death of a President*, p.67.

108. O'Donnell and Powers with McCarthy, *Johnny, We Hardly Knew Ye*, pp.26–27.

109. 11:40: CE 1024, 18 H 724, 730, 733; Angel: Manchester, "Death of a President," *Look*, p.36.

110. U.S. Department of Commerce, Weather Bureau, Surface Weather Observations, Dallas, Texas, Love Field, November 22, 1963, p.3.

111. O'Donnell and Powers with McCarthy, *Johnny, We Hardly Knew Ye*, p.27.

112. 2 H 67, WCT Roy H. Kellerman.

113. Hlavach and Payne, *Reporting the Kennedy Assassination*, p.72.

114. Connally and Herskowitz, *From Love Field*, p.2.

115. CE 705, 17 H 458–459; Sawyer Exhibit A, 21 H 389; CE 1974, 23 H 909.

116. "Discovering History with a Car Collector," p.46; United Press International, November 23, 1963; *New York Times*, November 23, 1963, p.9; Manchester, *Death of a President*, p.134.

117. 2 H 66, WCT Roy H. Kellerman; 2 H 129, WCT William Robert Greer.

118. 2 H 129, WCT William Robert Greer.

119. 2 H 65, WCT Roy H. Kellerman; 2 H 114, WCT William Robert Greer; 5 H 107, WCT Hon. J. Edgar Hoover; retractable running boards: Model and Groden, *JFK: The Case for Conspiracy*, p.163.

120. 7 H 445–446, WCT Kenneth P. O'Donnell; 4 H 349, WCT Winston G. Lawson; Manchester, *Death of a President*, p.122.

121. 3 H 163–164, WCT Bonnie Ray Williams.

122. 3 H 165, WCT Bonnie Ray Williams.

123. 6 H 352–354, WCT Charles Douglas Givens.

124. 6 H 349, WCT Charles Douglas Givens.

125. 3 H 168, WCT Bonnie Ray Williams.

126. 3 H 171, WCT Bonnie Ray Williams.

127. McMillan, *Marina and Lee*, p.537; WFAA-TV Collection, November 22, 1963, PKT-2; KRLD-TV Collection, November 22, 1963, reel 1, Sixth Floor Museum at Dealey Plaza.

128. WFAA-TV Collection, November 22, 1963, PKT-2; KRLD-TV Collection, November 22, 1963, reel 1, Sixth Floor Museum at Dealey Plaza; Manchester, *Death of a President*, p.129; *New York Times*, December 5, 1963, p.32; Gun, *Red Roses from Texas*, p.100.

129. Newseum with Trost and Bennett, *President Kennedy Has Been Shot*, p.16.

130. 2 H 134, WCT William Robert Greer.

131. Bishop, *Day Kennedy Was Shot*, p.125; WFAA-TV Collection, November 22, 1963, PKT-2; KRLD-TV Collection, November 22, 1963, reel 1, Sixth Floor Museum at Dealey Plaza; 2 H 63, WCT Roy H. Kellerman.

132. WFAA-TV Collection, November 22, 1963, PKT-2; KRLD-TV Collection, November 22, 1963, reels 1 and 21, Sixth Floor Museum at Dealey Plaza.

133. Bishop, *Day Kennedy Was Shot*, p.126; Manchester, *Death of a President*, p.128.

134. 7 H 460, WCT Lawrence F. O'Brien; Manchester, *Death of a President*, pp.37–38, 130–131.

135. Newseum with Trost and Bennett, *President Kennedy Has Been Shot*, p.15.

136. WFAA-TV Collection, November 22, 1963, PKT-2; KRLD-TV Collection, November 22, 1963, reels 1 and 21, Sixth Floor Museum at Dealey Plaza.

137. 7 H 333–334, WCT Forrest V. Sorrels.

138. 4 H 162, 168, 170, WCT Jesse E. Curry; 7 H 218, WCT F. M. Turner.

139. Manchester, *Death of a President*, p.37.

140. Todd Wayne Vaughan, *Presidential Motorcade Schematic Listing*, 1993; Trask, *Pictures of the Pain*, pp.616–617; 2 H 135, WCT Clinton J. Hill; Manchester, *Death of a President*, pp.133–135.

141. Connally, "Why Kennedy Went to Texas," p.104; Manchester, *Death of a President*, p.135.

142. 6 H 350–351, WCT Charles Douglas Givens.

143. 6 H 351, WCT Charles Douglas Givens.

144. 6 H 351, WCT Charles Douglas Givens; 7 H 385–386, WCT Roy Sansom Truly.

145. Manchester, *Death of a President*, pp.135–136; 2 H 135, WCT Clinton J. Hill.

146. 3 H 168–173, WCT Bonnie Ray Williams; CD 1245, p.82, FBI interview of Bonnie Ray Williams by Agents A. Raymond Switzer and Eugene F. Petrakis on May 25, 1964.

147. CE 2003, 24 H 203; CE 2006, 24 H 406; Brennan with Cherryholmes, *Eyewitness to History*, pp.4–6.

148. 2 H 165–167, WCT Arnold Louis Rowland.

149. 2 H 168–169, WCT Arnold Louis Rowland.

150. 2 H 168, WCT Arnold Louis Rowland.

151. 2 H 175, WCT Arnold Louis Rowland.

152. NAS-CBA DPD tapes, C2, 12:15–16 p.m.

153. 2 H 172, WCT Arnold Louis Rowland.

154. 2 H 166, WCT Arnold Louis Rowland.

155. 2 H 170–172, WCT Arnold Louis Rowland.

156. 2 H 174, WCT Arnold Louis Rowland; 6 H 181–182, WCT Barbara Rowland.

157. 3 H 172–173, WCT Bonnie Ray Williams.

158. WR, p.113; 5 H 134, WCT Thomas J. Kelley; CE 875, 17 H 881–895.

159. 3 H 173–174, WCT Bonnie Ray Williams.
160. NAS-CBA DPD tapes, C2, 12:20 p.m.; CE 1974, 23 H 911.
161. Connally, "Why Kennedy Went to Texas," pp.103–104; *Dallas Morning News*, November 23, 1963, sec. 4, p.5.
162. Interview of Charles F. Brehm by author on April 20, 1986; CE 1425, 22 H 837–838.
163. NAS-CBA DPD tapes, C2, 12:22 p.m.
164. O'Donnell and Powers with McCarthy, *Johnny, We Hardly Knew Ye*, pp.27–28; *Dallas Morning News*, November 23, 1963, p.1; 2 H 115–116, WCT William Robert Greer.
165. 4 H 131, WCT John B. Connally Jr.
166. 7 H 583–584, WCT Perdue D. Lawrence; largest and friendliest: *Dallas Morning News*, November 23, 1963, p.1.
167. NAS-CBA DPD tapes, C2, 12:23 p.m.
168. Savage, *JFK First Day Evidence*, p.362; CE 1024, 18 H 753.
169. NAS-CBA DPD tapes, C2, 12:23 p.m.
170. Manchester, *Death of a President*, p.137.
171. 3 H 142–144, WCT Howard Leslie Brennan; CE 477, 478, 17 H 197; CD 205, p.16, FBI interview of Howard Leslie Brennan on December 18, 1963; Brennan with Cherryholmes, *Eyewitness to History*, pp.6–8.
172. 7 H 570, WCT Abraham Zapruder; Trask, *Pictures of the Pain*, pp.57–58, 60; Interview of Marilyn Sitzman by Josiah Thompson on November 29, 1966.
173. Gun, *Red Roses from Texas*, p.16.
174. Interview of James Hosty by author on May 28, 1986; 4 H 461, WCT James P. Hosty Jr.; NAS-CBA DPD tapes, C2, 12:26 p.m.
175. Interview of Ralph Yarborough, *The Men Who Killed Kennedy, Part 1: Coup d'Etat*, Central Independent Television, 1988, History Channel, DVD AAE-70341.
176. 2 H 156–158, WCT Robert Hill Jackson.
177. NAS-CBA DPD tapes, C2, 12:26–12:28 p.m.; Sawyer Exhibit A, 21 H 390.
178. 6 H 203–204, WCT Robert Edwin Edwards; 6 H 193, WCT Ronald B. Fischer.
179. 6 H 193–194, 197, WCT Ronald B. Fischer; Fischer Exhibit No. 1, 19 H 650; 6 H 204, WCT Robert Edwin Edwards.
180. 6 H 171–172, WCT James N. Crawford; 6 H 175–176, WCT Mary Ann Mitchell.
181. Bedside interview of Governor John Connally at Parkland Hospital by CBS's Martin Agronsky most likely on the Wednesday or Thursday following the assassination; see also 4 H 147, WCT Mrs. John B. Connally Jr.
182. 5 H 179, WCT Mrs. John F. Kennedy.
183. Trask, *Pictures of the Pain*, pp.60–61.
184. NAS-CBA DPD tapes, C2, 12:30 p.m.
185. CE 1024, 18 H 734.
186. CE 1425, 22 H 837.
187. 8 HSCA 21.
188. 2 H 133–137, WCT Clinton J. Hill.
189. 3 H 175, WCT Bonnie Ray Williams; 3 H 191, WCT Harold Norman.
190. Trask, *Pictures of the Pain*, pp.62, 64, 476.
191. 3 H 175, WCT Bonnie Ray Williams; 3 H 191, WCT Harold Norman.
192. 7 H 509–510, WCT Mrs. Donald Baker; CE 354, 16 H 949.
193. Paul E. Landis Jr.: CE 1024, 18 H 754–755; John D. Ready: CE 1024, 18 H 749–750.
194. 2 H 149, WCT Rufus Wayne Youngblood; 5 H 562, WC statement of President Lyndon Baines Johnson.
195. 4 H 132–133, WCT Governor John B. Connally Jr.; 1 HSCA 43.

196. 5 H 180, WCT Mrs. John F. Kennedy.

197. 4 H 147, WCT Mrs. John B. Connally Jr.

198. 3 H 246–247, 258–60, 267–268, WCT Marrion L. Baker.

199. 2 H 192–193, WCT James Richard Worrell Jr.; CE 360, 16 H 957.

200. 2 H 203–205, 209, WCT Amos Euins; CE 365, 366, 16 H 961–962.

201. 3 H 143–144, 154, WCT Howard Leslie Brennan.

202. 3 H 175, WCT Bonnie Ray Williams.

203. CE 1425, 22 H 837.

204. CE 1024, 18 H 760.

205. CE 1024, 18 H 760, 763.

206. CE 1024, 18 H 742.

207. 2 H 73–75, WCT Roy H. Kellerman.

208. 2 H 73–75, WCT Roy H. Kellerman; Kellerman turns to left: Z frames 268–270, Trask, *National Nightmare*, p.52.

209. 4 H 133–134, 138, WCT Governor John B. Connally Jr.; 1 HSCA 43, 46.

210. 4 H 147, WCT Mrs. John B. Connally Jr.; 1 HSCA 40–41.

211. 5 H 180, WCT Mrs. John F. Kennedy.

212. 2 H 117–118, WCT William Robert Greer; 2 H 74, WCT Roy H. Kellerman; CE 1024, 18 H 725.

213. 2 H 150, WCT Rufus Wayne Youngblood; 5 H 562, WC statement of President Lyndon Baines Johnson.

214. 7 H 571, WCT Abraham Zapruder.

215. 6 H 206–207, WCT Jean Lollis Hill.

216. CE 363, 16 H 959; 2 H 194, 200, WCT James Richard Worrell Jr.; CE 361, 16 H 957.

217. 2 H 204–205, WCT Amos Euins.

218. 3 H 154, WCT Howard Leslie Brennan.

219. 7 H 571, WCT Abraham Zapruder.

220. Taped interview of Marilyn Sitzman by Josiah Thompson on November 26, 1966, p.2.

221. 5 H 180, WCT Mrs. John F. Kennedy.

222. 2 H 138–139, WCT Clinton J. Hill.

223. CE 1024, 18 H 725.

224. CE 1024, 18 H 755.

225. Interview of John B. Connally, *Men Who Killed Kennedy, Part 1: Coup d'Etat*, Central Independent Television, 1988; 4 H 134, WCT Governor John B. Connally Jr.; 4 H 148, WCT Mrs. John B. Connally Jr.; 1 HSCA 41, HSCA testimony of John B. Connally.

226. CE 1024, 18 H 725; 2 H 74, WCT Roy H. Kellerman.

227. 2 H 74, 76, WCT Roy H. Kellerman; Greer doesn't accelerate until after third shot: HSCA Record 180-10082-10454, HSCA staff interview of Secret Service agent William McIntyre on January 31, 1978; CE 1425, 22 H 838, FBI interview of Charles F. Brehm on November 24, 1963; CE 1426, 22 H 838, FBI interview of Mary Ann Moorman on November 22, 1963.

228. CE 1024, 18 H 734, 749–750.

229. CE 1024, 18 H 731–732.

230. 2 H 138–139, WCT Clinton J. Hill.

231. 2 H 138–140, WCT Clinton J. Hill.

232. 6 H 207, WCT Jean Lollis Hill; CE 1426, 22 H 838–839; JFK Exhibit F-129, Moorman Photo No. 5, 1 HSCA 109; slumps to grass: Wilma Bond photo in Trask, *Pictures of the Pain*, p.251.

233. CE 1425, 22 H 837–838; Testimony of Charles Brehm, Transcript of *On Trial: Lee*

Harvey Oswald, London Weekend Television, July 23, 1986, vol.1, pp.103, 109; *Men Who Killed Kennedy, Part 2: Forces of Darkness*, Central Independent Television, 1988.

234. 7 H 571, WCT Abraham Zapruder.
235. 2 H 194–195, WCT James Richard Worrell Jr.
236. 3 H 144, WCT Howard Leslie Brennan; Brennan with Cherryholmes, *Eyewitness to History*, pp.13–15.
237. 2 H 159–162, WCT Robert Hill Jackson; Testimony of Robert Jackson, Transcript of *On Trial*, July 23, 1986, pp.56–57.
238. 6 H 156–158, WCT Malcolm O. Couch; CD 5, p.18, FBI interview of Malcolm Couch on November 27, 1963; CD 5, p.15, FBI interview of Robert Jackson on November 22, 1963; 2 H 159, WCT Robert Hill Jackson.
239. 6 H 171–174, WCT James M. Crawford; 6 H 175–176, WCT Mary Ann Mitchell.
240. CE 1024, 18 H 742; 2 H 141, WCT Clinton J. Hill.
241. CE 1024, 18 H 742.
242. CE 1024, 18 H 755.
243. CE 1024, 18 H 755.
244. Savage, *JFK First Day Evidence,* p.363.
245. 4 H 161, WCT Jesse E. Curry; Curry, *JFK Assassination File,* p.30.
246. NAS-CBA DPD tapes, C2, 12:30 p.m.; CE 1974, 23 H 913.
247. CE 1358, 22 H 605; 6 H 251, WCT J. W. Foster.
248. 3 H 246–249, WCT Marrion L. Baker.
249. 3 H 259, WCT Marrion L. Baker; 3 H 221, WCT Roy Sansom Truly.
250. 3 H 222, WCT Roy Sansom Truly; 3 H 249, WCT Marrion L. Baker.
251. 6 H 297–298, WCT Clyde A. Haygood; CE 1426, 22 H 833; Trask, *Pictures of the Pain,* pp.426–427.
252. 6 H 259, WCT Joe E. Murphy; Murphy Exhibit A [No. 7], 20 H 638; Trask, *Pictures of the Pain,* p.266; 7 H 106, WCT Seymour Weitzman; CE 1428, 22 H 840, FBI interview of Jack Franzen on November 22, 1963; CE 2098, 24 H 531, FBI interview of Lillian Mooneyham on January 8, 1964; WR, p.76; 3 H 205, WCT James Jarman Jr.
253. 3 H 175, WCT Bonnie Ray Williams.
254. 3 H 191, WCT Harold Norman; 3 H 204, 211, WCT James Jarman Jr. CD 87, pp.9–11, Control No. 491, Secret Service interviews of Harold Norman, Bonnie Ray Williams, and James Jarman Jr., date of report December 7, 1963.
255. 3 H 205, WCT James Jarman Jr.; see also 7 H 542, WCT Welcome Eugene Barnett; CE 354, 16 H 949.
256. 3 H 211, WCT James Jarman Jr.; 3 H 175, WCT Bonnie Ray Williams; 3 H 191, WCT Harold Norman.
257. Testimony of Harold Norman, Transcript of *On Trial,* July 23, 1986, p.76.
258. NAS-CBA DPD tapes, C2, 12:31 p.m.; CE 1974, 23 H 913.
259. White, *In Search of History,* pp.521–522.
260. NAS-CBA DPD tapes, C2, 12:32 p.m.
261. 2 H 164, WCT Robert Hill Jackson.
262. Interview of Merriman Smith by Jack Fallon, Southwest Division News Manager, United Press International, Dallas, Texas, on December 17, 1963, p.1, Columbia University Collection; Manchester, *Death of a President,* pp.167–168; Bishop, *Day Kennedy Was Shot,* pp.182–183; United Press International, *Four Days,* p.22.
263. 7 H 546, WCT Eddy Raymond Walthers; 3 H 292, WCT Eugene Boone.

264. 3 H 223; WCT Roy Sansom Truly; 3 H 249–250, WCT Marrion L. Baker.

265. 3 H 250, 255–256, WCT Marrion L. Baker; location of Baker when he saw Oswald inside lunchroom: CE 1118, 22 H 85; see also CE 497, 17 H 212.

266. 3 H 252, 263, WCT Marrion L. Baker.

267. 3 H 224–225, WCT Roy Sansom Truly.

268. 3 H 225, WCT Roy Sansom Truly; 3 H 251, WCT Marrion L. Baker.

269. 3 H 252–253, WCT Marrion L. Baker; 3 H 225, WCT Roy Sansom Truly.

270. CD 1066, pp.61–62, FBI interview of Thomas Alyea by FBI SAs Neil Quigley and R. J. Robertson on March 26, 1964; Trask, *Pictures of the Pain*, pp.520–521; Hlavach and Payne, *Reporting the Kennedy Assassination*, pp.38–39.

271. MacNeil, *Right Place at the Right Time*, pp.198, 206–209; photo of MacNeil at railroad overpass: Trask, *Pictures of the Pain*, p.405.

272. 3 H 274, 276–278, WCT Mrs. Robert A. Reid; CD 5, p.27, FBI interview of Mrs. Robert A. Reid by Dallas SA Richard Harrison on November 26, 1963.

273. 3 H 258–259, WCT Marrion L. Baker.

274. Sneed, *No More Silence*, pp.146–147.

275. 2 H 149, WCT Rufus Wayne Youngblood; 5 H 562, WC statement of President Lyndon Baines Johnson; CE 1024, 18 H 768; Manchester, *Death of a President*, p.167.

276. 7 H 440, Affidavit of Ralph W. Yarborough; Interview of Ralph Yarborough, *Men Who Killed Kennedy, Part 1: Coup d'Etat*, Central Independent Television, 1988.

277. Manchester, *Death of a President*, p.163.

278. Sneed, *No More Silence*, pp.129, 135, 157.

279. Sneed, *No More Silence*, pp.130, 146–147, 156.

280. United Press International, *Four Days*, p.22; Newseum with Trost and Bennett, *President Kennedy Has Been Shot*, pp.19, 30–33; Bishop, *Day Kennedy Was Shot*, p.192.

281. Manchester, *Death of a President*, p.189; Morin, *Assassination*, p.78.

282. 6 H 282, WCT James Elbert Romack.

283. 7 H 546, 550, WCT Eddy Raymond Walthers.

284. NAS-CBA DPD tapes, C2, 12:35 p.m.

285. NAS-CBA DPD tapes, C2, 12:35 p.m.; 6 H 298–299, WCT Clyde A. Haygood.

286. 2 H 205, WCT Amos Euins; 6 H 310, WCT D. V. Harkness.

287. 6 H 311, WCT D. V. Harkness; amateur footage in *President Kennedy's Final Hour*, Dallas Cinema Associates, 1964.

288. 6 H 313, WCT D. V. Harkness.

289. 6 H 170, WCT James Robert Underwood.

290. NAS-CBA DPD tapes, C2, 12:36 p.m.

291. 6 H 315–316, WCT J. Herbert Sawyer.

292. 6 H 317, WCT J. Herbert Sawyer.

293. 6 H 320, WCT J. Herbert Sawyer.

294. 6 H 317, WCT J. Herbert Sawyer; 6 H 311, WCT D. V. Harkness.

295. 3 H 143, 145, 158–159, WCT Howard Leslie Brennan; CE 477, 17 H 197; 7 H 542–543, WCT Welcome Eugene Barnett.

296. 6 H 318, 297.320, WCT J. Herbert Sawyer.

297. 6 H 170, WCT James Robert Underwood.

298. Price Exhibit No. 31, 21 H 241.

299. 2 H 79, WCT Roy H. Kellerman.

300. 4 H 354, WCT Winston G. Lawson; Price Exhibit No. 12, 21 H 203; Price Exhibit No. 27, 21 H 226.

301. CE 1024, 18 H 756; Manchester, *Death of a President*, p.170; O'Donnell and Powers with McCarthy, *Johnny, We Hardly Knew Ye*, p.31; Savage, *JFK First Day Evidence*, p.363.

302. Interview of Ralph Yarborough, *Men Who Killed Kennedy, Part 1: Coup d'Etat*, Central Independent Television, 1988.

303. CE 1024, 18 H 735; Manchester, *Death of a President*, p.170; Connally and Herskowitz, *From Love Field*, p.9; Savage, *JFK First Day Evidence*, p.363.

304. Manchester, *Death of a President*, p.170.

305. 4 H 143, WCT Governor John B. Connally Jr.

306. 6 H 136, WCT Diana Hamilton Bowron.

307. 2 H 79, WCT Roy H. Kellerman; Savage, *JFK First Day Evidence*, p.363.

308. CE 1024, 18 H 756.

309. 2 H 79, 82, WCT Roy H. Kellerman; 2 H 142, WCT Clinton J. Hill; Manchester, *Death of a President*, pp.170–172; CE 1024, 18 H 756; 6 H 145, WCT Doris Mae Nelson; Price Exhibit No. 22, 21 H 217; Savage, *JFK First Day Evidence*, p.363.

310. Interview of Merriman Smith by Jack Fallon, December 17, 1963, p.1, Columbia University Collection; Manchester, *Death of a President*, p.168.

311. 2 H 80, WCT Roy H. Kellerman.

312. *Highlights: The History of Parkland Hospital*, p.36.

313. NAS-CBA DPD tapes, C2, 12:39 p.m.

314. NAS-CBA DPD tapes, C2, 12:39 p.m.

315. 2 H 262 264, 269, WCT Cecil J. McWatters.

316. 2 H 264, 270–271, WCT Cecil J. McWatters; Aynesworth and Grove, "Oswald Planned to Ride by Scene," *Dallas Morning News*, November 28, 1963, p.21.

317. 6 H 400–408, WCT Mary E. Bledsoe; CE 2189, 24 H 870.

318. 6 H 409–412, WCT Mary E. Bledsoe.

319. Recollections of Harry McCormick, 1964, *Dallas Morning News* Collection; 7 H 571–572, WCT Abraham Zapruder.

320. Thomas, "At War over a Tragic Film," p.39; Stolley, "Shots Seen Round the World."

321. 7 H 553, WCT James Thomas Tague; 7 H 546, WCT Eddy Raymond Walthers.

322. 7 H 553, WCT James Thomas Tague; CE 354, 16 H 949 (number 6).

323. 21 H 475, Shaneyfelt Exhibit No. 27.

324. 7 H 553–555, WCT James Thomas Tague; 7 H 546–547, WCT Eddy Raymond Walthers.

325. "America's Long Vigil," pp.23–24; CBS Television Archives.

326. 3 H 366–367, WCT Dr. Malcolm O. Perry; 6 H 52, WCT Dr. Ronald C. Jones; 6 H 105, WCT Dr. George T. Shires.

327. McMillan, *Marina and Lee*, pp.537–538; 3 H 68–70, WCT Ruth Hyde Paine; 1 H 73–74, WCT Marina N. Oswald.

328. 3 H 358, WCT Dr. Charles James Carrico.

329. 3 H 359–361, WCT Dr. Charles James Carrico; see also 6 H 40, WCT Dr. Charles Rufus Baxter.

330. 3 H 360, WCT Dr. Charles James Carrico.

331. 3 H 360, WCT Dr. Charles James Carrico; CE 392, 17 H 4.

332. 3 H 366–369, WCT Dr. Malcolm O. Perry; 3 H 360, WCT Dr. Charles James Carrico; Breslin, "Death in Emergency Room No. One," p.30.

333. 6 H 40, WCT Dr. Charles Rufus Baxter.

334. 3 H 367–368, WCT Dr. Malcolm O. Perry.

335. 3 H 368, WCT Dr. Malcolm O. Perry; Breo, "JFK's Death, Part II," p.2805; Breslin, "Death in Emergency Room No. One," p.30, Manchester, *Death of a President*, p.184.

336. FBI Record 124-10012-10169, Hoover to Tolson, November 22, 1963, 1:43 p.m. (EST), p.1; Schlesinger, *Robert Kennedy and His Times*, pp.607–608; RFK meets with U.S. attorneys: Davidson, "Profile in Family Courage," p.32b.

337. *New York Times*, November 23, 1963, p.6; Manchester, *Death of a President*, pp.197–198.

338. Goldsmith, *Colleagues*, p.99.

339. 6 H 84, WCT Robert Roeder Shaw; 6 H 146–147, WCT Doris Mae Nelson.

340. 3 H 360, WCT Dr. Charles James Carrico.

341. 3 H 361–362, WCT Dr. Charles James Carrico; 7 HSCA 268.

342. Breo, "JFK's Death, Part II," p.2805.

343. 6 H 20, WCT William Kemp Clark.

344. 6 H 40–41, WCT Dr. Robert N. McClelland; 6 H 40, WCT Dr. Charles Rufus Baxter; 6 H 69 WCT Paul C. Peters; 3 H 370–371, WCT Dr. Malcolm O. Perry; 6 H 46–47, WCT Dr. Marion T. Jenkins; 6 H 73–74, WCT Dr. Adolph H. Giesecke Jr.

345. 3 H 370, WCT Dr. Malcolm O. Perry.

346. 6 H 59, WCT Dr. Don Teel Curtis; 6 H 81, WCT Dr. Kenneth Everett Salyer; 6 H 82, WCT Martin G. White; Crenshaw with Hansen and Shaw, *JFK: Conspiracy of Silence*, p.84.

347. 6 H 54, WCT Dr. Ronald C. Jones; 6 H 70, WCT Paul C. Peters.

348. 6 H 20, WCT William Kemp Clark; Manchester, *Death of a President*, p.186.

349. CE 1126, 22 H 94; "Three Patients at Parkland," p.61.

350. 6 H 69, WCT Paul C. Peters.

351. CE 1126, 22 H 94; ARRB MD 67, Oral history interview with Admiral George G. Burkley for the John Fitzgerald Kennedy Library, October 17, 1967, p.16; HSCA Record 180-10104-10271, Affidavit of George G. Burkley, November 28, 1978, pp.1–2.

352. 7 H 452, WCT Kenneth P. O'Donnell.

353. Breo, "JFK's Death, Part II," p.2806.

354. 6 H 145, WCT Doris Mae Nelson; CE 1126, 22 H 94; Manchester, *Death of a President*, p.186.

355. 2 H 264–265, WCT Cecil J. McWatters; 6 H 410–411, WCT Mary E. Bledsoe; CE 2189, 24 H 870.

356. NAS-CBA DPD tapes, C2, 12:43 p.m.

357. NAS-CBA DPD tapes, C2, 12:44 p.m.

358. DPD tapes, C1 and 2, 12:45 p.m.

359. 1 H 67, 74, WCT Marina N. Oswald; CE 2003, 24 H 219; 9 H 432–433, WCT Ruth Hyde Paine; McMillan, *Marina and Lee*, p.538.

360. 2 H 255, WCT William Wayne Whaley; description of Whaley: Hugh Aynesworth and Larry Grove, "Oswald Planned to Ride by Scene," *Dallas Morning News*, November 28, 1963, p.21.

361. 2 H 255–256, 261, WCT William Wayne Whaley.

362. CE 2003, 24 H 228.

363. 2 H 256, 293, WCT William Wayne Whaley.

364. 2 H 293, WCT William Wayne Whaley.

365. 2 H 257–258, WCT William Wayne Whaley.

366. CE 2645, 25 H 911–915.

367. Transcript of *CBS News Inquiry: The Warren Report*, part III, June 27, 1967, p.3, CBS Television Archives.

368. DPD tapes, C1, 12:46 p.m.; 7 H 80–81, WCT Calvin Bud Owens; Putnam Exhibit No. 1, 21 H 274.

369. HSCA Record 180-10103-10353, Interview of Murray J. Jackson on October 20, 1977, p.2; Interviews of Murray J. Jackson by Dale K. Myers on March 9, 1985, November 15, 1999, and February 1, 2000.

370. Sneed, *No More Silence*, p.463, interview of Donald Flusche.

371. CE 2985, 26 H 485–490; lunch: *Dallas Morning News*, Noveber 23, 1963; Aynesworth with Michaud, *JFK: Breaking the News*, pp.25, 40; "78 clear": Savage, *JFK First Day Evidence*, p.375.

372. 7 H 348, WCT Forrest V. Sorrels.

373. 7 H 348, WCT Forrest V. Sorrels.

374. 7 H 347–348, WCT Forrest V. Sorrels.

375. 7 H 348, WCT Forrest V. Sorrels.

376. 7 H 349, WCT Forrest V. Sorrels.

377. 7 H 350, WCT Forrest V. Sorrels.

378. 6 H 429, WCT William Wayne Whaley.

379. 2 H 256, WCT William Wayne Whaley.

380. 2 H 254–256, WCT William Wayne Whaley; CE 382, 16 H 975.

381. NBC News, *Seventy Hours and Thirty Minutes*, Introduction and p.1; "America's Long Vigil," pp.23–24.

382. DPD tapes, C1, 12:54 p.m.; CE 1974, 23 H 849–850.

383. Myers, *With Malice*, pp.28–37; CE 2985, 26 H 485–489; *Dallas Morning News*, November 23, 1963, sect.4, p.5.

384. Giesecke Exhibit No. 1, 20 H 6.

385. 4 H 102, 6 H 85, WCT Dr. Robert Roeder Shaw.

386. 4 H 104–108, WCT Dr. Robert Roeder Shaw; 4 H 117–120, 6 H 97–98, WCT Charles F. Gregory; 6 H 105–106, WCT Dr. George T. Shires; Giesecke Exhibit No. 1, 20 H 6–7.

387. 4 H 204–205, WCT John Will Fritz; Sims Exhibit A, 21 H 511; CE 2003, 24 H 285.

388. Manchester, *Death of a President*, pp.214–215.

389. Manchester, *Death of a President*, pp.109–110, 136, 215.

390. 6 H 438–440, WCT Earlene Roberts; Roberts told Hugh Aynesworth, the first reporter to interview her on the afternoon of the assassination, that Oswald had come in "running like the dickens." Aynesworth with Michaud, *JFK: Breaking the News*, p.67.

391. 6 H 436–437, WCT Earlene Roberts.

392. 6 H 439–440, WCT Earlene Roberts.

393. 6 H 443–444, WCT Earlene Roberts; CE 1125, 22 H 93.

394. 6 H 20, WCT William Kemp Clark.

395. 6 H 9, 3 H 371, WCT Dr. Malcolm O. Perry; 6 H 20, WCT William Kemp Clark.

396. 3 H 371, WCT Dr. Malcolm O. Perry; Manchester, *Death of a President*, p.186.

397. 3 H 372, WCT Dr. Malcolm O. Perry; WR, p.4; HSCA Report, p.40; Breo, "JFK's Death, Part II," p.2806; Manchester, *Death of a President*, pp.186, 188; white sheet covering the face: *Philadelphia Sunday Bulletin*, November 23, 1963, p.3.

398. 3 H 372, WCT Dr. Malcolm O. Perry.

399. 3 H 365, WCT Dr. Charles James Carrico.

400. Semple, *Four Days in November*, p.595.

401. Breo, "JFK's Death, Part II," p.2806.

402. Manchester, *Death of a President*, pp.216–217; Breslin, "Death in Emergency Room No. One," p.30; *Philadelphia Sunday Bulletin*, November 24, 1963, p.3; *New York Times*, November 23, 1963, p.9.

403. Manchester, *Death of a President*, pp.217–218.

404. FBI Record 124-10012-10169; FBI memorandum, Hoover to Tolson, November 22,

1963, 2:10 p.m. EST, pp.2–3, Manchester, *Death of a President*, pp.217–218; Schlesinger, *Robert Kennedy and His Times*, p.608; Bishop, *Day Kennedy Was Shot*, p.189.

405. Thomas, *Robert Kennedy: His Life*, pp.276, 282.

406. FBI Record 124-10062-10262, FBI Briefing Book, "Texas School Book Depository: Photographs, Floor Plans, Parking Lots," photograph 37 and diagram of seventh floor; also CD 496.

407. 3 H 284, WCT Luke Mooney; 7 H 46, WCT Gerald Lynn Hill 4 H 204–205, WCT John Will Fritz.

408. 4 H 204–205, WCT John Will Fritz; 7 H 46–47, WCT Gerald Lynn Hill; 7 H 121, WCT Elmer L. Boyd; 7 H 160–161, WCT Richard M. Sims; CE 2003, 24 H 319.

409. 4 H 205, WCT John Will Fritz; 7 H 97, WCT L. D. Montgomery; 7 H 101, WCT Marvin Johnson; 7 H 122, WCT Elmer L. Boyd; 7 H 160–161, WCT Richard M. Sims; CE 2003, 24 H 285, 307, 319.

410. *New York Herald Tribune*, November 23, 1963, p.21.

411. CD 1, p.2, December 9, 1963, Tippit was "presumably acting on the basis of a broadcast over the police radio"; CE 2146, 24 H 767; channel 1: CE 1974, 23 H 843–845, 850.

412. CE 705, 17 H 406.

413. 5 H 563, WC statement of President Lyndon Baines Johnson.

414. Manchester, *Death of a President*, p.234.

415. Manchester, *Death of a President*, p.236; 5 H 566, WC statement of Mrs. Lyndon Baines Johnson.

416. Manchester, *Death of a President*, pp.219–220.

417. O'Donnell and Powers with McCarthy, *Johnny, We Hardly Knew Ye*, pp.32–34; Bishop, *Day Kennedy Was Shot*, p.248.

418. 2 H 152–153, WCT Rufus Wayne Youngblood; CE 2554, 25 H 786–787.

419. 3 H 323–325, WCT William W. Scoggins; description of neighborhood: Aynesworth with Michaud, *JFK: Breaking the News*, pp.32, 36.

420. 3 H 306, 317, WCT Helen Louise Markham.

421. Interview of Helen Markham by Hugh Aynesworth on November 22, 2003, in Aynesworth with Michaud, *JFK: Breaking the News*, p.32.

422. 3 H 325, WCT William W. Scoggins.

423. 3 H 307, WCT Helen Louise Markham; CD 630(c), pp.7–8, FBI interview of Helen Markham on March 16, 1964.

424. HSCA Record 180-10087-10355, Interview of Jack Ray Tatum on February 1, 1978; Interview of Jack Tatum by London Weekend Television staff on May 13, 1986, pp.1–2; Telephone interview of Jack Tatum by author on June 1, 1986; Testimony of Jack Tatum, Transcript of *On Trial*, July 23, 1986, pp.193–194.

425. 6 H 446–447, WCT Domingo Benavides.

426. 3 H 307–308, 315–316, WCT Helen Louise Markham; CD 630(c), p.2, FBI interview of Helen Markham on March 16, 1964.

427. 3 H 325, WCT William W. Scoggins; CE 2003, 24 H 225, Dallas Sheriff Department affidavit of William W. Scoggins, November 22, 1963; Secret Service affidavit of William W. Scoggins, December 2, 1963, p.1.

428. 6 H 447–448, WCT Domingo Benavides.

429. HSCA Record 180-10087-10355, Interview of Jack Ray Tatum on February 1, 1978; Interview of Jack Tatum by London Weekend Television staff on May 13, 1986, p.2; Telephone interview of Jack Tatum by author on June 1, 1986; Testimony of Jack Tatum, Transcript of *On Trial*, July 23, 1986, pp.195–196, 199.

430. 3 H 308, WCT Helen Louise Markham; CE 2003, 24 H 215.

431. Interview of Jack Tatum by London Weekend Television staff on May 13, 1986, p.2; Interview of Jack Tatum by author on June 1, 1986.

432. 3 H 308, WCT Helen Louise Markham.

433. 3 H 342–345, 347, WCT Barbara Jeannette Davis; 6 H 454–461, WCT Virginia Davis; Davis Exhibit Nos. 1–3, 19 H 428–430.

434. 3 H 325–327, WCT William W. Scoggins; CE 2003, 24 H 225.

435. Interview of Ted Callaway by Dale K. Myers on April 9, 1996; 3 H 352, WCT Ted Callaway.

436. 3 H 351–354, WCT Ted Callaway; CD 735, pp.262–263, FBI interview of Ted Callaway on February 26, 1964; HSCA Record 180-10091-10128, HSCA testimony of Ted Callaway, July 26, 1978, pp.4–5; Telephone interview of Ted Callaway by author on May 17, 1986; Testimony of Ted Callaway, Transcript of *On Trial*, July 23, 1986, pp.205–210.

437. 3 H 354, 356, WCT Ted Callaway.

438. 11 H 435, WCT Warren Reynolds; CE 2523, 25 H 731, FBI interview of Warren Reynolds on January 21, 1964; Lewis (L. J.) Exhibit A, 20 H 534; Russell Exhibit A, 21 H 383; CD 173, pp.271–272, FBI interview of Harold Russell on February 23, 1964; Patterson (B. M.) Exhibit A, 21 H 25.

439. 3 H 309, 317, 320, WCT Helen Louise Markham; CD 630(c), p.2, FBI interview of Helen Markham on March 17, 1964; half a block away: Interview of Helen Markham by Hugh Aynesworth, in Aynesworth with Michaud, *JFK: Breaking the News*, p.33.

440. CD 7, p.411, Interview of Frank Cimino by FBI agents Henry J. Oliver and David H. Barry on December 3, 1963.

441. 6 H 448, WCT Domingo Benavides.

442. DPD tapes, C1, 1:16 p.m.; CE 705, 17 H 407; CE 1974, 23 H 857; CE 2003, 24 H 202; HSCA Record 180-10113-10400, HSCA interview of Temple Ford Bowley on November 12, 1977, pp.1–2; 6 H 449, WCT Domingo Benavides.

443. 3 H 354, WCT Ted Callaway; 7 H 396–398, WCT Sam Guinyard.

444. 3 H 354, WCT Ted Callaway; CD 735, pp.262–263, FBI interview of Ted Callaway on February 26, 1964; 7 H 80, WCT Calvin Bud Owens.

445. Newseum with Trost and Bennett, *President Kennedy Has Been Shot*, p.71.

446. CE 2003, 24 H 202; HSCA Record 180-10113-10400, HSCA interview of Temple Ford Bowley on November 12, 1977, pp.1–2; Interview of T. F. Bowley by Dale K. Myers on March 16, 1983, pp.1–4.

447. DPD tapes, C1, 1:17:41 p.m.; CE 1974, 23 H 857–858; Sawyer Exhibit A, 21 H 394–395.

448. 7 H 47, WCT Gerald Lynn Hill; *Dallas Morning News*, November 20, 1983, p.6G.

449. 7 H 47, WCT Gerald Lynn Hill; Interview of Gerald L. Hill by Dale K. Myers on October 30, 1986.

450. Interview of Gerald L. Hill by Dale K. Myers on October 30, 1986, p.11; Jack Beers photograph, Richard E. Sprague Collection, No. 85PA1-149-21.

451. DPD tapes, C1, 1:19 p.m.

452. CE 1974, 23 H 920.

453. Interview of Hugh Aynesworth by Dale K. Myers on May 14, 1997; Interview of James Ewell by Dale K. Myers on February 24, 1986; *Dallas Morning News*, November 20, 1983, p.6G; 15 H 348, WCT Victor F. Robertson Jr.

454. 3 H 354, WCT Ted Callaway; 7 H 398, WCT Sam Guinyard; time of ambulance arrival almost 1:19 p.m.: CE 1974, 23 H 858; Interview of William Kinsley by Dale K. Myers on November 6, 1986; Nash and Nash, "Other Witnesses," p.8; HSCA Record 180-10107-10180, Interview of Jasper Clayton Butler on September 25, 1977, p.3; 12 H 201, WCT Kenneth Hudson Croy.

455. 6 H 129–131, WCT Darrell C. Tomlinson; Thompson, *Six Seconds in Dallas*, p.158 footnote.

456. CE 2011, 24 H 412.

457. Transcript of *CBS News Inquiry: The Warren Report*, part IV, June 28, 1967, p.7, CBS Television Archives; Thompson, *Six Seconds in Dallas*, pp.155–156; CE 1024, 18 H 799–800.

458. DPD tapes, C1, 1:20 p.m.

459. 3 H 354, WCT Ted Callaway; CD 735, p.263, FBI interview of Ted Callaway on February 26, 1964; 6 H 452, WCT Domingo Benavides; 3 H 332–333, WCT William W. Scoggins; CE 2003, 24 H 202; Russell Exhibit A, 21 H 383.

460. Brock (Mary) Exhibit A, 19 H 181; Brock (Robert) Exhibit A, 19 H 182; Patterson (B. M.) Exhibit A, 21 H 25; Patterson (B. M.) Exhibit B, 21 H 27; Russell Exhibit A, 21 H 383; 11 H 436, WCT Warren Reynolds; CE 2523, 25 H 731.

461. FBI Record 124-10012-10167, November 22, 1963, p.1.

462. FBI Record 124-10012-10033, FBI memorandum, Belmont to Tolson, 2:20 p.m. EST, November 22, 1963, p.1; Reprint from *Assignment: Oswald* by James P. Hosty, Jr., p.14, published by Arcade Publishing, New York, New York. Copyright © 1996 by James P. Hosty, Jr.

463. 3 H 292–293, WCT Eugene Boone.

464. Kent Biffle, "Reporter Recalls the Day Camelot Died in Dallas," *Dallas Morning News*, April 5, 1981, pp.1AA, 3AA.

465. Sims Exhibit A, 21 H 511; CE 2003, 24 H 286.

466. 7 H 107, WCT Seymour Weitzman; 3 H 292–293, WCT Eugene Boone; Weitzman Exhibits D–F, 21 H 723–724; Transcript of *CBS News Inquiry: The Warren Report*, part I, June 25, 1967, pp.9–10, CBS Television Archives.

467. Sims Exhibit A, 21 H 512; CE 2003, 24 H 286, 307, 314; 7 H 102–103, WCT Marvin Johnson; 7 H 143, WCT Robert Lee Studebaker; 7 H 162, WCT Richard M. Sims.

468. 3 H 292–295, WCT Eugene Boone; Sims Exhibit A, 21 H 512.

469. 4 H 205, WCT John Will Fritz; 4 H 253, WCT J. C. Day; CE 3145, 26 H 833–834; clip being empty: HSCA Record 180-10075-10175, September 10, 1964.

470. 3 H 392–399, WCT Robert A. Frazier; Cormack, *World Encyclopedia of Modern Guns*, pp.106, 120.

471. Interview of William Alexander by author on December 8, 2000.

472. 7 H 47, WCT Gerald Lynn Hill.

473. DMA Document 01-04-006, DPD Supplementary Offense Report, undated; Interview of Robert A. Davenport by Dale Myers on March 7, 1983; Interview of Paul C. Moellenhoff by Dale K. Myers on March 4, 1983.

474. Interview of Roy W. Walker by Dale K. Myers on April 2, 1983.

475. DPD tapes, C1, 1:22 p.m.

476. DPD tapes, C1, 1:23 p.m.

477. 7 H 47–48, WCT Gerald Lynn Hill; 7 H 79, WCT Calvin Bud Owens; Interview of William Alexander by author on December 8, 2000.

478. Myers, *With Malice*, p.118.

479. 12 H 202, WCT Kenneth Hudson Croy; 3 H 333, WCT William W. Scoggins; CD 735, p.263, FBI interview of Ted Callaway on February 26, 1964.

480. DMA Document 01-04-006, DPD Supplementary Offense Report prepared by R. A. Davenport and W. R. Bardin, undated; CD 5, p.81, FBI interview of Richard A. Liquori on November 29, 1963; Myers, *With Malice*, pp.116–117.

481. 4 H 461, WCT James P. Hosty Jr.; Hosty with Hosty, *Assignment: Oswald*, pp.14–16.

482. 7 H 48, WCT Gerald Lynn Hill; Aynesworth with Michaud, *JFK: Breaking the News*, p.42.

483. 7 H 115–117, WCT W. R. Westbrook; Interview of W. R. Westbrook by Larry A. Sneed on June 21, 1988, p.2; Sneed, *No More Silence*, p.314.

484. 7 H 30, 33, WCT Thomas Alexander Hutson.

485. DPD tapes, C1, 1:25 p.m.

486. NAS-CBA DPD tapes, C2, 1:30 p.m.

487. 2 H 153, WCT Rufus Wayne Youngblood; 12 H 29, WCT Jesse E. Curry; Manchester, *Death of a President*, p.238.

488. Bishop, *Day Kennedy Was Shot*, pp.264–265; Manchester, *Death of a President*, p.220.

489. CE 1974, 23 H 922.

490. O'Donnell and Powers with McCarthy, *Johnny, We Hardly Knew Ye*, pp.34–35; Bishop, *Day Kennedy Was Shot*, p.241; *New York Times*, December 5, 1963, p.32; Manchester, *Death of a President*, pp.292–294.

491. 6 H 137, WCT Diana Hamilton Bowron; Price Exhibit No. 12, 21 H 203–204; 6 H 141–142, WCT Margaret M. Henchliffe; Price Exhibit No. 30, 21 H 239; 6 H 146, WCT Doris Mae Nelson; Nelson Exhibit No. 1, 20 H 641; Price Exhibit No. 31, 21 H 242; Price Exhibit No. 21, 21 H 216.

492. Articles 49.01 and 49.03 of Chapter 49 of the Texas Code of Criminal Procedure.

493. 2 H 96–97, WCT Roy H. Kellerman; 15 H 504, 509, WCT, David L. Johnston; Manchester, *Death of a President*, pp.297–302; O'Donnell and Powers with McCarthy, *Johnny, We Hardly Knew Ye*, pp.35–36; Breo, "JFK's Death, Part II," pp.2804–2807.

494. 3 H 230, WCT Roy Sansom Truly.

495. 3 H 230, 7 H 382–384, WCT Roy Sansom Truly.

496. 3 H 230, WCT Roy Sansom Truly; Sims Exhibit A, 21 H 512.

497. *New York Times*, November 23, 1963, p.2; Manchester, *Death of a President*, pp.220–221, 244; Bishop, *Day Kennedy Was Shot*, pp.265–266; Semple, *Four Days in November*, p.28.

498. DPD tapes, C1, 1:34 p.m.; CE 1974, 23 H 866; Myers, *With Malice*, p.137; 7 H 118, WCT W. R. Westbrook.

499. 7 H 36, WCT C. T. Walker; 7 H 69, WCT J. M. Poe; DPD tapes, C1, 1:35 p.m.; Sawyer Exhibit A, 21 H 396–397.

500. KLIF, Dallas, radio log, November 22, 1963, reel 5, p.8, entry 23, Gerald R. Ford Presidential Library.

501. 7 H 2–4, WCT Johnny Calvin Brewer; CD 87, Control No. 474, U.S. Secret Service interview of Johnny Brewer on December 5, 1963, pp.1–2; Interview of Johnny Brewer by author on May 13, 1986; Transcript of *On Trial*, July 23, 1986, pp.239–240.

502. CE 147, 16 H 514; Moore Exhibit No. 1, 20 H 636.

503. 7 H 2–7, WCT Johnny Calvin Brewer; Transcript of *On Trial*, July 23, 1986, p.240; Hill (Gerald L.) Exhibit C, 20 H 157.

504. 7 H 10–11, WCT Julia Postal.

505. 7 H 11, WCT Julia Postal.

506. 7 H 10, WCT Julia Postal.

507. 7 H 4, WCT Johnny Calvin Brewer.

508. 7 H 10, WCT Julia Postal; 7 H 4, WCT Johnny Calvin Brewer.

509. Telephone interview of Ken Holmes by author on March 11, 2004; Sketch of theater drawn by Johnny Brewer for author in June 1986; Visit to theater, being renovated at the time, by author on September 22, 2004.

510. 7 H 5 WCT Johnny Calvin Brewer.

511. 7 H 10, WCT Julia Postal.

512. CBS Television Archives; "America's Long Vigil," p.25.

513. Gates, *Air Time*, p.4.

514. White, *Making of the President, 1964*, pp.5–6.

515. Hope with Shavelson, *Don't Shoot, It's Only Me*, p.244.

516. Wicker, *JFK and LBJ*, p.159.

517. Morin, *Assassination*, pp.78–79.

518. *New York Times*, November 23, 1963, p.5. Copyright © 1963 by The New York Times Co. Reprinted with permission.

519. Morin, *Assassination*, pp.88–90, 95–96; Brandt and Churchill: *New York Times*, November 23, 1963, pp.1, 8.

520. *New York Times*, November 23, 1963, p.8.

521. Manchester, *Death of a President*, pp.249–250.

522. *Fourth Decade*, November 1995, p.4.

523. McGill, "Hate Knows No Direction," p.8.

524. *New York Times*, November 23, 1963, pp.6, 8.

525. *New York Times*, November 23, 1963, p.13.

526. McGill, "Hate Knows No Direction," p.8.

527. 3 H 69–70, WCT Ruth Hyde Paine; McMillan, *Marina and Lee*, pp.538–539.

528. 7 H 36–37, WCT C. T. Walker; DPD tapes, C1, 1:38 p.m.; CE 1974, 23 H 925; Myers, *With Malice*, pp.139, 145–147.

529. FBI Record 124-10013-10003, p.2; U.S. Congress, Senate, *Final Report of the Select Committee to Study Governmental Operations with Respect to Intelligence Activities*, Book V: *The Investigation of the Assassination of President John F. Kennedy: Performance of the Intelligence Agencies*, 94th Congress, 2nd session, Report 94-755 (hereinafter "Church Committee Report"), p.39.

530. TerHorst and Albertazzie, *Flying White House*, p.213.

531. Youngblood, *20 Years in the Secret Service*, p.121.

532. 5 H 563, WC statement of President Lyndon Baines Johnson.

533. Schlesinger, *Robert Kennedy and His Times*, p.609; Manchester, *Death of a President*, pp.266–269; Bishop, *Day Kennedy Was Shot*, pp.270–271; 5 H 563, WC statement of President Lyndon Baines Johnson.

534. Manchester, *Death of a President*, pp.271–272; 5 H 564, WC statement of President Lyndon Baines Johnson.

535. Youngblood, *20 Years in the Secret Service*, pp.124–125.

536. 5 H 563–564, WC statement of President Lyndon Baines Johnson; Schlesinger, *Robert Kennedy and His Times*, p.609; Manchester, *Death of a President*, pp.270–272, 275.

537. 7 H 398–399, WCT Sam Guinyard; 6 H 449–450, WCT Domingo Benavides.

538. 7 H 68–69, WCT J. M. Poe (Hill erroneously testified that he received three shells from Poe); 7 H 48–49, WCT Gerald Lynn Hill.

539. DPD tapes, C1, 1:41 p.m.

540. CE 1974, 23 H 925.

541. 7 H 49, WCT Gerald Lynn Hill.

542. Sneed, *No More Silence*, p.296, interview of Gerald L. Hill.

543. WFAA-TV Collection, November 22, 1963, PKF-10, Sixth Floor Museum at Dealey Plaza; 7 H 111, WCT W. R. Westbrook.

544. 7 H 272, WCT W. E. Barnes.

545. NAS-CBA DPD tapes, C2, 1:45 p.m.

546. 7 H 5, WCT Johnny Calvin Brewer.

547. 7 H 11, WCT Julia Postal.

548. 12 HSCA 36; Myers, *With Malice*, pp.37, 39.

549. DPD tapes, C1, 1:46 p.m.

550. 7 H 111, WCT W. R. Westbrook.

551. 7 H 11–12, WCT Julia Postal.

552. *Dallas Morning News*, November 23, 1963, sect.1, p.6.

553. 7 H 12, WCT Julia Postal.

554. 7 H 49, WCT Gerald Lynn Hill.

555. 7 H 5, WCT Johnny Calvin Brewer.

556. 7 H 6, WCT Johnny Calvin Brewer.

557. 7 H 30, WCT Thomas Alexander Hutson; 7 H 6, WCT Johnny Calvin Brewer; 3 H 299, WCT M. N. McDonald.

558. 3 H 299–300, WCT M. N. McDonald; location of Oswald: 7 H 30–31, WCT Thomas Alexander Hutson.

559. 3 H 300–301, 303, WCT M. N. McDonald; 7 H 32, WCT Thomas Alexander Hutson.

560. 3 H 300, WCT M. N. McDonald; CE 2003, 24 H 241; 7 H 32, WCT Thomas Alexander Hutson; Interview of M. N. McDonald by Dale K. Myers on November 12, 1996.

561. 7 H 40, WCT C. T. Walker.

562. 3 H 300–301, WCT M. N. McDonald; hears snap of the hammer: CE 2003, 24 H 241, Letter from M. N. McDonald to Chief of Police J. E. Curry, December 3, 1963; 7 H 32, WCT Thomas Alexander Hutson; 15 H 591, WCT Thayer Waldo; DMA negative 91-001/029; CE 744, 17 H 515.

563. 7 H 112, WCT W. R. Westbrook.

564. 7 H 112–113, WCT W. R. Westbrook; Interview of W. R. Westbrook by Larry A. Sneed on June 21, 1988, p.7; 3 H 301, WCT M. N. McDonald.

565. Interview of Robert M. Barrett by Dale K. Myers on February 19, 1996.

566. 7 H 51–52, WCT Gerald Lynn Hill; HSCA Record 180-100084-10157, Interview of Bob K. Carroll on June 12, 1978, p.2; WFAA-TV Collection, November 22, 1963, PKF-10, Sixth Floor Museum at Dealey Plaza.

567. 7 H 9, 12–13, WCT Julia Postal.

568. Decker Exhibit No. 5323, 19 H 519, Report of Dallas deputy sheriff Buddy Walthers; Hill (Gerald L.) Exhibits B and C, 20 H 156–157; not sympathetic: Sneed, *No More Silence*, p.287; Myers, *With Malice*, pp.179–180.

569. 7 H 12 WCT Julia Postal; CD 735, pp.265–266, Interview of Julia Postal on February 27, 1964; CE 2003, 24 H 221–222.

570. 7 H 54–55, WCT Gerald Lynn Hill.

571. DPD tapes, C1, 1:52 p.m.

572. 7 H 56–58, WCT Gerald Lynn Hill; CE 2003, 24 H 240, Report of Dallas police officer K. E. Lyon to J. E. Curry.

573. 7 H 58, WCT Gerald Lynn Hill; 7 H 40–41, WCT C. T. Walker.

574. 7 H 58, 61, WCT Gerald Lynn Hill; 7 H 40, 41, WCT C. T. Walker; CE 2003, 24 H 240.

575. FBI Record 124-10012-10033, FBI memorandum, Belmont to Tolson, 2:20 p.m. EST, November 22, 1963, pp.2–3.

576. 7 H 59, WCT Gerald Lynn Hill.

577. 7 H 59, WCT Gerald Lynn Hill; WFAA-TV Collection, November 22, 1963, PKF-10; KRLD-TV Collection, Sixth Floor Museum at Dealey Plaza.

578. Recollections of Harry McCormick, 1964, *Dallas Morning News* Collection.
579. 7 H 352, WCT Forrest V. Sorrels.
580. 7 H 352, WCT Forrest V. Sorrels; Trask, *Pictures of the Pain*, pp.76–77; Wrone, *Zapruder Film*, pp.19–20.
581. Sims Exhibit A, 21 H 512; 7 H 123, WCT Elmer L. Boyd; 4 H 206, WCT John Will Fritz.
582. 7 H 248–249, WCT C. W. Brown.
583. 7 H 228, WCT Guy F. Rose.
584. 7 H 248, WCT C. W. Brown; 7 H 123, WCT Elmer L. Boyd.
585. Hampton, *Kennedy Assassinated!* pp.31, 62.
586. Greenstein, "Diffusion of News of the Kennedy Assassination," a study by the National Opinion Research Center of the University of Chicago.
587. 7 H 452–453, WCT Kenneth P. O'Donnell; 2 H 96–97, WCT Roy H. Kellerman; Manchester, *Death of a President*, pp.297–305; O'Donnell and Powers with McCarthy, *Johnny, We Hardly Knew Ye*, pp.35–36, 45; Bishop, *Day Kennedy Was Shot*, pp.287–289.
588. Manchester, *Death of a President*, pp.308–309; O'Donnell and Powers with McCarthy, *Johnny, We Hardly Knew Ye*, p.37; Telephone interview of Lem Johns by author on June 28, 2005.
589. Hosty with Hosty, *Assignment: Oswald*, p.16.
590. FBI Record 124-10012-10353, FBI memorandum, Belmont to Tolson, November 22, 1963, 3:50 p.m. EST; 4 H 461–462, WCT James P. Hosty Jr.; Hosty with Hosty, *Assignment: Oswald*, pp.16–17.
591. Sims Exhibit A, 21 H 514; WR, p.600; CE 2003, 24 H 286; 7 H 188, WCT Richard S. Stovall; 7 H 229, WCT Guy F. Rose.
592. 7 H 454, WCT Kenneth P. O'Donnell.
593. Manchester, *Death of a President*, p.310.
594. O'Donnell and Powers with McCarthy, *Johnny, We Hardly Knew Ye*, pp.37–39; 7 H 454, WCT Kenneth P. O'Donnell.
595. 5 H 566, WC statement of Mrs. Lyndon Baines Johnson; see also 7 H 470, WCT Lawrence F. O'Brien.
596. Sims Exhibit A, 21 H 514; 7 H 135, WCT Elmer L. Boyd.
597. HSCA Record 180-10112-10160, November 14, 1977, p.2.
598. Two lieutenants and twenty detectives: Batchelor Exhibit No. 5002, 19 H 145; three days' suspension: *JFK/Deep Politics Quarterly*, July 2005, p.7.
599. Telephone interviews of William Alexander by author on December 20, 2000, and March 8, 2004; Bonner, *Investigation of a Homicide*, pp.121–122.
600. Sneed, *No More Silence*, p.345, interview of Guy Rose.
601. Sneed, *No More Silence*, pp.354, 366, interview of Harry Holmes; Telephone interview of William Alexander by author on March 8, 2004.
602. Interview of James R. Leavelle by Dale K. Myers on July 1, 1996.
603. CE 2003, 24 H 265; 4 H 209, 213, 221–222, WCT John Will Fritz.
604. 4 H 207, 210, 214, WCT John Will Fritz.
605. CE 2003, 24 H 286.
606. Interview of T. L. Baker by Dale K. Myers on November 13, 1999.
607. O'Donnell and Powers with McCarthy, *Johnny, We Hardly Knew Ye*, p.39; United Press International, *Four Days*, p.27.
608. United Press International, *Four Days*, p.33; Manchester, *Death of a President*, pp.324–326.
609. Manchester, *Death of a President*, p.327, 349–351.

610. Manchester, *Death of a President*, pp.323, 327, 348–350.

611. 1 H 141–142, WCT Marguerite Oswald.

612. Schieffer, *This Just In*, pp.4, 7–8; Michael Young, "He Didn't Know It, but History Was Calling Him," *Dallas Morning News*, November 21, 2002, pp.29A, 33A.

613. Schieffer, *This Just In*, pp.8–9; 1 H 137, WCT Marguerite Oswald; however, she did cry: Statement of Bob Schieffer to AP on day of assassination, *Dallas Morning News*, November 23, 1963, p.6.

614. Oswald with Land and Land, *Lee*, pp.11–13.

615. Oswald with Land and Land, *Lee*, pp.13–15.

616. 7 H 292–293, WCT Harry D. Holmes; CE 1799, 23 H 419.

617. Holmes Exhibit No. 1, 20 H 172.

618. 7 H 293, WCT Harry D. Holmes; CE 1799, 23 H 419.

619. 7 H 352, WCT Forrest V. Sorrels; Recollections of Harry McCormick, 1964, *Dallas Morning News* Collection; Trask, *Pictures of the Pain*, p.79.

620. United Press International, *Four Days*, p.33.

621. 5 H 36, WCT Jack Revill.

622. 4 H 463, WCT James P. Hosty Jr.; Hosty with Hosty, *Assignment: Oswald*, pp.17–18.

623. 4 H 462–465, WCT James P. Hosty Jr.; 5 H 37, WCT Jack Revill; Hosty with Hosty, *Assignment: Oswald*, pp.18–19; time of conversation between Hosty and Revill: 17 H 495; but see also 4 H 463.

624. 5 H 35, WCT Jack Revill; 5 H 50, WCT V. J. Brian.

625. 10 H 295, WCT Mrs. Arthur Carl Johnson; 10 H 305, WCT Arthur Carl Johnson; 7 H 197, WCT Walter Eugene Potts; CE 2003, 24 H 324.

626. CE 2003, 24 H 317, 324, 327.

627. 10 H 295, WCT Mrs. Arthur Carl Johnson; 10 H 305, WCT Arthur Carl Johnson.

628. 6 H 441, WCT Earlene Roberts.

629. 6 H 441, WCT Earlene Roberts.

630. CE 2003, 24 H 324; 5 by 13½ feet: CE 2046, 24 H 460.

631. FBI Record 124-10012-10170, November 22, 1963.

632. 4 H 209, 238, WCT John Will Fritz; CE 2003, 24 H 265.

633. 4 H 153, WCT Jesse E. Curry.

634. CE 2003, 24 H 265.

635. 4 H 466–467, WCT James P. Hosty Jr.; 7 H 124, WCT Elmer L. Boyd; 7 H 310, WCT James W. Bookhout; Hosty with Hosty, *Assignment: Oswald*, p.20.

636. CE 832, 17 H 785; 4 H 210, WCT John Will Fritz.

637. 4 H 449–454, WCT James P. Hosty Jr.; 3 H 97–103, WCT Ruth Hyde Paine.

638. U.S. Congress, House of Representatives, *Hearings before the Subcommittee on Civil and Constitutional Rights of the Committee on the Judiciary, House of Representatives, on FBI Oversight*, 94th Congress, 1st and 2nd sessions, 1973–1974, p.145 (hereinafter "*FBI Oversight*"); Hosty with Hosty, *Assignment: Oswald*, p.185.

639. Hosty with Hosty, *Assignment: Oswald*, pp.21–22, 185.

640. CE 832, 17 H 785; 4 H 214, WCT John Will Fritz.

641. CE 2064, 24 H 488; 4 H 240, WCT John Will Fritz; 7 H 135, WCT Elmer L. Boyd.

642. CE 832, 17 H 785; Hosty with Hosty, *Assignment: Oswald*, p.25.

643. 4 H 214, WCT John Will Fritz.

644. CE 2003, 24 H 265; Fritz's handwritten notes of November 22, 1963.

645. CE 2003, 24 H 265; Fritz's handwritten notes of November 22, 1963; CE 832, 17 H 785; Hosty with Hosty, *Assignment: Oswald*, p.24.

646. CE 2003, 24 H 265–266; Hosty with Hosty, *Assignment: Oswald*, pp.24–25.

647. 7 H 124–125, WCT Elmer L. Boyd; Hosty with Hosty, *Assignment: Oswald*, p.25.

648. 4 H 212, WCT John Will Fritz; FBI Record 124-10167-10013, Letter, Lloyd Hill to J. E. Curry, November 27, 1963.

649. 7 H 262, WCT James R. Leavelle; Interview of James R. Leavelle by Dale K. Myers on July 1, 1996.

650. Parkland Memorial Hospital Pathology Laboratory Autopsy Report, Autopsy No. M63-352, November 22, 1963; removal of three bullets from body: U.S. Secret Service report, December 11, 1963, File CD-2-34030.

651. Beschloss, *Taking Charge*, pp.17–18.

652. ARRB MD 41, "At the White House with Wayne Hawks," transcript of the press conference at Parkland Hospital commencing at 3:16 p.m. on November 22, 1963; CE 1415, 22 H 832.

653. Manchester, *Death of a President*, p.222; MacNeil, *Right Place at the Right Time*, p.212.

654. 7 H 352, WCT Forrest V. Sorrels; Kodak Technical Report, "Analysis of Selected Motion Picture Photographic Evidence," Study 3, by Roland J. Zavada, 1998, p.2; Wrone, *Zapruder Film*, p.281.

655. CE 2003, 24 H 292; CE 2003, 24 H 286.

656. 7 H 548, WCT Eddy Raymond Walthers.

657. CE 2003, 24 H 292; Decker Exhibit No. 5323, 19 H 520; 3 H 78–79, WCT Ruth Hyde Paine; 7 H 229, WCT Guy F. Rose; 7 H 548, WCT Eddy Raymond Walthers; 7 H 188, WCT Richard S. Stovall.

658. 7 H 189, WCT Richard S. Stovall.

659. 7 H 229, WCT Guy F. Rose.

660. 7 H 229, WCT Guy F. Rose.

661. 1 H 74, WCT Marina N. Oswald.

662. 7 H 229–230, WCT Guy F. Rose; Sneed, *No More Silence*, p.340, interview of Guy F. Rose; 7 H 548, WCT Eddy Raymond Walthers.

663. 1 H 26, 52–53, 67, 74, WCT Marina N. Oswald; CE 2003, 24 H 219, Affidavit of Marina Oswald, State of Texas, County of Dallas, November 22, 1963.

664. 1 H 74, WCT Marina N. Oswald.

665. 3 H 79–80 WCT Ruth Hyde Paine; Sneed, *No More Silence*, p.340.

666. 7 H 230, WCT Guy F. Rose; McMillan, *Marina and Lee*, p.541; 1 H 73–75, WCT Marina N. Oswald; 3 H 80, WCT Ruth Hyde Paine; Decker Exhibit No. 5323, 19 H 520, 530; CE 2003, 24 H 292.

667. 7 H 205, WCT John P. Adamcik.

668. 4 H 210, WCT John Will Fritz.

669. CE 832, 17 H 785; CE 2003, 24 H 265; 4 H 209, WCT John Will Fritz; Fritz's handwritten notes of November 22, 1963.

670. CE 832, 17 H 785; CE 2003, 24 H 266; 4 H 210–211, WCT John Will Fritz; Fritz's handwritten notes of November 22, 1963.

671. CE 832, 17 H 785–786.

672. CE 832, 17 H 786.

673. CE 832, 17 H 786; CE 2003, 24 H 265; 4 H 213–214, WCT John Will Fritz; Fritz's handwritten notes of November 22, 1963.

674. Hosty with Hosty, *Assignment: Oswald*, photo section, Hosty's handwritten notes of November 22, 1963.

675. CE 832, 17 H 785–786; 4 H 213, WCT John Will Fritz; Fritz's handwritten notes of

November 26, 1963; Hosty with Hosty, *Assignment: Oswald*, pp.22–23, photo section—Hosty's handwritten notes of November 22, 1963.

676. CE 832, 17 H 786.
677. Hosty with Hosty, *Assignment: Oswald*, p.25.
678. 7 H 354, WCT Forrest V. Sorrels.
679. 7 H 353, 13 H 57, WCT Forrest V. Sorrels.
680. 7 H 353, WCT Forrest V. Sorrels.
681. 7 H 353–354, WCT Forrest V. Sorrels; 4 H 356–357, WCT Winston G. Lawson; 4 H 470, WCT James P. Hosty Jr.
682. 4 H 212, WCT John Will Fritz; 7 H 233, WCT W. E. Perry; 7 H 236, WCT Richard L. Clark.
683. Hunt-Jones, *JFK: For a New Generation*, p.70, photograph.
684. 7 H 136, 126, WCT Elmer L. Boyd.
685. 7 H 173, WCT Richard M. Sims.
686. CE 2003, 24 H 320; 7 H 180, WCT Richard M. Sims.
687. CE 2003, 24 H 345.
688. FBI Record 124-10009-10017, FBI memorandum, Belmont to Tolson, November 22, 1963 5:10 p.m. EST.
689. Report from Tippit to C. F. Hanson, April 28, 1956, Report from W. F. Dyson to C. F. Hanson, April 8, 1957; Letters from Harold A. Mattson, M.D., November 7 and December 27, 1956—all in Texas Attorney General's Files on the Kennedy Assassination, vol.12.
690. CE 709, 17 H 495; 5 H 39–40, WCT Jack Revill; 5 H 50, WCT V. J. Brian.
691. CE 709, 17 H 495; 7 H 405–407, WCT Mary Jane Robertson.
692. CE 2003, 24 H 316, 327; 7 H 213, WCT Henry M. Moore; 7 H 221–222, WCT F. M. Turner; Johnson Exhibit No. 1, 20 H 314; Telephone interview of William Alexander by author on December 8, 2000.
693. 7 H 167, WCT Richard M. Sims; 7 H 254, WCT L. C. Graves.
694. 7 H 127, WCT Elmer L. Boyd; 7 H 167, WCT Richard M. Sims.
695. 7 H 262, WCT James R. Leavelle; 4 H 212, WCT John Will Fritz; DPD lineup notes, DMA, box 1, folder 10, item 3, p.1; CE 2003, 24 H 287, 301.
696. Sims Exhibit A, 21 H 514.
697. 7 H 254, WCT L. C. Graves; 3 H 311, WCT Helen Markham.
698. 7 H 168, WCT Richard M. Sims; DPD lineup notes, DMA, box 1, folder 10, item 3, p.1.
699. 3 H 310–312, WCT Helen Markham; 7 H 254, WCT L. C. Graves; 7 H 263, WCT James R. Leavelle; 4 H 212, WCT John Will Fritz; 4 H 176, WCT Jesse E. Curry.
700. Sims Exhibit A, 21 H 514.
701. Bonner, *Investigation of a Homicide*, pp.144–145; 7 H 198, WCT Walter Eugene Potts; Telephone interview of William Alexander by author on August 20, 2004.
702. 7 H 198–199, WCT Walter Eugene Potts; Potts Exhibits A-1 and A-2, 21 H 141–142; CE 2003, 24 H 316–318, 324–325, 327, 341–344; Telephone interview of William Alexander by author on December 11, 2000.
703. Manchester, *Death of a President*, p.341.
704. 5 H 567, WC statement of Mrs. Lyndon Baines Johnson.
705. "Growing Rift of LBJ and Kennedy," p.26.
706. Morin, *Assassination*, pp.133–134; *Los Angeles Times*, November 22, 1966, p.10; quote of Manchester regarding LBJ: *New York Times*, January 23, 1967, p.26; Manchester, *Death of a President*, pp.316–317; Roberts, *Truth about the Assassination*, pp.106, 116; "Growing Rift of LBJ and Kennedy," p.26; Valenti's observation: *New York Times*, November 22, 1998, editorial section, p.17.

707. Morin, *Assassination*, pp.132, 135.

708. Manchester, *Death of a President*, p.346.

709. *USA Today*, August 26, 2005, p.A4.

710. Manchester, *Death of a President*, p.342.

711. ARRB MD 67, Oral history interview with Admiral George G. Burkley for the John Fitzgerald Kennedy Library, October 17, 1967, p.16; Manchester, *Death of a President*, pp.349–350; Bishop, *Day Kennedy Was Shot*, pp.355–356.

712. O'Donnell and Powers with McCarthy, *Johnny, We Hardly Knew Ye*, p.44.

713. O'Donnell and Powers with McCarthy, *Johnny, We Hardly Knew Ye*, pp.41–43; Manchester, *Death of a President*, p.8.

714. O'Donnell and Powers with McCarthy, *Johnny, We Hardly Knew Ye*, pp.43–44.

715. Breo, "JFK's Death—The Plain Truth from the MDs Who Did the Autopsy," p.2796; 2 H 348, WCT Dr. James J. Humes.

716. ARRB Transcript of Proceedings, Deposition of Dr. J. Thornton Boswell, February 26, 1996, pp.17–18.

717. 7 HSCA 190; 2 H 348, WCT Dr. James J. Humes; 2 H 377, WCT Dr. J. Thornton Boswell.

718. CE 1024, 18 H 757; Presidential Diary, "Backup file," November 22, 1963, LBJ Library.

719. O'Donnell and Powers with McCarthy, *Johnny, We Hardly Knew Ye*, p.44.

720. Manchester, *Death of a President*, p.387.

721. ARRB MD 163, After Action Report, joint casket team state funeral, President John Fitzgerald Kennedy, Samuel R. Bird, December 10, 1963, p.2.

722. KRLD-TV Collection, November 22, 1963, 5:08 p.m. CST, reel 5, Sixth Floor Museum at Dealey Plaza; Manchester, *Death of a President*, pp.389–390.

723. KRLD-TV Collection, November 22, 1963, 5:10 p.m. CST, reel 5, Sixth Floor Museum at Dealey Plaza; Manchester, *Death of a President*, p.391.

724. KRLD-TV Collection, November 22, 1963, 5:14 p.m. CST, reel 5, Sixth Floor Museum at Dealey Plaza; Youngblood, *20 Years in the Secret Service*, pp.134–135; Manchester, *Death of a President*, pp.344–345, 401.

725. "America's Long Vigil," p.24.

726. 3 H 80–81, WCT Ruth Hyde Paine; McMillian, *Marina and Lee*, p.542; Stoval Exhibit A, 21 H 596; CE 2003, 24 H 292–293.

727. CE 460, 17 H 179–180; Secret Service File CD-2-34, 030, November 28, 1963, p.1.

728. NBC News, *Seventy Hours and Thirty Minutes*, pp.26; 33–34; Morin, *Assassination*, p.138; *New York Times*, November 23, 1963, pp.1, 11; Bishop, *Day Kennedy Was Shot*, pp.428–429.

729. Manchester, *Death of a President*, pp.405–406; *New York Times*, November 26, 1963, p.5.

730. Law with Eaglesham, *In the Eye of History*, pp.235–236; 6:10 p.m. and 6:55 p.m.: CE 1024, 18 H 744, 757.

731. CE 1024, 18 H 744, 757.

732. *Washington Post*, November 23, 1963, p.A11; Posner, *Case Closed*, p.300; Manchester, *Death of a President*, p.397.

733. Solid mass of humanity: Law with Eaglesham, *In the Eye of History*, p.8.

734. 2 H 98–99, WCT Roy H. Kellerman; CE 1024, 18 H 744, 757; FBI Report of SAs Francis X. O'Neill and James W. Sibert, November 22, 1963, p.1, File 89-30; ARRB MD 189, Undated Report, "Assassination of President John F. Kennedy and Aftermath," by Francis X. O'Neill, pp.4–5; Manchester, *Death of a President*, pp.396–398.

735. Shaw, *White House Nannie*, pp.14, 20–21; *New York Times*, November 23, 1963, p.9; *New York Times*, November 24, 1963, p.3.

736. 2 H 143–144, WCT Clinton J. Hill; CE 1024, 18 H 744, 757; Manchester, *Death of a President*, pp.395, 397.

737. Morin, *Assassination*, p.140; Heymann, *Woman Named Jackie*, pp.123, 141–142; "inquiring photographer": Adler, *Eloquent Jacqueline Kennedy Onassis*, p.22.

738. Adler, *Eloquent Jacqueline Kennedy Onassis*, pp.1, 3.

739. ARRB MD 189, Undated Report, "Assassination of President John F. Kennedy and Aftermath," by Francis X. O'Neill, pp.4–5.

740. ARRB MD 44, FBI Report of O'Neill and Sibert, November 26, 1963, p.2; ARRB MD 46, Affidavit of James W. Sibert, October 24, 1978, p.2; ARRB MD 47, Affidavit of Francis X. O'Neill Jr., November 8, 1978, p.1.

741. ARRB MD 44, FBI Report of O'Neill and Sibert, November 26, 1963, pp.1–2; ARRB MD 189, Undated Report, "Assassination of President John F. Kennedy and Aftermath," by Francis X. O'Neill, pp.4–5; ARRB MD 47, Affidavit of Francis X. O'Neill Jr., November 8, 1978, p.2; ARRB MD 46, Affidavit of James W. Sibert, October 24, 1978, p.2; HSCA Record 180-10105-10405; ARRB MD 87, Interview of Richard A. Lipsey, January 18, 1978, p.2.

742. ARRB Deposition of James W. Sibert, September 11, 1997, p.45.

743. ARRB MD 163, After Action Report, joint casket team state funeral, President John Fitzgerald Kennedy, Samuel R. Bird, December 10, 1963, p.2.

744. ARRB MD 189, Undated Report, "Assassination of President John F. Kennedy and Aftermath," by Francis X. O'Neill, pp.4–5; Manchester, *Death of a President*, pp.399–400; Law with Eaglesham, *In the Eye of History*, p.37.

745. ARRB MD 189, Undated Report, "Assassination of President John F. Kennedy and Aftermath," by Francis X. O'Neill, pp.4–5.

746. HSCA Record 180-10105-10405; ARRB MD 87, Interview of Richard A. Lipsey, January 18, 1978, p.2.

747. ARRB MD 163, After Action Report, joint casket team state funeral, President John Fitzgerald Kennedy, Samuel R. Bird, December 10, 1963, p.2.

748. CE 2003, 24 H 293.

749. 9 H 106, WCT Ilya A. Mamantov; CE 2003, 24 H 287, 291, 293. Note: The name J. A. Brourantus in CE 2003, 24 H 287, may refer to a second translator or may be a very poor transcription of Ilya Mamantov's name.

750. CE 2003, 24 H 287, 291; 4 H 264, WCT J. C. Day; 9 H 116–117, WCT Ilya A. Mamantov.

751. CE 2003, 24 H 287, 297; 2 H 268, WCT Cecil J. McWatters.

752. 7 H 354, WCT Forrest V. Sorrels.

753. 3 H 355, WCT Ted Callaway.

754. Sims Exhibit A, 21 H 514.

755. 7 H 167, WCT Richard M. Sims.

756. 7 H 396, 400, WCT Sam Guinyard.

757. 2 H 270, WCT Cecil J. McWatters; but see 7 H 151–152, WCT C. N. Dhority.

758. Leavelle Exhibit A, 20 H 501; Testimony of Ted Callaway, Transcript of *On Trial*, July 23, 1986, p.214.

759. 2 H 349, WCT Dr. James J. Humes; ARRB MD 26, Memorandum, Andy Purdy to Jim Kelly and Kenneth Klein, August 17, 1977, Notes of interview with Dr. J. Thornton Boswell, pp.2–3; ARRB MD 44, FBI Report of O'Neill and Sibert, November 26, 1963, p.3; ARRB MD 189, Undated Report, "Assassination of President John F. Kennedy and Aftermath," by Francis X. O'Neill, p.5.

760. HSCA Record 180-10107-10448, Memorandum, Jim Kelly and Andy Purdy to Ken

Klein, August 29, 1977, re: interview of Paul K. O'Connor on August 25, 1977, p.3, ARRB MD 64; HSCA Record 180-10096-10391, HSCA Outside Contact Report, May 27, 1978, 3:15 p.m., pp.1–2.

761. Breo, "JFK's Death—The Plain Truth from the MDs Who Did the Autopsy," p.2797; 2 H 349, WCT Dr. James J. Humes; ARRB Deposition of Francis X. O'Neill, September 12, 1997, pp.59–61; ARRB MD 189, Undated Report, "Assassination of President John F. Kennedy and Aftermath," by Francis X. O'Neill, p.5; Kennedy's height (72½ inches) and weight: autopsy report, CE 387, 16 H 978.

762. 2 H 349, WCT Dr. James J. Humes; ARRB MD 44, FBI Report of O'Neill and Sibert, November 26, 1963, p.2.

763. ARRB MD 19, Memorandum to File, Andy Purdy, August 17, 1977, pp.13, 17; 7 HSCA 261, Interview of Drs. James J. Humes and J. Thornton Boswell by the Forensic Pathology Panel, September 16, 1977; ARRB MD 26, Memorandum, Andy Purdy to Jim Kelly and Kenneth Klein, August 17, 1977, Notes of interview with Dr. J. Thornton Boswell, p.3; ARRB Transcript of Proceedings, Deposition of Dr. James Joseph Humes, February 13, 1996, p.31; 7 HSCA 263.

764. ARRB MD 44, FBI Report of O'Neill and Sibert, November 26, 1963, p.3; ARRB MD 189, Undated Report, "Assassination of President John F. Kennedy and Aftermath," by Francis X. O'Neill, p.5.

765. 2 H 372, WCT Dr. James J. Humes; ARRB MD 189, Undated Report, "Assassination of President John F. Kennedy and Aftermath," by Francis X. O'Neill, p.6.

766. Interview of William Alexander by author on December 11, 2000.

767. 7 H 130, WCT Elmer L. Boyd; 4 H 215, 225, WCT John Will Fritz.

768. Interview of William Alexander by author on December 11, 2000.

769. CE 2003, 24 H 298.

770. 7 H 354, WCT Forrest V. Sorrels.

771. CE 2003, 24 H 298.

772. ARRB MD 44, FBI Report of O'Neill and Sibert, November 26, 1963, p.3.

773. 2 H 349, WCT Dr. James J. Humes; ARRB Transcript of Proceedings, Deposition of Dr. J. Thornton Boswell, February 26, 1996, pp.17–18.

774. ARRB Transcript of Proceedings, Deposition of Dr. J. Thornton Boswell, February 26, 1996, pp.212–213.

775. AFIP Record 205-10001-10002, Memorandum, Dr. Finck to Brigadier Gen. J. M. Blumberg, Personal notes on the Assassination of President Kennedy, February 1, 1965 (hereafter "Memorandum, Finck to Blumberg"), p.1; also ARRB MD 28; Breo, "JFK's Death, Part III," p.1749.

776. 4 H 157, WCT Jesse E. Curry; 15 H 506, WCT David L. Johnston; Johnston Exhibit Nos. 1 and 3, 20 H 314, 319–320; 5 H 229–230, WCT Henry Wade; Telephone interview of William Alexander by author on December 11, 2000.

777. CE 2003, 24 H 287; Sims Exhibit A, 21 H 514–516; 4 H 216–217, WCT John Will Fritz; Interview of William Alexander by author on December 12, 2000.

778. Posner, *Case Closed*, p.348; "Oswald Arrogance Irks Prosecutor," *Dallas Morning News*, November 24, 1963; Interview of William Alexander by author on December 12, 2000.

779. Johnston Exhibit No. 3, 20 H 319–320; 15 H 506, WCT David L. Johnston.

780. 4 H 216–217, WCT John Will Fritz.

781. Johnston Exhibit No. 1, 20 H 314.

782. Interview of William Alexander by author on December 12, 2000.

783. Oswald with Land and Land, *Lee*, pp.14–20; CE 323, 16 H 892–893.

784. 5 H 218, WCT Henry Wade.

785. 5 H 216–217, WCT Henry Wade.

786. Bonner, *Investigation of a Homicide*, pp.33–34.

787. Oswald with Land and Land, *Lee*, p.21.

788. Oswald with Land and Land, *Lee*, p.22.

789. Oswald with Land and Land, *Lee*, pp.22–23.

790. 7 H 319, WCT Manning C. Clements.

791. 7 H 320, WCT Manning C. Clements; 4 H 217, WCT John Will Fritz; Sims Exhibit A, 21 H 514, 516.

792. 7 H 321, WCT Manning C. Clements; DMA negatives 91-001/155, 156, 157.

793. CE 1991, 24 H 21–22; 7 H 321, WCT Manning C. Clements.

794. KRLD-TV Collection, November 22, 1963, 7:38 p.m. CST, reel 9, Sixth Floor Museum at Dealey Plaza.

795. 2 H 353–354, WCT Dr. James J. Humes; 2 H 94, 100, WCT Roy H. Kellerman; ARRB MD 47, Affidavit of Francis X. O'Neill Jr., November 8, 1978, pp.4–5.

796. ARRB MD 44, FBI Report of O'Neill and Sibert, November 26, 1963, p.4.

797. 2 H 354, WCT Dr. James J. Humes; ARRB MD 19, Memorandum to File, Andy Purdy, August 17, 1977, p.17; AFIP Record 205-10001-10002, Memorandum, Finck to Blumberg, p.2; also ARRB MD 28; Breo, "JFK's Death—The Plain Truth from the MDs Who Did the Autopsy," p.2798.

798. CE 391, 16 H 981, 987.

799. AFIP Record 205-10001-10002, Memorandum, Finck to Blumberg, p.1; also ARRB MD 28; ARRB MD 61, Memorandum, Jim Kelley and Andy Purdy to Ken Klein, August 29, 1977, p.6; Breo, "JFK's Death, Part III," p.1749.

800. 2 H 352, WCT Dr. James J. Humes.

801. ARRB MD 19, Memorandum to File, Andy Purdy, August 17, 1977, p.15; 2 H 352, WCT Dr. James J. Humes.

802. 2 H 355, WCT Dr. James J. Humes; Breo, "JFK's Death—The Plain Truth from the MDs Who Did the Autopsy," p.2798; Breo, "JFK's Death, Part III," pp.1749, 1752, 1754; AFIP Record 205-10001-10002, Memorandum, Finck to Blumberg, pp.2, 15; also ARRB MD 28; ARRB Transcript of Proceedings, Deposition of Dr. J. Thornton Boswell, February 26, 1996, p.195.

803. Hosty with Hosty, *Assignment: Oswald*, pp.42–52; Telephone interview of James Hosty by author on April 12, 2006.

804. Hosty with Hosty, *Assignment: Oswald*, pp.29–31.

805. 7 H 131–132, WCT Elmer L. Boyd; 7 H 171–172, WCT Richard M. Sims.

806. 6 H 461–462, WCT Virginia Davis.

807. Brennan with Cherryholmes, *Eyewitness to History*, pp.19–21; 3 H 160, WCT Howard Leslie Brennan.

808. 7 H 354, WCT Forrest V. Sorrels.

809. 7 H 354, WCT Forrest V. Sorrels.

810. 7 H 250, WCT C. W. Brown.

811. 3 H 349, WCT Barbara Jeannette Davis.

812. 6 H 462, WCT Virginia Davis.

813. Brennan with Cherryholmes, *Eyewitness to History*, p.25; 3 H 148, 155, 160, WCT Howard Leslie Brennan.

814. 3 H 155, 160, WCT Howard Leslie Brennan.

815. 7 H 354, WCT Forrest V. Sorrels; 4 H 357, WCT Winston G. Lawson.

816. 7 H 355, WCT Forrest V. Sorrels.

817. CE 2011, 24 H 420.
818. 7 H 296, WCT Harry D. Holmes; CE 817, 818, 17 H 697; 7 H 431, WCT James C. Cadigan.
819. 7 H 296, WCT Harry D. Holmes.
820. KRLD-TV Collection, November 22, 1963, 7:55 p.m. CST, reel 9, Sixth Floor Museum at Dealey Plaza; Kantor Exhibit No. 3, 20 H 366.
821. Sims Exhibit A, 21 H 516.
822. CE 1991, 24 H 21–22.
823. 7 H 130, WCT Elmer L. Boyd; 7 H 321, WCT Manning C. Clements.
824. 7 H 321, WCT Manning C. Clements.
825. FBI Record 124-10018-10310, FBI memorandum, Belmont to Tolson, November 22, 1963, 9:18 p.m. EST.
826. AFIP Record 205-10001-10002, Memorandum, Finck to Blumberg, pp.2–3; also ARRB MD 28; HSCA Record 180-10097-10183, Testimony of Pierre A. Finck, State of Louisiana vs. Clay L. Shaw, February 24, 1964, pp.12–13; Breo, "JFK's Death, Part III," p.1752.
827. ARRB MD 19, Memorandum to File, Andy Purdy, August 17, 1977, p.15; ARRB Transcript of Proceedings, Deposition of Dr. J. Thornton Boswell, February 26, 1996, pp.149–150.
828. ARRB MD 26, Memorandum, Andy Purdy to Jim Kelly and Kenneth Klein, August 17, 1977, Notes of interview with Dr. J. Thornton Boswell, p.6; ARRB MD 44, FBI Report of O'Neill and Sibert, November 26, 1963, p.4.
829. Breo, "JFK's Death, Part III," p.1750.
830. AFIP 205-10001-10002, Memorandum, Finck to Blumberg, pp.3, 16; also ARRB MD 28; 2 H 361, WCT Dr. James J. Humes; Breo, "JFK's Death, Part III," p.1754.
831. ARRB MD 156, FBI memorandum, SA Sibert and O'Neill to SAC, Baltimore, November 26, 1963, p.1.
832. HSCA Record 180-10097-10185, Testimony of Pierre A. Finck, State of Louisiana vs. Clay L. Shaw, February 25, 1969, pp.15–16.
833. 7 H 135, WCT Elmer L. Boyd.
834. CE 2003, 24 H 266; 4 H 217, WCT John Will Fritz.
835. 4 H 225, WCT John Will Fritz.
836. Sneed, *No More Silence*, pp.248–249, interview of Vincent Drain.
837. 4 H 195, WCT Jesse E. Curry.
838. FBI Record 124-10013-10000, November 22, 1963, p.2.
839. 7 H 286, WCT W. E. Barnes.
840. 7 H 278, WCT W. E. Barnes; Sims Exhibit A, 21 H 516; CE 2003, 24 H 287.
841. 7 H 279, WCT W. E. Barnes.
842. Savage, *JFK First Day Evidence*, p.199.
843. 3 H 486–487, WCT Cortlandt Cunningham.
844. WR, p.561.
845. 7 H 271, 281, 283, WCT W. E. Barnes; 3 H 492, WCT Cortlandt Cunningham; 4 H 276, WCT J. C. Day.
846. Sims Exhibit A, 21 H 516; CE 2003, 24 H 287.
847. 7 H 279, 282–283, WCT W. E. Barnes; Savage, *JFK First Day Evidence*, p.197.
848. 7 H 282–283, WCT W. E. Barnes.
849. 7 H 283, WCT W. E. Barnes.
850. 7 H 284–285, WCT W. E. Barnes.
851. 7 H 285, WCT W. E. Barnes.

852. NBC News, *Seventy Hours and Thirty Minutes*, p.48.
853. CE 2003, 24 H 293.
854. 4 H 218–219, WCT John Will Fritz.
855. 9 H 117, WCT Ilya A. Mamantov.
856. 4 H 218, WCT John Will Fritz.
857. 4 H 218–219, WCT John Will Fritz.
858. 9 H 103–104, 106, WCT Ilya A. Mamantov.
859. Oswald with Land and Land, *Lee*, p.24.
860. 1 H 346–347, WCT Robert Edward Lee Oswald.
861. 1 H 143–144, WCT Marguerite Oswald.
862. Oswald with Land and Land, *Lee*, p.24; 1 H 456–457, WCT Robert Edward Lee Oswald; CE 323, 16 H 894.
863. 1 H 144, WCT Marguerite Oswald.
864. Oswald with Land and Land, *Lee*, p.24.
865. "America's Long Vigil," p.29; Oswald with Land and Land, *Lee*, p.25.
866. Oswald with Land and Land, *Lee*, p.25.
867. Bonner, *Investigation of a Homicide*, pp.151–152.
868. Bonner, *Investigation of a Homicide*, pp.152–154; Telephone interview of William Alexander by author on December 12, 2000.
869. 3 H 83, WCT Ruth Hyde Paine; McMillan, *Marina and Lee*, pp.543–544.
870. 3 H 83, WCT Ruth Hyde Paine.
871. 1 H 146, WCT Marguerite Oswald.
872. 3 H 83–84, WCT Ruth Hyde Paine; 1 H 144–145, WCT Marguerite Oswald.
873. 1 H 145, WCT Marguerite Oswald.
874. 1 H 145, WCT Marguerite Oswald; 3 H 83–84, WCT Ruth Hyde Paine.
875. McMillan, *Marina and Lee*, p.543.
876. 1 H 146, WCT Marguerite Oswald.
877. Allen Grant, "Life Catches Up to Marina Oswald," *Los Angeles Times*, November 22, 1988, part V, p.8.
878. 1 H 457–458, WCT Robert Edward Lee Oswald; CE 323, 16 H 895; Oswald with Land and Land, *Lee*, p.27.
879. Sneed, *No More Silence*, pp.550–551, interview of William F. Alexander; Telephone interview of William Alexander by author on December 12, 2000.
880. 4 H 195 WCT Jesse E. Curry.
881. 11 H 205, WC affidavit of Louis Feldsott.
882. 11 H 206, WC affidavit of J. Philip Lux; 11 H 207, WC affidavit of Albert C. Yeargan Jr.
883. 11 H 205, WC affidavit of Louis Feldsott.
884. 7 H 364–365, WCT William J. Waldman; 7 H 370–371, WCT Mitchell J. Scibor; Bishop, *Day Kennedy Was Shot*, p.671.
885. 2 H 364, WCT Dr. James J. Humes; HSCA Record 180-10097-10185, Testimony of Pierre A. Finck, State of Louisiana vs. Clay L. Shaw, February 25, 1969, pp.15–16.
886. ARRB MD 44, FBI Report of O'Neill and Sibert, November 26, 1963, p.4.
887. ARRB MD 47, Affidavit of Francis X. O'Neill Jr., November 8, 1978, p.6.
888. ARRB MD 44, FBI Report of O'Neill and Sibert, November 26, 1963, p.4; ARRB MD 46, Affidavit of James W. Sibert, October 24, 1978, p.3.
889. ARRB MD 44, FBI Report of O'Neill and Sibert, November 26, 1963, pp.4–5; 2 H 367–368, WCT Dr. James J. Humes.
890. Telephone interview of Eva Grant by author on June 10, 1986; see also WR, p.338.
891. WR, pp.293–295.

892. CE 1470, 22 H 889, FBI interview of Irving Katz on November 25, 1963; CE 1485, 22 H 907; 14 H 417, WCT Earl Ruby; 15 H 224, WCT Edward J. Pullman.

893. CE 1479, 22 H 900.

894. 15 H 224, WCT Edward J. Pullman.

895. CE 1711, 23 H 207.

896. 5 H 184, WCT Jack L. Ruby.

897. 15 H 624, WCT Lawrence V. Meyers; CE 1747, 23 H 355.

898. 14 H 484–485, WCT Eva Grant.

899. Grant Exhibit No. 1, 20 H 9–10.

900. Grant Exhibit No. 1, 20 H 9–10; 15 H 42, WCT Hyman Rubenstein.

901. CE 2408, 25 H 406–407; 15 H 579–581, WCT Richard L. Saunders; 15 H 575, WCT Billy A. Rea; see also 15 H 541, WCT John Newnam.

902. 5 H 185, WCT Jack L. Ruby; 15 H 324, WCT Eva Grant.

903. 15 H 542, WCT John Newnam.

904. 5 H 185, WCT Jack L. Ruby.

905. 5 H 185, WCT Jack L. Ruby.

906. CE 2303, 25 H 245; 13 H 333, WCT Andrew Armstrong Jr.

907. 13 H 452, WCT Curtis LaVerne Crafard.

908. CE 2303, 25 H 245.

909. 14 H 151, WCT Ralph Paul.

910. 15 H 283, WCT Eileen Kaminsky.

911. CE 2003, 24 H 230; Wills and Demaris, *Jack Ruby*, p.20.

912. 15 H 31–32, WCT Hyman Rubenstein.

913. CE 2243, 25 H 143.

914. 14 H 559–560, WCT Jack L. Ruby; CE 1620, 23 H 98, FBI interview of Gayle M. Tippit on December 16, 1963; Hall (C. Ray) Exhibit No. 3, 20 H 57; CE 2430, 25 H 530; Tippit in Special Services Bureau: Batchelor Exhibit No. 5002, 19 H 20.

915. Grant Exhibit No. 1, 20 H 11–12.

916. WR, pp.337–338; 5 H 186, WCT Jack L. Ruby; 15 H 328, WCT Eva Grant; CE 2273, 25 H 197, FBI interview of Donald Safran on December 27, 1963; first time Carousel dark: Wills and Demaris, *Jack Ruby*, p.46.

917. 14 H 468, 15 H 327, 329, 331, WCT Eva Grant.

918. CE 2282, 25 H 206; WR, p.340.

919. CE 2281, 25 H 205.

920. 1 HSCA 478–480.

921. Hall (C. Ray) Exhibit No. 3, p.7, 20 H 52.

922. 5 H 187, WCT Jack L. Ruby; 13 H 324, WCT Andrew Armstrong Jr.; 14 H 485, WCT Eva Grant.

923. Joyce Gordon, Carousel stripper, on *Peter Jennings Reporting: The Kennedy Assassination: Beyond Conspiracy*, ABC News Special, November 20, 2003.

924. 5 H 187, WCT Jack L. Ruby; CE 2248, 25 H 146, FBI interview of Dallas police detective Richard Sims, November 28, 1963; eight black cherries and two celery tonics: CE 2252, 25 H 176.

925. 5 H 188, WCT Jack L. Ruby; CE 2252, 25 H 176, FBI interview of John Frickstad on November 30, 1963; Hall (C. Ray) Exhibit No. 3, 20 H 51; 14 H 434, WCT Eva Grant.

926. 5 H 188, WCT Jack L. Ruby; 15 H 484, WCT William Glenn Duncan Jr.

927. 5 H 188, WCT Jack L. Ruby; 15 H 616–618, WCT Roy E. Standifer; Standifer Exhibit No. 1, 21 H 549.

928. 13 H 182–184, 187–188, WCT A. M. Eberhardt; 5 H 188–189, WCT Jack L. Ruby; CE

2410, 25 H 477–479, Testimony of *Dallas Morning News* reporter John Rutledge at Jack Ruby trial, March 4, 1964; Ruby steps inside room: 15 H 351, WCT Victor F. Robertson Jr.

929. Oswald with Land and Land, *Lee*, pp.26–27; CE 323, 16 H 895.

930. 5 H 218, 240, WCT Henry Wade.

931. 5 H 219, WCT Henry Wade.

932. 5 H 259, WCT Waggoner Carr.

933. 5 H 219, 236, 240, WCT Henry Wade.

934. 5 H 229, WCT Henry Wade.

935. 5 H 218–219, WCT Henry Wade; 5 H 259, WCT Waggoner Carr.

936. Bishop, *Day Kennedy Was Shot*, pp.599–600.

937. 7 H 323, WCT Gregory Lee Olds.

938. Bishop, *Day Kennedy Was Shot*, p.600.

939. CE 2003, 24 H 293.

940. Excerpts from unpublished memoir of Horace Busby in *Los Angeles Times Magazine*, November 16, 2003, pp.23, 25, 27.

941. 3 H 83–84, WCT Ruth Hyde Paine.

942. McMillan, *Marina and Lee*, p.341.

943. McMillan, *Marina and Lee*, p.544; 1 H 79, WCT Marina N. Oswald; 1 H 146, WCT Marguerite Oswald; CE 1787, 23 H 398.

944. McMillan, *Marina and Lee*, p.544; 1 H 72–73, WCT Marina N. Oswald.

945. McMillan, *Marina and Lee*, p.545.

946. 5 H 219–220, WCT Henry Wade.

947. Stolley, "Shots Seen Round the World"; Trask, *Pictures of the Pain*, pp.81–83.

948. 2 H 354, WCT Dr. James J. Humes; but see ARRB 56 (two pieces of skull) and ARRB 259 (one piece); however, Dr. Finck also believes there were at least three pieces of skull—see AFIP 205-10001-10002, unnumbered p.2.

949. 2 H 354, WCT Dr. James J. Humes.

950. 2 H 355, WCT Dr. James J. Humes.

951. 2 H 379–380, WCT Lt. Col. Pierre A. Finck; AFIP Record 205-10001-10002, Memorandum, Finck to Blumberg, pp.2, 15; also ARRB MD 28; ARRB MD 44, FBI Report of O'Neill and Sibert, November 26, 1963, p.5; Breo, "JFK's Death, Part III," pp.1752, 1754.

952. ARRB MD 44, FBI Report of O'Neill and Sibert, November 26, 1963, p.5; CE 387, 15 H 978.

953. ARRB MD 44, FBI Report of O'Neill and Sibert, November 26, 1963, pp.2–3.

954. ARRB MD 78, Memorandum, Capt. J. H. Stover to Roy H. Kellerman, November 22, 1963.

955. ARRB MD 190, Memorandum, Cmdr. John H. Ebersole to Roy H. Kellerman, November 22, 1963.

956. HSCA Record 180-10109-10368, Letter, James J. Rowley, Secret Service, to Assistant Attorney General Barefoot Sanders, February 23, 1967, attachment p.1, ARRB MD 122.

957. Manchester, *Death of a President*, pp.433, 435.

958. ARRB MD 182, ARRB Meeting Report, Interview of Joseph E. Hagan, May 17, 1996, p.3; ARRB Transcript of Proceedings, Deposition of Dr. James Joseph Humes, February 13, 1996, p.91.

959. ARRB MD 181, ARRB Meeting Report, Interview of John VanHoesen, September 26, 1996, p.2.

960. ARRB MD 182, ARRB Meeting Report, Interview of Joseph E. Hagan, May 17, 1996, p.3.

961. ARRB MD 181, ARRB Meeting Report, Interview of John VanHoesen, September 26, 1996, p.2; ARRB MD 182, ARRB Meeting Report, Interview of Joseph E. Hagan, May 17, 1996, p.3; Manchester, *Death of a President*, p.433.

962. Manchester, *Death of a President*, pp.431–432.

963. Oswald with Land and Land, *Lee*, pp.27–28; CE 323, 16 H 895–896.

964. 7 H 323, WCT Gregory Lee Olds; Bishop, *Day Kennedy Was Shot*, p.601.

965. Curry, *JFK Assassination File*, pp.78–79.

966. CE 2003, 24 H 288; Johnston Exhibit No. 1, 20 H 314; Johnston Exhibit No. 4, 20 H 321–322.

967. Sims Exhibit A, 21 H 516; 7 H 175, WCT Richard M. Sims; 7 H 132, WCT Elmer L. Boyd.

968. 4 H 195, WCT Jesse E. Curry.

969. 5 H 231–232, WCT Henry Wade.

970. 4 H 195, WCT Jesse E. Curry.

971. 4 H 260, WCT J. C. Day.

972. Bishop, *Day Kennedy Was Shot*, pp.614–615; Sneed, *No More Silence*, pp.248–249, interview of Vincent Drain.

973. 4 H 260, WCT J. C. Day; CE 139, 16 H 512; CE 2003, item K1, 24 H 262.

974. 4 H 254, WCT J. C. Day; CE 543, 544, 17 H 241; CE 545, 17 H 241; CE 2003, items Q6 and Q7, 24 H 262.

975. CE 545, 17 H 241.

976. DMA, folder 7, box 10, item 9; CE 2003, 24 H 347; CE 545, 17 H 241; 4 H 254–256, WCT J. C. Day.

977. CE 141, 16 H 513; CE 2003, item Q8, 24 H 262.

978. 4 H 267, WCT J. C. Day; CE 142, 16 H 513; CE 2003, item Q10, 24 H 262.

979. 4 H 267, WCT J. C. Day.

980. 4 H 267, WCT J. C. Day.

981. Sneed, *No More Silence*, p.238, interview of Vincent Drain.

982. *Four Days in November*, television documentary, David Wolper Productions, 1964; Sneed, *No More Silence*, p.249.

983. CE 2142, 24 H 750–753; CE 2173, 24 H 846–847; WFAA-TV Collection, November 22, 1963, PKT-11, Sixth Floor Museum at Dealey Plaza.

984. WFAA-TV Collection, November 22, 1963, PKT-11; KRLD-TV Collection, November 22, 1963, reel 23, Sixth Floor Museum at Dealey Plaza.

985. CE 2142, 24 H 750–753; CE 2173, 24 H 846–847; WFAA-TV Collection, November 22, 1963, PKT-11; KRLD-TV Collection, November 22, 1963, reel 23, Sixth Floor Museum at Dealey Plaza.

986. CE 2142, 24 H 750–753.

987. NBC News, *Seventy Hours and Thirty Minutes*, pp.46–47; Bishop, *Day Kennedy was Shot*, p.604.

988. 7 H 322–323, WCT Gregory Lee Olds; Bishop, *Day Kennedy Was Shot*, pp.601–603.

989. 4 H 232, WCT John Will Fritz.

990. 4 H 166, WCT Jesse E. Curry; Curry, *JFK Assassination File*, p.76.

991. 4 H 153, 157, WCT Jesse E. Curry.

992. 4 H 219, WCT John Will Fritz.

993. Sims Exhibit A, 21 H 516; 7 H 175, WCT Richard M. Sims; 7 H 132, WCT Elmer L. Boyd.

994. 5 H 188, 189, 199, WCT Jack L. Ruby; Hall (C. Ray) Exhibit No. 3, 20 H 52; CE 2410, 25 H 476, Testimony of John Rutledge at Ruby trial; 15 H 257, WCT Russell Lee Moore (Knight); 15 H 484, WCT William Glenn Duncan Jr.

995. 5 H 189, WCT Jack L. Ruby; CE 2424, 25 H 524.

996. CE 323, 16 H 896.

997. Oswald with Land and Land, *Lee*, p.28.

998. Waldman Exhibit No. 5, 21 H 701.

999. Waldman Exhibit No. 3, 21 H 698; 7 H 362–363, WCT William J. Waldman.

1000. Waldman Exhibit No. 2, 21 H 693.

1001. Waldman Exhibit No. 4, 21 H 699; 7 H 371, WCT Mitchell J. Scibor.

1002. Waldman Exhibit No. 4, 21 H 700; 7 H 364, WCT William J. Waldman.

1003. 7 H 364–365, WCT William J. Waldman; Bishop, *Day Kennedy Was Shot*, p.671.

1004. 7 H 370, WCT Mitchell J. Scibor.

1005. 4 H 219, WCT John Will Fritz; KRLD-TV Collection, November 23, 1963, reel 23, Sixth Floor Museum at Dealey Plaza; CE 2151, 24 H 785.

1006. WFAA-TV, November 23, 1963, PKT-26, PKF-3; KRLD-TV Collection, November 23, 1963, reel 23, Sixth Floor Museum at Dealey Plaza.

1007. KRLD-TV Collection, November 23, 1963, reel 54, Sixth Floor Museum at Dealey Plaza; CE 2166, 24 H 817.

1008. Sims Exhibit A, 21 H 516–517; CE 2003, 24 H 288.

1009. Lianne Hart, "City Makes a Date with JFK History," *Los Angeles Times*, November 14, 2004, p.A21.

1010. 4 H 153–154, WCT Jesse E. Curry; 7 H 328, WCT H. Louis Nichols; Bishop, *Day Kennedy Was Shot*, pp.386–387.

1011. CE 2169, 24 H 829–831; WFAA-TV Collection, November 23, 1963, PKT-27; KRLD-TV Collection, November 23, 1963, reel 23, Sixth Floor Museum at Dealey Plaza.

1012. 4 H 248, WCT T. L. Baker; Savage, *JFK First Day Evidence*, pp.72–75; Curry, *JFK Assassination File*, pp.76, 78; Bishop, *Day Kennedy Was Shot*, pp.641, 645.

1013. Telephone interview of William Alexander by author on December 8, 2000; 6 H 368–371, WCT Joe R. Molina; CE 1381, 22 H 664; CE 2036, 24 H 447–450; CE 3132, 26 H 810–811; CE 2162, 24 H 807.

1014. CE 2169, 24 H 829–831; WFAA-TV Collection, November 23, 1963, PKT-27, Sixth Floor Museum at Dealey Plaza; 5 H 189, WCT Jack L. Ruby; 5 H 223, WCT Henry Wade.

1015. CE 2169, 24 H 832–835; WFAA-TV Collection, November 23, 1963, PKT-27; KRLD-TV Collection, November 23, 1963, reel 23, Sixth Floor Museum at Dealey Plaza.

1016. CE 2169, 24 H 838–839; WFAA-TV Collection, November 23, 1963, PKT-27; KRLD-TV Collection, November 23, 1963, reel 23, Sixth Floor Museum at Dealey Plaza.

1017. CE 2169, 24 H 841; WFAA-TV Collection, November 23, 1963, PKT-27; KRLD-TV Collection, November 23, 1963, reel 23, Sixth Floor Museum at Dealey Plaza.

1018. 5 H 189–190, WCT Jack L. Ruby; 15 H 484–486, WCT William Glenn Duncan Jr.; 15 H 254–256, WCT Russell Lee Moore (Russ Knight).

1019. 15 H 508, 513, WCT David L. Johnston.

1020. Curry, *JFK Assassination File*, p.79; Savage, *JFK First Day Evidence*, pp.75–77; 4 H 221, WCT John Will Fritz; 4 H 155–157, WCT Jesse E. Curry; 4 H 248, WCT T. L. Baker.

1021. Bishop, *Day Kennedy Was Shot*, p.651.

1022. 4 H 156, WCT Jesse E. Curry; 4 H 221, WCT John Will Fritz; 12 H 95–96, WCT M. W. Stevenson; 15 H 507–508, 513, WCT David L. Johnston; Savage, *JFK First Day Evidence*, pp.75–76.

1023. Johnston Exhibit Nos. 1 and 4, 20 H 315, 321–322; 15 H 508, WCT David L. Johnston.

1024. 4 H 156, WCT Jesse E. Curry.

1025. 15 H 508, WCT David L. Johnston.

1026. CE 2003, 24 H 288; 4 H 156–157, WCT Jesse E. Curry.

1027. 15 H 529–534, WCT Danny Patrick McCurdy; McCurdy Exhibit No. 1, 20 H 552–553; 15 H 252–254, 257–261, 264–265, WCT Russell Lee Moore (Russ Knight); 15 H 222–231, WCT Edward J. Pullman; 15 H 484–488, WCT William Glenn Duncan Jr.; CE 2294, 25 H 228 (Glenn Duncan); CE 2285, 25 H 211–212 (*Life Line*); 15 H 365–366, WCT Icarus M. Pappas.

1028. Newseum with Trost and Bennett, *President Kennedy Has Been Shot*, p.168.

1029. CE 2003, 24 H 288; Johnston Exhibit No. 1, 20 H 315; 12 H 95, WCT M. W. Stevenson.

1030. ARRB MD 130, Embalmers Personal Remarks.

1031. 5 H 191, WCT Jack L. Ruby; 14 H 626–633, 636, WCT Harry N. Olsen; 14 H 643–647, WCT Kay Helen Olsen.

1032. ARRB MD 134, Funeral Arrangements for John Fitzgerald Kennedy, November 22, 1963, p.2.

1033. ARRB MD 163, After Action Report, joint casket team state funeral, President John Fitzgerald Kennedy, Samuel R. Bird, December 10, 1963, p.2.

1034. ARRB MD 182, ARRB Meeting Report, Interview of Joseph E. Hagan, May 17, 1996, p.3; ARRB MD 134, Funeral Arrangements for John Fitzgerald Kennedy, November 22, 1963, p.2.

1035. ARRB MD 236, Memorandum, R. E. Boyijian to CO, Marine Corps Institute Company, November 26, 1963; AFIP Record 205-10001-10002, Memorandum, Finck to Blumberg, pp.3–4; also ARRB MD 28.

1036. Manchester, *Death of a President*, p.440.

1037. ARRB Transcript of Proceedings, Deposition of Dr. James Joseph Humes, February 13, 1996, p.81.

1038. Breo, "JFK's Death—The Plain Truth from the MDs Who Did the Autopsy," p.2799.

1039. ARRB MD 134, Funeral Arrangements for John Fitzgerald Kennedy, November 23, 1963, p.2.

1040. Manchester, *Death of a President*, p.440.

1041. Bishop, *Day Kennedy Was Shot*, pp.676–678; Manchester, *Death of a President*, pp.441–443; Schlesinger, *Robert Kennedy and His Times*, pp.610–611; ARRB MD 134, Funeral Arrangements for John Fitzgerald Kennedy, November 23, 1963, p.2.

1042. Schlesinger, *Robert Kennedy and His Times*, pp.610–611.

1043. Telephone interview of William Alexander by author on December 8, 2000; CE 2036, 24 H 447; CE 3132, 26 H 811.

1044. 7 H 364–365, WCT William J. Waldman; 7 H 370–371, WCT Mitchell J. Scibor.

1045. 7 H 362–363, 368, WCT William J. Waldman; Waldman Exhibit No. 1, 21 H 692.

1046. 7 H 368, WCT William J. Waldman.

1047. 7 H 369, WCT William J. Waldman.

1048. 7 H 367, WCT William J. Waldman.

1049. CE 785, 17 H 675; routinely destroyed: CE 3137, 26 H 819.

1050. CE 788, 789, 17 H 677–678.

1051. 7 H 364–367, WCT William J. Waldman.

1052. Waldman Exhibit No. 8, 21 H 704; CE 785, 17 H 675.

1053. 5 H 191, 194, WCT Jack L. Ruby; CE 2816, 26 H 237–242, Testimony of Gadash at Jack Ruby trial; WR, p.339, Ads of Carousel and Vegas being closed; advertising sketch of twistboard: CE 2791, 26 H 180; CE 2297, 25 H 231–232, FBI interviews of *Dallas Herald* employees Kennedy E. Griffith and Roy A. Pryor; 15 H 565–570, WCT Arthur William Watherwax; 15 H 559, 561, WCT Roy A. Pryor.

1054. 14 H 168–193, WCT George Senator; CD 106, p.87, FBI interview of George Senator on December 19, 1963; Wills and Demaris, *Jack Ruby*, p.45.

1055. 13 H 407–413, 420, 463–466, 14 H 87–90, WCT Curtis LaVerne Crafard; Crafard Exhibit No. 5226, 19 H 353–354, 357–358; 14 H 218–221, WCT George Senator; 5 H 203, WCT Jack L. Ruby.

1056. 14 H 219–224, WCT George Senator; CE 2003, 24 H 225; Hall (C. Ray) Exhibit No. 3, 20 H 53–54; Ruby's crying in the apartment and being out in space: Testimony of Senator at Ruby's murder trial: Holloway, *Dallas and the Jack Ruby Trial*, p.54.

1057. CE 323, 16 H 897–898; Oswald with Land and Land, *Lee*, pp.135–136.

1058. Hosty with Hosty, *Assignment: Oswald*, pp.35–37; 11 H 468, WC affidavit of Bardwell D. Odum; Odum Exhibit No. 1, 20 H 691.

1059. Bonner, *Investigation of a Homicide*, p.173.

1060. Manchester, *Death of a President*, pp.453–454; Holland, *Kennedy Assassination Tapes*, pp.67–68.

1061. Holland, *Kennedy Assassination Tapes*, pp.217–218; *New York Times*, November 24, 1964, p.33.

1062. 1 H 148, WCT Marguerite Oswald; 3 H 84, WCT Ruth Hyde Paine.

1063. 1 H 148, WCT Marguerite Oswald.

1064. 3 H 85, WCT Ruth Hyde Paine.

1065. 3 H 84, WCT Ruth Hyde Paine; 1 H 148, WCT Marguerite Oswald.

1066. 3 H 84, WCT Ruth Hyde Paine.

1067. Stolley, "What Happened Next . . . ," pp.134–135; Wrone, *Zapruder Film*, pp.33–34; see also 5 H 138 WCT Lyndal L. Shaneyfelt.

1068. 7 H 293–294, WCT Harry D. Holmes.

1069. ARRB MD 58, Interview of Malcolm Perry by Andy Purdy and T. M. Flanagan on January 11, 1978, p.9; 7 HSCA 257.

1070. 2 H 363, WCT Dr. James J. Humes; ARRB MD 19, Memorandum to File, Andy Purdy, August 17, 1977, p.8.

1071. Telephone interview of William Alexander by author on December 12, 2000.

1072. CE 323, 16 H 898; Oswald with Land and Land, *Lee*, pp.135–136.

1073. 5 H 225, WCT Henry Wade; 1 H 148, WCT Marguerite Oswald.

1074. 5 H 225–226, WCT Henry Wade; CE 323, 16 H 898; Oswald with Land and Land, *Lee*, pp.136–137.

1075. 5 H 225–226, WCT Henry Wade.

1076. Manchester, *Death of a President*, pp.209, 248, 501; NBC News, *Seventy Hours and Thirty Minutes*, p.101; Davis, *Kennedys: Dynasty and Disaster*, p.527.

1077. CE 2146, 24 H 763–766, 768; WFAA-TV Collection, November 23, 1963, PKT-12; KRLD-TV Collection, November 23, 1963, reels 4 and 10, Sixth Floor Museum at Dealey Plaza.

1078. CE 2145, 24 H 760; WFAA-TV Collection, November 23, 1963, PKT-12; KRLD-TV Collection, November 23, 1963, reels 4 and 10, Sixth Floor Museum at Dealey Plaza.

1079. CE 2146, 24 H 765–766, 768–769; WFAA-TV Collection, November 23, 1963, PKT-12; KRLD-TV Collection, November 23, 1963, reels 4 and 10, Sixth Floor Museum at Dealey Plaza.

1080. Extremely desirous: Letter from J. E. Curry to Earl Warren of May 28, 1964; had not interviewed Oswald in Dallas or had him under surveillance: Letter from J. Gordon Shanklin to Jesse E. Curry of October 13, 1964.

1081. Committee to Investigate Assassinations, *Assassination of JFK by Coincidence or Conspiracy?* pp.253, 411.

1082. 2 H 253, 260, WCT William Wayne Whaley; CE 2003, 24 H 267, 288.

1083. FBI Record 124–10013–10012, November 23, 1963; Church Committee Report, p.39.

1084. *New York Times*, November 24, 1963, pp.1, 2, 6, 8–9; "America's Long Vigil," pp.31–32; Manchester, *Death of a President*, p.368; United Press International, *Four Days*, pp.46–49; Grosvenor, "Last Full Measure," pp.312, 319; "Sorrow Rings a World," pp.117–126.

1085. WFAA-TV Collection, November 23, 1963, PKT-14; KRLD-TV Collection, November 23, 1963, reels 4 and 10, Sixth Floor Museum at Dealey Plaza.

1086. 10:35 a.m. time for start of interrogation: Fritz's handwritten notes; Kelley Exhibit A, 20 H 440; Sims Exhibit A, 21 H 517; CE 1988, 24 H 18; CE 2003, 24 H 272.

1087. Kelley Exhibit A, 20 H 440; CE 1988, 24 H 18; CE 2003, 24 H 267.

1088. 4 H 218–219, WCT John Will Fritz; Kelley Exhibit A, 20 H 440; CE 2003, 24 H 267.

1089. CE 1988, 24 H 18.

1090. 4 H 219, WCT John Will Fritz.

1091. 4 H 223, WCT John Will Fritz; Kelley Exhibit A, 20 H 440; CE 1988, 24 H 18–19; CE 2003, 24 H 267.

1092. 1 H 148–149, WCT Marguerite Oswald; Oswald with Land and Land, *Lee*, pp.137–139.

1093. 4 H 224, WCT John Will Fritz; CE 2003, 24 H 267; Kelley Exhibit A, 20 H 440; but see CE 1988, 24 H 19, where FBI agent James W. Bookhout says Oswald said he ate alone, and two Negro employees, one named Junior, possibly walked through the lunchroom while he was eating.

1094. Kelley Exhibit A, 20 H 440; CE 1988, 24 H 19; CE 2003, 24 H 267.

1095. CE 2003, 24 H 267.

1096. CE 1988, 24 H 19.

1097. CE 1988, 24 H 19.

1098. Kelley Exhibit A, 20 H 440–441; CE 1988, 24 H 19; CE 2003, 24 H 267.

1099. Kelley Exhibit A, 20 H 440–441; CE 1988, 24 H 19.

1100. Kelley Exhibit A, 20 H 441; CE 1988, 24 H 19; CE 2003, 24 H 268.

1101. 4 H 215, 225, WCT John Will Fritz; 7 H 356, WCT Forrest V. Sorels; Kelley Exhibit A, 20 H 441; CE 1988, 24 H 19.

1102. Kelley Exhibit A, 20 H 441; CE 1988, 24 H 19.

1103. Kelley Exhibit A, 20 H 441; CE 1988, 24 H 19.

1104. Kelley Exhibit A, 20 H 441; CE 1988, 24 H 19.

1105. CE 796, 17 H 682.

1106. Kelley Exhibit A, 20 H 441; CE 1988, 24 H 19.

1107. CE 1988, 24 H 20.

1108. WR, p.627; Kelley Exhibit A, 20 H 441; CE 1988, 24 H 20.

1109. 7 H 357, WCT Forrest V. Sorels.

1110. Sneed, *No More Silence*, p.363, interview of Harry D. Holmes.

1111. CE 1937, 23 H 732; WFAA-TV Collection, November 23, 1963, PKT-14; KRLD-TV Collection, November 23, 1963, reel 4, Sixth Floor Museum at Dealey Plaza.

1112. CE 2162, 24 H 807–809; WFAA-TV Collection, November 23, 1963, PKT-14; KRLD-TV Collection, November 23, 1963, reel 4, Sixth Floor Museum at Dealey Plaza.

1113. 1 H 149, WCT Marguerite Oswald.

1114. McMillan, *Marina and Lee*, p.546.

1115. 1 H 149, WCT Marguerite Oswald.

1116. 1 H 450, WCT Robert Edward Lee Oswald; CE 323, 16 H 899; Oswald with Land and Land, *Lee*, pp.139–140.

1117. Sims Exhibit A, 21 H 517; CE 2003, 24 H 288; CE 2003, 24 H 348; 7 H 439, WCT Earlene Roberts; 7 H 134, WCT Elmer L. Boyd; 7 H 177, WCT Richard M. Sims.

1118. CE 2144, 24 H 754–757; CE 2146, 24 H 766–767; WFAA-TV Collection, November 23, 1963, PKT-14; KRLD-TV Collection, November 23, 1963, reel 73, Sixth Floor Museum at Dealey Plaza.

1119. CE 2002, 24 H 97.

1120. Sneed, *No More Silence*, p.383; Bonner, *Investigation of a Homicide*, pp.175–177.

1121. Kelley Exhibit A, 20 H 442.

1122. Kelley Exhibit A, 20 H 442; 7 H 230–231, WCT Guy F. Rose; CE 2003, 24 H 268–269.

1123. CE 2003, 24 H 394; Oswald with Land and Land, *Lee*, p.139.

1124. 1 H 149, WCT Marguerite Oswald; Oswald with Land and Land, *Lee*, p.139.

1125. 1 H 149, WCT Marguerite Oswald; WFAA-TV Collection, November 23, 1963, PKT-21; KRLD-TV Collection, November 23, 1963, reels 16 and 73, Sixth Floor Museum at Dealey Plaza.

1126. CE 2172, 24 H 843–845; WFAA-TV Collection, November 23, 1963, PKT-25; KRLD-TV Collection, November 23, 1963, reel 26, Sixth Floor Museum at Dealey Plaza.

1127. *Newsday*, November 25, 1963; Joesten, *Oswald: Assassin or Fall Guy?* p.44.

1128. CD 1444, Affidavit of Dallas police officer J. R. Stacy, August 13, 1964; CE 2003, 24 H 289; Oswald with Land and Land, *Lee*, p.142.

1129. McMillan, *Marina and Lee*, pp.546–547.

1130. 1 H 78, WCT Marina N. Oswald.

1131. 1 H 78–79, WCT Marina N. Oswald; McMillan, *Marina and Lee*, pp.546–547.

1132. 1 H 149, WCT Marguerite Oswald.

1133. McMillan, *Marina and Lee*, p.547; 1 H 150, WCT Marguerite Oswald.

1134. 1 H 78–79, WCT Marina N. Oswald; McMillan, *Marina and Lee*, pp.547–548.

1135. CE 1999, 24 H 34–35; CE 2187, 24 H 859–860.

1136. CE 2003, 24 H 288.

1137. 7 H 193, WCT Richard S. Stovall; 3 H 85, WCT Ruth Hyde Paine.

1138. 7 H 194–195, WCT Richard S. Stovall; 7 H 231, WCT Guy F. Rose; Stovall Exhibit B, 21 H 598; Stovall Exhibit C, 21 H 603; 7 H 209, WCT John P. Adamcik.

1139. 7 H 195, WCT Richard S. Stovall; CE 2003, 24 H 346; CD 578, FBI Exhibit D-85, March 7, 1964.

1140. 7 H 195, WCT Richard S. Stovall; CE 796, 17 H 682.

1141. 3 H 85, WCT Ruth Hyde Paine; CE 2003, 24 H 290; 7 H 193–194, WCT Richard S. Stovall; 7 H 209, WCT John P. Adamcik; 7 H 215–216, WCT Henry M. Moore; 7 H 231, WCT Guy F. Rose.

1142. WFAA-TV Collection, November 23, 1963, 2:05 p.m. (hallway clock), PKT-25; KRLD-TV Collection, November 23, 1963, 2:05 p.m., reel 20-1, Sixth Floor Museum at Dealey Plaza; NBC News, *Seventy Hours and Thirty Minutes*, p.67; CE 2153, 24 H 787–788.

1143. CE 2003, 24 H 299, 311; 7 H 155, WCT C. N. Dhority; 7 H 265, WCT James R. Leavelle.

1144. CE 2003, 24 H 305; Leavelle Exhibit A, 20 H 502.

1145. KRLD-TV Collection, November 23, 1963, 2:14 p.m., reel 20-1, Sixth Floor Museum at Dealey Plaza.

1146. 3 H 334, 337, WCT William W. Scoggins.

1147. 2 H 261, WCT William Wayne Whaley.

1148. 2 H 260, 266, WCT William Wayne Whaley.

1149. 7 H 265, WCT James R. Leavelle; 7 H 246, WCT Daniel Gutierrez Lujan.

1150. 7 H 266, WCT James R. Leavelle; 2 H 261, WCT William Wayne Whaley.

1151. 3 H 337, WCT William W. Scoggins; 7 H 266, WCT James R. Leavelle.

1152. Interview of James R. Leavelle by Dale K. Myers on July 1, 1996; 7 H 266, WCT James R. Leavelle.

1153. CE 2003, 24 H 299.

1154. CE 2023, 24 H 437.

1155. KRLD–TV Collection, November 23, 1963, 2:25 p.m. CST, reel 20-2, Sixth Floor Museum at Dealey Plaza.

1156. 1 H 151–152, 157, WCT Marguerite Oswald; 1 H 79, WCT Marina N. Oswald.

1157. CE 323, 16 H 900; Oswald with Land and Land, *Lee*, pp.140–141.

1158. CE 2003, 24 H 394.

1159. CE 323, 16 H 900–901; Oswald with Land and Land, *Lee*, pp.142–146.

1160. Oswald with Land and Land, *Lee*, pp.147; CE 323, 16 H 901.

1161. NBC News, *Seventy Hours and Thirty Minutes*, p.71; *New York Times*, November 24, 1963, p.1.

1162. CD 1444, unnumbered p.19, Affidavit of J. L. Popplewell on August 20, 1964; Curry, *JFK Assassination File*, p.74, Affidavit of Dallas police officer Thurber L. Lord on August 20, 1964; 3 H 85–86, WCT Ruth Hyde Paine.

1163. 3 H 85–86, WCT Ruth Hyde Paine; notation of 4:22 p.m. phone call: CE 2187, 24 H 860; CD 1444, Affidavit of Dallas police officer J. L. Popplewell on August 20, 1964.

1164. 7 H 326–332, WCT H. Louis Nichols; Nichols (H. Louis) Exhibit A, 20 H 684–686; 4 H 154–155, 158–159, WCT Jesse E. Curry; CE 2165, 24 H 814.

1165. WFAA–TV Collection, November 23, 1963, PKT-25; KRLD–TV Collection, November 23, 1963, reel 36, Sixth Floor Museum at Dealey Plaza; CE 2165, 24 H 813–816; NBC News, *Seventy Hours and Thirty Minutes*, p.75.

1166. 15 H 508, WCT David L. Johnston; Johnston Exhibit No. 5, 20 H 315; Affidavit in Johnston Exhibit No. 5, 20 H 323.

1167. Johnston Exhibit No. 1, 20 H 315.

1168. WFAA–TV Collection, November 23, 1963, PKT-25; KRLD–TV Collection, November 23, 1963, reel 38, Sixth Floor Museum at Dealey Plaza.

1169. Sims Exhibit A, 21 H 517; CE 2003, 24 H 272, 289, 306.

1170. 7 H 316, WCT James W. Bookhout.

1171. 7 H 231, WCT Guy F. Rose.

1172. WR, p.608; 7 H 231, WCT Guy F. Rose; Savage, *JFK First Day Evidence*, pp.127–130.

1173. 7 H 316, WCT James W. Bookhout.

1174. 7 H 231, WCT Guy F. Rose.

1175. Kelley Exhibit A, 20 H 442; CE 2003, 24 H 269, 289; 4 H 226, WCT John Will Fritz; 7 H 231, WCT Guy F. Rose; 7 H 316, WCT James W. Bookhout.

1176. 4 H 226, WCT John Will Fritz; CE 2003, 24 H 269.

1177. Kelley Exhibit A, 20 H 442; CE 2003, 24 H 269, 289.

1178. WFAA–TV Collection, November 23, 1963, PKT-21; KRLD–TV Collection, November 23, 1963, reel 38, Sixth Floor Museum at Dealey Plaza; CE 2145, 24 H 759–760.

1179. 5 H 115–116, WCT Hon. J. Edgar Hoover.

1180. CE 1789, 23 H 419; 4 H 373, WCT Alwyn Cole.

1181. 4 H 228, WCT John Will Fritz; Kelley Exhibit A, 20 H 442.

1182. CE 2003, 24 H 268; 4 H 228, WCT John Will Fritz.

1183. Kelley Exhibit A, 20 H 442.

1184. WFAA–TV Collection, November 23, 1963, PKT-8, Sixth Floor Museum at Dealey Plaza; Sims Exhibit A, 21 H 517; CE 2003, 24 H 272.

1185. WFAA–TV Collection, November 23, 1963, PKT-8; KRLD–TV Collection, November 23, 1963, reel 44, Sixth Floor Museum at Dealey Plaza.

1186. 1 H 152–153, WCT Marguerite Oswald; 11 H 468, WC affidavit of Bardwell D. Odum; photo: Odum Exhibit No. 1, 20 H 691.

1187. NBC News, *Seventy Hours and Thirty Minutes*, p.80.

1188. 3 H 87–89, WCT Ruth Hyde Paine; 1 H 153, WCT Marguerite Oswald; 8:00 p.m. time of call: CE 2187, 24 H 860; CD 1444, unnumbered p.19, Affidavit of J. L. Popplewell on August 20, 1964.

1189. 1 H 153–154, WCT Marguerite Oswald.

1190. 12 H 2, WCT Charles Batchelor.

1191. 12 H 35, WCT Jesse E. Curry; CE 2002, 24 H 97; 4 H 242, WCT John Will Fritz.

1192. 12 H 2, WCT Charles Batchelor; 1 H 35, WCT Jesse E. Curry.

1193. WFAA–TV Collection, November 23, 1963, PKT-8; KRLD–TV Collection, November 23, 1963, reel 44, Sixth Floor Museum at Dealey Plaza; CE 2150, 24 H 782–785.

1194. Hlavach and Payne, *Reporting the Kennedy Assassination*, p.92; but see King Exhibit No. 5, 20 H 468, saying that a large number of newsmen remained in the third-floor hallways throughout the night.

1195. Hlavach and Payne, *Reporting the Kennedy Assassination*, pp.93–94.

1196. Hlavach and Payne, *Reporting the Kennedy Assassination*, pp.93–94.

1197. 15 H 127, WCT Jesse E. Curry.

1198. CE 2013, 24 H 429.

1199. CE 2013, 24 H 429; CE 2018, 24 H 434; 12 H 48–51, WCT J. E. Decker; 12 H 110, WCT Cecil E. Talbert.

1200. Frazier Exhibit No. 5086, 19 H 770.

1201. Frazier Exhibit No. 5087, 19 H 772.

1202. Frazier Exhibit No. 5086, 19 H 770; 4 H 233–234, WCT John Will Fritz; 12 H 48–51, WCT J. E. Decker.

1203. Frazier Exhibit No. 5086, 19 H 770; 12 H 48–51, WCT J. E. Decker.

1204. Frazier Exhibit No. 5086, 19 H 770–771; 15 H 127, WCT Jesse E. Curry.

1205. Frazier Exhibit No. 5086, 19 H 770; 12 H 53–55, WCT W. B. Frazier; 12 H 48–51, WCT J. E. Decker; 15 H 127, WCT Jesse E. Curry; Stevenson Exhibit No. 5053, 21 H 587; 12 H 4, WCT Charles Batchelor.

1206. CE 2003, 24 H 295, 298, 312.

1207. Talbert Exhibit No. 5065, 21 H 653.

1208. 1 H 155, WCT Marguerite Oswald; CE 323, 16 H 902.

1209. 2 H 337–338, WCT Peter Paul Gregory.

1210. 1 H 155, WCT Marguerite Oswald.

1211. 1 H 156, WCT Marguerite Oswald.

1212. 1 H 156, WCT Marguerite Oswald.

1213. 2 H 344, WCT Peter Paul Gregory.

1214. 1 H 156, WCT Marguerite Oswald; 2 H 344, WCT Peter Paul Gregory.

1215. 2 H 344, WCT Peter Paul Gregory.

1216. 12 H 4–6, WCT Charles Batchelor; 15 H 128, WCT Jesse E. Curry.

1217. NBC News, *Seventy Hours and Thirty Minutes*, p.88.

1218. CE 2003, 24 H 312.

1219. 7 H 296, WCT Harry D. Holmes; Sneed, *No More Silence*, p.359, interview of Harry D. Holmes.

1220. Stevenson Exhibit No. 5053, 21 H 587.

1221. Stevenson Exhibit No. 5053, 21 H 587; 12 H 7, WCT Charles Batchelor; 12 H 36–37, 15 H 126, WCT Jesse E. Curry.

1222. 12 H 7–8, 12, WCT Charles Batchelor.

1223. Fleming Exhibit No. 1, 19 H 651; 15 H 162, WCT Harold J. Fleming.

1224. 12 H 8, WCT Charles Batchelor; Stevenson Exhibit No. 5053, 21 H 588.

1225. 12 H 109–112, 128, 15 H 183–185, WCT Cecil E. Talbert; 12 H 338, WCT Rio Sam Pierce; Pierce (Rio S.) Exhibit No. 5077, 21 H 131; Pierce (Rio S.) Exhibit No. 5078, 21 H 133–134; Pierce (Rio S.) Exhibit No. 5079, 21 H 135–136.

1226. 12 H 338, WCT Rio Sam Pierce; 12 H 420, Patrick Trevore Dean.

1227. HSCA Record 180-10073-10050, HSCA interview of Patrick Dean, November 15, 1977; 12 H 141, WCT Charles Oliver Arnett.

1228. Sneed, *No More Silence*, p.420.

1229. 12 H 420–421, 423, WCT Patrick Trevore Dean; sketch of garage: CE 2179, 24 H 851.

1230. 12 H 173–175, WCT Alvin R. Brock; Brock (Alvin R.) Exhibit No. 5113, 19 H 177.

1231. 12 H 422, 424, WCT Patrick Trevore Dean; 12 H 173–174, WCT Alvin R. Brock.

1232. CE 2003, 24 H 289.

1233. 14 H 236, WCT George Senator; CE 1810, 23 H 461.

1234. 13 H 466–471, WCT Curtis LaVerne Crafard.

1235. 5 H 198, WCT Jack L. Ruby.

1236. 15 H 196, WCT Marjorie R. Richey.

1237. CE 2341, 25 H 315; but see Hall (C. Ray) Exhibit No. 2, 20 H 42, for Ruby leaving his apartment in the morning. Hall (C. Ray) Exhibit No. 3, 20 H 54, would indicate it was very unlikely Ruby left his apartment before the early afternoon.

1238. Hallmark Exhibit No. 1, 20 H 68–69; 15 H 491–492, WCT Garnett Claud Hallmark.

1239. 15 H 434, WCT Kenneth Lawry Dowe.

1240. CE 2407, 25 H 402–403.

1241. Bellocchio Exhibit No. 1, 19 H 161–162; 15 H 468–472, WCT Frank Bellocchio.

1242. Hall (C. Ray) Exhibit No. 3, 20 H 54, FBI interview of Ruby on December 21, 1963; CE 2324, 25 H 284, FBI interview of James Chaney on November 28, 1963; CE 2413, 25 H 498–500, Testimony of Wes Wise at Jack Ruby's trial; Grant Exhibit No. 1, 20 H 13; CE 2407, 25 H 402–403.

1243. 15 H 334, 336–339, 14 H 434–435, WCT Eva Grant; Grant Exhibit No. 1, 20 H 12–13; 15 H 262, WCT Russell Lee Moore (Knight).

1244. 15 H 514, 519–522, WCT Stanley M. Kaufman; Grant Exhibit No. 1, 20 H 12–13; 15 H 337–338, WCT Eva Grant.

1245. 14 H 485, WCT Eva Grant; sides: CE 1227, 22 H 335; CE 1696, 23 H 169.

1246. 13 H 209–211, WCT Karen Bennett Carlin; 13 H 203–204, WCT Bruce Ray Carlin; CE 2287, 25 H 214; Grant Exhibit No. 1, 20 H 13; WR, p.348.

1247. 15 H 631–635, WCT Lawrence V. Meyers; CE 2267, 25 H 191.

1248. CE 2334, 25 H 297, FBI interview of Huey Reeves on December 17, 1993; CE 2287, 25 H 214, Affidavit of Huey Reeves on June 9, 1964.

1249. CE 2307, 25 H 251, Telephone records of calls to Paul and Wall; 15 H 670–672, WCT Ralph Paul; 14 H 600, 605–607, WCT Breck Wall.

1250. 15 H 547, 551–552, WCT Robert L. Norton; Norton Exhibit No. 1, 20 H 687.

1251. CE 2337, 25 H 306; WR, pp.351–352.

1252. "My Dear Caroline" letter from Newman R. McLarry to Caroline Kennedy in Hyannis Port, Massachusetts, *Dallas Times Herald*, November 24, 1963, p.2A.

1253. *Dallas Times Herald*, November 24, 1963, p.5A.

1254. 5 H 198–199, WCT Jack L. Ruby; Sorrels Exhibit No. 1, 21 H 537; 13 H 65–68, WCT Forrest V. Sorrels.

1255. 5 H 198, 14 H 532, 536, WCT Jack L. Ruby; Hall (C. Ray) Exhibit No. 2, 20 H 42–43.

1256. 13 H 229–236, WCT Elnora Pitts; Wills and Demaris, *Jack Ruby*, pp.46–47.

1257. 7 H 296–297, WCT Harry D. Holmes; Sneed, *No More Silence*, pp.359–360, interview of Harry D. Holmes.

1258. CE 2003, 24 H 289.

1259. Sneed, *No More Silence*, p.360, interview of Harry D. Holmes.

1260. 7 H 267, WCT James R. Leavelle.

1261. Kelley Exhibit A, 20 H 443.

1262. CE 2064, 24 H 488; 7 H 303, WCT Harry D. Holmes.

1263. 4 H 154, WCT Jesse E. Curry.

1264. 12 H 8–9, WCT Charles Batchelor.

1265. 12 H 113, WCT Cecil E. Talbert; 12 H 428, WCT Patrick Trevore Dean.

1266. 4 H 187, 12 H 35, 15 H 126–127, WCT Jesse E. Curry; 21 H 587, 589, Stevenson Exhibit No. 5053; CE 2002, 24 H 85; 15 H 162, WCT Harold J. Fleming.

1267. 21 H 588, Stevenson Exhibit No. 5053; 15 H 184, 189, WCT Cecil E. Talbert.

1268. CE 2064, 24 H 489.

1269. CE 2064, 24 H 489; Sneed, *No More Silence*, pp.361–362, interview of Harry D. Holmes.

1270. CE 2064, 24 H 489; 7 H 298–299, WCT Harry D. Holmes.

1271. CE 2064, 24 H 489.

1272. 7 H 303, WCT Harry D. Holmes.

1273. CE 2064, 24 H 489.

1274. CEs 817 and 818, 17 H 697.

1275. CE 2064, 24 H 489; 7 H 299, WCT Harry D. Holmes.

1276. 7 H 267–268, WCT James R. Leavelle.

1277. 7 H 299, WCT Harry D. Holmes.

1278. CE 2064, 24 H 488; 7 H 297, WCT Harry D. Holmes.

1279. 12 H 338, WCT Rio Sam Pierce; Pierce (Rio S.) Exhibit No. 5077, 21 H 131; Pierce (Rio S.) Exhibit No. 5078, 21 H 133–134; Pierce (Rio S.) Exhibit No. 5079, 21 H 136.

1280. CE 397, 17 H 30–44; 1 HSCA 330; ARRB Transcript of Proceedings, Deposition of Dr. James Joseph Humes, February 13, 1996, p.135; 2 H 374, WCT Dr. James J. Humes; 7 HSCA 258; AFIP Record 205-10001-10002, Memorandum, Finck to Blumberg, p.4.

1281. CE 387, 16 H 983.

1282. 13 H 211–212, WCT Karen Bennett Carlin; 13 H 203–204, WCT Bruce Ray Carlin; 14 H 236, WCT George Senator; CE 2019, 24 H 434, Records of Southwestern Bell Telephone Company; 14 H 532, WCT Jack L. Ruby.

1283. CE 2147, 24 H 771–779; CE 2052, 24 H 467–468; CE 2053, 24 H 470; KRLD-TV Collection, November 24, 1963, reel 15, Sixth Floor Museum at Dealey Plaza.

1284. CE 2053, 24 H 470, FBI interview of Jeremiah O'Leary Jr. on December 4, 1963; Kantor, *Ruby Cover-Up*, pp.131, 134–135; Hlavach and Payne, *Reporting the Kennedy Assassination*, p.123.

1285. CE 2064, 24 H 489.

1286. CE 2064, 24 H 489–490; 7 H 301, WCT Harry D. Holmes.

1287. CE 2064, 24 H 490; 7 H 301–302, WCT Harry D. Holmes.

1288. Kelley Exhibit A, 20 H 443.

1289. Kelley Exhibit A, 20 H 443; 7 H 302, WCT Harry D. Holmes.

1290. 7 H 267, WCT James R. Leavelle; Kelley Exhibit A, 20 H 443; CE 2003, 24 H 269.

1291. Kelley Exhibit A, 20 H 443; CE 2064, 24 H 490; 7 H 298, WCT Harry D. Holmes.

1292. Kelley Exhibit A, 20 H 443.

1293. Stevenson Exhibit No. 5053, 21 H 588; 12 H 12–13, WCT Charles Batchelor; 15 H 164–165, WCT Harold J. Fleming.

1294. CE 2002, 24 H 119.

1295. 12 H 117, WCT Cecil E. Talbert; Talbert Exhibit No. 5067, 21 H 658–659; Talbert Exhibit No. 5069, 21 H 664; Steele Exhibit Nos. 5097 and 5098, 21 H 557–558.

1296. 12 H 14, WCT Charles Batchelor.

1297. CE 2064, 24 H 490; 4 H 228, WCT John Will Fritz; 7 H 298, WCT Harry D. Holmes.

1298. Kelley Exhibit A, 20 H 444.

1299. 4 H 228, WCT John Will Fritz.

1300. CE 2064, 24 H 490; Oswald with Land and Land, Lee, p.139.

1301. CE 2064, 24 H 490–491; Kelley Exhibit A, 20 H 444; 7 H 298, WCT Harry D. Holmes.

1302. CE 2002, 24 H 69; CE 2002, 24 H 127.

1303. 12 H 15, WCT Charles Batchelor; CE 2002, 24 H 49; 12 H 146, WCT Charles O. Arnett.

1304. 12 H 320, WCT William J. Newman; CE 2002, 24 H 70, 166; 12 H 147, WCT Charles O. Arnett; 12 H 15, WCT Charles Batchelor.

1305. CE 2064, 24 H 491; 4 H 218, WCT John Will Fritz.

1306. CE 2064, 24 H 491; 7 H 302, 306, WCT Harry D. Holmes.

1307. CE 2064, 24 H 491; 7 H 302, 306, WCT Harry D. Holmes.

1308. 7 H 357, WCT Forrest V. Sorrels; 12 H 36, WCT Jesse E. Curry.

1309. 7 H 357, WCT Forrest V. Sorrels.

1310. 4 H 154, WCT Jesse E. Curry; CE 2064, 24 H 491; 7 H 300, WCT Harry D. Holmes.

1311. CE 2064, 24 H 491; 7 H 299, WCT Harry D. Holmes.

1312. CE 2064, 24 H 491.

1313. Kelley Exhibit A, 20 H 444.

1314. 14 H 211, 239–240, WCT George Senator; Hall (C. Ray) Exhibit Nos. 2 and 3, 20 H 43, 52, 55; 5 H 199, WCT Jack L. Ruby, "right hip pocket."

1315. 5 H 199, WCT Jack L. Ruby; $873.50 in trunk: Smart Exhibit No. 5021, 21 H 524; 13 H 272–274, WCT Vernon S. Smart; Hall (C. Ray) Exhibit No. 3, 20 H 56; 14 H 83–85, WCT Curtis LaVerne Crafard; 13 H 311–312, WCT Andrew Armstrong Jr.; 14 H 211, WCT George Senator; $2,015.33 in cash found on Ruby's person: CE 1322, 22 H 498.

1316. CE 2002, 24 H 119–120; CE 2002, 24 H 61; CE 2002, 24 H 75–76; 12 H 17, WCT Charles Batchelor; CE 2002, 24 H 54; 13 H 7, WCT L. C. Graves.

1317. 12 H 100, WCT M. W. Stevenson.

1318. 15 H 151, WCT John Will Fritz; 15 H 136, WCT M. W. Stevenson; 13 H 62, WCT Forrest V. Sorrels; CE 2002, 24 H 171.

1319. 15 H 150, WCT John Will Fritz.

1320. 4 H 233, 15 H 148, 150, WCT John Will Fritz; 12 H 38, WCT Jesse E. Curry.

1321. 12 H 38, WCT Jesse E. Curry.

1322. 12 H 38, 15 H 125–126, WCT Jesse E. Curry; 4 H 233–234, 15 H 148, WCT John Will Fritz; WR, p.215; Telephone interview of James Leavelle by author on August 24, 2006.

1323. 15 H 150, WCT John Will Fritz.

1324. 15 H 150, WCT John Will Fritz.

1325. 13 H 17, WCT James R. Leavelle.

1326. 13 H 17, WCT James R. Leavelle; see also 15 H 132, WCT Jesse E. Curry.

1327. Telephone interview of James Leavelle by author on August 24, 2006; CE 2003, 24 H 289, 295. Note: The reference on page 295 to Preston is in error. Leavelle told me that "the street was Central. Preston was nowhere near there. It was 35 to 40 blocks away." See also Stevenson Exhibit No. 5053, 21 H 590, and 12 H 339 for correct street of Central.

1328. 12 H 100, WCT M. W. Stevenson.

1329. Stevenson Exhibit No. 5053, 21 H 590; 12 H 339, WCT Rio Sam Pierce; Telephone interview of James Leavelle by author on August 24, 2006.

1330. 15 H 152, WCT John Will Fritz.

1331. CE 2003, 24 H 270; CE 2064, 24 H 491–492 ; 7 H 357, WCT Forrest V. Sorrels; 13 H 5, WCT L. C. Graves.

1332. CE 2003, 24 H 270; 13 H 27, WCT L. D. Montgomery.

1333. 12 H 100, WCT M. W. Stevenson; 12 H 16–17, WCT Charles Batchelor; 12 H 68, WCT O. A. Jones.

1334. 13 H 225–226, WCT Doyle E. Lane.

1335. 13 H 221–226, WCT Doyle E. Lane; Lane Exhibit Nos. 5118 and 5119, 20 H 481; CE 2420 and 2421, 25 H 523.

1336. 15 H 151, WCT John Will Fritz; 12 H 38, WCT Jesse E. Curry.

1337. 13 H 63, WCT Forrest V. Sorrels.

1338. 12 H 38, WCT Jesse E. Curry.

1339. KRLD-TV Collection, November 24, 1963, 11:18 a.m. CST, reel 14, Sixth Floor Museum at Dealey Plaza; CE 2002, 24 H 174; CE 2002, 24 H 176; CE 2002, 24 H 178.

1340. Interviews of James R. Leavelle by Dale K. Myers on April 7, 1983, and November 13, 1999; Leavelle's statement on *Peter Jennings Reporting: The Kennedy Assassination: Beyond Conspiracy*, ABC News Special, November 20, 2003.

1341. 12 H 117–119, WCT Cecil E. Talbert; 12 H 339, WCT Rio Sam Pierce.

1342. 12 H 18–19, WCT Charles Batchelor.

1343. CE 2003, 24 H 289; CE 2002, 24 H 171; two lines: CE 2002, 24 H 54.

1344. CD 1314; CD 1314-A; CE 2052, 24 H 468; CE 2059, 24 H 477–478; Pappas Exhibit No. 4, 21 H 23–24.

1345. CE 2003, 24 H 289; 12 H 391–392, WCT Woodrow Wiggins; Wiggins Exhibit No. 5074, 21 H 729; Wiggins Exhibit No. 5075, 21 H 731–732.

1346. 12 H 339, WCT Rio Sam Pierce; Pierce (Rio S.) Exhibit No. 5077, 21 H 131; Pierce (Rio S.) Exhibit No. 5078, 21 H 133–134; Pierce (Rio S.) Exhibit No. 5079, 21 H 136–137; 12 H 344–347, WCT James A. Putnam; 12 H 360–364, WCT Roy Eugene Vaughn.

1347. Hall (C. Ray) Exhibit No. 3, 20 H 56; 14 H 538–539, polygraph examination of Ruby; 5 H 199, WCT Jack L. Ruby; 4 H 244, WCT John Will Fritz; 12 H 412, WCT Barnard S. Clardy; 12 H 339–340, WCT Rio Sam Pierce; 12 H 287, WCT Billy Joe Maxey; 12 H 345–347, WCT James A. Putman; Dean Exhibit No. 5008, 19 H 436–437; CE 2002, 24 H 136.

1348. 12 H 119, WCT Cecil E. Talbert; Talbert Exhibit No. 5070, 21 H 668; 12 H 68–69, WCT O. A. Jones; 12 H 18–19, WCT Charles Batchelor.

1349. CE 2052, 24 H 468; CE 2059, 24 H 477–478; Pappas Exhibit No. 4, 21 H 23–24.

1350. WFAA-TV Collection, November 24, 1963, 11:20 a.m., PKF-7, Sixth Floor Museum at Dealey Plaza; Wiggins Exhibit No. 5075, 21 H 731.

1351. WFAA-TV Collection, November 24, 1963, PKT-10, Sixth Floor Museum at Dealey Plaza.

1352. "America's Long Vigil," p.33; NBC News, *Seventy Hours and Thirty Minutes*, p.92.

1353. 15 H 151, WCT John Will Fritz; CE 2003, 24 H 289; 12 H 391–392, WCT Woodrow Wiggins; Wiggins Exhibit No. 5074, 21 H 729; Wiggins Exhibit No. 5075, 21 H 731–732.

1354. Cutchaw Exhibit No. 5042, 19 H 411; 15 H 151, WCT John Will Fritz; WFAA-TV Collection, November 24, 1963, 11:21 a.m., PKF-7; KRLD-TV, November 24, 1963, 11:21 a.m., Sixth Floor Museum at Dealey Plaza; CBS Television Archives.

1355. 15 H 150–151, WCT John Will Fritz; officers blinded by lights: CE 2002, 24 H 54; James Leavelle, Transcript of "Who Was Lee Harvey Oswald?" *Frontline*, PBS, November 16, 1993, p.41; Sneed, *No More Silence*, p.415.

1356. KRLD-TV Collection, November 24, 1963, 11:21 a.m., reel 57, Sixth Floor Museum at Dealey Plaza.

1357. 13 H 8, WCT L. C. Graves; CD 1314a, Icarus M. "Ike" Pappas recording, available at National Archives.

1358. 12 H 399, WCT Don Ray Archer.

1359. Testimony of James Leavelle at Jack Ruby's bond hearing on December 23, 1963, in Holloway, *Dallas and the Jack Ruby Trial*, p.53; CE 2163, 24 H 810–811, Interview of James Leavelle on WFAA-TV Dallas on November 24, 1963.

1360. Combest Exhibit No. 5101, 19 H 350; 12 H 20, WCT Charles Batchelor; 15 H 381, WCT John McCullough; 12 H 399, WCT Don Ray Archer; *New York Times*, November 25, 1963, p.1; Sneed, *No More Silence*, p.415; *Pittsburgh Post-Gazette*, November 25, 1963, p.3.

1361. 13 H 8–9, WCT L. C. Graves.

1362. CE 2003, 24 H 315.

1363. "America's Long Vigil," p.33; NBC News, *Seventy Hours and Thirty Minutes*, p.92.

1364. KRLD-TV Collection, November 24, 1963, 11:21 a.m., reel 57, Sixth Floor Museum at Dealey Plaza; 12 H 120, WCT Cecil E. Talbert.

1365. 13 H 122, WCT Robert S. Huffaker Jr.; KRLD-TV Collection, November 24, 1963, 11:21 a.m., reel 57, Sixth Floor Museum at Dealey Plaza; Huffaker, Mercer, Phenix, and Wise, *When the News Went Live*, p.55; 12 H 120, WCT Cecil E. Talbert.

1366. Huffaker, Mercer, Phenix, and Wise, *When the News Went Live*, pp.56–57.

1367. 12 H 184–185, WCT B. H. Combest; WFAA-TV Collection, November 24, 1963, 11:21 a.m., PKF-7, Sixth Floor Museum at Dealey Plaza.

1368. 12 H 70, WCT O. A. Jones; 12 H 20, WCT Charles Batchelor.

1369. 12 H 70, WCT O. A. Jones.

1370. 12 H 120, WCT Cecil E. Talbert; KRLD-TV Collection, November 24, 1963, 11:21 a.m., reel 57, Sixth Floor Museum at Dealey Plaza.

1371. 12 H 20, WCT Charles Batchelor.

1372. CE 2053, 24 H 470.

1373. 12 H 38, WCT Jesse E. Curry.

1374. 13 H 64, WCT Forrest V. Sorrels.

1375. 12 H 120–121, WCT Cecil E. Talbert; 12 H 153, WCT Charles Oliver Arnett; 12 H 308, WCT Louis D. Miller.

1376. 12 H 184–185, WCT B. H. Combest.

1377. 12 H 349–350, WCT Willie B. Slack.

1378. 13 H 90–92, WCT Frances Cason; Cason Exhibit No. 5135, 19 H 324–325.

1379. 13 H 96, WCT Michael Hardin; Hardin Exhibit Nos. 5125, 5126, and 5127, 20 H 81; 13 H 101, WCT C. E. Hulse; CE 1974, 23 H 891; CE 705, 17 H 441.

1380. 12 H 217, WCT Wilbert Jay Cutchshaw.

1381. Bieberdorf Exhibit No. 5123, 19 H 163–164; 13 H 83–89, WCT Fred A. Bieberdorf; Wiggins Exhibit No. 5075, 21 H 732.

1382. 13 H 8, WCT L. C. Graves; 12 H 20, WCT Charles Batchelor; 12 H 120–121, WCT

Cecil E. Talbert; 12 H 153, WCT Charles Oliver Arnett; 13 H 30, WCT L. D. Montgomery.

1383. 12 H 400, WCT Don Ray Archer; CE 2002, 24 H 107; CE 2002, 24 H 156; 12 H 308, WCT Louis D. Miller; CE 2409, 25 H 411, 430.

1384. CE 2002, 24 H 105.

1385. 12 H 121, WCT Cecil E. Talbert.

1386. 12 H 20, WCT Charles Batchelor.

1387. 12 H 121, WCT Cecil E. Talbert.

1388. 13 H 64–65, WCT Forrest V. Sorrels; Sorrels Exhibit No. 1, 21 H 536.

1389. 13 H 67, WCT Forrest V. Sorrels.

1390. 15 H 369, WCT Icarus M. Pappas; CD 1314a, Icarus M. "Ike" Pappas recording; KRLD-TV Collection, November 24, 1963, 11:24 a.m., reel 14, Sixth Floor Museum at Dealey Plaza.

1391. 13 H 128, WCT George R. Phenix.

1392. 15 H 381, WCT John G. McCullough; McCullough Exhibit No. 2, 20 H 547–551.

1393. KRLD-TV Collection, November 24, 1963, 11:21 a.m., reel 14, Sixth Floor Museum at Dealey Plaza.

1394. Archer Exhibit No. 5093, 19 H 22–23; Clardy Exhibit No. 5061, 19 H 332; McMillon Exhibit No. 5017, 20 H 557; 13 H 49, 51, WCT Thomas Donald McMillon.

1395. 12 H 401, WCT Don Ray Archer.

1396. 12 H 413, WCT Barnard S. Clardy.

1397. 12 H 412, WCT Barnard S. Clardy; 12 H 401, WCT Don Ray Archer; 5 H 245, WCT Henry Wade.

1398. 12 H 412–413, WCT Barnard S. Clardy; Clardy Exhibit No. 5063, 19 H 336–338.

1399. CE 2159, 24 H 800.

1400. "America's Long Vigil," p.35.

1401. 7 H 588–589, WCT Perdue D. Lawrence; Huffaker, Mercer, Phenix, and Wise, *When the News Went Live*, pp.122–124; Kantor Exhibit No. 4, 20 H 419.

1402. KRLD-TV Collection, November 24, 1963, 11:25 a.m., reel 14, Sixth Floor Museum at Dealey Plaza.

1403. CD 1314a, Icarus M. "Ike" Pappas recording; KRLD-TV Collection, November 24, 1963, 11:26 a.m., reel 14, Sixth Floor Museum at Dealey Plaza.

1404. CE 5126, 20 H 81; KRLD-TV Collection, November 24, 1963, 11:27 a.m., reel 14, Sixth Floor Museum at Dealey Plaza.

1405. CE 2003, 24 H 290, 295–296, 302, 315.

1406. 13 H 31–33, WCT L. D. Montgomery.

1407. CD 1314a, Icarus M. "Ike" Pappas recording.

1408. 15 H 364–365, WCT Icarus M. Pappas.

1409. CD 1314a, Icarus M. "Ike" Pappas recording.

1410. 1 H 157, WCT Marguerite Oswald.

1411. Oswald with Land and Land, *Lee*, pp.148–149.

1412. 1 H 157–158, WCT Marguerite Oswald.

1413. CE 323, 16 H 903–904; Oswald with Land and Land, *Lee*, pp.149–150.

1414. 2 H 344–345, WCT Peter Paul Gregory.

1415. 1 H 159, WCT Marguerite Oswald; 2 H 345, WCT Peter Paul Gregory.

1416. 13 H 97, WCT Michael Hardin.

1417. Bieberdorf Exhibit No. 5123, 19 H 164.

1418. WFAA-TV Collection, November 24, 1963, 1:31 p.m., PKF-6, Sixth Floor Museum at Dealey Plaza; Hardin Exhibit No. 5126, 20 H 81; CE 705, 17 H 444.

1419. Price Exhibit No. 8, 21 H 183.

1420. Price Exhibit No. 34, 21 H 265.

1421. Price Exhibit No. 7, 21 H 171–172.

1422. 3 H 384, WCT Dr. Malcolm O. Perry; 6 H 112, WCT Dr. George T. Shires; Telephone interview of James Leavelle by author on November 19, 2004; *Los Angeles Times*, November 14, 2004, p.A21.

1423. 3 H 384, WCT Dr. Malcolm O. Perry; Price Exhibit No. 32, 21 H 253, 266.

1424. 6 H 113, WCT Dr. George T. Shires.

1425. Price Exhibit No. 7, 21 H 172.

1426. Manchester, *Death of a President*, pp.515–517; Caroline's letter: Heymann, *Woman Named Jackie*, p.587.

1427. 13 H 67, WCT Forrest V. Sorrels.

1428. 12 H 430–431, WCT Patrick Trevore Dean; 7 H 358, WCT Forrest V. Sorrels.

1429. 12 H 433, WCT Patrick Trevore Dean.

1430. 13 H 74, 83, WCT Forrest V. Sorrels.

1431. 12 H 431–432, WCT Patrick Trevore Dean; 13 H 67, WCT Forrest V. Sorrels.

1432. 13 H 67, WCT Forrest V. Sorrels.

1433. Dean Exhibit No. 5010, 19 H 440.

1434. 13 H 67–68, WCT Forrest V. Sorrels.

1435. Dean Exhibit No. 5010, 19 H 440.

1436. 12 H 432, WCT Patrick Trevore Dean.

1437. 13 H 67–69, WCT Forrest V. Sorrels; Sorrels Exhibit No. 1, 21 H 536–538; Sorrels Exhibit No. 3a–c, 21 H 543–545.

1438. Dean Exhibit No. 5008, 19 H 435.

1439. 12 H 432–433, WCT Patrick Trevore Dean; CE 2002, 24 H 136; 12 H 412–413, WCT Barnard S. Clardy; Clardy Exhibit No. 5063, 19 H 336–338.

1440. 12 H 433, WCT Patrick Trevore Dean.

1441. Hosty with Hosty, *Assignment: Oswald*, pp.56–58.

1442. 3 H 385–386, WCT Dr. Malcolm O. Perry; 6 H 112–113, WCT Dr. George T. Shires; CE 392, 17 H 21–22.

1443. Newseum with Trost and Bennett, *President Kennedy Has Been Shot*, pp.222–223.

1444. *New York Times*, November 25, 1963, pp.1–4; NBC News, *Seventy Hours and Thirty Minutes*, pp.93–98; Manchester, *Death of a President*, pp.536–542; nine-man casket team: *Life*, December 6, 1963, p.40.

1445. 15 H 63, WCT C. Ray Hall.

1446. Hall (C. Ray) Exhibit No. 1, 20 H 37–40.

1447. CE 323, 16 H 904–905; Oswald with Land and Land, *Lee*, p.151.

1448. 3 H 385–386, WCT Dr. Malcolm O. Perry; 6 H 112–113, WCT Dr. George T. Shires; CE 392, 17 H 21–22.

1449. CD 1317, FBI SA Raymond P. Yelchak's interview of Guy Rose on July 23, 1964; CD 1317, FBI SA Raymond P. Yelchak's interview of Lieutenant J. C. Day on July 17, 1964; *Dallas Times Herald* photograph: CE 2426, 25 H 525; see also Kaplan and Waltz, *Trial of Jack Ruby*, pp.165–166.

1450. Price Exhibit No. 8, 21 H 186–187.

1451. WFAA-TV Collection, November 24, 1963, PKT-17, Sixth Floor Museum at Dealey Plaza.

1452. CE 323, 16 H 905; Oswald with Land and Land, *Lee*, pp.151–152.

1453. Price Exhibit No. 8, 21 H 186–187.

1454. Oswald with Land and Land, *Lee*, p.152.

1455. 3 H 90–91, WCT Ruth Hyde Paine; 2 H 345, WCT Peter Paul Gregory.

1456. 3 H 90, WCT Ruth Hyde Paine.

1457. 1 H 159–160, WCT Marguerite Oswald; McMillan, *Marina and Lee*, p.556.

1458. 2 H 345, WCT Peter Paul Gregory.

1459. "America's Long Vigil," p.39; NBC News, *Seventy Hours and Thirty Minutes*, p.98.

1460. KRLD-TV Collection, November 24, 1963, 1:29 p.m., reels 28 and 66, Sixth Floor Museum at Dealey Plaza; CE 2148, 24 H 780.

1461. Kantor Exhibit No. 4, 20 H 419.

1462. Sneed, *No More Silence*, p.292.

1463. Hall (C. Ray) Exhibit No. 4, 20 H 63; 15 H 64–65, WCT C. Ray Hall.

1464. Hall (C. Ray) Exhibit No. 4, 20 H 63; 15 H 64, WCT C. Ray Hall; 13 H 87–88, WCT Fred A. Bieberdorf; Bieberdorf Exhibit No. 5123, 19 H 165.

1465. Manchester, *Death of a President*, p.562; *New York Times*, November 26, 1963, p.10; United Press International, *Four Days*, p.99.

1466. "America's Long Vigil," pp.40, 42; Manchester, *Death of a President*, pp.556–557.

1467. *New York Times*, November 25, 1963, pp.1, 6–7; Manchester, *Death of a President*, pp.530, 557, 605.

1468. NBC News, *Seventy Hours and Thirty Minutes*, p.105.

1469. *New York Times*, November 25, 1963, p.10.

1470. *New York Times*, November 25, 1963, p.2.

1471. Manchester, *Death of a President*, pp.562–565.

1472. "America's Long Vigil," p.40.

1473. Price Exhibit No. 31, 21 H 244; Price Exhibit No. 6, 21 H 157.

1474. Price Exhibit No. 28, 21 H 228; Price Exhibit No. 23, 21 H 221.

1475. 1 H 162, WCT Marguerite Oswald.

1476. McMillan, *Marina and Lee*, p.557.

1477. 1 H 162, WCT Marguerite Oswald.

1478. CE 323, 16 H 905.

1479. Price Exhibit No. 8, 21 H 188.

1480. 1 H 162, WCT Marguerite Oswald.

1481. Price Exhibit No. 8, 21 H 188; CE 323, 16 H 906.

1482. 1 H 162–163, WCT Marguerite Oswald.

1483. Price Exhibit No. 8, 21 H 189; 1 H 163, WCT Marguerite Oswald.

1484. Price Exhibit No. 8, 21 H 189.

1485. Oswald with Land and Land, *Lee*, p.153; CE 323, 16 H 906.

1486. Hall (C. Ray) Exhibit No. 2, 20 H 43–44; 15 H 68, WCT C. Ray Hall.

1487. Hall (C. Ray) Exhibit No. 2, 20 H 43–44.

1488. Hall (C. Ray) Exhibit No. 2, 20 H 44.

1489. Hall (C. Ray) Exhibit No. 2, 20 H 44.

1490. 13 H 70–71, WCT Forrest V. Sorrels; 21 H 536–545, Sorrels Exhibit Nos. 1, 2-A–D, and 3-A–C.

1491. Hall (C. Ray) Exhibit No. 4, 20 H 63; 15 H 64, WCT C. Ray Hall.

1492. Sorrels Exhibit No. 1, 21 H 537.

1493. 4 H 243, WCT John Will Fritz.

1494. 4 H 243, WCT John Will Fritz.

1495. 4 H 243, WCT John Will Fritz; Sorrels Exhibit No. 1, 21 H 537–538.

1496. 4 H 244, WCT John Will Fritz.

1497. Sorrels Exhibit No. 1, 21 H 538.

1498. 4 H 244, WCT John Will Fritz.

1499. Sorrels Exhibit No. 1, 21 H 538; 13 H 74, WCT Forrest V. Sorrels.

1500. NBC News, *Seventy Hours and Thirty Minutes*, p.103.

1501. WFAA-TV Collection, November 24, 1963, PKT-17; KRLD-TV Collection, November 24, 1963, reels 19 and 25, Sixth Floor Museum at Dealey Plaza; CE 2154, 24 H 788–789.

1502. Hall (C. Ray) Exhibit No. 2, 20 H 41–42. Note: The date of this interview was November 24 (a continuation at 4:30 p.m. of the interview that was temporarily discontinued at 3:15 p.m.), not November 25, as the FBI report says; "25" was a "typographical error." 15 H 66, WCT C. Ray Hall; Memo from Assistant Director Alex Rosen to Assistant Director Al Belmont dated February 7, 1964; see CE 2325, 25 H 285, FBI interview of Thomas J. O'Grady on November 25, 1963.

1503. Hall (C. Ray) Exhibit No. 2, 20 H 42.

1504. Hall (C. Ray) Exhibit No. 2, 20 H 42.

1505. Hall (C. Ray) Exhibit No. 2, 20 H 43.

1506. Hall (C. Ray) Exhibit No. 2, 20 H 43.

1507. Oswald with Land and Land, *Lee*, pp.153–156; CE 323, 16 H 906–907.

1508. Hosty with Hosty, *Assignment: Oswald*, pp.59–61; Church Committee Report, p.97; Gentry, *J. Edgar Hoover*, pp.545–546; *FBI Oversight*, p.134.

1509. FBI Report, Interview of Charles B. Miller by SA B. Tom Carter and Robley D. Madland, November 25, 1963, File DL 89-43; Oswald with Land and Land, *Lee*, pp.156–157.

1510. *New York Times*, November 26, 1963, p.12.

1511. *New York Times*, November 25 (Dateline, Miami, November 24), 1963, p.7.

1512. 5 H 236–237, WCT Henry Wade.

1513. WFAA-TV Collection, November 24, 1963, PKT-27, 16, PKF-1; KRLD-TV Collection, November 24, 1963, reels 17 and 35, Sixth Floor Museum at Dealey Plaza; CE 2168, 24 H 819–829; NBC News, *Seventy Hours and Thirty Minutes*, p.117.

1514. 5 H 237, WCT Henry Wade.

1515. FBI Report, Interview of Charles B. Miller by SA B. Tom Carter and Robley D. Madland, November 25, 1963, File DL 89-43; Oswald with Land and Land, *Lee*, pp.157–158; Price Exhibit No. 32, 21 H 248–249.

1516. NBC News, *Seventy Hours and Thirty Minutes*, pp.119–120.

1517. *New York Times*, November 26, 1963, p.10; Grosvenor, "Last Full Measure," p.316.

1518. Oswald with Land and Land, *Lee*, pp.158–160, 165; CE 323, 16 H 910–911; 1 H 166, WCT Marguerite Oswald.

1519. "America's Long Vigil," p.41; *New York Times*, November 26, 1963, pp.4–5, 8; Manchester, *Death of a President*, pp.576–578; NBC News, *Seventy Hours and Thirty Minutes*, pp.130–132.

1520. *New York Times*, November 25, 1963, p.6; *New York Times*, November 26, 1963, pp.1–2, 4; NBC News, *Seventy Hours and Thirty Minutes*, pp.134–135; Manchester, *Death of a President*, pp.579–581.

1521. Grosvenor, "Last Full Measure," p.346.

1522. "America's Long Vigil," pp.41–42; United Press International, *Four Days*, pp.108–109.

1523. Grosvenor, "Last Full Measure," pp.330, 346; last public appearance: "Pages from a Family Album," p.113.

1524. *London Evening Standard*, November 25, 1963, p.1; *Dallas Morning News*, November 26, 1963, p.28.

1525. NBC News, *Seventy Hours and Thirty Minutes*, p.135; "America's Long Vigil," p.42; Manchester, *Death of a President*, pp.8, 37, 581–582, 584; ARRB MD 134, Funeral Arrangements for John Fitzgerald Kennedy, November 25, 1963, p.4, Kennedy family arrives at cathedral at 11:57 a.m. EST.

1526. "America's Long Vigil," p.42.

1527. Grosvenor, "Last Full Measure," pp.312, 346, 353.

1528. 13 H 19–20, WCT James R. Leavelle; Leavelle Exhibit No. 5089, 20 H 507; 4 H 234, WCT John Willis Fritz; Ruby running and lying on floorboard: Telephone interview of James Leavelle by author on November 19, 2004.

1529. *New York Times*, November 26, 1963, p.2; "America's Long Vigil," p.42; Grosvenor, "Last Full Measure," pp.343, 350.

1530. *New York Times*, November 26, 1963, p.1.

1531. "America's Long Vigil," p.42.

1532. "America's Long Vigil," p.43; *New York Times*, November 26, 1963, p.4; Manchester, *Death of a President*, pp.586, 590; United Press International, *Four Days*, p.115; NBC News, *Seventy Hours and Thirty Minutes*, p.136.

1533. "America's Long Vigil," pp.43–44; *New York Times*, November 26, 1963, pp.8, 10; *Life*, December 6, 1963, pp.44–45; ARRB MD 134, Funeral Arrangements for John Fitzgerald Kennedy, November 25, 1963, p.4, cortege departs from cathedral for Arlington cemetery at 1:17 p.m. EST.

1534. "America's Long Vigil," p.44; United Press International, *Four Days*, pp.116–119; Grosvenor, "Last Full Measure," pp.336–337.

1535. Grosvenor, "Last Full Measure," p.350.

1536. *New York Times*, November 24, 1963, p.3.

1537. Grosvenor, "Last Full Measure," p.350; Manchester, *Death of a President*, pp.596–597; *New York Times*, November 26, 1963, p.5.

1538. "America's Long Vigil," p.44; Manchester, *Death of a President*, p.598.

1539. "America's Long Vigil," p.44; Manchester, *Death of a President*, pp.599–600; Grosvenor, "Last Full Measure," p.350; ARRB MD 134, Funeral Arrangements for John Fitzgerald Kennedy, November 25, 1963, p.4, ceremonies at grave site commence at 2:47 p.m. EST.

1540. "America's Long Vigil," pp.44–45; *New York Times*, November 26, 1963, p.5; Manchester, *Death of a President*, pp.552, 600–602; United Press International, *Four Days*, pp.120–125; NBC News, *Seventy Hours and Thirty Minutes*, pp.138–139; lips trembling: "Historic Photo Report," p.57.

1541. *New York Times*, November 26, 1963, p.4.

1542. Grosvenor, "Last Full Measure," pp.346, 350.

1543. Walk down into darkness: Manchester, *Death of a President*, pp.619–620; *New York Times*, November 26, 1963, p.2.

1544. Oswald with Land and Land, *Lee*, pp.157–158; 1 H 167, WCT Marguerite Oswald; FBI Report, Interview of C. J. Price by SA James W. Swinford, November 25, 1963, p.2, File DL 44–1639.

1545. Oswald with Land and Land, *Lee*, pp.160–161; 1 H 167, WCT Marguerite Oswald; FBI interview of C. J. Price by SA James W. Swinford, November 25, 1963, p.2, File DL 44–1639.

1546. Hall (C. Ray) Exhibit No. 3, 20 H 57.

1547. "Policemen Pay Tribute to Heroic Officer Tippit," *Dallas Times Herald*, November 26, 1963, p.4-A; Thompson, "In Texas a Policeman and an Assassin Are Laid to Rest Too," pp.52B, 52C; Kent Biffle, "Heroic Patrolman Lauded at Rites," *Dallas Morning News*, November 26, 1963, sect.1, p.1; WFAA-TV Collection, November 25, 1963, PKT-18;

KRLD–TV Collection, November 25, 1963, reels 47-1 and 47-2, Sixth Floor Museum at Dealey Plaza; Kent Biffle, "Marie Tippit: A Policeman's Widow," *Dallas Morning News*, November 20, 1983.

1548. Lewis Harris, "Policeman's Family Not Forgotten," *Dallas Morning News*, November 24, 1963, sect.1, p.1; Kent Biffle, "Marie Tippit: A Policeman's Widow," *Dallas Morning News*, November 20, 1983; "Donations Pour in for Tippit Family," *Dallas Morning News*, November 27, 1963, sect.4, p.5; Detroit Lions, New York stockbroker, and Walter H. Annenberg: *New York Times*, November 28, 1963, p.23.

1549. Brad Kellar, "Oswald's Other Victim Recalled as Brave and Dedicated Police Officer," *Dallas Morning News*, November 23, 1996; Kent Biffle, "Marie Tippit: A Policeman's Widow," *Dallas Morning News*, November 20, 1983; *New York Times*, November 25, 1963, p.9; Manchester, *Death of a President*, p.635; NBC News, *Seventy Hours and Thirty Minutes*, pp.80–81.

1550. *Pittsburgh Post-Gazette*, November 25, 1963, p.2.

1551. Kent Biffle, "Heroic Patrolman Lauded at Rites," *Dallas Morning News*, November 26, 1963, sect.1, p.1.

1552. "Dallas Echoes JFK Dirge as Police Officer Buried," *Tulsa Daily World*, November 26, 1963, p.18; HSCA Record 180-10124-10413; WFAA-TV Collection, November 25, 1963, PKT-18; KRLD-TV Collection, November 25, 1963, reels 47-1 and 47-2, Sixth Floor Museum at Dealey Plaza.

1553. WFAA-TV Collection, November 25, 1963, PKT-22, Sixth Floor Museum at Dealey Plaza.

1554. "Service Held in Texas for Policeman and Oswald," *Flint Journal*, November 26, 1963; Thompson, "In Texas a Policeman and an Assassin Are Laid To Rest Too," p.52B.

1555. Thompson, "In Texas a Policeman and an Assassin Are Laid to Rest Too," pp.52B, 52C; Oswald with Land and Land, *Lee*, p.163.

1556. Oswald with Land and Land, *Lee*, pp.161, 163–164, 165; six reporters: Aynesworth with Michaud, *JFK: Breaking the News*, p.120.

1557. Oswald with Land and Land, *Lee*, pp.163–164; Thompson, "In Texas a Policeman and an Assassin Are Laid to Rest Too," pp.52C, 52D; *New York Times*, November 26, 1963, p.14.

Bibliography

Editor's's Note: The following is the complete Bibliography from *Reclaiming History*. Some of the sources may be cited in that text but not in *Four Days in November*.

Books

Adamson, Bruce Campbell. *Oswald's Closest Friend: The George de Mohrenschildt Story*. Santa Cruz, Calif.: Self-published, 2001.

Adelson, Alan. *The Ruby Oswald Affair*. Seattle: Romar Books, 1988.

Adler, Bill. *The Eloquent Jacqueline Kennedy Onassis: A Portrait in Her Own Words*. New York: William Morrow, 2004.

Agee, Philip. *Inside the Company: CIA Diary*. New York: Stonehill, 1975.

Aguilar, Luis. *Operation Zapata: The "Ultrasensitive" Report and Testimony of the Board of Inquiry on the Bay of Pigs*. Frederick, Md.: Aletheia Books, 1981.

Alsop, Stewart. *The Center: People and Power in Political Washington*. New York: Harper & Row, 1968.

Andrew, Christopher, and Vasili Mitrokhin. *The Sword and the Shield: The Mitrokhin Archive and the Secret History of the KGB*. New York: Basic Books, 1999.

Anslinger, Harry J., and Will Oursler. *The Murderers: The Story of the Narcotic Gangs*. New York: Farrar, Straus & Cudahy, 1961.

Anson, Robert Sam. *"They've Killed the President!" The Search for the Murderers of John F. Kennedy*. New York: Bantam Books, 1975.

Arévalo, Juan José. *The Shark and the Sardines*. New York: Lyle Stuart, 1961.

Armstrong, John. *Harvey and Lee: How the CIA Framed Oswald*. Arlington, Texas: Quasar, 2003.

Ashley, Clarence. *CIA Spy Master*. Gretna, La.: Pelican, 2004.

Associated Press. *The Torch Is Passed: The Associated Press Story of the Death of a President*. New York: Associated Press, 1963.

Austin, Anthony. *The President's War: The Story of the Tonkin Gulf Resolution and How the Nation Was Trapped in Vietnam*. Philadelphia: Lippincott, 1971.

Aynesworth, Hugh, with Stephen G. Michaud. *JFK: Breaking the News: A Reporter's Eyewitness Account of the Kennedy Assassination and Its Aftermath*. Richardson, Texas: International Focus Press, 2003.

Ayton, Mel. *The JFK Assassination: Dispelling the Myths.* Bognor Regis, West Sussex, United Kingdom: Woodfield Publishing, 2002.

Baden, Michael M., with Judith Adler Hennessee. *Unnatural Death: Confessions of a Medical Examiner.* New York: Ivy Books, 1989.

Baker, Judyth Vary. *Lee Harvey Oswald: The True Story of the Accused Assassin of President John F. Kennedy by His Lover.* Victoria, British Columbia, Canada: Trafford, 2006.

Bamford, James. *Body of Secrets: Anatomy of the Ultra-Secret National Security Agency.* New York: Doubleday, 2001.

Bane, Bernard M. *Is President John F. Kennedy Alive—and Well?* Boston: BMB Publishing, 1997.

Barron, John. *Operation Solo: The FBI's Man in the Kremlin.* Washington, D.C.: Regnery, 1996.

Belin, David W. *Final Disclosure: The Full Truth about the Assassination of President Kennedy.* New York: Scribner's, 1988.

Belin, David W. *November 22, 1963: You Are the Jury.* New York: Quadrangle, 1973.

Belli, Melvin M., with Maurice C. Carroll. *Dallas Justice: The Real Story of Jack Ruby and His Trial.* New York: McKay, 1964.

Belli, Melvin M., with Robert Blair Kaiser. *Melvin Belli: My Life on Trial; An Autobiography.* New York: Popular Library, 1977.

Benson, Michael. *Encyclopedia of the JFK Assassination.* New York: Facts on File, 2002.

Benson, Michael. *Who's Who in the JFK Assassination: An A-to-Z Encyclopedia.* Secaucus, N.J.: Carol Publishing Group, 1993.

Bergreen, Laurence. *Capone: The Man and the Era.* New York: Simon & Schuster, 1994.

Beschloss, Michael R. *The Crisis Years: Kennedy and Khrushchev, 1960–1963.* New York: Edward Burlingame, 1991.

Beschloss, Michael R. *Reaching for Glory: Lyndon Johnson's Secret White House Tapes, 1964–1965.* New York: Simon & Schuster, 2001.

Beschloss, Michael R., ed. *Taking Charge: The Johnson White House Tapes, 1963–1964.* New York: Simon & Schuster, 1997.

Bethell, Tom. *The Electric Windmill: An Inadvertent Autobiography.* Washington, D.C.: Regnery Gateway, 1988.

Bickman, Leonard, and Thomas Henchy. *Beyond the Laboratory: Field Research and Social Psychology.* New York: McGraw-Hill, 1972.

Biles, Joe G. *In History's Shadow: Lee Harvey Oswald, Kerry Thornley and the Garrison Investigation.* San Jose, Calif.: Writers Club Press, 2002.

Bird, Kai. *The Chairman: John J. McCloy and the Making of the American Establishment.* New York: Simon & Schuster, 1992.

Bishop, Jim. *The Day Kennedy Was Shot.* New York: Funk & Wagnalls, 1968.

Bissell, Richard. *Recollections of a Cold Warrior.* New Haven: Yale University Press, 1996.

Blair, Joan, and Clay Blair Jr. *The Search for JFK.* New York: Berkley, 1976.

Blakey, G. Robert, and Richard N. Billings. *Fatal Hour: The Assassination of President Kennedy by Organized Crime.* New York: Berkley Books, 1992.

Blakey, G. Robert, and Richard N. Billings. *The Plot to Kill the President.* New York: Times Books, 1981.

Blinkov, Samuil, and Il'ya I. Glezer. *The Human Brain in Figures and Tables.* Translated from Russian by Basil Haigh. New York: Basic Books, 1968.

Block, Alan A. *Perspective on Organizing Crime: Essays in Opposition.* Dordrecht, The Netherlands: Kluwer Academic, 1991.

Block, Lawrence, ed. *Gangsters, Swindlers, Killers, and Thieves: The Lives and Crimes of Fifty American Villains.* New York: Oxford University Press, 2004.

Blow, Richard. *American Son: A Portrait of John F. Kennedy Jr.* New York: Henry Holt, 2002.

Bonavolonta, Jules, and Brian Duffy. *The Good Guys: How We Turned the FBI 'round—and Finally Broke the Mob.* New York: Simon & Schuster, 1996.

Bonner, Judy Whitson. *Investigation of a Homicide: The Murder of John F. Kennedy.* Anderson, S.C.: Droke House, 1969.

Brandt, Charles. *"I Heard You Paint Houses": Frank "the Irishman" Sheeran and the Inside Story of the Mafia, the Teamsters, and the Last Ride of Jimmy Hoffa.* Hanover, N.H.: Steerforth Press, 2004.

Brener, Milton. *The Garrison Case: A Study in the Abuse of Power.* New York: Clarkson N. Potter, 1969.

Brennan, Howard L., with J. Edward Cherryholmes. *Eyewitness to History: The Kennedy Assassination as Seen by Howard L. Brennan.* Waco, Texas: Texian Press, 1987.

Breuer, William B. *Vendetta! Fidel Castro and the Kennedy Brothers.* New York: Wiley, 1997.

Brown, Anthony Cave. *Treason in the Blood.* Boston: Houghton Mifflin, 1994.

Brown, Madeleine. *Texas in the Morning: The Love Story of Madeleine Brown and President Lyndon Baines Johnson.* Baltimore: Conservatory Press, 1997.

Brown, Thomas. *JFK: History of an Image.* Bloomington: Indiana University Press, 1988.

Brown, Walt. *The Guns of Texas Are Upon Us.* Williamsport, Penn.: Last Hurrah Press, 2005.

Brown, Walt. *The People v. Lee Harvey Oswald.* New York: Carroll & Graf, 1992.

Brown, Walt. *Treachery in Dallas.* New York: Carroll & Graf, 1995.

Brown, Walt. *The Warren Omission: A Micro Study of the Methods and Failures of the Warren Commission.* Wilmington, Del.: Delmax, 1996.

Buchanan, Thomas G. *Who Killed Kennedy?* New York: G. P. Putnam, 1964.

Bugliosi, Vincent, with Curt Gentry. *Helter Skelter: The True Story of the Manson Murders.* New York: W. W. Norton, 1994.

Burleigh, Nina. *A Very Private Woman: The Life and Unsolved Murder of Presidential Mistress Mary Meyer.* New York: Bantam, 1998.

Butwell, Richard. *Southeast Asia: A Political Introduction.* New York: Praeger, 1975.

Califano, Joseph A., Jr. *Inside: A Public and Private Life.* New York: Public Affairs, 2004.

Callahan, Bob. *Who Shot JFK? A Guide to the Major Conspiracy Theories.* New York: Simon & Schuster, 1993.

Campbell, Rodney. *The Luciano Project: The Secret Wartime Collaboration of the Mafia and the U.S. Navy.* New York: McGraw-Hill, 1977.

Canal, John A. *Silencing the Lone Assassin.* St. Paul, Minn.: Paragon House, 2005.

Caro, Robert A. *The Path to Power.* New York: Alfred A. Knopf, 1982.

Carter, Lauren. *The Most Evil Mobsters in History.* New York: Barnes & Noble Books, 2004.

Castañeda, Jorge G. *Compañero: The Life and Death of Che Guevara.* New York: Vintage, 1998.

Castro, Fidel. *Che: A Memoir.* New York: Ocean Press, 1994.

Chandler, David Leon. *Brothers in Blood: The Rise of the Criminal Brotherhoods.* New York: Dutton, 1975.

Chang, Laurence, and Peter Kornbluh, eds. *The Cuban Missile Crisis, 1962: A National Security Archive Documents Reader.* New York: New Press, 1992.

Chapman, Gil, and Ann Chapman. *Was Oswald Alone?* San Diego: Publishers Export, 1967.

Cirules, Enrique. *The Mafia in Havana: A Caribbean Mob Story.* Melbourne, Australia: Ocean Press, 2004.

Claflin, Edward B., ed. *JFK Wants to Know: Memos from the President's Office, 1961–1963*. New York: Morrow, 1991.

Clarke, James W. *American Assassins: The Darker Side of Politics*. Princeton, N.J.: Princeton University Press, 1990.

Clemente, Carmine D. *Anatomy: A Regional Atlas of the Human Body*. 3rd ed. Baltimore: Urban & Schwarzenberg, 1987.

Colby, William, and Peter Forbath. *Honorable Men: My Life in the CIA*. New York: Simon & Schuster, 1978.

Collier, Peter, and David Horowitz. *The Kennedys: An American Drama*. New York: Summit Books, 1984.

Colson, Charles W. *Loving God*. Grand Rapids, Mich.: Zondervan, 1983.

Committee to Investigate Assassinations, under the direction of Bernard Fensterwald Jr. and compiled by Michael Ewing. *Assassination of JFK by Coincidence or Conspiracy?* New York: Zebra Books, 1977.

Connally, Nellie, and Mickey Herskowitz. *From Love Field: Our Final Hours with President John F. Kennedy*. New York: Rugged Land, 2003.

Cook, Fred J. *The FBI Nobody Knows*. New York: Macmillan, 1964.

Cooper, Milton William. *Behold a Pale Horse*. Sedona, Ariz.: Light Technology, 1991.

Cormack, A. J. R. *The World Encyclopedia of Modern Guns*. London: Octopus Books, 1979.

Corry, John. *The Manchester Affair*. New York: Putnam, 1967.

Corson, William R. *The Armies of Ignorance: The Rise of the American Intelligence Empire*. New York: Dial Press, 1977.

Corson, William R., and Robert T. Crowley. *The New KGB: Engine of Soviet Power*. New York: Morrow, 1985.

Craig, John R., and Philip A. Rogers. *The Man on the Grassy Knoll*. New York: Avon, 1992.

Crenshaw, Charles A., with Jens Hansen and J. Gary Shaw. *JFK: Conspiracy of Silence*. New York: Signet, 1992.

Crenshaw, Charles A., with J. Gary Shaw, Gary Aguilar, and Brad Kizzia. *Trauma Room One: The JFK Medical Coverup Exposed*. New York: Paraview Press, 2001.

Curry, Jesse E. *Retired Dallas Police Chief Jesse Curry Reveals His Personal JFK Assassination File*. Dallas: Self-published, printed by American Poster and Printing Company, 1969.

Cutler, Robert B. *The Umbrella Man*. Beverly Farms, Mass.: Self-published, 1975.

Dallek, Robert. *Flawed Giant: Lyndon Johnson and His Times, 1961–1973*. New York: Oxford University Press, 1998.

Dallek, Robert. *An Unfinished Life: John F. Kennedy, 1917–1963*. Boston: Little, Brown, 2003.

Dankbaar, Wim, ed. *Files on JFK: Interviews with Confessed Assassin James E. Files and More New Evidence of the Conspiracy That Killed JFK*. The Netherlands: Self-published, 2005.

Davis, John H. *The Kennedys: Dynasty and Disaster, 1848–1983*. New York: McGraw-Hill, 1984.

Davis, John H. *Mafia Kingfish: Carlos Marcello and the Assassination of John F. Kennedy*. New York: McGraw-Hill, 1989.

Davison, Jean. *Oswald's Game*. New York: W. W. Norton, 1983.

Davy, William. *Let Justice Be Done: New Light on the Jim Garrison Investigation*. Reston, Va.: Jordan, 1999.

DeLoach, Cartha. *Hoover's FBI: The Inside Story by Hoover's Trusted Lieutenant*. Washington, D.C.: Regnery, 1995.

Demaris, Ovid. *Director: An Oral Biography of J. Edgar Hoover*. New York: Harper's Magazine Press, 1975.

Demaris, Ovid. *J. Edgar Hoover, as They Knew Him*. New York: Carroll & Graf, 1975.

Demaris, Ovid. *The Last Mafioso: The Treacherous World of Jimmy Fratianno.* New York: Times Books, 1981.

Dempsey, John Mark, ed. *The Jack Ruby Trial Revisited: The Diary of Jury Foreman Max Causey.* Denton: University of North Texas Press, 2000.

Denton, Sally, and Roger Morris. *The Money and the Power: The Making of Las Vegas and Its Hold on America, 1947–2000.* New York: Alfred A. Knopf, 2001.

De Stefano, George. *An Offer We Can't Refuse: The Mafia in the Mind of America.* New York: Faber & Faber, 2006.

DiEugenio, James. *Destiny Betrayed: JFK, Cuba, and the Garrison Case.* New York: Sheridan Square Press, 1992.

DiEugenio, James, and Lisa Pease, eds. *The Assassinations: Probe Magazine on JFK, RFK, MLK and Malcolm X.* Los Angeles: Feral House, 2003.

Donovan, James. *Strangers on a Bridge: The Case of Colonel Abel.* New York: Atheneum House, 1964.

Douglas, Gregory. *Regicide: The Official Assassination of John F. Kennedy.* Huntsville, Ala.: Monte Sano Media, 2002.

Duffy, James R. *Who Killed JFK? The Kennedy Assassination Cover-Up, the Web.* New York: Shapolsky Publishers, 1988.

Dulles, Allen. *The Craft of Intelligence.* New York: Harper & Row, 1963.

Eddowes, Michael. *The Oswald File.* New York: Clarkson N. Potter, 1977.

Eisenberg, Dennis, Uri Dan, and Eli Landau. *Meyer Lansky: Mogul of the Mob.* New York: Paddington Press, 1979.

Eisenhower, Dwight D. *The White House Years.* Vol. 2: *Waging Peace, 1956–1961.* Garden City, N.Y.: Doubleday, 1965.

Epstein, Edward Jay. *The Assassination Chronicles.* New York: Carroll & Graf, 1992.

Epstein, Edward Jay. *Inquest: The Warren Commission and the Establishment of Truth.* New York: Viking, 1966.

Epstein, Edward Jay. *Legend: The Secret World of Lee Harvey Oswald.* New York: Reader's Digest Press, 1978.

Escalante, Fabian. *The Cuba Project: CIA Covert Operations 1959–1962.* Melbourne, Australia: Ocean Press, 2004.

Estes, Billie Sol. *Billie Sol Estes: A Texas Legend.* Granbury, Texas: BS Productions, 2005.

Evans, Monte. *The Rather Narrative: Is Dan Rather the JFK Conspiracy's San Andreas Fault?* Barrington, R.I.: Barbara Books, 1990.

Evica, George Michael. *And We Are All Mortal: New Evidence and Analysis in the John F. Kennedy Assassination.* West Hartford, Conn.: Self-published, printed by the University of Hartford, 1978.

Exner, Judith, as told to Ovid Demaris. *My Story.* New York: Grove Press, 1977.

Fairclough, Adam. *Race and Democracy: The Civil Rights Struggle in Louisiana, 1915–1972.* Athens: University of Georgia Press, 1995.

Feldman, Harold. *Fifty-one Witnesses: The Grassy Knoll.* San Francisco: Idlewild, 1965.

Fenster, Mark. *Conspiracy Theories: Secrecy and Power in American Culture.* Minneapolis: University of Minnesota Press, 1999.

Fetzer, James H., ed. *Assassination Science: Experts Speak Out on the Death of JFK.* Chicago: Catfeet Press, 1998.

Fetzer, James H., ed. *The Great Zapruder Film Hoax: Deceit and Deception in the Death of JFK.* Chicago: Catfeet Press, 2003.

Fetzer, James H., ed. *Murder in Dealey Plaza: What We Know Now That We Didn't Know Then about the Death of JFK.* Chicago: Catfeet Press, 2000.

Fite, Gilbert C. *Richard B. Russell, Jr., Senator from Georgia*. Chapel Hill: University of North Carolina Press, 1991.

Flammonde, Paris. *The Kennedy Conspiracy: An Uncommissioned Report on the Jim Garrison Investigation*. New York: Meredith Press, 1969.

Fonzi, Gaeton. *The Last Investigation*. New York: Thunder's Mouth Press, 1993.

Ford, Gerald R., and John R. Stiles. *Portrait of the Assassin*. New York: Simon & Schuster, 1965.

Fox, Sylvan. *The Unanswered Questions about President Kennedy's Assassination*. New York: Award Books, 1965.

Franqui, Carlos. *Family Portrait with Fidel: A Memoir*. New York: Random House, 1984.

Freed, Donald, with Fred Simon Landis. *Death in Washington: The Murder of Orlando Letelier*. Westport, Conn.: Lawrence Hill, 1980.

Freedman, Lawrence. *Kennedy's Wars: Berlin, Cuba, Laos, and Vietnam*. New York: Oxford University Press, 2000.

Fritz, Will. *The Kennedy Mutiny*. Akron, Ohio: Self-published, 2002.

Fuhrman, Mark. *A Simple Act of Murder: November 22, 1963*. New York: William Morrow, 2006.

Furiati, Claudia. *ZR Rifle: The Plot to Kill Kennedy and Castro; Cuba Opens Secret Files*. Melbourne, Australia: Ocean Press, 1994.

Fursenko, Aleksandr, and Timothy Naftali. *"One Hell of a Gamble": The Secret History of the Cuban Missile Crisis*. New York: W. W. Norton, 1997.

Galanor, Stewart. *Cover-Up*. New York: Kestrel Books, 1998.

Gambino, Richard. *Vendetta: The True Story of the Largest Lynching in U.S. History*. Toronto: Guernica, 2000.

Garrison, Jim. *A Heritage of Stone*. New York: Berkley, 1972.

Garrison, Jim. *On the Trail of the Assassins: My Investigation and Prosecution of the Murder of President Kennedy*. New York: Warner Books, 1988.

Gates, Gary Paul. *Air Time: The Inside Story of CBS News*. New York: Harper & Row, 1978.

Gedney, John Forrester. *The Making of a Bum: From Notoriety to Sobriety*. Melbourne, Fla.: Gami Publishing, 2001.

Gellman, Barton. *Contending with Kennan: Toward a Philosophy of American Power*. New York: Praeger, 1984.

Gentry, Curt. *J. Edgar Hoover: The Man and the Secrets*. New York: W. W. Norton, 1991.

Gertz, Elmer. *Moment of Madness: The People vs. Jack Ruby*. Chicago: Follett, 1968.

Giancana, Antoinette, John R. Hughes, and Thomas H. Jobe. *JFK and Sam: The Connection between the Giancana and Kennedy Assassinations*. Nashville: Cumberland House, 2005.

Giancana, Sam, and Chuck Giancana. *Double Cross: The Explosive, Inside Story of the Mobster Who Controlled America*. New York: Warner Books, 1992.

Gibson, Donald. *The Kennedy Assassination Cover-Up*. New York: Nova Science Publishers, 2005.

Goldberg, Robert Alan. *Enemies Within: The Culture of Conspiracy in Modern America*. New Haven: Yale University Press, 2001.

Goldman, Albert. *Ladies and Gentlemen—Lenny Bruce!!* New York: Random House, 1974.

Goldsmith, John A. *Colleagues: Richard B. Russell and His Apprentice, Lyndon B. Johnson*. Macon, Ga.: Mercer University Press, 1998.

Gosch, Martin A., and Richard Hammer. *The Last Testament of Lucky Luciano*. New York: Dell, 1976.

Greene, A. C. *Chance Encounters: True Stories of Unforeseen Meetings, with Unanticipated Results*. Albany, Texas: Bright Sky Press, 2002.

Griffin, Joe, with Don DeNevi. *Mob Nemesis: How the FBI Crippled Organized Crime.* Amherst, N.Y.: Prometheus Books, 2002.

Groden, Robert J. *The Killing of a President: The Complete Photographic Record of the JFK Assassination, the Conspiracy and the Cover-Up.* New York: Viking Studio Books, 1993.

Groden, Robert J. *The Search for Lee Harvey Oswald: The Comprehensive Photographic Record.* New York: Penguin Studio Books, 1995.

Groden, Robert J., and Livingstone, Harrison Edward. *High Treason: The Assassination of President John F. Kennedy; What Really Happened.* New York: Conservatory Press, 1989.

Grolier's Encyclopedia. Danbury, Conn.: Grolier, 1993.

Grose, Peter. *Gentleman Spy: The Life of Allen Dulles.* Amherst: University of Massachusetts Press, 1996.

Gun, Nerin E. *Red Roses from Texas.* London: Frederick Muller, 1964.

Guth, DeLloyd J., and David Wrone. *The Assassination of John F. Kennedy: A Comprehensive and Legal Bibliography, 1963–1979.* Westport, Conn.: Greenwood Press, 1980.

Haig, Alexander M., Jr., with Charles McCarry. *Inner Circles: How America Changed the World; A Memoir.* New York: Warner Books, 1992.

Haldeman, H. R., with Joseph DiMona. *The Ends of Power.* New York: Times Books, 1978.

Haley, J. Evetts. *A Texan Looks at Lyndon: A Study in Illegitimate Power.* Canyon, Texas: Palo Duro Press, 1964.

Hampton, Wilborn. *Kennedy Assassinated! The World Mourns; A Reporter's Story.* Cambridge, Mass.: Candlewick Press, 1997.

Hanson, William H. *The Shooting of John F. Kennedy: One Assassin, Three Shots, Three Hits— No Misses.* San Antonio, Texas: Naylor, 1969.

Hartogs, Renatus, and Lucy Freeman. *The Two Assassins.* New York: Thomas Y. Crowell, 1965.

Hatcher, Julian S., Frank Jury, and Jac Weller. *Firearms Investigation, Identification, and Evidence.* Harrisburg, Penn.: Stackpole, 1957.

Heiner, Kent. *Without Smoking Gun: Was the Death of Lt. Cmdr. William B. Pitzer Part of the JFK Assassination Cover-Up Conspiracy?* Walterville, Ore.: TrineDay, 2004.

Helms, Richard, with William Hood. *A Look over My Shoulder: A Life in the Central Intelligence Agency.* New York: Random House, 2003.

Hemingway, Mary Welsh. *How It Was.* New York: Alfred A. Knopf, 1976.

Hepburn, James. *Farewell America: The Plot to Kill JFK.* Roseville, Calif.: Penmarin Books, 2002.

Hersh, Seymour M. *The Dark Side of Camelot.* Boston: Little, Brown, 1997.

Heymann, C. David. *A Woman Named Jackie.* New York: Carol Communications, 1989.

Higgins, Trumbull. *The Perfect Failure: Kennedy, Eisenhower, and the CIA at the Bay of Pigs.* New York: W. W. Norton, 1987.

Highlights: The History of Parkland Hospital. Dallas: Parkland Memorial Hospital, March 2000.

Hinckle, Warren, and William W. Turner. *Deadly Secrets: The CIA-Mafia War against Castro and the Assassination of J.F.K.* New York: Thunder's Mouth Press, 1992.

Hlavach, Laura, and Darwin Payne, eds. *Reporting the Kennedy Assassination: Journalists Who Were There Recall Their Experiences.* Dallas: Three Forks Press, 1996.

Hoensch, Jörg K. *A History of Modern Hungary, 1867–1986.* London: Longman Group, 1988.

Hofstadter, Richard. *The Paranoid Style in American Politics and Other Essays.* New York: Alfred A. Knopf, 1965.

Holland, Max, ed. *The Kennedy Assassination Tapes.* New York: Alfred A. Knopf, 2004.

Holloway, Diane, ed. *Dallas and the Jack Ruby Trial: Memoir of Judge Joe B. Brown, Sr.* San Jose, Calif.: Author's Choice Press, 2001.

Holloway, Diane, ed. *The Mind of Oswald: Accused Assassin of John F. Kennedy.* Victoria, British Columbia, Canada: Trafford, 2000.

Hoover, J. Edgar. *Persons in Hiding.* Boston: Little, Brown, 1938.

Hope, Bob, with Melville Shavelson. *Don't Shoot, It's Only Me: Bob Hope's Comedy History of the United States.* New York: Putnam, 1990.

Hosty, James P., Jr., with Thomas Hosty. *Assignment: Oswald.* New York: Arcade Publishing, 1996.

Houts, Marshall. *Where Death Delights: The Story of Dr. Milton Helpern and Forensic Medicine.* New York: Coward-McCann, 1967.

Huffaker, Bob, Bill Mercer, George Phenix, and Wes Wise. *When the News Went Live: Dallas 1963.* Lanham, Md.: Taylor Trade Publishing, 2004.

Hughes, J. W. *Square Peg for a Round Hole.* Concord, Calif.: Self-published, 1993.

Hunt, Howard. *Give Us This Day.* New Rochelle, N.Y.: Arlington House, 1973.

Hunter, Diane, and Alice Anderson. *Jack Ruby's Girls.* Atlanta: Hallux, 1970.

Hunt-Jones, Conover. *JFK: For a New Generation.* Dallas: The Sixth Floor Museum and Southern Methodist University Press, 1996.

Hurt, Harry, III. *Texas Rich: The Hunt Dynasty, from the Early Oil Days through the Silver Crash.* New York: W. W. Norton, 1981.

Hurt, Henry. *Reasonable Doubt: An Investigation into the Assassination of John F. Kennedy.* New York: Holt, Rinehart & Winston, 1985.

Israel, Lee. *A Biography of Dorothy Kilgallen.* New York: Delacorte, 1979.

James, Rosemary, and Jack Wardlaw. *Plot or Politics: The Garrison Case and Its Cost.* New Orleans: Pelican Publishing, 1967.

Jennings, Dean. *We Only Kill Each Other: The True Story of Mobster Bugsy Siegel, the Man Who Invented Las Vegas.* New York: Pocket, 1967.

Joesten, Joachim. *The Dark Side of Lyndon Baines Johnson.* London: Dawnay, 1968.

Joesten, Joachim. *Oswald: Assassin or Fall Guy?* New York: Marzani & Munsell, 1964.

Johnson, Haynes, with Manuel Artime and others. *The Bay of Pigs: The Leaders' Story of Brigade 2506.* New York: W. W. Norton, 1964.

Johnson, Sam Houston. *My Brother Lyndon.* New York: Cowles, 1969.

Jones, Penn, Jr. *Forgive My Grief: A Critical Review of the Warren Commission Report on the Assassination of President John F. Kennedy.* Vol. 1. Midlothian, Texas: Midlothian Mirror, 1966.

Jones, Penn, Jr. *Forgive My Grief: A Critical Review of the Warren Commission Report on the Assassination of President John F. Kennedy.* Vol. 2. Midlothian, Texas: Midlothian Mirror, 1967.

Jones, Penn, Jr. *Forgive My Grief: A Critical Review of the Warren Commission Report on the Assassination of President John F. Kennedy.* Vol. 3. Midlothian, Texas: Midlothian Mirror, 1969.

Kantor, Seth. *The Ruby Cover-Up.* New York: Kensington Publishing, 1978.

Kantor, Seth. *Who Was Jack Ruby?* New York: Everest House, 1978.

Kaplan, John, and Jon R. Waltz. *The Trial of Jack Ruby.* New York: Macmillan, 1965.

Karnow, Stanley. *Vietnam: A History.* New York: Viking, 1983.

Kearns, Doris. *Lyndon Johnson and the American Dream.* New York: Harper & Row, 1976.

Kelley, Kitty. *His Way: The Unauthorized Biography of Frank Sinatra.* New York: Bantam Books, 1986.

Kennan, George. *Memoirs, 1925–1950.* Boston: Atlantic Monthly Press, 1967.

Kennedy, John F. *The Strategy of Peace.* Edited by Allan Nevins. New York: Harper & Brothers, 1960.

Kennedy, Robert F. *The Enemy Within*. New York: Harper & Brothers, 1960.

Kennedy, Robert F. *Thirteen Days*. New York: W. W. Norton, 1969.

Kirkpatrick, Lyman B., Jr. *The Real CIA*. New York: Macmillan, 1968.

Kirkwood, James. *American Grotesque: An Account of the Clay Shaw–Jim Garrison Kennedy Assassination Trial in the City of New Orleans*. New York: Simon & Schuster, 1970.

Knight, Peter Z., ed. *Conspiracy Theories in American History: An Encyclopedia*. Santa Barbara, Calif.: ABC-CLIO, 2003.

Koepke, Jim. *Chasing Ghosts: The Remarkable Story of One Man's Investigation into the Assassination of President John F. Kennedy*. Baltimore: PublishAmerica, 2004.

Kornbluh, Peter, ed. *Bay of Pigs Declassified: The Secret CIA Report on the Invasion of Cuba*. New York: New Press, 1998.

Kornbluh, Peter, ed. *The Pinochet File: A Declassified Dossier on Atrocity and Accountability*. New York: New Press, 2003.

Kroth, Jerome. *Conspiracy in Camelot: The Complete History of the Assassination of John Fitzgerald Kennedy*. New York: Algora, 2003.

Kuntz, Tom, and Phil Kuntz, eds. *The Sinatra Files: The Secret FBI Dossier*. New York: Three Rivers Press, 2000.

Kurtz, Michael L. *Crime of the Century: The Kennedy Assassination from a Historian's Perspective*. Knoxville: University of Tennessee Press, 1982.

Lacey, Robert. *Little Man: Meyer Lansky and the Gangster Life*. Boston: Little, Brown, 1991.

La Fontaine, Ray, and Mary La Fontaine. *Oswald Talked: The New Evidence in the JFK Assassination*. Gretna, La.: Pelican Publishing, 1996.

Lambert, Patricia. *False Witness: The Real Story of Jim Garrison's Investigation and Oliver Stone's Film* JFK. New York: M. Evans, 1998.

Landis, C., and W. Hunt. *The Startle Reaction*. New York: Holt, Rinehart, 1939.

Lane, Mark. *Plausible Denial: Was the CIA Involved in the Assassination of JFK?* New York: Thunder's Mouth Press, 1991.

Lane, Mark. *Rush to Judgment*. New York: Dell, 1966.

Lane, Mark. *Rush to Judgment*. New York: Dell, 1992.

Lattimer, John K. *Kennedy and Lincoln: Medical and Ballistic Comparisons of Their Assassinations*. New York: Harcourt Brace Jovanovich, 1980.

Law, William Matson, with Allan Eaglesham. *In the Eye of History: Disclosures in the JFK Assassination Medical Evidence*. Southlake, Texas: JFK Lancer Publications, 2005.

Lawrence, Lincoln. *Were We Controlled?* New Hyde Park, N.Y.: University Books, 1967.

Lazo, Mario. *Dagger in the Heart: American Policy Failures in Cuba*. New York: Funk & Wagnalls, 1968.

Leaming, Barbara. *Jack Kennedy: The Education of a Statesman*. New York: W. W. Norton, 2006.

Leonard, Jerry. *The Perfect Assassin: Lee Harvey Oswald, the CIA and Mind Control*. Bloomington, Ind.: 1st Books Library, 2002.

Lewis, Richard Warren. *The Scavengers and Critics of the Warren Report: The Endless Paradox. Based on an Investigation by Lawrence Schiller*. New York: Delacorte Press, 1967.

Lifton, David S. *Best Evidence: Disguise and Deception in the Assassination of John F. Kennedy*. New York: Macmillan, 1980.

Livingstone, Harrison Edward. *High Treason 2: The Great Cover-Up; The Assassination of President John F. Kennedy*. New York: Carroll & Graf, 1992.

Livingstone, Harrison Edward. *Killing Kennedy and the Hoax of the Century*. New York: Carroll & Graf, 1995.

Livingstone, Harrison Edward. *Killing the Truth: Deceit and Deception in the JFK Case*. New York: Carroll & Graf, 1993.

Livingstone, Harrison Edward. *The Radical Right and the Murder of John F. Kennedy: Stunning Evidence in the Assassination of the President.* Baltimore: Conservatory Press, 2004.

Loftus, Elizabeth F. *Eyewitness Testimony.* Cambridge, Mass.: Harvard University Press, 1996. .

Loken, John. *Oswald's Trigger Films: The Manchurian Candidate, We Were Strangers, Suddenly.* Ann Arbor, Mich.: Falcon Books, 2000.

Lorenz, Marita, with Ted Schwarz. *Marita: One Woman's Extraordinary Tale of Love and Espionage from Castro to Kennedy.* New York: Thunder's Mouth Press, 1993.

Lubin, David M. *Shooting Kennedy: JFK and the Culture of Images.* Berkeley: University of California Press, 2003.

Ludwig, Jurgen. *Current Methods of Autopsy Practice.* Philadelphia: W. B. Saunders, 1979.

Luttwak, Edward. *Coup d'Etat: A Practical Handbook.* New York: Alfred A. Knopf, 1969.

Maas, Peter. *The Valachi Papers: The First Inside Account of Life in the Cosa Nostra.* New York: G. P. Putnam's Sons, 1968.

MacNeil, Robert. *The Right Place at the Right Time.* Boston: Little, Brown, 1982.

Mahoney, Richard D. *Sons and Brothers: The Days of Jack and Bobby Kennedy.* New York: Arcade, 1999.

Mailer, Norman. *Oswald's Tale: An American Mystery.* New York: Random House, 1995.

Mallon, Thomas. *Mrs. Paine's Garage and the Murder of John F. Kennedy.* New York: Pantheon, 2002.

Manchester, William. *The Death of a President.* New York: Harper & Row, 1967.

Mangold, Tom. *Cold Warrior: James Jesus Angleton: The CIA's Master Spy Hunter.* New York: Simon & Schuster, 1991.

Mankiewicz, Frank, and Kirby Jones. *With Fidel: A Portrait of Castro and Cuba.* Chicago: Playboy Press, 1975.

Mann, Robert. *Legacy to Power: Senator Russell Long of Louisiana.* New York: Paragon House, 1992.

Marchetti, Victor, and John D. Marks. *The CIA and the Cult of Intelligence.* New York: Alfred A. Knopf, 1974.

Marcus, Raymond. *The Bastard Bullet: A Search for Legitimacy for Commission Exhibit 399.* Los Angeles: Self-published, 1966.

Marks, John. *The Search for the "Manchurian Candidate": The CIA and Mind Control.* New York: Times Books, 1979.

Marrs, Jim. *Alien Agenda: Investigating the Extraterrestrial Presence among Us.* New York: HarperCollins, 1997.

Marrs, Jim. *Crossfire: The Plot That Killed Kennedy.* New York: Carroll & Graf, 1989.

Martin, David C. *Wilderness of Mirrors: How the Byzantine Intrigues of the Secret War between the CIA and the KGB Seduced and Devoured Key Agents James Jesus Angleton and William King Harvey.* New York: Harper & Row, 1980.

Matthews, James P. *Four Dark Days in History.* Los Angeles: Special Publications, 1963.

May, Ernest R., and Philip D. Zelikow, eds. *The Kennedy Tapes: Inside the White House during the Cuban Missile Crisis.* Cambridge, Mass.: Harvard University Press, 1997.

McCarthy, Dennis V. N., with Philip W. Smith. *Protecting the President: The Inside Story of a Secret Service Agent.* New York: William Morrow, 1985.

McClellan, Barr. *Blood, Money and Power: How LBJ Killed JFK.* New York: Hanover House, 2003.

McClellan, John L. *Crime without Punishment.* New York: Duell, Sloan & Pearce, 1962.

McConnell, Brian. *The History of Assassination.* Nashville: Aurora Publishers, 1970.

McCoy, Alfred W. *The Politics of Heroin in Southeast Asia: CIA Complicity in the Global Drug Trade.* New York: Harper & Row, 1972.

McDonald, Hugh C. *Appointment in Dallas: The Final Solution to the Assassination of JFK.* New York: Zebra Books, 1992.

McKeever, Porter. *Adlai Stevenson: His Life and Legacy.* New York: William Morrow, 1989.

McKnight, Gerald. *Breach of Trust: How the Warren Commission Failed the Nation and Why.* Lawrence: University of Kansas Press, 2005.

McMillan, Priscilla Johnson. *Marina and Lee.* New York: Harper & Row, 1977.

McNamara, Robert S., with Brian VanDeMark. *In Retrospect: The Tragedy and Lessons of Vietnam.* New York: Times Books, 1995.

Meagher, Sylvia. *Accessories after the Fact: The Warren Commission, the Authorities, and the Report.* New York: Vintage, 1976.

Meagher, Sylvia. *Subject Index to the Warren Report and Hearings and Exhibits.* New York: Scarecrow Press, 1966.

Meagher, Sylvia, in collaboration with Gary Owens. *Master Index to the J. F. K. Assassination Investigation: The Reports and Supporting Volumes of the House Select Committee on Assassinations and the Warren Commission.* Metuchen, N.J.: Scarecrow Press, 1980.

Mellen, Joan. *Farewell to Justice: Jim Garrison, JFK's Assassination, and the Case That Should Have Changed History.* Dulles, Va.: Potomac Books, 2005.

Meneses, Enrique. *Fidel Castro.* New York: Taplinger Publishing, 1966.

Menninger, Bonar. *Mortal Error: The Shot That Killed JFK.* New York: St. Martin's Press, 1992.

Méray, Tibor. *Thirteen Days That Shook the Kremlin: Imre Nagy and the Hungarian Revolution.* New York: Praeger, 1959.

Messick, Hank. *Lansky.* New York: Berkley, 1971.

Miller, Merle. *Lyndon: An Oral Biography.* New York: Putnam, 1980.

Model, F. Peter, and Robert J. Groden. *JFK: The Case for Conspiracy.* New York: Manor Books, 1976.

Moenssens, Andre A., and Fred E. Inbau. *Scientific Evidence in Criminal Cases.* Mineola, N.Y.: Foundation Press, 1978.

Moldea, Dan E. *Dark Victory: Ronald Reagan, MCA, and the Mob.* New York: Viking, 1986.

Moldea, Dan E. *The Hoffa Wars: Teamsters, Rebels, Politicians, and the Mob.* New York: Paddington Press, 1978.

Moldea, Dan E. *The Killing of Robert F. Kennedy: An Investigation of Motive, Means and Opportunity.* New York: W. W. Norton, 1997.

Moore, Jim. *Conspiracy of One: The Definitive Book on the Kennedy Assassination.* Fort Worth, Texas: Summit Group, 1991.

Morin, Relman. *Assassination: The Death of President John F. Kennedy.* New York: Signet, 1968.

Morrow, Robert D. *First Hand Knowledge: How I Participated in the CIA-Mafia Murder of President Kennedy.* New York: S.P.I. Books, 1992.

Mosby, Aline. *The View from No. 13 People's Street.* New York: Random House, 1962.

Moss, Armand. *Disinformation, Misinformation, and the "Conspiracy" to Kill JFK Exposed.* Hamden, Conn.: Archon Books, 1987.

Myers, Dale K. *With Malice: Lee Harvey Oswald and the Murder of Officer J. D. Tippit.* Milford, Mich.: Oak Cliff Press, 1998.

Nagle, John M. *A Guide to the Sites of November 22, 1963: Facts, Questions, Pictures, and History.* Dallas: Self-published, 2005.

NASA, Nazis, and JFK: The Torbitt Document and the Kennedy Assassination. With a foreword by David Hatcher Childress and an introduction by Kenn Thomas. Kempton, Ill.: Adventures Unlimited Press, 1996.

Navasky, Victor S. *Kennedy Justice.* New York: Atheneum, 1971.

NBC News. *Seventy Hours and Thirty Minutes, as Broadcast on the NBC Television Network by NBC News*. New York: Random House, 1966.

Nechiporenko, Oleg. *Passport to Assassination: The Never-Before-Told Story of Lee Harvey Oswald by the KGB Colonel Who Knew Him*. New York: Carol Publishing, 1993.

Nelli, Humbert S. *The Business of Crime: Italians and Syndicate Crime in the United States*. New York: Oxford University Press, 1976.

Newcombe, Fred T., and Perry Adams. *Murder from Within*. Santa Barbara, Calif.: Probe, 1974.

Newman, Albert H. *The Assassination of John F. Kennedy: The Reasons Why*. New York: Clarkson N. Potter, 1970.

Newman, John M. *JFK and Vietnam: Deception, Intrigue, and the Struggle for Power*. New York: Warner Books, 1992.

Newman, John M. *Oswald and the CIA*. New York: Carroll & Graf, 1995.

Newseum, with Cathy Trost and Susan Bennett. *President Kennedy Has Been Shot: Experience the Moment-to-Moment Account of the Four Days That Changed America*. Narrated by Dan Rather. Naperville, Ill.: Sourcebooks, 2003.

Nixon, Richard. *Six Crises*. New York: Doubleday, 1962.

Norris, W. R., and R. B. Cutler. *Alek James Hidell, Alias Oswald*. Manchester, Mass.: GKG Partners, 1985.

North, Mark. *Act of Treason: The Role of J. Edgar Hoover in the Assassination of President Kennedy*. New York: Carroll & Graf, 1991.

Noyes, Peter. *Legacy of Doubt*. New York: Pinnacle, 1973.

O'Brien, Michael. *John F. Kennedy: A Biography*. New York: Thomas Dunne Books, 2005.

O'Donnell, Kenneth P., and David F. Powers with Joseph McCarthy. *Johnny, We Hardly Knew Ye: Memories of John Fitzgerald Kennedy*. Boston: Little, Brown, 1972.

Oglesby, Carl. *The Yankee and the Cowboy War: Conspiracies from Dallas to Watergate*. Mission, Kansas: Sheed Andrews & McMeel, 1976.

O'Leary, Brad, and L. E. Seymour. *Triangle of Death: The Shocking Truth about the Role of South Vietnam and the French Mafia in the Assassination of JFK*. Nashville: WND Books, 2003.

Oliver, Beverly, with Coke Buchanan. *Nightmare in Dallas*. Lancaster, Penn.: Starburst Publisher, 1994.

O'Neill, Tip, with William Novak. *Man of the House: The Life and Political Memoirs of Speaker Tip O'Neill*. Boston: G. K. Hall, 1988.

Oswald, Robert L., with Myrick Land and Barbara Land. *Lee: A Portrait of Lee Harvey Oswald by His Brother*. New York: Coward McCann, 1967.

O'Toole, George J. A. *The Assassination Tapes: An Electronic Probe into the Murder of John F. Kennedy and the Dallas Coverup*. New York: Penthouse, 1975.

Palamara, Vince. *The Third Alternative—Survivor's Guilt: The Secret Service and the JFK Murder*. Pittsburgh: Self-published, 1993.

Pantaleone, Michele. *The Mafia and Politics*. London: Chatto & Windus, 1966.

Parmet, Herbert S. *Jack: The Struggles of John F. Kennedy*. New York: Dial Press, 1980.

Parmet, Herbert S. *JFK: The Presidency of John F. Kennedy*. New York: Penguin Books, 1984.

The Pentagon Papers: The Defense Department History of United States Decisionmaking on Vietnam. Senator Gravel edition. Boston: Beacon Press, 1971–1972.

Persons, Albert C. *Bay of Pigs*. Jefferson, N.C.: McFarland, 1990.

Phelan, James. *Scandals, Scamps, and Scoundrels: The Casebook of an Investigative Reporter*. New York: Random House, 1982.

Phillips, David Atlee. *The Night Watch*. New York: Atheneum, 1977.

Piper, Michael Collins. *Final Judgment: The Missing Link in the JFK Assassination Conspiracy.* Liberty Lobby, 1998.

Popkin, Richard H. *The Second Oswald.* New York: Avon, 1966.

Posner, Gerald. *Case Closed: Lee Harvey Oswald and the Assassination of JFK.* New York: Random House, 1993.

Powers, Francis Gary, with Curt Gentry. *Operation Overflight: The U-2 Spy Pilot Tells His Story for the First Time.* New York: Holt, Rinehart & Winston, 1970.

Powers, Richard G. *Broken: The Troubled Past and Uncertain Future of the FBI.* New York: Free Press, 2004.

Powers, Richard G. *Secrecy and Power: The Life of J. Edgar Hoover.* New York: Free Press, 1986.

Powers, Thomas. *The Man Who Kept the Secrets: Richard Helms and the CIA.* New York: Pocket Books, 1979.

President John F. Kennedy: Assassination Report of the Warren Commission. FlatSigned Rare Books, FlatSigned.Com, 2004.

Prouty, L. Fletcher. *JFK: The CIA, Vietnam, and the Plot to Assassinate John F. Kennedy.* New York: Birch Lane Press, 1992.

Raab, Selwyn. *Five Families: The Rise, Decline, and Resurgence of America's Most Powerful Mafia Empires.* New York: Thomas Dunne Books, 2005.

Ragano, Frank, and Selwyn Raab. *Mob Lawyer.* New York: Scribner's, 1994.

Ramsay, Robin. *Who Shot JFK?* London: Pocket Essentials, 2002.

Ranelagh, John. *The Agency: The Rise and Decline of the CIA.* New York: Simon & Schuster, 1986.

Rather, Dan, with Mickey Herskowitz. *The Camera Never Blinks: Adventures of a TV Journalist.* New York: William Morrow, 1977.

Reeves, Richard. *President Kennedy: Profile of Power.* New York: Simon & Schuster, 1993.

Reid, Ed. *The Grim Reapers: The Anatomy of Organized Crime in America.* Chicago: Henry Regnery, 1969.

Reppetto, Thomas. *American Mafia: A History of Its Rise to Power.* New York: Henry Holt, 2004.

Reston, James. *Deadline: A Memoir.* New York: Random House, 1991.

Reynolds, Quentin James. *Courtroom: The Story of Samuel S. Leibowitz.* New York: Farrar, Straus, 1950.

Richards, David. *Played Out: The Jean Seberg Story.* New York: Random House, 1981.

Roberts, Charles. *The Truth about the Assassination.* New York: Grosset & Dunlap, 1967.

Roberts, Craig. *Kill Zone: A Sniper Looks at Dealey Plaza.* Tulsa, Okla.: Consolidated Press International, 1997.

Roberts, Craig, and John Armstrong. *JFK: The Dead Witnesses.* Tulsa, Okla.: Consolidated Press International, 1995.

Robertson, Jerry. *Documents and Photos for John Armstrong's Book Harvey and Lee.* Lafayette, Ind.: Self-published, 2004.

Robison, John. *Proofs of a Conspiracy against All the Religions and Governments of Europe, Carried on in the Secret Meetings of Free Masons, Illuminati, and Reading Societies.* New York: George Forman, 1789.

Rodriguez, Felix I., and John Weisman. *Shadow Warrior: The CIA Hero of a Hundred Battles.* New York: Simon & Schuster, 1989.

Rodríguez Cruz, Juan Carlos. *The Bay of Pigs and the CIA.* New York: Ocean Press, 1999.

Roffman, Howard. *Presumed Guilty.* London: Associated University Presses, 1975.

Ross, Robert Gaylon, Sr. *The Elite Serial Killers of Lincoln, JFK, RFK, and MLK.* Spicewood, Texas: RIE, 2001.

Rupp, Rebecca. *Committed to Memory: How We Remember and Why We Forget.* New York: Crown, 1998.

Russell, Dick. *The Man Who Knew Too Much: Hired to Kill Oswald and Prevent the Assassination of JFK.* New York: Carroll & Graf/Richard Gallen, 1992.

Russo, Gus. *Live by the Sword: The Secret War against Castro and the Death of JFK.* Baltimore: Bancroft Press, 1998.

Russo, Gus. *The Outfit: The Role of Chicago's Underworld in the Shaping of Modern America.* New York: Bloomsbury, 2001.

Sahl, Mort. *Heartland.* New York: Harcourt Brace Jovanovich, 1976.

Salandria, Vincent J. *False Mystery: Essays on the Assassination of JFK.* Louisville, Colo.: Square Deal Press, 2004.

Salerno, Ralph, and John S. Tompkins. *The Crime Confederation: Cosa Nostra and Allied Operations in Organized Crime.* New York: Doubleday, 1969.

Sample, Glen, and Mark Collom. *The Men on the Sixth Floor.* Garden Grove, Calif.: Sample Graphics, 2001.

Sauvage, Léo. *The Oswald Affair: An Examination of the Contradictions and Omissions of the Warren Report.* Cleveland: World Publishing, 1966.

Savage, Gary. *JFK First Day Evidence.* Monroe, La.: Shoppe Press, 1993.

Schacter, Daniel L. *The Seven Sins of Memory: How the Mind Forgets and Remembers.* Boston: Houghton Mifflin, 2001.

Scheim, David E. *Contract on America: The Mafia Murders of John and Robert Kennedy.* Silver Spring, Md.: Argyle Press, 1983.

Schieffer, Bob. *This Just In: What I Couldn't Tell You on TV.* New York: Putnam, 2003.

Schlesinger, Arthur M., Jr. *Robert Kennedy and His Times.* Boston: Houghton Mifflin, 1978.

Schlesinger, Arthur M., Jr. *A Thousand Days: John F. Kennedy in the White House.* Boston: Houghton Mifflin, 1965.

Schlesinger, Stephen, and Stephen Kinzer. *Bitter Fruit: The Untold Story of the American Coup in Guatemala.* Garden City, N.Y.: Doubleday, 1982.

Schlott, Joseph L. *No Left Turns.* New York: Praeger, 1975.

Schotz, E. Marlin. *History Will Not Absolve Us: Orwellian Control, Public Denial and the Murder of President Kennedy.* Brookline, Mass.: Kurtz, Ulmer & Delucia Book Publishers, 1996.

Sciacca, Tony. *Luciano: The Man Who Modernized the American Mafia.* New York: Pinnacle Books, 1975.

Scott, Peter Dale. *Crime and Cover-Up: The CIA, the Mafia, and the Dallas-Watergate Connection.* Santa Barbara, Calif.: Open Archives Press, 1993.

Scott, Peter Dale. *Deep Politics and the Death of JFK.* Berkeley: University of California Press, 1993.

Seigenthaler, John. *A Search for Justice.* Nashville: Aurora Publishers, 1971.

Semple, Robert B., Jr., ed. *Four Days in November: The Original Coverage of the John F. Kennedy Assassination by the Staff of the* New York Times. New York: St. Martin's Press, 2003.

Shannon, William V. *The Heir Apparent: Robert Kennedy and the Struggle for Power.* New York: Macmillan, 1967.

Shaw, J. Gary, with Larry R. Harris. *Cover-Up: The Governmental Conspiracy to Conceal the Facts about the Public Execution of John Kennedy.* Cleburne, Texas: Self-published, 1976.

Shaw, Maud. *White House Nannie: My Years with Caroline and John Kennedy, Jr.* New York: New American Library, 1966.

Sheridan, Walter. *The Fall and Rise of Jimmy Hoffa.* New York: Saturday Review Press, 1973.

Shesol, Jeff. *Mutual Contempt: Lyndon Johnson, Robert Kennedy, and the Feud That Defined a Decade.* New York: W. W. Norton, 1997.

Sirica, John J. *To Set the Record Straight: The Break-in, the Tapes, the Conspirators, the Pardon.* New York: W. W. Norton, 1979.

Sloan, Bill. *JFK: Breaking the Silence.* Dallas: Taylor Publishing, 1993.

Sloan, Bill, with Jean Hill. *JFK: The Last Dissenting Witness.* Gretna, La.: Pelican, 1992.

Smith, Earl E. T. *The Fourth Floor: An Account of the Castro Communist Revolution.* Washington, D.C.: Selores Foundation Press, 1987.

Smith, Matthew. *Conspiracy: The Plot to Stop the Kennedys.* New York: Citadel Press, 2005.

Smith, Matthew. *JFK: The Second Plot.* Edinburgh: Mainstream, 1992.

Smith, Matthew. *Say Goodbye to America: The Sensational and Untold Story behind the Assassination of John F. Kennedy.* Edinburgh: Mainstream, 2001.

Smith, R. Harris. *OSS: The Secret History of America's First Central Intelligence Agency.* New York: Delta Books, 1973.

Smith, W. H. B. *Small Arms of the World: The Basic Manual of Military Small Arms, American, Soviet, British, Czech, German, French, Belgian, Italian, Swiss, Japanese, and All Other Important Nations.* 10th ed. Harrisburg, Penn.: Stackpole Books, 1973.

Sneed, Larry A. *No More Silence: An Oral History of the Assassination of President Kennedy.* Dallas: Three Forks Press, 1997.

Sondern, Frederic. *Brotherhood of Evil: The Mafia.* New York: Farrar, Straus, & Cudahy, 1959.

Sparrow, John. *After the Assassination: A Positive Appraisal of the Warren Report.* New York: Chilmark Press, 1967.

Specter, Arlen, with Charles Robbins. *Passion for Truth: From Finding JFK's Single Bullet to Questioning Anita Hill to Impeaching Clinton.* New York: William Morrow, 2000.

The Speeches of Senator John F. Kennedy's Presidential Campaign of 1960. Washington, D.C.: Government Printing Office, 1961.

Sprague, Richard E. *The Taking of America 1-2-3.* Rev. ed. Self-published, 1979.

Stafford, Jean. *A Mother in History.* New York: Farrar, Straus & Giroux, 1966.

Steinberg, Alfred. *Sam Johnson's Boy: A Close-up of the President from Texas.* New York: Macmillan, 1968.

Stone, Oliver, and Zachary Sklar. *JFK: The Book of the Film.* New York: Applause, 1992.

Sturdivan, Larry M. *The JFK Myths: A Scientific Investigation of the Kennedy Assassination.* St. Paul, Minn.: Paragon House, 2005.

Sullivan, William C., with Bill Brown. *The Bureau: My Thirty Years in Hoover's FBI.* New York: W. W. Norton, 1979.

Summers, Anthony. *Conspiracy.* New York: McGraw-Hill, 1980.

Summers, Anthony. *Goddess: The Secret Lives of Marilyn Monroe.* New York: Macmillan, 1985.

Summers, Anthony. *Not in Your Lifetime.* New York: Marlowe, 1998.

Summers, Anthony. *Official and Confidential: The Secret Life of J. Edgar Hoover.* New York: Putnam, 1993.

Summers, Anthony, with Robbyn Swan. *The Arrogance of Power: The Secret World of Richard Nixon.* New York: Viking, 2000.

Summers, Anthony, and Robbyn Swan. *Sinatra: The Life.* New York: Alfred A. Knopf, 2005.

Tagg, Eric R. *Brush with History: A Day in the Life of Deputy E. R. Walthers.* Garland, Texas: Shot in the Light Publishing, 1998.

Tague, James T. *Truth Withheld: A Survivor's Story.* Dallas: Excel Digital Press, 2003.

Taylor, Maxwell D. *Swords and Plowshares.* New York: W. W. Norton, 1972.

TerHorst, Jerald F., and Ralph Albertazzie. *The Flying White House: The Story of Air Force One.* New York: Coward, McCann & Geoghegan, 1979.

Theoharis, Athan G., ed. *Culture of Secrecy: The Government versus the People's Right to Know.* Lawrence: University Press of Kansas, 1998.

Theoharis, Athan G., with Tony G. Poveda, Susan Rosenfeld, and Richard Gid Powers, eds. *The FBI: A Comprehensive Reference Guide*. Phoenix: Oryx Press, 1999.

Thomas, Evan. *Robert Kennedy: His Life*. New York: Simon & Schuster, 2000.

Thomas, Evan. *The Very Best Men: Four Who Dared: The Early Years of the CIA*. New York: Simon & Schuster, 1995.

Thomas, Hugh. *Cuba; or, Pursuit of Freedom*. London: Eyre & Spottiswoode, 1971.

Thomas, Ralph D. *Missing Links in the JFK Assassination Conspiracy*. Austin, Texas: Thomas Investigative Publications, 1992.

Thomas, Ralph D. *Photo Computer Image Processing and the Crime of the Century*. Austin, Texas: Thomas Investigative Publications, 1992.

Thompson, Josiah. *Six Seconds in Dallas: A Micro-study of the Kennedy Assassination*. New York: Bernard Geis Associates, 1967.

Thornley, Kerry W. *The Idle Warriors*. Avondale Estates, Ga.: IllumiNet Press, 1991.

Thornley, Kerry W. *Oswald*. Chicago: New Classics House, 1965.

Toplin, Robert Brent. *Oliver Stone's USA: Film, History, and Controversy*. Lawrence: University Press of Kansas, 2000.

Torcia, Charles E. *Wharton's Criminal Law*. 15th ed. Deerfield, Ill.: Clark Boardman Callaghan, 1993–1996.

Trask, Richard B. *National Nightmare on Six Feet of Film: Mr. Zapruder's Home Movie and the Murder of President Kennedy*. Danvers, Mass.: Yeoman Press, 2005.

Trask, Richard B. *Photographic Memory: The Kennedy Assassination, November 22, 1963*. Dallas: Sixth Floor Museum, 1996.

Trask, Richard B. *Pictures of the Pain: Photography and the Assassination of President Kennedy*. Danvers, Mass.: Yeoman Press, 1994.

Trask, Richard B. *That Day in Dallas: Three Photographers Capture on Film the Day President Kennedy Died*. Danvers, Mass.: Yeoman Press, 1998.

Trento, Joseph J. *The Secret History of the CIA*. Roseville, Calif.: Prima, 2001.

Tully, Andrew. *CIA, the Inside Story*. New York: William Morrow, 1962.

Turner, William W. *Rearview Mirror: Looking Back at the FBI, the CIA, and Other Tails*. Granite Bay, Calif.: Penmarin Books, 2001.

Turner, William W., and Jonn G. Christian. *The Assassination of Robert F. Kennedy: A Searching Look at the Conspiracy and Cover-Up, 1968–1978*. New York: Random House, 1978.

Twyman, Noel. *Bloody Treason: The Assassination of John F. Kennedy, on Solving History's Greatest Murder Mystery*. Rancho Santa Fe, Calif.: Laurel, 1997.

Unger, Irwin, and Debi Unger. *LBJ: A Life*. New York: John Wiley, 1999.

United Press International. *Four Days: The Historical Record of the Death of President Kennedy*. New York: American Heritage, 1964.

Valentine, Douglas. *The Strength of the Wolf: The Secret History of America's War on Drugs*. New York: Verso, 2004.

Voltaire. *Dissertation sur la mort de Henri IV.* Vol. 2. Ed. Furne, 1835.

Waldron, Lamar, with Thom Hartmann. *Ultimate Sacrifice: John and Robert Kennedy, the Plan for a Coup in Cuba, and the Murder of JFK*. New York: Carroll & Graf, 2005.

Warren, Earl. *The Memoirs of Earl Warren*. Garden City, N.Y.: Doubleday, 1977.

Weberman, Alan J., and Michael Canfield. *Coup d'État in America: The CIA and the Assassination of John F. Kennedy*. San Francisco: Quick American Archives, 1992.

Wecht, Cyril H. *Cause of Death*. New York: Penguin, 1994.

Weisberg, Harold. *Case Open*. New York: Carroll & Graf, 1994.

Weisberg, Harold. *Never Again! The Government Conspiracy in the JFK Assassination*. New York: Carroll & Graf, 1995.

Weisberg, Harold. *Oswald in New Orleans: Case of Conspiracy with the CIA.* New York: Canyon Books, 1967.

Weisberg, Harold. *Photographic Whitewash: Suppressed Kennedy Assassination Pictures.* Hyattstown, Md.: Self-published, 1967.

Weisberg, Harold. *Post Mortem: JFK Assassination Cover-Up Smashed!* Frederick, Md.: Self-published, 1975.

Weisberg, Harold. *Whitewash: The Report on the Warren Commission.* Hyattstown, Md.: Self-published, 1965.

Weisberg, Harold. *Whitewash II: The FBI-Secret Service Cover-Up.* Hyattstown, Md.: Self-published, 1966.

Weisberg, Harold. *Whitewash IV: Post Assassination Transcript.* Hyattstown, Md.: Self-published, 1966.

White, Stephen. *Should We Now Believe the Warren Report?* New York: Macmillan, 1968.

White, Theodore H. *In Search of History: A Personal Expedition.* New York: Harper & Row, 1978.

White, Theodore H. *The Making of the President, 1964.* New York: Atheneum, 1965.

Whitehead, Don. *The FBI Story: A Report to the People.* New York: Random House, 1956.

Wicker, Tom. *JFK and LBJ: The Influence of Personality upon Politics.* New York: William Morrow, 1968.

Williams, James Doyle. *The Dolphus Starling, Minnie Lee Williams Family, An Autobiography, Family-Careers.* Self-published, October 1990.

Williams, T. Harry. *Huey Long.* New York: Alfred A. Knopf, 1969.

Wills, Garry, and Ovid Demaris. *Jack Ruby.* New York: Da Capo Press, 1994.

Wilson, Kirk. *Unsolved Crimes: The Top Ten Unsolved Murders of the 20th Century.* New York: Carroll & Graf, 2002.

Windchy, Eugene G. *Tonkin Gulf.* Garden City, N.Y.: Doubleday, 1971.

Wise, David. *The American Police State: The Government against the People.* New York: Random House, 1976.

Wise, David, and Thomas B. Ross. *The Invisible Government.* New York: Random House, 1964.

Wofford, Harris. *Of Kennedys and Kings: Making Sense of the Sixties.* New York: Farrar, Straus & Giroux, 1980.

Wrone, David R. *The Zapruder Film: Reframing JFK's Assassination.* Lawrence: University Press of Kansas, 2003.

Wyden, Peter. *Bay of Pigs: The Untold Story.* New York: Simon & Schuster, 1979.

Yeltsin, Boris. *The View from the Kremlin.* London: HarperCollins, 1994.

Youngblood, Rufus W. *20 Years in the Secret Service: My Life with Five Presidents.* New York: Simon & Schuster, 1973.

Zelizer, Barbie. *Covering the Body: The Kennedy Assassination, the Media, and the Shaping of Collective Memory.* Chicago: Chicago University Press, 1992.

Zirbel, Craig. *The Texas Connection: The Assassination of President John F. Kennedy.* Scottsdale, Ariz.: Texas Connection, 1991.

Zubin, David M. *Shooting Kennedy: JFK and the Culture of Images.* Berkeley: University of California Press, 2003.

Articles in Magazines and Journals

Aguilar, Gary L. Letter to editor. *Federal Bar News & Journal*, June 9, 1994.

Aguilar, Gary L., Cyril H. Wecht, and Rex Bradford. "A Neuroforensic Analysis of the Wounds of President John F. Kennedy: Part 2—A Study of the Available Evidence, Eyewitness

Correlations, Analysis, and Conclusions." *Neurosurgery-Online.com*, vol. 57, no. 3, September 2005.

Alvarez, Luis W. "A Physicist Examines the Kennedy Assassination Film." *American Journal of Physics*, vol. 44, no. 9, September 1976.

"America's Long Vigil." *TV Guide*, issue 565, vol. 12, no. 4, January 25, 1964.

Ansen, David. "A Troublemaker for Our Times." *Newsweek*, December 23, 1991.

Anson, Robert Sam. "The Shooting of *JFK*." *Esquire*, November 1991.

Armstrong, Ken. "Dallas Puzzle—By a Canadian Eyewitness." *Liberty*, July 15, 1964.

"As the Book Appears: A Close Look at the Facts." *U.S. News & World Report*, January 23, 1967.

"The Assassination: History's Jury." *Newsweek*, December 16, 1963.

Attwood, William. "In Memory of John F. Kennedy." *Look*, December 31, 1963.

Auchincloss, Kenneth, with Ginny Carroll and Maggie Malone. "Twisted History." *Newsweek*, December 23, 1991.

Aynesworth, Hugh. "The JFK 'Conspiracy'." *Newsweek*, May 15, 1967.

Bardach, Ann Louise. "The Spy Who Loved Castro." *Vanity Fair*, November 1993.

Beck, Melinda, and Anne Underwood. "I Wanted to Be a Hero." *Newsweek*, November 22, 1993.

Berendt, John. "Name: Igor 'Turk' Vaganov." *Esquire*, August 1967.

Berquist, Laura. "John Fitzgerald Kennedy, 35th President of the United States." *Look*, November 17, 1964.

Beschloss, Michael. "An Assassination Diary." *Newsweek*, November 23, 1998.

Beschloss, Michael. "The Day That Changed America." *Newsweek*, November 22, 1995.

"Best of '86." *Time*, January 5, 1987.

Bethell, Tom. "Conspiracy to End Conspiracies." *National Review*, December 16, 1991.

Bethell, Tom. "Jim Garrison's Great Escape." *American Spectator*, December 1998.

Bethell, Tom. "Was Sirhan Sirhan on the Grassy Knoll?" *Washington Monthly*, March 1975.

"Birch View of JFK." *Newsweek*, February 24, 1964.

Blythe, Myrna, and Jane Farrell. "Marina Oswald, Twenty-five Years Later." *Ladies' Home Journal*, November 1988.

"The Bold and the Beautiful." *U.S. News & World Report*, December 26, 1966.

"The Book That Has Backfired." *U.S. News & World Report*, December 26, 1966.

Branch, Taylor, and George Crile III. "The Kennedy Vendetta: How the CIA Waged a Silent War against Cuba." *Harper's Magazine*, August 1975.

Breo, Dennis L. "JFK's Death—The Plain Truth from the MDs Who Did the Autopsy." *Journal of the American Medical Association*, vol. 267, no. 20, May 27, 1992.

Breo, Dennis L. "JFK's Death, Part II—Dallas MDs Recall Their Memories." *Journal of the American Medical Association*, vol. 267, no. 20, May 27, 1992.

Breo, Dennis L. "JFK's Death, Part III—Dr. Finck Speaks Out: 'Two Bullets, from the Rear'." *Journal of the American Medical Association*, vol. 268, no. 13, October 7, 1992.

Breslin, Jimmy. "A Death in Emergency Room No. One." *Saturday Evening Post*, December 14, 1963.

Bunton, Judge Lucius. "Texas Judge Offers Perspectives on Presiding at Oswald's Trial." *Texas Bar Journal*, November 1988.

Cartwright, Gary. "I Was Mandarin." *Texas Monthly*, December 1990.

Cartwright, Gary. "The Old Soldier." *Texas Monthly*, February 1991.

Cartwright, Gary. "Who Was Jack Ruby?" *Texas Monthly*, November 1975.

Chandler, David. "The 'Little Man' Is Bigger Than Ever." *Life*, April 10, 1970.

Chevigny, Bell Gale. "Surviving Revolution and Obscurity." *Ms.*, April 1987.

Chomsky, Noam. "Vain Hopes, False Dreams." *Z Magazine*, September 1992.

Christensen, Dan. "JFK, King, the Dade County Links." *Miami Magazine*, December 1976.

"Clay Shaw: An Exclusive Penthouse Interview." *Penthouse*, September 1969.

Connally, John. "Why Kennedy Went to Texas." *Life*, November 24, 1967.

Corliss, Richard. "Who Killed JFK?" *Time*, December 23, 1991.

Corn, David, and Gus Russo. "The Old Man and the CIA: A Kennedy Plot to Kill Castro?" *Nation*, March 26, 2001.

Crenshaw, Charles A., and J. Gary Shaw. "Commentary on JFK Autopsy Articles." *Journal of the American Medical Association*, vol. 273, no. 20, May 24, 1995–May 31, 1995.

Cushman, Robert F. "Why the Warren Commission?" *New York University Law Review*, vol. 40, May 1965.

Daly, Steve. "Camera Obscura." *Entertainment Weekly*, January 17, 1992.

Daniel, Jean. "When Castro Heard the News." *New Republic*, December 7, 1963.

Davidson, Bill. "A Profile in Family Courage." *Saturday Evening Post*, December 14, 1963.

"The De-briefing Process for the U.S.S.R's Defectors." *Newsweek*, February 24, 1964.

"The Demise of a Don." *Time*, June 30, 1975.

Devlin, Lord. "Death of a President, the Established Facts." *Atlantic*, March 1965.

"Did This Man Happen upon Kennedy's Assassins?" *Maclean's Reports*, November 1967.

"A Different Look at Dallas, Texas." *U.S. News & World Report*, February 3, 1964.

"Discovering History with a Car Collector: Feature Car: The Kennedy Lincoln." *Car Collector*, April 2005.

Dudman, Richard. "Commentary of an Eyewitness." *New Republic*, December 21, 1963.

Epstein, Edward. "Reporter at Large." *New Yorker*, July 13, 1968.

Epstein, Edward. "The Second Coming of Jim Garrison." *Atlantic*, March 1993.

"Fateful Two Hours without a President." *U.S. News & World Report*, November 14, 1966.

"FBI: Shaken by a Cover-Up That Failed." *Time*, November 3, 1975.

Fisher, Bob. "The Why and Hows of JFK." *American Cinematographer*, February 1992.

Fonzi, Gaeton. "Seduced by the Web-Weavers." *Pennsylvania Gazette*, November 1993.

Fonzi, Gaeton. "Who Killed JFK?" *Washingtonian*, November 1980.

Freese, Paul L. "The Warren Commission and the Fourth Shot: A Reflection on the Fundamentals of Forensic Fact-Finding." *New York University Law Review*, vol. 40, May 1965.

Gage, Nicholas. "The Little Big Man Who Laughs at the Law." *Atlantic*, July 1970.

Gates, David, with Howard Manly, Donna Foote, and Frank Washington. "Bottom Line: How Crazy Is It?" *Newsweek*, December 23, 1991.

Gavin, James M. "We Can Get Out of Vietnam." *Saturday Evening Post*, February 24, 1968.

Gelb, Leslie. "Would Defeat in Iraq Be So Bad?" *Time*, October 23, 2006.

Gertz, Elmer. Review of "My Life as a Radical Lawyer." *Real Crime Digest*, August 30, 1993.

Gertz, Elmer. "The 30th Anniversary of the Kennedy Assassination." *Real Crime Book Digest*, October–November 1995.

Gest, Ted, and Joseph Shapiro with David Bowermaster and Thom Geier. "JFK: The Untold Story of the Warren Report." *U.S. News & World Report*, August 17, 1992.

Goldman, Peter, with John J. Lindsay. "Dallas: New Questions and Answers." *Newsweek*, April 28, 1975.

Goldman, Peter, with Elaine Shannon, Diane Camper, and Lee Donosky. "Rush to Judgment." *Newsweek*, January 15, 1979.

Golz, Earl. "Confidential: The FBI's File on JFK." *Gallery*, November 1982.

Golz, Earl. "Confidential: The FBI's File on JFK—Part Two." *Gallery*, December 1982.

"Good-by Belli." *Newsweek*, March 30, 1964.

Goodhart, Arthur. "The Mysteries of the Kennedy Assassination and the English Press." *Law Quarterly Review*, vol. 83, January 1967.

Goodhart, Arthur. "The Warren Commission from the Procedural Standpoint." *New York University Law Review*, vol. 40, May 1965.

Goodman, Craig G. "History of the U.S. Petroleum Depletion Allowance, Part III." *Oil and Gas Quarterly*, vol. 39, March 1991.

Greenstein, Fred I. "Diffusion of News of the Kennedy Assassination." *Public Opinion Quarterly*, Summer 1965.

Groden, Robert. "A New Look at the Zapruder Film." *Rolling Stone*, April 24, 1975.

Grosvenor, Melville Bell. "The Last Full Measure." *National Geographic*, March 9, 1964.

"Growing Rift of LBJ and Kennedy." *U.S. News & World Report*, January 2, 1967.

Guinn, Vincent. "JFK Assassination: Bullet Analysis." *Analytical Chemistry*, vol. 51, no. 4, April 1979.

Hall, Kermit. "The Virulence of the National Appetite for Bogus Revelation." *Maryland Law Review*, vol. 56, no. 1, 1997.

Hansen, Mark. "Truth Sleuth or Faulty Detector." *American Bar Association Journal*, May 1999.

"Historic Photo Report." *U.S. News & World Report*, December 9, 1963.

Holland, Max. "The Demon in Jim Garrison." *Wilson Quarterly*, Spring 2001.

Holland, Max. "The JFK Lawyers' Conspiracy." *Nation*, February 20, 2006.

Holland, Max. "The Key to the Warren Report." *American Heritage*, vol. 46, no. 7, November 1995.

Holmes, John Clellon. "The Silence of Oswald." *Playboy*, November 1965.

"In the Works: Tighter Laws on Gun Sales." *U.S. News & World Report*, December 9, 1963.

"Investigations." *Time*, December 13, 1963.

Isaacson, Walter. "If Kennedy Had Lived." *Time*, April 13, 1992.

"Jack Kennedy's Other Women." *Time*, December 29, 1975.

Jackson, Donald. "The Evolution of an Assassin." *Life*, February 21, 1964.

Janos, Leo. "The Last Days of the President: LBJ in Retirement." *Atlantic*, January 1973.

"JFK: The Death and the Doubts." *Newsweek*, December 5, 1966.

Johnson, Priscilla. "Oswald in Moscow." *Harper's Magazine*, April 1964.

Kaiser, Robert Blair. "The Mystery Tramps in Disguise?" *Rolling Stone*, April 24, 1975.

Kaplan, David A. "The JFK Probe—25 Years Later." *National Law Journal*, November 28, 1988.

Katz, Bob. "Mark Lane, the Left's Leading Hearse Chaser." *Mother Jones*, August 1979.

Kelley, Kitty. "The Dark Side of Camelot." *People*, February 29, 1988.

Kempton, Murray. "Jack Ruby on Trial." *New Republic*, March 7, 1964.

Kempton, Murray, and James Ridgeway. "Romans." *New Republic*, December 7, 1963.

"Kiss of Death." *Newsweek*, October 7, 1963.

Knebel, Fletcher. "J. Edgar Hoover, the Cop and the Man." *Look*, May 31, 1955.

Knebel, Fletcher. "A New Wave of Doubt." *Look*, July 12, 1966.

Kornbluh, Peter. "JFK & Castro: The Secret Quest for Accommodation." *Cigar Aficionado*, October 1999.

Lacayo, Richard. "How Sick Was J.F.K.?" *Time*, December 2, 2002.

Lattimer, J. K. "Additional Data on the Shooting of President Kennedy." *Journal of the American Medical Association*, vol. 269, no. 12, March 24, 1993.

Lattimer, J. K., J. Lattimer, and G. Lattimer. "An Experimental Study of the Backward Movement of President Kennedy's Head." *Surgery, Gynecology, and Obstetrics*, February 1976.

Lattimer, John K. "Observations Based on a Review of the Autopsy Photographs, X-rays and Related Materials of the Late President John F. Kennedy." *Resident and Staff Physician*, May 1972.

Lattimer, John K., Angus Laidlaw, Paul Heneghan, and Eric J. Haubner. "Experimental Duplication of the Important Physical Evidence of the Lapel Bulge of the Jacket Worn by Governor Connally When Bullet 399 Went through Him." *Journal of the American College of Surgeons*, vol. 178, May 1994.

Lattimer, John K., and Jon Lattimer. "The Kennedy-Connally Single Bullet Theory." *International Surgery*, vol. 50, no. 6, December 1968.

Lattimer, John K., Edward B. Schlesinger, and H. Houston Merritt. "President Kennedy's Spine Hit by First Bullet." *Bulletin of the New York Academy of Medicine*, Second Series, vol. 53, no. 3, April 1977.

Lemann, Nicholas. "The Case against Jim Garrison." *GQ*, January 1992.

Levine, Jack. "Hoover and the Red Square." *Nation*, October 20, 1962.

Levy, Michael L., Daniel Sullivan, Rodrick Faccio, and Robert Grossman. "A Neuroforensic Analysis of the Wounds of President John F. Kennedy: Part 2—A Study of the Available Evidence, Eyewitness Correlations, Analysis, and Conclusions." *Neurosurgery*, vol. 54, no. 6, June 2004.

Lewis, Flora. "The Tragedy of Bertrand Russell." *Look*, April 4, 1967.

Lundberg, George D. "Closing the Case in JAMA on the John F. Kennedy Autopsy." Editorial. *Journal of the American Medical Association*, vol. 268, no. 13, October 7, 1992.

Macdonald, Dwight. "A Critique of the Warren Report." *Esquire*, March 1965.

Magnusen, Ed, edited by Ronald Krise. "The Truth about Hoover." *Time*, December 22, 1975.

Mailer, Norman. "The Amateur Hit Man." *New York Review of Books*, May 11, 1995.

Mailer, Norman. "Oswald in the U.S.S.R." *New Yorker*, April 10, 1995.

Manchester, William. "The Death of a President." *Look*, January 24, 1967.

Manchester, William. "William Manchester's Own Story." *Look*, April 4, 1967.

Mandel, Paul. "End to Nagging Rumors: The Six Critical Seconds." *Life*, December 6, 1963.

Marchetti, Victor. "CIA to Admit Hunt Involvement in Kennedy Slaying." *Spotlight*, August 14, 1978.

"Marina's Turn." *Time*, September 21, 1992.

Martin, Harold H. " 'Help Us Fight!' Cry the Angry Exiles." *Saturday Evening Post*, June 8, 1963.

Martindale, David. "The Bizarre Deaths following JFK's Murder." *Argosy*, March 1977.

"A Matter of Reasonable Doubt." *Life*, November 25, 1966.

McGill, Ralph Emerson. "Hate Knows No Direction." *Saturday Evening Post*, December 14, 1963.

McKinley, James. "Cries of Conspiracy." Part V of "Playboy's History of Assassination in America." *Playboy*, May 1976.

McKinley, James. "The End of Camelot." Part IV of "Playboy's History of Assassination in America." *Playboy*, April 1976.

McNamara, Robert. "The Lessons of October." *Newsweek*, February 13, 1989.

Morgenthau, Tom, with Elaine Shannon. "Tales of Conspiracy." *Newsweek*, July 30, 1979.

Morley, Jefferson. "The Good Spy: How the Quashing of an Honest C.I.A. Investigator Helped Launch 40 Years of JFK Conspiracy Theories and Cynicism about the Feds." *Washington Monthly*, December 2003.

Morrow, Lance, and Martha Smilgis. "Plunging into the Labyrinth." *Time*, December 23, 1991.

Mosk, Richard M. "Conspiracy Theories and the JFK Assassination: Cashing in on Political Paranoia." *Los Angeles Lawyer*, November 1992.

"Murder of Innocence." *Reporter*, October 1992.

Nash, George, and Patricia Nash. "The Other Witnesses." *New Leader*, October 12, 1964.

Nichols, John. "President Kennedy's Adrenals." *Journal of the American Medical Association*, vol. 201, no. 2, July 10, 1967.

Nichols, John. "The Wounding of Governor Connally of Texas." *Maryland State Medical Journal*, October 1977.

Norton, Linda, James A. Cottone, Irvin M. Sopher, and Vincent J. M. DiMaio. "The Exhumation and Identification of Lee Harvey Oswald." *Journal of Forensic Science*, January 1984.

"A Note from Jack Ruby." *Newsweek*, March 27, 1967.

Oliver, Revilo P. "Marksmanship in Dallas." *American Opinion*, February 1964.

Olson, Don, and Ralph F. Turner. "Photographic Evidence and the Assassination of President John F. Kennedy." *Journal of Forensic Sciences*, vol. 16, no. 4, October 1971.

O'Toole, George, and Paul Hoch. "Dallas: The Cuban Connection." *Saturday Evening Post*, March 1976.

"Pages from a Family Album." *Look*, November 17, 1964.

Petty, Charles. "JFK—An Allonge." *Journal of the American Medical Association*, vol. 269, no. 12, March 24, 1993.

Phelan, James. "Rush to Judgment in New Orleans." *Saturday Evening Post*, May 6, 1967.

Phelan, James. "The Vice Man Cometh." *Saturday Evening Post*, June 8, 1963.

Phillips, Kevin. "Fat City." *Time*, September 26, 1994.

"Pike Committee Report." *Village Voice*, February 16 and 23, 1976.

"Playboy Interview: Jesse Ventura." *Playboy*, November 1999.

"Playboy Interview: Jim Garrison." *Playboy*, October 1967.

"Playboy Interview: Mark Lane." *Playboy*, February 1967.

Posner, Gerald. "Cracks in the Wall of Silence." *Newsweek*, October 12, 1998.

Prouty, Fletcher. "President Kennedy Was Killed by a Murder, Inc." *Executive Intelligence Review*, February 7, 1992.

Rahn, K. A., and L. M. Sturdivan. "Neutron Activation and the JFK Assassination, Part I, Data and Interpretation." *Journal of Radioanalytical and Nuclear Chemistry*, vol. 262, no. 1, October 2004.

Randall, Teri. "Clinicians' Forensic Interpretations of Fatal Gunshot Wounds Often Miss the Mark." *Journal of the American Medical Association*, vol. 269, no. 16, April 28, 1993.

Randich, Eric, Wayne Duerfeldt, Wade McLendon, and William Tobin. "A Metallurgical Review of the Interpretation of Bullet Lead Compositional Analysis." *Forensic Science International*, April 2002.

Randich, Eric, and Patrick M. Grant. "Proper Assessment of the JFK Assassination Bullet Lead Evidence from Metallurgical and Statistical Perspective." *Journal of Forensic Sciences*, vol. 51, no. 4, July 2006.

Raskin, Marcus. "JFK and the Culture of Violence." *American Historical Review*, April 1992.

Reeves, Richard. "JFK: Secrets & Lies." *Reader's Digest*, April 2003.

"The Right to Be Wrong." *Newsweek*, March 30, 1964.

Rogers, Warren. "The Persecution of Clay Shaw." *Look*, August 26, 1969.

Saunders, Charles J., and Mark S. Zaid. "The Declassification of Dealey Plaza: After Thirty Years, a New Disclosure Law at Last May Help to Clarify the Facts of the Kennedy Assassination." *South Texas Law Review*, vol. 34, October 1993.

Schonfeld, Maurice W. "The Shadow of a Gunman." *Columbia Journalism Review*, July–August 1975.

Schwartz, Sorrell L. Letter to editor. *Time*, February 16, 1981.

"Seventy-five Year Secrecy for Exhibits in JFK Killing." *U.S. News & World Report*, January 4, 1965.

Sidey, Hugh. "All the Way with JFK." *Time*, May 26, 2003.

Sidey, Hugh. "When It Counted, He Never Faltered." *Time*, December 2, 2002.

"$650,000 for Family of Man Killed by Oswald." *U.S. News & World Report*, November 2, 1964.

Smith, Sandy. "Carlos Marcello, King Thug of Louisiana." *Life*, September 8, 1967.

Smith, Sandy. "The Crime Cartel." *Life*, September 1, 1967.

Smith, Wayne. "JAMA Knows Best: The Medical Journal Called the JFK Case Closed—and the Verdict Went Unchallenged." *Columbia Journalism Review*, September–October 1993.

Solomon, Jolie. "True Disbelievers." *Newsweek*, November 22, 1993.

"Sorrow Rings a World." *Life*, December 6, 1963.

Sprague, Richard E. "The Assassination of President John F. Kennedy: The Application of Computers to the Photographic Evidence." *Computers and Animation*, vol. 19, May, June, and July 1970; vol. 20, March and May 1971.

Stetler, Russell. "Can Congress Crack the Kennedy Assassination?" *Inquiry*, March 16, 1978.

"Still Secret: The KGB's Oswald File." *Newsweek*, July 5, 1999.

Stolley, Richard. "Shots Seen Round the World: A Journalist's Behind-the-Scenes Story of the Most Historic Home Movie Ever." *Entertainment Weekly*, January 17, 1992.

Stolley, Richard. "What Happened Next . . ." *Esquire*, November 1973.

Stone, Oliver. "Oliver Stone Talks Back." *Premiere*, January 1992.

Stone, Oliver. "Was Vietnam JFK's War?" *Newsweek*, October 21, 1996.

Sturdivan, Larry M., and K. A. Rahn, "Neutron Activation and the JFK Assassination, Part II, Extended Benefits." *Journal of Radioanalytical and Nuclear Chemistry*, vol. 262, no. 1, October 2004.

Sullivan, Daniel, Rodrick Faccio, Michael L. Levy, and Robert Grossman. "The Assassination of President John F. Kennedy: A Neuroforensic Analysis—Part 1: A Neurosurgeon's Previously Undocumented Eyewitness Account from Trauma Room 1." *Neurosurgery*, vol. 53, no. 5, November 2003.

Summers, Anthony. "Hidden Hoover." *Vanity Fair*, March 1993.

Summers, Anthony, and Robbyn Summers. "The Ghosts of November." *Vanity Fair*, December 1994.

Szulc, Tad. "Cuba on Our Mind." *Esquire*, February 1974.

Talbot, David. "Fatal Flaw." *Image*, March 29, 1992.

Thomas, D. B. "Echo Correlation Analysis and the Acoustic Evidence in the Kennedy Assassination Revisited." *Science & Justice*, vol. 41, no. 1, 2001.

Thomas, Evan. "At War over a Tragic Film." *Newsweek*, January 17, 1992.

Thomas, Evan. "Bobby at the Brink." *Newsweek*, August 14, 2000.

Thomas, Evan. "The Real Cover-Up." *Newsweek*, November 22, 1993.

Thompson, Thomas. "In Texas a Policeman and an Assassin Are Laid to Rest Too." *Life*, December 6, 1963.

Thomson, J. Anderson, Jr., Joy Boissevain, and Clare Aukofer. "Lee Harvey Oswald—Another Look." *Mind and Human Interaction*, vol. 8, no. 2, Spring/Summer 1997.

Thorburn, William. "Cases of Injury to the Cervical Region of the Spinal Cord." *Brain, a Journal of Neurology*, vol. IX, 1887.

"Three Patients at Parkland." *Texas State Journal of Medicine*, vol. 60, January 1964.

"To Help You Keep the Record Straight about That Book." *U.S. News & World Report*, February 6, 1967.

Trillin, Calvin. "The Buffs." *New Yorker*, June 10, 1967.

"The Truth about Hoover." *Time*, December 22, 1975.

"Truth about Kennedy Assassination." *U.S. News & World Report*, October 10, 1966.

Vanocur, Sander. "Kennedy's Voyage of Discovery." *Harper's Magazine*, April 1964.

Viorst, Milton. "The Mafia, the CIA, and the Kennedy Assassination." *Washingtonian*, November 1975.

"The Warren Commission Report." *Time*, October 2, 1964.

Wecht, Cyril. "The Medical Evidence in the Assassination of President John F. Kennedy." *Forensic Science Gazette*, vol. 4, no. 4, September 1973.

Wecht, Cyril, and Robert P. Smith. "The Medical Evidence in the Assassination of President John F. Kennedy." *Forensic Science*, vol. 3, fig. 2, 1974.

Welsh, David. "The Legacy of Penn Jones." *Ramparts*, November 1966.

West, Jessemyn. "Prelude to Tragedy: The Woman Who Sheltered Lee Oswald's Family Tells Her Story." *Redbook*, July 1966.

Whalen, Richard J. "The Kennedy Assassination." *Saturday Evening Post*, January 14, 1967.

"What Does Oliver Stone Owe History?" *Newsweek*, December 23, 1991.

Wheeler, Keith. "Cursed Gun—The Track of C2766." *Life*, August 27, 1965.

"Who Killed JFK? Just One Assassin." *Time*, November 24, 1975.

"Who Knew about 'Bugging' . . . RFK's Story—and the FBI's." *U.S. News & World Report*, December 26, 1966.

Will, George F. "Eleven Men and Sic 'Em." *Newsweek*, November 7, 2005.

Wilson, Richard. "What Happened to the Kennedy Program?" *Look*, November 17, 1964.

Wrone, David R. "Review of Gerald Posner, *Case Closed*." *Journal of Southern History*, vol. 6, February 1995.

Zoglin, Richard. "What If Oswald Stood Trial?" *Time*, December 1, 1986.

Government Reports

Alleged Assassination Plots Involving Foreign Leaders, An Interim Report of the Select Committee to Study Governmental Operations with Respect to Intelligence Activities, United States Senate, Together with Additional, Supplemental, and Separate Views. 94th Congress, 1st session, Senate Report No. 94-465. Washington, D.C.: Government Printing Office, 1975. (*Alleged Assassination Plots*)

Covert Action in Chile 1963–73. Church Committee Staff Report. Washington, D.C.: Government Printing Office, 1975.

Drugs, Law Enforcement and Foreign Policy: A Report Prepared by the Subcommittee on Terrorism, Narcotics and International Operations of the Committee on Foreign Relations. 100th Congress, 2d session, Senate. December 1988. Washington, D.C.: Government Printing Office, 1989.

Final Report of the Assassination Records Review Board. Washington, D.C.: Government Printing Office, 1998. (Final Report of the ARRB)

Final Report of the Select Committee on Assassinations, U.S. House of Representatives, Ninety-fifth Congress, Second Session, Summary of Findings and Recommendations. House Report 95-1828. Washington, D.C.: Government Printing Office, 1979. (HSCA Report)

Foreign Relations of the United States, 1961–1963. Vol. 2: *Vietnam, 1962.* Washington, D.C.: Government Printing Office, 1990.

Foreign Relations of the United States, 1961–1963. Vol. 4: *Vietnam, August–December 1963.* Washington, D.C.: Government Printing Office, 1991.

Foreign Relations of the United States, 1961–1963. Vol. 11: *Cuban Missile Crisis and Aftermath.* Washington, D.C.: Government Printing Office, 1996.

Forensic Analysis: Weighing Bullet Lead Evidence. Committee on Scientific Assessment of Bullet Lead Elemental Composition Comparison, Board on Chemical Sciences and Technology, National Research Council. Washington, D.C.: National Academies Press, 2004.

Hearings before the Legislative and National Security Subcommittee of the Committee on Government Operations, House of Representatives. 103rd Congress, 1st session, November 17, 1993. Washington, D.C.: Government Printing Office, 1994. (Conyers Committee Hearing)

Hearings before the Subcommittee on Civil and Constitutional Rights of the Committee on the Judiciary, House of Representatives, on FBI Oversight. 94th Congress, 1st and 2nd sessions, 1973–1974. Washington, D.C.: Government Printing Office, 1976. (*FBI Oversight*)

The Investigation of the Assassination of President John F. Kennedy: Performance of the Intelligence Agencies. Book V. *Final Report of the Select Committee to Study Governmental Operations with Respect to Intelligence Activities.* 94th Congress, 2nd session, Senate Report No. 94-755. Washington, D.C.: Government Printing Office, 1976. (Church Committee Report)

"1968 Panel Review of Photographs, X-Ray Films, Documents, and Other Evidence Pertaining to the Fatal Wounding of President John F. Kennedy on November 22, 1963, in Dallas, Texas." (Clark Panel Report)

Report of the Committee on Ballistic Acoustics. Commission on Physical Sciences, Mathematics, and Resources, National Research Council. Washington, D.C.: National Academies Press, 1982. (CBA Report)

Report of the President's Commission on the Assassination of President Kennedy. Warren Commission. Washington, D.C.: Government Printing Office, 1964. (Warren Report)

Report to Accompany S. 3006, The President John F. Kennedy Assassination Records Collection Act of 1992. 102nd Congress, 2nd session, Senate Report No. 102-328. Washington, D.C.: Government Printing Office, 1992. (1992 Senate Report)

Report to the President by the Commission on CIA Activities within the United States. New York: Manor Books, June 1975. (Rockefeller Commission Report)

"Review Requested by the Department of Justice of the Acoustical Reports Published by the House Select Committee on Assassinations." Technical Services Division, Federal Bureau of Investigation, November 19, 1980. (TSD Report)

Sklar, Barry. *U.S. Cuban Relations, 1959–1964: An Analysis.* Washington, D.C.: Library of Congress, Congressional Research Service, 1978.

Supplementary Detailed Staff Reports on Intelligence Activities and the Rights of Americans. Book III. *Final Report of the Select Committee to Study Governmental Operations with Respect to Intelligence Activities.* 94th Congress, 2nd session, Senate Report No. 94-755. Washington, D.C.: Government Printing Office, 1976. (*Supplementary Detailed Staff Reports*)

Texas Supplemental Report on the Assassination of President John F. Kennedy and the Serious Wounding of Governor John B. Connally, November 22, 1963 [by Attorney General Waggoner Carr]. Austin, Texas: Attorney General's Office, 1964. (*Texas Supplemental Report*)

Acknowledgments

There are very few people who manage to complete a long and difficult journey without having a lot of help along the way, and I am no exception. But the list of names of those who have helped me in some way, if only to answer one question among the thousands I have asked since I first started work on this book in 1986, is unmanageably long for an acknowledgments section. So to those of you whom I do not mention in this section, and you know who you are, I say thank you so very much.

I can tell those who have not seriously studied the assassination of President John F. Kennedy that it is a bottomless pit. With every project that we take on in our lives, we intuitively know, without even giving it a thought, that if we work long and hard enough we will reach the bottom of the pile. But I found, as others also have, that there is no bottom to the pile in the Kennedy case. It is endless, and I say this not as a casual turn of phrase. At the very moment I am writing these words on my yellow pad, I'm aware that there are at least a hundred people in the United States alone who are dedicating their lives to this case, examining every word and paragraph in every document they can find (the millions of pages on the case at the National Archives alone would take a lifetime to read) to come up with some inconsistency, discrepancy, or hint of a conspiracy in the assassination. And when there are a hundred or more intelligent minds working almost full-time on something (and, in the Kennedy case, thousands of others working part-time), they can create a lot of mischief. For many years during the writing of this book, I've been responding to their findings. But alas, most things, good and bad, come to an end in life, and at least for me, this book will be the end of my immersion in the Kennedy case, as I must go on to other endeavors. For me to continue to address the mostly imaginary issues of this case would be to sacrifice the rest of my life inasmuch as the allegations are, and will continue to be, without end.

The following people have helped me the most in this terribly long journey I am now bringing to an end. I must start with my erudite editor—by my lights, the best in the business—Starling Lawrence. Star's limitless patience and unconditional support, always saying yes, never no, to whatever I needed, coupled with the sagacious advice and guidance he gave me through the many years, elevates him to a very special position on my list. No one has a better ear, if you will, for the right or wrong word in a sentence. And the times were very numerous when Star immediately caught that word, or told me I was going over the top on some point. And when someone as highly critical as I am (I'd find fault with a beautiful morning sunrise) accepts the advice of someone over 90 percent of the time, that person has to be special. And Star is. I've been so blessed to have him as my editor on this monumental odyssey of mine.

And I want to thank Mary Babcock, a hardworking and meticulous copy editor who helped me so very much in rounding my manuscript into its final form.

And then there is Rosemary Newton, who has been like my secretary for this book. Though Rosemary works freelance, typing this book has been her main job, occupying most of her working day for many years. (And in the last several years the times have been many when I have also asked Rosemary to search for something on the Internet for me.) I wrote and dictated at my home and then made literally hundreds of trips to Rosemary's home in the hills, picking up drafts of sections she had typed and dropping off new work for her. Rosemary has had a very tough job working with me on this book, yet she was always competent and extraordinarily reliable. In a way, she worked more closely with me than anyone else and became the person on whom I relied the most.

In addition to transcribing, from my audio dictation, the contents of 72 sixty-minute and 8 ninety-minute tapes, during which she had to listen to my less-than-dulcet voice and my speaking a mile a minute, Rosemary had to decipher and type at least a thousand (maybe many more) inserts of mine handwritten in pencil on yellow legal paper. Though resulting from much dictation, the book you have read is, much more than dictation, a book of inserts. By that I mean the first drafts of sections I wrote (e.g., Zapruder film, wounds to the president, CIA, Oliver Stone, etc.), which I then dictated, were not overly long. But they all increased far beyond their original size in the many subsequent drafts with the addition of yellow-page inserts (as well as inserts on the top, sides, bottom, and between the lines of the pages). If you could read some of these inserts you would have great compassion for Rosemary. While still within an insert on the handwritten yellow or typewritten white page, she would be very apt to get directions like this: "Now to Insert 36 [arbitrary number] on the seventh yellow page following page 67." Fine. But when she gets there she sees I've inserted a five-page handwritten endnote which has three footnote inserts in it, any one of which could itself contain an endnote or direct her to one or more other places. And then back to where she left off on the original insert perhaps an hour earlier. Often the pages and flow of the point I was trying to make got so garbled with inserts, deletions, arrows, et cetera, that it was impossible for me, the architect of the madness, to follow. Yet Rosemary never complained and more than once figured out my own labyrinth for me. As if the above were not enough, a great number of times I would write so small on a page (to squeeze in what I wanted in the only space available) that without a magnifying glass only the world's most myopic person could read what I had written. I don't have to tell Rosemary how very grateful I am to her. She deserves some type of medal.

This book, as you know, is itself broken down into two books, Book One being on *what happened*, the non-conspiracy part, and Book Two, on *what did not happen*, the conspiracy allegation part of this sweeping story. For Book One, I was fortunate to have two people who made noteworthy writing contributions. Even though he worked with me for a relatively short part of my long journey, no one helped me as much as Dale Myers, the Emmy Award–winning computer animation specialist and superb student of the assassination from Detroit, Michigan. Dale helped me in the writing of several sections of Book One, most notably on acoustics, "Four Days in November" (particularly in the Oswald interrogations), and all matters dealing with still photography. I am deeply grateful to Dale for lending his time, energy, and considerable expertise to this literary project.

The other person who played a writing role, though a smaller one, was Fred Haines, a soft-spoken and extremely well-read intellectual. Fred's fine hand has survived in several places of the "Lee Harvey Oswald" and "Four Days in November" sections. And it was Fred's suggestion, a great one, I feel, and one for which I am indebted to him, to have the latter section, and to a lesser extent the Oswald biography (as opposed to every other part of the book), written in a narrative style normally reserved for fiction, giving this part of this nonfiction book a literary quality it would not have had without it. Very few nonfiction books can be written in such a narrative style without resorting to invention, but the unprecedented richness of the historical record on every single incident in this case has permitted it. Thus, as opposed to "Rimma accompanied Oswald to the train station, where he departed for Minsk," this: "Always faithful Rimma saw him off at the station. He was depressed and wanted her to accompany him on the overnight train trip, but by now he understands that such things were not as simple in the Soviet Union as they might have been in the states. It was snowing as they said their good-byes. Both of them were crying."

I also want to thank Patrick Martin for all the work he put into the graphics in the photo section of the book to help make them what they are, and Douglas Martin, Fred Kuentz, and Michael McDermott for the similar contributions they made with their respective graphics.

Other individuals who stand out among the many who have helped me along the way include Dr. Michael Baden, the great pathologist who headed up the forensic pathology panel of the House Select Committee on Assassinations. With his many duties (he's still a pathologist, he lectures, serves as a consultant on important criminal cases, even appears as a regular on a television reality series) he still always got back to me when I called, and took the time to answer my many questions dealing with the medical aspects of the assassination. Though I did not rely on him quite as much, whenever I did call on Dr. Baden's friend and counterpart in this case, Dr. Cyril Wecht, the famed pathologist and coroner (up to January of 2006) of Allegheny County in Pittsburgh, he unfailingly found time in his very busy day, or in the evenings or on weekends, to answer my questions.

And then there were two people in Dallas, both of whom I could invariably count on to make me laugh in response to their dry, homespun Texas humor, but more importantly, to help me get to the bottom of several problem areas in the case I was exploring. I'm speaking of Bill Alexander, the former top prosecutor in the Dallas DA's office who was the lead prosecutor in the trial of Jack Ruby for killing Lee Harvey Oswald, and was scheduled to prosecute and put Oswald away if Ruby hadn't gotten to him first, and former Dallas County sheriff James C. Bowles, who probably was a member of Dallas law enforcement (fifty-three years) longer than anyone else in Dallas history. Alexander, in his mid-eighties, is still practicing law, and Bowles just retired in 2005. Though both were always busy—especially Bowles when he was still sheriff—they always found time in their day to answer my many questions. Together, the two of them were part of Dallas law enforcement for a great number of years and know it as well or better than any two other people alive. They graciously shared their accumulated knowledge and wisdom with me, and even helped me to the extent of putting me in contact with former members of Dallas law enforcement I had been unable to locate.

The main source for this book on the assassination is, of course, as it must be, the twenty-seven volumes of the Warren Commission, the granddaddy of all literature on the assassination. Not too far behind are the thirteen volumes of the HSCA. The next great source, among so many others, is the collection of countless documents on the assassination stored at the National Archives, the temple to America's past, in College Park, Maryland. There simply is no way that this book ended up being the book I think it is without the wonderful cooperation I received from Steven D. Tilley, up until April of 2004 (he has since been elevated) the chief person in charge of these documents (the JFK Assassination Records Collection) at the archives, and his staff, particularly his able assistant James R. Mathis. Tilley and his staff, more than once, went above and beyond the call of duty to locate obscure but important documents for me. My requests for specific documents, several of which alone contained over a hundred pages each (e.g., the testimony of a witness before the HSCA), were continuous. I kept wondering whether I'd soon be getting a letter from Steve or one of his assistants saying, "Vince, please. Enough is enough," but I never did. What I always got, never accompanied by a complaint, was a very large envelope in the mail containing everything I had requested that they could find. I of course am very grateful to Steve and his staff for all the tremendous assistance they gave me.

Although I am proud to say that I have done 99.9 percent of my own research for everything I wrote in this book (which is typical for me, not feeling comfortable relying on others to do research for me), I want to give very special thanks to four individuals, three of whom are avid students of the assassination, who have helped me in so many diverse ways. Having no official connection to the case like a Bill Alexander, Dr. Michael Baden, or Steven Tilley, just their friendship and their desire to help me, they were always there for me, without hesitation, whenever I needed them—whether it was to take a photo of an angle at Dealey Plaza I needed, secure someone's phone number for me, loan me one of their many books on the assassination, in some cases get a document for me they had ready access to, or whatever. They are Jack Duffy of Fort Worth (who has been with me on this book the longest), David Phinney of Los Angeles, Jim Agnew of Chicago, and Bill Drenas of Lowell, Massachusetts. I'll never forget the help these four gave me and will always be especially grateful to them.

And then there is Gary Mack, the curator of the Sixth Floor Museum at Dealey Plaza in Dallas since 1994 and a student of the assassination since 1975. Gary carries in his head an enormous wealth of knowledge about the case—much of it not the type one would find in the Warren Report or the report of the HSCA—which he is generous to share with whoever asks. If I called Gary once in the past years, I called him thirty times, always for his input on some arcane issue, and nearly always he was able to help me, for which I am, of course, very appreciative and indebted. I also want to thank Gary's research colleague, fellow Texan David Perry, a former insurance investigator from Grapevine, Texas, who was also very helpful to me on the many occasions I called him for assistance. Dave has made a specialty out of debunking (sometimes in league with Mack) people like Ricky White and Madeleine Brown who come out of the woodwork with their phony assassination-related tales. The story I like to tell about David is the time I found a reference to a nut in a conspiracy book, one I had never heard of before and about whom there was no reference in any other book on the assassination that I was aware of. I called Dave to find out what he knew about the kook and his allegation, but a small part of me was hoping that Dave, too, had never heard of him, enabling me to say to him, "I finally found a nut you've never heard of." But before I could even get the second syllable of the man's name out of my mouth, Dave started bombarding me with a blizzard of information on him. He knew all about this guy and his allegation and had already debunked the man's story.

Thanks are also in order to John H. Slate, the very diligent chief of the Dallas Municipal Archives who was invariably helpful to me whenever I needed his assistance, and the many members of the reference staff at the Dallas Public Library. I must not forget the staff of the Pasadena Public Library, where I spent literally hundreds of hours on their machines looking at microfilm and to a lesser extent microfiche. Since up to last year, when they got new machines, the machines were in terrible condition from overuse, and I'm not proficient with mechanical things, I would frequently need their help to fix or adjust a malfunctioning unit, and not once were the staff members anything but helpful and pleasant. And then there were the virtually hundreds of books the library staff got for me that were not at their library but at one of their branches, and the considerable number they got for me through their interlibrary loan service—most out of print and several very obscure—from libraries not only throughout California, but in other states, like one published in 1798, a copy of which they located for me at Brigham Young University in Provo, Utah.

I also want to express my appreciation, ironically, to three people who, unlike those already mentioned, had no conscious intent to help me but nevertheless did. I'm referring to the publishers of the three main conspiracy community publications, which I subscribed to and carefully read through the years. They are Jerry Rose's monthly *Decade* series, Jim DiEugenio's bimonthly *Probe*, and Walt Brown's *JFK/Deep Politics Quarterly*. (The *Decade* series, ending in the fourth decade after the assassination, and *Probe* are no longer in existence.) Although I usually didn't agree with the conclusions set forth in the articles in these publications, I found all three to be scholarly and informative, and here and there I picked up valuable points from Rose, DiEugenio, and Brown (as well as from the many private assassination researchers who contributed to their publications) that I hadn't come across in my own research and that had been overlooked by the Warren Commission and HSCA. Also, I learned from these publications the principal areas of interest in the mainstream conspiracy community, which I knew I would have to address in my book if it was going to be the book I wanted it to be.

And lastly, but certainly not the least, I want to thank my wonderful wife Gail—who has always brought sunlight to my darkest hours—for the tremendous support and encouragement (and for sacrifices too numerous to mention) she gave me over the many years it took me to write this book.

Although I have done far, far more work on this book than any other book I've ever written, I can honestly say I enjoyed my labor, because apart from the terrible tragedy of Kennedy's death (other than that, Mrs. Lincoln, how was the play?), the case, as any longtime assassination researcher will tell you, is endlessly intriguing and fascinating. Only one section, Oswald's biography, was pure pain for me to write. One reason is that I am a nonfiction, true-crime writer normally working with trial transcripts, police and autopsy reports, witness statements, et cetera, and writing someone's biography is not my cup of tea. Secondly, I was dealing with a subject (Oswald) who moved no fewer than seventeen times in a sixteen-year period before joining the Marines, and had been in the military and in Russia. Nearly every day while writing this section I spent a good part of it with a magnifying glass looking at sketchy, faint, and often difficult-to-decipher grade school, military, and other records, and trying to reconcile conflicting memories of chronological events with documentary evidence that just didn't seem to fit. So it was an unpleasant task, but I had no choice but to "bite the bullet" and do it. I questioned when it would ever end, at one point envisioning a large, empty tub that I knew would one day be full of water, but only because of my putting one drop of water into it at a time. I took to telling people I was on a "lead diet" (biting the bullet) and working "eight days a week," because it was the only section of the book I wrote in which almost without exception, I worked on the case throughout the night in my dreams. I thought the "eight days a week" line was original and clever and so did those I used it on until one day someone reminded me, "Hey, that's a Beatles song," and it rang a distant bell to me. It was a great relief to finally finish this section and return to the luxury of working only seven days a week.

I've always been able to work seven days a week for months on end, sometimes, when required, a hundred or more hours a week, without manifesting any physical problems. In other words, I find work easy. When I was a prosecutor, trying a two- or three-month murder case before a jury wasn't fatiguing at all, although I knew some trial lawyers who, after a two- or three-day drunk driving case, would say they had to go to Palm Springs to recuperate. For whatever reason, I always seemed to be immune to the deprivations of hard work. But I had never encountered the Kennedy assassination before. Although I feel I can still get up and run around the block without any problem, for the first time in my life I feel (I'm not sure and certainly hope it's not true) that the research and writing of this book may have taken a toll on me. And one reason is that, as I've indicated, there simply is no end to the case, and more than once I wondered if I had bitten off more than I could chew.

What I can say with a lot more confidence is that without all the help I got from so many people along the way in this long journey of mine, not only wouldn't this book be the book it is, but I would have had a much more difficult time reaching the finish line to write these acknowledgments.

Index

ABC (American Broadcasting Company), 43, 263
  at Dallas county jail, 435
  JFK mourners and, 340, 473, 492
  on JFK shooting, 89, 106
  at Love Field, 57, 225
Ables, Don, in police lineups, 214, 253
Abt, John, 240, 310, 347, 350, 357–58, 367, 372–73, 374, 385
  LHO's calls to, 369–70, 406
  Ruth Paine's attempt to reach, 370n
Abundant Life Temple, 150, 162–63
ACLU, *see* American Civil Liberties Union
Acme Brick, 188–90, 244
acoustic evidence, *see* ballistic acoustics
Adamcik, John P., 227, 233–34
  in Paine residence searches, 179, 203, 360–61
  rifle shown to Marina Oswald and, 234
  in Ruby apartment search, 465
Addison's disease, 13–14
adrenal glands, 13–14
Air Force, U.S., 460
Air Force One, 34, 62n, 191, 216–26
  friction between JFK and LBJ factions in, 216–17
  Irish wake on, 219–20
  JFK coffin in, 175–76, 179–80, 187–88, 218–23
  JFK's funeral and, 502
  LBJ's swearing-in on, 184–87, 217, 226

  LBJ's use of, 119–20, 120n, 143, 160–61, 179–80, 201, 216–20
  RFK's boarding of, 222
Air Force Two, 119n–20n, 121, 191n
Air Time (Gates), 436n
Alabama, 340
Alcohol and Tobacco Tax Unit, *see* Treasury Department, U.S.
Alessandri Rodriguez, Jorge, 157
Alexander, William, 287, 290
  at Book Depository, 129–30
  Communist conspiracy feared by, 215, 270, 282–83
  criminal complaint forms filled out by, 239, 242, 290
  LHO indictment sought by, 331
  LHO's interrogation and, 183n, 239–40
  at Majestic Steak House, 266
  Molina and, 304–5, 319, 331
  police lineup and, 361–62
  in search of LHO's room, 215
  search warrant prepared by, 213
  "Smokey Joe" Smith incident and, 138
  Tippit murder and, 129–30, 137–42, 239–45
Alger, Bruce, 158
Allen, Jim, 235, 266
Allman, Pierce, 417n
Alyea, Thomas P., 74
Amagiri (Japanese destroyer), 92n, 218
Amarillo, Tex., 157
American Broadcasting Company, *see* ABC

Index

as potential criminal informant (PCI),
457–58

reaction to JFK assassination of, 273–80,
315, 320–24, 396–403, 455, 480–81,
482–84, 505

revolver of, *see* Colt Cobra pistol, of
Ruby

sandwiches purchased by, 277–79, 280,
307–11, 482

temper of, 8–10, 315, 324, 396, 399–400

at *Times Herald* building, 314

Tippit murder and, 275

transfer of, 497–99

troubles of, 8–10, 32–33

Vegas Club of, *see* Vegas Club

at Webb's Waffle shop, 323–24

Rudnicki, Jan G. (Nick), 237*n*

Rusk, Dean, 473

Russell, Harold, 126

Russia, *see* Soviet Union

Rutledge, John, 386

Ryan, Bill, 226

Safran, Don, 276

St. Matthew's Cathedral, 494–95, 496–97,
499–500

Saint Patrick's Cathedral, 338

Salinger, Pierre, 22, 24*n*

Salyer, Kenneth Everett, 97

San Antonio, Tex., 16, 17, 36

Sandburg, Carl, 280*n*–81*n*

Sanders, Barefoot, 18, 184, 282

Sardar (bay gelding), 460

Saunders, Rev. Louis, 509–11

Sawyer, J. Herbert, 35, 129

Brennan as source of, 100–101

Elm command post of, 139

in search of Book Depository, 80–81

Schieffer, Bob, 188–89

Schlesinger, Arthur M., Jr., 318

Schrank, John, 187*n*

Schwartz, Erwin, 171–72, 191

Scibor, Mitchell, 271, 297–98, 319

Scoggins, William:

police lineups and, 361–63

Tippit murder and, 121–25, 131, 133,
140, 336

on Tippit's following of LHO, 117*n*

Scott, Foresman & Company, 27

Scrap Iron and Junk Handlers Union, 463

Scudder, Gene, 313

Searcy, B. D., 125–26

Secret Service, U.S., 183*n*, 212, 380

on Air Force One, 175–76, 185

autopsy photos and X-rays acquired by,
288–89

at Bethesda Hospital, 230, 231–33,
237–38*n*, 241–42, 258–59, 288–89,
315–16

at Book Depository, 104–6

Box 6225 surveillance and, 190

erroneous report of death in, 133–34

at Executive Inn, 448–50

FBI cooperation with, 245, 486

FBI file on LHO and, 177–78

FBI offer of help to, 134

in Fort Worth, 11, 23, 25, 37, 508–11

Gregory contacted by, 392

at Inn of the Six Flags, 484–85, 491,
493–94, 505

JFK's funeral and, 495, 500, 501, 504

JFK's personal style as concern of, 40*n*

JFK's restriction of, 42, 57–58, 92*n*

JFK threats recorded by, 20

jurisdiction issues and, 134, 291–92

at LBJ's residence, 218, 284

LHO murder and, 440, 443, 453–54,
467–69

LHO-release password and, 491–92

LHO's funeral and, 487, 508–11

LHO's interrogation and, 208–9, 210,
341, 349, 375, 380, 406, 409, 417,
419–20, 423–24

LHO's transfer and, 426, 430

at Love Field, 160, 175–76

Marina Oswald protected by, 448–50,
467–69, 474–77, 484–85, 508–11

Parkland bullet and, 132

at Parkland Hospital, 82–85, 99, 113,
119, 120–21, 132, 143–46, 175, 464,
466–67, 474–77

police lineups and, 235, 241, 253–55

in presidential motorcade, 36–37, 39–44,
50, 51, 56–58, 92*n*

radio contact of, 62*n*, 64

RFK and, 115